Introductory psychology

The Dorsey Series in Psychology
Editor   HOWARD F. HUNT   *Columbia University*

Introductory psychology

MARVIN L. SCHROTH, Ph.D.
University of Santa Clara

and

DERALD WING SUE, Ph.D.
California State University, Hayward

1975

 The Dorsey Press   Homewood, Illinois   60430

Irwin-Dorsey International   London, England   WC2H 9NJ
Irwin-Dorsey Limited   Georgetown, Ontario   L7G 4B3

First Printing, February 1975

ISBN 0-256-01710-7
Library of Congress Catalog Card No. 74–24455

Printed in the United States of America

LEARNING SYSTEMS COMPANY—
a division of Richard D. Irwin, Inc.—has developed a
PROGRAMMED LEARNING AID
to accompany texts in this subject area.
Copies can be purchased through your bookstore
or by writing PLAIDS,
1818 Ridge Road, Homewood, Illinois 60430.

Preface

Our primary goal in this text is to motivate student interest in the field of psychology. We have attempted to do this by focusing our attention on what students want to know: altered states of consciousness (drugs, sleep, hypnotism, transcendental meditation, and ESP), biofeedback studies, sexuality, aging and death, abnormal behavior, psychotherapy, racism, and sexism. These are all topics of high interest to the student not usually given comprehensive coverage in other introductory psychology textbooks. In many cases, we have devoted whole chapters to the above subjects. In addition, we have tried to make the content of psychology relevant to the lives of our students by constantly relating psychological knowledge and theory to practice and applications. We recognize that most students will have no formal exposure to advanced psychology courses and will profit most from a highly practical and meaningful presentation of the subject.

Although the text may best be characterized as possessing a "social-adjustment" emphasis, we have not neglected traditional areas such as perception, memory, learning, and the biological basis of behavior. Our goal has been to present these fields as clearly and simply as possible without resorting to excessive technical jargon. Since our concern is to present a molar picture of human behavior, we have purposely deemphasized the more molecular study of man. We have not, however, compromised the integrity of science nor have we been overly simplistic. Our selective topical approach has allowed us to write a text much shorter than many others. The relative brevity of this text plus the selection and coverage of topics will provide an unhurried and lively one-term course in psychology.

Another concern of ours was to organize and write chapters that would aid the student in integrating and understanding concepts. To accomplish this goal we have provided comprehensive summaries for each chapter. In addition, each chapter is preceded by a detailed outline. These outlines will provide a general overview for the student and serve to help him organize and learn the material.

This text is written in such a fashion as to allow the instructor flexibility in designing his own course. Although our approach has been to add continuity to each topic by first presenting basic psychological principles before broader and more complex issues are presented, we have purposely made each chapter more or less independent of the others. Although it is helpful to read our text in a particular sequence, it is not essential. Instructors may elect to delete certain chapters or to rearrange them in a manner consistent with their lecture plans. Several colleagues have suggested that a strong case can be made for reversing the sequence of study by exposing students to the section on Social Psychology and Social Issues first in order to give them a broad and meaningful overview of the field immediately. Many instructors may desire to use this approach. In any case, the semi-independent nature of the chapters provides the instructor with greater flexibility in fitting the course content to his unique interests and style.

The writing of this text has been a massive undertaking and would not have been possible without the help of skilled reviewers. We are especially indebted to Howard F. Hunt, John Clark, Marc Marcus, and Joel M. Cohen for their appraisal of the manuscript and helpful comments in improving it. We would also like to acknowledge the help and support provided by Roland C. Lowe. Finally, special thanks are due to Paulina Wee Sue, a supportive, patient, and encouraging wife who helped in the typing of the entire manuscript and who put up with both authors' irritations and frustrations during the manuscript preparation.

January 1975   MARVIN L. SCHROTH
                                       DERALD WING SUE

Contents

cal stress. Alternative views of mental illness. Treatment of emotional disorders: *Physical therapies. Psychotherapy.* The effectiveness of psychotherapy. Summary.

SECTION ONE

What is psychology?

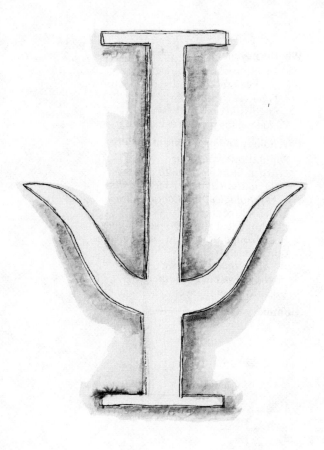

1

The nature
of psychology

From the beginning of time, man has been fascinated with himself and the world around him. When faced with situations that go beyond the limits of his comprehension, he has resorted to the use of supernatural explanations. The early writings and art forms of primitive civilizations indicate that many people attempted to explain man's actions as the work of good or evil spirits. Demons were seen as possessing man's body and influencing his behavior. Certain forms of behaviors such as headaches, convulsive attacks, or bizarre actions were seen as the work of spirits who had possessed the person's body. It was believed that these spirits could even leave the body and visit other places during dreams or visions. Although many of us believe that we have come a long way from the superstitious explanations of human behavior, much of our current pseudoscientific theories still exist to account for man's feelings, experiences, and behaviors. For example, note the rebirth of interest in witch cults, satanism, possessions *(The Exorcist)* and astrology.

While there is nothing new about man's attempt to understand human behavior, the science of psychology is a relatively new field. *Psychology is the science which studies the behavior of man and other animals.* It is a science because it attempts to discover new and useful information in the form of verifiable data obtained under controlled conditions. This allows others to make similar observations and obtain the same results. What psychology tries to do is to *describe, understand, predict,* and at times *control* behavior. To accomplish this task, psychologists seek to discover facts and establish general laws or principles without resorting to explanations of divine intervention or supernatural forces.

Although we may be able to define psychology in a broad sense for you, psychology means different things to different people. To the clinical psychologist it is the diagnosis and treatment of mental disorders while for the social psychologist it is the study of social factors (family, friends, peers, institutions, and so on) as they affect one's development and personality. The ultimate decision as to what psychology is, and can be for you, will develop in the course of your studying it. However, it may be helpful for us to discuss some common methods that psychologists use to study their subject matter. Table 1–1 outlines some of the major fields in psychology.

Methods of psychology
Subjectivity versus objectivity

We all have the tendency to consider things in the light of our own point of view and to make evaluations from this framework. The natural tendency toward subjectivity and evaluation can be illustrated by the following experiment (Sanford & Wrightsman, 1970). Students in a psy-

TABLE 1–1
Fields of psychology

Clinical psychology: Activities of the clinical psychologist center around psychological testing and diagnosis, psychotherapy with the maladjusted or mentally ill, and research on mental disorders and personality.

Counseling psychology: Many of the activities of the counseling psychologist tend to be similar to that of the clinician. However, his work is generally with individuals having less serious problems. A major part of his work includes vocational and educational counseling.

Experimental psychology: The oldest field of specialization within psychology is experimental psychology, which is closely associated with physics, chemistry, and biology. The work of the experimental psychologist tends to be oriented toward the use of controlled experiments in investigating behavior.

Psychometric psychology: The design and application of tests, rating scales, and other methods of measuring abilities, personality, and behavior are the concerns of the psychometrician.

Educational psychology: These psychologists are especially concerned with increasing the efficiency of learning in school through the application of psychological knowledge about learning and motivation. In addition, their activities may involve counseling, diagnosis of abilities, achievement and curriculum building.

School psychology: School psychologists (counseling psychologists in school settings) are more involved in the testing of and guidance of individual students than educational psychologists, although activities do overlap. A large part of their work consists of working with students who need some sort of special attention.

Social psychology: Social psychologists are concerned with social factors that affect one's development and personality, such as the many groups we belong to—our family, peers, cliques, social class, and so on. Among social problems of interest to social psychologists are prejudice, propaganda, crime and delinquency, and the use of drugs.

Developmental psychology: Developmental psychologists are interested in how behavioral changes take place with increasing age. Since behaviors and abilities change most rapidly during the first few years of life, a major part of developmental psychology is child psychology. Old age, however, is also the concern of developmental psychologists as many changes take place at the opposite end of life.

Personality psychology: Personality psychologists, like clinical psychologists, are interested in the individual as well as in general laws of behavior. The main difference between these two fields of psychology would be that while clinical psychologists are interested in the deviant behavior of the individual, personality psychologists are largely concerned with "normal" individuals.

chology class were asked *(a)* to listen to the story of a man who murdered his wife and then committed suicide, and *(b)* to write down the first words that occurred to them. Most of the words the students listed were evaluative or subjective adjectives: *distressful, horrible, sad, bad, terrible,* and *pathetic.* These words all describe the students' attitudes and feelings about the act, not the act itself. Only a few of the students gave relatively neutral and objective adjectives, such as *fatal, bloody, mortal, extreme,* and *violent.*

Evaluation is natural and often necessary for living. We have to deal with people, events, and act on problems. But while evaluation is a friend of action, it is an enemy of science. Science attempts to be objective and the scientist, as such, must look at the world as if he had no emotion, biases, or prejudices. At work, he tries to see the world as if it had no goodness or evil, beauty or ugliness, and joy or sadness.

Although not always successful in controlling subjectivity, the psychologist uses safeguards that tend to preserve his objectivity. To make sure that he sees something that is actually there, and not a figment of his imagination, he follows certain techniques. He makes *repeated observations* of the same event. He brings in other observers to watch so he can be sure that his own perceptions are not fooling him. In addition, he is alert to poor sampling, the danger that what he sees in a few people will not be true of most people. Much of the methodology in psychology consists of devices to guard against subjectivity.

Casual versus controlled observation

Few problems in everyday life or the scientific world can be solved without observation. Medical doctors have to rely on observing symptoms in diagnosing the illnesses of patients. Even Einstein had to observe the many facts furnished him by hundreds of experimental physicists before coming up with his original theories.

However, in the many decisions we make in our daily lives, observation plays a relatively minor role. We do not examine carefully all of the facts regarding two political candidates before we vote. We do not read all of the available reviews about the different movies in town before we decide which one to attend. We do not examine carefully the state of lubrication of the joints of a car before we decide it's time for a lube job. If we do any observing before leaping to action, it is apt to be quite casual without consideration of all the facts. In contrast, the psychologist has many methods available for making *controlled observations* that we ordinarily do not employ in everyday life. Let us look at two of these.

The *experiment* (Figure 1–1) is considered the best of the controlled observations used by psychologists. In its simplest form, it is made up of an *independent variable* (defined as the factor manipulated by the scientist in order to discover what effect, if any, it has) and a *dependent variable* (defined as the behavior the scientist seeks to understand). In addition, any other variables (events) that could affect the behavior under observation are controlled so that they will not influence the results. The following experiment will help illustrate a few of the most basic principles and give a clearer picture of how an experiment is conducted.

Suppose that you are interested in the effects of alcohol on reaction time. Through many observations, you have noticed that intoxicated people respond very slowly to timed tasks and you are interested in scientifically confirming or disconfirming this observation. You decide that you will have one group of students drink a given amount of alcohol and then compare their reaction time to another group which was not given alcohol. In this case, the independent variable is the amount of alcohol and the dependent variable is the reaction times of the students. In addition, a number of other variables such as age, sex, and practice of the subjects could contaminate your study. For example, if two groups

FIGURE 1–1
Reaction time experiment. The subject's reaction
time is being measured by this apparatus. On each
separate trial one of the panel lights comes on.
The subject presses the button underneath the light
as fast as he can, the elapsed time being
electronically recorded.

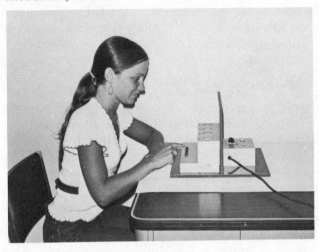

of subjects differ in age, 18 versus 65 year olds, you could not be sure
that the slower responses of the older group was not because of age instead of alcohol consumption. For that reason, scientists attempt to control these variables. One way you could do this is to match both groups
as to age, sex, and amount of practice each subject has had on the task.
Your problem, then, is to manipulate the independent variable, measure
the dependent variable, and hold constant or control the other variables
that could contaminate the results. All this is done with two groups, the
experimental group, which received the independent variable (alcohol)
and a *control group*, which did not.

The results of your experiment show that alcohol slows reaction
times since the control group performed faster on the reaction time
task than did the experimental subjects. You are able to come to this
conclusion because the possible effects of other variables have been
controlled. If the subjects in the experimental and control groups had
not been equated before the study began, alternative interpretations of
the results become possible and the results would be partly ambiguous.

Although the experiment is the best manifestation of a controlled observation, it is frequently not possible or practical to use. As a result,
psychologists frequently resort to other techniques such as the *field
study method*. Essentially, the researcher goes into a natural setting to
observe his subjects without any effort to control their behavior under
investigation. For example, in 1954, a group of psychologists were in-

trigued by the beliefs of a Mrs. Kreech who claimed she had received messages from superior beings on a planet called "Clarion." These beings who had visited the earth in flying saucers predicted that a great flood and cataclysm would strike the earth on December of that year. She gathered about her a group of dedicated believers who went into seclusion to prepare for the event. In order to study what happens when people's beliefs are disconfirmed, a number of psychologists joined the group and pretended to be believers. They diligently and carefully observed and recorded the believers' actions and attitudes as they naturally occurred. The results of their study have been published in a fascinating book entitled *When Prophesy Fails* (Festinger, Riecken, & Schachter, 1956). Investigators that engage in the use of natural observations are trained to observe and record accurately in order to avoid reading their own wishes and biases into the report.

Vague versus precise use of language

A major aspect of both scientific and practical thought involves the use of language. If we are going to make sense out of our observations and communicate them to others, the language must be very precise with no ambiguities. The well-known communication gap that exists between people often involves the vague use of words.

For example, consider the following statement: "Jane is a sexy girl." This represents an opinion, not fact, and other people may disagree. The person who made the above statement is really not talking about Jane. He is talking about himself and the fact that Jane arouses him sexually. There is nothing wrong with this except that he should realize that if others take issue with this statement, the argument is over personal evaluations and not facts.

In psychology and other sciences, we are not satisfied just to describe facts. We relate observed facts together through the use of the *language of constructs*. We can examine the nature of psychological constructs by considering the matter of hunger. While all of us have had what seems to be some direct and indirect experience with our own hunger, we have never observed directly the hunger of anyone else. We can only observe directly behavior in the presence or absence of food. We can hear an individual talking about food, expressing his hunger, and watch him grow restless when it is time for his dinner. From this behavior we invent the construct of hunger, *a hypothetical concept to account for his actions*. However, we do not observe hunger. This also holds true for other matters such as emotions, values, personality traits, intelligence, or for many terms frequently used by psychologists.

Constructs are usually given *operational definitions* to give them a clearer meaning. This can be illustrated by taking an experiment on motivation. We can make hunger more meaningful by describing in detail the *operation* of food deprivation. The experimental rats, we say, were deprived of food for 24 hours before the experiment began. Later, with their hunger clearly defined, we can describe how they behaved in learning a maze; it took an average of 30 trials before they made no wrong turns (errors). Thus, an operational definition is *a definition of an abstract concept framed in terms of the operations for observing it.*

It may sound at this point that the psychologist is a person devoid of feelings, emotions, and involvement in world affairs. Nothing could be further from the truth. Although psychologists use many methods to guard against subjectivity in their study of behavior, many are now applying their talents and knowledge to the social problems of our time.

Psychology and problems of society

George Miller (1969) gave a presidential address to the American Psychological Association (APA) in which he strongly urged making psychology more relevant to the social scene. It is particularly significant that a man like Miller would devote his address to making such a plea. He is a very distinguished experimental psychologist who has many outstanding publications in a broad range of areas such as physiological and mathematical psychology and the psychology of audition. He completely skipped over the tradition of previous APA presidents by not giving a technical lecture on his own research findings. Miller ended his statement by proposing that psychologists must discover the best way to teach laymen how to make use of psychology based on scientific principles. Hopefully, this will change people's conception of themselves and will contribute to the promotion of human welfare.

Likewise, Edward Walker (1969) proposed a new set of obligations that experimental psychology owes society. They amount to a formulation of a new set of social and political goals in which psychologists have the responsibility of interpreting its research findings to society as a whole, and of stepping up their attacks on pressing social problems.

We shall now turn our attention to some of the problems brought on by a changing world, in which psychologists are playing an increasingly important role. These are essentially worldwide problems which will command the attention of experts in many fields if we are going to find solutions. Thus, we have the emergence of a new interdisciplinary approach: psychologists, engineers, sociologists, biologists, and experts from many other different fields, all working together in a common effort.

The population explosion

The United Nations has recently estimated the world population to be slightly more than 3½ billion persons. The population of the United States is about 210 million. Approximately 2 billion people live in Asia with the People's Republic of China, alone, having about 800 million and India 500 million. If these figures do not boggle the mind, consider this. The United Nations has projected the world population at the end of the century to be 7 billion persons or double the number there are now. For the United States, Frejka (1970) estimates that the population will grow about 50 percent by the year 2000, making a total of 300 million. His projection is based on the assumption that childbearing will continue to decline at a slow pace. The reasons for his rather dismal prediction, in spite of a marked decline in the overall birthrate, lie in the present increase in the number of persons of childbearing age.

Recognizing the responsibility of psychologists in this area of growing social concern, the APA established a Task Force on Psychology, Family Planning, and Population Policy in October 1969. They were charged with preparing a review of psychological activities related to population growth and with finding ways of stimulating psychologists to offer their professional services to this area. Evidence is accumulating which shows that psychologists are definitely becoming interested in the problems of the population explosion. For instance, since July 1968, more than 500 psychologists have sought out information and application forms from the Center for Population Research of the National Institute of Child Health and Human Development (APA Task Force, 1972).

Psychologists are currently providing several services in the population area including: the counseling for family-size planning; the development of sex education programs; the education of the public on the dangers of overpopulation; and the service as legislative consultants in formulating governmental policies. In addition, many psychologists are involved in active research on population problems. The APA Task Force conducted a questionnaire survey on the specific areas of research activities commanding their attention; the results are shown in Table 1–2.

ATTITUDES TOWARD BIRTH CONTROL. A recent study by Buckhout (1972) on attitudes toward birth control is a good example of the type of research psychologists can do on population growth. Buckhout administered an attitude questionnaire to a sample of 267 unmarried undergraduate students at California State University, Hayward. The main sample group was stratified by race according to the population distribution in California. This resulted in a sample in which 80.9 percent were white, 9.1 percent blacks, 5.3 percent Chicanos, 3 percent Orientals, and 1.5 percent native Americans. There were an equal number of men and women; the average age (mean) was 22 years.

The most surprising result of the survey was the finding that the ideal number of children wanted was 2.6; with men reporting 2.4 and women, 2.7. These results are dramatically lower than the usual figures of 3.0 to 3.5 which have consistently shown up since 1936 (Eisner, 1970). Presumably, this may reflect the effects of the recent heavy ecology publicity. Additionally, Chicanos and blacks significantly desired more chil-

TABLE 1–2
Areas of research activity as indicated in the Task Force questionnaire responses

Topic	N	Percent
Family planning and reproduction— Psychological, physiological, and psychosomatic factors related to (a) present and planned size and composition of family; (b) use or nonuse of contraceptive methods; (c) choice of abortion, (d) sterilization, or (e) pregnancy	88	39
Family roles and sex roles— (a) Sex-role stereotyping, (b) human sexuality, (c) population control and changing family styles, (d) population control and changing roles of women	55	25
Population policy— Methods of influencing opinion for or against population control: (a) conditioning, (b) incentives, (c) mass media campaigns, (d) religious influences, (e) governmental policies, (f) legal alternatives under the United States Constitution and Bill of Rights	11	5
Environmental effects of increasing population— (a) Effects of crowding and high-density living on animal and human populations, (b) environmental impact of increasing population	30	13
Curriculum development in psychology and population	25	11
Cross-cultural studies in family planning and population study, including studies in demography and migration	16	6
Total	225	99

Source: After APA Task Force Survey on Psychology, Family Planning and Population Policy, *American Psychologist*, January 1972, p. 28. Copyright 1972 by the American Psychological Association. Reprinted by permission.

TABLE 1–3
Attitudes toward family planning

Item	Main sample	Chicanos	Blacks
Probability of marriage	75%	78%	76%
Probability of having children	71%	76%	77%
Importance of children (0–10)	6.5	7.8	7.3
Ideal number of children desired	2.63	4.0	4.1

Source: Robert Buckhout, "Toward a two-child norm: Changing family planning attitudes," *American Psychologist*, 1972, 27, 16–26. Copyright 1972 by the American Psychological Association. Reprinted by permission.

dren than did whites; 4.0 and 4.1 children, respectively. These data, along with other findings, are summarized in Table 1–3.

In subsequent sample surveys conducted only six to nine months later, Buckhout reported a continuation of the rapid decline in desired number of children and a marked increase in the favorability toward using birth control measures. However, the difference in number of children wanted by ethnic groups remained relatively the same.

POPULATION AND THE MEGALOPOLIS. The human problems brought on by overpopulation can best be seen in the United States in congested cities. Enormous urban centers have developed with large concentrations of people in a relatively small area.

Megalopolis is a term used to describe these huge metropolitan areas in which large cities have engulfed the smaller towns around them. About 75 percent of the population live in super cities such as New York and Los Angeles. The projection to the end of this century is that about 90 percent of Americans will live in urban areas.

The advantages of living in megalopolis are well known. These advantages are principally economic, such as a wider range of job opportunities provided by the development of many business and service enterprises. In addition, there are the often-mentioned bonus features of more complete welfare services and greater cultural opportunities, including the theater arts and sporting events. The disadvantages are equally well known; housing is crowded, traffic jams are a common occurrence, and air pollution is widespread thus creating a new source of respiratory illness and disease. These problems, as well as the greater amount of crime, are adding to the irritations and tensions individuals feel in the megalopolis.

PSYCHOLOGICAL IMPLICATIONS. Not so well known are the effects on human values and dignity, the price we pay for population growth, as exemplified by the crowded conditions in the cities. Large concentrations of people make individuality harder to achieve and to recognize. Such questions as, "Who am I?"; "What difference does my being alive make?"—all reflect the loss of personal identity. Large numbers of people tend to become anonymous members of groups and numbers rather than individuals. Consider how many numbers you have for various purposes, such as registration in college, social security, and credit cards. The list goes on and on; small wonder that psychiatrists report handling more and more cases of alienation and "identity crisis."

Antagonistic behavior appears to be yet another consequence of overcrowding. Some experiments on how people react to crowded rooms indicate that men become very competitive and hostile to one another (Johnson, 1972). Interestingly enough, women respond more positively to crowded conditions and mixing the sexes appears to help negate the effects of crowding.

These same effects may also be found within different families. Viel (1971) examines infanticides among South American children and finds that the larger the family the less likelihood of infantile deaths caused by disease and other biological factors. His findings show that the death rate of children in families with ten or more children is five times as high as in families with only one child. Hence, the parents may tend to neglect any given child when there are too many children under the same roof.

Obviously, we all will pay a terrible price for an overpopulated world, and our survival may be at stake. For instance, carefully controlled studies on animals show a dramatic increase in violence with increases in population growth (Johnson, 1972). By analogy, we may be seeing the same thing happen in human societies, considering the crime rate, ghetto riots, and number of wars or quasi wars that continue to plague mankind. There is no longer any question about whether man's position in relation to his environment will change; the only question is whether this will be brought about by his own restraints or by the catastrophic results of an unbalanced ecology.

Man and technology

Man has, for the first time in history, obtained the power to completely design the environment in which he will live. This dramatic state of affairs has been brought about by man's ingenious development of technology. Although these technological breakthroughs typically do not make the headlines of the day, with the exception of space exploration feats, they have a far greater and more lasting impact on the daily lives of people than the actions of any well-known political leader. Just think about the impact of the development of automobiles, television, airplanes, computers, insecticides, and new medical techniques, including surgery and psychopharmacology, on your own daily life. There is no way you can avoid being affected in some manner by these technological achievements; not even if you drop out of society. Technology is and will continue to be the greatest fundamental producer of change.

It is just in the last few years that people have become increasingly aware of the mixed blessings that technology has brought upon them. DDT (the wonder of all insecticides) which was the cure for all farming difficulties in the last decade now threatens man and animal alike over the next decade by polluting the environment with poison. The car that makes one so mobile, so independent, also produces dangerous air pollution and, indeed, in some instances even strangles our mobility; just witness the familiar 5 o'clock traffic jam in any large city.

It is because of the basic effects of technological inventions on our environment and hence, on ourselves, that the field of psychology is establishing a position of ever-increasing importance in evaluating the application of new scientific discoveries. What if technology creates environments that people generally accept, but are not suitable in the long run for fulfilling the basic biological and psychological needs of human nature?

Richard Landers (1966), voices the fears of many in articulating the human need for resisting identification with and domination by machines we construct. It is his provocative thesis that our ready acceptance of the material luxuries and comfort provided by machines opens up the possibility of our being taken over and made totally dependent on them; the roles will be reversed in which we become the slaves instead of masters. In fact, he envisions the day when machines can create their own technology and art forms. These machines will be used to replace man, not to aid him. The views of Landers can be seen in current science fiction thrillers such as *I Have No Mouth, and I Must Scream* (Ellison, 1967).

Not all scientists are as pessimistic as Landers about man having created a "Frankenstein Monster" in technology. But certainly, psychologists have an important role to play in helping to identify the basic human psychobiological needs in order for the effective planning and realization of suitable man-made environments.

Van Cott and Spector (1968) illustrate that with proper planning and direction, technology can be used to bring material benefits, and not social disorganization or personal demoralization. They believe that the so-called emerging nations, not yet fully industrialized, offer human engineers a unique opportunity for the designed introduction of social change without disruption of society. In part, their system for change is based upon establishing effective communication channels with the residents, determining community characteristics and needs, and careful selection and training of community development workers.

EDUCATIONAL TECHNOLOGY. Many psychologists have become active agents for social change by utilizing technology to facilitate education. The use of technology is not actually a recent development. Even the "objective teaching methods" of over 100 years ago were dependent on technology for guiding learning (Wilbur, 1865).

The *Montessori methods* in the United States, which are currently very popular, owe part of their success to the use of well-developed equipment and materials. Pictures of children in early Montessori schools show the students engaged with blocks, cubes, gardening, lacing frames and the like (Montessori, 1964). At any rate, they resemble in many ways modern-day children engaged in computer-assisted instruction seated at the console of some machine.

The actual forerunner of using the computer as a tutor was embodied in the pioneering efforts of S. L. Pressey in 1926. He developed the original teaching machine. It was really a testing machine which presented a series of multiple-choice questions to the student, which he was to answer by pushing the proper key. The series of items would be repeated until the student answered correctly.

The techniques of *programmed learning* were developed by B. F. Skinner, the well-known psychologist whose contributions to psychology are discussed in detail in Chapter 5. Skinner used the teaching machine for original learning rather than just as a device for review and testing of material already learned. Basically, the contents of a course are broken down into a series of small steps, and require active responding by the student at each step. New terms or new ideas are introduced one at a time, or material that has been covered previously is reviewed. As soon as the student has made his response, he will be given immediate feedback or *knowledge of results*. This informs him whether he has responded correctly or not.

Figure 1–2 shows an excerpt from a programmed textbook in psychology. In this program, the student proceeds through the material responding to each question and looking at the correct answer. If the

FIGURE 1-2
A programmed textbook. Frames from a programmed psychology
textbook discussing topics from the chapter on learning. The
students fills in the blank in each frame and then looks at the
correct answer (on the next page). Then the student moves on to
the next frame after getting the correct answer. The obvious
advantages of a programmed learning technique are that it allows
each student to work at his own pace while providing immediate
feedback as to the correctness of his answer.

SENTENCE TO BE COMPLETED	WORD TO BE SUPPLIED
With reference to the influence of the temper tantrum on the mother's behavior, the tantrum is a negative (1) reinforc-____; its cessation is a negative (2) reinforc-____. 10-3	(1) (reinforc-)er (2) (reinforc-)ement
If temper tantrums have been previously conditioned, the mother can (1) ____ the response by consistently not (2) ____ it. 10-8	(1) extinguish (2) reinforcing
We call a man a golf "enthusiast" if he frequently ____ the operant behavior of playing golf. 10-13	emits
When a pigeon is reinforced for pecking a key, the (1) ____ at which the response is (2) ____ increases. 10-18	(1) rate (frequency) (2) emitted
There *is no* eliciting stimulus for ____ behavior. 10-23	operant
Most (1) ____ behavior involves the activity of smooth muscles and glands. Most (2) ____ behavior involves the activity of striated muscles. 10-28	(1) respondent (2) operant

From *The Analysis of Behavior* by James G. Holland and B. F. Skinner.
Copyright 1961, McGraw-Hill Book Company. Used with permission of
McGraw-Hill Book Company.

program is presented in a machine, the student may have to make the
response before the machine will move on to the next frame or question.
If the program is being presented by a computer, the student may sit at
a terminal in which the questions are typed out; he then types his
answer and the computer tells him in a printout whether he is right or
wrong. Or, the program may be presented on a type of television screen
on which the student indicates his answer with a pen.

The advantages of computer-assisted instruction are that it can optimize many of the necessary conditions for learning and allow the student to work at his own pace (Figure 1–3). The display boxes can catch and hold the attention of a student, in whom the novelty of the computer produces high levels of motivation. In addition, it provides for the prompt and immediate knowledge of results necessary for efficient learning. One drawback of computer instruction is that the use of a computer is expensive, in comparison to a teacher who oversees many students at a time (Seltzer, 1971).

FIGURE 1–3
Results of computer-assisted instruction. This table shows the results of an experiment in teaching arithmetic by computer-assisted instruction in a group of schools where achievement levels were below grade level. The pupils were given a standard test at the beginning of the school year; then some were taught by programmed instruction via the computer and others by standard teaching methods. When the pupils were tested again at the end of the year, those taught by the computer were found to have made significantly more improvement than those taught by the standard classroom methods.

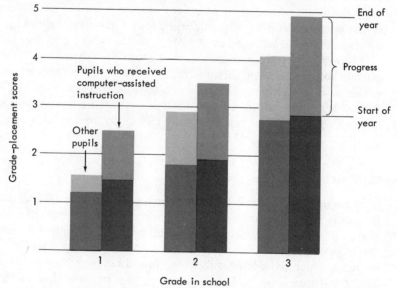

Source: After P. Suppes and M. Morningstar, in F. F. Korten, et al. (eds.), *Psychology and the Problems of Society* (Washington, D.C.: American Psychological Association, 1970), pp. 225–27. Copyright 1970 by the American Psychological Association. Reprinted by permission.

One study on computer instruction yielded some fascinating and unexpected results. A group of junior high school students from impoverished backgrounds in San Jose were taught by both programmed instruction and an actual teacher. After the experiment on the two types of instruction was finished, the children were asked to rate the computer and the teacher on such scales as warmth, fairness, and intelligence. To the surprise of the investigators, the computer was given superior ratings rather than the teacher on all these scales (Hess & Tenezakis, 1970). Apparently the children not only liked the computer better than the teacher but were attributing human properties to it. These findings are sobering, to say the least, in light of the fears expressed by many learned people that machines are becoming more like us, and humans are becoming more machinelike.

Psychological studies of social discord

The rapid changes, spurred on by technology and population, in our society and others have brought forth much social disharmony and protest. As we have already indicated, psychologists are in the vanguard of investigators who are studying the causes of social strife in an effort to find solutions as seen in an article on social unrest by Tiffany and Tiffany (1973). The civil rights movement of the 1960s, the Vietnam War, and the ensuing protests of college students have confronted psychology with the issue of social involvement versus scientific detachment. An example of this conflict are studies of social activism, "should psychologists take up the banner and champion the causes of various protestors or keep an objective detachment and study the social conflicts as important phenomena in themselves?" There is, of course, no right or wrong answer to such a theoretical question; it is a matter of different values. What we shall do at this point is to examine the findings of various studies on student activism and attempt to interpret its causes and goals.

The background of student activism

Students have played an important role as agents of social change for many years. Historians can point to the significant role that students played in 19th-century Europe in fostering social change and revolutionary action. Student action has clearly dominated Latin American universities which have commonly been shut down for long periods of time. This condition is so widespread that it can be said that the familiar clashes between the police and students have become institutionalized in many Latin American universities as well as in various other undeveloped nations. In the first half of this century, it appeared that activism would not be significant in the industrialized countries, and particularly not in the United States.

This state of affairs began to change rapidly beginning in the 1950s when student protest and sit-ins apparently reached their apex in the 1960s (Figure 1–4). Many interpretations have been given to account for the worldwide explosions of student protest that have made the headlines. Among the best known are the protests that rocked San Francisco, Berkeley, West Berlin, Tokyo, Madrid, Calcutta, Rio de Janeiro, and

FIGURE 1-4
Demonstrations on college campuses were common in the 1960s and early 1970s, as pictured here in this demonstration at the University of Santa Clara.

Courtesy of Paul Fry, *The Santa Clara*, University of Santa Clara

Cairo. Various psychologists, sociologists, and political scientists in dealing with different nations and university situations have suggested specific explanations relevant to the particular time and place.

From our current perspective, many of these explanations now seem to be somewhat simple and naïve although valid to some degree. Some people have suggested that student tension reflects a lack of participation in the affairs of the university and lack of power to determine the course of their own lives. Therefore, if students were given more power in the university structure, the potential for strong confrontation tactics would be reduced. Although this viewpoint undoubtedly has some validity, it cannot be the sole or even primary cause of activism. One needs only to look at some leading universities in the world and in the United States, in which students do have considerable power. Institutions such as the Free University of Berlin and many Latin American universities have been rocked by student protests. Co-government has not made the students more docile or more conciliatory in their demands.

Other authorities have attributed student protest to the large size of classes and the impersonality of huge universities such as those at Berkeley and Madison. Again, there is undeniably some truth to this thesis. On the other hand, a number of small, elite, private colleges have also been strongholds of political activism—i.e., Reed, Brandeis, and Chicago. Thus, it is apparent we must look for additional sources, such as characteristics of activists themselves, that contribute to student dissatisfaction as well as internal factors within the various institutions. Lipset (1970), who has done much research on student protest, stresses the role politics play in activism. Students are more responsive to political trends, and to opportunities for action than almost any other group in society, except possibly intellectuals. As a result, they become agents for social change and strife by effectively communicating their causes and ideologies to the general public.

Studies assessing the intellectual dispositions, personality characteristics, and value systems of young activists are being amassed by psychologists and sociologists. An intensive research effort was carried out by Block, Haan, and Smith (1969) that involved samples of students recruited from the University of California at Berkeley and from San Francisco State College, plus several groups of Peace Corps trainees. Activists, according to their definition, were those people concerned with the plight of their fellow beings and who worked to alleviate pain, poverty, and injustice. At the same time, they were disillusioned with the status quo and involved themselves in protest against policies and institutions that did not accord with their image of a just society.

Block, Haan, and Smith were particularly interested in the parent-child relationship of activists versus nonactivists. As perceived by their children, they found that parents of activists tended to emphasize independency, responsibility, and maturity at an early age; the activist's parents were similar to those of other parents in these child-rearing practices. However, the parents of activists diverged from other parents in de-emphasizing achievement and competition. As might be expected, the parents of activists were much lower in their demands for conformity, tending to encourage the individualization and independent judgment of the child. They were also perceived as being much more tolerant of the child's secrecy and privacy needs, and accepting of sexual curiosity. In general, the parents of activists stressed discipline less than other parents and were more interested in encouraging inner-directed goals and values as opposed to externally defined roles.

These results are consistent with those gained from studies of the parents themselves (Flacks, 1967; Schedler, 1966). Schedler found activists' parents to be more permissive and significantly more tolerant of unconventional behavior than were parents of nonactivists. Flacks, in his study, reported that parents of student activists strongly stressed self-expression in their children while de-emphasizing personal achievement, traditional morality, and conventional religiosity. In contrast, parents of nonactivists expressed the conventional middle-class American values on achievement, material success, sexual morality, and religion.

Closely paralleling the above quoted studies of the importance of parental child-rearing practices on student activism is the study by Zellman and Sears (1971) on the origin of tolerance for dissent. The results illustrate a close relationship between parental value systems and the behavior of the young. Most of the children expressed strong support for the abstract principle of free speech in slogan form. But, like their parents, they were less tolerant in concrete situations. Their support for free speech in these instances was dictated largely by the child's attitude toward the dissenting outgroup in question and only rarely by the general principle of free expression. Thus, general political attitudes and their implications for subsequent tolerance of free speech and participation in activism can be shown to originate early in life. They stem primarily from the child-rearing practices of parents and by families transmitting their own values.

CHARACTERISTICS OF ACTIVISTS. Much has been written about the personal characteristics of student activists. Too much of this work, however, has been largely anecdotal, journalistic, and devoid of facts. Baird (1970) conducted a large study on students in many diverse colleges. The data included information on students' interests, achievements, and personalities. Overall, there were 12,432 students from 31 institutions in the sample.

Compared to other students, both male and female activists described themselves as socially ascendant and capable; they rated themselves high on leadership, popularity, and aggressiveness. They also considered themselves to be very sociable and sensitive to the needs of others. These personal descriptions coincide with the fact that student activists gave higher values to becoming a community leader, playing an important role in public affairs, and to keeping more up to date politically than nonactivists. Their strong social orientation is also reflected in the high rating they gave to helping others in difficulty. Surprisingly, the activist students did not give significantly lower ratings to life goals we might expect them to reject. They did not differ from nonactivists on such values as being well off financially, making their parents proud of them, being successful in their own business, or following a formal religious code.

Two results of Baird's finding are in disagreement with the impressions of many writers. One of these findings concerns the social class backgrounds of youthful dissenters, who have often been described as affluent youth in revolt. To the contrary, student activists did not come from wealthier backgrounds than nonactivists; there were no differences. However, further analysis of their home life did show that their homes had provided more intellectual resources, and that they had a wider range of experiences.

The second finding, at variance with popular conception, involves the academic achievement of activists. In terms of achievement in classroom studies, they were not better students than nonactivists. However, they were talented in many other nonacademic areas. They had notably greater achievements in leadership, social service, humanities, and social science. For example, they held student offices, participated in voluntary on-campus and civic improvement projects, and thrived on independent study programs.

In summary, student activists in the Baird study were found to be both altruistic and strongly power motivated (desiring to be community leaders). Finally, they are more distinguished by their leadership abilities from nonactivists than by academic achievements or general alienation from society at large.

In looking at student activism it must be remembered that the vast majority of youths are not activists. For instance, in Baird's study only 2.7 percent of the men and 2.5 percent of the women were out and out activists. About a quarter of the students displayed moderate activism in which they were involved in a few activities. The remainder of the students had not engaged in any activist activities. In the 1970s, it appears that student activism is taking the form of participating in cultural institutions to bring about change rather than becoming involved in mass sit-ins and demonstrations. This can be seen by the number of students choosing law as a career or by the number of young people working within the major political parties.

Consumer psychology

In the past, psychologists interested in consumer behavior were employed by business firms or governmental agencies wanting to know the buying habits of the American public. It was the task of the psychologist to conduct studies to determine the needs, desires, and motives behind potential buyers. An example of this type of approach is the Shepherd-Bayton study (1951), for the U.S. Department of Agriculture. This study began by using six values which were obtained from the literature: comfort, orderliness, economy, pleasure, social approval, and recognition. From interviews, the investigators found that these values were closely associated with four attributes of men's suits which provided a means of attaining these goals: style, material, color, and fit. As expected, they also found differences between socioeconomic groups and their preferences for clothing.

A more recent experiment was undertaken by the Psychological Corporation, a consulting firm often commissioned by business firms to determine the effectiveness of advertising. They were hired by Union Carbide and Carbon to investigate the readership and comprehension of their newspaper advertising (Gilmer, 1971). Interviewers questioned 363 men and women on the Sunday and following Monday in which their advertisements appeared in the two local papers. Of those who reported having read the newspapers, 74 percent reported having seen the advertisement, and 40 percent of that group reported reading it. Of these latter cases, 84 percent were able to give at least one idea which showed a good understanding of the advertising. Thus, the company had good evidence that their advertising methods were indeed reaching the consumer.

SUBLIMINAL ADVERTISING. One of the most lively controversies in the area of advertising and consumerism has directly involved psychologists. The dispute concerns the use of *subliminal advertising,* the presentation of advertising material without the viewer's knowledge. For example, newspapers reported that a command to "Buy popcorn," or "Drink Coca-Cola," flashed on a movie screen so rapidly that the audience could not consciously see them led to a significant increase in the sale of these products. Such perceptions are called *subliminal* because they apparently take place below the level of our conscious perceptual thresholds. Adherents of this technique believed that in some manner, these advertisements stimulated an unconscious desire to purchase popcorn or Coca-Cola. These initial claims appear to be exaggerated, but public concern ran high because of the possibility that people's behavior might be influenced by subliminal messages displayed without their awareness.

Psychologists were called upon to investigate this phenomenon and have given subliminal stimulation careful scientific scrutiny. In one controlled study, two groups of subjects watched the same experimental film (Gilmer, 1970). While the film was being shown, the experimenter projected a slide on the movie screen for 0.01 second at 10 second intervals. For the experimental group, the slide showed a spoon of rice with the words "Wonder Rice," presented below it. For the control group, the slide contained lines that were arranged in a meaningless or jumbled fashion.

At the end of the film, all subjects were shown a picture of the spoon of rice without the name and asked if they had ever seen it before in an experiment. Interestingly enough, there were a few subjects in the control group, as well as in the experimental group, who said that they had seen it before. Next, all subjects were asked which of two brands (Wonder or Monarch) was more likely to be associated with the picture; both groups chose Monarch more often than Wonder. Previous subliminal exposure of the words "Wonder Rice" to the experimental subjects failed to have any effects at all on their association of this brand name with the picture. Thus, psychologists have cast strong doubts on the effectiveness of subliminal advertising. To the contrary, it would appear that the consumer would be fortunate, indeed, if most advertising was presented in this fashion; obnoxious commercial messages would then probably go undetected.

NEW TRENDS IN CONSUMERISM. As we have seen, psychologists have developed research methods to evaluate the effectiveness of advertising. These findings have primarily benefited leading industrial companies and business firms in trying to reach the consumer. With the emerging social concern of psychologists, research methods are being now used to help the consumer instead of just the advertiser. Psychologists are helping to lead this revolution among consumers over poor quality products and shoddy service, with the intent of forcing businessmen to revise their approach to consumer needs.

Pressure is being applied to industry at both the local and the national levels to stop making false advertising claims and to evaluate the quality of their products. Governmental agencies such as the Food and Drug Administration are increasingly being influenced by consumer groups to regulate the unethical manufacturer who feels no responsibilities to the public. Actually, there appears to be no sector of the buyer-seller relationship that is not embroiled with consumer complaints, ranging from excessive automobile repair charges to unwanted credit cards. Psychologists using their techniques may well discover more basic human wants by focusing on consumer complaints, possibly giving new ideas to well-established research on man's hierarchy of motives.

Vocational guidance

> Bruce B. had been a very good student throughout high school. He won a scholarship to a large university. However, his first year was a disaster and he was in danger of flunking out. The main problem was that he had no future vocation plans. Hence, all of his courses seemed irrelevant and he could not get interested in studying. His problem was complicated by the fact that his father, a leading physician, was strongly urging him to become a doctor.

This case history is introduced to illustrate another widespread problem within our society that psychologists are called upon to help solve. The choice of a vocation is one of the major decisions we have to make in our lives. When one considers that the average person will spend more than 40 years of his life working, the crucial significance of a vocational choice is immediately apparent. It is also generally true that people stay within the general field of work that they first enter upon completion of education. Thus, decisions you make in regard to initial vocational choice set the general direction your life will take. This does not mean that vocational decisions cannot be, or are not, changed. For example, with the decreasing employment opportunities taking place in the aerospace industry, many engineers have been forced to take up new careers, such as that of bartending or sales.

WHAT AM I GETTING INTO? The first problem concerning a choice of career involves knowing what any vocational field entails. What does an executive really do on the job? What are the actual demands made on lawyers? Is the job of being an airline steward/stewardess all that glamorous? Too often people blindly make a vocational choice without knowing anything about the requirements of the job. They may have been urged by their parents or a friend to strongly consider a certain career without having any intrinsic interests in that line of work.

> Many young women have a very faulty idea of what being an actress means and what the actual work entails. It is represented to them as romantic, exciting work filled with individual expression and adventure. Prestige and fame are particularly stressed and, indeed, there are a few girls who become prominent world figures. When a young lady examines the actual job requirements, however, she finds it may mean many long hours of memorizing lines or spending several weeks on a remote location without the usual conveniences of civiliza-

tion. Even more likely, an aspiring young actress may be without work for long periods of time since there are more would-be starlets than roles or parts available in the movies. Consequently, she may have to support herself by taking any part-time jobs offered to her. Even if she happens to be one of the few lucky ones to make it big, it does not necessarily guarantee a happy fulfilling life. Witness the sad personal case histories of Marilyn Monroe and Judy Garland, both of whom committed suicide.

Perhaps the best way to learn realistically about a job is to visit people who have taken it up as a career. If this isn't possible then one should make a strong effort to see a personnel psychologist or vocational counselors who make available various job descriptions. They can provide needed information on the following questions concerning many fields of work. What are the actual things I will do on the job? How will my general life-style be affected by this job? What are the benefits offered by the job? What are the opportunities for growth and advancement?

KNOW THYSELF. One of the concerns of the field of psychology is helping people to better understand themselves. Psychologists know that job dissatisfaction often leads to emotional problems manifested in depression, unhappiness, and anxiety. It can even cause physical difficulties such as the development of ulcers. Thus, the second problem in making a vocational choice is knowing yourself. The better you understand yourself, the more likely you are to select a vocation which will bring a feeling of fulfillment and satisfaction.

First, you should know what your abilities are. You should keep a record of your strengths and weaknesses and see if they are compatible with the vocation which you find interesting. There is no point in trying to pursue a career in medicine if you lack the ability to handle basic science courses. Second, know what your interests are. Your hobbies are often a good guide to your interests. The counseling centers in most leading colleges can also help you here. One of their services is to make available various psychological tests such as the *Strong Vocational Interest Blank* (SVIB). This is an inventory which compares the subject's interest patterns with those of persons engaged in various fields of work.

Summary

Psychology is the science which studies the behavior of man and other animals. It is a science because it seeks to discover facts which form the basis for establishing general principles that describe and predict events.

Reliance on the scientific approach avoids the many pitfalls of common sense (biases) through the use of three approaches: (1) Objectivity is characteristic of the scientist who attempts to check the human tendency (subjectivity) to see the desired rather than the real world. (2) Controlled observations through experiments and field studies are frequently used. (3) To be scientific, the precise use of language must be used to communicate our observations without ambiguity or vagueness.

Many contemporary psychologists have begun to stress the importance of using psychological knowledge to attack pressing social problems of our society. Several major areas are outlined in which psychologists have begun and must play an increasingly important role.

One particular area in which psychologists have become increasingly involved is in the population explosion which has psychological implications for birth control programs and increasing urban living. The term "megalopolis" has been coined to describe large cities which have engulfed masses of people. Although "super" cities have many advantages, the effects of overcrowding on human values and dignity raises many problems (identity conflicts, antagonistic behaviors, crime, and so on).

The development of technology, to the point in which it has the power to completely design man's environment, has great impact on our lives. For example, technology has been applied to education via computers (programmed learning) or computer-assisted instruction. While the results have been encouraging, many have expressed fears that we will become slaves to machines or that they will destroy our environment (insecticides and cars). Psychologists are giving serious considerations to these fears.

One of the areas in which psychology has been involved is that of social discord (civil rights movement, crime, and group protests). What are the goals and causes of social strife? The student protest movements of the 1960s provide a fascinating look at how psychology has provided some answers to this question.

Many explanations have been proposed for the student protests that rocked campuses throughout the United States (San Francisco State, Berkeley, Kent State, and so forth). Among these are lack of student power and participation in the affairs of the university, and large impersonal classes. Although these explanations hold some validity, they tend to be too simplistic. Some psychologists believe we also have to look at characteristics of the activists to adequately explain these protests.

In general, studies indicate that social activists (people concerned with the plight of their fellow beings) have different parent-child relationships than nonactivists. The former group perceive parents as emphasizing independence, responsibility, and maturity at an early age, while de-emphasizing achievement and competition. They were also much lower in their demand for conformity, stressed discipline less, and were much more tolerant of a child's privacy. Such practices seem to result in the activist seeing themselves as being socially ascendant, high in leadership, sociable and sensitive to others, and possessing a strong interest in working with people (social service, humanities, social science, and extracurricular civic endeavors). Student activists are not so much distinguished from nonactivists via academic achievements, socioeconomic status, or alienation from society, as much as they desire to enter leadership roles.

Consumer behavior is also another fascinating province of psychology.

Psychologists are often asked to determine the needs, desires, and motives behind potential buyers in order to facilitate the selling of products. One of the most controversial areas in advertising concerns the use of subliminal advertising; that is, the presentation of subconscious advertising material to the general public. The effects of subliminal messages seem greatly exaggerated. Nevertheless, psychologists need to be aware of the dangers inherent in unethical advertising.

Last, the problem of vocational choice is an important area of study. To make rational career choices, it is important that everyone (a) obtain a thorough and actual job description of the occupations they are considering, and (b) become aware of their strengths and limitations with respect to interests, abilities, and personality traits.

References

APA Task Force on Psychology. Population and family planning: Growing involvement of psychologists. *American Psychologist*, 1972, **27**, 27–30.

Baird, L. L. Who protests: A study of student activists. In J. Foster and K. Long (Eds.), *In Protest! Student activism in America*. New York: William Morrow, 1970, 123–133.

Block, J. H., Haan, N., & Smith, M. B. Socialization correlates of student activism. *Journal of Social Issues*, 1969, **24**, 143–177.

Buckhout, R. Toward a two-child norm: Changing family planning attitudes. *American Psychologist*, 1972, **27**, 16–26.

Eisner, T. Population control, sterilization and ignorance. *Science*, 1970, **167**, 337.

Ellison, H. *I Have No Mouth, and I Must Scream*. Berkeley, Calif.: Galaxy Publishing Co., 1967.

Festinger, L., Riecken, H. W., & Schachter, S. *When prophesy fails*. Minneapolis: University of Minnesota Press, 1956.

Flacks, R. The liberated generation: An exploration of the roots of student protest. *Journal of Social Issues*, **23**, 1967, 52–75.

Frejka, T. United States: The implication of zero population growth. *Studies in Family Planning*, 1970, **60**, 1–4.

Gilmer, H. V. B. *Psychology*. New York: Harper & Row, 1970.

Gilmer, H. V. B. *Industrial and organizational psychology*, New York: McGraw-Hill, 1971.

Hess, R. D., & Tenezakis, M. Guess what (who?) is most believable. Reported in the *Stanford Observer*, 1970, **4**(8), 11.

Johnson, R. N. *Aggression in man and animals*. Philadelphia: W. B. Saunders, 1972.

Landers, R. R. The good life. In R. R. Landers, *Man's place in the Dybosphere*. Englewood Cliffs, N.J.: Prentice-Hall, 1966.

Lipset, S. M. American student activism in comparative perspective. *American Psychologist*, 1970, **25**, 675–693.

Miller, G. A. Psychology as a means of promoting human welfare. *American Psychologist*, 1969, **24**, 1063–1075.

Montessori, Maria. *The Montessori method*. Cambridge, Mass.: Robert Bentley, 1964.

Sanford, F. H., & Wrightsman, L. S. *Psychology: A scientific study of man*. Belmont, Calif.: Brooks/Cole Publishing Co., 1970.

Schedler, P. Parental attitudes and political activism of college students. Unpublished master's thesis, University of Chicago, 1966.

Seltzer, R. A. Computer-assisted instruction —What it can and cannot do. *American Psychologist*, 1971, **26**, 373–377.

Shepherd, J. A., & Bayton, J. A. Men's preferences among wool suits, coats and jackets. *Agricultural Information Bulletin*, No. 64 Washington, D.C.: U.S. Department of Agriculture, 1951.

Tiffany, D. W., & Tiffany, P. G. Social unrest: Powerlessness and/or self direction? *American Psychologist*, 1973, **28**, 151–154.

Van Cott, H. P., & Spector, P. The human engineer as an agent of change in industrializing nations. *Human Factors*, 1968, **10**, 641–648.

Viel, B. The social consequences of population growth. In W. Jackson (Ed.), *Man and the environment*. Dubuque, Iowa: W. C. Brown, 1971.

Walker, E. I. Experimental psychology and social responsibility. *American Psychologist*, 1969, **24**, 862–868.

Wilbur, H. B. Object system of instruction. *American Journal of Education*, 1865, **15**, 189–208.

Zellman, G. C., & Sears, D. O. Childhood origins of tolerance for dissent. *Journal of Social Issues*, 1971, **26**, 109–136.

SECTION TWO

Biological aspects of behavior

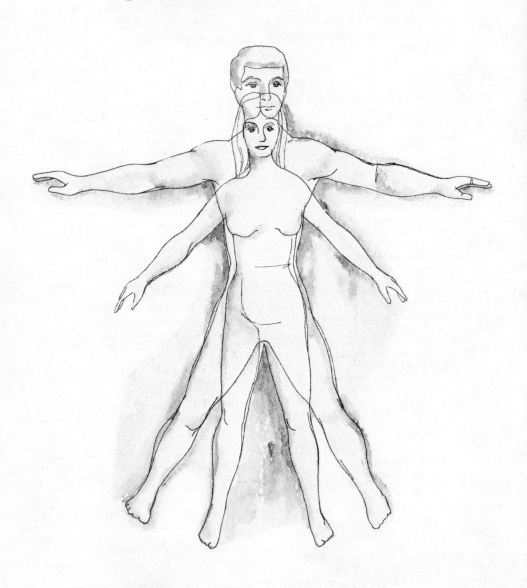

Many of you will be surprised to find a section of this book devoted to the biological aspects of behavior. After all, you may ask, aren't we taking a course in psychology? Why should we study a topic in the biological sciences? To answer, let us use an example.

Many Americans are very concerned about the energy crisis because of the widespread implications it has for the production of heating oil and gas. Recognizing that Americans now demand that their cars obtain maximum utilization of fuel, car manufacturers are increasingly producing compact or economy cars. Likewise, we have begun to think of ways to increase our gas mileage: getting a tuneup, driving slower, and driving at a constant speed. Indeed, the energy crisis has made many Americans more conscious of how their cars operate.

Like cars, our bodies can operate without any understanding of what goes on under the "hood." However, the more familiar we are with the engine, transmission, brakes, and accessories, the better we can understand the limitations of our car, care for it, and extend its efficiency. Likewise, knowledge of our body's internal and external characteristics gives us understanding of how we behave. Although the car analogy is an oversimplification, we study biology because it is impossible to understand man's behavior and mental processes without a thorough knowledge of his biological makeup. Man is a product not only of his environment, but also his biological equipment. Like a car which cannot go faster than it was designed to go, we cannot rise above our biological limitations—the kinds of muscles, glands, and nervous system which we have inherited.

For example, all of us are born with different sizes, colors, shapes, and abilities. What impact does this have on us? Chapter 14 suggests the possibility that biological differences between men and women have contributed to the development of traditional sex roles. Chapter 7 discusses a controversial issue dealing with heredity, intelligence, and race. Studies of behavior pathology presented in Chapter 9 suggest that many abnormal behaviors may be due to defective biological equipment.

In addition, the study of the nervous system and its functions has produced invaluable data with broad implications. We now know that our emotions are partially regulated by hormones secreted by certain glands. Pleasure and pain centers have been identified in the brain which can be used as a means of psychotherapy. Biofeedback studies indicate that man can consciously control respiration, acid secretions of the gastrointestinal tract, heart rate, and many other biological functions. The implications for treating ulcers, migraine headaches, and hypertension are fascinating. Studies dealing with the biochemical bases of learning and memory may lead to maximized learning.

As you read this text we hope that you will constantly relate what you have learned in this chapter to the rest of the book.

2

Biological foundations of behavior

In order to truly understand ourselves and our behavioral potentialities, it will be necessary to recognize our biological connection with all other forms of life. Are we something special in the animal kingdom—"just a little bit lower than the angels"—or are we just another ape? While we can never answer philosophical questions such as these, we can, however, determine in what ways we are similar and different from all other organisms. Success in understanding our ascent from lower animals will provide us with greater ability to understand the mechanisms of our bodies.

Our goal in this chapter is to understand the individual within a biological perspective. We naturally view man as a rather special creature—with undeniable justification. However, man's achievements are accomplished by means of a nervous system and body which are in continuity with the rest of the animal kingdom. Consider this! What would happen if you were to receive extensive brain damage as a result of an accident? Needless to say, your life would change drastically, which illustrates in dramatic fashion the underlying role of the nervous system in all behavior.

Modern psychologists now believe that all mental processes have a physiological basis. Accordingly, physiological-response "machinery" of the human body consists of the sense organs (receptors), the nervous system (connectors), and the muscles and glands (effectors).

The cell

The fundamental structural unit of all living organisms is what is called the *cell*. The three principal parts of the cell (Figure 2–1) are the membrane, the cytoplasm, and the nucleus. Each of these elements carries on the metabolic activities which are necessary for the life of the cell as a whole.

The single cell of original life had to perform all of the metabolic and behavioral acts necessary for life. Eventually these cells grouped together and later began to specialize according to structure and function. Groups of cells began to lose their general, nondifferential functions and develop highly specialized ones.

In man, the life of an individual cell greatly depends upon the functions carried out by a tremendously large number of cells elsewhere in the body. Every other cell in the body dies if such cells, which comprise the lungs, heart, kidneys, and nervous system, fail to carry out their vital functions.

Psychologists are especially interested in those cells which through differentiation and specialization came to constitute the physiological response machinery of all higher organisms.

FIGURE 2–1
Diagram of a cell

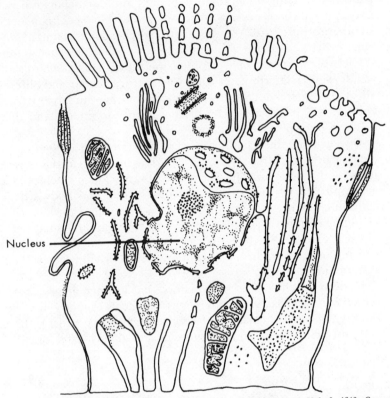

Nucleus

Source: *McGraw-Hill Encyclopedia of Science and Technology*, Vol. 2, 1960. Copyright 1960 McGraw-Hill Book Company. Used with permission of McGraw-Hill Book Company.

The receptors

The receptor cells are specialized to respond to physical energy such as heat, light, mechanical, and chemical stimuli. The heat or thermal receptors are located in the skin. Mechanical receptors are involved in hearing, balance, movement, and touch. The chemical receptors are responsible for taste and smell while light receptors function in the eye. In addition, the receptors for pain respond to a wide variety of thermal, mechanical, and chemical stimuli.

In the receptor cells, physical energy is transformed into electrical activity. This has tremendous implications for us. The brain actually receives changes in the electrochemical activity of millions of single cells, conveyed to it through neural pathways, which it transforms into sensations. One very important area of current research is directed toward understanding the relationship between these physical energy changes and the resulting changes in the activities of single receptor cells.

The effectors

The effectors consist of muscles and glands enabling us to react to our environment. In fact, behavior (what an organism is observed to be doing) consists of the actions of muscles and glands. Physical tasks are accomplished by contractions of various sets of muscles; fear involves excessive secretions of the sweat and other glands; and tears are the secretions of the tear glands. Common behavior is composed of these basic physiological processes organized into complex patterns.

Muscles

Movements such as calisthenics, walking, lifting a suitcase, or driving a car are alike in one important way. They all result from contractions of *skeletal muscles*. Skeletal muscles are made of living cells that function in the same way: they contract (meaning they tighten up and get shorter), and then relax again. There are nearly 700 skeletal muscles in the human body, named by virtue of the fact that they are attached to the bones of the skeleton by tendons.

Smooth muscles constitute a second group of muscles in the body, and are found especially in the lining of soft internal organs and the walls of the blood vessels. One common example which illustrates the operation of smooth muscles is the pupil reflex. The size of the pupil of the eye is controlled by the actions of the smooth muscles that make up the iris. Among other examples, too many to enumerate, are the wave-like contractions of smooth muscles in the lining of the esophagus which push food along to the stomach. Unlike skeletal muscles, we have little or no control over their functioning; in addition, most of these movements are not visible.

Endocrine glands

Among the important determinants of behavior are the endocrine glands. They are also known as ductless glands, as depicted in Figure 2–2, because they secrete small amounts of chemical substances known as *hormones* directly into the bloodstream or lymph system, instead of ducts. The hormones trigger and control many kinds of bodily activities and behavior, including that of playing a crucial role in maintaining the constancy of our internal environment. For instance, our lives would cease if the amount of water, oxygen, or the degree of temperature and chemical balance of our bodies were not kept within certain limits.

Of particular interest to psychologists is the role the endocrine glands play in regulating behavior in times of emergency. When we are threatened by danger, they rapidly secrete hormones that make the heart beat faster, raise the blood pressure, lift the blood sugar level, and in many other ways prepare us for immediate and drastic action. These internal

FIGURE 2–2
Location of endocrine glands

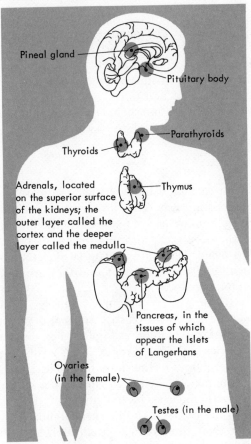

Pineal gland

Pituitary body

Parathyroids

Thyroids

Adrenals, located on the superior surface of the kidneys; the outer layer called the cortex and the deeper layer called the medulla

Thymus

Pancreas, in the tissues of which appear the Islets of Langerhans

Ovaries (in the female)

Testes (in the male)

changes are closely related to the emotions of fear and anger. People have been known to perform extraordinary feats of physical activity when the endocrine system is working at top speed.

The pituitary gland, about the size of a kernel of corn, is of particular importance because it not only secretes hormones which act directly on many parts of the body, but it secretes hormones which affect the activities of other endocrine glands. Thus, it is known as the master gland.

In the early years, the pituitary secretes a hormone that regulates growth. As is illustrated in Figure 2–3, if the gland produces too much of this hormone the child will grow into a giant, while too little of the hormones causes the child to become a dwarf. At the time of puberty, the pituitary begins to secrete another hormone which activates the sex glands, or gonads, which changes the child into a physically mature man or woman.

FIGURE 2–3
The results of overactivity or underactivity of the pituitary gland are dramatically illustrated in this photograph of a giant and a dwarf.

Another gland which plays an important role is the thyroid gland. In general, it controls the metabolic process, thereby influencing the general level of bodily activity. People with an underactive thyroid gland tend to be placid, tire easily, are often sleepy, and have little "get up and go." In addition, they often gain weight and become fat and "lazy."

People suffering from an overactive thyroid gland present a marked contrast in their behavior patterns. They tend to be excitable, overactive, and often lose weight. Their "nerves are on edge" and they have trouble sleeping. By being either under- or overactive, this small but important gland causes tremendous and important changes in behavior.

The nervous system

Any behavioral act such as walking or talking is made possible by the activities of many effector mechanisms. However, none of these mechanisms would operate without the nervous system, which literally connects the effectors with the sources of stimulation. Unlike one-celled animals that can respond to stimulation without a nervous system, we would be completely helpless without one.

All of the more complicated animals possess specialized nerve cells that convey messages from one part of the body to another. Even the lowly jellyfish has a primitive nervous system known as a *nerve net*. It is simply a network of nerves functioning somewhat independently of one another and located in different parts of the body without any particular central point. Animals higher up on the evolutionary scale possess more complex nervous systems. Especially important is the development of a central nervous system: the brain and spinal cord. It is man's brain that has made him the dominant organism on earth and is responsible for all mental events such as ideas, images, and sensations.

The nerve cell

Before we can discuss the brain and other parts of the nervous system, it is necessary to examine in detail its basic unit, the *neuron* or nerve cell. You will notice in Figure 2–4 that the neuron has three parts: the dendrites, cell body, and axon.

The neuron's *cell body* is responsible for maintaining the metabolism of the cell necessary for life. Most conspicuous in the differentiation of the nerve cell are the two kinds of fibers, the *dendrites* and the *axon*.

The dendrites and axons have their separate features and are different in two main ways. (1) The dendrites are to be found in positions where they can be excited by environmental stimuli or by activities of other cells. Therefore, the dendrite is the "receiving" end of the neuron. The axon, on the other hand, is connected to effectors or to other neurons to which it sends the "nervous impulse" it carries. The area of contact be-

FIGURE 2-4
Diagram of the parts of a neuron

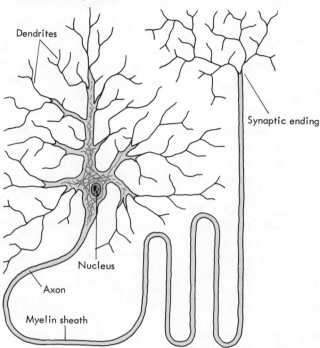

tween the axon of one neuron and the dendrite of another is called the *synapse*. It is the point where neural impulses are transmitted from the axon of one neuron to the dendrite of another. (2) A neuron usually has several dendrites, branching much like a tree, while it has only one axon.

The main function of the neurons is to transmit a *neural impulse* which is both electrical and chemical in nature. Neural impulses underlie all behavior and the neurons are constantly firing, sending, and receiving messages set off by different stimuli from the beginning of life until death. Actually, neural activity as it is transmitted from a neuron to a neighboring one is organized by the structure of our nervous system. Of necessity, neural impulses are transmitted along *pathways* dictated by the location and distribution of individual neurons. Each neuron runs alongside many other neurons, the whole collection forming a *nerve*. In a similar way, telephone wires are bound together forming a cable.

The human brain

The nervous system has many divisions; the main one is the brain and spinal cord, called the central nervous system (CNS). In principle, the nervous system is simple but actually it is very complex. It looks like a hollow tube which has some bulges in it, constituting the brain, and some tiny branches growing out of it (nerves), making up the *peripheral nervous system.*

The human brain, itself, consists of approximately 14 billion nerve cells woven together into an incredibly complex pattern. The nervous cells are so tightly packed together that one cell is probably never active without influencing some of its neighboring cells. The activity patterns of the brain may involve many different combinations of individual neurons.

The brain does not operate independently of other parts of the body. Such essentials as food and oxygen are necessary to keep it functioning normally. For example, interruption of the blood supply for a few seconds will stop brain activity and can cause a person to faint. In addition, one cannot go longer than five minutes without oxygen before permanent brain damage normally occurs.

The brain has three major subdivisions: the *hindbrain*, the *midbrain*, and the *forebrain*. They are "bumps" on the "hollow tube" which constitutes the nervous system. The human brain is shown in Figure 2–5.

THE HINDBRAIN. The three major parts within the hindbrain are the medulla, cerebellum, and pons. Actually there is no clear separation between the spinal cord and the brain since they are woven together.

FIGURE 2–5
Diagram of major parts of the human brain

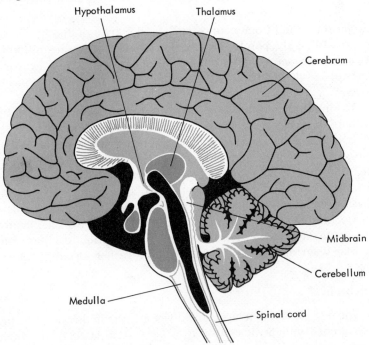

The spinal cord, which conducts neural impulses to and from the brain and mediates certain reflexes, enters into the *medulla*. The medulla, besides being a connecting tract for nervous impulses to and from the brain, regulates many important physiological functions. It is known as the vital center because it regulates breathing, heartbeat, and blood pressure. Damage to this part of the hindbrain causes death.

The *cerebellum* controls body posture, coordinates body movements and equilibrium. Even slight damage to the human cerebellum from injury or disease can seriously interfere with motor activities requiring coordination, such as walking. The cerebellum reaches its greatest size, in proportion to other areas of the brain, in birds. Apparently, from an evolutionary viewpoint, it developed its great size in birds because flying activities are so dependent on excellent coordination.

The *pons* is a group of nerve fibers which connects the two sides of the cerebellum together and also transmits impulses upwards and downwards within the central nervous system. Recent evidence indicates that the pons also helps regulate breathing and is responsible in part for the rapid eye movements that take place while dreaming (Kleitman, 1964).

THE MIDBRAIN. The midbrain contains tracts which connect the cerebral cortex with lower structures in the brain known as the brain stem. It also contains "primitive" centers, a collection of neurons, for visual and hearing functions. These are primitive in the sense that there are higher centers in the cerebral cortex which are very important for these vital sensory functions. Although they play a larger role in controlling visual and hearing functions for lower organisms than for humans, they do help our eyes to follow a moving target.

THE FOREBRAIN. The forebrain can be divided into three main parts: the thalamus, the limbic system, and the cerebrum.

The *thalamus* is the brain's major relay station, connecting the cerebrum with the lower structures of the brain and spinal cord. Also, nervous impulses that originate in the senses arrive eventually at the thalamus and from there are sent on to the cerebrum. Disruption of the operations of the thalamus stops impulses such as various sounds and lights, carried by the nerves of the body, from reaching consciousness.

The *limbic system* is a complex organization of neural structures and pathways involved in such complex psychological phenomena as motivation and emotion. It is sometimes called the *visceral brain* because it also regulates the functioning of internal organs such as the heart and stomach.

The term was first used by Broca in 1878 to designate the old cortex, the first part of the cortex to evolve in lower organisms, which surrounds the upper portions of the brain stem. It presents a common denominator of brain tissue of all the mammals. Figure 2–6 shows the area of the brain which is called the limbic system in the rabbit, cat, and monkey. The farther up the phylogenetic scale we move, the smaller the size of brain tissue in the limbic system when compared to the neocortex. The neo-

FIGURE 2-6
Diagram of the limbic system and its major parts

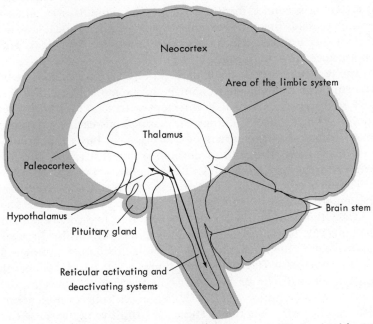

Source: Edward J. Murray, *Motivation and Emotion,* © 1964. Reprinted by permission of Prentice-Hall, Inc., Englewood Cliffs, N.J.

cortex is the last part of the brain to evolve and is distinct from the old cortex because of the number of layers of cell bodies it has.

In research with lower animals, electrical stimulation of certain areas in the limbic system excites rage. Stimulation of other areas seems to produce pleasure. For instance, Olds (1960) found that animals will cross a painfully charged electric grid in order to receive stimulation of the pleasure areas in the limbic system. In fact, they seem more willing to endure a greater amount of pain in order to electrically stimulate their brain than they will to reach food when hungry. In man, lesions (injuries) to various sections of the limbic system can produce many dramatic symptoms as *hallucinations* (false sensory impressions), epilepticlike seizures, and disordered memory. We also know it plays a large role in our emotions, as is also true of lower animals.

One particular part of the limbic system that deserves special attention because of its important functions is the *hypothalamus*. It is located at the base of the cerebrum below the thalamus and is the size of a lump of sugar. The hypothalamus controls our sleep-waking cycles, heart action, and digestion as well as other vital processes. It also acts as a control center for hunger, thirst, sex, and body temperature.

The *cerebrum* is divided into two halves, the left and right cerebral hemispheres. These two hemispheres are connected by a large tract of fibers, the *corpus callosum*. The whole outer surface of the cerebrum (called the *cerebral cortex*) is covered mainly by the cell bodies of neurons which form a gray mantle ⅛ to ¼-inch thick. The cortex is corrugated into a complex pattern of convolutions giving it a wrinkled appearance. The pattern's complexity varies in mammals from species to species. It is very striking in monkeys and apes, and particularly so in man. This portion of the brain is so important in behavior that it will be discussed later in detail.

Beneath the cortex lies the remainder of the cerebrum, consisting mainly of white nerve fibers. These subcortical cells in the cerebral hemispheres connect various parts of the nervous system together. Some connect areas of the separate hemispheres while still others connect the cerebral cortex with some of the lower centers in the brain stem, or spinal cord.

The cerebral cortex in man

The two large hemispheres at the top of the human brain represent man's new brain, as illustrated in Figure 2–7. It is the cerebral cortex more than any other part of the brain that distinguishes man from lower animals. The fact that it is so large and highly developed has resulted in what we consider distinctively human behavior. All complex psychological activities take place inside the cerebral cortex.

The evolutionary development of the cortex can be readily seen when comparing different species of animals. The cortex in mammals has undergone great development compared with birds or other lower animals, and in man it constitutes about one-half the weight of the entire

FIGURE 2–7
Top view of the cerebral cortex and its
two hemispheres

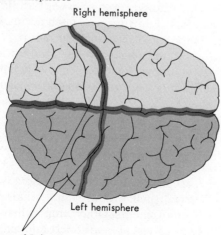

Right hemisphere

Left hemisphere

Fissure of Rolando

nervous system. It has expanded so greatly in man that it appears to have folded over inside the skull giving it the appearance of convolutions or wrinkles.

Certain convolutions serve as landmarks in describing areas of the *cerebral hemispheres.* The two hemispheres are symmetrical and, in general, functions of the left side of the body are controlled by the right hemisphere while the left hemisphere controls the right side. Each hemisphere is divided into four parts or *lobes* which have different functions: the *frontal, parietal, occipital,* and *temporal* lobes. The landmarks dividing these lobes are shown in Figure 2–8. The *fissure of*

FIGURE 2–8
Fissures and lobes of the cerebral cortex

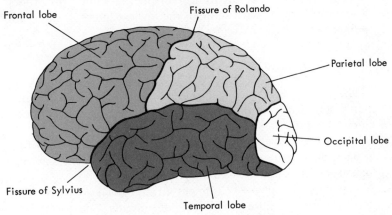

Rolando, or *central fissure,* runs almost vertically, dividing the frontal lobe from the parietal. The increased development of the cortex of man as compared with lower animals is particularly evident in the development of the frontal lobes. For example, even allowing for differences in the sizes of the brains, man has eight times as much cortex in this forward part of his brain as has the cat. A second major fissure is the *fissure of Sylvius,* or *lateral fissure.* It runs diagonally, separating the temporal lobe below it from the frontal and parietal lobes above it. The occipital lobe lies at the back of each hemisphere and is not clearly demarked.

Functions of the cerebral cortex

Our clearest knowledge of the cortex has to do with psychological functions that are related to specific areas of the brain. These are known as *localized functions* which are mapped on the cortex. Some areas of the cortex when stimulated electrically will produce different kinds of *motor responses* such as arm or leg movements. Other areas when stimulated will yield *sensory effects* such as visual, auditory, or touch sensations and are known as *sensory projection areas*. Still other areas are involved in speech or other complex mental activities (*association areas*).

THE MOTOR AREA. An area of special importance in producing muscle movements lies immediately in front of the central fissure. It is known as the executive area for muscle movements since it controls all movements of the body. When it is stimulated electrically different parts of the body will move, and if these different areas of the motor cortex are damaged, the same parts of the body will be paralyzed. Movements on the right side of the body originate through stimulation of the motor area of the left hemisphere, movements on the left side through stimulation of the right hemisphere.

SENSORY PROJECTION AREAS. When we see a light or hear a sound, the first thing that happens in the cortex is that a large neural impulse arrives via neural pathways from the sense organs; these particular places in the brain are known as sensory projection areas. The *visual area* is located in the occipital lobes. Whenever we see a pretty girl or bright colors, these visual impressions from the eyes are relayed to this particular area by way of the thalamus. Direct electrical stimulation or a blow on the head at the location of the occipital lobes can cause visual sensations such as flashes of light or "stars." If this area should be badly damaged, blindness results.

The *auditory center* is located in the temporal lobes. All auditory sensations are conveyed to this part of the cortex, by neural pathways via the thalamus, from the ears. There is some spatial distribution in that the part sensitive to high tones is distinct from the one sensitive to low tones. In the auditory areas, both ears are totally represented on both sides, so that the loss of one temporal lobe has very little effect upon hearing.

The other major sense organs also have sensory projection areas within the cortex. The parietal lobe serves as that part of the brain responsible for touch and taste. A person who suffers an injury to an area situated right behind the central fissure may lose the ability to tell the positions of his arms or hands when his eyes are closed or to recognize objects by touch. Other parts of the parietal lobe yield sensations of taste upon stimulation although other areas such as the underside of the brain near the temporal lobe also seems to be involved.

Finally, the sense of smell has its primary projection center in the temporal lobe. When excited by stimuli such as onions or perfume, nerve pathways carry these neural impulses back to an area of the cortex distinct from the auditory area.

THE ASSOCIATION AREAS. In terms of function, some areas of the cortex when stimulated yield sensations; other areas produce movement. However, three fourths of the human cortex does not cause sensation or movement when stimulated. Thus, these areas have become known as the silent or association areas. When biologists removed these areas from animals, studies have shown that they could still see, hear, and move about actively. Removal of these areas, at first, seemed to have little effect on the animal's behavior. But it is now clear that these areas of the brain play a vital role in such high-level mental functions as learning, memory, and thought.

The human cortex has two main association areas which are much larger than in lower organisms: the frontal and POT (parietal, occipital, and temporal) association areas.

Frontal lobe association areas. Interest in the frontal association area, located in front of the motor area, was first aroused in 1848, in the celebrated case of Phineas P. Gage (Harlow, 1848).

> Phineas P. Gage was injured on September 13, 1848 when a tamping iron was blown through the frontal region of his brain. Prior to the accident, he was considered an efficient and capable foreman. However, his personality underwent such a radical change that friends and acquaintances no longer recognized him. He would indulge in the grossest profanity, and exhibited impulsivity, obstinancy and vascillation. He would devise many plans for future implementation but would abandon them without apparent reason. In addition, he was fitful, irreverant, and manifested little deference to friends.

This interesting case is one of the earliest reports of mental change as a result of damage to the frontal association areas. More recently, based on preliminary results of experiments with chimpanzees, an operation called the frontal lobotomy was developed in the 1930s. This operation involves severing most of the neural connections between the frontal association areas and the rest of the brain. It has been used chiefly to relieve anxiety and depression in certain types of human mental illnesses. However, a debate, reminiscent of the movie *A Clockwork Orange* and the book *One Flew over the Cuckoo's Nest* (Kesey, 1962), has been raging over the use of psychosurgery, and other medical methods to control violent persons in prison (Chorover, 1974; Holden, 1973; Science News, 1972a) and mental illness.

Although there have been more than 65,000 frontal lobotomies performed, the results are not encouraging. While doctors have reported considerable improvement in some mentally ill patients and violent inmates, other patients and violent-prone prisoners have not been helped by this operation. As a consequence of these mixed findings we still have no coherent picture of the functions of the frontal association areas.

Some investigations have noted that among the subtle changes in a person's thinking that often appear with a frontal lobotomy is a lack of concern for the immediate or distant future. For instance, some lobotomized patients are unable to even plan their daily activities. However, this lack of planning or foresight does not always appear in patients who have undergone a frontal lobotomy.

POT association area. The other large association area of the cortex includes parts of the parietal, occipital, and temporal lobes that do not cause either movement or sensation when stimulated in a conscious human patient. We do not know the exact functions of the POT association area but certain types of behavior changes do occur after damage to it.

A somewhat humorous case history of a British soldier wounded during World War II (as reported in Kimble, 1963) illustrates well what can happen after damage to the POT association area (parietal area):

> Since doctors could find little or nothing wrong with his bodily senses after his wound had healed, the soldier was discharged from the hospital as cured. Shortly thereafter, he paid a visit to his girlfriend and her mother. While seated on the sofa with his girl, the soldier casually placed his arm around the girl while continuing to converse with the mother. Some time into the conversation, both the girl and mother became increasingly embarrassed and angry. Finally, the young man was ordered from the house for "taking liberties" with the girl in plain view of the mother. Doctors soon realized that the young man had lost the ability to *recognize* familiar objects by their feel. He was simply unaware of what his hands were doing.

If a person suffers damage to the association area near the occipital lobe, the individual can still "see" objects but cannot recognize them. He is not blind but cannot recognize previously familiar or simple objects; they appear not to have any meaning to the victim. This inability to recognize familiar objects is called visual *agnosia* and may include any of the sensory modalities depending on the exact location of the injury, as evidenced in the case history above.

Another example of this type of defect is the case of a 49-year-old nurse, as reported by Neilson (1946) in his book, *Agnosia, Apraxia, Aphasia*. She suffered damage to the POT association area as the result of a brain infection:

> Results of her brain infection revealed some astounding changes in perception and memory. This came to light one day when she commented about how strange it was that nurses had begun to wear black instead of white uniforms. When asked to read letters, she claimed that she could not see them even when they were written two and one half inches high. However, she could identify the letters if allowed to trace them with her finger. Her ability to trace them proved that she could see. When shown a bunch of keys, she could not say what they were until they were shaken. She was also unable to recognize an orange until she was allowed to smell it.

Agnosia involves more complex psychological processes than pure sensation involving the primary projection areas in the cortex. Thus, as these case histories illustrate, the POT association area is involved in memory, perception, and other complex mental processes.

A second type of behavioral impairment related to damage to this association area are *aphasias*. The major symptom of aphasia is loss of speech, but the term also refers to any disturbances caused by brain damage affecting thought processes involving language. The patient is labeled according to the area of language most affected—speech, comprehension of oral speech, reading, or writing. However, "pure" forms of aphasia, involving just one defect, almost never exist.

It is important to note that aphasics can move their lips, tongue, and vocal cords in a normal manner; there is no actual muscular paralysis of the speech organs. Instead, their difficulty is that they cannot seem to remember how to talk. Sometimes aphasics can recover, but usually only after a long relearning process.

SPLIT BRAIN: TWO DIFFERENT ME's? The cerebral cortex, as already indicated, has two halves or hemispheres connected together by tissue called the corpus callosum. Ordinarily, these two halves function as one organ. Although each hemisphere is mainly associated with one side of the body, the right brain presiding over the left side and the left brain over the right side, their influence is not always restricted in this way. If an area in one hemisphere is damaged, the corresponding area in the other often takes over its work and controls the functions involved for both sides of the body.

Recently, much interest has occurred as to what purpose the corpus callosum serves. As a result, a new type of operation has been developed known as *split-brain preparations*. The hemispheres of different animals are separated at the level of the corpus callosum by cutting through the structure. These experiments usually involve not only cutting the corpus callosum but also a structure called the *optic chiasm*, in which half the nerve fibers from each eye cross over to the brain hemisphere on the opposite side of the head. The effect of this combined operation is to leave each eye feeding its messages solely to the hemisphere on the same side of the head (Sperry, 1968).

Monkeys, after this operation, have then been trained to solve a problem presented only to one eye while the other eye was covered. The problem, for example, might consist of making a discrimination between a square and a circle. If the animal responded to the correct form, it received a reward of food. After it had learned to make the correct choice with one hemisphere, the problem was then presented to the other eye and hemisphere, the first eye now covered with a patch.

The results proved to be very exciting. When the animal used the second eye, it reacted as if it had never been faced with the problem before. In other words, the transfer of learning and memory from one hemisphere to the other did not take place in these animals with the corpus callosum cut, unlike normal subjects. Each hemisphere, and its associated eye, was independent of the other.

This was demonstrated even more strikingly when the two hemispheres were trained to make opposite choices; for one eye, the square was the correct solution, while for the opposite eye and hemisphere, the circle was correct. This reversed training through the separate eyes gave rise to no sign of interference or conflict, as it does in an animal with a corpus callosum intact.

In short, it appears that the corpus callosum has the important function of allowing the two hemispheres to share learning and memory. Furthermore, bisection of the brain leaves each hemisphere virtually undisturbed. Each retains its full set of cerebral control centers and the potentiality for performing nearly all the functions of a whole brain. These results apparently are also true for man as evidenced from cases in which patients have had to have the corpus callosum removed for medical reasons.

One case has been reported of a 49-year-old man whose corpus callosum had to be cut for medical reasons; some rather strange results occurred (Sperry, 1967).

> It appeared on the surface that the man's personality, intelligence, and general behavior were unaffected by severing the corpus callosum. However, psychological tests indicated in many ways that the man seemed to possess two separate and independent brains. Whenever motor tasks were performed by his left hand, which is controlled by the right hemisphere, he was unable to recall what he had done. The dominant left hemisphere had no memory for the activities of the right one. This was also supported by the fact that when touched on one side of the body, the other side was unable to locate the touched spot.

Even stranger in cases of hemisphere disconnection, some people apparently were able to learn two different tasks simultaneously (Gazzaniga, Bogen, & Sperry, 1965). These patients, as in the above case, were behaving as if they had two consciousnesses or minds, in which two different processes of thinking were taking place.

Peripheral nervous system

The term peripheral means "outlying," and the peripheral nervous system includes all the nerve cells and nerve fibers that lie outside the central nervous system. As previously stated, the central nervous system is composed of the brain and spinal cord.

The peripheral nervous system serves primarily to conduct impulses to and from the central nervous system; the fibers conducting these impulses are the sensory and motor neurons. The sensory fibers run from receptors into the central nervous system; the motor fibers run out from the central nervous system to excite muscles and glands. Some of these fibers are quite long. For example, the nerve fibers extending from the spinal cord to the toe may be 4 feet long.

While the neurons of the peripheral nervous system have been identified as sensory or motor in function, they also have been identified on the basis of location. Twelve pairs of nerves connect directly with the brain. Since the portion of the skull which contains the brain is the cranium, these nerves are called *cranial nerves*. The remaining 31 pairs are called *spinal nerves* and extend outward from spaces between the vertebrae in the spinal cord to various parts of the body.

CRANIAL NERVES. Typical cranial nerves serve the receptors and effectors of the head. They are connected to such structures as the eyes, ears, mouth, and neck. Some of the cranial nerves have distinctly sensory functions and are involved in vision, hearing, smell, and taste. Others have motor and/or sensory functions. The motor fibers carry the nerve impulses which enable one to move various parts of the head such as the tongue, jaw, eyes, and parts of the neck. Therefore, when one moves his neck and eyes, or is eating, motor fibers of the cranial nerves are involved.

THE SPINAL NERVES. The 31 pairs of spinal nerves serve other parts of the body such as the neck, chest, trunk, arms, and legs. They are very important because impulses traveling over sensory fibers give rise to such sensations as warmth, cold, pain, and pressure. The motor fibers, on the other hand, carry impulses involved in moving the arms and legs as well as the trunk. When one is dancing, walking, or running, for instance, innumerable motor fibers in the spinal nerves are activated. If the room feels too cold or somebody touches you, impulses for these sensations are transmitted by sensory fibers of the spinal nerves.

To summarize, the main role of the peripheral nervous system is to transmit impulses to and from the central nervous system. The coordinating centers within the central nervous system take these impulses coming in from the receptors via the sensory nerves and send out impulses via the motor nerves to the appropriate effectors. Thus, this is how we are able to physiologically react and adjust to our environment.

Physiological mechanisms in learning

Structural changes

Among the most exciting newer developments within psychology is the search for the *engram*, the lasting physiological changes associated with learning. There is no better way of demonstrating to psychology students the justification for studying physiology than by showing how such knowledge increases one's understanding of learning and other behavioral processes. The crucial information we seek, in searching for the physiological basis of learning, is some mechanism of permanent change in the nervous system. How else can we account for all of the many memories we have accumulated during the years? Many questions are being raised about what to do with our knowledge as we continue to discover more facts about the biological basis for learning and memory.

Synaptic changes

For a long time, the only mechanisms seriously considered as candidates for the physiological or biochemical basis of long-term memory were purely structural ones. The assumption was made that the ease with which activity in an axon can excite activity in an adjoining neuron depends upon the facility with which the appropriate synapse can be traversed. According to this viewpoint, learning might simply consist of the development of more or larger axon terminals from many neurons converging on synapses. Hence, the reason you might recognize somebody you have seen before is because the particular neurons involved were previously stimulated upon prior perception of him. Each time you see him, it would have the effect of increasing the size of the axon terminals. This would facilitate transmission across the synapses, and physiologically would be the basis for recognition.

By analogy, the connecting parts of neurons would grow larger with usage in the same manner that physical exercise stimulates the growth of muscle cells. At this time, there is no direct evidence for this explanation of memory; however, there are some interesting observations that may support the plausibility of this theory.

ENVIRONMENT AND BRAIN GROWTH: HOW TO DEVELOP A SMART BRAIN. Among the most pertinent experiments are those that provide evidence that an enriched environment can increase the size and weight of the cerebral cortex. Mark Rosenzweig and associates (1969), indeed, found that enriched rats, who have been raised with problems to solve such as mazes, have heavier brains and a thicker cortex than impoverished animals. Analysis of their brains revealed more activity of biochemical substances such as *acetylcholine* (ACH), which is believed to aid in the transmission of neural impulses at the synaptic junction. These findings implicate biochemical as well as structural mechanisms in memory.

Chemical changes inside the neuron

So far we have emphasized changes in the synapse as a possible explanation for the crucial physiological mechanism in learning and memory. Now we shall consider the possibility that changes take place during the learning process *within* neurons, rather than between neurons. This possibility is not in conflict with the theory on synaptic changes because chemical changes inside the neuron may cause the former to take place.

The intraneural hypothesis is very important because it suggests that the "memory" storage mechanism of the brain may be found within the chemical nature of its individual nerve cells. The major hypothesis concerning changes within the neuron states that "individual memory" (the consequences of learning within a single lifetime of a person) is carried by the structure of a biochemical substance known as ribonucleic acid (RNA). This substance is found within each living cell, and is involved in controlling many of its activities.

RNA AND THE CANNIBALISTIC WORMS. What is the nature of the evidence for the role of RNA in memory storage? Many students will be surprised to know that some of the original evidence came from the lowly flatworm, planaria. In a famous experiment (McConnell, 1962), planaria were taught to respond to light. RNA was taken from the ground-up bodies of the educated planaria and fed to other planaria without this training. The untrained planaria were reported to have shown a memory of what the first worms had learned.

Imagine the excitement that this discovery created in scientific circles, as well as among students on college campuses. Here at last was a use for old professors: simply grind them up and feed them to students. Unfortunately, these provocative findings have not been well substantiated to date. However, more recent evidence does support the hypothesis that learning experiences can change the detailed chemical structure of RNA within the neurons.

CURRENT STATUS OF RNA HYPOTHESIS. Some studies have been reported to show that administration of RNA (or of a drug that increases its manufacture in the brain) produces better learning and memory in experimental animals. For example, James McGaugh has been using drugs (such as strychnine and Metrazol) to increase the level of RNA in the brains of mice. He has been very successful in increasing the learning abilities or intellectual level of hundreds of mice by this technique (Krech, 1971). He even found in one of his experiments that hereditarily stupid mice were able to turn in better maze performances than their hereditarily superior but untreated fellows. Here we have a "chemical memory pill" which not only improves memory and learning, but can serve to make all mice equal when genetics has created inequality. Can anybody fail to see the implications of these startling results for human beings?

Additional evidence supporting the role of RNA in learning and memory comes from two sources: (1) definite changes in the composition of RNA in rats, given various learning tasks, has been found, and (2) exposure of the brain to biochemical materials that *break down RNA* causes memory losses in cats, rats, and planaria.

Although the aforementioned studies indicate that in some way RNA is involved in the activities of the neuron that make learning possible, the exact details still have to be worked out. For instance, it is possible that the structure of RNA is not specially related to learning as suggested by the RNA hypothesis (Science News, 1972b). An equally plausible alternative theory is that RNA is essential to the general well-being and functioning of the cell; and, on the assumption that "if a little is good, a lot more is better," a generally better functioning neuron will "learn" more efficiently than one that does not function as well. Another explanation (Science News, 1973) is that rather than direct memory transfer, RNA simply alters the motivational status of the animal by increasing activity, sensitization and may facilitate learning. For our purposes, it is not necessary to know the exact details, but only to be aware that learning modifies the chemistry of the brain; RNA being involved in some manner.

Brave New Worlds: Biochemistry and mankind

Although caution must be exercised in interpreting and extrapolating these findings, many scientists and interested laymen have speculated about the glorious future of mankind. Just think about the ramifications of get-smart pills (a la McGaugh) or specific knowledge pills (a la McConnell). A race of intellectual giants like Einstein may be developed or, in the future, instead of going to conventional classes and absorbing knowledge the hard way, students may just select pill A for chemistry and pill B for psychology. However, sober reflection brings to mind the tremendous social, educational, ethical, and political problems that would arise.

Who is going to tell the Brave New World scientists what type of human minds to manufacture? We are, of course, talking about goals, values, and aims. Shall we raise or lower artistic ability, aggressiveness, plasticity, scientific ability, motor skills, or intellectual functioning? Is it desirable to have people differing in their abilities or for everyone to be geniuses? In fact, are we even wise enough to predict the consequences of altering people's minds?

Before we let our speculations get out of hand, we can place these new developments in their proper perspective by reviewing David Krech's (1971) summation of his two decades of research on the biochemistry of learning. He and his colleagues have found that not every experience or variation in environment contributes equally to the development of the brain. They discovered the existence of species-specific enrichment experiences. What this means can be best demonstrated in the case of rats. Through natural selection a rat has developed a particular type of brain that enables it to learn its way through tunnels and dark passages. The "effective" rat brain is one which is a "space brain," not a language or arithmetic-reasoning brain. As a consequence, the most effective stimulating environment for rats is one which makes spatial learning demands on that brain, like maze learning. Other types of environmental experiences are not as efficient in developing its brain.

To generalize these findings on animals to human beings is tempting. This would suggest that we can expect the existence of species-specific environments for man as well. What the maximal efficient environments would be for developing children's brains is not clear. Krech personally believes that part of the answer lies in the language arts, those environments which emphasize language. After all, it is speech which first and foremost distinguishes man from the great apes and lower organisms. Further implications of the existence of maximal efficient environments are that psychochemical treatments would change *specific abilities* rather than general "intellectual functioning." For example, we might expect to develop proficiency in arithmetic, verbal intelligence, or motor skills, but not all of these. It would depend upon the type of brain an individual had already inherited.

Physiological mechanisms in motivation and emotions

The attainment of pleasure and the avoidance of pain are sometimes cited as the primary motivators of human behavior. This view of motivation, which is called *hedonism,* can be traced back to the ancient philosophers, but it was most prominent in the 18th and 19th centuries. Psychologists have traditionally tended to reject this explanation for many reasons, among the most important being the necessity of depending upon people's subjective reports and many exceptions to the general premise.

Nevertheless, there has been a resurgence of interest in the hedonistic theory in psychology. Scientists now use objective measures of approach and avoidance behavior in place of subjective reports to test sophisticated modern versions of hedonism. In addition, new discoveries of brain mechanisms have made hedonism more plausible.

Pleasure and pain centers

One of the larger scientific finds within psychology in the 1950s was that an electrode implanted deep in the brain of an experimental subject, with small amounts of electricity passing through it, acts as a reward for animals. Rats were found to learn various responses when followed by brain stimulation. Hence we had the discovery of pleasure centers, soon followed by the discovery of pain centers. Both of these centers are localized in regions deep within the brain, close to the hypothalamus.

Hungry rats, when given the choice of pleasurable stimulation to the brain or of food, will run faster to the electrical lever than to a lever that would give them something to eat. In fact, some rats have been known to self-stimulate themselves up to 2,000 times an hour for 24 hours straight; a remarkable feat of endurance if nothing else. On the other hand, direct stimulation of the pain centers will result in the learning of responses to turn off the stimulation.

Biofeedback

The function of the *autonomic nervous system* (ANS) is to control basic physiological or visceral responses, including heart rate, blood pressure, dilating of blood vessels, perspiration, and digestive secretions. The traditional view, for many years, has been that we cannot learn to exercise voluntary control over these responses in the same way we can skeletal responses; i.e., running, walking, moving your arms up and down, and talking. However, a major breakthrough by Neal Miller (1971) has shown this is not true: both animals and human subjects have actually learned to control visceral responses mediated by the ANS.

Various procedures have been devised for use with subjects in modification of visceral responses (Figure 2–9). They are designed primarily to prevent skeletal responses, such as moving, which might affect ANS mediated responses. This is achieved by administering drugs which block all motor responses, but which do not affect the level of consciousness. In addition, the procedures are designed to deliver reinforcement instantaneously, following a visceral response, which do not evoke overt behavior as would be the case in eating. This is accomplished by delivering electric shock directly to certain areas of the brain which bring pleasure to animals or human subjects, appropriately named pleasure centers.

Although there has been some difficulty in replicating these findings, Neal Miller (1971) reports using electric stimulation in teaching rats to increase or decrease their rate of urine formation, blood pressure, heart rate, and intestinal contractions. Furthermore, other experiments have shown that the voltage of the rat's brain waves can be increased or decreased through reinforcement (Carmona, 1967). Similar findings have been obtained for human patients (Razvan, 1961), and it is even conceivable, in the case of some patients, that abnormal brain wave patterns can be modified by learning. Practitioners of transcendental medi-

FIGURE 2–9
Experiment on biofeedback. The subject is being taught to modify or control her own brain wave patterns as they are monitored by a physiograph which measures the electrical activity of the brain.

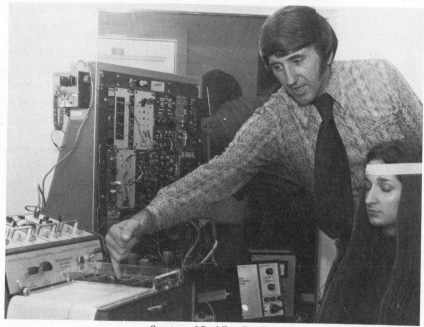

Courtesy of Paul Fry, *The Santa Clara*, University of Santa Clara

tation also seem to possess the ability to control the ANS (Schwartz, 1974).

HUMAN PATIENTS. Pleasure and pain centers have also been located in human brains and have been put to practical use. Many patients with various afflictions have undergone brain stimulation for therapeutic purposes. In many of these cases, electrodes to the pleasure centers have alleviated or blocked out pain. Heath (1971) reports the treatment of a 25-year-old epileptic patient who suffered from uncontrollable periods of impulsive behavior and feelings of discomfort. Almost instantly, upon stimulation, his behavior would change from one of disorganization and rage to one of happiness and mild euphoria. Interestingly enough, he described his subjective feelings to be like the beginnings of a general sexual arousal.

In a few cases, even patients with cancer who are under extremely heavy dosages of morphine may get relief from self-stimulation. By using electrical current, some patients have been able to do without narcotic drugs for as long as three months (Murray, 1969). Presently, such success is the exception rather than the rule. But with new and improved techniques, we can look forward to greater success in the future.

The discovery of electrical stimulation of the brain has not only proven useful in treating pain, but also has great potential for the relief of other types of human suffering. For example, paralyzed limbs can be moved and there is even a possibility that some day people may be able to move artificial limbs via electrical stimulation.

The physiological effects of stress

Medical men are well aware that our emotions can be disruptive as well as adaptive and, in fact, can make us physically ill. Physical illnesses brought on predominantly by emotional stress are known as *psychosomatic disorders*. There is always physical damage of some type involved in which the clinical picture is dominated by changes in the structure and function of the internal organs. Many investigators have found striking correlations between physical and emotional disturbances. This strongly supports the view that we must take into consideration "the whole person" in evaluating an illness rather than compartmentalizing maladaptive patterns into "mind" or "body."

The correlation between physical and emotional disturbances is well illustrated in the report by Jacobs et al. (1971) of 179 college students. One hundred and six of the students sought medical help for respiratory infections. The ill subjects were significantly more likely than the "well" students to perceive the year preceding their illness as characterized by failure and disappointment; the more severely ill they were, the more frequent and intense were their reports of frustrating and stressful events.

DYNAMICS OF PSYCHOSOMATIC DISORDERS. Five common types of psychosomatic reactions are peptic ulcers, migraine headaches, asthma, eczema (skin disruptions), and hypertension (elevated blood pressure). These specific types of reactions occur from prolonged psychological stress and intense emotion, usually accompanied by bodily changes including an increased heartbeat, secretions of adrenalin, and high blood pressure. These visceral reactions prepare the individual to deal with emergencies of some type, but over a period of time change the internal environment of the body. The dynamics of a psychosomatic disorder are best known in the case of peptic ulcers, which develop in the following manner.

Ulcers are formed when, under stress, there is an increased secretion of hydrochloric acid and increased stomach motility. The acid erodes away a part of the lining of the stomach wall, thereby creating the ulcer. Patients who develop ulcers tend to have a history of a high rate of gastric secretion, and stress acts to increase the flow of digestive juices.

Ulcers have been produced in the laboratory by various means showing the interaction of physiological and psychological factors. For instance, Brady (1958) experimented with pairs of monkeys that were placed in similar compartments. Both monkeys would receive an electric shock every 20 seconds unless the animal in the "control" compartment (the "executive" monkey) pressed a lever (Figure 2–10). The monkey in the other compartment had no control over the shock. When the monkeys were placed on a schedule of six hours out of the apparatus, the "executive" monkey showed an increase in the production of stomach acid and ultimately developed a duodenal ulcer. In contrast, the other monkey never developed ulcers.

In this experiment, the actual occurrence of electric shock was rare because the "executive" monkey became so skilled in pushing the lever. Thus, the stress was psychological in nature. There was pressure to maintain attention and the ever-present fear that the shock would not be avoided. On the other hand, the monkey who had no control of the shock had little fear to cope with. Only very rarely did he experience any discomfort and he was not subjected to the pressure of maintaining vigilance at the lever.

Since psychosomatic disorders involve both true bodily damage and psychological problems, their treatment necessitates medical and psychological approaches. Medical therapy can alleviate and control physical symptoms such as stomach acidity with drugs or clear the bronchial passageways in asthma. However, to stop the conditions from recurring, the psychological stress producing the condition must also be treated. This might involve psychotherapy to help the patient resolve the problem which is producing the emotional tension. Or, changes might be made in the environment.

BIOFEEDBACK AND PSYCHOSOMATIC ILLNESSES. A hope for the future in the treatment of psychosomatic disorders is the use of biofeedback. It is

FIGURE 2–10
Ulcers in "executive" monkeys. Both animals received electric shocks administered at 20-second intervals. The "executive" monkey, at the left, learned to press its lever every 20 seconds to prevent shocks to both animals. The lever, however, for the monkey on the right is a dummy. Although both animals received the same number of shocks, only the "executive" monkey developed the ulcers.

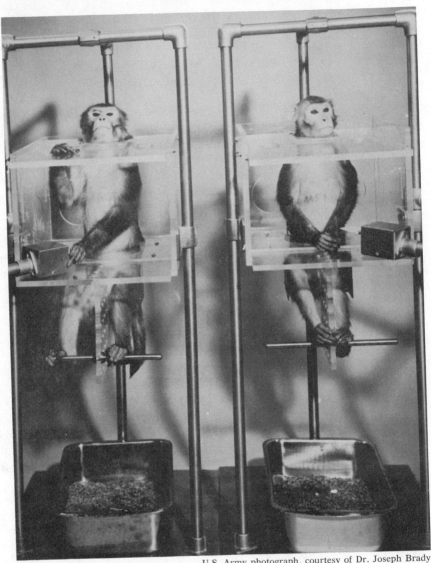

U.S. Army photograph, courtesy of Dr. Joseph Brady

plausible that these techniques can be applied to help people with *psychosomatic* disorders, particularly because subjects may be taught to control the operation of their intestines and the expansion or contraction of their blood vessels.

Sometime in the past, people with these problems may have learned to respond with these symptoms under stress. For example, a person may have been conditioned to expand blood vessels in the brain, causing migraine headaches. These headaches, in return, could have proven useful in getting out of doing something unpleasant, so the body repeats the process the next time the person faces a problem and the psychosomatic illness continues.

Since these physiological reactions can be controlled by learning, it is possible that patients can be taught to control the destruction to their own bodies. For example, perhaps patients in the future may be able to stop the expansion of blood vessels in the brain, thereby avoiding migraine headaches. People with heart trouble may learn to control their blood pressure or heart rate and ward off heart attacks. When one considers all of these possibilities, it is not surprising that so much current research is being devoted to biofeedback and its medical applications.

Heredity

Every once in a while a person is born and becomes recognized by the world as a genius or a great man. We are speaking of the Bachs, Newtons, Einsteins, or da Vincis. To understand what factors are involved in the development of these outstanding individuals, requires a basic understanding of genetics. These famous individuals are in part the result of a special combination of genetic materials, *chromosomes* and *genes*, that occur with a low probability.

Everyone begins life as a single cell, a *zygote*, that is formed when the male sperm penetrates the female egg *(ovum)*. The sperm and egg, known as *germ cells*, or *gametes*, are different from all other cells in the human body because they contain only 23 separate and distinctively different chromosomes; all other cells in the body contain 46 chromosomes (23 pairs). This difference can be explained by the process of cell division that takes place within gametes, in which the number of chromosomes is reduced in half to 23. However, in the zygote, the chromosomes of the sperm and ovum combine to give the fertile egg 23 pairs of chromosomes, thereby restoring the normal complement of 46. Each cell in the millions that make up a person's body will carry a carbon copy of the original 23 pairs of chromosomes that come together at conception.

Genes

Each chromosome is subdivided into hundreds of thousands of genes, which are the determiners of hereditary traits. The genetic makeup of any individual is determined largely by chance and that is why there are only a few geniuses born every generation. For example, half of one's genes comes from one sperm cell, out of a possible several million, that penetrates one of the hundreds of egg cells produced by the female during her reproductive life. Each sperm and egg cell differs in the genes it carries from all other gametes. By the random combination of the genes from a given sperm and ovum, a human being is formed. He will be both unique and like his fellowmen in many ways.

One can gain an appreciation of why we have a great diversity of individuals, including surprising differences within siblings, by examining the following staggering statistic. The chance of two children of parents inheriting the same chromosomal constitutions is less than 1 in 70 trillion (with the exception of identical twins).

DOMINANT AND RECESSIVE GENES. At conception, a gene from the father will be paired with its counterpart from the mother, and it is one of the rules of genetics that these genes work together to produce a certain characteristic. If both members of a pair dictate identical characteristics, the condition is called *homozygous*. If the genes should dictate different characteristics, the condition is called *heterozygous*. What happens in the latter case is that one gene becomes dominant over the other (said to be recessive) and produces its own characteristics. The concept of dominant and recessive traits can best be seen in the case of inherited eye color.

If a man who is homozygous for blue eyes marries a woman homozygous for brown eyes, all of their children will have brown eyes, since brown is dominant over blue. In genetics, it is common to call the genes determining this characteristic eye color Bb (brown) and bB (blue), the capital letter designating the dominant trait and the small letter the recessive one. The children of the homozygous couple, after the process of reduction division in the gametes, will have one gene for brown eyes (Bb) and another for blue eyes (bB). What will happen if a heterozygous man marries a heterozygous woman? Figure 2–11 shows the outcome of this union. The distribution of children will be one-fourth homozygous for brown eyes (BB), one-half heterozygous (Bb), and one-fourth homozygous for blue eyes (bb). Hence, three-fourths will have brown eyes, and one-fourth will have blue eyes. It is interesting to note that there is a possibility that blue-eyed children can result from this marriage even though both parents are brown-eyed. Also, inheritance of eye color is not a single factor trait so that it is possible to have a brown-eyed student with two blue-eyed parents.

Actually, most characteristics are determined by the interaction of several pairs of genes that have small accumulative effects. This explains why characteristics of men and animals tend to vary continuously along a dimension, such as intelligence. In other words, we do not find a cluster of bright people and a cluster of stupid people, but a normal distribution of intelligence with most people around average and less at the extremes (see Chapter 8).

DETERMINATION OF SEX. The sex of a child is determined by the composition of a single pair of chromosomes. Females have two similar X

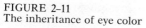

FIGURE 2–11
The inheritance of eye color

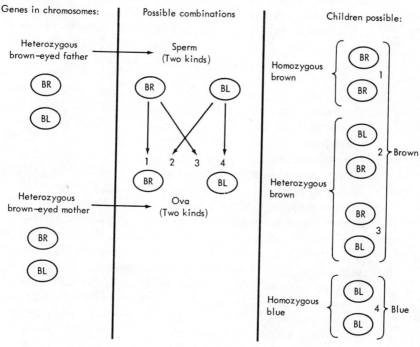

chromosomes, while males have an X and a smaller Y chromosome. Since the female has two chromosomes, her egg will always have one X chromosome to pass on after reduction division. The same process occurs in the male, except that he has either an X or Y chromosome to pass on via his sperm. When a sperm carrying an X chromosome unites with the egg, the zygote will contain the XX combination, and the offspring will be a female. When a sperm carrying a Y chromosome fertilizes the egg, the offspring will be a male because it will carry the XY pair.

Thus, it is the male sperm that determines the sex of a child, not the egg. This is interesting from a historical viewpoint since kings in the past were known to do away with their wives when the union resulted in a procession of female children. Of course, in order to serve justice, if someone had to be put away, it should have been the kings not their unfortunate spouses.

GROSS GENETIC DEFECTS. Genetic defects account for almost one-fifth of all birth imperfections (Rogers, 1969). One of the best known defects that results from the addition of an extra chromosome is *mongolism*, better known as *Down's syndrome;* mongoloids, in contrast to most humans who have 46 chromosomes, are born with 47. Unfortunately, the excess genetic material harms rather than helps the child by, perhaps, throwing the body's carefully regulated growth processes off balance (Bishop & Davis, 1966). This condition is always associated with severe mental retardation and physical abnormalities. Typically, the mongoloid will have a prominent epicanthal fold across the corner of the eye, a short neck, and stubby hands and feet. Children suffering from Down's syndrome also tend to age prematurely and are "old" by the time they reach their 30s.

Another genetic anomaly, which is fairly common, occurs when a male inherits an extra female sex chromosome (XXY). These infants look normal but will fail to mature sexually. This condition is known as *Klinefelter's syndrome*. Another situation is the case of males who are born with an additional male chromosome (XYY).

There are many questions and issues centered around this latter condition that are not completely and clearly resolved yet (Jarvik, Klodin, & Matsuyama, 1973; Shaw & Borgoankar, 1974). Some research has indicated that men who have the additional male sex chromosome are taller than average and are more disposed toward violent actions against society or other people than most men. The example of Richard Speck comes to mind who was convicted for slaying eight nurses in Chicago. However, a report from National Institute of Mental Health conference of scientists has concluded "The demonstration of the XYY karotype in an individual does not, in our present state of knowledge, permit any definite conclusions to be drawn about the presence of mental disease or mental defect in that individual. A great deal of further scientific evidence is needed" (*Medical World News*, 1971).

Among women, Turner's syndrome results from a genetic defect when only one X chromosome is inherited. Victims of this defect have a defective body structure in addition to mild mental retardation. They are typically characterized by a short stature, webbing of the neck, and sexual infantilism. Unfortunately, in the case of women who inherit an additional female chromosome, they are not "superfemales" as men might expect or hope, but are usually mentally retarded.

Heredity and intelligence

The role of heredity in influencing psychological characteristics has been most thoroughly investigated in the development of intelligence. The relative contributions made by genetics and environmental factors in determining one's level of intelligence has been argued back and forth for many years. The controversy in recent years has taken on an added dimension because of its possible implications for racial differences, which will be discussed in a separate section.

The evaluation of the contribution of heredity to intelligence is best made, in the case of humans, by the study of twins, raised together and apart. There are two types of twins: identical twins who come from the same egg (monozygotic) and fraternal twins who come from different eggs (dizygotic). Basically, this means the twins who come from the same egg, will have the same inherited characteristics. But in the case of fraternal twins, their genetic makeup is no more similar than the usual brothers and sisters. Studies have been conducted on both types of twins, reared together and apart. *Correlation coefficients,* which are statistical devices for measuring the degree of relationship between two variables have been reported for these twins. A perfect correlation would be 1.00 and no relationship would be .00. Researchers have found a .15-point correlation difference between identical twins reared apart and those reared together in a similar environment. The differences in correlations between identical twins reared separately or together is produced by the effects of different environments.

The importance of heredity can be seen by examining the difference between fraternal twins reared together and identical twins reared apart; the result is a striking .22 points difference in correlation. This suggests that entirely separate environments do not alter intelligence as much as the different heredity of fraternal or nonidentical twins. The role of heredity is further suggested when comparing siblings (who have some hereditary components in common) with unrelated children living together; brothers and sisters living together correlated .53 as compared with correlations only in the .20s for unrelated children.

Many investigators might quarrel with the above conclusions as to the relative merits of environment and heredity in determining intelligence. However, after many years of study we can safely conclude that: (1) basic intellectual potential is something inherited from one's parents and (2) environment is a critical variable in determining how much of this potential is developed and utilized.

RACE AND INTELLIGENCE. An emotionally laden issue is the question as to whether or not there are differences between races in intelligence (Dobzhansky, 1973; Jensen, 1973; Rice, 1973; Williams, 1974). For many reasons, this is an extremely complex question to answer. Some of these being the difficulties in defining race and the emotional reactions of many people to this topic. Recently the issue of racial differences has received widespread publicity from an article published by A. R. Jensen (1969). He argued that available research has shown intelligence to be inherited and concluded that compensatory education cannot do much to raise the intellectual level of disadvantaged children. Moreover, he maintained that the intelligence of whites in America is probably inherently superior to that of blacks.

Some psychologists, in response, argue that Jensen has made a number of questionable assumptions in reaching his conclusions about the measurement of intelligence. Among the assumptions he made are: (1) research on the intelligence of whites can be generalized to blacks; (2) middle-class and lower-class blacks grow up in similar environments to middle- and lower-class whites; and (3) test instruments are valid for both white and black subjects. While scores of black people are generally below those of whites, there are many factors that could explain their difference which are related to the doubtful assumptions made by Jensen. It is generally agreed that most intelligence tests are culturally biased in regard to the pictures they show or the questions they ask. Thus, the test items will be more familiar to one population than another, giving one group a built-in advantage. Furthermore, differences between blacks and whites in regard to early experiences, home atmosphere, career goals, and aspiration are all going to affect performance on intelligence tests, to what extent, nobody can say for sure.

More important, we should recognize that the "average values" of different populations tell us nothing about any one individual. Heritability is a function of the population not of a trait. Both black and white populations have individuals ranging from bright to mentally retarded; to think of any racial group in terms of a single stereotype goes against all we know about the mechanics of heredity. We will return to this controversial issue later in Chapter 8.

Instinctive behavior

One of the popular views which dominated American psychology until the 1930s was the belief that many behavioral responses seen in man and lower organisms were due to instincts, an innate unlearned action. Certain behaviors such as the aggressive stinging response of bees, ritualistic mating behavior of some fishes, migratory behavior of birds, web weaving of spiders, nest building of birds, and maternal behavior of female rats have all been called instinctive because they share four characteristics. (1) They are *unlearned;* a black widow spider does not have to learn how to weave a web. (2) The behavior is rigidly *patterned.* There does not seem to be much variability in the nest building of a robin. (3) Instinctive behavior is found within all members of a species *(species-specific).* For example, spiders of a particular species weave webs with identical patterns. (4) The behavior is relatively complex, involving the whole organism, in contrast to a simple reflex. Such is the case of the migratory behavior of birds and their uncanny ability to find far away locations.

Modern ethologists, scientists who study innate behavior as it occurs in its natural setting, have given the instinct concept new respectability through their careful observational studies. They have been able to increase our understanding of *species-specific* or instinctive behavior by uncovering the internal and external stimuli which elicit the rigid and stereotyped sequence of responses.

An example of this type of approach which has paid off in practical dividends for man is the discovery of stimuli that release the aggressive behavior of bees. After observing the effects of a variety of stimuli provoking stinging by bees, Free (1964) was able to make suggestions on how to avoid bee stings. Bees are incited to attack humans wearing unclean, dark clothing of a rough texture. In addition, he discovered that rapid movements, such as running, and perspiration will increase the chances of being stung.

A second example of the work of ethologists is their examination of the mating behavior of the stickleback fish. The male stickleback will engage in certain stereotyped behavioral patterns which are associated with the courtship cycle. He assumes command over a portion of the bottom of his pond and will defend it from any other male intruders. When a female comes into his territory he will engage in a zigzag dance around the female. These actions help to squeeze the eggs from the female and result in their fertilization.

What are the cues that trigger this courting behavior? Tinbergen (1951) found the answer to this question in experiments when he introduced various shaped objects into the water near the male stickleback. Only a few characteristics were determined to be responsible for the elicitation of their innate behavior. The actual cues for the zigzag dance are protruding underportions of a figure that need only be vaguely fishlike. The cues responsible for eliciting the aggressive behavior appropriate to a male intruder are the color and size of the underbelly of a fishlike form. As a matter of fact, Tinbergen's manufactured models, with their enlarged cues, proved to be more effective in eliciting instinctive responses than those provided in nature.

A third example of fieldwork on instinctive behavior is the migratory habits of birds. Some crows that live in the midwestern United States fly in the fall from Alberta, Canada, to Kansas. The migratory behavior of these birds is in part a response to certain light stimuli and can be modified in experiments (Rowan, 1931). A large number of crows were captured in Canada during the early fall and exposed to an artificially lit environment. Here they received a daily *increase* in illumination in place of the normal decrease in sunlight that results when autumn days become progressively shorter. Many of the crows that had been banded and then released in November, were subsequently found not to have migrated south in contrast to "normal" birds. This knowledge on the migratory behavior of birds has proved to be useful in artificially increasing the egg production among chickens.

INSTINCT AND MAN. How applicable are these findings to man? Is much of our behavior controlled by innate forces? In early psychology, instincts were postulated as an explanation for almost any conceivable trait or activity. Man was said to have aggressive, belonging, loving, security, and so on, instincts. As a result, many social scientists became disenchanted with this viewpoint. First, labeling behavior as instinctive made apparent the *nominal* fallacy, that by naming something you have explained it. Calling something instinctive did not bring psychologists closer to an understanding of what the crucial variables were in determining when, where, and how behavior would occur. Second, learning theorists or environmentalists were able to show that much of man's behavior was under the control of environmental forces. If we stick to a rigid definition of instinctive behavior, as implied by the previously stated four criteria, it would be very difficult to find any in man. The development of our brain makes us much more able than lower species to adapt to variations in environmental stimulation. Whatever instincts we may possess are modified by the effects of learning.

As pointed out by many modern psychologists, however, the development of behavior in the higher organisms is best understood by not setting up a false dichotomy of learned versus instinctive behavior. Instead we should recognize that much behavior depends on both the genetic endowment of an organism and its past experiences. When examining human behavior in this context, we can certainly recognize some species-specific action patterns in man. Vocal expressions and the range of emotional reactions both testify to man's innate behavioral repertoire.

The development of temper tantrums serves as a case in point. Human babies do not need to learn how to manifest this emotional reaction (Hebb, 1972). Babies do not have to practice a temper tantrum, nor observe others having one, in order to produce one. Although this part of the emotional reaction is innate, it is not independent of learning. The baby must have learned to want something out of his reach and to see that it is being withheld from him.

IMPRINTING. The complex interaction of innate factors and learning in the development of behavior can be seen in *imprinting*. For some time, it has been known that when certain animals are exposed for a period of time after birth to various objects in the environment, strong social attachments occur. Apparently, the species identity and social attachment are imprinted on the organism during this time of exposure. Under natural conditions, the young of many species develop strong attachments to their parents; the example of a group of goslings following a mother goose is common enough in many rural areas. However, in Figure 2–12, we find a group of confused goslings following the ethologist, Dr. Konrad Lorenz, just as naturally as they would their own mothers. What psychological processes are at work which cause this strange behavior? The answer to this question is provided by experiments which tell us how young animals get to know their parents and later their appropriate sexual mates.

What is seen in the picture of Lorenz and goslings is an extraordinary instinctive response among fowls. The young birds, soon after hatching, are prepared to follow and seek contact with any stimulus-object, providing that the overall conditions of stimulation are right. The range of stimuli that young birds can be imprinted is wide, although some objects are more easily imprinted than others. In the first 24 hours or so after hatching, this exposure has a lasting effect and is a determinant of the bird's identity and behavior at maturity.

Normally, chicks are exposed to the adult of their own species and

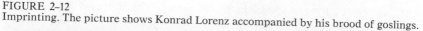

FIGURE 2–12
Imprinting. The picture shows Konrad Lorenz accompanied by his brood of goslings.

Nina Leen, Time-Life Picture Agency

proper early learning occurs. This produces the normal species-predict-able behavior such as the type of song sung by the bird. But what will happen if the young birds are imprinted on an adult of another species instead of their own? In most cases, the birds respond to this other species as it normally would to its own, as in the case of Lorenz's goslings. The degree of this effect varies from one kind of bird to another. When greylag geese are exposed only to human beings at birth, they will prefer man over their own kind at maturity. Indeed, the ganders will tend to make their sexual advances to people and not to females of their own species. Many farmers, much to their own surprise, have reported that they are a sex object to some of their own barnyard fowls.

IMPRINTING IN MAMMALS: DOGS' LOVE OF MAN. Much of the research on imprinting has been concerned with its generality. This early social learning can be seen in its clearest and most dramatic form in birds, but the same kind of effect may appear in mammals too. It has been reported that deer, goats, sheep, and guinea pigs raised by men act like pets only and do not associate with members of their own species. Female chimpanzees brought up in a nursery by human caretakers differ markedly from those raised by their own mothers. In general, they tend to prefer human company to their own kind and are less sexually responsive to male chimpanzees.

One of the best examples of imprinting in mammals can be seen in domestic dogs. Scott (1960) in his studies found that dogs seem incapable of forming attachments to humans unless they have been given opportunities to do so when very young. Apparently these animals have a six- to nine-week critical period in which social attachments can be formed. After about 12 weeks, puppies raised together away from humans or dogs do not become devoted pets. In the former case, puppies exhibit a greater attachment to dogs than humans and, in the latter case, they remain undomesticated. Thus, as a general rule, a person would not want to purchase a puppy older than 12 weeks, especially if the dog is a potentially dangerous and highly sensitive breed such as a Doberman pinscher. It is important to keep in mind that critical periods for socialization depends on the species.

CRITICAL LEARNING PERIODS IN HUMANS. As we have seen, many animals have different periods of time in their life in which they are much more susceptible to certain learning influences. Indeed, if learning does not occur at this time, much of the animal's later learning may be irreversible. This is what we mean by critical periods. It seems likely that humans have similar learning periods. For instance, an analogy has been made between the wagging of a dog's tail, which occurs at a specific time and the smiling response which elicits a social response from others. It has been suggested, in regard to human social development, that there are two critical periods (Nash, 1970). The first is an imprinting one, lasting from about six weeks to six months, and the second one, from about three months to three years. Extensive affectional and social relationships are formed during these periods. While the periods overlap in their ranges for groups, they necessarily do not in individual cases. The disproportionate number of orphans, who have been reared in impersonal orphanages, with "personality problems" and difficulty in forming social relationships lends some credence to this view.

Learning a foreign language with a correct and natural accent is another example of a critical learning period. In spite of the fact that foreign languages are primarily offered at the high school and college levels, research suggests that learning to speak a language like a native is only possible with young children (Hurlock, 1972). Some changes seems to occur beyond this age which makes it almost impossible to speak a foreign language correctly. Even within our own nation, it is often possible to tell what section of the country an adult was born in by the regional accent he has developed.

Along the same lines is the importance of critical periods in the development of motor skills. The well-known experiments by McGraw (1935) showed that there are times in the development of motor skills when practice produces rapid acquisition and at other times little effect. To convince yourself of this, observe the difficulty adults have in learning sports such as swimming, golf, or tennis in contrast to children. It is no accident that world champions like Jack Nicklaus in golf, and Rod Laver in tennis learned their prospective skills early in their lives. Furthermore, the training techniques utilized to develop world class swimmers are most efficient with young children and not with adults or even adolescents.

Summary

The fundamental unit of all living organisms is the cell. In many organisms such as man, cells have become highly specialized. Receptor cells transform physical energy such as heat, light, mechanical, and chemical stimuli into electrical activity that are sent to the brain. Effector cells are involved in the muscles (skeletal and smooth) and glands which enable us to react in our environment. Among the important determinants of behavior are the endocrine glands which secrete hormones that influence many bodily activities and behavior such as in emergency situations. Two of the glands, the pituitary (master gland) and thyroid seem to regulate growth and metabolism, respectively.

In man, the receptors and effectors are bridged by the nervous system. The basic unit of the nervous system is the neuron, composed of (1) a cell body responsible for maintaining metabolism, (2) dendrites which receive excitation, and (3) an axon which sends impulses. The central nervous system is divided into two major parts: the brain and spinal cord. The brain has three major subdivisions: the hindbrain, midbrain, and forebrain.

The hindbrain is composed of the medulla, which is a connecting tract for impulses to and from the brain and also regulates many important physiological functions; the cerebellum which controls body posture and coordinates movement; and the pons. The midbrain connects the cerebral cortex to the brainstem and is also concerned with visual and hearing functions. The forebrain is divided into (1) the thalamus, which is the brain's major relay station; (2) the limbic system, which is involved in motivational and emotional reactions; and (3) the cerebrum, two hemispheres connected by the corpus callosum. It is the cerebral cortex that most distinguishes man from other species. The two hemispheres are symmetrical and control opposite sides of the body. Each hemisphere may be divided into four lobes which have different functions: frontal, parietal, occipital and temporal. Certain areas of the cortex produce motor responses, sensory effects, and other complex activities such as speech (association areas). The cortex has two main association areas: the frontal and POT (parietal, occipital, and temporal). The exact function of these areas are not well known. Psychosurgery of frontal lobes (lobotomy) for violent behaviors and mental illness has been conducted with mixed results. However, damage to the POT can cause agnosia, inability to recognize a familiar object; and aphasia, a disturbance of speech and language. Recent interest has centered around the split-brain phenomena, severing the corpus callosum which connects the two hemispheres. When this occurs, the two halves seem to function independently of one another.

The peripheral nervous system includes all nerve cells and fibers that lie outside the CNS. Its main function is to conduct impulses to and from the CNS system. As a result, the coordinating centers of the CNS take impulses via the sensory nerves and send out impulses via the motor nerves to the appropriate receptors. Thus, we can react and adjust to our environment.

One of the exciting areas in psychology has been the search for the engram, the lasting physiological changes associated with learning. According to one viewpoint, the basis of memory lies in certain structural changes in the neurons such as thickening of the axon terminals. Another view postulates biochemical changes within the neuron which become stored. The belief is that a chemical substance, RNA, plays an important role in memory. Studies on planaria and other organisms seem to indicate that better learning and memory are promoted when organisms are injected with RNA. Because of these discoveries, much speculation about producing "get-smart" pills for humans has been rampant.

There has been a resurgence of interests in studying the physiological mechanisms of motivation and emotion. First, pleasure and pain centers have been identified in which electrical stimulation of certain parts of the brain are pleasurable and others are painful. Brain stimulation has been used for therapeutic purposes to block out pain, discomfort, and to control rage.

Second, biofeedback studies now reveal that the autonomic nervous system (brain waves, heart rate, blood pressure, digestive secretions) may be voluntarily controlled. The implications for the treatment of psychosomatic patients are vast. Psychosomatic disorders are intimately associated with psychological stress and are manifested as peptic ulcers, migraine headaches, hypertension, and so forth.

Many of our characteristics are determined by heredity. All our cells contain 46 chromosomes except the sperm and egg cells which contain only 23. During fertilization, the sperm and egg combine to make 46. Each chromosome is divided into hundreds of thousands of genes which are the determiners of heredity. Genes which are dominant will generally win over recessive ones. Gross genetic defects can account for many birth imperfections. Among those discussed were (1) Down's syndrome (mongolism), which is caused by the presence of an extra chromosome; (2) Klinefelter's syndrome, caused by males inheriting an extra female sex chromosome; (3) a condition in which males inherit an extra male chromosome; and (4) Turner's syndrome, caused when only one X chromosome is inherited.

Heredity also affects intelligence. Studies of identical (homozygotic) and fraternal (heterozygotic) twins indicate a strong hereditary component although environment also determines how much this potential will develop. An emotionally laden issue concerns race and intelligence. Jensen argues that blacks are intellectually inferior to whites and that this is caused by heredity. However, he makes a number of questionable assumptions that are not warranted.

An important concept in the biological and behavioral sciences is that of the instinct. Certain behaviors in lower organisms such as web weaving by spiders, nest building by birds, and maternal behavior in rats are considered innate. Instincts are species-specific behavioral patterns that are complex, rigid, and unlearned. As we move up the phylogenetic scale, behavior becomes less instinctive and is more influenced by learning or environmental influences. Nevertheless, certain analogies can be drawn between some human behaviors and instincts. The complex interaction of innate factors and learning in the development of behavior can be seen in imprinting. Social attachment or species identification in lower organisms is strongly determined by consistent exposure to certain objects at birth. Normally, animals are exposed to adults of their own species but can be imprinted to other ones. Imprinting is most effective during certain critical periods that vary with the species. In man, this analogy can be applied to certain behaviors such as affectional and social development, motor skills, and the learning of foreign languages.

References

Bishop, J., & Davis, D. M. *New horizons in medicine*. Princeton, N.J.: Dow Jones Books, 1966.

Brady, J. V. Ulcers in executive monkeys. *Scientific American*, 1958, **199**, 95–100.

Carmona, A. Trial-and-error learning of the votage of the cortical EEG activity. Doctoral dissertation, Yale University, New Haven, Conn., 1967.

Chorover, S. L. The pacification of the brain. *Psychology Today*, 1974, **7**(12), 59–69.

Dobzhansky, T. Differences are not deficit. *Psychology Today*, 1973, **7**(7), 97–101.

Free, J. B. The stimuli releasing the stinging response of honeybees. In S. C. Rattner & M. R. Denny (Eds.), *Comparative psychology, research in animal behavior*. Homewood, Ill.: Dorsey Press, 1964.

Gazzaniga, M. S., Bogen, J. E., & Sperry, R. W. Observations on visual perception after disconnection of the cerebral hemisphere in man. *Brain*, 1965, **88**, 221–236.

Harlow, J. M. *Boston Medical Surgery Journal*, 1848, **39**, 389.

Heath, R. G. Electrical self-stimulation of the brain in man. In M. Karlins (Ed.), *Psychology and society*. New York: John Wiley & Sons, 1971.

Hebb, D. O. *Textbook of psychology*. (3d ed.) Philadelphia: W. B. Saunders, 1972.

Holden, C. Psychosurgery: Legitimate therapy or laundered lobotomy? *Science*, 1973, **179**, 1109–1112.

Hurlock, E. B. *Child development*. (5th ed.) New York: McGraw-Hill, 1972.

Jacobs, M. A., Spilken, A. Z., Norman, M. M., & Anderson, L. S. Life stress and respiratory illness. *Journal of Psychosomatic Research*, 1971, **15**(1), 63–72.

Jarvik, L. F., Klodin, V., & Matsuyama, S. S. Human aggression and the extra Y chromosome: Fact or fantasy? *American Psychologist*, 1973, **28**, 674–482.

Jensen, A. R. How much can we boost IQ and scholastic achievement? *Harvard Educational Review*, 1969, **39**, 1–123.

Jensen, A. R. The differences are real. *Psychology Today*, 1973, **7**(7), 80–86.

Kesey, K. *One flew over the cuckoo's nest*. New York: Viking Press, 1962.

Kimble, D. P. *Physiological psychology: A unit for introductory psychology*. Reading, Mass.: Addison-Wesley, 1963.

Kleitman, N. Patterns of dreaming. In *Frontiers of psychological research: Readings from Scientific American*, San Francisco: W. H. Freeman and Co., 1964, 236–242.

Krech, D. Psychoneurobiochemeducation. In Robert V. Guthrie (Ed.), *Psychology in the world today: An interdisciplinary approach*. (2d ed.) Reading, Mass.: Addison-Wesley, 1971, 93–101.

McConnell, J. V. Memory transfer through cannibalism in planaria. *Journal of Neuropsychiatry*, 1962, **3**, 45.

McGraw, M. B. *Growth: A study of Johnny and Jimmy*. New York: Appleton, 1935.

Medical World News. Reprinted from Medical World News. Copyright © 1971 McGraw-Hill, Inc.

Miller, N. E. Psychosomatic effects of specific types of training. In L. W. Schmaltz (Ed.), *Scientific psychology and social concern.* New York: Harper & Row, 1971.

Murray, J. B. The puzzle of pain. *Perceptual and Motor Skills,* 1969, **28,** 887–889.

Nash, J. *Developmental psychology: A psychobiological approach.* Englewood Cliffs, N.J.: Prentice-Hall, 1970.

Neilson, J. M. *Agnosia, apraxia, aphasia.* (2d ed.) New York: Hoeber Co., 1946.

Olds, J. Pleasure centers in the brain. *Scientific American,* 1956, **195**(4).

Olds, J. Approach-avoidance dissociations in rat brain. *American Journal of Physiology,* 1960, **199,** 965–968.

Razvan, G. The observable unconscious and the inferable conscious in current Soviet psychophysiology: Interoceptive conditioning and the orienting reflex. *Psychological Review,* 1961, **68,** 81–147.

Rice, B. The high cost of thinking the un-unthinkable. *Psychology Today,* 1973, **7**(7), 89–93.

Rogers, D. *Child psychology.* Belmont, Calif.: Brooks & Cole, 1969.

Rowan, W. *The riddle of migration.* Baltimore: Williams and Wilkens, 1931.

Rosenzweig, M. R., Bennett, E. L., Diamond, M. L., Suyu, W. M., Alagle, R. W., & Saffran, E. Influences of environmental complexity and visual stimulation of development of occipital cortex in rats. *Brain Research,* 1969, **14,** 427–445.

Schwartz, G. E. TM relaxes some people and makes them feel better. *Psychology Today,* 1974, **7**(11), 39–44.

Science News, 1972, **101**(11), 174–175. (a)

Science News. Pro-and-con-debate over the chemical transfer of learning. 1972, **102**(7), 97–112. (b)

Science News. The biology of memory. 1973, **104**(14), 218–219.

Scott, J. P. Comparative social psychology. In R. H. Walters, D. A. Rethlingshafer, & W. E. Caldwell (Eds.), *Principles of comparative psychology.* New York: McGraw-Hill, 1960.

Shah, S. A., & Borgaonkar, D. S. The XXY chromosomal abnormality. *American Psychologist,* 1974, **29,** 357–359.

Sperry, R. W. The great cerebral commissure. In *Psychobiology, the biological bases of behavior: Readings from Scientific American,* San Francisco: W. H. Freeman & Co., 1967, 240–250.

Sperry, R. W. Hemisphere deconnection and unity in conscious awareness. *American Psychologist,* 1968, **23,** 723–733.

Tinbergen, N. *The study of instinct.* New York: Oxford University Press, 1951.

Williams, R. L. Scientific racism and IQ. *Psychology Today,* 1974, **7,** 32–34, 37–41, 101.

SECTION THREE

The perceptual process

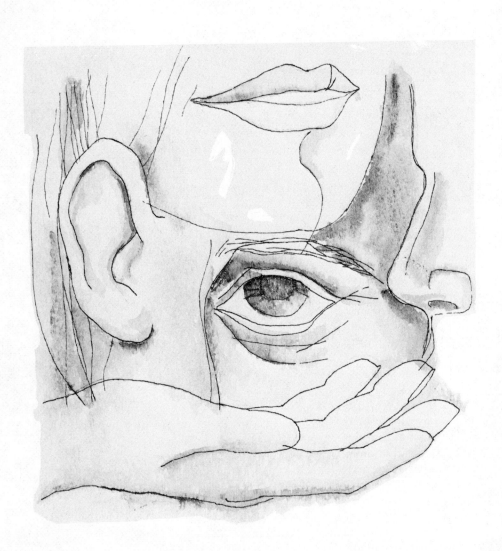

While writing this book, the authors have had the common experience of staying up late into the night and early into the twilight hours. One of us can recall vividly the sensation of dozing off at his desk and the fearful dream he had concerning grotesque evil spirits chasing him about the house. The content of the dream, no doubt, was affected by his experience of seeing the movie *The Exorcist*, from the previous night. Upon awakening, he discovered that it was now early morning. Besides being relieved that he had awakened from such a frightful experience, he got up from his desk and drew the curtain back from the window. Before him was one of the most glorious and beautiful sights to fall on his eyes. The sun had just risen from the horizon and its rays cast different colors through the clouds in the sky. Shades of blue, orange, and yellow were reflected throughout the sky. Being somewhat of an amateur photographer, he quickly ran to his storage cabinet and took out his camera. The pictures which he took with his polaroid camera that early morning, however, did not seem as brilliant and beautiful as the scene from his window.

This short tale serves to introduce us to a most important topic, that of the perceptual process. How was it possible for one of the authors to actually see what he saw? Did the discrepancy between what he saw and that recorded by the camera indicate a faulty camera or sensory apparatus? Our sense organs, eyes, ears, nose, and skin, may place limitations on what and how we perceive. However, much of what we see is influenced by our immediate situation and learning experiences. For example, a 6-foot, 4-inch basketball player standing next to a group of 6-foot men will appear taller than the same person standing near a group of 6-foot, 8-inch players. It is possible that the rarity of viewing a sunrise and its contrast to a frightening dream made the scene more brilliant and beautiful than it actually was. On the other hand, the camera simply recorded what was out there and was unaffected by previous experiences or emotions. Chapter 3 deals with how our sensations may be modified by our perceptions. It discusses the workings of our sensory apparatus. As discussed in the preceding chapter, our sense organs frequently affect our behaviors. Although we can be tricked by our senses, we generally behave in accordance with what we perceive. For that reason, it is important that we understand those factors affecting perception.

Perception involves seeing and sensing the world around us as well as what is occurring inside our bodies. Many events that we sense occur apart from what we call waking state consciousness. For example, the dream experienced by one of the authors is just such an event. Man has always been fascinated by sleep and dreams. Why does man dream? How does it occur? These are questions covered in Chapter 4 and involves what we call altered states of consciousness. Such topics as use of drugs, meditation, hypnotism, and extrasensory perception are examples.

3

Awareness of the world

Most of us move around our world confidently, secure in the belief that we perceive and comprehend reality. For example, John's perception of Mary is that of a beautiful and desirable woman. However, Peter looks at Mary and perceives an unattractive and slightly overweight woman. Both men are sure they are perceiving the "real" Mary. Which one is right? We now know that beauty and desirability are in the "eyes of the beholder." Furthermore, many serious errors in perception often take place. This is well illustrated by the following experiment (Science News Letter, 1954).

> In order to test the observational powers of a group of law students Erle Stanley Gardner, a lawyer and famous mystery writer, was reported to have conducted the following experiment. Midway through a legal lecture given by Gardner, a woman burst into the room and shouted "You got my brother hung!" Consequently, she rushed at and attacked him with a pointed can opener. She was stopped from accomplishing this task and escorted from the room by another person. Students were then told that this incident was a hoax and asked to describe in detail the appearance and clothing of the woman. Of the 34 members of the class, 3 students described her complexion as dark; 2 ruddy; 1 medium; 5 fair; 7 pale; 3 heavily powdered and rouged; 13 said they did not know. In addition, the woman wore an old-fashioned, high-laced, and high-heeled shoe on her right foot with a low-heeled shoe on the other. This gave her a noticeable limp. However, 25 of 34 students failed to mention her outlandish appearance and limp.

How do so many errors occur in our observations (further illustrated in Figures 3–1 and 3–2)? This is not a question to which there are simple

FIGURE 3–1
The Müller-Lyer illusion. The vertical line
B is seen by most observers as longer
than vertical line A, although they are
actually the same length.

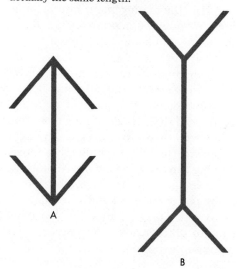

A

B

FIGURE 3–2
The Sander parallelogram illusion. The *AC* diagonal often seems as long or longer than *BC*, but it is, in reality, about 16 percent shorter.

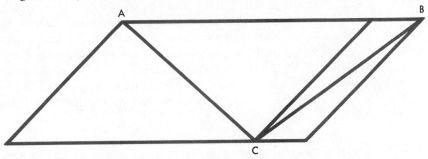

answers. It is the purpose of this chapter to examine the various factors that influence our awareness of the world and to understand the process of perception and sensation.

Perception

The modes of contact with our environment are through the various senses such as vision, hearing, touch, smell, and taste. The receptors in these senses are constantly being bombarded by many kinds of stimuli or physical energies from the outside world such as light waves, sound waves, the mechanical energy of pressure, and the chemical energy of the things we smell and taste. As we saw in Chapter 2, these excitations are carried back by sensory neural pathways to the highest centers in the brain for interpretation. When this final step takes place, we speak of sensations. It is the experiencing of such excitations as sounds, colors, odors, and many others.

What then is perception? It is the arrangement into meaningful patterns of incoming sensations. Through perception we are able to understand the many stimuli impinging on us and to maintain the experience of a continuing and stable environment.

To realize how perception modifies pure sensations, you need only glance at a building. Look first to the left of the building, then move your gaze slowly to the right. As you do this, the image of the building that reaches your eyes definitely moves; the stimuli coming from the building fall first on one part of your eye, then cross over to another part. As far as your sense of vision is concerned, that building has moved just as surely as if it were a dog passing across your field of vision. However, the building does not seem to move and stays in place. Your perception of the world says that a building is a motionless and stationary object and this is the way it appears to you. This is something you have *learned* which points out another major difference between perception and sensation. The former depends upon experience while the latter does not.

Perceptual development

The question psychologists frequently ask is whether we are born with some ability to perceive objects and space in our environment or whether these abilities are completely learned. The general answer seems to be that for some aspects of perception, important limitations arise from the nervous system and maturation of its structures. For others, learning is important. For still others, there is an interaction between learning processes and the perceptual abilities developed through maturation. Let us examine some of the areas of research that shed light on the roles of maturation (innate factors) and learning in perception.

VISUAL DEPRIVATION. Suppose that a man is born blind and has been taught by touch to distinguish between a wooden triangle and a wooden square; and now, as an adult, he suddenly has his vision restored. Could he tell the difference between the triangle and square on the basis of sight? Those who stress innate factors in perception would argue he could, while those who stress learning would certainly predict the opposite.

Evidence on this question is provided by studies of individuals who were born with cataracts on both eyes and whose vision was restored by surgical means when they were adults. What are the perceptual worlds of these newly seeing people like?

Most specific accounts of perception of such patients show that when the bandages are removed for the first time from their eyes, they are overwhelmed by the bewildering array of visual stimuli. At first, such patients are able to distinguish vague figures from the background (apparently in much the same way as normally sighted people). In addition, they can see colors and follow moving figures with their eyes. These abilities then appear to be innate.

On the other hand, these patients cannot distinguish between common shapes such as triangles and squares on the basis of vision alone, nor can they tell which of two uneven sticks is longer. They can eventually learn to recognize the difference between triangles and squares, but visual recognition of shape and other common objects requires weeks or months of visual experience. Perceptual organization gradually improves and vision becomes almost normal.

THE VISUAL CLIFF. One of the areas which have been most thoroughly investigated is the perception of height, which is a special case of distance or depth perception. Experiments on the ability to perceive height have been performed with the aid of an apparatus called a "visual cliff" (Walk & Gibson, 1961). The visual cliff consists of two surfaces, both displaying the same pattern, which are covered by a sheet of thick glass. One surface is directly under the glass; the other is dropped several feet. To a person with depth perception, there appears to be a sharp drop-off from the deep or cliff side. Inducements are offered to the subject to venture to the "shallow" or to the "deep" side. The assumption is that the subject's ability to perceive depth will be reflected in his preference for the shallow side.

Most parents assume that the ability to perceive height is something the child must learn. However, a study by Gibson and Walk (1960) casts doubts on this assumption. They tested some 36 infants ranging in age from 6 to 14 months by placing them on the center board of the visual cliff. The mother then called to the child from the deep and shallow side, successively. Almost all of the infants crawled off on the shallow side and refused to crawl on the deep side.

Since the infants could not be tested until they were old enough to crawl, the experiment does no prove conclusively that depth perception is present at birth. However, in a more recent experiment by Bower (1971), infants less than three months old were able to perceive depth although crude by adult standards. However, the results with other organisms such as chickens, goats, and kittens (Hein, Held, & Gower, 1970) indicate that depth perception is present as soon as the animal is able to locomote.

Previous experiences and perception

PERCEPTUAL CONSTANCY. Perhaps the most dramatic impact of previous experience on perception can be seen in perceptual constancies (the tendency for characteristics of an object in our environment to be perceived as constant). The world appears stable to us. A man does not appear to change much in size as he walks toward or away from us. Visual objects also appear constant in their degree of whiteness, blackness, or grayness. This probably does not seem very surprising to you.

However, the physical stimuli from objects are not constant. For example, the size of the image of an object on the eye depends upon how far away the object is. The farther away the object, the smaller the image. Therefore, we might expect the perceived size of an object to change as we approach it. At 50 feet, a man should appear much larger than at 100 feet. Nevertheless, this is not the case; within limits, a man does not look like a midget at a distance or a giant when he is near to you. This illustrates the phenomenon of *size constancy*.

The development of size constancy depends largely on experience. A three-year-old child looking at mountains in the distance will see them as small hills and often insist that they cannot be large. His size constancy is not yet developed for objects in the distance. Adult-size constancy commonly breaks down when objects are viewed from great heights, as from an airplane. But the adult makes an intellectual correction that a young child does not make (Meneghini & Leibowitz, 1967).

As you might expect, the constancy of object size is closely related to the perception of distance. When depth or distance cues are artificially reversed, familiar objects that ordinarily appear constant in size are perceived as vastly different in size. In the case of an unfamiliar object, the perception of its size corresponds to the image on the eye if the cues to depth or distance are gradually eliminated.

Another perceptual constancy dependent in part on experience is *brightness constancy*. For instance, even though we are receiving different sensations from a piece of coal, it continues to look black in bright sunlight or in dim illumination. Similarly, snow continues to look white even at night.

The phenomena of brightness constancy can be demonstrated in the following manner. A spotlight is focused on the black circle so that the entire area is illuminated with no light being allowed to fall on the background. Next, the ceiling light and others in the room are dimmed until both of the circles are of equal brightness. Each circle reflects the same amount of light, and to a person who walks into the room unaware of the concealed spotlight, they look identical. But the moment the observer becomes aware of the spotlight, he suddenly sees that one circle is black. It looks completely and strikingly different. However, when his attention is directed away from the spotlight beam, the two circles again look alike.

Other perceptual constancies are equally well known. Just as we tend to perceive objects to be of the same brightness regardless of the actual amount of light they reflect, we also tend to perceive colored objects as displaying color constancy. In addition, we also perceive known objects as constant and unchanging in shape and location. *Shape constancy* is illustrated by the common example that we perceive the dinner plate as round even though its image seldom reaches our eyes as a circle. *Location constancy* refers to the fact that we perceive objects in a setting that remains essentially fixed although we live in a kaleidoscopic world which sends us a myriad of changing impressions as we move about. The world does not seem to whirl by us in the opposite direction when we move our heads. Why doesn't this occur? The following experiments conducted on the psychology of perception gives us some answers to this important question.

Experiments with visual distortion

In a classic study of perception, a psychologist wore a specially designed pair of goggles which inverted the images on his eyes (Stratton, 1897). The effects being that he not only saw the world upside down but also reversed so that objects perceived on the left were actually on the right, and vice versa. Stratton reported that at first the world seemed to lose its stability: "When I moved my head or body so that my sight swept over the scene, the movement was not felt to be solely in the observer, as in normal vision, but was referred both to the observer and to objects beyond. . . . I did not feel as if I were visually ranging over a set of motionless objects, but the whole field of things swept and swung before my eyes" (Stratton, 1897, p. 342). In addition, the world looked upside down, which made even the simplest tasks such as washing and eating extremely difficult and laborious. However, after a few days objects began to right themselves and eventually the world began to look absolutely normal. When he stopped wearing the goggles, the world again looked upside down but returned to normal in a few days.

In the last 60 years, similar experiments have been repeated with comparable results (Kohler, 1962; Snyder & Pronko, 1952). A newer technique for studying displaced vision which has fewer disturbing side effects (such as nausea) for the subject, involves the use of closed-circuit television. For instance, the subject performs tasks such as tracking a moving target, assembling an object, tracing geometrical figures or mazes, and writing. The subject views his performance not directly but by means of a television screen. The television camera is adjusted so that the subject's view of his movements is reversed, inverted, or rotated to any desirable angle. Also, the apparent size of the television image can be increased or decreased. Smith and Smith (1962) using this new methodology compared the effects of inversion, reversal, and a combination of both on a series of manual tasks. They found that inversion of the visual image definitely produced more difficulty in performance than reversal and usually more than combined inversion and reversal.

Influences upon perception

ATTENTION. Our perceptions are selective. We focus and consciously react to only a few of the stimuli impinging upon us—only those that are related to our present needs and interests. For example, when we are deeply engrossed in an interesting movie, we usually are not much aware of the temperature and furnishings of the theater or people down the row from us. This process of psychological selectivity or perceptual focusing is called *attention.*

ATTENTION AS A SET TOWARD ACTION. Attention may also be regarded as a *set* or readiness to respond in a particular way to some stimulus situation for which there are a variety of possible responses. For example, when a sprinter is listening for the sound of a gun, his set includes not only the readiness to hear the gun but also the readiness to jump forward and run in the race.

Another example would be if we were to take an intelligent student for whom simple arithmetical operations are automatic and give him a problem to solve. We seat him before a screen, tell him that pairs of numbers will be flashed on it, and instruct him to multiply them as quickly as possible. We then present a series which is made up of combinations such as 6, 2, and so on. To each he always gives a correct and rapid response. The 6, 2 combination produces the response 12 every time—until we give the subject a different set by saying, "Now add, divide, or subtract"; whereupon the same stimulus pattern produces, with equal speed and reliability, the response 8, 3, or 4. It is, therefore, clear that the response is not determined by the present stimulus alone but also by the preparatory set.

SOCIAL MOTIVES. The importance of *social motives* as a factor in perception has been demonstrated in experiments with sex. Clark (1952), using college students, investigated the effects of sexual needs by using sexually arousing stimuli (pictures of female nudes or the presence of an attractive, perfumed female test administrator). He then had the subjects write stories to TAT slides (see Chapter 7). His results, in contrast to what might be expected, indicated that control groups, which had been shown a series of slides of landscape scenes revealed more sexual responses in the written stories than the experimental groups. These findings can be interpreted as indicative of the "puritan morality," that under the circumstances, the guilt evoked by sexual arousal was sufficient to inhibit the expression of sexual responses.

Lindner (1953), on the other hand, using similar techniques, obtained significantly more sexual responses from sexual offenders than from prisoners who were incarcerated for other offenses. These results show clearly the importance of the sex drive on perception and also the differences in the moral attitudes of the prisoners and the college students in the first study.

Another important factor is the influence of *social suggestion* upon our perception of various objects. The following well-known experiment has shown the influence of social suggestion on the perception of movement (Sherif, 1935).

> The experiment made use of the well-known "autokinetic effect." When subjects are seated in a darkened room and shown a stationary pinpoint of light, the light appears to move. Subjects tested individually showed wide variations in reported movements. However, when tested in groups of two or three and each subject heard the estimates of others, the judgements tended to be influenced toward the group average.

More recent experiments have corroborated the finding that social pressure often influences perceptual organization. For instance, do you think you can accurately identify your favorite brand of cola from other brands if blindfolded? The odds are you cannot. Manufacturers spend millions of dollars on advertisements telling you that their brand is tastier than others. In other words, they are using social suggestion to make you think that large differences exist between their product and competing brands. In reality, the differences are so minimal you could not tell the difference when blindfolded. An experiment of this type was actually conducted which demonstrated these findings (Pronko & Herman, 1950).

Similar results are obtained when blindfolded subjects are given different brands of beer to identify (Meeker & Bettencourt, 1973). Twenty students, who considered themselves experienced beer drinkers, were given four brands of beer varying widely in price. None of the students who said they liked or disliked a certain beer could identify the brand. Meeker and Bettencourt also indicated that they obtained similar results for bourbon and scotch. Wine drinkers, although they could discriminate white from red, failed in discriminating between wines that cost $4 a fifth and those costing $2 a jug. In the interest of thrift, the fact that you cannot tell *Iron City* from a *Michelob* is something to keep in mind.

PERSONAL NEEDS AND VALUES. Many investigators have been interested in examining the influence of personal needs and values on perception. The value an individual places on an object may affect such direct impressions as those of size. In one interesting study (Ashley, Harper & Runyon, 1951), subjects were hypnotized, and an artificial life history which stressed either a poor or rich economic status was induced. The subjects were then instructed to adjust the size of a spot of light until it looked to them to be the size of a penny, nickel, dime, or quarter. In one phase of the study, subjects had to make judgments based upon the remembered size of each of the four coins, while in the second phase, the coin was present on a card and the judgment was made from this. Results indicated that the size of the light spot that the subject set as equal to the coins, differed markedly between the rich and poor subjects in both the present and remembered size of the coins. A second part of their experiment consisted of using a gray metal slug as the experimental disk with the subjects being told that it was made of either lead, silver, white gold, or platinum. Again the task was to adjust the spot of light until it appeared to be the size of the slug. Results indicated that the size of the slug increased with the increased cost of the metal.

Another experiment using the tachistoscope was performed with six groups of subjects who highly valued religion, politics, economics, society, the arts, or theory. It was found that most of them were quicker to recognize words relating to these special fields than other words. The subjects interested in religion were quick to recognize *sacred*, for example, and those interested in economics were quick to recognize *income*.

As has been said, we tend to perceive what we expect to perceive and we see what we value most highly. In everyday life, our perceptual expectations are dependent upon our state of mind. Nowhere is this better illustrated than to listen to people with different political viewpoints discuss various controversial issues. They seem to be perceiving entirely different worlds since their values and biases influence what they see.

Perceptual illusions

The perceptual process organizes physical stimulation. Sometimes, however, it organizes physical stimulation so that the resulting perception fails to correspond with reality as shown in Figure 3–1. Such false perceptions are called *perceptual illusions*. It is not difficult to produce a large number of examples of situations in which perception becomes conspicuously inaccurate.

THE HORIZONTAL-VERTICAL ILLUSION. Figure 3–3 presents two examples of the vertical-horizontal illusion, one with simple lines, the other with a drawing of a familiar object. When most observers see a vertical line next to a horizontal line of the same length, they perceive the vertical line as longer.

There is no simple explanation of this illusion but the best known theory has been put forth by a Swedish psychologist, Kunnapas (1955). He has hypothesized that the shape of our field of vision is responsible for the horizontal-vertical (H-V) illusion. Although our field of vision does not have sharp borders like a picture frame, its shape is generally similar to that of a football with flattened ends, a horizontal ellipse. A horizontal line must extend further in both directions to reach the edge of the field of vision than a vertical line. To put it another way, a horizontal line in our field of vision is comparable to a line on a large card; therefore it appears smaller than it is. Conversely, the vertical line is similar to a small card and appears larger.

FIGURE 3–3
The vertical-horizontal illusion.
Although the vertical
dimensions seem greater than
the horizontal dimensions, they
are actually the same length.

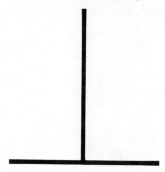

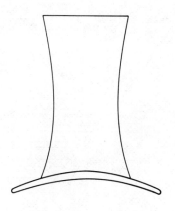

MOON ILLUSION. The moon illusion has fascinated men since the time of the ancient Greeks. It refers to the fact that, near the horizon, the moon appears to be two to three times as large as it does when it is high in the sky. Although the illusion does not look nearly as impressive with pictorial materials as it does in the natural setting, most people see the same effect in Figure 3–4. It will be seen more clearly at a distance of several feet rather than at arm's length and is essentially the same as the Ponzo illusion.

Throughout history there have been numerous varied explanations of this phenomenon. The best known theory was first put forth by Ptolemy, the astronomer, who suggested an apparent distance hypothesis which has been supported by modern psychologists (Kaufman & Rock, 1962). According to this interpretation you see the horizon moon in relation to cues of the terrain—houses, behind trees, and hills—and, therefore, it appears farther away than the zenith moon which you see against an empty sky. As a result, you automatically apply the rule that when two objects form images on the eye of equal size and one is more distant than the other, the one furthest away must actually be larger. Thus, you judge the horizon moon to be larger and perceive it in that manner.

This theory is supported by research findings which show that the size of the horizon moon decreases when the landscape is masked, and that the size of the zenith moon increases when, by means of a mirror, it is seen immediately above the terrain.

TRAPEZOIDAL ILLUSION. The trapezoidal illusion is one of the most familiar of illusions used for demonstrational purposes. It consists of rotating a trapezoidal window. The subject tends to perceive the longer end as always closer to him when the window appears to oscillate or

FIGURE 3–4
The moon illusion. The moon overhead appears to be smaller than the moon on the horizon. This illusion is seen better in real life than in drawings or photographs.

sway rather than to rotate. Most Americans are subject to this illusion which is related to early environmental experiences, as shown by the following comparison of Zulus reared in two settings.

> A group of urban Zulus and a group of herd boys—youngsters aged ten to fourteen who had not been off the native reserves—were tested for the illusion. Only 45 percent of the rural group saw it as compared with 88 percent of the urban group. In the rural Zulu environment, all huts and enclosures are round, and the straight lines and square corners so common in an urban environment are virtually nonexistent. Evidently previous experience with rectangles is a factor in the perception of this particular illusion (Allport & Pettigrew, 1957).

Perception under unusual conditions

SUBLIMINAL PERCEPTION. The term *subliminal perception* implies that there is a threshold or intensity level below which a stimulus cannot be detected consciously, but that "observers" respond to a stimulus which is below that threshold. In other words, we respond to something in our environment even though we are not aware of what is causing us to act in a certain way.

A dramatic example of this concept is the early claims made for the effectiveness of subliminal stimulation in advertising. As we saw in Chapter 1 on the section on consumer psychology, there was a reported increase in buying particular products, such as popcorn, when movie or television audiences were repeatedly exposed to below-threshold advertisements requesting the audience to purchase the products. As a matter of fact, this was brought to the attention of the U.S. Congress as an unethical method of influencing buying habits. How effective is subliminal advertising? The best source for a review of the evidence is a paper by McConnell, Cutler, and McNeil (1958). To summarize their findings, there is no scientific evidence that subliminal stimulation can initiate subsequent action, to say nothing of commercially or politically significant action. In addition, there is certainly nothing to suggest that such action can be produced "against the subject's will," or more effectively than through normal, recognized messages.

Nevertheless, in spite of the lack of evidence of the effectiveness of subliminal perception in advertising, the concept of subliminal perception is a useful one. For instance, Bricker and Chapanis (1953) did a study in which they flashed nonsense words on a screen for very short exposure times and had the subjects guess what the words were. Interestingly enough, many of the subjects correctly guessed what the words were even though they stated that they could not "see" them. The results of this experiment and others show quite clearly that the human nervous system responds to extremely low levels of stimulation. But, much more work is needed to determine the nature of this response and the conditions under which it occurs.

EXTRASENSORY PERCEPTION. Probably no topic in all of psychology is more fascinating to the student than extrasensory perception (ESP). Are there forms of perception that circumvent all the known sensory channels? The answer to this question is the source of a major controversy within contemporary psychology. Although some psychologists believe that the evidence for the existence of certain forms of ESP is now incontrovertible, most remain unconvinced. For a thorough critical review of evidence on ESP, see Hansel (1966). We will discuss ESP more fully in Chapter 4.

Sensation

In the last section, we saw how learning and experience affects our perceptions. We now turn our attention to a discussion of our sensory apparatus and their functioning. We will be concerned with the biological functioning of our sensory organs apart from experience factors. This is the study of sensation.

Most of us take for granted the infinite number of sensations delivered to us by our senses from our environment; the fantastic variety of sights, sounds, smells, and feelings. Consider for a moment how it would feel to be born deaf and blind like Helen Keller (see Figure 3–5); how could you make contact with your environment and learn to communicate? In Helen Keller's case, the answer arrived in the form of a gifted teacher, Anne Sullivan, who herself was plagued by

FIGURE 3–5
Miss Helen Keller (left) is shown observing her 81st birthday in 1961 during a visit with Katherine Cornell. Miss Keller talked to her hostess with her hands and listened by placing her fingers on Miss Cornell's lips.

Wide World Photos

poverty, isolation, prejudice, and half-blindness. Helen's father hired Anne to teach his young daughter to communicate with other people. Anne began her new duties by spelling into Helen's hand, certain symbols that stood for actions, objects, and events. The young child responded by imitating the finger motions like an intelligent and inquisitive animal (Keller, 1955). After a month of such intensive efforts by Anne Sullivan, Helen's mind had been reached; she made contact with reality. It occurred one day when water was being pumped over Helen's hand, and in a flash she realized what the finger motions on her palm meant—water! In that thrilling moment, she found the key to her kingdom. Everything had a name and she now had a way to learn their names. For example, she formed a question by pointing to Anne Sullivan. "Teacher," was the reply.

From that time on, Helen's progress was rapid, and at the age of ten she learned to talk with her mouth instead of with her fingers. Helen entered Radcliffe College when she was 20 years old and graduated four years later with a cum laude degree, won in open competition with girls who could see and hear.

In contrast to the inspiring story of Helen Keller, people with normally intact sensory systems are able to make contact with their worlds with minimal conscious efforts. But, the intriguing question is how? How are we able to see things? Why do some cars appear black while others look red? Why does the trunk of a nearby tree look brown and its leaves green? Even though you may wish not to hear a boring lecture from your professor, how are you able to hear him? Why does a piano sound different from a guitar, and a guitar from a saxophone? Philosophers and scientists have wrestled with such questions for many centuries.

We now know that there are two principles involved in the operation of all our sensory modalities. First, there must be a *stimulus*, a physical energy of some type impinging upon our bodies. Second, there must be *receptors*, as discussed in Chapter 2, that are sensitive to the stimulus. We shall illustrate these basic principles by focusing on our two major senses, vision and hearing.

Vision

We can gain some insight into the nature of energy transmission necessary for the sensation of vision by considering the following example. Suppose that you are lying on the beach one hot summer day when you decide to wade into the ocean for a refreshing swim. You suddenly become aware of the intensity and power of the waves being generated in the water. A wave is a form of energy transmission that is analogous to what happens when you "crack the whip"; the energy starts at the snap of the wrist and is transmitted in the form of a wave to the end of the whip. Now, by keeping in mind the examples of the ocean and whip, you have a basic image of a representative form of energy transmission, the wave.

THE VISUAL STIMULUS. The physical energy, necessary for all visual sensations (seeing), is any electromagnetic wave (packets of energy called protons) between 400 and 700 millimicrons ($m\mu$). Wavelengths determine the color of the light; short ones sensitive to our eyes are seen as blue or violet (ultraviolet) while long ones are seen as red (infrared). While most scientists generally accept this as the usual range of visible wavelengths, experiments have been conducted which demonstrate that if we are willing to endure some damage to our eyes by exposing them to powerful ultraviolet or high intensity infrared lights, we can see wavelengths considerably below 400 or above 700 $m\mu$ in length. Ultraviolet rays, which have an extremely high frequency and a very short wavelength, have a penetrating power so great that people use ultraviolet lamps to get a suntan. Of course, they must cover up their eyes while doing so in order to avoid injury.

WHAT DETERMINES COLOR VISION? There is a very close relationship between the perceived color and the wavelength of light. One method that demonstrates the visible spectrum of light is to take sunlight (white light) and pass it through a prism. Hold the prism so that the sunlight passes through it onto a neutral light gray paper. The long waves will refract, or bend the least as they pass through the prism, and the short waves will bend the most. As a consequence, there will be a nice orderly arrangement of the entire visible spectrum spread out on the gray paper.

THE QUALITIES OF COLOR. In making distinctions between one color and another, three qualities of color discrimination are used: *hue, saturation,* and *brightness.*

If you have normal vision you will see some cars as blue and others as green, red, yellow, and so on. You are able to discriminate between these colors because of the different frequencies of the light waves reflected from those objects. Hence, wave frequency (how often photons are emitted in a given time) is the physical stimulus and *hue* is the resulting sensation.

You are likewise able to discriminate between colors on the basis of their *saturation,* even if they are of the same hue. When you say Jane's dress is of a dull, grayish blue, this means that the color is not highly saturated with blue. The rich green of her scarf, on the other hand, is a saturated color. In terms of light waves, the saturation of a color is determined by the *complexity* of the light being reflected off an object. The light waves coming from the dull-blue dress contain not only light waves which would produce the sensation of a blue hue but also some light waves which, by themselves, would produce a gray. Thus, the color appears to be a relatively unsaturated blue.

Still a third quality of color you are able to distinguish is shown in the striped shirt worn by Jack. The three colors of the stripes all appear different: one is maroon (a dark red), the second, a rose color (a medium shade of red), and the third, pink (a light shade of red). Since the stripes are all of the same hue and the same degree of saturation, they differ only in the amount of *brightness*—that is, the strength of the light waves emanating from the stripes which is called the *intensity*. A 100-watt electric light bulb produces light waves of stronger intensity than a 50-watt bulb and thus objects look brighter.

The intensity of light waves, however, does not fully account for all the degrees of brightness we see. Our eyes are most sensitive to the green and yellow at the middle of the spectrum and, hence, look brighter than reds or blues of equal intensity.

MIXING THE HUES. It is a common notion that there are *three primary colors*, out of which all other hues can be derived by mixing them in appropriate proportions. Every schoolchild who owns a paint set knows that when blue and yellow are mixed together you get the hue of green. However, if you combine the wavelength of a blue light with the wavelength of a yellow light you do not obtain green but gray. The reason for this apparent discrepancy lies in the fact that color mixtures can be accomplished by one of two techniques—*subtraction* or *addition*. When you mix two paint pigments, the resultant color is produced by the process of subtraction. However, when two or more colored spotlights converge on a background, the new color that emerges is the consequence of addition.

You can conduct a simple demonstration, with the proper equipment, which will illustrate the additive rules of color mixture. Place good quality filters of blue, yellow, and red into separate projectors; next, project the beam from each source onto a previously unlighted background. The result will be a white light.

You can demonstrate the subtractive process, on the other hand, by making use of the same filters (blue, yellow, and red) in a different fashion. Place the blue filter between your eyes and a pure white paper; when this is done, the paper seen through the filter will appear blue to you. If you then place a yellow filter in contact with the blue filter, the paper seen through the two filters will appear greenish. When you placed the blue filter alone over the paper, the red and most of the green wavelengths were subtracted (filtered out); however, some of the green wavelengths came through with the blue. Now when you placed the yellow filter and blue filter in tandem over the paper, the yellow filter subtracted (filtered out) the blue wavelengths, again letting some green sneak through.

The structure of the eye

So far in our discussion on vision, we have been focusing upon the nature of the stimulus, light, and the resultant sensations. In order to understand the processes of vision, however, it is equally important to understand how our eyes work. Unfortunately, few people really ever appreciate the wonderful workings of these valuable possessions of ours until vision is lost, temporarily or permanently.

THE EYE AS A CAMERA. Camera fans will be quick to recognize certain resemblances between the eye and the camera. Consequently, the camera analogy of the inner workings of the eye has been and is a useful one for certain purposes, as illustrated in Figure 3–6. Each has an adjustable opening to regulate the amount of light coming in, a lens for focusing, and a sensitive surface to receive the image.

Looking at the anatomy of the eye (Figure 3–7), light passes from the outside through the transparent covering over the eye known as the *cornea*. It next passes through the *pupil*, an opening in the *iris*, which adjusts in size to regulate the amount of light entering the eye, thus affecting the brightness and clarity of the image. After this adjustment of the pupil, the light rays making up the image penetrate the *lens* (an oval-shaped structure). They, in turn, focus the light rays onto the sensitive surface of the *retina*, the back portion of the eyeball which lies behind the pupil. The retina corresponds to the film in the camera and contains the receptors for vision.

RODS AND CONES: RECEPTORS IN THE EYE. The actual receptors for vision, located in the retina, are the *cones* and *rods*. The cones are receptor cells which function only in the light; they are responsible for color vision and high visual acuity (sharpness of vision). In darkness, a second visual system, that of the rods, takes over as the cones are no longer being stimulated. The rods are capable of producing sensations of whites, grays, and black, but not of hues. In contrast to cones, they are effective during both day and night vision.

There are more than seven million cones in the human retina. They

FIGURE 3–6
Comparison of how the eye and camera work. Each has an adjustable opening to regulate the light coming in, a line for focusing, and a sensitive surface to receive the image.

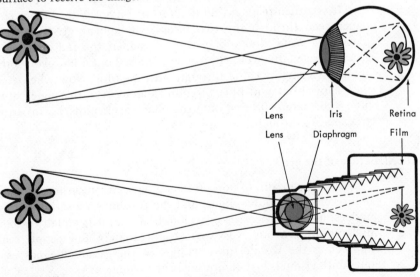

| Lens | Iris | Retina |
| Lens | Diaphragm | Film |

FIGURE 3-7
The anatomy of the eye. In order to see anything in the external world, light reflected from an object must pass first through the cornea, a transparent protective covering in front, and then through the pupil. The pupil is a small opening in the iris, which reflexively adjusts in size to regulate the amount of light entering the eye. In this manner, the brightness and the clarity of the image are controlled. Next, the light rays penetrate the lens, which focuses them on to the retina where the receptors are located. This causes chemical reactions to take place in the receptors, initiating nerve impulses which travel through the optic nerve to the occipital lobes at the back of both hemispheres of the brain.

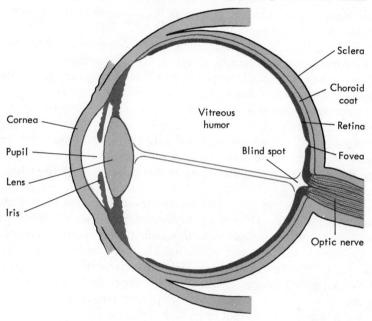

are packed most closely together in the center of the retina, an area called the *fovea*. There are no rods in the fovea, which is located toward the periphery of the retina.

Dark adaptation. Although we cannot see in total darkness, the human eye is remarkable in its ability to adjust to an extremely wide range of illumination. A case in point is the following example which most people have experienced in their lives. When you enter a theater (where there is little light) from broad daylight, you cannot see very well. You are likely to have trouble distinguishing which seats are empty and which ones are not, and, much to your embarrassment, may end up sitting unintentionally on somebody's lap. However, after you have been in the theater awhile, you find that you can clearly see the aisles, the seats, and the people around you. What has happened is that the eyes have undergone the process known as *dark adaptation*. Full adjustment to dark conditions takes about half an hour, and at this point, the eye has become at least 100,000 times more sensitive than during the day, although visual acuity has decreased because the cones are not operating.

Light adaptation. This term refers to a gradual decrease in sensitivity in bright illumination. This phenomenon occurs because the rods lose their sensitivity in bright light and it takes a few minutes for the cones to take over. A common example of this process is the painful glare of light we experience when coming from a movie theater into daylight. Another example is that skiers emerging into the intense glare of sunlight on icy snow gradually become accustomed to this condition and see better after a time.

Visual acuity. The doctor's eye chart, designed to determine your need for glasses, is a test of visual acuity or sharpness of vision. Your vision is considered 20:20 when you can distinguish a standardized block of letters on a chart at a distance of 20 feet what the normal eye distinguishes at that distance. If you can only distinguish at 20 feet or less what the normal eye can see at 40 feet, your vision is 20:40, one half of normal and you should be fitted with corrective lenses. On the other hand, if you can read letters on the chart at a distance at 20 feet what the normal eye can read only at 10 feet, you have 20:10 vision or two times normal.

Psychologists use other techniques besides the block-letter charts to study visual acuity. Of interest is how acuity varies when the image is projected on different parts of the retina. As previously discussed, vision is sharpest at the center of the retina, the fovea, and drops sharply when you focus slightly to the left or right of the stimulus. To put it another way, your vision looking straight ahead may be 20:20, but for objects off in the periphery, your vision is much poorer, similar to the 20:200 vision of a near-sighted person for objects in direct focus.

VISUAL DEFECTS. There are several types of visual defects that are commonplace and of interest to psychologists. We shall focus in our discussion on three common types of defects.

Nearsightedness. The condition of nearsightedness, technically called myopia, is caused by too great a curvature in the lens of the eye. Because the lens bulges out too far, the light rays come into focus slightly in front of the surface of the retina, and spread out again so that the image is fuzzy. If you suffer from this condition, you will find that you must hold a book close to your eyes in order to improve the focus. Myopia, fortunately, is readily corrected with glasses.

Farsightedness. Farsightedness, or hyperopia, is a visual disorder in which the individual sees objects at a distance quite well, but has trouble distinguishing nearby objects, which appear blurred. This person often holds his newspaper at arm's length in order to bring it into better focus. This condition may be caused by the lens not bulging out for close vision, or because the muscles controlling its shape are too weak. As a consequence, the image comes into focus behind the retina.

Farsightedness, which also may be corrected by glasses, does not result in superior distant vision for the afflicted person. In fact, the far-sighted person cannot see any farther than a normal person.

Color blindness. Huddart (1777) published one of the first articles, in a philosophical magazine, to describe the reactions of people who are unable to distinguish colors. One such person happened by accident to discover a child's stocking in a street. He took it to a neighboring house to inquire who was the owner. He was quite surprised when the people called it a red stocking having thought that he, himself, had adequately described the article in calling it a stocking.

Such cases, as the above, are very rare in which the individual is totally color blind. Such people can only see the world in shades of gray, such as a black and white photograph. We do not know whether this condition is caused by malfunctioning cones or by their absence altogether.

Much more common are cases of partial color blindness. Many people are color blind for two colors, of which the most frequent encountered is red-green color weakness. It is estimated that approximately 8 percent of the male population has a red-green color blindness of some degree. As discussed in Chapter 14, it is a sex-linked trait almost always transmitted from a male grandparent through his daughter (who herself is rarely color blind) to her son. Thus if you are a male who is red-green blind, your maternal grandfather is to be "blamed." The red-green blind person typically sees these hues as poorly saturated yellows or browns, but is able to see yellows and blues as well as those who have normal vision. This suggests that the red-green blind, unlike the totally color-blind person, has a complete set of cones. Their cones operate differently from those of people with complete color vision.

Many people, who have a red-green color weakness use the words *red* and *green* freely without being aware of their defect. They refer to "green grass" and "red bricks." However, this does not mean that they can discriminate between red and green stimuli in the same manner as people with normal color vision. It merely indicates that they have learned to describe their environment as others do. Typically they have learned to use other cues to make up for this color deficiency. For example, a red-green, color-blind male does not have any trouble discriminating between red and green traffic lights. He may have learned that the red light is above the green and is not as bright. In addition, in order to help him discriminate between the traffic lights, blue has been added to the green, and yellow to the red.

Seeing the world in three dimensions

One of the most fascinating topics in the study of vision is how we are able to perceive the third dimension, distance and depth, even though the retina is only a two-dimensional surface. Since we use many cues in obtaining the perception of distance, the answer is not simple.

STEREOSCOPIC VISION. If you have ever viewed pictures through a *stereoscope* you have had the experience of perceiving depth in flat pictures. In *stereoscopic vision*, both eyes operate together to yield the experience of solidity and distance. The technique involves two flat pictures which are presented before each eye and combine to yield the effect of three dimensions, very different from that received from a single, flat picture. The depth or distance appears real as though you were viewing objects right around you.

The cue which stereoscopic vision utilizes, unlike flat pictures, is known as *retinal disparity*. Because our eyes are separated in our head, we get two slightly different views of an object. This is unlike a person with vision only in one eye. The stereoscopic effect results from the combination of these slightly different pictures in one view. You can demonstrate retinal disparity to yourself without having a stereoscope. Close one eye and hold a pencil in front of you. Now, without changing the position of your head or eyes, close your other eye instead. Notice that the pencil will appear to have moved from your first view. With the right eye you see more of the right side of the pencil; with the left eye, more of the left side. You interpret distance by automatically comparing the two slightly different retinal images.

Three-dimensional movies involve the same principle, providing you with slightly different pictures of the same object. These movies were prominent in the 1950s in which moviegoers wore special glasses, provided by the theater, which had a different colored plastic lens on each half of the spectacles. Two overlapping images were projected onto the screen which were separated slightly from each other and of different colors. Because the glasses had colored filters, each eye received a slightly different image through the appropriately colored lens, giving the viewer a very lifelike effect of depth. Monsters could be seen creeping about scaring audiences in such three-dimensional films as *I Was a Teen-Age Werewolf*. More recently the presentation of "sex" in three-dimensional movies has proved to be a highly successful commercial adventure as exemplified by the movie, *The Stewardesses*.

MONOCULAR CUES. A person with one functioning eye is also able to perceive depth because other cues give us this effect besides retinal disparity. There are many monocular cues—visual cues involving one eye —for depth and distance. These cues are made use of by the artist in painting on a two-dimensional surface, some of which were first noted by Leonardo da Vinci. *Linear perspective* is a monocular cue often used by artists. It refers to the tendency for parallel lines to appear to converge in the distance and can be readily demonstrated by looking down a railroad track. The painter also uses the cue of *size* to enhance the three-dimensional effect. Closeup objects cast a much larger image on the retina than objects at a distance. We can also see more detail in nearby objects as opposed to distant ones, and near objects are seen more clearly than are far ones. This cue of *aerial perspective* is especially important when viewing objects at great heights or distances. Two other important monocular cues described by da Vinci are interposition and shading. *Interposition* is the phenomenon of nearer objects imposing themselves between our eyes and the more distant objects, blocking out part of the image. *Shadowing*, in which the pattern of light and shadow on an object varies, is often used in painting to enhance the three-dimensional effect.

Audition

Most of us would probably agree that our eyes are our most important source of information about the environment. Second, if not equally important, is our sense of hearing, or audition. Most of us do not realize just how sensitive are our ears. In fact, if they were only slightly more acute, we could hear the collision of molecules in the air about us. This is further illustrated by the fact that blind people, like bats and porpoises, can learn to avoid obstacles by listening to the sounds reflected from obstructions.

THE DIMENSIONS OF SOUND AND THEIR PHYSICAL BASIS. We all know that when lightning flashes, we soon hear the accompanying sound of thunder. From this observation we know that light travels faster than sound. To put it another way, light waves, the physical basis for vision, travel faster than sound waves, the stimuli for hearing. The latter travel at about the speed of 750 miles an hour while the former travel at a speed of 186,000 miles a second, the fastest speed known. As mentioned previously, light travels via electromagnetic waves while sound travels by the mechanical movement of particles. *Sound waves* are normally the changes in air pressure produced by vibrations, or movements, of the sound source. The vibrations created by striking the keyboard of the piano or firing a pistol are carried through the air similar to the visible ripples of water spreading out from where a fish has jumped.

Frequency/pitch. Pitch refers to how high or low a note sounds. It is related to the frequency of the sound wave: the higher the vibration frequency, expressed in *cycles per second* (cps), the higher the perceived pitch. The range of frequencies that we can hear is between about 20 to 20,000 cps. Our ability to detect differently pitched sounds is meager in comparison to some animals. For example, a porpoise can hear sounds four times as high as what we are able to hear. A dog can also hear sounds considerable higher than human beings; this principle has made possible the development of high-pitched dog whistles that are inaudible to man.

Intensity/loudness. Loudness is determined primarily by the height of the waves. It is that aspect of sound that we describe in terms of "weak" and "strong." Sound intensity is measured by a unit we call a *decibel;* the decibel scale is shown in Figure 3–8. It should be noted that this is not an absolute scale. For example, the sound of a large pneumatic

FIGURE 3–8
The decibel scale. The loudness of various common
objects are illustrated in decibels.

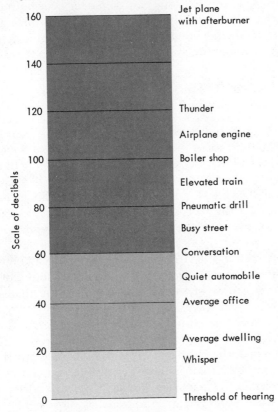

riveter of 120 decibels is far more than twice as loud as a conversation
at 60 decibels. Zero decibels has been arbitrarily set as the absolute
threshold for hearing a 1,000 cps tone.

Complexity/timbre. Just as the colors we see are seldom pure, so
the sounds that we hear are seldom pure tones. In fact, outside of the
laboratory, the closest thing to a pure tone is the sound made by a simple
musical instrument, the flute.

The third quality of the sound waves that reach our ears in addition to
frequency and intensity is called *complexity.* When you strike a guitar
string that produces the sound of middle C, the string is vibrating at a
frequency of 256 cycles a second. However, it also vibrates in other
ways. Not only will the string vibrate up and down through its entire
length, but it also vibrates in halves, thirds, quarters, and so on, with
each partial vibration producing its own frequency. These *overtones* are
multiples of the fundamental tone of 256 cps.

It is the nature of the overtones that makes one musical instrument
sound differently from another. Some instruments produce a greater

number of overtones than others and also may differ in construction, which enhance certain overtones and deaden others. This characteristic quality of a musical tone we hear is called *timbre*. It is the timbre of a tone that tells us whether it comes from a piano or a saxophone. Timbre, as well as pitch, also helps us distinguish one voice from another.

An analogy between the dimensions of sound and those of color can be drawn as follows:

Dimensions of color	*Dimensions of tone*
Hue	*Pitch*
Brightness	*Loudness*
Saturation	*Timbre*

Hue and pitch are produced by the wave frequency; brightness and loudness are functions of wave intensity; saturation and timbre are the result of wave complexity (mixture of different frequencies).

The structure of the ear

THE EAR AS A MICROPHONE. To demonstrate the inner workings of the eye, we compared it with the functions of a camera. Similarly, the ear can be compared with the way a microphone works. A microphone receives, amplifies, and transmits sounds in an electrical form to their destination. The ear functions in an analogous way. It receives, amplifies, and transmits the vibration movements of the air (sound waves) so that they yield information to the nervous system. In order to understand how, we must know something of the anatomy of the ear. The structures of the ear (Figure 3–9) which perform these tasks may be divided into three parts: the *outer, middle,* and *inner* ears.

FIGURE 3–9
Anatomy of the ear. This diagram shows the course of the sound wave as it goes from the outer ear, to the eardrum, through the ossicles of the middle ear, and eventually to the oval window.

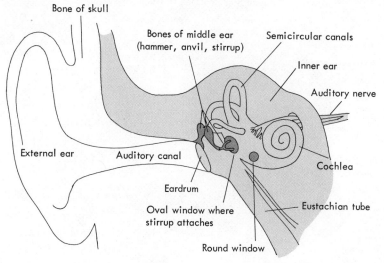

Bone of skull

Bones of middle ear
(hammer, anvil, stirrup)

Semicircular canals

Inner ear

Auditory nerve

External ear

Auditory canal

Cochlea

Eardrum

Oval window where
stirrup attaches

Eustachian tube

Round window

The two major features of the outer ear, which receives or collects the sound, are the auditory canal and the tympanic membrane. When sound waves travel through the *auditory canal*, they strike the *tympanic membrane* (eardrum), causing it to vibrate. These vibrations are passed on and activate the structures of the middle ear.

The middle ear is the chief amplifying system with the ear. The vibrating tympanic membrane activates three small bones, the *ossicles*, within the middle ear, these in turn press against the oval window, which marks the beginning of the inner ear. The three ossicles are activated by the eardrum in the following sequence: the *hammer, anvil* and *stirrup*. The stirrup, which has a muscle attached to it sends the vibrations against the oval window.

In the inner ear, movements of the oval window exert pressures on a very important structure, the *cochlea*. The cochlea consists of liquid-filled canals which allow waves to travel up and down it. These waves then activate the receptors located on the cochlea, which transmit nerve impulses to the brain. Thus, the inner ear may be seen as a converting system, which serves to change a signal from one type of energy to another. In this case, mechanical motions of the oval window become electrochemical signals.

The cochlea. Upon closer examination, it becomes evident that the cochlea has three canals and that the movement of the liquid in the two outer canals stimulates the membranes which separate them from the inner canal called the cochlear canal (Figure 3–10). Attached to one of these membranes, known as the basilar membrane, located in the cochlear canal, is the *Organ of Corti* (see Figure 3–10). It consists of

FIGURE 3–10
The cochlea. Two views of the snail-shaped cochlea are illustrated in these drawings. The auditory receptors are located in the organ of Corti, which rests upon the basilar membrane. When the basilar membrane is bent, this activates the hair cells and produces impulses in the auditory nerve which are carried to the temporal lobe.

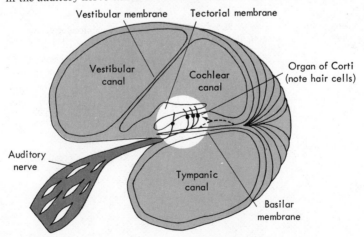

about 23,000 hair cells which move in response to movements of the basilar membrane. It is these *hair cells* which are analogous to the rods and cones in vision as they are the receptors for hearing. The movement of these hair cells initiate neural impulses in the nerve fibers to which they are connected. These nerve fibers join together to form the *auditory nerve* that travels to the auditory center in the brain.

Hearing defects

Deafness is, of course, a great handicap in working and in going about our everyday lives. In fact, a person who is born deaf is perhaps under more of a handicap than a congenitally blind person because he cannot learn the symbolic uses of sound in language—so vital for human communication. Even a person who becomes deaf after he has thoroughly learned a language has great difficulty communicating because even the most skilled lip-reader fails to respond to the subtle tonal inflections. Conversation with the deaf is usually a slow and difficult process which requires a lot of patience and understanding.

There are two major types of deafness that are generally recognized. Both types usually occur primarily as a matter of degree.

INTENSITY DEAFNESS. Many people are "hard-of-hearing" in the sense that they cannot hear weak sounds easily heard by people with normal hearing. This type of partial deafness tends to be caused by aging and, in addition, is produced by the particular working conditions of different occupations. Pilots, boilermakers, and rock-and-roll musicians, for example, often become partially deaf from the loud noises to which they are constantly subjected.

Intensity deafness can be caused by some defect in structures of the ear, such as the eardrum, or ossicles, of the inner ear, which are responsible for conducting sound waves to the cochlea and hence to the auditory nerve. Deafness of this type can often be remedied by devices that amplify sound vibrations and transmit them directly through the bones of the skull to the inner ear. Most hearing aids, however, merely magnify the sound stimulus so that it can be sent through regular channels with enough intensity to overcome structural defects.

TONE DEAFNESS. Some people have hearing problems in which they cannot perceive differences in tone; one note sounds like another to them. This kind of deficiency in hearing is usually the result from damage to the nerves themselves. The ability to discriminate between notes is a matter of degree. People with so-called normal hearing differ in their ability to distinguish between different pitched sounds. Most frequently, the person with a loss of auditory discrimination is unable to hear the high-frequency sounds as well as he can hear low-frequency.

People with this type of deafness can never become good singers or musicians. More seriously, such deafness causes problems in hearing speech sounds, many of which are of high frequency. The individual with tone deafness also has trouble in distinguishing between certain words such as "ice" and "eyes" or between "seal" and "zeal."

Other sensory modalities

Man possesses many more senses than just that of sight and hearing. We have senses that allow us to *taste, touch* (pressure, pain, warmth, cold), detect movement and position of our body in space *(kinesthesis)*, and *balance*. These senses also operate under the same principles as that of sight and audition. Without these additional senses providing us feedback from the environment, we would either lead a very drab existence (no sense of smell or taste) or be unable to function adaptively (kinesthesis and balance). Students interested in pursuing the study of these other senses should ask their instructor for further resource materials.

Summary

Most of us believe that we are able to perceive and comprehend our world accurately. However, many serious errors in perception frequently occur. That is because *sensations*, the reception of physical stimulation through our senses, must be arranged into meaningful patterns through the process of *perception*. Our sensations are frequently modified by perception. The latter is strongly influenced by learning experiences and may cause false impressions.

One of the controversies in visual perception is whether our ability to see objects is innate or learned. Studies on the visual cliff and the perception of height, seem to indicate that depth perception may be present at birth. However, many studies also indicate that previous experience (learning) can play an important role in perception.

Perhaps the most dramatic impact of previous experience on perception can be seen in perceptual constancies (the tendency for characteristics of an object in our environment to be perceived as constant, regardless of the actual stimulus properties). Many specific factors tend to influence our perceptions: (1) attention, (2) social motives, and (3) personal needs and values.

Oftentimes, our perceptual processes do not correspond with reality and provide perceptual illusions or false impressions. Among these are the *(a)* horizontal-vertical illusion, the perception that a horizontal line is longer than a vertical one of the same length; *(b)* moon illusion, the impression that the moon is larger near the horizon than when high in the sky; and *(c)* trapezoidal illusion, the phenomenon of a rotating trapezoidal window appearing to oscillate or sway.

Perceptions also occur under highly unusual conditions. Such is the case of subliminal perceptions which imply the detection of stimuli below one's level of awareness and extrasensory perception.

Psychologists now know that although many perceptual processes are learned and may be influenced by unidentifiable forces, it is important to study the physical characteristics of sensations in order to determine the extent of these influences. Just how do our senses function? To answer this question two major senses were discussed: vision and hearing.

Electromagnetic waves produce the sensation of seeing. The lengths of the light waves that reach our eyes determine the color we see: short ones produce blue or violet, while longer ones produce red. Color vision is determined by three qualities: (1) hue or wavelength; (2) saturation, the presence or absence of different wavelengths; and (3) brightness, the intensity of the light waves. Color perception is also affected by the mixing of colors. When two colors are mixed it is important to determine whether subtraction or addition is being used.

The eye has been likened to a camera. Light travels through the transparent covering over the eyes called the cornea, then through the pupil, an opening in the iris, which adjusts to regulate the amount of light entering. This affects the brightness and clarity of images which pass through the lens and onto the retina, the back portion of the eyeball. Two types of receptors are present on the retina: cones and rods. Cones are receptor cells which function only in the light and are responsible for color vision and visual acuity. Rods function best in darkness when the cones no longer operate. Dark and light adaptation as well as visual acuity depends on the differential function of these two receptors.

Several types of visual defects were discussed. Nearsightedness (myopia) is caused by too great a curvature of the lens in the eye. Farsightedness (hyperopia) is caused by either weak muscles controlling the len's shape or lack of lens curvature. Total color blindness is rare but partial blindness for colors is frequent. The most common form is for the red-green color. Lack of cones in the former and sex-linked genes have been used to explain the latter form of color blindness.

Even though the retina is two dimensional, we are able to perceive distance and depth, the third dimension. Stereoscopic vision, like our eyes, operate under the principle of retinal disparity, reception of two slightly different views of the same object. Other cues used to see depth are linear perspective, size, aerial perspective, interposition and shadowing.

Sound waves have three properties which parallel those of light. Pitch, like hue, is determined by frequency. Loudness, like brightness, is determined by intensity or the height of the waves. The timbre, like saturation, depends on the complexity or the pureness of wavelengths that reach us.

To receive the stimuli and give us the sensation of sound, our ear receives, amplifies, and transmits them. The three parts of the ear are the outer, middle, and inner ear. The outer ear collects sounds via the auditory canal and tympanic membrane (eardrum) which causes it to vibrate. The middle ear which amplifies these stimuli via the ossicles (hammer, anvil, and stirrup) presses against the oval window and exerts pressure in the inner ear. The cochlea (liquid filled canals) is important in transmitting nerve impulses to the brain.

Two types of hearing defects often occur. In intensity deafness, weak sounds are difficult to hear. Aging and working conditions with loud noises can damage the ear structures. Tone deafness occurs when a person has problems perceiving one tone from another. Damage to the nerves is usually the cause.

References

Allport, G. W., & Pettigrew, T. F. Cultural influences on the perception of movement: The trapezoidal illusion among Zulus. *Journal of Abnormal and Social Psychology*, 1957, **55**, 104–113.

Ashley, W. R., Harper, R. S., & Runyon, D. L. The perceived size of coins in normal and hypnotically induced economic states. *American Journal of Psychology*, 1951, **64**, 564–572.

Bower, T. G. R. The object in the world of the infant. *Scientific American*, 1971, **225**, 30–38.

Bricker, P. D., & Chapanis, A. Do incorrectly perceived tachistoscopic stimuli convey some information? *Psychological Review*, 1953, **60**, 181–188.

Clark, R. A. The projective measurement of experimentally induced levels of sexual motivation. *Journal of Experimental Psychology*, 1952, **44**, 391–399.

Gibson, E. J., & Walk, R. D. The "visual cliff." *Scientific American*, 1960, **202**, 66–71.

Hansel, C. M. *ESP: A scientific evaluation*, New York: Scribners, 1966.

Hein, A., Held, R., & Gower, E. C. Development and segmentation of visually controlled movement by selective exposure during rearing. *Journal of Comparative and Physiological Psychology*, 1970, **73**, 181–187.

Huddart, J. An account of persons who could not distinguish colours. *Philosophical Transactions*, 1777, **67**, 260–265.

Kaufman, E. L., & Rock, I. The moon illusion. *Scientific American*, 1962, **207**(1), 120–130.

Keller, H. *Helen Keller, teacher: Anne Sullivan Macy*. New York: Doubleday, 1955.

Kohler, I. Experiments with goggles. *Scientific American*, 1962, **206**, 62–72.

Kunnapas, T. M. Influence of frame size on apparent length of line. *Journal of Experimental Psychology*, 1955, **50**, 168–190.

Lindner, H. Sexual responsiveness to perceptual tests in a group of sexual offenders. *Journal of Personality*, 1953, **21**, 364–374.

McConnell, J. V., Cutler, R. L., & McNeil, E. B. Subliminal stimulation: An overview. *American Psychologist*, 1958, **13**, 229–242.

Meeker, F. B., & Bettencourt, R. D. Perceptual learning of discriminations in beer tasting: Effects of the subject's belief in his ability to discriminate. Paper presented at the meeting of the Western Psychological Association, 1973.

Meneghini, K. A., & Leibowitz, H. W. The effect of stimulus distance and age on shape constancy. *Journal of Experimental Psychology*, 1967, **74**, 241–248.

Pronko, N. H., & Herman, D. T. Identification of cola beverages: IV. *Journal of Applied Psychology*. Postscript, 1950, **34**, 68–69.

Science News Letter. Eye witnesses can get facts twisted. 1954, **66**, 68.

Sherif, M. A study of some social factors in perception. *Archives of Psychology*, 1935, **27**, 127.

Smith, K. V., & Smith, W. M. *Perception and motion: An analysis of space-structured behavior*. Philadelphia: Saunders, 1962.

Snyder, F. W., & Pronko, N. H. *Vision with spatial inversion*. Wichita, Kans.: McCormick-Armstrong, 1952.

Stratton, G. M. Vision without inversion of the retinal image. *Psychological Review*, 1897, **4**, 341–360, 463–481.

Walk, R. D., & Gibson, E. J. A comparative and analytical study of visual depth perception. *Psychological Monograph*, 1961, 75 (Whole No. 519).

4

Altered states
of consciousness

I f you were to thumb at random through various psychology textbooks, you would find that most authors do not devote much space to the discussion of consciousness. This is particularly true in the case of textbooks devoted primarily to the experimental areas of psychology. As a matter of fact, philosophers and theologians have traditionally shown more interest in awareness than the behavioral scientists. Even though some early psychologists were interested in the content of consciousness, the emphasis was quite different. One objection to accepting consciousness as a subject matter for science lies in the rejection of an alleged dualism between the mind and the body, the belief that there are both physical and mental facts. More specifically, dualism implies that the mind is somehow separate from the brain. However, a way of combating this objection as currently accepted in scientific circles, is not to deny any fundamental dualism, but to accept the convenience of a double language. The language of mental activities includes private experiences and intentions, on the one hand, and the language of physics and physiology, on the other. The use of this double language can be illustrated by the following example. When you describe a dream to a psychologist, the first language is used; when your dreaming is described in terms of brain waves, the other language is used.

What is consciousness?

What we typically consider to be the normal waking consciousness, the ability to report accurately what is happening in the environment around us, is not itself a single, simple state. We may be looking, listening, talking, or planning the future—sometimes all at once. One of the best ways to illustrate the complexity of normal wakefulness is for you to reflect on what is currently happening. As you read this page, you may be listening to a record or carrying on a conversation simultaneously with your roommate. Although you can attend fully to only one activity at a time, information from a second activity also registers.

The above examples all involve or imply a certain amount of alertness, but not all waking states are this alert. Consider this the next time you drive a car on a long trip. Are you totally aware of steering as you drive for several hours at a time? You will discover the answer is not simple because the state of consciousness is not an all-or-nothing phenomenon. It is a matter of degree and waxes and wanes from moment to moment. At one extreme you are very alert to all the details of an event that arouses you; i.e., a car bearing down on you from the opposite direction. At the other extreme, your mind may be almost a complete blank as is commonly associated with long, monotonous hours of driving.

Many other examples could be cited. However, this will be made clearer when we discuss below the psychological and physiological criteria for consciousness. The discussion on indicators of consciousness will be followed by sections on the various techniques used to modify consciousness, such as drugs and meditation. This chapter will be concluded by a presentation of special altered states of consciousness including sleep and dreaming and different forms of extrasensory perception.

Psychological indicators

One of the best methods developed for denoting consciousness was formulated by Donald Hebb (1972). He has effectively translated a strictly mental event, which can never be seen, into behavioral terms. One behavioral sign of consciousness in humans or animals can be seen in the purposefulness of one's reactions. Behavior is classified as purposive when it varies with circumstances in such a manner as to achieve a definite goal, or end. When the situation changes, the behavior changes accordingly. For example, if a student wants a certain course but finds the class is already filled up, he varies his behavior accordingly. He may visit the instructor to see if he will be given special permission to sit in on the course. If this doesn't work, he may vary his behavior by waiting to see if one of the registered students may later decide to drop the class. All of his modified responses are designed to produce the effect of achieving his goal; gaining admittance to the class.

In much of the purposive behavior of man, we encounter long, unified chains of action with a definite end in sight. To a lesser degree, we find similar behavioral actions in the higher animals, a sign of consciousness. Consider the family dog that becomes hungry. He may first try to arouse the owner by whining and barking. If this does not work, plan B goes into operation in which the family pet may sit by the refrigerator. The dog has changed his behavior in order to obtain his goal of food.

A more humorous example, concerning the purposefulness of behavior in animals took place at the San Antonio zoo. A group of psychologists were touring the zoo after attending a conference. They happened to stop by a large cage to observe a gorilla. The animal seemed to be greatly annoyed by the group of people standing next to his cage and staring at him. He reacted by making threatening gestures toward the tourists, attempting to frighten them away. This didn't work, so the gorilla changed his behavioral patterns. He disappeared briefly. All of a sudden he returned with his hand full of feces, which he threw at the onlookers, hitting several. The deadly aim of the gorilla achieved its purpose; the people scattered in several directions, thereby leaving him alone in peace.

Closely related to purposefulness as a function of consciousness is the second process of Hebb's schemata, *mediating processes*. They may be roughly defined as thoughts and ideas, which determine a subject's response to a stimulus. Mediating processes make complex and flexible behavior possible, as opposed to reflexive responses that are invariant. Scientifically, there is no reason for ascribing consciousness to any lower organism, such as houseflies or jellyfish, whose behavior is entirely reflexive or instinctive (see Chapter 2). Even the remarkable behavior of the social insects, such as bees and ants, has been shown to be nothing more than reflexive adaptation to the environment (Figure 4–1). On the other hand, it is not possible to avoid the inference of mediating processes, and hence consciousness, in the higher animals such as the chimpanzee, dog, or cat. This is well documented in problem-solving studies testing thought processes (see Chapter 5, section on "Insight").

A third criterion laid down by Hebb for consciousness is *immediate memory* (memory for the immediate past). Normally, a person remembers what he has just said and done, and does not unnecessarily repeat the same action that is already completed. Nor would we bore our friends by telling them the same joke twice within a time span of a few minutes. Immediate memory makes it possible to coordinate past experience and action with future action.

Consciousness as a matter of degree

As noted before, consciousness is not an all-or-nothing matter. Instead, it exists as a matter of degree and consists of several processes. Consider the following case. One of the authors participated in a touch football game a few years ago, and late in the game, one of the players fell to the ground hitting his head. He continued playing, and as far as anyone could tell, he was all right. However, the next day he could recall no de-

FIGURE 4–1
This bee is going through the complex behavioral process of collecting pollen from a flower, and later it will communicate the location of the flower to other bees back at the beehive.

Courtesy of Dennis L. Briggs,
Staff Research Associate,
Department of Entomology,
University of California, Davis

tails about the game following his fall, nor could he even remember driving himself home after the game. What had happened was that he received a concussion as a result of his fall, unbeknown to anyone. The important thing about this case, is that it illustrates that consciousness consists of several functions, not just one. The football player was conversing in an apparently normal fashion with his teammates, but did not know where he was and later could not remember how he got home. Some of the processes normally present in the conscious subject were present in this case, but others were absent or impaired.

This actual case is worth consideration because it tells us something about the nature of consciousness. It varies greatly from one time to another, even in normal subjects, and consists of several functions. Responsiveness, in itself, does not necessarily indicate consciousness because reflexes are present in people in a comatose state (who, by definition, are unconscious) or even in lowly insects. It is the variability and degree of responsiveness, as well as to what the organism or subject responds, from which we infer consciousness.

Physiological indicators

Scientists have known for many years that complex electrical activity is constantly taking place within the brain. However, it remained for a German psychiatrist, Hans Berger, to first publish in 1929 some strange little pictures consisting only of wavy lines, known as *brain wave patterns*. His research was not taken seriously at the time, because scientists felt that it was impossible to isolate and measure the individual functions of the complex human brain. Today, we know that Berger was indeed measuring the electrical activity of the brain, and presently there are several hundred laboratories in the United States and Europe recording these electrical patterns. The science of measuring brain waves is called *electroencephalography*. The machines that record the electrical rhythms of the brain wave have become very elaborate, consisting of hundreds of components (Figure 4–2). A really elaborate research apparatus may have several hundred controls, set and adjusted by a team of highly skilled researchers before and during each experiment. Figure 4–2 shows the general method of recording brain activity in man.

The standard electroencephalogram (EEG) which results from the recording, shows a set of eight or more wavy lines, each line being a graph of the electrical signals from one area in the brain. It is a kind of overall average of what many thousands of nerve cells in the brain are doing. Two measurements are commonly used to analyze an EEG record: the *amplitude* or size of the waves and the *frequency* or number of waves per second.

A striking example of this information is conveyed by the EEG, and is important in determining the state of consciousness. Small, fast waves mean a very alert state; large, slow waves indicate a deep state of sleep

FIGURE 4–2

EEG records from a human infant 90 hours old. The waking record of the infant
has slow waves, in comparison with awake adults, though of much lower amplitude
than in the two sleep records. There is a marked absence of both alpha and beta
frequencies.

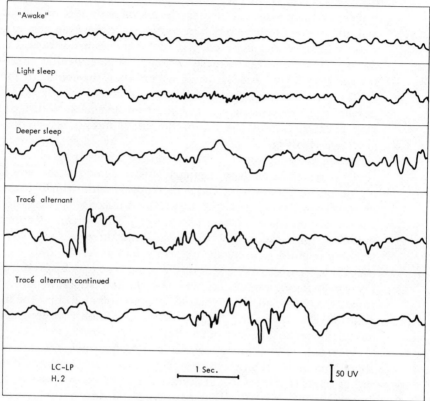

"Awake"

Light sleep

Deeper sleep

Tracé alternant

Tracé alternant continued

LC–LP
H.2

1 Sec.

50 UV

Courtesy of A. K. Bartoshuk, Hunter Laboratory, Brown University

and are also found when the brain function is impaired by disease or
anesthesia. They are called *beta* and *delta rhythms*, respectively. The
alpha rhythm represents an intermediate state of alertness or consciousness and appears when the subject is instructed to close his eyes and
relax.

EEG RECORD OF INFANTS. It is interesting and informative to compare
the EEG records of human babies with adults. A 90-hour-old baby is characterized by slow, low amplitude waves while he is awake. Also noticeable is a marked absence of alpha and beta frequencies. This means that
in spite of certain romantic and nostalgic writings to the contrary, the
infant is not conscious in the same way as an adult. Furthermore, it
explains why we cannot remember early postnatal events; such aware-
nesses are not simply forgotten, they never existed. It is likely that
the newborn infant is not fully conscious and only gradually becomes so
in the first five to eight months of life.

Current perspectives

All of us experience states of consciousness different from our ordinary waking state, as exemplified by sleep, daydreaming, meditation, trance, and hypnosis. All of these forms of nonordinary consciousness and others seem to have much in common. Primarily, a person's awareness is focused and directed inward rather than outward. Currently, there is much interest in these various mental states because of their relationship to the use of drugs which alter the mind. In fact, Weil (1972) contends that the desire to alter consciousness is an innate psychological drive arising out of the neurological structure of the human brain and, hence, is the predominant motive behind the use of psychoactive drugs.

Strong evidence for this inborn motive comes from observations of very young children who regularly use techniques of consciousness alteration on themselves. These methods include whirling until dizziness ensues, hyperventilating to produce unconsciousness, and being choked around the neck to cause fainting. Such practices appear to be culturally universal, and occurs in two- and three-year-olds when social learning is unlikely to be an important factor. As children grow older, they discover that experiences of the same type may be produced chemically by being exposed to a general anesthesia via operations, or inhaling fumes from gas and other volatile solvents found around the house. In addition, they typically have several chances to observe the behavior of adults under the influence of alcohol.

According to Weil, since the need to alter consciousness is innate, one should pay more attention to how people are satisfying their inborn drive rather than attributing drug taking to foreign wars or domestic tensions. In this manner, the altered state of consciousness becomes a phenomenon to be investigated in its own right rather than just as a by-product of drugs. This approach will be discussed in this chapter. We shall focus on the mind-altering effects of drugs and other techniques, rather than the related moral or sociological issues. However, we must keep in mind that not everyone would agree with Weil that an inborn need to alter consciousness is present in man.

Altered states of consciousness: External control

We shall now refer to those modulating influences on our states of consciousness that are external, or come from outside our body. As already indicated, the most popular external agents for altering awareness are drugs. Alcohol has been the perennial favorite among American adults. However, marijuana, which has been used in some cultures for centuries, is a rapidly growing contender for first place among the young. Other popular drugs for altering the mind, which we shall discuss, are LSD, amphetamines, barbiturates, and heroin.

Chemicals are not the only external methods for the altering of awareness. Consciousness, for example, can be changed by distorting the visual input to the brain. This is accomplished by the use of special prism goggles which require the brain to make adjustments in order to cope with the visual world. This technique will be subsequently discussed in detail.

Alcohol

Scholars are agreed that alcohol has been used as an intoxicant since prehistory. Wine, for example, has been known long before recorded history, and beer since the ancient Egyptian civilization. The Egyptians were beholden to more than seven varieties of wine and beer, and a 17th-century Egyptian tomb bore hieroglyphics which translates: "Be of festive disposition, urged a servant to his mistress. She replied, give me 18 vessels of wine. You see, I love drunkenness" (J. Cohen, 1970).

Not surprisingly, we find many references to the excessive use of alcohol in many of man's earliest written records. Cambyses, King of Persia in the sixth century B.C., has the dubious distinction of being one of the first alcoholics on record. Since his time, many notable historical figures have been reported to have had alcoholic problems. In fact, alcoholism has been a major problem for several entire societies.

GENERAL EFFECTS OF ALCOHOLISM. Contrary to the belief of many people, alcohol is not a stimulant but a depressant which attacks and numbs the higher brain centers such as the association areas which lessens their normal inhibiting control. As a consequence, more primitive emotional responses appear and the drinker indulges in acts he ordinarily holds in check. Typically, he experiences a sense of warmth, expansiveness, and well-being in which the unpleasant realities of life are screened out. Casual acquaintances become his best friends and are sympathetic to his problems.

Many drinkers have deluded impressions of "mind-sharpening" under the influence of emotional boldness. However, psychological tests demonstrate that alcohol, even in small amounts, damages judgmental and perceptual functions. Next, motor coordination is impaired by the progressive effects of alcohol. This can be seen in the difficulty people have in walking a straight line or driving a car after a few drinks.

In general, the behavioral effects of alcohol are correlated roughly with the alcoholic content of the bloodstream. When the blood alcohol reaches approximately 0.05 percent, the highest nervous centers are affected and the drinker loses his inhibitions and judgment. At 0.15 percent, the deeper motor areas are affected as manifested by slurred speech and staggering. Progressively, deeper areas are affected with continued drinking until the last stage of death is reached. Fortunately, this final stage is seldom reached as the individual normally passes out when the blood alcohol reaches 0.6 percent. Concentrations above 0.8 percent are usually lethal because of the stoppage of heartbeat and respiration.

ALCOHOL ADDICTION AND DETERIORATION. Prolonged immoderate drinking can result in both physical and mental deterioration. Gross physical symptoms such as sluggish pupillary action, extreme nausea, and functional mental retardation often occur among alcoholics. The latter condition is the result of the destruction of brain cells and cerebral dysfunction (Claeson & Carlsson, 1971). The continued excessive use of alcohol can also result in cirrhosis of the liver, heart damage, ulceration of the stomach, and internal bleeding.

Recently, evidence has been accumulated which indicates that once excessive use of alcohol is established, it is maintained by physiological addiction (*Science News*, 1972). Although the exact mechanisms of alcohol's chemical reactions in the brain are unknown, Robert D. Meyers theorizes that the chemical pathways of electrical transmission are affected. To support his conclusion, he effectively diminished the rate of consumption of alcohol by "alcoholic" rats by lowering the level of one of the brain's transmitter substances, serotonin.

Psychological addiction and mentally aberrant reactions parallel the above physical effects. Besides the general intellectual deterioration that results from the chronic overuse of alcohol, there is often an overall deterioration of the personality and a moral decline. The individual's behavior typically becomes coarse; he neglects his family, takes no interest in his personal appearance, and finds it difficult to hold down a job because of his irresponsibility.

PHASES OF ALCOHOLISM. E. M. Jellinek (1971) cataloged the common behavioral symptoms of 2,000 alcoholics. He divided the development of alcoholism into four stages, varying widely from user to user.

1. *The pre-alcoholic phase.* The candidate for alcoholism begins by drinking in the company of others at various social occasions and finds the sensations provided by alcohol to be a rewarding experience. Tension is reduced, inhibitions dissolve, and repressed emotions emerge. He gradually increases his rate of alcohol consumption until he is drinking every day in order to relieve his tensions. After a period ranging from several months up to two years, he reaches the point where he often forgets his drunken interlude. In this fashion, he distinguishes himself from normal, social drinkers who are able to recall their drunken interludes.

2. *The prodromol (precursory) phase.* This period is marked by the drinker's compulsive search for the stimulation provided by alcohol. His tolerance has increased considerably; hence, he has to increase his rate of drinking in order to get the desirable effects such as psychic anesthesia.

Sudden blackouts also commonly occur during this stage, during which the drinker may show few, if any, signs of intoxication and may even carry on a reasonable conversation. Such amnesic episodes sometimes happen to average social drinkers when they drink too much during emotional or physical exhaustion. However, Jellinek considers amnesia without loss of consciousness to be a danger signal of alcoholism only when it happens on a regular basis, not just on rare occasions.

3. *The crucial phase.* This stage is characterized by the drinker losing control over his alcoholic consumption. He now takes to drinking alone, usually consuming more than he had planned. He suffers modest physiological dependence, hangovers (headache, vomiting, diarrhea, thirst) plague him, and more alcohol is required to dispel these symptoms. By now, the alcoholic has begun to feel that he cannot start the day without a drink "to steady his nerves."

4. *The chronic phase.* The alcoholic has now abandoned himself to stupors of intoxication which may last for several weeks. These long, drawn-out drinking bouts are usually associated with a marked impairment of thought processes and powerful physiological dependence manifested in tremors and explosive vomiting. In addition, he is susceptible to convulsions, the fearful *delirium tremens*—full-blown hallucinations of small animals; i.e., insects, rats, and snakes seem to attack him. These fears become especially pronounced as soon as the alcohol disappears from his system. At this point he is unable to help himself. However, some alcoholics admit defeat and become amenable to outside treatment.

Marijuana

Marijuana is the least toxic of the various psychoactive or hallucinogenic drugs that are commonly in use (Coleman, 1972; Grinspoon, 1972). Although it produces many of the same effects, it does not alter consciousness to nearly so great an extent as the other drugs, nor does it lead to increasing tolerance to the drug usage. Moreover, marijuana smokers can usually learn to gauge the effects accurately and, hence, control the intake of the drug to the amount needed to produce the desired mind-altering effects. In spite of the fact that marijuana is a relatively mild drug, many questions are still left unanswered concerning the possible physical or psychological harm in its prolonged usage. However, many studies have been conducted that furnish evidence in regard to its immediate effects.

The specific physiological and psychological effects of marijuana smoking depend upon the strength of the dosage, the personality and mood of the user, and the past experience of the individual with the drug. The marijuana normally used in this country is relatively mild in comparison to *hashish*, a related drug ten times as strong commonly used in Europe and Asia. Most of the following findings are based on the milder forms of the drug.

PHYSIOLOGICAL EFFECTS. Marijuana, in contrast to alcohol, stimulates various pathways in the brain, producing the typical "high" which will be reported later. However, the various physiological effects, if present at all, are very mild. The most consistently reported reaction is a moderate increase in heartbeat (Grinspoon, 1972). This increase in the heart rate normally occurs about 15 minutes after smoking regardless of the strength of the dosage used; chronic users show a greater increase than naïve subjects. Other noticeable but slight physiological effects are slower reflexes, bloodshot and itchy eyes, dry mouth, and increased appetite (Coleman, 1972). The effect of marijuana on respiratory rates varies with the past history of the subjects. Chronic users show a small increase in rate of breathing after smoking, but nonusers do not and contrary to popular opinion, marijuana does not affect the size of the pupil.

Unlike heroin and other related drugs, marijuana does not lead to a physiological dependence in which discontinuance of the substance causes withdrawal symptoms. Neither is its continued usage accompanied by an increased tolerance. Although studies conducted in Eastern countries have found evidence of increased tolerance to hashish over long periods of time, studies in the United States—which have involved lower dosages for shorter time periods—have failed to find evidence of increased tolerance (HEW, 1971). In fact, habitual users often show "reverse" tolerance wherein greater effects with the same dosages can be observed. This is apparently because of the drug remaining in the body for long periods and being available to enhance the effects of the next dose.

SUBJECTIVE EFFECTS. There is considerable agreement among regular users that when marijuana is smoked and inhaled, they get "high." This form of altered state of consciousness is characterized by euphoria in which the smoker has increased feelings of well-being and pleasant feelings of relaxation. This is often accompanied by sensations of drifting and floating away. Sensory inputs in many cases are enhanced: colors seem brighter, foods taste better, enjoyment of music is increased, smells seem richer, and sexual feelings in intercourse seem more intense. As noted before, the previous experience of the individual is important in determining the extent of his reactions to marijuana, including these subjective effects. Most first users report few or no effects with mild dosage (0.5 gram). Weil et al. (1968) found that even with high intake of the drug (2 grams) experienced users reacted differently than nonusers. In their study involving college subjects, nonusers reported minimal subjective effects with little euphoria; in contrast, all of the experienced users got "high."

It should be noted that marijuana may lead to unpleasant as well as pleasant experiences. If an individual takes the drug in depressed or angry moods, he tends to feel all the worse. Emotionally unstable or susceptible persons quite often suffer intense anxiety, confusion, depression, and unpleasant perceptual distortions. Keeler (1970) found about a fourth of the subjects in a study reported spontaneous occurrence of visual effects in later drug-free states. Fortunately, acute psychotic episodes (see Chapter 9) are only rarely triggered by marijuana.

This appears to occur only in very susceptible individuals who use moderate to heavy doses (HEW, 1971).

OBJECTIVE BEHAVIORAL EFFECTS OF MARIJUANA. Many researchers have been interested in determining the effect of marijuana on intellectual and psychomotor tasks, which can be objectively measured in contrast to the above subjective experiences. On tasks designed to measure a subject's capacity for sustained attention, the performance has been found to be unaffected for groups of both users and nonusers, regardless of the amount of dosage. However, on a simple cognitive or intellectual task, the *Digit Symbol Substitution Test,* marijuana was found to affect performance. There were gross decrements in the performance of naïve college subjects following both low and high doses. Chronic users, in contrast, improved slightly in performance, which would suggest they can turn on and off the effects of marijuana whereas nonusers cannot (Weil, Zinberg, & Nelson, 1968).

In the same study, muscular coordination was measured by use of the rotary pursuit task. The subjects' task was to keep a stylus in contact with a small spot on a moving turntable. Decrements in the performance for nonusers occurred after both high and low doses of marijuana, 15 and 90 minutes later, respectively. As was found in the case of the Digit Symbol Test, chronic users improved in their performance after smoking marijuana. However, Weil and associates believe this is probably due largely to practice with the task, rather than the drug.

One other notable finding is that smoking marijuana temporarily affects the individual's ability to estimate time (Coleman, 1972). His sense of time is distorted, so that often an event that lasts but a few seconds may seem to cover a much longer time span.

EFFECTS OF MARIJUANA ON SPEECH. Weil and Zinberg (1969) did a detailed study of the effects of marijuana on speech, testing chronic users and naïve subjects. In most instances, the verbal behavior of the chronic users changed grossly after smoking the drug, in contrast to the nonusers. Although the kinds of changes varied from individual to individual, overall there was greater and more vivid imagery, shifting of time orientation from past or future to present, increased number of rambling free associative thoughts, and lesser awareness of a listener in their speech patterns.

Weil and Zinberg hypothesize that this speech retardation is probably the result of the subjects' having to work harder to remember the logical content of what they are saying. This can be seen in the subjects forgetting what they are going to say next and in their strong tendencies to go off on irrelevant tangents as they lose their train of thought. In all probability, according to Weil and Zinberg, these speech patterns are a manifestation of a more general acute effect of marijuana on a specific mental function: an interference with immediate memory (ultra-short-term recall).

COMPARISON OF MARIJUANA AND ALCOHOL ON DRIVING PERFORMANCE. One of the few attempts to compare the effects of marijuana and alcohol was conducted by Crancer and associates (1969). Subjects, experienced with both marijuana and alcohol, were given a simulated driving performance test after a marijuana "high" on one occasion and alcohol intoxication on another. The strength of dosage of the two drugs was carefully regulated for all of the subjects: 1.7 grams of marijuana cigarettes; blood alcoholic concentration was brought to 0.10 (considered to be a fairly high level of intoxication). The driver-training simulator used in the experiment was specifically designed to obtain data on the effects of the treatments. A test film was used which gave the subject a driver's view of the road as he simulated driving in a mockup containing all the control and instrument equipment relevant to the driving task. Driving mistakes were recorded as follows: (1) speedometer, (2) steering, (3) brake, (4) accelerator, (5) signal, and (6) total errors.

Overall, the results showed that there was a significantly greater deterioration in driving performance following the use of alcohol than with marijuana. In comparison with their normal states, the subjects using marijuana accumulated more speedometer errors on the simulator, but there were no significant differences in accelerator, brake, signal, steering, and total errors. However, under the influence of alcohol, the same subjects accumulated significantly more accelerator, brake, signal, speedometer, and total errors than when not intoxicated. There was no significant difference in steering errors. The authors concluded, on the basis of a review of other studies, that deterioration in the driver-simulated task implies deterioration in actual driving performance. Hence, alcohol appears to impair driving ability more than marijuana under similarly controlled conditions.

OTHER KEY FINDINGS CONCERNING MARIJUANA. As previously indicated, the long-range effects of chronic marijuana smoking is not yet well known. It took many years before it was documented that prolonged cigarette smoking was hazardous to one's health; this could also be true in the case of marijuana. One chronic physical effect directly linked to its long-term use, so far, is permanent congestion of some of the ciliary vessels of the eyes with yellow discoloration (HEW, 1971). A potentially more disturbing finding is that marijuana has been found to weaken the role of certain blood cells in fighting viruses (Nahas, Suciu-Foca, Armand, & Morishima, 1974). They found that the white cells' ability to divide—to reproduce—was 40 percent less than in nonsmokers. On the basis of their findings, the researchers argue that marijuana should not be legalized without further analysis of the facts. In addition, some evidence has been found that heavy use of marijuana can have a depressing effect on a man's production of male sex hormones and sperms (*Science News*, 1974).

A key question concerning the use of marijuana is whether or not it leads to the use of hard drugs. Several investigators have found in answer to this question that there is no inevitable progression from marijuana to such drugs as heroin. Only a small percentage of frequent users become chronic users or go on to stronger drugs (Massett, 1970).

Finally, there is no evidence that marijuana stimulates sexual desire or power (Grinspoon, 1972). Although some users report that the "high" enhances the enjoyment of sexual intercourse, this is probably true only in the same sense that the enjoyment of art and music is apparently enhanced.

Heroin

Of all the addictive drugs, heroin is its own best salesman, which is what makes it so difficult to control. It is also very attractive to those who traffic in drugs. In order to obtain enough money to support his habit, the addict will usually push the drug onto someone else. The appeal of heroin is the escape feeling it provides—a feeling that "all's well with the world."

Heroin and related opium drugs, such as morphine, are commonly introduced into the body by hypodermic injection, inhaling, smoking, or eating. Typically, the young addict progresses from inhaling the bitter powder to hypodermic injections. The addiction process normally advances through three transitional stages:

In the first stage, addicts-to-be enjoy the pleasant, relaxed feelings brought on by comparatively small doses. Jack B., a San Francisco addict, reported his first heroin experience. "I had this awful pain following removal of my wisdom teeth and was given a shot. It took the pain away and I felt very good and peaceful. I enjoyed the junk so much I started taking it myself. Although I knew what junk can do to you, I couldn't help myself and I was hooked."

In the second stage, the addict becomes psychologically dependent on the drug as his tolerance increases. More and more heroin is required to achieve the desired euphoriclike state, sometimes compared to the sexual orgasm. The "high" may last for several hours during which the addict typically is in a lethargic, withdrawn state and in which bodily needs, including those for sex and food, are markedly diminished.

During this period, opium addicts are continuously concerned with the next drug dose, and all behavior is directed to this end. While in this state of reverie, addicts seek contacts for more drugs and sympathetic companionship with other addicts.

In the third stage, the addict's homeostatic balance becomes adjusted to the presence of the drug. Heroin seems to act on certain specific neurons in the brain which become dependent on the drug, and terrible agonies result if it is not provided. The user has become hooked. A fundamental change in his biochemistry has taken place, and when this happens it becomes extremely difficult to reverse. A simple act of will is insufficient because of the appalling withdrawal symptoms.

Withdrawal sickness accompanying heroin addiction may be summarized as follows. About four to six hours after the last heroin dose, the addict begins to grow uneasy or feel sick. He yawns, shivers, and sweats profusely, while a watery discharge pours from inside his nose. As time passes, the symptoms grow progressively worse, usually reaching a peak at about 48–72 hours, at which time the addict enters the lower depths of his personal hell. More watery mucous pours from his eyes as they dilate widely, and his skin resembles a plucked turkey, appropriately termed "goose flesh" or "cold turkey." His stomach and bowels react with violence as manifested in vomiting and diarrhea. Occasionally there may also be delirium, manic activity, and other symptoms of mental illness. If heroin is administered at any point along the way, the physiological symptoms are arrested and equanimity is restored in about 5 to 30 minutes.

The severity of withdrawal symptoms following total abstinence actually varies somewhat for different opiates, as shown in Figure 4–3. Withdrawal is shortest and most severe following morphine and heroin addiction, but longest and least severe for methadone addiction.

THE CONTROVERSY OVER METHADONE. Drug addiction has always been very difficult to cure because of both psychological and physiological dependencies that result from the frequent usage of opiates. In the search for a heroin "cure," methadone has been used by doctors as a substitute for heroin. Its main advantage over the other opiates is that it creates an even feeling of peace by not causing sporadic euphorias and stupors, thereby allowing the addict to function in society and hold a job. Although tolerance to methadone eventually develops, its main advantages over heroin is that it can be easily taken orally, is not needed in increasingly large doses, and is far less expensive. But the prescribed use of methadone does have its critics (Arehart, 1972). The first object of their attack is the widespread notion that the drug addiction problem can be solved with another drug. The critics maintain that all that is being accomplished is that physicians are substituting one problem for another in which heroin addiction is replaced by methadone addiction. They further point out that most methadone maintenance subjects eventually revert back to heroin use, and in fact some youngsters are dying in the ghettoes from methadone overdoses. They are able to obtain the drug either from members of their own household on methadone maintenance or from a rapidly growing black market.

In an effort to solve some of the problems associated with methadone use, the government has formulated new guidelines for methadone-maintenance programs. Plans are underway to reclassify the 450 or more programs and to take it out of the hands of private practitioners. Then, the methadone-maintenance system will be greatly expanded (Arehart, 1972). It is likely that future treatment of heroin addiction will continue to combine the use of methadone (until better nonaddicting drugs are discovered) with some form of psychotherapy. In addition, the govern-

FIGURE 4-3

Severity of withdrawal symptoms, following total abstinence, differs for different opiate drugs. Withdrawal is shortest and most severe following morphine addiction, while longest and least severe following methadone addiction. After morphine addiction, gradual reduction of the drug reduces withdrawal symptom (see upper curve at right). The gradual reduction of substituted methadone, following morphine addiction, reduces withdrawal symptoms even further (see lower curve at right).

A—Temporary withdrawal period   C—Drug reduction
B—Restabilization period   D—Drug abstinence

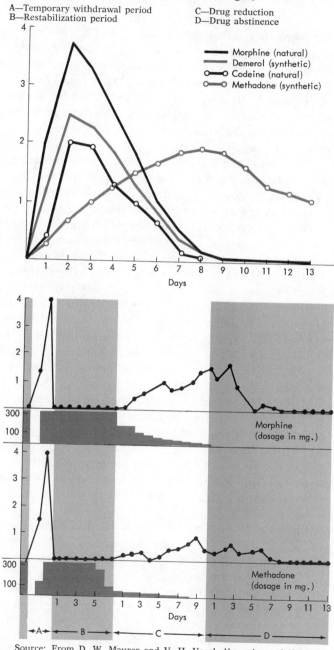

Source: From D. W. Maurer and V. H. Vogel, *Narcotics and Narcotic Addiction*, 3d ed., 1967. Courtesy of Charles C Thomas, Publisher, Springfield, Illinois.

ment can be expected to continue to crack down on the importation of various opiate drugs and growth of opium poppies.

The hallucinogenic drugs: LSD and mescaline

The so-called hallucinogenic drugs, including LSD and mescaline, are powerful mind-altering substances. They are thought to induce hallucinations, but actually do not "create" sensory images so much as to distort them. Thus, the individual commonly sees, hears, and smells things in a different manner from that in which he is accustomed to experiencing. LSD, or lysergic acid diethylamide, is a chemically synthesized drug, whereas mescaline is derived from the peyote cactus. In this discussion we shall concentrate on LSD, the more powerful of the two drugs.

Albert Hoffman, a Swiss biochemist, was the first to synthesize LSD in the laboratory and also the first to discover its strange psychological effects. His discovery of LSD's mind-altering effects came while working on the drug and makes an interesting story in itself (Hoffman, 1971). One April afternoon in 1943, Hoffman was forced to stop his work and go home. He was seized by a peculiar restlessness and sensations of dizziness. Once home, he immediately laid down and sank into a strange state of drunkenness which was characterized by lively imaginations. He was aware of fantastic images of extraordinary vividness, accompanied by a kaleidoscopelike display of colors. Dr. Hoffman and others followed up his initial experiences with scientific studies of LSD as a research tool to investigate experimental psychoses (see Chapter 9). In addition, some investigators studied the mind-altering effects of LSD. This side of LSD became extremely controversial in light of the dispute started by a few Harvard professors such as Timothy Leary. They had taken the drug themselves and were so overwhelmed by the experience that they proclaimed it as a cure for everyone's psychological problems. Indeed, even the problems of the world could be solved if everyone would only "turn on." This seductive message was given wide publicity via the news media and in the 1960s it became a fad for some high school and college students on campuses to drop acid. Today, its usage is not nearly as common as before, which may be due to the discovery of its potential dangers.

PHYSICAL EFFECTS OF LSD. As previously noted, LSD is a very powerful drug although it is colorless, odorless, and tasteless. It is active in amounts so small as to be almost invisible, 25 micrograms (1/40,000th of a gram). The average dose, usually taken in sugar cubes, is 100 micrograms but up to 10,000 micrograms have been taken by some subjects with recovery. The lethal dose for man is considered to be about 15,000 micrograms (Cohen, 1971). Tolerance develops within a few days, but no withdrawal symptoms are evident. It evidently enhances neural pathways within the sympathetic nervous system. Hence, it causes dilation and partial paralysis of the iris and increases body temperature, blood pressure, and blood sugar.

Studies by Rorvik (1970) and others have suggested that chronic usage of LSD may cause chromosomal damage as well as congenital malformations. However, other investigators have failed to find such effects at moderate dosage levels (Aase, Laestadius, & Smith, 1971). Much more research needs to be done in regard to possible chromosomal malformations and, likewise, other possible physiological effects. For example, S. Cohen (1971) reports, on the basis of preliminary work in his laboratory, that certain changes in the functioning of brain cells occurs. But the question of brain damage still cannot be satisfactorily answered in our present state of knowledge.

PSYCHOLOGICAL EFFECTS. After taking LSD, a person typically goes through about eight hours of tremendous intensification of sensory perception, the most important psychic effect. The visual effects are particularly striking. When the eyes are open, the perception of light and space is affected: colors seem much more vivid, surface details appear to be more sharply defined, and the space between objects becomes more apparent. Many people feel a new awareness of the physical beauty of the world in light of the visual harmonies, colors, and the exquisiteness of details of perceived objects.

The visual effects are even more intensified when the eyes are closed. The subjective effects range in content from abstract forms to dramatic scenes involving imagined people, sometimes in ancient times. Different individuals report they have seen bright wavy lines, landscapes, checkerboard designs, diamonds, chariots, Christ, and "the mythical dwelling places of the Greek or Roman gods." The content of the hallucinations are to a great extent determined by the personality and current mood of the LSD user. For example, a religious-oriented individual is apt to have visions of God, whereas an artist is likely to perceive abstract or landscape scenes.

The changes in visual perception are not always pleasant as can be seen by the "bum trips" some drug users have. They may experience "hellish" hallucinations in which contradictory sensations are induced by the drug. For instance, an individual may have an impression of blackness accompanied by feelings of depression and isolation, or perceive sickly greens and ugly "nightmarish" reds. When a person closes his eyes he may feel his body is greatly distorted or that his legs and arms are decaying. Imaginary ghouls may seem to be chasing him, in situations in which he cannot run.

Besides the visual effects, other sense modalities are affected in a similar manner. Often there are complex auditory hallucinations in which lengthy conversations are held between imaginary people. Some subjects hear perfectly orchestrated musical compositions they have never heard before; others experience voices speaking foreign languages unknown to them. There have also been many reports of hallucinatory odors and tastes and of other bodily sensations. Frequently, there is a crossover or association of sensations between the sensory modalities. The subject, upon hearing music, may see beautiful colored lights, and the pricking of his skin with a pin may evoke visual impressions of dazzling geometric designs.

In addition to the intensity of basic perceptual reactions and accompanying emotional changes, many other subjective reactions are reported. In some individuals, one of the most basic constancies is a loss of ability to estimate time. The passage of time may seem to go very slowly, in which minutes seem like hours, or vice versa. The subject may even feel outside of or beyond time, or time and space may seem infinite.

Some subjects lose the ability to distinguish between self and object, characterized by a loss of personal identity. This happens because one's sense of identity depends on knowing accurately the borders of the self and on being able to distinguish what is inside from what is outside. Mystical and transcendental experiences are marked by the loss of this basic constancy. A feeling of "all is one and one is all" is an example of such experiences. While such "holy" and mystical feelings bring ecstasy to some subjects, they are unpleasant to others. In the latter cases, such individuals have a sense of being completely undifferentiated, as though it were their personal consciousness that had been "emptied," leaving none of the usual discriminations on which the functioning of the self depends. One man who had this experience thought later that it was like being nothing, or not alive, and that the world had come to an end. While under the influence of the drug he was unable to recall any personal experiences.

THE "FLASHBACK." One of the possible unpleasant effects of using LSD is that the individual may experience intrusive recurrent hallucinatory images which are known as "flashbacks." They happen to approximately 1 in 20 drug users and are usually of a negative and frightening nature (Horowitz, 1969). One 19-year-old user, who on a "bad trip" had been terrorized by images of small insects attacking him, continued to have flashbacks of the insects ten weeks later. A 17-year-old coed who had hallucinations of a decaying man during a "bum trip" had the same image reappear a month later about five times a day. Nobody today knows for sure why they happen, but fortunately flashbacks ordinarily can be worked through in brief psychotherapy sessions, after which they may cease to reoccur.

CHANGES IN PERFORMANCE. In addition to the various subjective effects of the hallucinogens, there are a number of changes in overt performance that can be measured or at least described objectively. Under the influence of LSD there is usually some reduction in performance on standard tests of reasoning, memory, arithmetic, spelling, and drawing (Barron, Jarvik, & Bunnell, 1972). It is difficult to determine whether the decline in performance on these tasks can be attributed to the pharmacological effects of the drug, which might impair problem-solving ability, or loss of motivation on the part of the subjects. It may be that after taking LSD many people simply refuse to cooperate with the tester; the very fact that someone should want to test them may seem absurd and spark hostility.

Barbiturates

The barbiturates are the primary sedative drugs prescribed by physicians to calm patients or to induce sleep. In small prescribed amounts, these drugs are not especially dangerous, though some vigorous physical exercise during the day is a safer route to drowsiness. Unlike marijuana, LSD, and other mind-expanding drugs which stimulate the arousal neural pathways in the brain, barbiturates depress the action of the brain, somewhat like alcohol. Barbiturate abuse is seen in many middle-aged people who use it as a chemical crutch.

Barbiturates are addictive as the user needs increasing amounts to get the desired results, thereby setting up a vicious circle. The oversedated brain grows forgetful, and the user may not remember he has just taken pills. He may swallow a second dose, and unfortunately combine the pills with some alcoholic beverage. The result, all too often, may be an accidental overdose which sedates the brain so severely that the centers controlling respiration and heartbeat stop functioning, and death results. Marilyn Monroe and Judy Garland are two unhappy victims illustrating the inherent dangers of oversedation.

GENERAL EFFECTS. In general, the barbiturates produce feelings of euphoria, in which the user reports a sense of inner peace and calmness. However, reliance on the drugs often results in a number of undesirable side effects. Among these are impairment of problem solving and memory, confusion, slow speech, uncoordination, and depression. Particularly noticeable in chronic users is the appearance of sudden uncontrollable changes in moods. This can be seen as some individuals abruptly shift from laughter into tears, and in some cases, may even engage in unprovoked violence.

If the barbiturate user becomes seriously addicted, he suffers withdrawal symptoms every bit as severe as the delirium tremens of an alcoholic. It is thought that these symptoms are caused by the neurons in the brain, depressed by the drug, attempting to compensate for this effect and to restore a normal balance by increasing their activity. Larger doses of the drug are then required to keep them in check. When the drug is withdrawn from the barbiturate addict, an explosive overactivity of the nerve cells ensues. Since, in general, withdrawal symptoms are the opposite of the effects a drug produces to begin with, euphoria quickly gives way to an incapacitating depression. Calmness yields to tremors and convulsions, accompanied by hostility and violent behavior toward others. Other symptoms include rapid heartbeat, elevated blood pressure, vomiting, and a general weakness.

Fortunately, the withdrawal symptoms can be minimized by the administration of increasingly smaller doses of the drug itself, providing that the barbiturate addiction is not complicated by alcoholism or dependence on other drugs, as is so often the case. The elimination of the psychological dependence on barbiturates is not so severe a problem as is opiate addiction. However, many barbiturate addicts do require professional help in the form of psychotherapy.

The amphetamines

These drugs, like the barbiturates, are widely prescribed by doctors for people who are mildly depressed. In contrast to the barbiturates, which depress or slow down the action of the brain, the amphetamines have chemical effects that stimulate or speed up the activity of the central nervous system. Taken in large doses or injected into the bloodstream, they first produce a euphoric "high" and a state of hyperalertness as the pleasure center within the brain is affected.

These drugs have been considered "wonder drugs" by many people because they have the effect of keeping an individual awake and temporarily functioning at a level beyond normal. Hence, night workers, long-distance truck drivers, students cramming for exams, and athletes striving to improve their performances have been attracted to the amphetamines. In regard to the latter case, athletes participating in the 1972 Olympics had to undergo medical tests to see if they were using these drugs.

GENERAL EFFECTS. The amphetamines are not only medically prescribed for cases of depression and maintaining alertness, but also for curbing the appetite when weight reduction is desirable. However, the American Medical Association (1968) has repeatedly emphasized that they are not a magical source of extra mental and physical energy, but rather serve to push the user toward a greater expenditure of his own resources—to the point of dangerous fatigue. An overdose results in heightened blood pressure, enlarged pupils, rapid or unclear speech, profuse sweating, and confusion.

As with the case of other drugs, the precise effects of amphetamines may vary with the type, the amount, the length of time they are used, and the psychological state of the individual user. The body rapidly builds up a tolerance for the drug so that the habitual user or "speed freak" needs more and more of the amphetamines to stay "high." The addict may become the complete captive of his habit and go on a "run" lasting from several days to a week or more, after which he collapses in total exhaustion.

This devotion to the habit has serious personality consequences for the addict. He ultimately lives in the present as the past and future recede in his mind. In addition, he gradually loses control over his behavior and, in fact, suicide, homicide, and assault are commonly associated with amphetamine usage (Ellinwood, 1971). The behavior of some habitual users deteriorates so badly that they develop a form of mental illness, known as *amphetamine psychosis*, which is literally indistinguishable from paranoid schizophrenia. The paranoid delusions and persecutions involved in amphetamine psychosis normally disappear when the drug is taken away, but in cases where brain damage has resulted from excessive use of the drug, residual effects may remain (Nelson, 1969). In such instances, there is an inability to concentrate and an impairment of memory and learning functions.

THE USE OF "SPEED" WITH HYPERACTIVE CHILDREN. Excessive hyperactivity among certain children is a condition commonly seen at child guidance clinics and elementary schools. The clinical picture in hyperactive, or *hyperkinetic*, children consists of exaggerated muscular activity, short attention span, impulsiveness, emotional instability, and lack of inhibition. The following case, involving a seven-year-old boy illustrates a somewhat typical clinical picture:

> Tom B. was referred to a child guidance clinic by a school psychologist because of overactive, disruptive, and emotionally unstable behavior. He was failing in class and creating a problem for the teacher and other students by constantly running around and yelling. Both at school and at home he had had periodic temper tantrums. Although his school performance was low, he had a high I.Q. He had been seen by several medical doctors, who were unable to find anything wrong with him such as brain damage. Hence, he was diagnosed as a hyperkinetic child.

One of the usual treatments for hyperactivity, in addition to the standard psychotherapeutic techniques, has been the employment of the amphetamines, although other drugs are used in current practice. Interestingly enough, these drugs, which are stimulants for adults, have been found to usually have a quieting effect on hyperkinetic children. They typically slow down in their overall activity and are better able to concentrate on any given task at the moment. As a result, their school performance increases and they do not hinder the working efforts of other children and the teacher.

In spite of the advantages of using these drugs, a number of questions have been raised concerning their usage. One question concerns which children will be selected for drug therapy. While the drugs are no doubt useful for children that are truely hyperkinetic, they should not be used for children that are merely restless or hyperactive because of hunger, boring curricula, or unfortunate home conditions. In the latter cases, most investigators feel it is unethical to use the amphetamines merely to keep children peaceful in the classroom or at home.

Another major question regarding drug therapy with hyperactive children is the possibility of side effects. Such undesirable symptoms as decreased appetite, dizziness, headache, and insomnia have been reported in some cases in which children are prescribed the amphetamines (Eisenberg, 1971). The consensus among physicians and other child experts seems to be that these drugs can be potentially dangerous and should be used only with extreme caution. Even then it is preferable that psychotherapy be tried first. At the same time, it is important that the public be well informed as to the beneficial effects of treatment with amphetamines, in order to avoid an exaggerated reaction against their use.

Altered states of awareness: Internal control

In this section we will be focusing on the factors that affect our states of consciousness which come from inside the body, and hence, are said to be internal. Many of the subjective effects and physiological changes associated with use of the various drugs can occur independently through dreaming, hypnosis, and meditation. For instance, perceptions under these states can be just as remarkable and different from normal perceptions as those we have seen with the use of drugs.

Also included in this section are critical evaluations of "extrasensory perception (ESP)," the possibility that some individuals can be aware of events or capable of influencing physical objects without the use of known senses.

Sleep and dreaming

As we noted at the beginning of the chapter, different brain waves are recorded when one is asleep as opposed to when one is awake. The question naturally has been raised concerning the nature of dreaming. These hallucinatory experiences have intrigued social scientists and soothsayers alike, and their bizarre contents have been variously interpreted as prophetic insights or cues to the personality. However, until fairly recently, there was no technique available with which dreaming could be investigated scientifically. The sole witness to the dream is the dreamer himself, and upon wakening, he may fail to recall dreaming.

However, a discovery was made which made it possible to investigate objectively what had been a subjective matter. Kleitman (1960) and his associates discovered that a sleeper's eyes continued to move under their closed lids for some time after all major body movements had ceased. The eye movements would stop and then begin several times during the course of sleeping. They have since become named rapid eye movements (REM) and are known to be a fairly reliable indicator that a person is dreaming. When a sleeper is not dreaming, the eye movements are not present, but when a subject is immediately awakened following REM, he does indeed remember and report that he had been dreaming. (See Figure 4-4.)

Coincident with the cycle of eye movements are fluctuations in brain wave patterns as measured by the EEG. Slow waves correlate with deep

FIGURE 4-4
Scientists have discovered that changes in brain wave patterns and rapid eye
movements (REM) are associated with dreaming, one form of altered state of
consciousness. As a result, researchers now have the methodology to objectively
study the process of dreaming.

Courtesy of Paul Fry, *The Santa Clara*, University of Santa Clara

states of sleep when the subject is not dreaming, while faster brain waves
are found when a person is dreaming. This latter condition has become
known as paradoxical sleep because it is difficult to wake a person while
he is dreaming, and yet, his brain wave patterns resemble those of a person awake.

The occurrence of the REM state or dreaming during a night's sleep
appears to follow a general sequence. Deep slow-wave sleep is usually
reached soon after falling asleep, followed by dreaming about an hour
later, which lasts perhaps ten minutes. During the night, the sleeper
waxes and wanes between periods of deep sleep and dreaming. The evidence strongly suggests, contrary to what some people report in the
morning, that everyone dreams. People who do not recall dreams in the
morning apparently dream just as often as those who do remember their
dreams (Lewis, Goodenough, Shapiro, & Sleser, 1966). Overall, adults
spend about 20 percent of a night's sleep in the REM state, although this
percentage decreases with age. Surprisingly, REM sleep is present in the
newborn, and in fact, infants spend up to 80 percent of their sleep in the
REM state. It is very doubtful whether they are dreaming in the sense
that children or adults do, because of their undeveloped cognitive capacity. The appearance of these REM states in infants and in lower animals, such as cats and dogs, complicates the usual interpretation of connecting eye movements with dreaming. In neither case can they verbalize
whether or not they had been dreaming after being awakened. However,
the notion that a dog is barking while asleep because he is dreaming
about chasing a cat may not be too farfetched.

The prevalence of REM early in life suggests that very primitive processes must be associated with this state of sleep. It logically follows, at least in Freudian theory (see Chapter 8), that the dreams associated with REM later in life are probably manifestations of illogical and primitive impulses. The fantasizing of the senile and of persons suffering certain disorders of the central nervous system may also be likened to dreaming.

THE CONTENT OF DREAMS. While eye movements tell us something about the process of dreaming, in regard to the physiological state of the brain, they do not necessarily reflect the content, what the dream is about. Interpretation of what dreams mean vary according to the theoretical orientation of the psychoanalyst and other dream researchers. A childhood dream that Marilyn Monroe recalled, later related to her analyst, is a case in point (Ansbacher & Adler, 1970).

She remembered a childhood dream in which she stood naked in the church while the congregation lay on the floor at her feet. Ansbacher (1970) does an interpretation of this dream in terms of Alfred Adler's individual psychology, a form of psychoanalysis. Adler believed that the life goal of the maladjusted is personal superiority and power over others, and this is reflected in the following interpretation. Marilyn's position above the congregation shows that she perceives herself as above others. She is untouchable and a goddess, in this dream, as can be seen by the fact that other people are lying prostrate at her feet.

The discerning reader will readily recognize that other meanings could be given to this dream, depending upon one's personal viewpoints and imagination. Although such interpretations are a matter of art more than science, some researchers have investigated in an objective manner whether external events can significantly influence the content of a subject's dreams, as commonly believed.

To test this idea, Dement and Wolpert (Kleitman, 1972) exposed a number of subjects to various stimuli of sound, light, and drops of water during periods of REM. Overall, elements suggestive of such stimuli appeared in only a minority of the dreams reported upon waking. Drops of water, falling on the skin, proved to be the most effective stimuli in influencing dream content. Falling water occurred in 6 out of 15 dreams reported following arousal by this stimulus, and water showed up in 14 narratives out of 33 sleepers who managed to sleep through this stimulus. Internal sensations associated with hunger and thirst surprisingly did not affect the content of dreams in most cases. Only a few subjects who had gone without food or water for 24 hours had elements in their dreams which were somewhat related to such stimuli. In no cases did the subjects' dream narratives involve drinking or eating.

THE EFFECT OF DREAM DEPRIVATION. As previously noted, much of the time during sleep is spent in dreaming. Since there appears to be no exception to this nightly occurrence in anyone, the question was raised of whether or not this amount of dreaming is in some way a necessary and vital part of our lives. What happens to people physiologically and psychologically if they go without dreaming during the course of sleep?

Dement (1971) in an attack on such problems performed an experiment in which sleeping subjects were awakened immediately after the onset of dreaming. This procedure was continued throughout the night, so that each dream period was artificially terminated at its beginning. The number of consecutive nights of dream deprivation arbitrarily selected for the study was five. A control group of subjects underwent a series of awakenings during nondream periods in order to see if the findings following dream deprivation were solely an effect of the denial of dreaming and not merely the result of awakening.

All of the subjects who were not allowed to dream manifested a progressive increase in the number of attempts to dream during the course of the study. Psychological disturbances such as anxiety, irritability, and poor concentration developed during the period of dream deprivation, but were not severe in most cases. However, of the eight subjects, one quit the study in an apparent panic and two insisted on stopping one night short of the goal of five nights of dream deprivation, presumably because they could not take the stress. One of the subjects did manifest serious agitation and anxiety, and five others developed a marked increase in appetite during this period of dream deprivation. The latter observation was supported by daily weight measurements which showed a gain in weight of 3 to 5 pounds in three of the subjects. All of these behavioral changes disappeared as soon as the subjects were again allowed to dream in a normal manner. It is important to note that none of these observed changes were seen for subjects in the control group, who were awakened only during non-REM sleep.

These results may be interpreted to indicate that a certain amount of dreaming each night is a necessity in order for a person to function normally. Apparently, pressure to dream builds up with the accumulation of dream deprivation, similar to the increase in hunger and thirst drives which result from food and water deprivation. The first evident signs of the effects of dream deprivation are increased attempts to dream and then, during the recovery period, there is a marked increase in total dreamtime. The fact that this increase in amount of dreaming was maintained over four or more successive recovery nights strongly suggests that there is a quantitative compensation for the deficit. Finally, it appears that temporary dream suppression causes psychological disturbances in some subjects and that, if the deprivation was carried on long enough, would probably result in a serious disruption of the personality.

Hypnosis

Hypnosis has excited the curiosity and imagination of man for many years, but despite this intense interest knowledge concerning this phenomenon has been slow in accumulating. Unfortunately, the student approaching the topic of hypnosis is likely to be baffled by the fickle nature of the data or "facts." He will find that what is considered to be a fact by one investigator is often relegated to the status of an artifact by another. Besides the undoubted complexity and the elusiveness of hypnotism to scientific scrutiny, a partial explanation resides in the strong resistances manifested by behavioral scientists and medical practitioners toward involvement in this field. Hypnosis has long been associated with the mystical, magical, and sensational, which has led many scientists to ridicule and discredit it rather than to attempt to study it. Hence, psychologists and others have been dissuaded from active inquiry because of the very real danger to their professional careers.

We shall attempt to present hypnosis in its proper perspective with the realization that much more research is necessary in order to answer many of the questions it poses. Above all, it is hoped that the student will recognize that hypnotic behavior can be experimentally investigated like other psychological phenomena and adheres to the same laws.

INDUCTION OF HYPNOSIS. Hypnosis is designed to bring about a state of selective attention at the suggestion of the hypnotist. The induction of hypnosis in a susceptible subject is ordinarily a straightforward and simple matter. One technique of inducing the hypnotic state consists of the hypnotist's use of verbal suggestions. The subject is told that he is becoming relaxed, drowsy, and sleepy in a gentle, sustained manner; however, occasionally the suggestions are strong and abrupt. Sometimes the process is augmented by the use of eye fixation in which the subject is asked to fix his gaze on a target, such as the *hypnodisk,* so that he must raise his eyes. This causes a strain on the eyelid muscles, producing fatigue. The hypnotist merely mentions that the eyelids will grow tired and heavy, eventually closing. He continues to comment on the eyelids becoming heavy and on the development of sleepy feelings throughout the fixation period. Some subjects close their eyes and are asleep immediately, but others require several repetitions of the suggestions before falling asleep.

The hypnotist or operator can deepen the trance by giving the subject a graded series of suggestions, beginning with an easy one such as closing of the eyes or arm heaviness and ending with a difficult one such as bizzare *posthypnotic suggestion.* The latter is not only used as an indicator of the depth of a trance, but can be used to induce the phenomenon of hypnosis. For example, the operator gives a suggestion to a hypnotized subject to be carried out during the waking state; he may be told that he will fall asleep when he hears keys being jingled. The subject, if so instructed, cannot remember consciously the origin of the suggestion and usually resorts to various excuses to account for his strange behavior. During a demonstration, one student was instructed as follows. When the hypnotist used the word "study" she was to rush from the lecture hall. She later returned and rationalized, "The room is very stuffy; I needed some fresh air."

The question "Can I learn to hypnotize is often raised concerning hypnotic induction and is phrased in a manner that indicates such a technique must involve the use of mysterious and potent powers. Actually, although it is not the intent to induce the reader to engage in hypnotism, the fact is that anyone can learn, with limited practice, how to hypnotize at least some subjects. The process, as stated above, simply involves the use of suggestion and perhaps the use of mechanical apparatuses that engender monotony. Thus, there is nothing magical or complicated about the induction processes. However, because of the possible dangers of trances, which will be discussed later, beginners should refrain from inducing hypnotic states in others.

Who can be hypnotized? Despite continued investigations over many years, little is known regarding hypnotic susceptibility, although it correlates with suggestibility. For instance, the normal waking state is characterized by reduced suggestibility and the artificial hypnotic state by heightened suggestibility which is progressive. However, approximately 15 percent of the general population are not suggestible enough to be hypnotized at all (J. Cohen, 1970). Therefore, suggestible scales have been devised in order to identify promising subjects. The items commonly included on such scales are listed as follows:

Postural Sway. The hypnotist suggests that the standing subject is falling. The suggestible subject sways back and forth and may fall.

Hand Lowering. The hypnotist suggests that the subject's hand is heavy. The suggestible subject reacts by lowering his hand at least six inches.

Finger Lock. The hypnotist suggests that the subject, with interlocked fingers, cannot unclasp his hands. The suggestible subject, in spite of spirited efforts, is unable to disengage his fingers.

Chevreul Pendulum. The hypnotist suggests that weights, hanging on a string from the subject's hands, will swing like a pendulum, back and forth in directions perpendicular to the wall. The suggestible subject will react by moving his hands enough to achieve the pendulum effect.

Arm Rigidity. The hypnotist suggests that the subject's arm is stiff and will not bend. The suggestible subject will keep his arm in a stiff or straight fashion as indicated.

Odor Identification. The hypnotist asks the subject to signal when he smells odors. However, inadequate stimuli are presented which produce no odor. The suggestible subject responds by reporting a perceived fragrance. For example, he may imagine that a bottle of water, labeled "My Sin," smells like perfume.

With the use of such items, it has been found that children are much more highly suggestible than adults. The minimum mental age required for hypnosis is about 5 to 6 years: susceptibility then increases with age and reaches a maximum between 9 and 14 years of age. Susceptibility then starts to decline with age and reaches the adult level at 15 (London, 1965). The sex of the subject, the operator, and the past experience of the operator have not been found to be critical variables (Hilgard, 1965).

Contrary to the opinion of many professionals, repeated inductions and other "deepening" techniques employed by experts do not increase susceptibility (Hilgard & Tart, 1966).

Is it possible to draw a composite picture of the hypnotizable person? In spite of the experiments reporting either little or no correlations with personality characteristics, a general picture of susceptible people has emerged from case histories. The hypnotizable person is one who has rich ideational interests as opposed to highly athletic ones. He welcomes new experiences and thus looks forward to the opportunity of being hypnotized. He tends to follow his inner impulses and is not afraid to withdraw from reality for the moment. In addition, he is "normal" in the sense that he is not overly troubled by personal problems as are neurotic individuals.

CHARACTERISTICS OF HYPNOSIS. Many intriguing alterations or distortions in perception of reality and body image have been reported during hypnotic states, or trances. Some subjects report feelings of sinking, floating, moving outside of their body, or undergoing a general anesthetic. Others report paralysis of major muscle groups, anesthesia (loss of sensation), and positive and negative sensory hallucinations. Sometimes these experiences are frightening and the subject awakens. In most cases, subjects have little difficulty in discriminating between trances and waking states, and they can also usually make meaningful distinctions between degrees of hypnosis.

Many of these experiences can be seen in the personal accounts of one very susceptible subject, a 19-year-old coed.

> I found that my mind was splitting: part of me was floating in space, the rest of me was hearing your voice. It was a pleasant experience as I felt so free, floating about.
>
> My arms felt so heavy that I couldn't move them even though I tried, but it wasn't unpleasant.
>
> I didn't seem to be aware of the walls in the room; it was like staring at them and not seeing anything. The whole experience was weird, difficult to relate.

Most hypnotized subjects also readily enact unusual roles which are suggested to them, such as being someone other than themselves. They may carry out various complex behaviors that are associated with the role they are playing. For example, during a trance a student may follow the suggestion and play the role of the teacher by starting to give a lecture, or a subject may start behaving like a doctor. It may well be that there is something of an actor in all of us, and hence, the permissiveness of the "hypnotic situation" allows subjects to put their ordinary restraints aside. In fact, one well-known theory of hypnosis affirms that people are simply engaged in role-playing during a trance. Therefore, according to this hypothesis, the hypnotic state consists of engaging in behavior we ordinarily would during waking states once inhibitions are removed. This is similar to what takes place under the influence of alcohol.

ANTISOCIAL BEHAVIOR. Much controversy has centered around the issue of whether or not people can be made to engage in antisocial or self-destructive acts during trances. Authorities have long been divided on the issue, taking extreme stands on both sides of the question. However, some of the confusion and discrepancy in the experimental literature can be cleared up when we examine the definitions of antisocial acts that have been used. They have been defined primarily in two different ways: (1) *recognized* antisocial acts, behavior understood as wrong or antisocial by the subject himself (goes against his code of morality); and (2) *unrecognized* antisocial acts consist of behavior which is wrong by consensus, but misperceived by the subject; the meaning of the antisocial act is disguised by the hypnotist as he makes use of suggested hallucinations, delusions, and illusions.

Generally, the investigators who have reported evidence for antisocial behavior have used the second definition, while researchers who report opposite findings have used the former category. In other words, subjects will engage in antisocial behavior only when it is disguised and unrecognized. For example, the literature reports the following case: "A subject was told when you slowly open your eyes you will see in front of you, your boss. He has just fired you because he does not like you; he even refuses to give you a letter of recommendation, which you need in order to get another job. You will have to attack and beat him up to change his mind." A man stood in front of the subject, and three other men had to pull him off the victim.

Cases such as this are considered to be unethical by other professionals; therefore, there are not many experiments of this type. In similar cases, hypnosis is primarily legitimizing behavior to which the subject is already inclined. A hypnotized subject with strong hostile impulses might engage in destructive behavior which he normally holds under control. Or a subject with strong exhibitionistic impulses might take off his clothes, an impulse which he holds in check otherwise.

There are no well-documented reports of crimes or other antisocial acts being committed under the influence of hypnosis, that are recognized as such by the subject himself. Subjects will refuse to part with their money or commit murder despite the fact that such behavior often occurs in fictional literature. Subjects are ordinarily capable of resisting the demands made by the hypnotist if they are too burdensome and are against their personal moral codes.

AGE REGRESSION. Much has been written about the use of hypnosis to recover lost memories, in which it is suggested to the subject that he traverse back in time to some younger age, to infancy, or even prior to birth. The subject typically exhibits some behavior consistent with the suggested age such as "baby talk," crawling on hands and knees, or nursing from a bottle. The subjects also report subjective feelings of being a child or baby again. But, nevertheless, there remains an unresolved controversy as to the genuineness of the phenomenon. The heart of the disagreement is whether the subject has really regressed to a previous age or is simply engaging in role-playing and behaving as he imagines a child to function at that earlier age.

Among the most convincing evidence that age regression is genuine and not just role-playing is the inducement of "old" physiological symptoms. One of the most often quoted studies is by Kupper (1945), who reported the case of a 24-year-old man who had suffered convulsive seizures of six years' duration. Diffuse irregularities, characteristic of epileptics, were manifested in his EEG recordings. When the patient was regressed to his 12th birthday the brain wave patterns became essentially normal and remained so during hypnotic progressive regression until his 18th year, when he had suffered his first convulsive attack.

A second often quoted study (Moody, 1946) describes the case of a 35-year-old woman under narcohypnotic treatment (drug-induced trance), who reexperienced a riding accident that had happened to her when she was 10 years old. According to reports she had suffered some broken ribs on the right side. During the hypnotic state, hemorrhages and bruising developed following the line of the right tenth rib, accompanied by a sharp pain in the original place of the injury. The organic or physical symptoms lasted for several hours.

Although the above cases and other physiological studies have been singled out as convincing proof of the age regression phenomenon by some (Pattie, 1956), other investigators have discounted the results for several reasons (Barber, 1962). For example, it is possible that the sudden reappearance of old organic symptoms may be explained by biofeedback data, previously discussed in Chapter 2. These patients could simply have gained control over autonomic functions of the brain, which can cause the appearance of irregular brain wave patterns and even bleeding or bruising.

MEDICAL APPLICATIONS. Hypnosis has been used medically as a general anesthesia during operations because it has no dangerous side effects, unlike the use of ether and other drugs. Moreover, with some patients it has effectively diminished surgical shock, reduced bleeding, accelerated healing, and greatly lowered pain intensity. Unfortunately, only the deepest levels of hypnosis can bring about such dramatic beneficial effects following surgery. Consequently, because of the time element and general safety of the regular anesthetic drugs, most physicians do not resort to the use of hypnosis. However, its effectiveness is well documented as illustrated in the following case from Esdaile (1850), who pioneered the use of hypnosis in surgery:

> The writer vividly describes using a long knife to cut open the person's face from the corner of the mouth through the cheek and nose to skin at the corner of the eye. "The pressure of the tumor had caused the

absorption of the anterior wall of the antrum, and on pressing my fingers between it and the bones, it burst, and a shocking gush of blood, and brain-like matter, followed." All during the time of this surgery the man did not move. The doctor was able to turn the patient's head in any direction without resistance. Except for an occasional indistinct moan, the man did not show any signs of life. However, during the operation the physician passed his fingers into his throat to detach part of the tumor but unfortunately a stream of blood was directed into the wind-pipe which caused the patient to cough. It was at this point that the patient apparently awoke and opened his eyes for the first time. However, the operation was finished at this point and the wound sewed up.

It is now generally recognized that such dramatic uses of hypnosis is effective with only a limited proportion of medical patients. Many advocates of the use of hypnosis, in fact, recommended that a dry run or rehearsal be tried before surgery. Even if hypnosis should fail to be effective as the sole anesthetic agent, it may reduce preoperative fear and postoperative discomfort.

OBSTETRICS. One of the most popular medical uses of hypnosis has been in connection with childbirth. One of the chief reasons for pain in childbirth is anxiety, which causes the mother-to-be to tense up. As a result, the sympathetic branch of the autonomic nervous system is stimulated which opposes the natural process of childbirth, under regulation of the neural centers. More specifically, the peristaltic action of the uterus propelling the fetus down the birth canal is opposed by the action of the sphincter muscles of the uterus when the woman is nervous or afraid. Pressure results which produces pain. Hence, relaxation through hypnosis effectively reduces pain similar to training in natural childbirth.

Reyher (1968) reports the use of the following procedure in childbirth if the expectant mother is capable of a very deep hypnosis. The doctor begins by producing a generalized state of muscular relaxation in the hypnotized patient, starting with the toes and working up to the muscles of the neck and forehead. This is followed by the suggestion that this state of relaxation can be achieved whenever she counts from one to five. Next, counting from one to five is paired with the inducement of a generalized anesthesia. When the doctor has ascertained that the general anesthesia is thoroughly effective, he introduces a hand anesthesia with instructions that it will become anesthetized whenever the physician strokes it three times. It is then suggested to the patient that any body part can be made equally anesthetic whenever the physician directs her to rub the part to be anesthetized. Finally, while still under the influence of hypnosis, she is asked if she would like to watch the birth of her baby. If she agrees, then every effort is made to assure her this will be done, if medical considerations permit.

The patient is hypnotized just prior to being brought into the delivery room and is told that she can open her eyes and watch if she so desires. When the operation is begun, the hand (covered with a sterile glove) can be used to strengthen the effects of the anesthesia at the place where the incision will be made to enable an easier exit for the baby. After the surgery, she is asked if she would like to walk back to her room, carrying her baby. Following this ordinary, exhilarating, and fulfilling experience, she is brought out of this "waking" hypnosis and induced to sleep. The doctor simply suggests that at the count of ten she will fall into a deep, natural state of sleep, which enhances the recovery process.

DANGERS AND LIMITATIONS OF HYPNOSIS. It should come as no surprise that the experts are divided on the issue of the possible dangers of hypnosis just as they are on every other aspect of this controversial subject. Some of its detractors consider it not to be a bona fide subject, and view it as a fraud, while others do not perceive any danger in it because the subject retains an ability to protect himself from its unethical applications. The possible limitations and dangers of hypnosis are well pointed out by Meares (1961):

1. *Unscrupulous use of hypnosis.* An unethical hypnotist may take advantage of the naïve subject and exploit him for his own purposes. This can be seen sometimes in stage shows during which the subject engages in silly acts during a trance. This is illustrated by one well-known case in which a subject stripped down to his shorts, following suggestions made to him during a trance. The subject afterwards was very upset by his own antics and angered because he had been made to look like a "fool." The hypnotist was guilty of using him to entertain the audience, apparently not worried about what the subject's later reactions would be.

2. *Traumatic insight.* The subject might suddenly recall previously repressed materials that he cannot accept. Thus he may become very agitated and require professional help in order to handle his problems.

3. *Precipitation of a psychosis.* The individual who has an underlying mental illness may have it triggered by various suggestions made during a trance. An untrained hypnotist is not well equipped to handle a crisis of this magnitude.

4. *Development of disabling substitute symptoms when the original symptoms have been removed by hypnotic suggestion.* This happens in cases in which patients want to get rid of some aberrant behavioral patterns such as thumbsucking, sometimes seen in older children. If the symptoms are based on unresolved emotional conflicts they may be replaced by other crippling symptoms. Psychotherapy is needed in such cases to get at the core of the problem.

5. *Sudden panic reactions occasioned by the experience of hypnosis itself.* Certain susceptible subjects have been badly frightened by the mind-altering experiences of hypnosis in a manner similar to the "bad trips" associated with LSD. It is not intrinsic to the hypnosis process itself; it is more likely caused by the emotional state of the subject.

6. *Difficulty in waking a subject.* Unfortnuately, there have been a few cases reported in the literature in which the practitioner has en-

countered difficulty in awakening the subject. However, this is much more likely to happen when trances are induced by inexperienced or unqualified hypnotists.

Thus, because of these problems associated with the use of hypnosis, Meares and others have concluded that its use by unskilled people represents a real danger.

Extrasensory perception (ESP)

One of the age-old questions which has always fascinated man has been "Does man possess 'supernatural' or 'parapsychological' powers?" The answer to this question has been a source of a major controversy within the field of psychology for several years. Although some psychologists believe that there is incontrovertible evidence for ESP, the majority maintain that the scientific data for such phenomena is unconvincing.

1. *Mental telepathy* is thought transference from one person to another or an ability to read someone else's mind.
2. *Clairvoyance* is the ability to perceive what is happening elsewhere without the use of the regular senses such as a train wreck far away.
3. *Precognition* is the ability to know what is going to happen before it occurs, such as perceiving one's future.
4. *Psychokinesis* (PK) is a mind over matter phenomena whereby a mental thought affects a physical body or an energy system (e.g., wishing for a certain horse to win at the racetrack).

Scientists conducting experiments on these mental events work in accordance with the usual rules of science and generally disavow any connection between their work and supernaturalism or spiritualism. A typical experiment consists of card guessing in which, under various controlled conditions, the subject attempts to guess the symbols on cards that have been shuffled. The ESP pack consists of 25 cards having five symbols so that by chance a subject should get five correct hits per pack. This is similar to the situation in which a coin flip by chance will come up heads 50 percent of the time and tails the other times. Even the most successful subjects in the various experiments seldom score as high as seven hits although they may score above five often enough so that chance alone cannot explain the results.

One of the more successful subjects was Mrs. Gloria Stewart who was studied in England over a long period of time (Table 4–1). As can be seen by the data, Mrs. Stewart responded above chance on the mental telepathy trials but not on clairvoyance. In regard to the former, her average scoring level of 6.8 hits (instead of 5) per pack of 25 is well above chance according to acceptable standards of statistical significance. However, her performance on the clairvoyance trials (average 4.9 hits per pack) is what would be predicted from chance alone.

In a study on mental telepathy, the experimenter or "sender" thinks

TABLE 4–1
**Experimental results of telepathy and clairvoyance with
one subject**

Chronological order of successive groups of 200 trials	Hits per 200 trials (Expected = 40)	
	Telepathy Trials	Clairvoyance Trials
1945	65	51
	58	42
	62	29
	58	47
	60	38
1947	54	35
	55	36
	65	31
1948	39	38
	56	43
1949	49	40
	51	37
	33	42
Total hits	707	509
Expected hits	520	520
Difference	+187	−11
Hits per 25 trials	6.8	4.9

Each group of 200 trials consisted of alternating blocks of 50 telepathy
and 50 clairvoyance trials.
Source: S. G. Soal and F. Bateman, *Modern Experiments in Telepathy* (New Haven, Conn.: Yale University Press, 1954), p. 352.

of the symbol of the card he has looked at and the subject attempts "to read his mind"; if the "sender" does not look at the card at all as it lies face down on the table, then the subject guesses what the symbol is, the experiment is on clairvoyance.

WHY PSYCHOLOGISTS FIND EVIDENCE FOR ESP UNCONVINCING. In a number of the original experiments, the results seemed to indicate the existence of ESP. However, upon reviewing these studies many errors have been discovered. For example, clerical errors in recording the data were made in one direction so that the accuracy of the subjects' guesses were reported to have been better than they actually were (Kennedy, 1939). In other research, there was considerable evidence that the experimenter was unintentionally whispering the correct response to the subject. This was discovered by placing a sound reflector behind the experimenter's head, which immediately resulted in the subject improving his score. In addition, when the experimenter was simply asked to think of a number between one and ten which the subject was asked to guess, the experimenter tended to choose certain numbers more often than others so that the subject had a better chance of guessing correctly. Another methodological error was found in other early studies in which defective cards were used. The printing on the backs of the cards actually showed through, although barely; hence, without realizing it, many subjects who thought they were really reading minds may instead have been reading the backs of the cards.

When these possible errors were removed in later studies, some experimenters still obtained positive results for ESP (the case of Mrs. Gloria Stewart, for example). However, most other investigators, using improved methods, report negative results (Girden, 1962). In fact it has been often stated, concerning research on ESP, that the poorer the conditions the better the results. This is the exact reverse of the trends in research on most scientific topics.

With the current state of knowledge, the arguments concerning the authenticity of ESP are not decisive on either side of the issue. All that can be said scientifically is that ESP has not been conclusively proven nor disproven; hence, it is desirable to keep an open mind in order for more research to be conducted. For those students who want to look further into the issues regarding ESP phenomena, excellent reviews are presented by McConnell (1949) and Hansel (1966).

Transcendental meditation

One of the most popular methods of altering consciousness is transcendental meditation (TM), also commonly referred to as the drugless high (Campbell, 1974). The procedure is extraordinarily simple, with the exercises calling for relaxation and controlled breathing, usually in a sitting or kneeling position on the floor. The important point is that the position must be conducive to relaxation without inducing sleep. There are several variations to this general procedure, but the following method is typical. The subject takes one clean handkerchief, three pieces of fresh, sweet fruit, and several fresh flowers. These various articles are symbolic offerings which are to be laid before a portrait of the Indian guru, who once taught the Maharishi Mahesh Yogi (Figure 4–5), founder of the International Meditation Society. The subject is alone with his teacher or mentor in an atmosphere made mystical by candlelight, the chanting of Sanskrit phrases, and incense. The recruit is specifically taught *mantra*, which is an ancient Hindu incantation that strikes uninformed observers as meaningless sounds.

After the above initiation, the beginner then takes three more two-hour lessons in order to learn how to relax, for which he generally pays a modest fee; however, college students usually only pay a fee of $45 in order to reap the alleged benefits of transcendental meditation. These techniques are not really new but have only recently been practiced by Western men, many of whom have become discontented with what they see as a corruption of life through material interests and technology. These practices have been part of Eastern religions for many, many years. Those exercises derived from Hindu philosophy are called *yoga* and the practices derived from Buddhism are referred to as Zen. Both yoga and Zen, which are similar, are used by the mentor to teach the subject to enjoy life more and to shed tension by letting the mind travel from mundane concerns.

EXPERIMENTAL MEDITATION. In contrast to the use of drugs or hyp-

FIGURE 4–5
Maharishi Mahesh Yogi, Indian philosopher

Wide World Photos

nosis to induce altered states of consciousness, TM does not seem to have any harmful effects. For this reason many people have been enthusiastic about its general usage. Some behavioral scientists have become interested in TM and have performed experiments in an attempt to investigate alleged claims of mind expansion, including the development of creative intelligence and subtler states of thought.

In one study involving 28 college recruits, 45-minute practice sessions, followed by short interviews, were held each weekday for a two-week period (Maupin, 1965). A Zen program was adhered to in which the principle instruction called for concentration on breathing:

> While you are sitting let your breath become relaxed and natural. Let it set its own pace and depth if you can. Then focus your attention on your own breathing: the movements of your belly, not your nose or throat. Do not allow extraneous thoughts or stimuli to pull your atten-

tion away from your breathing. This may be hard to do at first, but keep directing your attention back to it. Turn everything else aside if it comes up (Maupin, 1965, p. 140).

The subjects were divided into three different-type response groups on the basis of the quality of their responses during the interviews. A "high-response" group was selected as having one or more experiences described as extreme detachment: a deeply satisfying state of consciousness in which the meditator is able to take a calmly detached view of any thoughts or feelings that happen to emerge. Low responders reported no mental effects except occasional dizziness, fogginess, relaxation, and calmness. Moderate responders frequently reported an intensification of pleasant bodily sensations and other sensations associated with breathing. The high responders reported all responses, including the previously described detachment except dizziness and fogginess.

In another experiment, a subject sat in an armchair in a pleasant, carpeted room looking at a blue vase 10 inches high on a table. The instructions consisted of telling the subject to concentrate on the blue vase and to try to see the vase as it exists in itself, without any connections to other things. He was also told to exclude all other thoughts or feelings as well as sounds or body sensations (Deikman, 1963).

After the session began, the subject's ability to concentrate without distractions was tested by the experimenter presenting a number of sounds by a tape recorder. Meditation consisted of 12 practice sessions, spread out over three weeks; the time of each session was gradually increased from 5 to 33 minutes. Some interesting altered states of consciousness took place as follows: (1) a more intense perception of the blue vase; (2) time periods appeared to the subject to be shorter than they actually were; (3) conflicting perceptions were noted, as the vase seemed to fill the visual field and not to fill it; this caused some agitation and was described as both pleasant and disturbing by the subject; (4) increasing ability of the subject to shut off awareness of external stimuli, such as sounds; and (5) a pleasurable state, the experiences of which were described as invaluable and rewarding by the subject.

In spite of the interesting results of the two studies above and of other similar findings, it is still difficult to evaluate the effectiveness of TM. Part of the problem in trying to document its psychological effects is that it is difficult to exclude the effects of suggestion. It is possible that its devotees are kidding themselves in their claims that TM has improved their sex lives, memories, and general alertness. However, there is undisputed evidence that meditation does produce physiological changes.

THE PHYSIOLOGY OF MEDITATION. We have already seen, in connection with biofeedback studies, that an individual can control his physiological reactions to psychological events. Among the most successful subjects in obtaining such control are practitioners of meditation systems such as yoga and Zen Buddhism. To be sure, some exaggerated claims have proven to be false such as voluntarily stopping the heartbeat, or surviving for extended periods in an "airtight" pit or in extreme cold without food. Two American physiologists, Drs. M. A. Wenger and B. K. Bagchi, conducted an extensive investigation of subjects at the All-India Institute of Medical Sciences in New Delhi. None of the yogis they studied showed a capability for stopping the heart; they did find, however, that some of the yogis could slow both heartbeat and respiration rate. Furthermore, other investigators found that meditation produced changes in the electrical activity of the brain. When Zen monks meditated with their eyes half-open, the EEG recordings showed a predominance of alpha waves (slow waves typically obtained when a person is thoroughly relaxed with his eyes closed).

A systematic study of the physiological effects or correlates of meditation was recently carried out in the United States by Wallace and Benson (1972). They used the "transcendental meditation" technique, previously described, with 36 subjects from Boston City Hospital and the University of California at Irvine. Their experience in meditation ranged from less than a month to nine years; the majority had from two to three years of experience. Apparatuses designed for continuous measurement of blood pressure, heart rate, skin resistance (GSR), and brain waves were attached to the subject.

The rate of oxygen consumption and carbon dioxide emissions decreased remarkably during periods of meditation in contrast to before and after periods as seen in Figure 4–6. Furthermore, there was a reduction in the rate of respiration and in the volume of air breathed. All of these physiological changes are the result of a reduced rate of metabolism.

The subjects' arterial blood pressure remained at a rather low level throughout the study. Measurements of the lactate concentration in the blood (an indication of metabolism in the absence of free oxygen) showed a marked decline in the subjects during meditation. Wallace and Benson interpret this as a sign that meditation has reduced the major activity of the sympathetic nervous system, so that its constriction of the blood vessels is absent. In other words, low blood lactate rates are associated with relaxed states, in which the activity of the sympathetic nervous system is reduced, as you will recall from Chapter 2. On the other hand, high blood lactate rates are correlated with stress, when the activity of the sympathetic nervous system is increased.

Other findings in this study confirmed the picture of a highly relaxed, although wakeful, condition. The heart rates of the subjects slowed by about three beats per minute on the average during meditation and their skin resistance to an electric current increased fourfold (in sleep, skin resistance normally rises). EEG recordings revealed a marked increase in alpha waves in all of the subjects; this was found in both the frontal and central regions of the brain.

Wallace and Benson sum up their physiological findings as indicating that subjects are in a "wakeful, hypometabolic" state during meditation

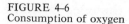

FIGURE 4–6
Consumption of oxygen

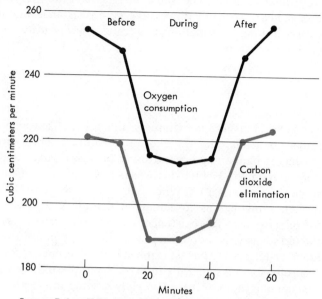

Source: Robert Keith Wallace and Herbert Benson, "The Physiology of Meditation," *Scientific American*, February 1972, p. 86.

which is reflected psychologically by the subjects' subjectively reporting that they feel very relaxed and "at peace." These physiological modifications in subjects' practicing the easily learned TM techniques are very similar to those that have been observed in highly trained experts in yoga and in Zen monks who have had from 15 to 20 years of experience in meditation.

COMPARISON OF EFFECTS OF MEDITATION WITH OTHER RELAXED STATES. Somewhat surprisingly, the physiological changes brought on by meditation are quite different from sleep and hypnosis (Wallace & Benson, 1972). Oxygen consumption drops rapidly within the first five or ten minutes of meditation. In contrast, hypnosis produces no noticeable change in this metabolic index, and during sleep the rate of consumption of oxygen is reduced only after several hours. The mixture of brain wave patterns during sleep consists of slow waves at 12 to 14 cycles per second and weaker waves at various frequencies—these patterns are not found during TM. One other difference between states of sleep and meditation that is frequently reported concerns the GSR. The rate and amount of electrical skin resistance during sleep is on a much smaller scale than is found in meditation.

Various changes during hypnosis are even less similar to those that take place during meditation. The brain wave patterns of the hypnotized subject take on the form of the mental activity that had been suggested to him; either alpha, beta, or delta waves can often be induced upon command of the hypnotist. The same is true of other physiological changes such as heart rate, blood pressure, skin resistance, and respiration. All of these autonomic functions in a trance merely adjust to reflect the suggested mental state.

Summary

The idea of consciousness is extremely difficult to discuss and define because it does not seem to be a single, simple state. An ability to report accurately what is happening around us (alertness) waxes and wanes from moment to moment. Hebb lists three behavioral signs of consciousness in humans and animals: (1) When behavior varies with the circumstances in such a manner as to achieve a definite goal, we infer the existence of *purpose*. (2) The existence of *mediating processes*, defined as thoughts and ideas which determine a subject's response to a stimulus, is a second criteria. (3) The last criteria is the presence of *immediate memory*. Consciousness is generally inferred from these three variables.

Electroencephalography (EEG) has shown some interesting physiological indicators of consciousness. Alpha rhythms are correlated with alertness, while beta and delta rhythms indicate sleep. Brain wave patterns of newborn babies indicate that they may not be fully conscious in the adult sense, even when awake.

All of us experience various states of consciousness much different from our waking state (sleep, dreams, meditation, trances, and so on). These nonordinary states have one common feature: awareness is focused inward rather than outward. Some evidence exists that indicates the desire to alter states of consciousness may be an innate motive. Altering consciousness can be accomplished by external (drugs) or internal (dreaming, hypnosis, meditation, and so forth) means.

Alcohol is one of the most widely used drugs in our society which alters consciousness. It is a depressant which numbs the higher brain centers and lessens inhibitory controls. Typically, a sense of warmth, expansiveness, and well-being is experienced. Alcohol, in even small amounts, damages judgmental and perceptual functions. Prolonged drinking can result in both physical and mental deterioration. Excessive use results in psychological and physiological addiction. Jellinek identifies four stages of alcoholism: the prealcoholic, prodromal, crucial, and chronic.

Marijuana is a relatively mild drug that does not seem to lead to physiological dependence or increased tolerance. The physiological and psychological effects seem to depend on the dosage, personality of the user, and the past experience of the individual with the drug. In contrast to alcohol, it stimulates the pathways to the brain in producing its "high." Physiologically, heartbeat and appetite increases, eyes become bloodshot and itchy, the mouth becomes dry, and reflexes are slower. Subjectively, regular users report increased feelings of well-being, relaxation, and enhanced sensory experiences. However, marijuana may also lead to unpleasant experiences. Behaviorally, much of the effects of marijuana depends upon whether the person is a naïve or chronic user. General findings indicate distortion in time estimation and effects on speech patterns. In a comparison of alcohol and marijuana usage on driving skills, it was found that the former impairs driving more than the latter.

Heroin is a highly addictive drug that can cause a fundamental change in the biochemistry of the body resulting in *severe* withdrawal symptoms if not taken. As a result, much of the addict's time is spent in supporting his habit. Another drug, methadone, has been used as a means of combating heroin addiction. Methadone is substituted for heroin because it provides a feeling of peace, can be taken orally, does not require larger doses, and allows the person to function in society. Nevertheless, methadone critics feel that substituting another drug in place of one, does not solve the problem.

Hallucinogenic drugs such as LSD and mescaline are powerful mind-altering substances that distort sensory images. Tolerance for these drugs increases but withdrawal symptoms are absent. There is some evidence that chronic use may cause chromosome damage, however, much more research is needed.

Barbiturates, which depress the action of the brain, are sedatives prescribed by physicians to calm patients or to induce sleep. Patients may become addicted and require increasing dosages to obtain the same results. Although barbiturates produce feelings of euphoria, undesirable side effects such as impairment of cognitive functioning and depression may result.

Amphetamines have chemical effects that stimulate the activity of the central nervous system and is prescribed for mildly depressed persons. They produce a state of hyperalertness beyond the normal level of the individual and, if taken constantly, can result in exhaustion. Like other drugs, many harmful side effects are also present. Amphetamines seem to have an opposite effect on hyperkinetic children by slowing down their overall activity.

Much of the subjective effects of drugs can be accomplished by internal controls which arise from within the body. Dreaming, which is correlated with REM and certain EEG patterns is such an experience. All of us dream and there is evidence to suggest that dreaming is necessary for our mental health. Studies on dream deprivation indicate the development of psychological disturbances (anxiety, irritability, poor concentration, and so on) if dreaming is not allowed.

Hypnosis is designed to bring about a state of selective attention to the suggestions of the hypnotist, who tells the subject that he is becoming drowsy, relaxed, and sleepy. Tests of suggestibility have been developed to determine people's susceptibility to hypnotism. Alterations in perception of reality and body image have been reported by subjects during the trance state. Two areas of controversy, having subjects perform antisocial behavior and the genuineness of age regression, were discussed. Beyond these controversies, hypnosis has medical applications such as in surgery and obstetrics. The use of hypnosis by unskilled people may lead to possible dangers such as unethical use, traumatic insight, precipitation of psychosis, development of disabling symptoms, panic reactions, and difficulty in awakening the subjects.

ESP is another fascinating area in the study of consciousness. However, the positive results of studies on mental telepathy, clairvoyance, precognition, and psychokinesis are questionable because of possible methodological errors in many experiments.

Transcendental meditation (TM), originating from Eastern philosophies, uses exercises that call for relaxation and controlled breathing. The psychological effects such as subjects' reporting a relaxed state and other phenomena are difficult to evaluate because it is hard to exclude the effects of suggestion. However, physiological changes during TM indicate a reduced metabolic rate (lower oxygen consumption and heart rate as well as increased skin resistance).

A comparison of sleep, hypnosis, and TM reveals different physiological patterns and strongly suggests that these three phenomena are not the same.

References

Aase, J. M., Laestadius, N., & Smith, D. W. LSD-dosed mothers have normal infants in Seattle. *Psychiatric News*, 1971, **6**(1), 6.

American Medical Association, Department of Mental Health. The crutch that cripples: Drug dependence, part I. *Today's Health*, 1968, **46**(9), 11–12, 70–72.

Ansbacher, H., & Adler, A. Individual psychology. *Psychology Today*, 1970, **3**(9), 42–45, 66.

Arehart, J. L. The search for a heroin cure. *Science News*, 1972, **101**(16), 250–251.

Barber, T. X. Hypnotic age-regression: A critical review. *Psychosomatic Medicine*, 1962, **24**, 286–299.

Barron, F., Jarvik, M., & Bunnell, D. S. The hallucinogenic drugs. In *Altered States of Awareness: Readings from Scientific American*, San Francisco: W. H. Freeman, 1972.

Campbell, C. Transcendence is as American as Ralph Waldo Emerson. *Psychology Today*, 1974, **7**(11), 37–38.

Claeson, E., & Carlsson, C. Swedish scientists link alcohol to brain disorder. *Psychiatric News*, 1971, **6**(4), 20.

Cohen, J. *Secondary motivation. I. Personal motives.* Chicago: Rand McNally, 1970.

Cohen, S. Pot, acid, and speed. In Robert Guthrie (Ed.), *Psychology in the world today: An interdisciplinary approach*, Reading, Mass.: Addison-Wesley, 1971.

Coleman, J. C. *Abnormal psychology and modern life.* Glenview, Ill.: Scott, Foresman, 1972.

Crancer, A., Jr., Dille, J. M., Delay, J. C., Wallace, J. E., & Haykin, M. D. Comparison of the effects of marijuana and alcohol on simulated driving performance. *Science*, May 16, 1969, **164**, 851–854.

Deikman, A. J. Experimental meditation. *Journal of Nervous and Mental Disease*, 1963, **136**, 329–373.

Dement, W. The effect of dream deprivation. In R. V. Guthrie (Ed.), *Psychology in the world today: An interdisciplinary approach*, Reading, Mass.: Addison-Wesley, 1971.

Eisenberg, L. Principles of drug therapy in child psychiatry with special reference to stimulant drugs. *American Journal of Orthopsychiatry,* 1971, 4(3), 371–379.

Ellinwood, E. H. Assault and homicide associated with amphetamine abuse. *American Journal of Psychiatry,* 1971, **127**(9), 90–95.

Esdaile, J. *Mesmerism in India and its practical application in surgery and medicine.* Hartford, Eng.: Silus Andrus and Son, 1850.

Girden, E. A review of psychokinesis. *Psychological Bulletin,* 1962, **59**, 353–388.

Grinspoon, L. Marijuana. In *Altered states of awareness: Readings from Scientific American.* San Francisco: W. H. Freeman, 1972.

Hansel, C. E. M. *ESP: A scientific evaluation.* New York: Scribners, 1966.

Hebb, D. O. *A textbook of psychology.* Philadelphia: W. B. Saunders, 1972.

HEW. Physical damage of pot yet unproven, says HEW. *Psychiatric News,* 1971, **6**(8), 23–26.

Hilgard, E. R. *Hypnotic susceptibility.* New York: Harcourt, Brace & World, 1965.

Hilgard, E. R., & Tart, C. T. Responsiveness to suggestion following waking and imagination instructions and following induction of hypnosis. *Journal of Abnormal Psychology,* 1966, **71**, 196–208.

Hoffman, A. LSD discovery disputes "chance" factor in finding. *Psychiatric News,* 1971, **6**, 23–26.

Horowitz, M. J. Flashbacks: Recurrent intrusive images after the use of LSD. *American Journal of Psychiatry,* 1969, **126**, 147–151.

Jellinek, E. M. Phases of alcohol addiction. In G. D. Shean (Ed.), *Studies in abnormal behavior.* Chicago: Rand McNally, 1971, 86–98.

Keeler, M. K. Search for insight in heavy marijuana users. *Psychiatric News,* 1970, **5**, 42.

Kennedy, J. L. A methodological review of extra-sensory perception. *Psychological Bulletin,* 1939, **36**, 60–61.

Kleitman, N. Patterns of dreaming. In *Altered states of awareness: Readings from Scientific American.* San Francisco: W. H. Freeman, 1972.

Kupper, H. I. Psychic concommitants in wartime injuries. *Psychosomatic Medicine,* 1945, **7**, 15–21.

Lewis, H. B., Goodenough, D. R., Shapiro, A., & Slesser, I. Individual differences in dream recall. *Journal of Abnormal Psychology,* 1966, **71**, 52–59.

London, P. Subject characteristics in hypnosis research. Part I. A survey of experience, interest, and opinion. *International Journal of Experimental Hypnosis,* 1965, **9**, 151–161.

Massett, L. Marijuana and behavior: The unfilled gaps. In R. V. Guthrie (Ed.), *Psychology in the world today.* Reading, Mass.: Addison-Wesley, 1970, 255–259.

Maupin, E. W. Individual differences in response to a Zen meditation exercise. *Journal of Consulting Psychology,* 1965, **29**, 139–145.

McConnell, R. A. ESP and credibility in science. *American Psychologist,* 1969, **5**, 531–538.

Meares, A. An evaluation of the dangers of medical hypnosis. *American Journal of Clinical Hypnosis,* 1961, **4**, 90–97.

Moody, R. L. Bodily changes during abreaction. *Lancet,* 1946, **2**, 934–935.

Nahas, G., Suciu–Foca, N., Armand, J.–P., & Morishima, A. *Science,* 1974, **183**, 419.

Nelson, H. Study compares drug dangers. *Los Angeles Times,* October 6, 1969.

Pattie, F. A. The genuineness of some hypnotic age regression. In R. M. Dorcus (Ed.), *Hypnosis and its therapeutic applications.* New York: McGraw-Hill, 1956.

Reyher, J. *Hypnosis.* Dubuque, Iowa: W. C. Brown, 1968.

Rorvik, D. M. Do drugs lead to violence? *Look,* April 7, 1970, 58–61.

Science News. Alcohol on the brain. April 8, 1972, 233.

Science News. Marijuana and sex, May 11, 1974.

Smith, K. V., & Smith, W. M. *Perception and emotions: An analysis of space-structured behavior.* Philadelphia: Saunders, 1962.

Snyder, F. W., & Pronko, N. H. *Vision with spatial inversion.* Wichita, Kans.: McCormick-Armstrong, 1952.

Stratton, G. M. Vision without inversion of the retinal image. *Psychological Review,* 1897, **4**, 341–360, 463–481.

Wallace, R. K., & Benson, H. The physiology of meditation. In *Altered states of awareness: Readings from Scientific American.* San Francisco: W. H. Freeman, 1972.

Weil, A. Altered states of consciousness. *New Scientist,* 1972, **53**, 696–698.

Weil, A. T., & Zinberg, N. E. Acute effects of marijuana on speech. *Nature,* 1969, **222**(5153), 434–437.

Weil, A. T., Zinberg, N. E., & Nelson, J. M. Clinical and psychological effects of marijuana in man. *Science,* 1968, 1234–1242.

SECTION FOUR

Learning and motivation

In the last two chapters, we have been concerned with exploring our innate biological equipment and its effects on our behavior. We now move to a more environmental explanation of behavior. As we saw in Chapter 3, various learning experiences may affect perception. How does this learning take place? This is an extremely important question for us to deal with. As we saw in Chapter 2, the behavior of lower animals is dictated largely by innate factors. In order to survive and adapt to the demands of a changing environment, we must profit from experience. Of all organisms, man is superior because he is the best learner. Our adaptability is based on our ability to predict future events from past experiences and to predict the consequences of our responses. For example, a track star knows that unless he practices and conditions his body properly, he may lose in a track meet. He is able to predict this from past meets and is aware of the consequences. The learning and storage in memory of new information and skills are crucial for our survival. Exactly how does this process occur? What principles underlie learning and how can we use them effectively? These are all questions which we will explore in Chapter 5.

The discussion of learning naturally leads into such topics as motivation and emotion. As pointed out in Chapter 6, motivation is frequently the key to learning. The efficiency to which you will learn concepts in psychology may depend on how motivated you are. What motivates a person varies greatly with the individual. Whether a person is motivated by grades or the acquisition of knowledge influences how he approaches a learning task or how hard he works. In addition, the emotions we experience such as love, hate, anger, fear, and frustration affects our behavior. The study of motivation and emotion attempts to tell "What directs human behavior."

5

Learning and memory

What is learning?

Classical conditioning.
Extinction and spontaneous recovery.
Uses of classical conditioning.

Instrumental learning and behaviorism.
Historical background.
Mechanical man?
Instrumental conditioning in animals and humans.

Cognitive learning.
Problem solving.
Insight.
Reasoning.

Reinforcement and habit patterns.

Imitation learning.

Memory and forgetting.
Methods of measuring memory.
The course of retention.

Improving our memories.

Why do we forget?

Special topics in learning.
How good can memory be?
Eidetic imagery.

Summary.

One night a college coed awakened other women in her dormitory with loud hysterical screams. In rushing to her aid, the coeds could find nothing in her room but a small cat. On the surface, this seems to be puzzling behavior. Why should the unfortunate lady be so terrified of a harmless house cat? The mystery to this unusual behavior disappears upon further inquiry and can be explained in terms of modern psychological theories of learning. Many of our strange fears (phobias) are, in reality, learned behavior that can be explained in the same way as the acquisition of other behaviors.

For example, two pigeons can be taught to bat a ball back and forth to each other. The principles involved in teaching a pigeon to play table tennis are the techniques used by all animal trainers in getting their animals to perform tricks in a zoo or circus. When you teach your dog to shake hands or to retrieve a stick, you are probably applying basic principles of learning.

The importance of learning

In order to gain an appreciation that learning has always been a crucial topic in psychology, consider this question: What would happen if you suddenly forgot everything that you had ever learned? You would be like a helpless newborn baby, completely dependent upon others for survival. You could not communicate with others because you would not have learned a language. You would be unable to recognize your friends and enemies. You would not even have the simplest skills such as being able to use a fork and spoon.

Unlike lower organisms, man has practically no strong instinctive behaviors that would automatically enable him to adjust to his environment. We must do it the hard way, by learning. As a generalization, the more complex the animal or organism is (higher on the evolutionary scale), the greater is the capacity for learning and the less reliance is placed on innate behavior. As we saw in Chapter 2, the behavior of a bee is much more rigid and stereotyped than the behavior of a dog. Man, of course, has the greatest capacity of all to learn. Humans can live and thrive in a diversity of environments and are even now engaged in the exploration of space, a totally foreign environment. Of all living creatures, man seems to be able to acquire the greatest store of information, to develop the greatest diversity of motor skills, and to adapt to the largest range of situations.

What is learning?

We can tentatively state that learning is a change in behavior or performance that occurs as a result of practice or experience. Thus, variability or change in behavior is implicit in this definition. However, a major difficulty with this definition is that changes occur in performance that are not due to practice or experience. We must be careful to rule out other factors that affect performance such as drugs, fatigue, maturation, motivation, or change in the environments before we can conclude that true learning has taken place.

You should also remember that the definition of learning is essentially neutral; the results of learning are not always beneficial. People can learn to be unhappy and this is one reason why society is confronted with a serious mental health problem. People can learn to be prejudiced and hate one another. In the United States, social problems have arisen because members of one religious or racial group have learned negative attitudes toward members of other groups (see Chapter 13 on "Racism").

You can also learn to do things the wrong way. For instance, you may have learned to hold your golf club incorrectly so that your swing tends to drive the ball toward the left or right rather than straight ahead. Or you may have developed poor study habits so that you find it very difficult to understand class materials and waste a great deal of time in ineffective reading.

Classical conditioning

At the beginning of the 20th century, a Russian physiologist, Ivan Pavlov, made what turned out to be a breakthrough in the psychology of learning. Pavlov was conducting basic research on the salivation response of dogs and noticed that he could stimulate the flow of digestive juices not only by placing food in a dog's mouth but also by simply showing it to the animal (Figure 5-1). He recognized that some psychic phenomenon was at work which soon proved to be one of the basic models of learning.

In Pavlov's famous experiment, a bell was rung just before meat powder was placed in a dog's mouth. At first, the dog did not salivate until it actually got the meat. After several pairings of the bell and meat, it salivated at the sound of the bell. Finally, the dog would continue to respond to the bell even if it was not followed by meat. The transfer of a response from one stimulus to another, such as in the example above, is called conditioning and is a form of learning. Pavlov's conditioning procedures are termed classical because of their historic significance in psychology. Perhaps one reason for the prominence of this particular type of conditioning is that most of us find ourselves similarly conditioned to a variety of sights and sounds—our mouths water at the sight, smell, or thought of our favorite foods.

The terms that describe classical conditioning can be illustrated by Pavlov's experiment. The meat powder that produced salivation without

FIGURE 5–1
A drawing of the apparatus used by Pavlov in his original studies of classical or respondent conditioning.

Source: R. M. Yerkes and S. Margulis, "The Method of Pavlov in Animal Psychology," *Psychological Bulletin*, 1909, 6. Copyright 1909 by the American Psychological Association. Reprinted by permission.

training was an *unconditioned stimulus* (UCS) producing saliva, an *unconditioned response* (UCR). After the conditioning procedure, the sound of the bell which now produces salivation is called a *conditioned stimulus* (CS). The *conditioned response*, (CR), salivation made to the CS in this case is the same as the UCR. A UCS is simply any exciting event to which animals and man automatically respond on its initial presentation. In contrast, a CS is a previously neutral event that will not produce a response until it has been paired or associated with the UCS. The responses in classical conditioning, such as eyeblinks, heartbeats, and perspiration, are essentially *reflexive* in nature.

EXTINCTION AND SPONTANEOUS RECOVERY. Pavlov's experiments demonstrated many of the principles of learning and provides much of our terminology in the field. The process through which the conditioned response (CR) tends to disappear because the UCS or reward is withdrawn or not presented with the conditioned stimulus (CS) is known as *extinction*. For example, if Pavlov only sounded the bell (CS) without introducing the meat (UCS) for several trials, the salivating (CR) of the dog would tend to disappear to the CS. However, Pavlov also discovered that even after extinction, the conditioned response tends to recur after a rest. This phenomenon in which there is a reappearance of an extinguished response (CR) is called spontaneous *recovery*.

CONDITIONED RESPONSES IN LIFE SITUATIONS. The conditioned response is far more than a strange phenomenon that takes place only in the laboratory. For example, consider the case of the college coed who was terrified of cats. Her fear or phobia of cats can be explained entirely in terms of classical conditioning. As a little girl she had been badly scratched by a cat and became afraid of it. Her fear (crying and trembling) then generalized from that particular cat to all cats. In the language of conditioning, the cat was a previously neutral stimulus, a CS. The UCS in this case was being badly scratched by the cat which automatically produced fear, the UCR. Thus a CR of fear was transferred to the cat on the basis of association and she developed her phobia.

A similar phobia was demonstrated by John Watson, one of the most famous of the early psychologists. One experiment that Watson helped conduct is the "Albert Study"—named after an 11-month-old child who served as the subject. Generally, a child automatically responds to an unexpected loud noise with fear. Watson wanted to see if this fear could be transferred or conditioned to other stimuli. He therefore showed little Albert a white rat. Displaying no fear at all, Albert tried to play with it. Watson then proceeded to present the animal several times to the child and immediately accompanied it with a loud noise (Figure 5–2). After several pairings, Albert showed fear whenever he saw the rat. The fear response set off automatically by the loud noise had now been conditioned to the white rat, a previously neutral stimulus. Little Albert generalized his fear to furry objects such as rats, rabbits, and even to men with beards (Watson & Rayner, 1920).

FIGURE 5–2
An illustration of how little Albert was conditioned to the fear response. As little Albert reaches for the rat (A) a loud noise is presented at the same time (B). After this conditioning, the child shows fear of the rat (C) and even a man's beard resembling a furry animal.

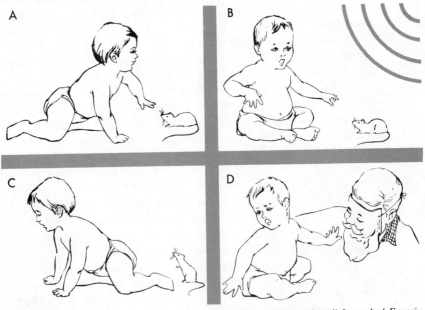

Source: J. B. Watson and R. Rayner, "Conditioned Emotional Reactions," *Journal of Experimental Psychology*, 1920, 3. Copyright 1920 by the American Psychological Association. Reprinted by permission.

Thus, many of our likes, dislikes, and fears are nothing but conditioned responses obtained similarly to the way conditioning takes place in the psychological laboratory. What appears to be very strange behavior is understandable once we know the circumstances surrounding it.

USES OF CLASSICAL CONDITIONING. Psychologists have made use of the classical conditioning model in order to understand more complex behaviors and to treat psychological problems. In the laboratory, it has been employed to investigate how the world appears to animals. What are dogs able to see and hear in our environment? The range of sounds dogs can hear was discovered in the following manner. First, a sound of medium pitch such as "middle" C was presented to an animal and followed by food. After "middle" C and food had been paired several times, a conditioned response developed and the dog salivated to "middle" C. The experimenter then presented successive sounds that were higher or lower in pitch than the original conditioned stimulus. The dog typically generalized his salivation response to the new sounds and eventually stopped salivating when the sounds were too high or too low in pitch for him to hear. Thus, we have an objective way to determine how the world appears to animals. By employing the classical conditioning model, we know dogs live in a rich world of odors and sounds but are relatively color blind.

In a similar manner, clinical psychologists and psychiatrists have used classical conditioning techniques to help their patients. This will be discussed in more detail in Chapter 9.

Instrumental learning and behaviorism

Historical background

While Pavlov was involved in working primarily with conditioned responses, other psychologists were also attempting to teach animals to act more purposefully instead of reflexively. The types of responses they were working with became known as operant behavior and their technique for modification was called instrumental conditioning.

Both humans and animals engage in operant behavior which appears to be much more variable than reflexes. As a start toward defining it, think about typical behaviors you do during the day. You shower, eat, drive a car, walk, and turn on the television. None of these actions is automatic nor is the basic stimulus a flash of light or a sound. These actions appear to be spontaneous in the sense that they are not directly elicited by some stimulus. As a matter of fact, you "operate" on your environment and change it. Hence, the phrase *operant behavior*.

One of the most important examples of operant behavior is human speech. There is nothing in our environment that will automatically make us say tree or car. In addition, we may use different words to refer to such an object. How do humans acquire a language? A start toward this answer is provided by discussing instrumental conditioning as it occurs in animals and then in man himself.

MAZES AND BOXES. A precursor to psychologists who were interested in instrumental conditioning was an American named Edward Thorndike. Like Pavlov, he was interested in the objective study of stimuli and responses. However, he viewed learning as problem solving. He was the forerunner of several generations of American psychologists who devoted themselves to studying the ways in which rats, cats, and dogs worked their way through mazes and out of boxes. In a typical Thorndike experiment, hungry cats were placed inside boxes. They were fed only after they had escaped. In order to escape, the animals had to release a catch over the front of the box. There were several ways they could do it. Typically, a cat would thrash about aimlessly; then by accident, it would spring the release. After being put back in the box again, its performance would not be very good. However, the cat would eventually learn the solution and escape in a matter of seconds.

Thorndike (1898) was not impressed with the problem-solving ability of cats and believed that they only learned through trial and error. He viewed trial and error as a process by which the cats developed mental associations or "connections" between stimuli and the responses that enabled them to solve problems.

THE ADVENT OF BEHAVIORISM. Following Thorndike's basic experiments on problem solving, an American, John B. Watson, came along to dominate psychology. He was greatly influenced by Thorndike's work and developed what became known as behavioristic psychology. It was Watson's view that the mind could not be studied scientifically and should be ignored by psychologists. Indeed, behaviorism was one of the main schools of psychology that downgraded the study of consciousness. As we saw in Chapter 4, its impact in this area was so great that only recently has interest in consciousness been revived. According to Watson, the only thing that could be studied scientifically was behavior. By observing behavior closely, we could learn everything necessary about the mind. It was the belief of behavioristic psychology that all seemingly complex behavior was nothing but combinations of reflexes or simple movements attached to stimuli.

Mechanical man?

It was Watson's contention that we are born with only three real emotions: anger at having our movements frustrated, fear of falling or loud noises, and love of being stroked. All other behavior is learned. He believed that he could teach children to avoid fears and prejudices and behave naturally through conditioning. We have already discussed Watson's "little Albert" experiment. He conducted many others along similar lines; for example, he eliminated the fears children had toward animals by letting his subjects see the animals while giving them, at the same time, something delicious to eat.

Watson's essentially "mechanical" view of man led him into many controversies. As a reaction to his antagonists he took more and more extreme positions. He warned parents against excessive display of affection toward children and stressed the importance of strict discipline. Probably his most famous pronouncement was:

> Give me a dozen healthy infants, well-formed, and my own specified world to bring them up in, and I'll guarantee to take any at random and train him to become any type of specialist I might select—doctor, lawyer, artist, merchant-chief, and yes, even beggarman and thief, regardless of his talents, penchants, tendencies, abilities, vocations, and race of his ancestors. I am going beyond my facts and I admit it, but so have the advocates of the contrary, and they have been doing it for many thousands of years (Watson, 1926, p. 10).

With pronouncements of this kind, is it any wonder that he was controversial?

Behaviorist psychology reached its peak in the 1920s, although Watson continued to write and lecture on behaviorism for many more years and to attract controversy. It is interesting to note that his own son, a psychiatrist, publicly attacked his views on rearing children in 1950. However, when Watson died in 1958 much more sophisticated behavioristic theories on learning had been developed. Their main emphasis continues to be to break the learning process down into its basic stimulus and response components.

Concepts of instrumental conditioning

The best known modern-day behaviorist is B. F. Skinner (Figure 5–3) who has become the center of a controversy by virtue of his recent book, *Beyond Freedom and Dignity* (1971). He argues that we no longer can afford to entertain the fictitious concept of freedom, and so we must replace it with conscious control over man's conduct and culture. The method of control would simply involve reinforcing or rewarding desired behavior. By the use of systematic reinforcement, men of good will can create a society in which everyone can work, love, and live in security. His ideas on how behavior can be controlled will become clearer as we discuss the basic concepts of instrumental conditioning.

Skinner provides the simplest and most direct explanation of how operant behavior is modified through learning or instrumental conditioning. A rat was placed in a box and began a series of random movements. It would sniff about, paw the air, scratch itself, and touch various parts of the box with its paws. By accident it would press a bar in the

FIGURE 5–3
B. F. Skinner

box and a pellet of food would drop into a dish. Eventually it would press the bar again and another pellet would drop into the dish. After this occurred several times, it would begin pressing the bar as fast as it could to get more pellets.

The process by which the rat learned to press the bar to obtain food is called instrumental conditioning. We could say in psychological language that the presentation of the food constituted *reinforcement* for the operant response of pressing the bar. The fundamental law of instrumental conditioning is that once an operant response is reinforced, it tends to occur again. Behavior that goes unreinforced tends to be extinguished.

Instrumental conditioning follows many of the same laws that Pavlov discovered for classical conditioning. An operant response can be extinguished by taking away reinforcement. For example, if a child continues to ask for ice cream and if his mother no longer lets him have any, this behavior tends to cease. However, she may discover that the next day he is asking for ice cream again: spontaneous recovery has occurred just as in classical conditioning.

Instrumental conditioning and animal behavior

Anyone who has ever tried to teach his pet a trick is basically applying techniques of instrumental conditioning. The example of pigeons playing table tennis illustrated operant behavior shaped by the use of reinforcement. The manner in which animals and human beings come to perform more complicated actions through instrumental conditioning is technically known as *shaping*. This can best be illustrated by describing the way pigeons are taught to play table tennis.

First of all, when the pigeon makes some random movements in the direction of a ball, it is immediately rewarded with food. After it learns this basic response, it is now required to peck the Ping-Pong ball before it will receive its reward. Once it has learned this second response, the rules of the game are again changed so that only when the ball is pecked hard enough to roll it across the table to another pigeon will food be given. Thus, an animal trainer requires his subject to perform increasingly difficult actions in order to receive a reward. The behavior of the pigeon has been shaped through use of *successive approximations;* that is, reinforcement is given to animals who perform behaviors somewhat similar to the desired act which we may wish them to perform. Once they have learned this, we reinforce only those behaviors that successively become more and more similar to the actual act, until the desired behavior is reached.

Anyone who tries to teach a dog to fetch a stick is engaged in the process of shaping. You start with the fact that dogs sometimes grasp objects in their mouths and then shape this simple operant behavior into something more complicated. Animals can be taught to perform very complicated acts such as those seen in circuses (Figure 5-4). All of these animal acts are the result of shaping. The key to the animals' learning all of these complex operations is that they have to be kept hungry so that food will act as a reinforcer. The amount of learning which takes place depends to a great extent on the kind of reinforcement that is provided and its timing. *Reinforcement* may simply be defined as *anything that happens after a response which affects the probability that it will occur again.* In other words, reinforcement is anything which increases the probability of a response. It corresponds roughly to what the layman calls reward and punishment.

Instrumental conditioning and human behavior

We have seen that one of the differences between instrumental and classical conditioning is the freedom of the learner to emit responses. Also, in the shaping of behavior the learner is led to the final response through the learning of a chain of simple responses leading to the final response. The key ingredient is the appropriate use of reinforcement.

FIGURE 5-4
Some results of shaping. These dolphins, shown high jumping, have been taught to perform this task by animal trainers, using the technique of "shaping."

It is obvious that the principles of instrumental conditioning and shaping are general and apply to human behavior as well as to lower animals. Many attitudes and beliefs, learned goals, customs, and certain aspects of the use of language are shaped by means of reinforcement or reward.

One example which took place in a mental hospital over a period of six to eight weeks illustrates this method (Isaacs, Thomas & Goldiamond, 1960). The psychologist selected chewing gum as the reinforcer after noticing that the subject was attracted to a package of gum. The subject had been mute for 19 years, and it was the psychologist's aim to induce him to talk. In addition, the process may illustrate how all children learn to talk. In the description that follows, E stands for experimenter and S for subject:

Weeks 1, 2. A stick of gum was held before S's face and E waited until S's eyes moved toward it. When this response occurred, E as a consequence gave him gum. By the end of the second week, response probability in the presence of the gum was increased to such an extent that S's eyes moved toward the gum as soon as it was held up.

Weeks 3, 4. The E now held the gum before S, waiting until he noticed movement in S's lips before giving it to him. Toward the end of the first session of the third week, a lip movement spontaneously occurred, which E promptly reinforced. By the end of this week, both lip movement and eye movement occurred when the gum was held up. The E then withheld giving S the gum until S spontaneously made a vocalization, at which time E gave S the gum. By the end of this week, holding up the gum readily occasioned eye movement toward it, lip movement, and vocalization resembling a croak.

Weeks 5, 6. The E held up the gum, and said, "Say gum, gum," repeating these words each time S vocalized. Giving S the gum was made contingent upon vocalizations increasingly approximating gum. At the sixth session (at the end of week 6), when E said, "Say gum, gum," S suddenly said, "Gum, please." This response was accompanied by . . . other responses of this class, that is, S answered questions regarding his name and age (Isaacs et al., 1960, p. 9).

Later, the patient responded to other questions and eventually he made spontaneous requests, saying, for example, "Ping-Pong" when he wished to play a game. Another example illustrates shaping the behavior of a seriously disturbed child (Wolf, Risley, & Mees, 1964).

For all practical purposes the boy was nearly blind at age two after a series of operations for cataracts. Since it was important for him to wear glasses, this behavior was shaped by successive approximation to the final response of wearing glasses. The boy was placed in a room with several glass frames scattered throughout the area. Whenever he picked up one of these, he was reinforced with candy. Next he was given bits of lunch whenever he brought the glasses closer and closer to a wearing position. Soon it was possible to shape his behavior of putting on and looking through the glasses. The boy was soon wearing his glasses throughout the entire day.

Cognitive learning

So far we have discussed relatively simple learning. Both classical and instrumental conditioning refer to the attaching of simple responses to simple stimuli. You might rightly ask whether there is not more to learning than that? Human thinking is certainly considered the most outstanding development in psychological evolution. For this reason, a number of psychologists view thinking and associated processes, collectively referred to as *cognitive processes*, as playing a vital role in man's capacity for complex learning.

Cognition is a difficult term to define. Its basic meaning is closest to knowledge or understanding but includes such processes as ideas, reasoning, judging, and problem solving. One of the features of cognitive behavior that distinguishes it from simple forms of behavior, such as a classically conditioned response, is a process in the mind of the organism that intervenes between the stimulus and the response (Ellis, 1972). We have ideas, for instance, that determine our overt behavior.

To illustrate cognitive processes at work, let us consider the oddity task as used in studies on the problem-solving ability of children (Schroth, 1968a, 1968b, 1972). Usually, two different pairs of identical stimuli such as two circles and squares are used, but only three of the four stimuli are presented together on a given trial. The odd stimulus is always rewarded. On an individual trial, the position, object, and single representation is rewarded. However, only the single representation is rewarded 100 percent of the time. The other stimulus and situational variables (the position of the reward and the particular object rewarded) must be disregarded by the subject if he is to master the problem.

One variation of the oddity problem, the *Weigl Principle Oddity Test*, is used clinically to test a patient's ability to engage in abstract thinking. In this problem, the patient chooses among three nonidentical stimuli, two of which are alike in color, and two alike in form. The object odd in respect to form is correct when placed on a cream-colored tray. The object odd in respect to color is correct when placed on an orange tray. The color of the board serves as an additional cue or sign to complicate the problem.

How do subjects solve such a problem? The problem itself is clear, but not the method for solving it. This problem and the behavior required for its solution illustrate two characteristics of cognitive processes. First, when attempting to solve such a problem, subjects have to manipulate symbols and concepts such as color, oddity, and form. Second, their behavior in reaction to the problem consists largely of covert responses: they may have started "talking to themselves" about various ways of solving it. Thus, many of the events underlying problem solving are hidden from immediate observation because they are inside the mind. Understanding the nature and functioning of these symbolic and usually covert mediating processes is essential to understanding how we think and reason.

PROBLEM SOLVING. Problem solving, deals with an organism's behavior in discovering a correct response to a new situation. As stated by H. H. Kendler (1968), there are three basic characteristics of problem solving. First, in a problem-solving situation the correct response is not obvious. If it were obvious, there would be no problem. Second, human problem-solving behavior consists mainly of ideas or other mediating processes. The phrase "mediating processes" simply means something is happening in the mind such as ideas or images which determine our overt response to a stimulus. Research in problem solving is directed at understanding those events which occur in the mind. Third, the subject may struggle for a while with the problem, seemingly getting nowhere, when all of a sudden the solution comes to him in a flash. This is known as *insight*.

INSIGHT. Wolfgang Kohler, a German psychologist, was studying apes on an island off the coast of Africa when World War I broke out. The outbreak of the war prevented him from returning home so he decided to utilize his time by studying the problem-solving ability of chimpanzees. In a typical experiment, Kohler would suspend a banana from the top of a cage out of the animal's reach. At the other end of the cage, he would place a box which the chimp could use to stand on and grasp the food if he moved it underneath the banana. Typically, the chimpanzee would jump for the banana repeatedly without any success. Then all of a sudden the animal would stop jumping beneath the banana and go over to the box. He would drag it underneath the banana, stand on it, and grab the fruit.

Kohler used the term *insight* to denote the process which the animal had used to solve the problem. It is an "ah-ha" experience we have when we suddenly grasp the solution to a problem with which we have been struggling. Typical of insight is that once the solution is achieved, no more errors are made. It involves putting together two or more aspects of a problem to arrive at the correct solution. In the previous example, the chimp had to perceive the relationship between the box and suspended banana. Just to illustrate how intelligent a chimpanzee is, some have been known to grab the experimenter by the hand and lead him over to the suspended banana and climb on top of the person to reach it.

To solve a problem of this nature requires an original response, one you have never made before. The originality of this type of response, called insight, is most striking in the cases of men such as Einstein and Darwin who formulated theories as brilliant or convincing as general relativity or natural selection in evolution. However, we all manifest, to a certain degree, the ability to give new solutions when faced with a problem to solve. Actually, we are much more unique and original in our behavior in new situations than we realize. Children, especially, are known to be very creative when faced with new problems and left to their own devices.

Reasoning

Related closely to the process of insight is that which psychologists call reasoning. The ability to solve problems by reasoning has made man dominant over all other organisms. It is considered such a vital function that specific problems designed to test one's ability to reason are included in most intelligence tests.

Before attempting to define it, let us look at an experiment that was conducted on reasoning with two groups of children; one of kindergarten age and the other in the third grade (Kendler & Kendler, 1962). They were trained to use an apparatus (Figure 5–5) with three distinctively colored panels. In the center of each of the side panels was a button and an opening. When the button on the left panel was pressed, a steel ball bearing dropped out of the opening; when the button on the right panel was pressed, a glass marble appeared.

Once the children had learned this difference, their attention was shifted to the center panel where there was a circular opening. They could insert either the ball bearing or the marble into this opening. They would receive a gold-colored charm if they inserted the ball bearing and nothing if the marble was inserted.

FIGURE 5–5
Design of apparatus to test reasoning. The button on
the left delivers a ball bearing, whereas the button
on the right releases a marble. If the ball bearing is
inserted into the circular opening of the center panel, a
charm is delivered into the trough near the bottom
of the panel.

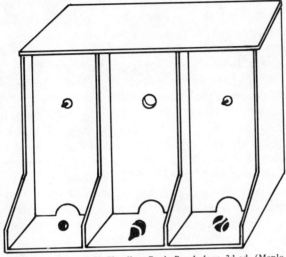

Source: Howard K. Kendler, *Basic Psychology*, 3d ed. (Menlo
Park, Calif.: W. A. Benjamin, Inc., 1974).

Once the children had become accustomed to the apparatus and how
it worked, the test of their reasoning began. The correct solution involved two steps. The first step consisted of the subjects' pressing the
button on the left panel, while the second step consisted of the subjects' dropping the ball bearing into the opening in the center panel.
Only 6 percent of the kindergarten children were able to solve the problem without making an incorrect response. The third graders, in contrast, discovered the correct procedure much more easily, half of them
solving the problem directly.

This is considered to be a test of reasoning because the children had
to be able to integrate two habits; the occurrence of the second habit
depended on the occurrence of the first. Thus, a *definition of reasoning*
is that which involves the ability to integrate two or more separate
habits; in other words, the second habit becomes conditioned to the re-
sponse-produced cues of the first habit.

This experiment in reasoning resembles the studies of insight in that
both processes depend on the integration of previously learned habits.
In human behavior this integration is often mediated by covert linguistic
responses. In animals, the nature of the mediating behavior is difficult to
identify. Nevertheless, in both cases something akin to ideas or other
thought processes function as the cues which determine overt behavior.

Learning and problem solving

Complex learning is normally differentiated from conditioning by noting the different psychological processes each emphasizes. With classical or instrumental conditioning, the major emphasis is upon learning a simple response to a stimulus known as an S-R connection. In problem solving, the emphasis is upon how S-R associations are linked together. This involves thought processes occurring in the mind, which are not observable.

It is impossible to draw a line separating problem solving from other kinds of learning. The difference is actually a matter of degree. There are mediating processes or covert behavior in conditioning as well as in complex learning tasks, but there is considerably more covert behavior or cognitive processes involved in problem solving. It would appear that as the learning process becomes more complex, it merges into problem solving.

Reinforcement and habit patterns

No discussion on learning would be complete without a closer examination of reinforcement and all its ramifications. Hence, we shall take a close look at various parameters of reinforcement because it is an important tool in the development and control of behavior.

As we have seen, the most important principle in operant conditioning is the application of reinforcement. In real life, behavior is not reinforced on every occasion. The fisherman does not catch a fish with every cast of the line; the basketball player does not make a basket every time he throws the ball at the hoop; the boy does not get a date everytime he asks a girl for one; and the rat does not get a pellet each time he presses the lever. The operant conditioner will often reinforce responses only occasionally: 1:1; 1:2; 1:3; and so on. Such conditions are called *partial reinforcement* as distinguished from *continuous reinforcement* in which rewards follow every response. Exactly how responses are selected for a payoff, known as *schedules of reinforcement*, is crucial for the determination of different habit patterns. Each payoff schedule has been found to have a characteristic effect on human and animal behavior.

Effects of partial reinforcement

In first training a subject to make a response, it is more effective to deliver reinforcement after every correct one rather than only occasionally. Once it has been learned, however, it is not necessary to continue using such a schedule of continuous reinforcement to maintain the behavior. The experimenter usually reinforces only selected responses. Before we discuss the specific effects of different schedules, it is important to know the most significant effect of partial reinforcement. Subjects trained under partial reinforcement schedules are much more resistant to extinction than subjects who have acquired a response under 100 percent reinforcement. These conditions are illustrated in representative experiments discussed by Mednick, Pollio and Loftus (1973). The practical importance of such findings should not be underestimated. For example, consider the training of children. When we first teach a child to do something such as learning to play the piano, we should reinforce him liberally. As the child increases his skill, reinforcement should not be given as often. By reinforcing only intermittently, we assure the response a longer life (playing the piano). Intermittent schedules of reinforcement make responses persistent and difficult to extinguish. The latter observation is illustrated by the case of the child who annoys his parents by constantly asking for ice cream or cookies between meals. It is highly probable that the parents contributed to this behavior by giving in on some occasions while denying the child on others. As a result, he continues to demand his favorite snacks while hoping that his parents will grant his requests. Psychologists have speculated for many years about why partial as opposed to continuous reinforcement increases resistance to extinction. However, there is no generally accepted explanation.

RATIO SCHEDULES. When we have a situation in which the same number of responses earns a reinforcement each time (such as a salesman receiving a commission for each ten sales), the schedule is called *fixed ratio*. In the laboratory, a rat may have to press the lever in a Skinner box one or more times before obtaining a single pellet. Use of a fixed ratio schedule produces a high rate of responding in organisms. Analogous observations at the human level are seen if one considers the behavior of workers who are paid a fixed amount of money for a given number of products produced.

A *variable ratio schedule*, the most likely to occur in everyday life, delivers *on the average* one reinforcement after so many responses. A 5:1 variable ratio schedule might "pay off" after 7, then 3, and then 5. Although the reinforcement varies with the number of responses, the average ratio winds up to be 5:1. Even though animals cannot predict when the reinforcement will come, they learn that a fast rate of responding brings more reinforcement than a slow one. Slot machines in gambling casinos operate under this principle. Gamblers never know when they might hit the jackpot and as a result feed coins into the machines at a high rate. A major reason that gambling behavior is so difficult to extinguish is that gamblers do not realize that they have been placed on a variable ratio schedule which produces the greatest payoff for the house. It is fascinating and often humorous to watch "little old ladies" playing three or more slot machines at once!

INTERVAL SCHEDULE. When the period between reinforcements is determined by time instead of number of responses, it is known as an *interval schedule*. In contrast to ratio schedules, it is not how much work the subject does that brings the reinforcement but when he does it. All that is required in the typical laboratory situation is that the subject make one correct response which is reinforced after a certain length of time. After another interval of time has passed, the next correct response is reinforced. If the interval is the same length each time, say every five minutes, it is called a *fixed interval* schedule. Laboratory animals gradually increase their rate of responding just before the time for each reinforcement as they learn to discriminate the time interval between reinforcements quite accurately. If your professor gives examinations every Friday he has placed you under a fixed interval schedule. Think about your own habit patterns when you know a regularly scheduled exam is coming up on Friday. If you behave similarly to many other students, studying will be minimal early in the week and will increase as time passes. You will probably "hit the books" (cram) hard on Thursday evening.

It is possible to maintain a consistent response rate by varying the interval around some average value, called a *variable interval*. For example, organisms respond steadily when they have been placed on a variable interval schedule. They may be required to respond for five minutes before receiving a reinforcement, and then they might receive a reinforcement for the first response just one minute later and so forth. The organism can never know when a reinforcement will appear and usually responds at a high steady rate. If you take a class in which the professor employs pop quizzes you will probably find yourself and other students being more consistent in studying for the course.

The four partial reinforcement schedules, illustrated with appropriate examples, are summarized in Table 5–1. There are two important ways in which they differ: (1) reinforcement is based on either the number of responses (ratio) or the time elapsed (interval) and (2) the schedule is either regular (fixed) or irregular (variable).

TABLE 5–1
The four basic partial reinforcement schedules

	Ratio *(depends on responses)*	Interval *(depends on time)*
Fixed (constant)	Piecework	Weekly quiz
Variable .... (average value)	Slot machine	Pop quiz

Source: A. Buss, *Psychology, Man in Perspective* (New York: John Wiley & Sons, Inc., 1973), p. 283.

Delay of reinforcement: Instant need gratification versus postponement

In the last few years, we have seen a gradual turning away from the puritanical belief that we should focus our attention on the future rather than living for the moment. Relating this to our discussion of reinforcement, we know that for reinforcers to be effective, they must be applied immediately after a response occurs. The general principle is that immediate reinforcement produces the most learning and that delay of reinforcement reduces the amount of learning. This generalization is based on many experiments with different organisms and has many practical implications. If you want to teach your dog a trick, you will have more success if you reward the animal immediately after his successful attempts rather than waiting until later.

Education is most effective when approaches involve a sufficient number of rewards with little delay. One technique that is being increasingly used by teachers, which we discussed in Chapter 1, is to employ teaching machines and programmed books. This procedure assures instantaneous feedback as to the correctness or incorrectness of a response.

Secondary reinforcement

Although we still are a long way from knowing the complete range of things that are or can become reinforcing to people, we have broadened our ideas considerably on what can reinforce behavior. There are some objects and events which are reinforcing without the need for previous learning experiences; these are referred to as primary reinforcement. Food, water, sexual behavior, and escape from painful situations are primary reinforcements. All of them provide satisfaction for physiological needs and drives, and their value to the organism does not have to be learned. In contrast, a period of learning is necessary before some things or events begin to have reinforcement value. Elementary school children can be taught to do almost anything to receive a small gold star from their teacher. An infant learns that the approaching footsteps of his mother is usually followed by warm milk and stops crying at the sound of the footsteps. When a previously nonreinforcing circumstance after being associated with a reinforcing one becomes reinforcing in its own right, it is called *secondary reinforcer*.

Secondary reinforcers are extremely important in the control of human behavior. Think about your own behavior in the course of a day and you will realize that little of what you do is reinforced by primary reinforcers. This is especially true for technologically advanced and affluent countries. A smile, a pat on the back, and good grades are all secondary reinforcers which are important to us.

THE CHIMP-O-MAT CAPER. Many experiments have been conducted in which animals have been taught complicated responses when conditioned with secondary reinforcers. In one well-known series of experiments (Cowles, 1937), chimpanzees were taught to work for poker chips as reinforcers rather than food. The chimpanzees later could use the poker chips to obtain food from a vending machine named "Chimp-o-mat" (Figure 5–6). After being conditioned, the animal would work as hard for a poker chip as for the food itself, occasionally saving up a few poker chips before converting them into the food reward of grapes.

FIGURE 5-6
Teaching a chimp the value of money. A chimpanzee uses tokens (secondary reinforcers) to obtain food (primary reinforcement). The animal has learned to place poker chips in the machine in order to get fruit. Chimps in this experiment would "work" to obtain chips, and would hoard them immediately.

Yerkes Regional Primate Research Center of Emory University

After the chimpanzees had learned to use the Chimp-o-mat, they were introduced to another apparatus that consisted of a lever attached by strong springs which the chimpanzees could push forward only by great effort. Their work was rewarded by a grape attached at the end of the lever. After the chimpanzees had learned to obtain grapes in this manner, the grape was replaced by a poker chip. Three out of the four chimpanzees strained as hard at the instrument for the poker chip as for the grape. They could later exchange the chips for grapes from the vending machine. The human parallel for a child is that candy may provide a strong reinforcement. However, since money can buy candy, it becomes a strong secondary reinforcer.

Imitation learning

All of the learning discussed so far has been *nonsocial*: classical conditioning, instrumental conditioning, and cognitive learning; that is, the stimuli may involve objects, events or other organisms. In contrast to these types of learning, *imitation learning* or *modeling* is *social* in that another organism must be involved. Many lower organisms and especially human beings often learn new behavioral patterns by simply observing and imitating others. This method of learning is so widespread that it is well expressed by the old saying, "Monkey see, monkey do." This is one popular adage that is well supported by scientific evidence.

Animal learning through imitation

Some of the best documented reports on imitation learning comes from researchers who have raised chimpanzees in a human environment. In one study, Viki, the chimpanzee reared with humans, spontaneously sharpened pencils and applied cosmetics to her face in front of a mirror (Hayes & Hayes, 1952). Viki learned to do this without her behavior being followed by reinforcement of any kind.

Similar results have been obtained in a study in which the chimpanzee, Washoe, learned to imitate additional human behavior:

> One day, during the 10th month of the project, she bathed one of her dolls in the way we usually bathed her. She filled her little bathtub with water, dunked the doll in the tub, then took it out, and dried it with a towel (Gardner & Gardner, 1969, p. 666).

Human learning through imitation

A well-known experiment by Bandura (1965) demonstrates imitation learning under the controlled conditions of the laboratory. Nursery school children watched a film of a man playing with a large doll in a highly aggressive manner, striking it with a mallet and kicking it about the room. When given the chance to play with the doll, the children behaved in a remarkably similar aggressive fashion (Figure 5–7). The implications of this and other experiments like it are obvious when one considers the number of hours children spend watching television. However, the social learning of aggression is not without its critics. A major question difficult to answer is whether a child who strikes a doll after viewing such a film is also more apt to hit another child.

Memory and forgetting

Some years ago, psychologist Harold Burtt (1941) spiced his infant son's daily reading diet of nursery rhymes with passages in Greek from

FIGURE 5-7
Imitation of aggression. Both the boy and girl are viciously striking a "Bobo" doll. What has caused this aggression? The answer is that they are imitating a woman who had behaved in this same manner in a movie they had just watched.

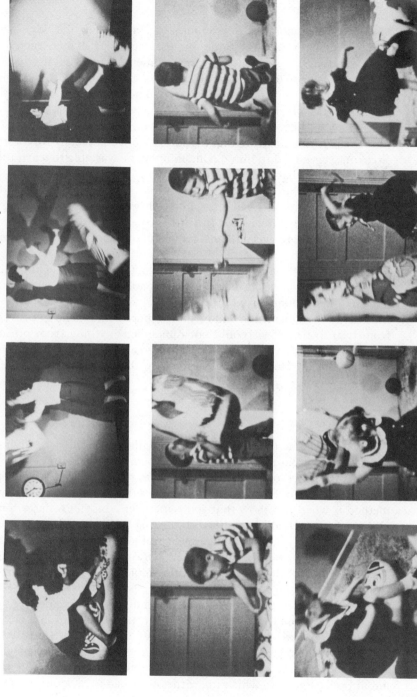

Source: From A. Bandura, E. B. Blanchard, and B. Ritter, in *Journal of Personality and Social Psychology*, 1969, 13. Copyright 1969 by the American Psychological Association. Reprinted with permission.

Sophocle's "Oedipus Rex (Tyrannus)." Starting when the boy was only 18 months old, he read the same three selections of 20 lines each to him every day for three months. Five years later, Burtt tested his son (now eight years old) on his memory of these passages by asking him to memorize some of the same passages as well as a number of other equally difficult ones with which he had no previous experience. It took the boy 435 repetitions to learn the new passages, but only 317 to learn the old ones. These results demonstrate that his son had not completely forgotten the Greek passages read to him during infancy; he was able to learn the old passages faster than the new ones.

This remarkable case demonstrates in a striking way how good our memories really are. Even though the original material was classical Greek (nonsense material for the little boy since he did not understand the language) there was still an obvious retention of some kind from the original exposure.

In this section, we will focus on those factors which affect our ability to retain material we have once learned and the various explanations put forth to account for why we forget. Obviously, there is a close relationship between learning and memory; there could be no improvement from trial to trial if we could not remember anything from preceding trials. In addition, what we have discovered about the processes of memory in the laboratory can be applied by the student in studying for tests.

Methods of measuring memory

RECALL. The method of recall is particularly useful for studying the retention of verbal material, such as a poem or a selection from a textbook. Your professors use this technique to test your memory whenever they give you an essay examination. Another example of the recall method is when you show that you remember a movie by describing its plot to a friend. Of all the methods of testing for memory, the recall technique yields the least amount of measurable retention. This is because this method furnishes the subject with only a minimum of cues and it is always more difficult to recall something "cold" than it is to relearn or to recognize something.

RECOGNITION. Recognition is a matter of discriminating between what you have seen from that which is new. Objective examinations consisting of multiple-choice questions are examples of this method. Students often prefer this type of test because it is easier to recognize the correct answer rather than to recall it. Another example of recognition is the familiar police lineup in which the witness is asked to pick out the suspect from a group.

RELEARNING. The *method of savings* is the technique most often used by psychologists for experimental studies of retention. The subject is simply asked to relearn a task that he had previously learned. The measure of retention is the difference in the number of trials required for original mastery and for the second learning. The savings from the first learning can be computed from the following formula:

$$\frac{\text{Number of trials to learn originally}}{\text{Number of trials to learn originally}} \times 100$$

If it took ten repetitions to learn to repeat a certain passage from reading material without making any errors but only five repetitions to relearn the passage a month later, the savings would be 50 percent.

An important point about the savings method, as illustrated in the story of Burtt's son, is it may show retention long after the other methods have ceased to indicate any retention. The importance of this principle is that you should not think that much of school is a waste of time because you cannot recall some of the material you have learned in your classes. You will probably discover considerable savings whenever you have the need to use that material again or the need to relearn it.

The course of retention

Just how much of what we learn stays with us after a period of time? Although the answer depends to some extent upon the nature of the learning task and type of method used to measure retention, the general form of the retention curve has been known to psychologists since the 19th century. The first psychologist to answer this question was Hermann Ebbinghaus (1885). He wanted to study memory in its purest form, unaffected by previous experience, emotional factors, or any other personality variables. He employed nonsense syllables, which consisted of two consonants separated by a vowel such as *zeb, bap, cax, rab,* and so on, as the learning materials. Psychologists have been using them ever since in experiments. What makes Ebbinghaus such as interesting individual is that he used himself as the subject. He would spend many long hours memorizing nonsense syllables as a young man, keeping track of the time it took him to learn them without error. He then waited for varying periods of time, from 20 minutes to 31 days, before setting out to relearn them.

Ebbinghaus' results are shown by the graph in Figure 5–8. This is the typical *curve of forgetting* for most kinds of learning and applies to motor skills, poems, and college courses we have taken. The most notable feature is the rapid decline in retention during the period that immediately follows learning and then a declining loss as time progresses. To put it another way: *We forget much of something new that we learned very quickly but we retain at least part of it for a long time.*

FIGURE 5–8
Retention curve. This retention curve, based on lists of nonsense syllables measured by relearning, illustrates the course of forgetting over time and is typical for most types of learning. The response measure is the saving score percentage.

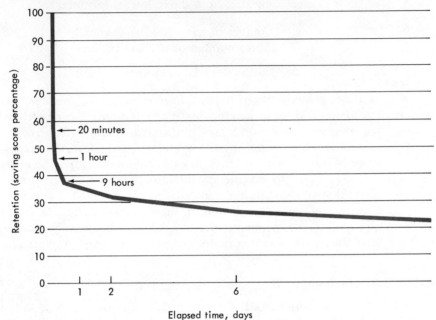

Elapsed time, days

Source: H. Ebbinghaus, *Memory*, 1885, translated by H. H. Ruger and C. E. Bussenius (New York: Teachers College, 1913).

Improving our memories

Is there anything psychologists have learned about memory that we can use to stop or slow down the inevitable processes of forgetting? The answer is a definite yes. Experimental studies have identified four major techniques for improving retention: overlearning, organization, self-recitation, and the use of mnemonic devices.

Overlearning

If we are to retain something we have learned, we must take advantage of the technique of *overlearning*—that is, we must continue to practice after the point of simple mastery has been reached. For example, you must not stop reading a chapter of a text when you are "satisfied" that you have learned the material. If you want to retain your knowledge for an examination, you must reread the chapter several times.

This is well illustrated in a classic study by Krueger (1929). Three groups of students were given lists of 12 nouns to learn to different degrees: 100 percent learning, 150 percent learning, and 200 percent learning. For subjects in the 100 percent learning group, practice was terminated at a criterion of a single correct repetition. For the 150 percent group, practice was continued beyond the point of mastery for half as many trials as were needed in the original learning; for the 200 percent group, twice as many trials were given—in other words, the materials were *overlearned*. Memory for the nouns was then tested by the relearning technique after varying numbers of days (1 to 28 days later). The results shown in Figure 5–9 indicate that the amount of retention depended upon the amount of overlearning; the greater the degree of overlearning, the greater the amount of retention.

FIGURE 5–9
The effects of overlearning on retention. Subjects learned a list of 12 nouns to three varying degrees of mastery and were tested for retention at later dates. Retention was measured as the saving score on subsequent relearning.

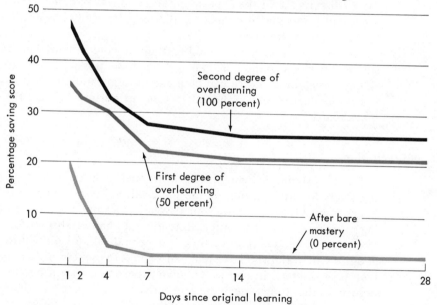

Source: W. C. F. Krueger, "The Effect of Overlearning on Retention," *Journal of Experimental Psychology*, 1929, 12. Copyright 1929 by the American Psychological Association. Reprinted by permission.

One major reason that we retain some of our skills learned in childhood is because of the considerable amount of overlearning involved in such skills as swimming or bicycling. Overlearning is also particularly important in learning and retaining information such as telephone numbers, names, and knowledge acquired on the job. We simply do not quit practicing skills and materials vital to our everyday lives once we have reached "mastery." Fortunately, overlearning keeps our memories from completely collapsing on us.

Organization

Memory is not just a collection of items thrown together in a haphazard fashion. In both simple and complex learning, we group items together by rules that impose varying degrees of *organization*. For example, in learning experiments involving the use of words, the greater the degree of organization that the learner can impose on the material, the better the subsequent recall (Fisher, 1971).

The following experiment illustrates how much easier it is to memorize facts when they are organized into a meaningful framework (Bower & Clark, 1969). Subjects in the control group were told to memorize a list of words, while subjects in the experimental group were instructed to devise a meaningful story from the words to be memorized. The median recall of words for the control group was only 13 percent; in contrast, the median recall for the experimental group was 94 percent. Organizing the words into a meaningful story, therefore, proved to be a valuable aid to the memorization process.

This is the reason that a good textbook includes many headings and subheadings in a chapter. This helps the student in organizing the material. A professor's lecture can be made more meaningful and easier for the students to learn if he takes time to outline his lecture on the blackboard.

Self-recitation

During original learning, reciting to oneself interspersed with reading tends to aid retention of the material. Suppose that you have two hours in which to study for your psychology exam and you do the reading assignment in 30 minutes. Rereading a chapter three times is less likely to be effective than reading it once and asking yourself questions about the material you have read (Morgan & Deese, 1969). As a matter of fact, it was shown in one well-known experiment that if as much as 80 percent of the study time is spent in active recitation, rather than in reading, the result is better retention (Gates, 1917). In order to be certain that you understand and remember, you should stop periodically and try to recall to yourself what you have read.

There are at least two good reasons for this emphasis on recitation. One is that self-recitation serves to keep your *attention* on the task: you cannot concentrate on recalling the material and daydream at the same time. The second reason is that it serves as a check on your *accuracy* in recall; it shows where you are the weakest, in terms of mistakes, and where you could benefit most by a second reading.

Mnemonic devices

The term *mnemonics* refers to a variety of techniques for organizing memory, many of which are employed by so-called memory experts. The theory behind most mnemonic devices is to use old information as starting points for new knowledge.

At one time or another we have all used simple mnemonics to help us remember things important to our daily learning. For example, the rhyme, "Thirty days hath September," helps us to remember the number of days in each month. Similar rhymes can be used in learning foreign languages, for instance, in remembering exceptions to grammatical rules. Then there are phrases and verses that have been devised to aid retention of names of U.S. presidents, planets, neural pathways in the body, and so on.

Some mnemonic systems are much more complicated as used by "memory experts." They are often the underlying basis for their impressive feats of memory as displayed on television and the stage. As discussed in the books by Norman (1969), they have in common means of enabling the learner to impose some organization on initially unstructured material and of relating the material to that which is already familiar and organized.

An additional characteristic of many mnemonic devices is that they may make use of *visual imagery*. This technique is particularly useful in building up one's vocabulary in a technical field or foreign language. The effectiveness of visual imagery in the latter case is demonstrated in a recent experiment by Kellogg and Howe (1971). Children between the ages of 9 and 11 were required to learn words in Spanish. Spanish words were spoken by a teacher while the English equivalents were shown either by displaying the written word or by showing a picture of the object. The results indicated that children learned the Spanish words at a faster rate with the pictures than with the written English equivalents. The implications of these findings for teachers are that they would be wise to resort to visual aids in the classroom when possible. In addition, the use of visual imagery is a very useful technique to employ in remembering people's names. The more vivid and specific the imagery of a person, the better it is for remembering.

Why do we forget?

The above subheading might surprise you at first glance because the answer seems rather elementary. Common sense would tell us that forgetting is due simply to disuse or lack of practice. Something once learned seems to fade away without practice. Therefore, the *theory of disuse* seems to be reasonable. However, many psychologists discount it as a serious explanation of forgetting. One argument against the theory is that disuse cannot explain forgetting if it implies only the passage of time without practice. Time in itself does not cause anything to happen. Events happen in time and changing conditions cause forgetting to occur. In a similar fashion, people do not simply die of old age; events occur in time which brings about death.

Besides the above philosophical objection to the theory of disuse, there is considerable evidence that argues against it. As a young man, Ebbinghaus once memorized some of the stanzas of Lord Byron's poem *Don Juan*. Some 22 years later, he brought the poem out to see if he could remember any of the stanzas. Even though he could not recall any of the stanzas, he had not completely forgotten them. He was able to relearn these stanzas much faster than it took him to learn others he had never memorized before.

A different type of evidence in regard to the theory of disuse comes from the work of the well-known brain surgeon, Wilder Penfield (1959). In the course of operations performed under local anesthetic, in which the patients are awake, he found that electrical stimulation of certain parts of the brain often resulted in "flashbacks," a vivid reliving of previous experiences long since forgotten. One woman reported hearing an orchestra playing a popular song when the electrode was held in place. Another patient cried out in astonishment, after stimulation, "Yes, Doctor; yes, Doctor. Now I hear people laughing—my friends in South Africa." When questioned about this he explained the reason for his strange reactions. He felt he was laughing with his cousins whom he had left on a farm in South Africa, although he realized that he was now on the operating table in Montreal.

Old memories are also sometimes recalled by subjects under hypnosis that have long been forgotten. One patient under hypnotic therapy recalled being abused by her older brother when she was only three. These findings indicate that forgetting cannot be explained by disuse. It is, of course, possible that some forgetting is due to a deterioration of neural tissues where memory is located and that the psychological causes of forgetting are superimposed on physiological processes.

Interference

One of the major psychological determinants of forgetting is the events that intervene between learning and a test of retention. It is apparent that when we learn something, our ability to remember it is interfered with by things we have learned previously and also by things we will learn in the future. Suppose that in a class on zoology you learned a list of technical names for organisms. After a week has passed, you are given an examination in class. However, during the week you have learned many new terms and names in your other classes. According to what we have learned from experiments in the laboratory, these new terms and names are likely to compete and interfere with your memory for the zoological items. On the other hand, if you could have avoided such postclass interfering experiences, a large share of this forgetting probably could have been prevented.

RETROACTIVE INHIBITION. One source of interference is *retroactive inhibition*, which occurs when new learning affects the retention of some previously learned task. An example of this is the problem professors have in remembering the names of former students; learning the names of new students interferes with their ability to recall the names of former ones.

Retroactive inhibition is demonstrated in an experiment by Jenkins and Dallenbach (1924). They arranged for two subjects to learn lists of nonsense syllables. One immediately went to sleep while the other continued his normal waking activities; both were tested for retention after the same intervals. As shown in Figure 5–10, the sleeping subject had higher retention scores at each testing point and his scores varied little after different intervals of sleep. On the other hand, the scores of the subject who remained awake declined as the intervals between learning and testing increased. The differences in retention between these subjects appear to be because the student who remained awake was exposed to the effects of new learning that competed with the retention of responses from the initial task. By analogy, this would suggest that as a student, you would have better retention if you went to sleep after studying for an examination rather than studying for another test. This is especially true if the exam is to take place the following day.

PROACTIVE INHIBITION. We have seen in retroactive inhibition that learning something new can interfere with our memory for the old. Equally important are the effects of previous learning on the new. When

FIGURE 5–10
Memory is better preserved after sleep. Retention is much better after sleep than following waking activity. Sleep is the best case of a low-interference activity in regard to memory.

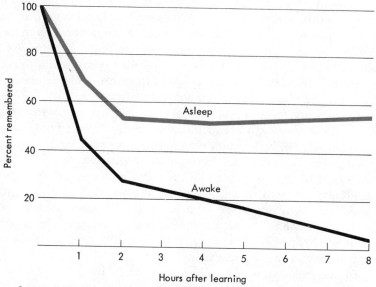

Source: E. B. Newman, "Forgetting of Meaningful Material During Sleep and Waking," *American Journal of Psychology*, 1939, 52. Reprinted by permission of University of Illinois Press.

what we have learned in the past interferes with our ability to retain something new, this process is called *proactive inhibition*. Proactive inhibition can be seen when people have to learn new habits to replace old ones. A familiar example is the case of the novice tennis player who learns to play tennis with bad form. Later on when he takes up the game seriously, he finds it difficult to learn to stroke the ball in the correct manner. His old responses are competing with new ones.

Fortunately, our memories do not completely break down in light of the cumulative effects of competing responses. One reason is that we are constantly practicing the most important responses. A second reason is that we acquire methods to make important memories distinctive which helps us to keep them from competing with others.

MOTIVATED FORGETTING. Most of us have had the experience of conveniently forgetting painful and unpleasant memories. Observations of this type have led some psychologists to conclude that we are simply motivated to remember the pleasant and to forget the unpleasant. The habitual gambler is a case in point; people who gamble are notoriously prone to remember the times they won and to forget the times they lost. Another example is that people who have strong political viewpoints often forget arguments detrimental to their theories but can remember favorable statements quite well.

Special topics in learning

How good can memory be?

Imagine how wonderful it would be if there were no limitations whatsoever on the amount of material your mind could retain. With such a perfect memory you could remember all of the materials you have studied in your classes, recall the names of everyone you have ever met, or remember every place you have ever been on vacations. Although there is no such thing as a perfect memory, there are a few case studies that have been made of people who are truly gifted memorizers.

LURIA'S GIFTED MNEMONIST. The Russian psychologist, Alexander Luria (1968), presents a semiclinical account of a mnemonic "superstar" known as S. He had been a newspaper reporter who came to the psychology laboratory at the University of Moscow. S. first came to the attention of his editor because of his habit of never taking notes at staff meetings, although everyone else took extensive notes. This naturally made the editor angry and he proceeded to bawl out S. for not paying attention. Much to the surprise of his boss, S. repeated the entire assignment word for word. Not only that but S. could recall assignments made long ago and what he had accomplished.

In one experiment, Luria presented him with a list of words. S. listened to them and then repeated the words back in exactly the same order in which they had been presented to him. S. was able to repeat back

70 words in exactly the same order. S. could handle lists of numbers or letters equally well and could also reproduce the lists in reverse order. One last observation of importance was that S. could retain these lists for weeks, months, and even as long as 20 years.

S. was apparently able to perform such feats of memory by converting words or numbers into graphic images. This explains why he was able to reproduce a series frontward or backward equally well. Having such a spectacular memory did have some bad consequences. S. had a lot of trouble in reading simple prose; every word had an image associated with it and often the image would be inappropriate for the passage as a whole. This caused him on many occasions to miss the main point of what he was reading; thus his reading comprehension was greatly affected by his remarkable memory.

THE CASE OF VP. A more recent case of a person with an amazing memory is reported by two psychologists at the University of Washington (Hunt & Love, 1972). The subject, who they called VP, was brought to their attention because of exhibitions of chess he gave in which he played up to seven games simultaneously blindfolded. Hunt and Love later found that VP could play as many as 60 correspondence games of chess without consulting written records.

Experimental studies in the laboratory provided further proof of VP's tremendous capacity to memorize various materials. In one study, he was asked to read Bartlett's (1932) "The War of the Ghosts," a special story designed to test one's memory. After one hour, in spite of being given other tasks to do, he was able to reproduce the story nearly verbatim. After six weeks, and without any practice, he was asked to write the story once again. His memory for the story, including nouns and verbs, was almost as good as it was after only one hour.

Another feat of memory was accomplished by VP when he was given a digit span test in which he was presented numbers at the rate of one per second. The test was similar to the one included on the WAIS intelligence test; college-level students have a span of about eight digits. However, VP with some practice was able to retain some 17 digits. When asked how he did it, VP reported that he formed associations to the digits and also grouped them together in order to improve his retention. Other subjects also have been found to increase their digit span when instructed to use these techniques; however, they were not nearly as successful.

Unlike the case of Luria's subject, VP did not use visual imagery to accomplish any of his feats of memory. Instead, as we have seen in the case of his digit span, he relied on recoding the information and formulating associations to it, which he learned as a child. In addition, he was found to have the ability to recognize details rapidly as indicated by his high score on a perceptual speed test that was given to him. Thus, VP's interest in memorizing for memory sake, as reflected by his learning how to improve his memory during childhood, in combination with his speed in the perception of details, appear to form the basis for his exceptional memory. Unlike the case of Luria's gifted memorizer, VP did not appear to suffer any undesirable side effects from his great memory. He was last reported to be content working as a store clerk although, by some standards, he might be considered to be an underachiever in light of his fairly high IQ of 136.

Eidetic imagery

In this chapter we have come across the topic of imagery and its importance for memory. We have discussed the point that most mnemonic techniques used to facilitate memory depend upon visual imagery. S. relied extensively on visual imagery to retain masses of information he had learned over the years.

Everybody has the ability to form images to a certain degree. However, a few individuals possess imagery which is almost like actual perception in its clarity and accuracy. These exceptionally detailed and vivid memory images are called *eidetic images*.

Eidetic imagery occurs rarely; S. was such a case. Another case is reported by Stollmeyer and Psotka (1970). They presented a paired set of stimuli containing the letter "T" in it, but only when viewed with both eyes, to a woman with remarkable visual imagery. One member of the pair was presented to her right eye. After a brief period, the other pattern was shown to her left eye, while she superimposed an image of the right-eye pattern. She immediately identified a "T" that appeared to be coming toward her. What is highly unusual about her response is that this is the usual perception of a person looking at both patterns *simultaneously*. Only a person with eidetic imagery can bridge the time gap like she did in order to see the "T."

At this point you are probably wishing you had such eidetic imagery or "photographic" memory, as it is often called. People with such a gift can form images of a page they have read which they may reproduce on examinations. However, it is very much a mixed blessing as we have seen in the case of S. It interfered with his ability to concentrate on simple abstract ideas and in other cases it seems to hamper real learning, such as comprehending what one has read.

ARE THERE REALLY PHOTOGRAPHIC MEMORIES? Eidetic imagery and photographic memories are terms that are often used interchangeably. People with eidetic imagery often explain their memories for verbal material by saying that they have just called up an image of a word to help them spell it.

If you have such a memory or know of such a person you can make an interesting test (Hebb, 1972). The image in these cases appears to be as vivid as a photograph. With an actual word or photograph of it to look at, one could read off the letters of a word accurately. Think of a long word such as Mississippi and form an image of it or have your friend with a photographic memory do it. Now try to spell the image forward and backward. You or your friend will discover that this is very difficult to do. This illustrates that the term "photographic memory" is really something of a misnomer. Although people with eidetic imagery actually can form very clear images, it is not quite the same as seeing the real thing or looking at a photographic record.

Summary

Of all organisms, man's behavior is determined least by instincts and most by learning. Learning may be defined as a change in behavior or performance as a result of practice or experience.

The psychology of learning received a great boost from a Russian physiologist, Ivan Pavlov, who studied classical conditioning. When a previously neutral stimulus (CS) is paired with one (UCS) that elicits a reflexive response (UCR) and is now able to produce that response (CR) when presented alone, we are talking about classical conditioning.

While classical conditioning involves reflexive behavior that is elicited, instrumental or operant conditioning is much more purposive and deals with emitted behaviors. Three men were important in developing concepts for the latter form of conditioning: Thorndike, Watson, and Skinner. Thorndike's major contribution was in viewing learning as problem solving and the establishment of stimulus-response connections. Watson developed the school known as behaviorism which stressed the study of observable behavior and the influence of environmental forces on the development of personality.

Perhaps the best known modern-day behaviorist is B. F. Skinner who believes that man's behavior can be controlled and shaped by systematic reinforcement. Reinforcement is anything which increases the probability of a response. Organisms can be taught behaviors through shaping procedures using successive approximations.

In both classical and instrumental conditioning, learned responses can be eliminated through the process of extinction. In the former, one simply presents the CS in the absence of the UCS over a number of trials. The CR will disappear when the CS is presented. In the latter case, reinforcement of a learned response is withdrawn and will generally result in the elimination of that behavior. Even after extinction, the extinguished response may reappear after some intervening time. This has been called spontaneous recovery.

While classical and instrumental conditioning refer to the attachment of simple responses to stimuli, thinking and associated processes (cognitive processes) gives man the capacity for complex learning. Man's cognition (knowledge and understanding) or the intervening covert process between stimulus and response allows him to think and reason.

Man has the capacity for problem solving or discovering a correct response to a new situation. Three basic characteristics are inherent in problem solving: (1) The correct response is not obvious; (2) human problem solving consists mainly of ideas or other covert mediating processes; and (3) the solution may occur in a flash after a period of struggle with the problem. This latter response has been termed insight because it occurs suddenly, eliminates errors, and is generally an original response. Closely related to insight is reasoning. This involves the ability to integrate two or more previously learned habits mediated by covert responses.

Schedules of reinforcement may be either continuous, delivered after every response, or intermittent. The latter is more likely to occur in real life and makes responses more difficult to extinguish. Four schedules and their consequent effects on behavior were discussed. In ratio schedules, reinforcement is delivered after a certain number of responses. When the same number of correct responses earns a reinforcement each time, we call this a fixed ratio. Responding occurs at a high rate under this schedule. When reinforcement occurs at some *average* number of responses, it is known as a variable ratio schedule. Again, a fast rate of responding brings more reinforcement.

In interval schedules, time is used to determine reinforcement rather than the number of responses. A fixed interval schedule is one in which reinforcement is delivered to the correct response after a certain length of time. Responses are generally slow in the beginning and pick up toward the end. When reinforcement is delivered around some average time interval to the correct response, it is called a variable interval. Responses tend to be constant and evenly spaced in this type of schedule.

Other parameters of reinforcement involve delay of reinforcement and the concept of secondary reinforcement. Reinforcement is most effective when delivered immediately after a correct response. When a previously nonreinforcing circumstance, after being associated with a reinforcing one, becomes reinforcing in its own right, it is called a secondary reinforcer. Much of what motivates us (money, prestige, grades, and so on) are secondary reinforcers.

Imitation learning or modeling is different from other forms because it is social and another organism must be involved. Many organisms learn behavioral patterns by observing and imitating others.

Memory and forgetting refers to retaining or forgetting previously learned materials or skills. Three means have been used to measure memory: recall, recognition, and relearning. Curves of forgetting indicate that we forget much new learned material quickly and retain part of it for a long time. Forgetting may be delayed and memories may be improved by overlearning, organization, self-recitation, and mnemonic devices. The latter technique refers to a variety of ways in which new knowledge is organized by old information. The use of visual imagery is very important.

Although it seems that one forgets because of lack of practice and disuse, this theory is too simplistic. We forget things because of interference; psychological processes that intervene between learning and a test of retention. Interference can occur when new learning affects the retention of previous learning (retroactive inhibition) or when what we have learned in part affects our ability to learn something new (proactive inhibition). Forgetting can also occur via motivated means because memories are too painful to recall.

People who are able to demonstrate outstanding memories make heavy use of mnemonic devices and especially visual imagery. Eidetic images is the term used to describe detailed and vivid memory images that a few exceptional individuals possess. Such people have been described as having a photographic memory although this is a misnomer.

References

Bandura, A. Influence of models' reinforcement contingencies on the acquisition of imitative responses. *Journal of Personality and Social Psychology*, 1965, **1**, 589–595.

Bartlett, F. C. *Remembering: A study in experimental and social psychology*. London: Cambridge University Press, 1932.

Bower, G. H., & Clark, M. C. Narrative stories as mediators for serial learning. *Psychonomic Science*, 1969, **14**, 181–182.

Burtt, H. E. An experimental study of early childhood memory. *Journal of Genetic Psychology*, 1941, **58**, 435–439.

Buss, A. *Psychology, man in perspective*. New York: Wiley, 1973.

Cowles, J. T. Food tokens as incentives for learning by chimpanzees. *Comparative Psychological Monographs*, 1937, **14**, 96.

Ebbinghaus, H. *Memory*, 1885. Translated by H. H. Ruger & C. E. Bussenius. New York: Teachers College, 1913.

Ellis, H. C. *Fundamentals of human learning and cognition*. Dubuque, Iowa: W. C. Brown Co., 1972.

Fisher, D. F. The effects of delay interval on word recall and clustering. *Journal of Psychology*, 1971, **77**, 67–77.

Gardner, R. A. & Gardner, B. T. Teaching sign language to a chimpanzee. *Science*, 1969, **165**, 664–672.

Gates, A. I. Recitation as a factor in memorizing. *Archives of Psychology*, 1917, **6** (Whole No. 40).

Hayes, K. J., & Hayes, C. Imitation in a home-raised chimpanzee. *Journal of Comparative and Physiological Psychology*, 1952, **45**, 450–459.

Hebb, D. O. *Textbook of psychology*, Philadelphia: W. B. Saunders Co., 1972.

Hunt, E., & Love, T. How good can memory be? In A. W. Melton & E. Martin (Eds.), *Coding processes in human memory*. New York: Wiley, 1972, 237–260.

Isaacs, W., Thomas, J., & Goldiamond, I. Application of operant conditioning to reinstate verbal behavior in psychotics. *Journal of Speech and Hearing Disorders*, 1960, **25**, 8–12.

Jenkins, J. G., & Dallenbach, K. M. Oblivescence during sleep and waking. *American Journal of Psychology*, 1924, **35**, 605–612.

Kellogg, G. S., & Howe, M. J. A. Using words and pictures in foreign language learning by children. *Alberta Journal of Educational Research*, 1971, **17**, 89–94.

Kendler, H. H. *Basic psychology*, 3d ed. Menlo Park, Calif.: W. A. Benjamin, Inc., 1974.

Kendler, T. S., & Kendler, H. H. Inferential behavior in children as a function of age and subgoal constancy. *Journal of Experimental Psychology*, 1962, **64**, 460–466.

Krueger, W. C. F. The effect of overlearning on retention. *Journal of Experimental Psychology*, 1929, **12**, 71–78.

Luria, A. R. *The mind of a mnemonist*. New York: Basic Books, 1968.

Mednick, S. A., Pollio, H. R., & Loftus, E. F. *Learning*. Englewood Cliffs, N.J.: Prentice-Hall, 1973.

Morgan, C. T., & Deese, J. *How to study*. New York: McGraw-Hill, 1969.

Norman, D. H. *Memory and attention: An introduction to human information processing*. New York: 1969.

Penfield, W. The interpretive cortex. *Science*. 1959, **129**, 1719–1725.

Schroth, M. L. The function of stimulus predifferentiation pretraining in complex problem-solving. *Psychonomic Science*, 1968, **12**, 123–124. (a)

Schroth, M. L. Transfer in oddity problems as a function of type and amount of pretraining. *Psychonomic Science*, 1968, **12**, 151–152. (b)

Schroth, M. L. The effects of informative feedback on problem solving. In J. F. Rosenblith, W. Allinsmith, & J. P. Williams (Eds.), *Readings in educational psychology.* Boston: Allyn & Bacon, 1972.

Skinner, B. F. *Beyond freedom and dignity.* New York: Knopf, 1971.

Stollmeyer, C. F., & Psotka, J. The detailed texture of eidetic images. *Nature*, 1970, **225**, 346–349.

Thorndike, E. L. ·Animal intelligence. *Psychological Review Monograph Supplement*, 1898, **2**(4, Whole No. 8).

Watson, J. B. Experimental studies on the growth of emotions. In C. Murchison (Ed.), *Psychologies of 1925.* Worcester, Mass.: Clark University Press, 1926.

Watson, J. B., & Rayner, R. Conditioned emotional reactions. *Journal of Experimental Psychology*, 1920, **3**, 1–14.

Wolf, M. M., Risley, T., & Mees, H. Application of operant conditioning procedures to the behavior problems of an autistic child. *Behavior Research and Therapy*, 1964, **1**, 305–312.

Yerkes, R. M. & Margulis, S. The method of Pavlov in animal psychology. *Psychological Bulletin*, 1909, **6**, 257–273.

6

What directs
human behavior

Professor Jones is busy lecturing on his favorite topic to students who are either dozing or daydreaming about something else. All of a sudden he hits upon the magic word "sex" and the drowsy students are suddenly wide awake.

Although the school psychologist says that John has an exceptionally high IQ, he continues to do poorly in class. Yet, one of his classmates, Jean, who possesses only an average IQ, is consistently out-performing John by earning A's and B's on all tests.

Both of the above examples raise certain questions. In the former, what caused the students' sudden and abrupt change in alertness? In the latter, how can someone with a lower intelligence score perform better than one with a higher one?

The answer to both of the questions is what psychologists term motivation or what is commonly known as being "turned on." It goes without saying that most young people have an interest in sex and all of us are alerted to things in our environment which are consistent with our current motives. The importance of motivation is further illustrated by the case of John and Joan, which is a situation you undoubtedly have experienced; courses which you enjoy are easy to concentrate on and subjects that do not naturally interest you are difficult to study. Thus, motivation is what gives behavior its push.

Motivation

Motivation in everyday life

The word motive is certainly one of the most popular words in the science of psychology and to the general public. When a young man is habitually getting into barroom scraps, we may conclude that his motives can be called aggressive. If we see a teen-age girl who often clings tenaciously to her mother rather than spending time with her friends, we label her dependent. Or if another young woman spends most of her time studying in order to get ahead and excel, we may infer that she is motivated by achievement needs.

Actually, motivation helps answer the "why" of behavior and is the key to understanding people. For example, some men have a strong motive to make a lot of money by becoming outstanding businessmen. Other men become politicians because they have an overpowering need to determine the governmental affairs of their city, state, or nation. Still others have predominant humanitarian interests and devote their lives to helping others. An outstanding example of this would be Albert Schweitzer (Figure 6-1). Here was a man who devoted most of his life to the practice of medicine among the natives of Africa. Certainly, he could have become richer by working in the United States. However, he

FIGURE 6–1
Albert Schweitzer

Wide World Photos

felt that he was greatly needed among these people who had little in the way of routine medical services.

The importance of motivation can be further illustrated by the fact that policemen always look for a motive in trying to solve a crime. In addition, convicted lawbreakers receive sentences which are to a great extent determined by their motives. The penalty for murder, for instance, is greater than the penalty for manslaughter. The difference in the nature of these crimes lies in the existence of motivation (malice) for the former and the lack of malice in the latter.

Although everybody feels free to examine the motives of others, it is extremely difficult to do so simply by observing overt behavior. As a matter of fact, motives may never result in observable behavior. A man who is an ardent moviegoer may have a strong desire to become an actor. Yet the goal is unreachable for him and he makes no attempt to attain it. On a more commonplace level, many people talk wistfully about a vacation in Europe yet neither try to save money nor to take the time for the trip. Many people say they want to get more exercise; they have a motive to lose weight or be in better physical shape. However, they seldom engage in physical activities. People who are strongly motivated by a need to dominate others may never show it except in hidden and devious ways.

Though motives are not always easy to identify, motivation is a key issue in psychology because it answers the "why" of behavior. Motives indicate a common concern with what *activates* and *directs* the organism. It denotes that behavior is directed toward a goal and implies a degree of regularity of function. The actual form of behavior may change on occasion but its function remains the same. For example, the individual in need of social status and recognition from others may try to excel in football during high school. After graduation, this motive may be expressed through participating in community affairs. The form of behavior has changed in each particular occurrence of the motive state. However, the goal remains the same, recognition from others.

The persistence of behavior often gives us a clue as to how motivated people really are. The student who continually calls up a certain coed for a date in the face of several refusals is strongly motivated. Take the case of Vincent Lombardi, former coach of the Green Bay Packers. Here was a man who did not give up his goal of becoming an outstanding professional football coach in spite of the fact that he was passed over for a head coaching position until he was in his forties. His level of motivation eventually paid off for him as he led several championship teams.

Classifying motives

There have been several classification systems proposed in the psychology of motivation. One method that is widely used to identify and organize motives is to group them together according to similarity of causes. In one classification system, motives are divided into three groups—survival, social, and self motives.

Survival motives are those directly affecting the survival of the individual. They may be either physiological or psychological. Physiologically based motives include hunger, thirst, need for oxygen, avoidance of pain, elimination, and sleep. These motives follow the deprivation-satiation cycle (such as thirst), and others depend upon some episodic stimulation (such as avoidance of pain). Psychologically based motives are those which orient the individual to particular stimuli in his environment. Among these needs are curiosity-exploration, manipulation, and the related phenomenon of sensory deprivation.

The *social* motives are those which depend upon interaction with others for their instigation or expression. Included in the social category are aggression, altruism, affiliation, and "contact comfort." There are, of course, physiological factors that play an important role in these motives, but the direction of the behavior is toward others.

Self motives are those related to the development and maintenance of the concept of self or ego. Self motives include the need to achieve, dominate, development of values, and related concepts such as praise, encouragement, failure, and threat. These similar motives all have in common the purpose of enhancing and defending the picture one has of himself.

It should be noted that these three categories of motives do not have perfectly sharp boundaries. They primarily serve as a useful framework in which to relate similar motives together.

Physiological survival motives

HUNGER. Probably the survival motive we know the most about is *hunger*. It occurs naturally as a response to the need for food. But did you ever wonder why you feel hungry? The commonsense notion is simply that hunger is a feeling of mild pain in the stomach known as hunger pangs. However, the explanation is not all that simple. For instance, people who have had their stomachs removed report that they feel hungry even though they do not experience hunger pangs. In controlled experiments, rats without stomachs behave very much like those with intact stomachs in learning situations that involve food as a reward.

In all probability there is more than one control system that influences our eating behavior. There is no doubt that blood chemistry and sugar utilization are part of the basic physiological mechanism that regulates eating behavior. For example, many people who "run out of sugar" while exercising on a hot day experience an overall weakness and report hunger.

In recent years, much research has been conducted in an attempt to find structures in the brain that affect motivated behavior. It has been found that the hypothalamus (see Chapter 2) acts as an eating control center. One important observation is that the destruction of a certain area within the hypothalamus causes rats, dogs, rabbits, and monkeys to become excessively fat. The animals overeat to such a great extent that they may double their normal weight. This condition is known as *hyperphagia* (overeating because of damage of the hypothalamus).

The opposite reaction can also be made to occur by destroying other tissues in the hypothalamus. In this condition, known as *hypophagia*, animals will starve to death in the midst of food. Thus, these data support the general assumption that there are two centers in the hypothalamus that control eating—one that initiates eating and another that terminates it.

However, damage to the hypothalamus and other related physiological factors do not explain normal cases of obesity in man. For instance, Stanley Schachter (1971) in a series of provocative studies has discovered that obese people apparently eat for different reasons than do persons of normal weight. Data from studies of hospital dieters, Jews fasting on Yom Kippur, students eating in campus dining halls, and studies of flight crews indicate that individuals of normal weight eat in response to internal physiological cues such as stomach contractions while obese persons eat in response to external cues such as the smell, taste, and sight of food. This explains why a person of normal weight will pass up a bakery after just eating a full meal in contrast to an overweight individual who, under the same circumstances, will respond to the external cues of the bakery and go inside. These findings help account for the notorious long-term ineffectiveness of virtually all attempts to treat obesity by lessening the intensity of the physiological symptoms or inner signals of food deprivation. An effective dieting program would necessitate blinding the obese dieter to food-relevant cues. For example, in the treatment of obesity, many psychologists suggest that the person eat in an isolated area away from friends, reading material, TV, music, and so on. The attempt here is to remove external cues that may reinforce eating. As mentioned in the previous chapter, these cues may be secondary reinforcers maintaining eating behavior. Their removal tends to repress excessive eating.

Also of special interest to psychologists are the psychological effects of going without enough food. A study was conducted during World War II in which conscientious objectors volunteered to restrict their intake of food from approximately 3,400 to 1,500 carories per day (Keys, Brozek, Heuschel, Mickelson, & Taylor, 1950). This study took place over a 24-week period.

The physiological effects were immense. On the average, the men lost 25 percent of their normal weight and became so weak that a routine task such as climbing stairs was difficult for them. However, the psychological consequences were even more devastating. The men became quite apathetic and took no interest in their surroundings. Other psychological changes were that these men became quarrelsome with one another. They argued at parties held for their benefit and also became quite sloppy in their physical appearance. One of the most noticeable changes in their behavior was their complete lack of interest in sex. They broke off romances with their girl friends and seemed to be completely incapable of displaying any affection toward them.

Near the end of this "semistarvation" study, most of their thoughts and daydreams revolved around food. They talked about changing their occupations to becoming cooks and bakers. Their favorite reading materials were recipes and cookbooks. Although their interests and other personality traits changed considerably during the study, the subjects suffered no overall loss in intelligence.

The importance of this experiment is that it illustrates in a dramatic fashion how strong the hunger drive is when it goes unsatiated. In our well-fed, modern Western world, most of us seldom see the full effect of the hunger drive. However, people who go on diets to lose weight may also suffer the same symptoms as the men in this study.

THIRST. Humans are capable of surviving for several weeks without food, but one cannot live more than a few days without water. When we go without drinking water for a period of time, the cells and tissues of our bodies suffer from the effect of losing too much moisture.

Thirst is very similar to hunger in many respects. Sensory messages from the dryness of the mouth, throat, blood, and stomach play a minor role in initiating drinking behavior in organisms. As in the case of hunger, the hypothalamus is the center within the brain that regulates the thirst drive.

SLEEP. Lesions in one area of the hypothalamus causes an animal to remain awake until it dies of exhaustion; destruction of another area of the brain (reticular center) causes an animal to sleep almost constantly. There appears to be a "sleep center" and a "wakefulness center" in the brain. In the case of the "wakefulness center," people sometimes suffer damage to this area as a result of a hard blow to the head which produces a coma. Boxers have been known to remain in a comatose state for long periods of time as a result of injuries suffered in the ring.

Normally, people require from six to nine hours of sleep a day. We ordinarily sleep when it is dark and are awake when it is daylight. However, people who live in the extreme north maintain almost the same rhythm of sleep and wakefulness during the months of almost total darkness as they do during the months of prolonged daylight.

The psychological effects of going without sleep have been found to produce a general decrement in motor skills performance. People who are forced to stay awake for 50 hours can usually continue to perform short and simple tasks efficiently. But, their ability to perform more complicated tasks, particularly of a mental nature, is seriously affected and their judgment impaired.

Unlike some basic drives such as hunger, recovery from extended sleep loss does not require that the total lost time be spent in sleep. Even after many days of sleep deprivation, people require only about 11 or 12 hours of sleep to regain the normal state of wakefulness.

OTHER PHYSIOLOGICAL MOTIVES. There are four other physiological motives which deserve mention. The motive to breathe air is not ordinarily important. However, it becomes the most intense of all motives if we should suddenly be cut off from air. It might become increasingly important in the future if we continue to overpollute the atmosphere.

The motive to avoid pain leads primarily to such reflex behavior as pulling one's hand away from a hot object. It also leads to learned be-havior such as taking aspirins for headaches. Certainly, the desire to avoid pain has led the field of medicine to discover better anesthetics to use for operations.

Elimination needs (to get rid of the body's waste materials) gain im-portance mostly because of social customs and taboos that have grown up around it. It is especially important in child rearing because of society's emphasis on toilet training.

Finally, the need to maintain a constant temperature is common to all warm-blooded animals and is also regulated by the hypothalamus. Studies show that damage to various regions of that structure leads to losses in temperature regulation. Its importance can be seen in the fact that a considerable amount of human activity is devoted to making clothing and building houses (including heating and air cooling systems) which satisfy our temperature needs.

Psychological survival needs

The needs discussed in this section all have in common the character-istic of sensory stimulation and stimulus variability. They seem to be as intrinsic or basic to animal and human behavior as the physiological drives.

CURIOSITY-EXPLORATION. Research with different species suggests that organisms are curious about their environment and will explore it with-out any reward such as food, sex, or water. Monkeys will learn to open a window just to be able to peer out. You may have noticed while visiting the cages of chimpanzees and monkeys at a zoo, that these animals may be staring at you while you look at them; they, too, are curious.

Man has the greatest curiosity of all organisms; his curiosity knows no bounds. We are not content just to explore the depths of the ocean or the highest mountains on our planet, but we are also exploring outer space. In fact one of the most important motives behind the space pro-gram is insatiable curiosity. Men like Einstein have tried to take on the whole universe in an attempt to understand it.

More commonplace is the fact that people get bored when doing the same thing. Imagine seeing the same movie (although some do) over and over again; it would lose its appeal. However, a new movie you hear about may immediately arouse your curiosity. In addition, many people will select a job that they find a challenge rather than select a boring one that pays well.

MANIPULATION. Closely related to the curiosity motive is a manipula-tion need as demonstrated by Dr. Harry Harlow in a series of experi-ments (Harlow, Blazek, & McClearn, 1965). In one study, it was shown that monkeys will solve over and over again a mechanical puzzle similar to the one in Figure 6–2. They continue to manipulate this puzzle in spite of the fact that no reward (such as water or food) is made available.

FIGURE 6–2
The monkey has opened the cage door, "manipulates" or plays with the blocks
placed in front of the cage. This behavior is not motivated by hunger or any
other physiological drive but appears to be an end in itself.

This suggests that playing with the puzzle is its own reinforcement. This
need to manipulate is seen even more clearly in the case of humans. Many
men enjoy tinkering with old cars in order to get them to run.

SENSORY DEPRIVATION AND MODERN SOCIETY. Some of the most interesting studies that demonstrate the importance of some type of external
stimulation are in the area of sensory deprivation. In a classic study
(Bexton, Heron, & Scott, 1954), male college students were deprived of
visual, auditory, and many tactile stimuli. The subjects were paid $20 a
day just to rest in a quiet room. This may sound like an easy way to earn
money but the catch is as follows. The subjects' hands and feet are encased in cardboard cylinders, goggles are placed over their eyes, and
foam rubber pads are placed over their ears. Such conditions were relaxed only in order to allow the subjects to eat or perform eliminative
functions. During the early part of the experiment, the students slept,
but later became restless, irritable, and began to have disturbing visual
hallucinations. Few of them could endure the conditions for more than
three days. Apparently, in order for the brain to function normally, it
needs a certain amount of external stimulation or it manufactures its
own stimulations (hallucinations).

Although everyday conditions are not so extreme, the effects of inadequate external stimulation often result in boredom. Ancient Rome made
the discovery that the populace needed entertainment, such as circuses
and food orgies to keep them from becoming restless. So they held glad-

iatorial contests and engaged in tremendous acts of brutality by tossing many Christians to the lions. We can look at our modern society in the same light and understand the widespread popularity of sports or other entertaining activities. The brutalities of modern-day football and boxing serve the same function of keeping us aroused. In addition, we can add movies, television, and amusement parks (Disneyland) which play a vital role in our lives. It needs to be stressed that such things are not luxuries but are necessities which satisfy the need for a certain level of external stimulation and arousal.

Finally, it might be mentioned that riots, demonstrations, and involvement in causes of many types may be partially understood in terms of the same psychological motive. It is possible that in our "well-to-do" Western societies increasing material wealth leads to social strife because people become bored and seek excitement.

Social motives

SEX AS A MOTIVE. Sex is commonly considered to be a physiological motive although there are also psychological and social factors involved. For most lower organisms, sexual behavior is unlearned; birds and other lower animals raised in isolation show normal sexual behavior at the first opportunity. However, higher animals such as monkeys and men do not. Among human beings, sex is not just a biological motive. Unlike lower organisms, sex is not completely dependent upon the flow of sexual hormones. We have devoted a chapter to sex (Chapter 10), in which its physiological aspects are discussed in detail. At this point, we shall discuss a learning theory approach to sex which stresses social forces.

One viewpoint on why sex is such a powerful motive is that sexual appetite has been slowly learned from the early years of life (Hardy, 1964). In our culture, exploration of the genital organs by children is treated in such a fashion that they expect something pleasant and exciting. Parents typically overract to the child's natural curiosity, thereby, strongly directing his attention to this behavior. Suppression of behavior connected with the pleasurable sensations of sexual arousal often increases interest in it. The sexual motive is constantly being aroused by emphasis in movies, plays, and magazines (*Playboy* and *Playgirl*). The advertisement industry also makes great use of sex-arousing cues such as handsome men and beautiful women in advertisements. (Note the "fly me" commercials of National Airlines.)

The importance of social and cultural factors in the sex motive is well illustrated by anthropological studies. The conceptions of feminine beauty vary widely from one society to another. Slim, slightly rounded women are considered most appealing in some societies, while in others plump and even obese women have all the honors. In the case of males, attractiveness frequently depends less on physical characteristics than on social features, such as their status in the group.

AGGRESSION. One of the most important social motives today is aggression. It may be defined as the desire to overcome opposition forcefully. It may take the form of a direct physical attack or occur in a more symbolic nature such as trying to destroy the opposition with words.

Recently, psychologists and biologists have increased their attempts to understand the nature of aggression; what are its causes? There are two opposing viewpoints on the relative contributions of innate and learned factors to aggressive behavior. An approach which emphasizes the role of instinctive, or innate, factors in behavior, including aggression, is the ethological movement. Konrad Lorenz, a leader of ethology, believes that man is innately aggressive. To illustrate this, he points to human history and the number of wars in which man has been engaged. To a great extent, the dominant societies in history have been those who are the most aggressive. In the history of our own country, it is easy to point out the amount of violence that has existed and which is still taking place. However, this is also true of most of the other nations and certainly is not limited only to the United States.

A major psychological theory in agreement with the ethological viewpoint is Freud's theory of personality (see Chapter 8). Freud linked aggression with his concept of the death instinct and was highly impressed with how aggressive mankind is.

However, other psychologists would disagree with Lorenz and Freud by emphasizing that aggression is a learned response. Neal Miller and John Dollard (1939) conducted several experiments on animals and humans in which they sought to prove aggression occurs as a result of frustration. They found that the more frustrated their subjects were, the greater would be the amount of their aggression. In their viewpoint, aggression is learned in situations where anger is elicited. More specifically, Berkowitz and associates (Berkowitz & Geen, 1966; Berkowitz & Le Page, 1967) have analyzed the nature of stimuli that elicit aggressive behavior. They found that observing others in violent acts, whether in the movies or in real life, provoked aggressive behavior in children. In addition, the perception of weapons also was found to stimulate aggressive behavior. Whether aggression is learned or innate is an issue which cannot be immediately resolved. Like many issues in psychology, it is possible that the two conflicting theories may have to be combined in some manner. Then the question might be, What are the relative contributions of these two factors?

ALTRUISM: PEOPLE HELPING PEOPLE. The section on aggression has indicated that man certainly possesses strong destructive tendencies toward his fellowman. However, is that the whole story? Recently, social psychology has become interested in a relatively new area of study called altruism. Altruism is defined as behavior where the helper goes out of his way to aid another person, particularly a stranger.

Safety in numbers. Surprising and puzzling as it may seem, the research is quite consistent in discovering that individuals in trouble are less likely to receive help from strangers the larger the audience observing their difficulties. These findings are reminiscent of the Kitty Genovese murder in New York City. The killing took more than half an hour, but not one of the 38 people who watched from their apartments came to her rescue. In fact, no one even phoned the police! We will return to discuss this phenomenon in Chapter 12, when we explore possible reasons for so many people failing to help individuals' experiencing a crisis situation.

Several investigations have focused on attempts to increase altruistic behavior in naturalistic settings. Bryan and Test (1967) demonstrated that auto drivers were more likely to stop and aid a lady in distress with a flat tire if they had just passed another lady being helped in a similar predicament. The authors conclude that altruism, like aggression, can be increased by appropriate modeling opportunities. Bryan and Test (1967) report a further experiment involving Salvation Army Kettle stations which seem to support the modeling hypothesis. At selected intervals, confederates of the experimenter would deposit money in the kettles in front of customers entering and leaving a department store. As compared with the no-model condition, the model condition produced significantly more donations.

Further research needs to be done to determine more accurately the conditions associated with helping behavior. One generalization seems to be supported by many studies, including a recent study by Wispe and Freshley (1971). Men seem to offer help more than women. Perhaps this is explainable by the observation that men are the doers in our society, a fact which seems to be more related to conditioning than to any genetic predisposition.

AFFILIATION. The desire to be with other similar individuals is termed an affiliative motive. Not all species engage in grouping behavior but it is considered to be most important for mankind. We generally consider it unusual when an individual completely isolates himself from others as in the case of hermits.

People who have a high affiliative motive tend to be more concerned with human relationships than with their work or other tasks. These people definitely prefer to work in a group rather than by themselves (Murray, 1964). Relating this to everyday life, we could expect this sort of person to find it difficult to study in his room alone; he would much rather be at a bull session or out on a date. We might also speculate that fraternity and sorority groups as well as other organizations that are entirely social in nature, provide an important function. They help satisfy the need for belonging or affiliation.

NEED FOR CONTACT OR MOTHER LOVE. A series of experiments conducted by Dr. Harry Harlow (1971) provide strong evidence for an innate basis to many social motives. Harlow took baby monkeys from their mothers and gave them substitutes known as "surrogate mothers." These infant monkeys based their preferences on the kind of tactual stimulation that the surrogates provided. They greatly preferred to snuggle up and cling to a "mother" made of sponge rubber and terry cloth, which provided softness and warmth, rather than one who provided them with food but less physical comfort. These experiments are very reminiscent of the way human babies cling to the softness of the mother's body or to the behavior of the young child who needs a "security" blanket and teddy bear before he is able to sleep. This inborn need or motive to seek something soft and warm is called *contact comfort*.

Some other important findings of these studies are that monkeys raised with wire mothers show an absence of affection, a lack of cooperation, exaggerated aggression, and almost total lack of sexual responsiveness to other monkeys. Thus, it is clear that the whole emotional development of the monkey is adversely affected. Those raised with cloth mothers show less aggression and some sexual responsiveness but of an immature nature. Although cloth surrogate mothers are superior to wire ones, emotional development is far more enhanced with a real, live mother monkey (Figure 6–3). However, Harlow later found that contact with other infant monkeys did make up for lack of mothering. Having close contact with monkeys their own age appears to be as important as having a mother.

The question arises, "Do Harlow's findings with animals have any implications for human behavior?" Since there is a remarkable correspondence between these findings and studies of human children who have been deprived of normal mothering and close contact with peers, the answer seems to be yes. The best evidence comes from a number of

FIGURE 6–3
Effects of lack of "mother love." This monkey, raised by a wire surrogate mother, shows exaggerated fear of strangers and lack of security in contrast to normally raised monkeys, that have been provided with "contact comfort."

Courtesy of Harry F. Harlow, University of Wisconsin Primate Laboratory

studies of children who have been placed in orphanages or foundling homes; typically these children received little physical or emotional stimulation.

Very young children and infants who have had little stimulation during the first year of life appear to be withdrawn and devoid of emotional feelings. Many of them seem to have permanently lost the capacity to form human attachments. Others, who had adequate mothering the first year and then were separated, show dramatic changes in their behavior. Many of these children become emotionless robots and show abnormal symptoms such as incessant rocking and a complete lack of social responsiveness.

Older children who have been brought up in these impersonal institutions may develop a type of personality known as "psychopathic" or "sociopathic." They tend to be unable to form close emotional ties and are highly aggressive and antisocial. In regard to other people, they appear to be motivated "to use them" for their own purposes. As we saw in Chapter 2, all of these studies can be summed up by noting the effects of lack of affection during these critical years. If humans do not receive adequate affection early in life, they do not seem to develop love and affection for others.

Self-motives

NEED TO ACHIEVE. The need to achieve may be defined as a motive to accomplish something difficult or to excel. McClelland and his associates (McClelland, 1955) have systematically researched this human motive. It has been found that high need achievers tend to try harder and attain more success in many different situations than other people of equal ability but weaker achievement motives. For example, they do better on mathematical and verbal tests (Lowell, 1952).

In general, high-achieving people seem to have many of the characteristics of the ambitious businessman. They tend to have self-confidence, prefer individual responsibility, choose experts rather than friends as working partners, and are resistant to outside social pressure. In addition, they enjoy taking moderate risks in situations that depend on their own ability, but dislike pure chance situations, such as betting at a racetrack.

An important question is, "How do people develop a motive for achievement?" Studies of people rated high in achievement motivation have shown that their parents highly valued and demanded independence. For instance, these individuals were expected to try new and difficult things on their own, to be active and energetic, and to do well in competition.

DOMINANCE: NEED TO MAINTAIN ONE'S POWER. The social motive of dominance is basic to vertebrate animal behavior. The existence of a dominant-subordinate hierarchy was first described in barnyard hens and has since been observed in such diverse species as sparrows, canaries, peacocks, turkeys, ducks, goats, elephant seals, mice, rats, rabbits, dogs, cats, monkeys, chimpanzees, and man.

In hens we find the familiar "pecking order." Pecks are always unidirectional. Henpecked hens cannot peck back but can only peck hens lower than themselves on the scale. The maximally dominant hen usually pecks all other hens but is herself never pecked; the maximally subordinate hen is pecked by all others but pecks none.

Among baboons dominance is expressed by grooming. Higher ranking baboons are groomed by those lower than themselves. If the individuals are close in rank two hands are used. If the ranking is far apart the lower baboon uses only one hand to groom the higher.

Among men the expressions of dominance are rather more complex. Dominance is usually expressed symbolically through expensive clothing, prestigious titles, property, and so forth rather than by direct physical expression such as pecking or grooming. Consider the uniforms worn by the police and military personnel. The blue cloth, shining buttons, and decorative striping serves no practical function, except one. It allows us to identify those dominant to us. In other cultures where clothing has been minimal, the same function has been served by body tattoos, by number or kind of feathers worn in the hair, or perhaps, by the size of a bone pierced through a lip or a nose.

Strip away all signs of dominance from human society or jumble these signs and chaos would result. How would a naked, fat, out-of-condition executive be distinguished from a naked, fat, out-of-condition hobo. Only by our possessions can dominance be told. He who smokes the most expensive cigar, has the biggest, shiniest car, sits at the head of the table, or has the fattest wallet, is dominant. But what benefits go to those who are dominant? Who would want the ulcers or long hours of the executive or the vast responsibility of a senator or president? To understand this, we must look back at the lower animals.

Dominant hens take precedence at water and food troughs, nests, and roosts. Dominant cocks take sexual precedence over subordinate cocks and sire more chicks. Food and sexual privileges are the prerogatives of dominant members of every species. So we find dominance to be a genetically fostered trait in every generation. Only those who are dominant live and reproduce. Natural selection, or rather group selection, plays its part and a need for dominance becomes an instinct, a trait of all individuals of a species, although naturally some succeed better than others.

This is only a theory, and the role of environment in fostering the competitive attitude among humans should not be minimized. However, sexual and neural bases of dominance have been discovered, such as the amygdala, within the temporal lobe—and experiments with rhesus monkeys have confirmed that removing this structure from a maximally dominant monkey causes him to become maximally subordinate. Applying this to humans, mind control 1984 style may be only a decade away.

OTHER SELF-MOTIVES. Other ego involved motives extensively studied are the value systems to which an individual identifies. Of particular note is the manner in which our different values affect what we perceive in our environment. In one of the classic studies in this area, Bruner and Goodman (1947) examined the influence of value on size estimation. Ten-year-old children, coming from poor or rich families adjusted a light source to the size of a variety of coins, presumed to be socially valued objects, and "neutral" gray disks. The results indicated that the coins were judged larger than the gray discs. In addition, the poor children overestimated the size of the coins more than the rich group.

Other studies, frequently conducted within school settings, have investigated the effects of ego-enhancing variables (such as praise and encouragement), as well as ego-threatening ones (failure and threat). Although the findings in this area are controversial, most investigators have found that some type of ego-involved variable can operate to affect performance of various types. For example, the studies of Sears (1937) and Lantz (1945) indicate that praise results in a performance increment and failure in decrement.

Maslow's motivational hierarchy

Abraham Maslow has developed a theory of motivation that helps tie together many of the basic motives that we have discussed in this chapter. He suggests that man has a number of primary innate motives ranging from *lower* to *higher* ones. These are arranged in a hierarchy that corresponds to an assumed evolutionary level of the motive as illustrated in Figure 6–4.

First comes the *physiological motives* such as hunger, thirst and sex, then the *safety motives* such as security, stability and order, then the *love motives* such as affection and affiliation, the *esteem motives* such as

FIGURE 6–4
Maslow's need hierarchy

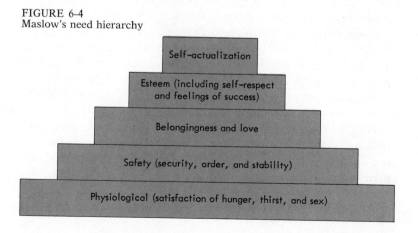

prestige, success, and self-respect, and finally the motives for *self-actualization*. The order of listing of these motives is significant because the lower the motive, the more crucial it is for survival and the earlier it appears in evolution. It is also the order in which such motives tend to appear in the normal development of the individual.

If these earlier motives are not satisfied, the person never gets around to doing much about the later motives. For instance, people in a poor society will be mostly concerned with physiological and security motives. However, a "wealthy" society will manage to satisfy the motives lower in the hierarchy so that the higher motives will emerge. Once the physiological motives are taken care of, then love motives emerge. When the love motives are satisfied by friends or family members, esteem motives appear. As may be the case, when a person needs love desperately he may sacrifice self-respect by crawling back to a tormenting love object. Finally, when all lower motives are satisfied, Maslow says the highest motive of all emerges, *self-actualization* (see Chapter 8).

Unconscious motivation

One of the most important postulates in current psychoanalytical thought, which comes largely from the theories of Sigmund Freud, is that much of human behavior is determined by unconscious forces within the person. People often act in ways which they, themselves, do not understand. Your explanation for your behavior, while self-satisfying, may not be the real motives which remain hidden in the *unconscious*.

According to psychoanalysts, the unconscious is a large segment of the mind which contains a great deal of "forgotten" material that cannot be recalled at will (Sarason, 1972). It contains ideas, wishes, and motives which were once conscious, but now have been buried or repressed. It may be viewed as a tremendous storehouse of forgotten memories and experiences. An analogy is often drawn between an iceberg and the way the human mind operates. Like the tip of an iceberg, about one-sixth of the human mind is exposed to consciousness and about five-sixths or more is below the surface.

Is there evidence that the unconscious exists? The answer is yes. Much of this evidence comes from clinical psychology and the phenomenon of hypnosis which was discussed in Chapter 4. People under hypnosis often recall many events of their past lives which they cannot remember in a normal state of consciousness. One patient, for example, was hypnotized during the course of psychiatric treatment after being arrested for child-beating. Under hypnosis she recalled being beaten by her mother for crying when she was two to three years old. Apparently, she failed to remember this traumatic event in her life because the material was repressed from consciousness.

We all make interesting slips of the tongue which can be funny or embarrassing, because they tell a partial truth and expose feelings which we may not wish to express consciously. A case in point is the politician who says: "Ladies and gentlemen, a vote for me is a vote against honesty —I mean, ha, ha—a vote against dishonesty in government." He may be revealing some of his underlying motives and should be watched. Another interesting but embarrassing slip of the tongue happened to one of the co-authors of this book. In counseling a beautiful coed, he advised her to take the "intercourse" in personality being offered the following term.

Selective forgetting is another evidence of the unconscious. The unconscious process of excluding unpleasant and unwanted thoughts from awareness is called repression. Laboratory studies have shown that the forgetting of unpleasant events do occur. Glucksberg and King (1967) administered electric shocks for certain words and not for others on a recall test. They found that the subjects recalled more readily nonshocked words than words associated with the unpleasant stimulus. Hence, experiments of this type support personal experiences we have all had in our daily lives such as the tendency to forget appointments we really didn't want to keep.

Other evidence of the unconscious is the change in peoples' behavior when they are under the influence of alcohol, drugs, or anesthesia. Under the influence of alcohol, a person who is normally shy may become bold and aggressive. A sweet, modest, young lady may become the *femme fatale*. And we have all heard of people doing funny things when coming out of an anesthesia such as crying over a long forgotten childhood event.

According to psychoanalysts, all behavior such as slips of the tongue and pen, accidents, lapses of memory, and dreams (see Chapter 9) have psychological significance. They are indicative of our unconscious thoughts and desires at work. Not all psychologists, however, are in agreement on the role of unconscious motives and some prefer alternative explanations.

The emotions

Imagine that you are walking by yourself late one night in a large city. You are completely alone in a dark alley that has no street lights. All of a sudden you hear footsteps behind you. You turn around and see a shadowy figure fast approaching. There is an accompanying loud cracking noise and you become badly frightened. You feel a sinking sensation in the pit of your stomach, and your muscles tense up. The effect on your behavior is dramatic—you immediately set out in full flight, running as fast as you can. However, as you look back once more to see if you are being followed, you perceive that the shadowy figure is a young child who has stopped walking. The loud bang you have heard, turns out to be a firecracker. You stop running and feel your fear turn to anger—this idiot has frightened you, scaring you out of the proverbial "ten years growth." Your anger also has dramatic effects on your behavior—you set your jaw and stride toward the child. Then you see that the young boy is injured with blood streaming from his hands and face: the firecracker exploded before being properly released. You are now overcome by nausea accompanied by a strong feeling of compassion. Once more your behavior is energized and you administer first aid and call for an ambulance.

We are talking about emotions—powerful physiological and psychological responses that influence perception, learning, and performance. Life without these stimulating reactions would certainly be most drab. If there were no joys and sorrows, no triumphs or failures, no hopes and dismays, human experience would lose its colorfulness and warmth.

The problem of emotion is complicated by the lack of consensus on a basic definition of the nature of the concept. There is no clear-cut distinction between emotional and nonemotional behavior, nor between one emotion and another. Certainly, the basic emotions such as love, fear, anger, and sadness combine into one another with various degrees to produce complex emotional patterns such as patriotism and contempt. Also, psychologists tend to concentrate on the different aspects of emotion. Some define emotion subjectively—in terms of the feelings or affective states experienced by the individual. Others see emotions as bodily changes; either overt behavior or physiological reactions in the internal visceral organs, as discussed in Chapter 2.

Emotional development

Anybody who has raised children or been around babies has to be impressed with the rapid changes that take place in emotional behavior with increasing age. It is important that parents and teachers be aware of the normal pattern of emotional development if they are to help the child use his emotions in a beneficial way. Genetic studies have yielded a great amount of information on normal development, including the roles of maturation and learning.

The ability to respond emotionally is present in every newborn baby. Consequently, it does not have to be learned: the infant is born with the capacity to cry and laugh. The first sign of emotional behavior is a state of general excitement which is brought about by any strong stimuli, such as a bright light shining directly into the eyes of the infant. This diffuse excitement is reflected in the newborn baby's mass activity (crying, straining and thrashing about). At birth, however, the infant shows no clear-cut responses that can be identified as specific emotional states such as love, fear, and anger (Riccinti, 1968).

The general excitement of the newborn gradually becomes differentiated into simple reactions that suggest pleasure and displeasure (Bakwin & Bakwin, 1966). First, the *unpleasant responses* occur, characterized by restrained movement and tenseness of the body. A little later the *pleasant responses* emerge which can be elicited by rocking, patting, and holding the baby. The baby shows his pleasure by a general relaxation of the entire body and cooing vocalizations.

This sequence of emotional responses can be seen in Figure 6–5. Before the infant is a year old his emotional responses are recognizably similar to those of adults. He displays an increasing repertoire of specific emotional responses—*joy, anger, fear, jealousy,* and *happiness.* These responses can be aroused by a wide range of stimuli, including people, objects, and situations, which in the younger infant were undifferentiated.

The regularity of the pattern of emotional development in children throughout the whole world indicates that emotions are part of our innate behavioral equipment. This is supported by a study of emotional expression in a ten-year-old child who was deaf and blind from birth. This child, because of her physical handicap, had no opportunity to learn

FIGURE 6–5
Emotional development in infancy. The graph shows one view of
the sequence in the development of various emotions in infancy.

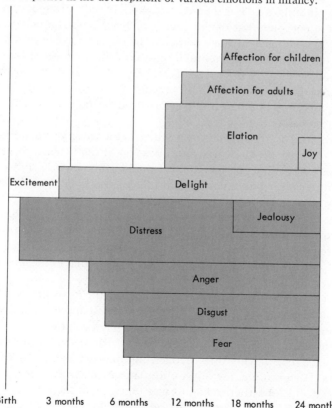

Source: K. M. Bridges, *The Social and Emotional Development of the Pre-School Child* (London: Kegan Paul, 1931).

the expression of emotions in other people except, possibly, by touch. In spite of the lack of opportunity to observe others, her facial expressions of laughter or crying, and her accompanying postures and gestures, were typical of the classical descriptions of emotions (Goodenough, 1932). Differences in heredity, health, and environment, however, do produce individual variations in the frequency, intensity, and duration of the different emotions. These early patterns of emotional behavior in children tend to persist unless they experience radical changes in environment and health. We can best illustrate the interaction of various variables working together affecting development by examining the intense emotions of fear and anger. Unfortunately, one limitation of the research on emotion is that it has concentrated primarily on the negative or unpleasant emotions while neglecting the positive emotions such as love. Hence, we shall necessarily be concerned with fear and anger.

FEAR. What causes fear? Besides being caused by learning, it can be produced in an animal, child, or adult by nearly any sudden and intense stimulus. Pain, sudden loud noises, and any abrupt loss of support cause fear in all mammals. However, as we go from lower to higher mammals we find an increasing number of other causes of fear which parallels increasing intelligence. For the rat, we need add only strange surroundings to have a complete list of the causes of fear. With the dog, the list becomes much longer: strange persons, the dog's owner in different clothing, a large statue of an animal, or even a balloon being blown up in front of the dog (Hebb, 1972). This, of course, does not mean that all dogs are equally affected. There are differences between dogs bred for intelligence, and bulldogs and terriers bred for pugnacity. The latter are much less susceptible to fear.

Chimpanzees are affected by a still greater variety of conditions than dogs. In addition, the degree and duration of disturbance is greater. In a series of studies conducted by Donald Hebb (1962) and others on chimpanzees, we gain much insight into the everyday fears exhibited by man.

THE CAUSES OF FEAR. Hebb, in his experiments on individual differences of fear among chimpanzees, presented test objects of three different categories to the animals: primate objects, pictures of primates, and nonprimate objects. The test objects were presented to the animals while they were in their own cages.

Nearly all adult subjects were terrified by the death mask of an adult and the life-size clay model of an infant chimpanzee's head. When the experimenter carried these objects in his hands and walked toward the cage, many screamed and ran out of sight. In addition, the adult subjects were made fearful when anesthetized chimpanzees were used as stimulus objects. For example, the adult chimpanzees were definitely frightened when a deeply anesthetized adult was taken up to their cages in a wheelbarrow. Strangeness seems to be the key factor.

These are all spontaneous fears, that cannot be explained by previous associative learning. The behavior of younger animals is much different. The same things that terrified the adults were exciting but not frightening to the half grown and not even noticed by the infants. Hebb attributes these results to psychological maturation and not associative learning, since none of the test objects or anything similar to them had been seen before by the animals.

IMPLICATIONS FOR MAN. There is much similarity between human emotional responses to the dead and distorted human bodies, such as a mutilated face and the fears of chimpanzees. The responses tend to be strongest on first experience and more typical of adults than children. Available evidence supports the view that such fears are more the result of maturation than learning. For example, just consider how difficult it is to train adults to drive a car carefully or to keep children from playing in dangerous places. It is easy to condition fear of some things, but very hard with others. Such demonstrations support the existence of emotional susceptibilities which are the basis of spontaneous or almost spontaneous fears.

Among the innate fears are those induced by strange persons and animals; the list being almost endless for man, who has the greatest susceptibility. Studies have shown fear of snakes, spiders, and small insects to be quite common.

To sum up this section on the causes of fear, the comparative evidence indicates that the capacity for emotion increases with intelligence. Also, it is the old rather than the young that are more fearful. Fortunately, in the case of man, the structure of "civilization" cushions the adult's sensitivities and protects him from the causes of fear.

ANGER. Fear and anger are notoriously related, and it is impossible to discuss any of the causes of anger which would not comprise causes of fear as well. As in the case of fear, we can find a progressive increase in the range of effective stimuli which will cause anger as we move up the phylogenetic scale (from rat to dog to man). In the rat, for example, there is little need of such a term as "anger" in describing the animal's behavior. The rat is aggressive or he is not, showing the same pattern in different circumstances. The same is generally true of the dog, although occasionally his behavior resembles the primate's sulking. But with the chimpanzee, the peculiarly human patterns of temper tantrum and sulking occur frequently (Hebb & Thompson, 1968). Jane Goodall, who is well known for her natural observation studies, reports a temper tantrum which a mature chimpanzee exhibited (Mark & Ervin, 1970). The episode occurred when a large male climbed a tree 10 feet above her head and worked himself into a rage, screaming and hitting the trunk. About five minutes later, the chimpanzee climbed down, moved behind her, and after a short yell hit her on the head. Many other observations of rage among primates have also been made.

Hebb reports cases of male chimpanzees having temper tantrums when denied access to female chimpanzees in heat; particularly if the male is led to expect, by the caretaker's actions, that he will be admitted to the female's cage (Hebb & Thompson, 1968). One chimpanzee, Pan, had a fit at the sight of two experimenters taking a vaginal smear from a female in heat in another cage. Another, Mimi, was driven to rage by the chimpanzees in the next cage, who would wait until her back was turned and then spring at her screaming, apparently startling her. Kohler (1929) in his studies on primate behavior, noted that noisemaking and begging may be causes of anger for a chimpanzee just as for man.

At first glance, the chimpanzee may appear to be in a state of perpetual uproar when one considers his many angers and hostilities. Actually, this is not the case; most of the time he is no more angry or agitated than his caretaker. For instance, Jane Goodall (1965) reports that chimpanzees in the wild are very peaceful. The important point is that as one moves up the phylogenetic scale there is an increasing number of situations that will evoke anger.

Man is also born with the capacity to be angered by many situations; fortunately, his reactions are ordinarily kept in check by society. The emotion of anger in humans has a clear set of observable responses, sometimes noticeable in facial expressions. Other times it takes the form of approach behavior directed toward the infliction of psychological or bodily harm—aggression. We have already commented on man's propensity for aggression but luckily, the emotions of love are ordinarily prepotent over anger; this makes it possible for various societies to function in a harmonious way (Harlow, McGaugh, & Thompson, 1971).

The initial manifestations of anger become modified very early in life. Goodenough (1931) noted that expression of anger changed from temper tantrums and outbursts of uncontrolled motor activity with infants to the directed motor and language responses of the child by the age of two. The conditions leading to the arousal of anger in the very young are primarily physical: restrictive clothing, denial of desirable play activities, and confinement are all situations eliciting anger.

In the case of adults, an increasingly large number of situations will cause anger. The antecedent conditions of anger for adults usually involve psychological or social limitations in addition to physical. Hence, there is a wealth of data supporting the position that anger, as well as fear, has innate components and develops over a considerable period of time, probably through puberty. However, many specific angers and fears are learned or at least modified by our experiences.

"GHOST IN THE MACHINE." Arthur Koestler points out well the predicament of mankind. While man is the most intelligent and creative organism on earth, he is also the most emotional and susceptible to irrational fears and angers. Koestler argues, in The Ghost in the Machine (1967), that intelligence and emotion are two sides of the same coin, the result of the evolutionary development of a large brain. The first is responsible for the wonders of our technology and the splendor of our cathedrals, the second for the wars and riots that dominate the headlines.

His hypothesis, based on neurological evidence (see Chapter 2), suggests that the explosive growth of the human brain resulted in a faulty coordination between old and recent brain structures. Hence, a pathological split between emotion and reason has developed. In essence, the "ghost in the machine" refers to the relatively unchanged old parts of the brain that are essentially reptilian in nature. It causes our perception of reality to be constantly disturbed by emotional reactions, thereby affecting our ability to reason. Koestler puts this in simple terms: nature has let us down in allowing this pathology of the human mind.

Not all psychologists and other scientists would accept Koestler's controversial ideas; many would prefer a more social learning interpretation of the nature of man. Nevertheless, Koestler's theories are in accord with the findings on spontaneous fears and angers.

Frustration

A major area of human behavior of concern to psychologists are the emotional changes provoked by frustrating events. Frustration, the blocking of our goals, is part of the price human beings must pay for the privilege of living together in any society. It is difficult to imagine any society that could survive if its members freely satisfied their acquisitive motives by totally disregarding the rights of others.

A golf tournament or a beauty contest provide good examples of frustration in the making. Several contestants in both events are strongly motivated to win, but there can be only one winner in each case. All the other contestants are bound to be frustrated. If we watch the losers closely, we will see a variety of emotional effects. Some will display depression and for days afterward will have a difficult time becoming interested in other events. Even those who shrug off defeat and smilingly congratulate the winners will have some kind of emotional twinges such as disappointment.

REACTIONS TO FRUSTRATIONS. Frustrations, by definition, are unpleasant. They result in disagreeable emotional reactions which appear to be universal; they have been observed in many different societies. However, there are significant differences in the types of reactions that can be observed. Moreover, there are individual differences in the intensity of these responses which begin in childhood. In one experiment, an intelligence test was given to two groups of children, one judged to be well adjusted and the other to be poorly adjusted (Hutt, 1947). It was hypothesized that poorly adjusted children would be frustrated by going in the usual progression from easy to difficult items, the latter which they cannot answer, and thus receive lower scores. Therefore, the test was administered twice—once in the ordinary way ("frustrating condition") and once by mixing up the easy and difficult questions and returning to an easy one every time the child experienced a failure ("nonfrustration condition"). The well-adjusted children made almost the same scores both times. But, the poorly adjusted children made substantially lower scores on the "frustrating" test—indicating that their performance on the test was indeed affected by a lower threshold for frustration.

Frustration and aggression. When frustrated by some obstacle, men often fight back. Dollard et al. (1939) hypothesized that aggression is man's natural response to frustration. Originally they argued that every act of aggression was preceded by a frustration; the greater the degree of frustration, the greater the amount of aggression. However, it soon became apparent that aggression can occur for other reasons than frustration (to demonstrate power, for example). As already mentioned, some observers believe aggression is part of man's inborn nature.

In a well-known experiment by Barker, Dembo, and Lewin (1941), young children were allowed to play for a time with a set of attractive toys. A frustrating wire screen was then introduced, which prevented the children from reaching the toys. As expected, the children showed furious aggressive behavior by kicking the barrier and threatening to hit the experimenter.

In many cases, displaced aggression is more likely to occur than a direct attack on the obstacle. The employee who cannot safely yell at his boss may go home and bawl his wife out—using her as a scapegoat. Scapegoating sometimes accounts for prejudice displayed against other people, who are viewed as different. A prime example of using members of an ethnic group as scapegoats occurred under Hitler in Germany. He blamed the Jews for all of the economic problems and political tensions that the nation suffered before World War II. As we will see in Chapter 13, the frustration-aggression hypothesis has been used to explain racial prejudice.

Frustration and other emotional reactions. Another reaction to frustration is to repeat some reaction over and over again, in spite of the fact that it does not serve any useful purpose. This is called *stereotyped behavior.* Karsh (1970) gave rats food for pressing the correct bar, and both food and shock for pressing the incorrect bar. They showed a high degree of fixated or stereotyped behavior when the position of the correct bar was reversed from day to day. They continued to press the same bar day after day regardless of whether it was correct or not.

It is quite possible that the results obtained in an experiment such as this one may explain some persistent behavior we see in humans. Thumbsucking or bed-wetting in young children may have become fixated because punishment and repeated frustration in efforts to get rid of them have intensified the undesirable behaviors. The persistence of reading or mathematics difficulties among bright children may be partially explained as a result of errors stereotyped by early frustration.

Another type of emotional response that may occur as a consequence of frustration is *regression.* This is a return to more primitive modes of behavior which characterize a younger age. This can be seen when an older child seeks the affection bestowed upon him in childhood by behaving once again as he did when younger: i.e., crying and seeking parental caresses. Extreme cases of regression are sometimes found among the severely emotionally disturbed. This is illustrated in Figure 6–6. The young psychiatric patient makes every effort to look as she did as a child.

DEFENSES AGAINST FRUSTRATION. Frustration tends to make one's behavior more emotional. Since the resultant emotions are not pleasant, *defense mechanisms* are developed in order to alleviate the stress. The purpose of these mechanisms are to protect the individual's self-esteem and defend him against excessive anxiety when confronted with continuing frustrations. All the mechanisms have in common the quality of self-deception and are to be found in the everyday behavior of "normal" people. In Chapter 8 we will discuss defense mechanisms in greater detail.

SENSITIVITY TRAINING: HELP IN HANDLING OUR FRUSTRATIONS. The past decade has seen the development of a rather new approach to helping people better understand the emotions and frustrations of their fellow-man including their own. This approach has become known as *sensitivity training*. Essentially, this involves a group of people who interact together on many different levels over an extended period of time. These sensitivity groups, also known as *encounter groups*, emphasize the expression of feeling and attitudes not usually displayed in public. The group leader encourages the participants to explore their own feelings as well as those of the other group members. The purpose is to stimulate an exchange between members that is not inhibited by defensiveness and which achieves a maximum of openness and honesty.

Sensitivity training, or encounter, sessions have been used in various settings involving people of vastly different backgrounds. There are encounter sessions between youth and their elders, the advantaged and the disadvantaged, and so forth. In addition, it has been used in business and educational organizations in an attempt to help people work better together (Gunther, 1968).

Various encounter groups differ in the specific techniques that are employed. In some groups, members may interact primarily on a physical basis by touching one another without verbal communication. In other groups, participants may emphasize speaking openly to each other telling how they feel. We shall discuss a few of the more prominent techniques below.

The nude marathon. One of the more radical attempts in light of conventional mores to get people over their emotional inhibitions is the nude marathon. It was first suggested by Abraham Maslow (1965) in his book, *Eupsychian Management.* He speculated in the book on what would happen if groups took off their clothes. Maslow hypothesized that people would go away a lot freer, more spontaneous, and less defensive. People would not only get over their hangups about the imperfections of their bodies but would also become less defensive about expressing feelings.

The nude marathon is usually conducted at a motel or private home

FIGURE 6–6
A case of regression. The 17-year-old girl (A) was brought to a clinic because of her temper tantrums and in general, childish behavior such as giggling incessantly. In addition, (C) she had shaved her eyebrows, cut her hair, and begun to affect the facial expression and sitting posture of the picture (B) she found of herself as a five-year-old child.

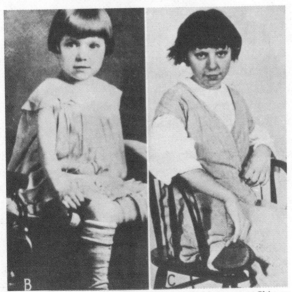

Courtesy Jules H. Masserman, Chicago

with a heated pool. The group ranges from 14 to 18 people and is balanced to include approximately half men and half women. Adults are carefully screened before admittance to the group; minors are excluded (Elliott, 1971). The participants' reactions to nudity fall into the following seven categories:

1. A sense of pleasure derived from the freedom to look at other persons' bodies and to be looked at.
2. A personal sense of comfort, exhilaration, and freedom.
3. The desire to touch and experience skin contact and a sense of being inhibited in this respect.
4. Pleasure arising from the sense of group closeness and the relaxed expressions on the faces of the other participants.
5. A sense of the naturalness of the nude condition, and a feeling of relief at not having reacted inappropriately.
6. The experience of being "high" or unable to sleep for the remainder of the night.
7. A sense of concern about one's physical body when comparing it with other members of the group.

Do people carry over their experiences to their life outside the group? There are no studies that give a clear-cut answer to this question. However, Paul Bindrim, a licensed psychologist who has led many nude encounters, reports that 50 percent of the people experience major changes in their lives (Elliott, 1971). They report a decrease in alienation, greater warmth, openness, and a greater degree of relatedness to other people.

The second-chance family. Dan Malamud (1971) describes a class program that has provided personal growth opportunities to a large number of students of all ages and backgrounds. The workshop is organized so that its members can create among themselves a second-chance family. Its explicit aim would be to provide new opportunities for the nourishment and development of the self which may not have been available in the actual childhood families.

After members become acquainted with each other, they form families of from six to ten members each which they work with throughout the course. Training exercises are introduced that focus on one or another aspect of how to be a good working family: how to share feelings, to confront and to give support in a constructive manner.

The Synanon Game. A unique type of encounter experience is provided in the *Synanon Game*. The techniques used are based on the premise: You are guilty of self-deceit until you either prove yourself innocent or confess (Enright, 1971). The purpose is to stimulate self-growth by obliterating any traces of resistance.

The Synanon Foundation is a residential situation with more than 1,000 full-time residents for whom it is a whole way of life. Many of these long-time members were habitual drug users who had become skilled liars, con men, and quite socially irresponsible. Their faults are attacked in a surgical fashion because the Synanon game players have absolutely no patience with resistance.

There are many other varieties of encounter groups too numerous to cite here. But it should be pointed out that some psychologists have become concerned about the sudden proliferation of encounter groups and the lack of training of some of the leaders. One of the dangers, they stress, is the possibility that an emotionally disturbed individual may be shocked into suicide or a severe mental illness when stripped of his psychological defenses. Therefore, it is important to determine the qualifications of encounter group leaders and to do follow-up studies on individual participants.

Only further research will determine how effective encounter groups are in helping people to better understand themselves, their emotional problems, and their relationships with one another. The long-term results will determine whether sensitivity training will survive as an institution or disappear as a passing fad.

Summary

The word motivation is one of the most popular words to psychologists and laymen alike. Motives answer the "why" of behavior and is what activates and directs the organism. Although, some motives may not be manifested directly through behavior, we generally infer motivation and its strength from observing an organism behave. Motives may be divided into three groups: survival, social, and self motives.

1. Survival motives are those directly affecting the survival of the individual and may be either physiological (hunger, thirst, sleep, elimination, and temperature regulation) or psychological (curiosity-exploration, manipulation, and need for stimulation).
2. The social motives (aggression, altruism, affiliation, and contact comfort) are those which depend upon interaction with others for their instigation or expression.
3. Self motives are those related to the development and maintenance of the concept of self.

Maslow's motivation hierarchy theory states that motives may be arranged from lower to higher ones and these correspond to an evolutionary level. In order of ranking, these are physiological, safety, love, esteem, and finally self-actualization needs. The lower the motive the more crucial it is for the organism's survival. One must satisfy lower motives before he can express or attend to the others.

A great many psychologists believe that many of our motivations remain hidden from consciousness. For a number of reasons (painful or traumatic experiences), ideas, wishes, and motives may be buried or repressed. However, our behavior is often dictated by these repressed impulses. Evidence for the existence of unconscious processes comes from clinical psychology, the phenomena of hypnosis, and laboratory studies.

Emotions are powerful physiological and psychological responses that influence perception, learning, and performance. The ability to respond emotionally is present at birth and does not have to be learned. Early emotional reactions consist of diffuse general excitement with no identifiable specific emotions (love, hate, and fear). With increasing age, specific emotional responses become differentiated. Two important emotions are fear and anger. In fear and anger, much evidence supports the position that innate components are present. However, many specific angers and fears are learned or modified by experience.

A major area of human behavior of concern to psychologists are emotional changes provoked by frustration. Frustrations result when we are blocked from reaching our goals. As a result, it is unpleasant and is often followed by aggression, stereotyped behavior in which the organism repeats a behavior over and over, regression or a return to more primitive modes of behavior, and the use of various defense mechanisms that involve self-deception.

The past decade has seen the development of a rather new approach to helping people better understand the emotions and frustrations of their fellowman. Sensitivity training or the use of encounter groups emphasize the expression of feelings and attitudes not usually displayed in public. Group members are encouraged to be honest with themselves and others as to how they feel. The method of group interaction may take the form of nude encounters (attempts to symbolically strip away inhibitions and free the person to be himself), the second-chance family (providing new opportunities for development and nourishment of the self not available in actual childhood families), and the Synanon games (interactions characterized by confrontation and attacking methods to break down resistance and defense). More research needs to be conducted on the effectiveness and dangers of these encounter group techniques.

References

Bakwin, H., & Bakwin, R. M. *Clinical management of behavior disorders in childhood.* Philadelphia: Saunders, 1966.

Barker, R. G., Dembo, T., & Lewin, K. Frustration and aggression: An experiment with young children. *University of Iowa Studies in Child Welfare,* **18,** No. 386, 1941.

Berkowitz, L., & Geen, R. G. Film violence and the cue properties of available targets. *Journal of Personality and Social Psychology,* 1966, **3,** 525–530.

Berkowitz, L., & LePage, A. Weapons as aggressive-eliciting stimuli. *Journal of Personality and Social Psychology,* 1967, **7,** 202–207.

Bexton, W. H., Heron, W., & Scott, T. H. Effects of decreased variation in the sensory environment. *Canadian Journal of Psychology,* 1954, **8,** 70–76.

Bruner, J. S., & Goodman, C. C. *Journal of Abnormal and Social Psychology,* 1947, **42,** 33–44.

Bryan, J. H., & Test, M. A. Models and helping: Naturalistic studies in aiding behavior. *Journal of Personality and Social Psychology*, 1969, **6**, 400–407.

Dollard, J. et al. *Frustration and aggression*. New Haven, Conn.: Yale University Press, 1939.

Elliott, J. The nude marathon. In L. Blank et al. (Eds.), *Confrontation: Encounters in self and personal awareness*. New York: Macmillan, 1971.

Enright, J. B. On the playing fields of synanon. In L. Blank et al. (Eds.), *Confrontation: Encounters in self and personal awareness*. New York: Macmillan, 1971.

Glucksberg, S., & King, L. J. Motivated forgetting mediated by implicit verbal chaining: A laboratory analog of repression. *Science*, 1967, **158**, 517–518.

Goodall, J. Chimpanzees of Combe Stream Reserve. In I. DeVore (Ed.), *Primate Behavior*. New York: Holt, Rinehart, & Winston, 1965.

Goodenough, F. L. *Anger in young children*. Minneapolis: University of Minnesota Press, 1931.

Goodenough, F. L. Expression of the emotions in a blind-deaf child. *Journal of Abnormal and Social Psychology*, 1932, **27**, 328–333.

Gunther, B. *Sense relaxation below your mind*. New York: Collier Books, 1968.

Hardy, K. R. An appetitional theory of sexual motivation. *Psychological Review*, 1964, **71**, 1–18.

Harlow, H. F. *Learning to love*. San Francisco: Albion Publishing Co., 1971.

Harlow, H. F., Blazek, N. C., & McClearn, G. E. Manipulatory motivation in the infant rhesus monkey. *Journal of Comparative and Physiological Psychology*, 1956, **49**, 444–448.

Harlow, H. F., McGaugh, J. L., & Thompson, R. F. *Psychology*. San Francisco: Albion Publishing Co., 1971.

Hebb, D. O. On the nature of fear. In Douglas K. Candland (Ed.), *Emotion: Bodily change*. New York: D. Van Nostrand Company, 1962.

Hebb, D. O., & Thompson, W. R. The social significance of animal studies. In G. Lindsey & E. Aronson (Eds.), *Handbook of Social Psychology*. Vol. 2. Reading, Mass.: Addison-Wesley Publishing Company, 1968.

Hutt, M. L. Consecutive and adaptive testing with the revised Stanford-Binet. *Journal of Consulting Psychology*, 1947, **11**, 93–103.

Karsh, E. B. Fixation produced by conflict. *Science*, 1970, **168**, 873–875.

Keys, A., Brozek, J., Heuschel, A., Mickelson, O., & Taylor, H. L. *The biology of human starvation*. Minneapolis: University of Minnesota Press, 1950.

Koestler, A. *The ghost in the machine*. New York: Macmillan, 1967.

Kohler, W. *The mentality of apes*. New York: Harcourt, Brace, 1929.

Lantz, B. Some dynamic aspects of success and failure. *Psychological Monographs*, 1945, **59**, 1.

Lowell, E. L. The effect of need for achievement on learning and speed of performance. *Journal of Psychology*, 1952, **33**, 31–40.

Malamud, D. I. The second-chance family: A medium for self-directed growth. In L. Blank et al. (Eds.), *Confrontation: Encounters in Self and Personal Awareness*. New York: Macmillan, 1971.

Mark, H. M., & Ervin, F. R. *Violence and the brain*. New York: Harper & Row, 1970.

Maslow, A. H. *Eupsychian management: a journal*. Homewood, Ill.: Dorsey, 1965.

McClelland, D. C. (Ed.). *Studies in motivation*. New York: Apple-Century-Crofts, 1955.

Miller, N. E., & Dollard, J. *Social learning and imitation*. New Haven, Conn.: Yale University Press, 1939.

Murray, E. J. *Motivation and emotion*. Englewood Cliffs, N.J.: Prentice-Hall, 1964.

Riccinti, H. N. Social and emotional behavior in infancy: Some developmental issues and problems. *Merrill-Palmer Quarterly*, 1968, **14**, 82–100.

Sarason, I. G. *Personality: An objective approach*. New York: Wiley, 1972.

Schachter, S. Obesity and eating. In M. Karlins (Ed.), *Psychology and society: Readings for general psychology*. New York: Wiley, 1971.

Sears, R. R. Initiation of the repression sequence by experienced failure. *Journal of Experimental Psychology*, 1937, **20**, 570–580.

Wispe, L. G., & Freshley, H. B. Race, sex, and helping behavior: The broken bag caper. *Journal of Personality and Social Psychology*, 1971, **17**(1), 59–65.

SECTION FIVE

Individuality and personality

W e, as human beings, are more than the sum total of our biological properties, perceptions, motivations, and emotions. One of our unique features, which sets us apart from other animals, is our ability to engage in intellectual and creative thinking. Just as we would all like to possess healthy emotions and fantastic memories, we all have strong desires to be intelligent and creative. These attributes have always occupied a central role in our thinking. But what exactly is intelligence and creativity? Chapter 7 will address itself to this question.

Following this chapter, we will begin to explore the many facets of personality in Chapter 8. The study of personality is that field most intimately associated with studying the whole person: you and me. This section will attempt to integrate and weave together many psychological principles into a global and comprehensive description of man. The focus of this approach is on our differences from one another: our uniqueness. Much emphasis will be given to theories of personality which attempt to explain and describe the individual's development, adjustment, survival, and motivations. As such, this section flows nicely from our earlier discussion of motivation. In addition, we will describe the characteristics of the normal healthy personality.

Unfortunately, personality does not always develop normally. Each year millions of people suffer from emotional problems that cause them and their friends much pain and misery. What causes mental illness? How can we recognize it? What can we do about it? These are all questions which Chapter 9 attempts to answer in its discussion of abnormal psychology.

219

7

Intelligence and creativity

O ne of the more familiar psychological terms to the general public is intelligence. For instance, you might have heard it said that John is not very bright or as intelligent as his brother Bill. Or that Mary is very intelligent because she gets outstanding grades in school. All of these statements imply that we not only know what intelligence is but that there exists individual differences.

However, intelligence is an abstract concept that is not easily defined even though it is used quite often. As we shall see, even psychologists do not agree entirely on the meaning of this concept and will define it in different ways.

Intelligence

Definitions of intelligence

Two general approaches have been used by psychologists in defining intelligence. If not altogether satisfactory, the first is simple, direct, and very practical. *Intelligence* is what intelligence tests measure. This type of definition is not as valueless as it sounds and must be interpreted in terms of the way intelligence tests are developed. The test constructor starts with the belief that we all have some ability to classify people according to their intelligence. In doing so, he relies partly on examples of what is generally considered to be clever or stupid behavior and partly on such external indices as school and job attainment. Unless there exists a fairly high correlation (degree of relationship between two variables) between a test and these criteria, we are not justified in calling it an intelligence test.

In general, we tend to have faith in intelligence tests because they have been found to work in predicting how well children will do in school or in selecting adults for particular types of vocational training. However, we also know that the value of the tests is limited because our predictions do not always work out. This seems to be especially true for various minority groups.

The second general definition is to define intelligence in abstract or theoretical terms. Examples of these are "Intelligence is the ability to think abstractly," or "Intelligence is the ability to solve problems" or, more broadly, "Intelligence is the ability to learn." But what do these impressive sounding phrases really mean? How do we decide whether one person is better able to think in abstract terms or solve problems better than someone else? And what is meant by ability to learn? Some people might learn to use drugs, but we would not necessarily consider this to be intelligent behavior. Although there seems to be some confusion over precisely how to define intelligence, there has been extensive use of such tests.

Intelligence tests

Intelligence testing began around the turn of the century when Alfred Binet, one of the great names in the history of psychology, was commissioned by the French government to devise some kind of test to determine which children were too dull to profit from ordinary schooling. He proceeded to construct the first systematic and successful test of intelligence, which serves as the direct ancestor of modern intelligence tests.

Binet made three critical assumptions which proved to be correct: (1) intelligence is complex and involves far more than simple sensory and motor abilities; (2) intelligence increases with age up to maturity; (3) a dull child would behave on tests like a normal child of a younger age.

After making these assumptions, Binet and his co-worker Simon proceeded to choose items to include in the test. In effect they were concerned with what bright students did that distinguished them from dull ones, other than those things which were the result of special training. When such items were found, they were used whether they looked like tests of intelligence or not. Binet handled the problem of validity by keeping only those items that older children did better on than their younger counterparts.

MENTAL AGE. Binet and Simon developed norms (average scores) with which any child's performance could be compared. Each item was assigned to an age level, namely the age at which a little over half of the children of a given age got the item correct. Once each item was assigned to an age level, each child could then be scored according to the age level of the items that he passed. His score was called his mental age (MA).

Thus the child who could pass the six-year tests but not those at the seven-year level was credited with a mental age of six years. The child of chronological age (CA) six who achieved an MA of six was regarded as having average intelligence. However, the child with an MA of six might be ten years old (CA) and, therefore, dull for his age, or he might be three years old (CA) and extremely bright. Consequently, the concept of mental age indicates the level of intelligence achieved, but without reference to chronological age it gives no indication of the brightness or dullness of the individual.

INTELLIGENCE QUOTIENT. Later it was suggested that an intelligence quotient (IQ) be used to serve as a convenient index of brightness. The IQ index expresses intelligence as a ratio of the mental age to the chronological age:

$$IQ = 100 \times \frac{\text{Mental age (MA)}}{\text{Chronological age (CA)}}$$

The 100 is used as a multiplier to remove the decimal point. This quotient shows the rate at which MA is increasing in relation to CA. Thus, a five-year-old child with an MA of six has an IQ of 120 while a ten-year-old child with an MA of nine has an IQ of 90. The first child would be a good risk for further education; the second child would be a poorer one. It should be noted that the brightness scale has about the same meaning from one age to another.

Now that we have discussed how Binet and Simon developed the first intelligence test we shall look at the best known and most widely used American tests of intelligence. These are known as individual tests be-cause the examiner tests only one person at a time. Many of the test items are presented orally, and the subject's answers are recorded verbatim.

THE STANFORD-BINET TEST. This test, so named because it was de-vised by psychologists at Stanford University following the procedures developed by Binet, has undergone three editions. The latest edition ap-peared in 1960 and incorporated the best items from the earlier scales (Terman & Merrill, 1960). By "best" items is meant those which have the greatest value in differentiating various age groups.

The wide variety of items of the Stanford-Binet test include measures of information and past learning, verbal ability, memory, perceptual-motor coordination, and logical reasoning. For example, at the sixth-year level the child must define at least six words, such as puddle, orange, and envelope; state the differences between a dog and a bird, slipper and boot; recognize parts that are missing in pictures of a shoe, wagon, and rabbit; count up to nine blocks; and trace the correct path through a maze.

Since the particular items a child is given on the Binet will depend on the range of his ability, no child will be administered all the items. The test has been developed to cover the years from two to adulthood, al-though it is no longer recommended for adults.

DISTRIBUTION OF IQs. Figure 7–1 shows the distribution of IQs in children for the population used in standardizing the Stanford-Binet. Nearly 3,000 youngsters constitute the standardization group; they serve as a reference population against which individual IQ scores on the Stanford-Binet may be compared. For example, a child who obtains an IQ of 100 is considered average because his performance equals the average of the standardization group. Similarly, individuals who ob-tain IQs of 50 and 150 are considered exceptional because a very small percentage of the reference group obtained such scores. Table 7–1 gives the adjectives commonly used to describe the various IQ levels along with a frequency distribution for those tested in the standardization group.

It is well to keep in mind, when interpreting the meanings of IQs, that this test was standardized on American-born white children who speak the same language and have similar general educational opportunities. Thus, it is extremely difficult to interpret the results of the test when it is given to children of different ethnic origin or subjects with little or no educational opportunity. We will return to this issue shortly.

FIGURE 7–1
A normal distribution of IQs. The distribution of IQs approximates
a normal distribution. The exact range of IQ scores, because of
statistical differences, varies from one test to another.

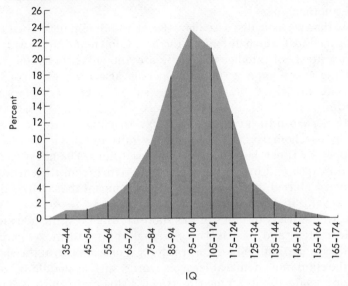

TABLE 7–1
Interpretation of intelligence quotients on the Stanford-Binet

IQ	Verbal description	Percent falling in each group (among 2904 subjects, ages 2 to 18)
140 and above	Very superior	1
120–139	Superior	11
110–119	High average	18
90–109	Average	46
80–89	Low average	15
70–79	Borderline	6
Below 70	Mentally retarded or defective	3
		100

Source: M. A. Merrill, "The Significance of IQ on the Revised Stanford-Binet
Scales," *Journal of Educational Psychology*, 1938, 26. Copyright 1938 by the American
Psychological Association. Reprinted by permission.

THE WECHSLER SCALES. The *Wechsler Adult Intelligence Scale*, commonly abbreviated *WAIS*, was designed by Dr. David Wechsler (1958) of
Bellevue Psychiatric Hospital to measure the intelligence of adults. Its
counterpart for children, the Wechsler Intelligence Scale for Children
(WISC), measures intelligence for persons from ages 5 to 15.

In contrast to the Sanford-Binet, the items on the Wechsler Scales are grouped according to different subtests rather than according to age level, although the items within a particular subtest are arranged in order of increasing difficulty. Thus, a person starts on the simpler items in each of the 11 subtests consisting of both the Verbal and Performance components listed below. He then continues to items of increasing difficulty until his limit for that subtest is reached. Next he goes on to another subtest. The 11 subtests on the WAIS (similar to the WISC) are:

Verbal subtests	*Performance subtests*
Information	Picture arrangement
General comprehension	Picture completion
Digit span	Block design
Arithmetic	Object assembly
Similarities	Digit symbol
Vocabulary	

The names of the tests in most cases suggest their content. The digit span subtest requires the subject to repeat to the tester a series of numerical digits that he recites aloud, such as 3–5–6–9–1, first in a forward direction, and then other series in a backward direction. His score depends upon the length of the series he gets correct. In the block design subtest, the subject must arrange blocks to match geometric designs. The object assembly subtest resembles a jigsaw puzzle; it calls for putting together parts to complete a figure such as an elephant, human profile, hand, or mannequin.

One great advantage of both Wechsler Scales is that separate IQ measures can be obtained from the verbal and performance subtests as well as an overall IQ score. This feature is helpful in testing people of foreign background or of cultural deprivation who have had little opportunity to develop their verbal abilities. In this way, an immigrant or a culturally deprived person who tests high on the performance subtests and low on the verbal ones probably had their verbal IQ affected by a language handicap that has nothing to do with intelligence. On the other hand, the IQ of a person who did poorly on the performance subtests may be depressed because of a physical handicap. Thus, the Wechsler Scales have a built-in warning device for identifying individuals who have handicaps which could affect IQ scores.

The method of computing IQs for the Wechsler Scales and the latest (1960) edition of the Stanford-Binet test is different from the old method. Instead of using MA and dividing by CA, which is appropriate only for children, a subject's performance is compared with other subjects in his own age group. His IQ is merely a function of his percentile rank in comparison with his peers. To illustrate, take the case of a child of six who obtains a WISC IQ of 79. This simply means (taken from the appropriate table in the WISC manual) that this particular child has done better on the test than about 10 percent of the six-year-olds in the standardization group, and less well than about 90 percent. However, interpretation of the IQ score remains the same.

GROUP TESTS. Individual intelligence tests such as the Stanford-Binet and Wechsler Scales are similar in that they are difficult to administer and can be given to only one person at a time. The usefulness of intelligence tests as predictors of performance in school and other situations became apparent almost immediately after the first Binet Scales appeared. As a result, a search began to find a way of applying the principles of the early Binet Scales on a large scale. Thus, *group tests* were invented and soon became indispensable.

Such tests, also referred to as paper and pencil tests, can be administered to many subjects at the same time. They can be given by almost anyone and can be scored quickly in contrast to the individual tests. Therefore, it is possible to test an entire population. The vast majority of American high school and college students, at some time in their lives, have taken a group test of mental ability.

Group tests, in general, are less reliable than individual tests because those who administer the former cannot be sure that each individual is in a fit condition to take the test at that time or that he is trying to do his best. However, if there is reason to believe that a student is not doing his best, an individual test is usually given.

The components of intelligence

For the most part, we have treated intelligence as a unitary global ability or a single trait because this is how it was originally conceived. When we think of Martha as being "bright" and Jim as being "dumb," we are applying unitary labels to a person. The fact that most of our tests of intelligence, such as the Stanford-Binet and Wechsler Scales, produce one overall score (IQ) further determines our thinking about intelligence in this manner. However, at an informal level, we know that Martha may be good at languages and poor at math while Jim may seem dull in school but bright about mechanical things. The question then arises, "Is there an overall intelligence, or does intelligence consist of a collection of specific abilities?"

Statistical methods have been devised which furnish a way of answering that question. These methods, known collectively as *factor analysis*, which have analyzed intelligence into their basic elements have suggested that intelligence is not one unitary ability but instead consists of different components. For our purposes, it is not necessary to know the mathematics of factor analysis but rather to understand the value of tests based on these statistical procedures.

TESTS BASED UPON FACTOR ANALYSIS. Spearman, an English psychologist, observed that similar results were obtained when the performance of various people on different intelligence tests were statistically compared. This finding suggested to him that the different tests and test items were measuring some common intellectual factor. He called this factor *general intelligence,* or *g.* Spearman claimed that many different skills, such as mechanical, musical, arithmetical, spelling, and many other abilities, are in part determined by this basic *g* factor. Many psychologists, however, take exception to this view that there is a single, general intelligence factor.

Spearman, in addition, postulated *specific intelligences*, or *ss*, which are also vital for each skill. Thus, a person's performance in mathematics would depend on the amount of *g* he possesses and his specific mathematical skills. His mechanical ability would also be the combined result of *g* and the mechanical *ss*.

Following Spearman, Thurstone developed a battery of intelligence tests with the aid of factor analysis. This battery is known as *Tests for Primary Abilities* (L. L. Thurstone, 1938), which we shall discuss as an example of factor analytic tests. He set out to find a few clusters of abilities that made up the composite tested by the regular intelligence tests. In other words, he was employing sophisticated statistical techniques to identify subtests or individual items that are very similar.

L. L. Thurstone (L. L. Thurstone & T. G. Thurstone, 1941) inferred from his elaborate analysis of some 60 different intelligence tests that there are seven independent factors or *primary abilities*. These seven factors are as follows:

1. *Verbal comprehension* (V). Ability to define and understand words. Vocabulary tests represent this factor.
2. *Word fluency* (W). This factor calls for the ability to think of words rapidly, as in contemporaneous speech or in solving crossword puzzles.
3. *Number* (N). This factor involves the ability to do simple arithmetic tests.
4. *Space* (S). Tests of this ability deal with visual form relationships, such as drawing a design from memory.
5. *Memory* (M). As the name implies, this factor involves the ability to memorize and recall material, such as pairs of items.
6. *Perception* (P). This factor is found in tests which measure the subject's ability to grasp visual details and to see similarities and differences among objects.
7. *Reasoning* (R). This ability is found in tests that call for finding general rules, principles or concepts in solving problems, such as in finding how a number series is constructed from a portion of that series.

With a battery of these tests, it is now possible to obtain a test profile for an individual which will indicate how well he performs on tests that demand each of the several abilities. More recently, the view of separate factors has been modified in the direction of Spearman's "two-factor" theory (Cronbach, 1970). The latest revision of The Primary Mentals Test (T. G. Thurstone, 1963) concludes that in addition to primary factors, there is a general factor of intelligence.

The important practical question remains whether or not primary abilities tests are better predictive instruments than general intelligence tests, such as the Stanford-Binet and Wechsler Scales. At present both appear to be equally valid in predicting scholastic achievement or job success. However, there is no doubt that factor analytic tests have provided a more complete map of intelligence and can be applied to aid people in making vocational decisions.

The extremes of intelligence

MENTAL RETARDATION. Intelligence tests were developed initially to discover those children who could not be expected to benefit from ordinary schooling. With the advent of the concept of IQ, it has become common to define *mental retardation,* or other commonly used terms such as *mental deficiency* and *mental subnormality,* in terms of individuals having scores below 70. However, it must be remembered that IQs vary continuously and, as a consequence, there is no sharp break between the subnormal and the normal. Many borderline cases exist. Furthermore, there are many kinds and degrees of mental subnormality. Calling all retarded children and adults by a common name, such as mentally deficient, can be misleading since they are not all alike.

The classification of anyone as subnormal depends to a great extent on his *social competence* in addition to his IQ. This criterion is particularly important in deciding which people who fall on the borderline are mentally retarded. It is possible that a person who is dull might function marginally in one environment but not in another. A man might be considered socially incompetent and, hence retarded, if he does not appear bright enough to hold down a job in the city. On the other hand, he may be able to live on a farm and do routine chores with supervision, and as a result, not be considered retarded.

CATEGORIES OF MENTAL RETARDATION. It is estimated that about 3 percent of the people in the United States are mentally deficient (Coleman, 1972). They fall into four categories: *mild* (IQ 52–67), *moderate* (IQ 36–51), *severe* (IQ 20–35), and *profound* (IQ below 20). The cutoff score of 67 and the range of the four categories is used because they reflect the amount of supervision required by retarded individuals.

The mild retardate's ultimate mental age is approximately 8–12 years. He is capable of some vocational adjustment and can profit from schooling up to the sixth-grade level. He can learn to read and write and may pass on jobs that require little ability in terms of intellect and social skills. His physical appearance is likely to be normal, although there is usually a minimal amount of retardation in his coordination and agility.

A moderately retarded individual reaches a mental age of from six to eight years as an adult. He can perform unskilled or semiskilled work with supervision which does not require much social awareness. He can learn functional academic skills to approximately the fourth-grade level by the late teens, if given special education. Physically, he often appears to be ungainly.

As adults, the severely retarded have mental ages ranging from three to six years. Although they can be trained in elementary health habits, they cannot learn functional academic skills. Some are able to perform simple unskilled tasks under complete supervision in a controlled environment. Poor motor coordination is prominent among these individuals who also may have various physical handicaps such as poor eyesight or poor hearing.

The profoundly retarded will only reach mental ages of three or below. The chances are that they will be unable to master the most simple tasks. If they talk at all, it will not be very well. They are totally incapable of self-maintenance and must have complete care and supervision. Sensory and motor handicaps, retarded growth, and various physiological anomalies are very common among the profoundly retarded.

CAUSES OF MENTAL RETARDATION. It was once believed that most mental deficiency was the result of faulty heredity because of defective genes. Deficient people tended to have deficient children. It is now clear that there are many specific causes of mental retardation besides the inheritance of a mental condition. Thus, we recognize two general classes of causes which bring about mental deficiency. The first class of causes is heredity—mental deficiency because of defective genes is called *primary mental retardation*. There is no obvious organic defect, no evidence of injury or disease that might have caused the intellectual deficit. The person seems quite normal in every respect except for low intelligence. In such cases there is often some record of mental deficiency occurring in other members of the family, which is why it is also called *familial mental retardation*.

The second general category consists of additional factors that may cause mental retardation by brain damage. Mental deficiency because of these conditions is called *secondary mental retardation*. There are many conditions which affect the developing fetus while in its mother's womb; excessive X-rays, certain deficiencies in the blood (which may be inherited), and illnesses of the mother.

In addition, birth injuries, dietary deficiencies, disorders of metabolism and endocrine gland functioning are secondary causes of mental retardation since they may damage or interfere with brain functioning. An example of mental deficiency associated with a malfunctioning endocrine gland is *cretinism*. The child is born either with a thyroid gland that does not secrete enough of the hormone thyroxin or without the gland itself. Without treatment, the child grows up as a retarded stocky dwarf with a large head. Fortunately, cretinism has become rather rare because the thyroid hormone can be replaced artificially. Figure 7–2 shows a mongoloid, discussed in Chapter 2, whose retardation is the result of an extra chromosome.

FIGURE 7–2
This mentally retarded little girl is a
victim of Down's syndrome. She has
the characteristic round head, slanting
eyes with thick eyelids, small mouth
with fissured lips, and short neck,
typical of mongoloids.

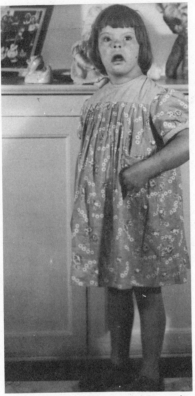

Courtesy of the State of Connecticut,
Southbury Training School

MANAGEMENT AND TRAINING. Many of the lower level mental deficients
have to be institutionalized because of the difficulty of physical care and
the emotional stress that their long-term presence at home would inflict
on the family. However, institutionalization as a permanent solution for
all mentally subnormals is certainly not necessary (Table 7–2).

For those classified as mildly or moderately retarded, there is no question about the benefits of special training techniques that have been devised. They can be taught to carry out many socially useful activities.
Whether the retardate becomes a community liability or asset depends
largely on whether he receives adequate supervision and the emotional
security and stability necessary to get along (Coleman, 1972).

While a great deal can be done for the mentally deficient in terms of

TABLE 7—2
Developmental characteristics of the mentally retarded

Degree of mental retardation	Preschool age 0–5 maturation and development	School age 6–20 training and education	Adult 21 and over social and vocational adequacy
Profound (IQ below 20)	Gross retardation; minimal capacity for functioning in sensori-motor areas; needs nursing care.	Some motor development present; may respond to minimal or limited training in self-help.	Some motor and speech development; may achieve very limited self-care; needs nursing care.
Severe (20–35)	Poor motor development; speech is minimal; generally unable to profit from training in self-help; little or no communication skills.	Can talk or learn to communicate; can be trained in elemental health habits; profits from systematic habit training.	May contribute partially to self-maintenance under complete supervision; can develop self-protection skills to a minimal useful level in controlled environment.
Moderate (36–52)	Can talk or learn to communicate; poor social awareness; fair motor development; profits from training in self-help; can be managed with moderate supervision.	Can profit from training in social and occupational skills; unlikely to progress beyond second-grade level in academic subjects; may learn to travel alone in familiar places.	May achieve self-maintenance in unskilled or semiskilled work under sheltered conditions; needs supervision and guidance when under mild social or economic stress.
Mild (53–69)	Can develop social and communication skills; minimal retardation in sensori-motor areas; often not distinguished from normal until later age.	Can learn academic skills up to approximately sixth-grade level by late teens. Can be guided toward social conformity.	Can usually achieve social and vocational skills adequate to minimum self-support but may need guidance and assistance when under unusual social or economic stress.

Source: Reprinted by permission of the President's Committee on Mental Retardation, Washington, D.C.

learning social habits, certain vocational skills with special training programs, this should not, however, be confused with raising their IQs. In many retarded individuals, a small increase in IQ comes with better social adjustment, but there is little reason to expect striking changes (Kirk, 1958).

THE MENTALLY GIFTED. At the opposite end of the scale from the mentally retarded are those who are mentally gifted. An unhappy error in the history of intelligence testing was made by psychologists who used the term *genius* to describe these individuals with very high IQs (usually above 140). This caused much confusion because it implied that everybody with high IQs would become famous by performing earthshaking intellectual accomplishments. Of course, most people with high IQs did not become famous, which then caused much unhappiness both to the parents and the alleged "genius" himself.

Now the term genius is most often used to refer to people who actually have performed tremendous intellectual feats while the adjective "gifted" is reserved for those children with very high IQs. Obviously, nurture (in the form of attention, concern, and opportunity) must be combined with nature (very high IQ) to produce a genius. Thus, a high level of motivation and appropriate environment are equally important.

Figure 7–3 shows a partial listing of men who have made great contributions to science, letters, art, philosophy, and politics, and also shows their estimated IQs (Cox, 1926). The IQs of these men of "genius" were based upon biographical data. From studies of these men and others like them we know that the popular conception of geniuses being "crazy" and stupid in everything but their narrow specialties is not true. Neither are they necessarily difficult to live with or lacking in common sense. These notions of genius simply do not correspond with the facts. The truth is that they do not have more idiosyncrasies than common people.

TERMAN'S STUDIES OF THE GIFTED. In the early 1920s, Lewis Terman and his associates began a long-range study of a group of gifted children in California (Terman & Oden, 1959). The group was chosen on the basis of IQs of 140 or above. About 1 out of every 100 children in the public schools have IQs that high. Fifteen hundred qualifying students were discovered, most coming from the homes of professional people and from those in higher business classes. The parental background and home environment probably contributed to the gifted children by way of both heredity and environment. The brighter parents are found in the superior occupational groups for the most part, and also tend to provide more stimulating environments for their children.

What did Terman find out about the gifted child? Many popular misconceptions were dispelled. One is that the very bright child is a weakling and unhealthy. He is neither and actually tends to be larger and medically superior to the average child. Second, he is better adjusted than the average child as revealed by personality tests and his social adaptibility. His school work was outstanding, as would be expected. Furthermore, marked unevenness in performance proved to be the exception rather than the rule. As the above findings point out, the very bright child is not the weakling and social misfit he is often characterized to be.

The follow-up studies on the gifted through their adult years are equally impressive. Educationally, they excelled on all accounts. About two-thirds went to college where they excelled in the number of honors they earned. By comparison with the average college graduate, six times as many of the gifted went to graduate school and received the Ph.D. degree. Occupationally, most found positions in professional and semiprofessional fields with many achieving international reputations. As a group, they were outstanding in publishing a great number of books, scientific, technical, and professional articles, and short stories and plays. The total record makes it unmistakably clear that a high IQ in childhood is correlated with outstanding achievement in adulthood. The relationship is not perfect, however, because some of the gifted wound up in undemanding jobs that did not tax their intellectual talents.

More recently, an interesting testing program has been carried out on

FIGURE 7-3

Estimated and corrected IQs of great men of the ages. The judgments were made by Cox, Terman, and Merrill on the basis of achievements of each man at the ages of 17 and 26. Many were "late bloomers" although all show evidence of great potential at an early age.

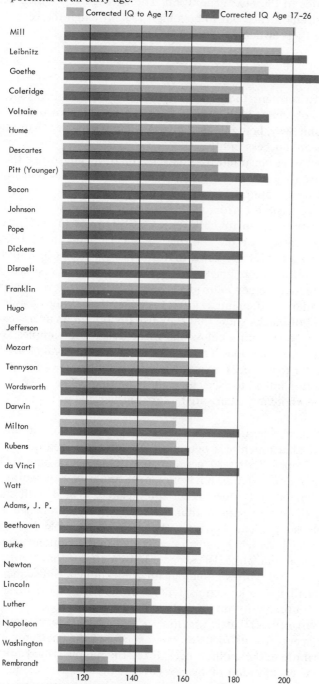

Corrected IQ to Age 17   Corrected IQ Age 17–26

Source: C. M. Cox, "Genetic Studies of Genius," vol. W. *The Early Mental Traits of Three Hundred Geniuses* (Stanford, Calif.: Stanford University, 1926).

the children of these intellectually gifted people to see if they passed on their abilities to the next generation. The average IQ of their offspring (1,571 children) turned out to be a high 133, although the scores ranged from mentally retarded to above 200 (Oden, 1968).

IQ and race

The early Terman studies contributed much to our beliefs about the desirability of having high IQs and the shame and disgrace at having low ones. In some way, being labeled gifted made you better than others because it meant success in life.

A number of ethnic minorities have begun to vocally attack the IQ concept because they feel that such tests are culturally biased against them and are being used unfairly in hiring and job promotion practices and in educational decisions (Williams, 1974). In the latter case, Dunn (1968) reports that ethnic minority children constitute over 50 percent of those enrolled in classes for the retarded in the United States. Likewise, a study by Mercer (1971) revealed that three times more Chicanos and two and one-half times more blacks in Riverside, California, tested at the borderline defective range (79 or less) than expected from their percentage in the population. Baughman (1971) reports that studies conducted on the IQ level of blacks show that they usually obtain an average of 85, or approximately 15 points below the mean for white samples. What do these findings mean? Does it mean that blacks and Chicanos are intellectually inferior to whites? Can we conclude from this type of evidence that genetic factors linked to race cause these findings? These are all difficult questions without any clear satisfactory answer. Let us explore this issue further.

THE GENETIC EXPLANATION. The genetic explanation of intelligence emphasizes that much of a person's IQ is due to hereditary factors. It has been proposed that 80 percent of intelligence is due to heredity while 20 percent is due to environment. Studies of behavioral genetics indicate that heredity does affect intelligence. Armed with this belief and other significant data, Arthur R. Jensen (1969) published a lengthy and highly sophisticated article "How Much Can We Boost IQ and Scholastic Achievement?" which created an uproar among social scientists and the public alike. In essence, Jensen claims that the IQ gap between blacks and whites is biologically determined. Subsequently, this position has become known as Jensenism and the emotional reactions to it have continued to run unabated.

THE ENVIRONMENTAL EXPLANATION. The nongenetic explanation of the IQ gap concentrates its focus on two aspects of the environment which may contribute to these differences. First, the impoverished cultural and educational background of blacks (detrimental effects of deprivation, malnutrition, teachers' low expectations, irrelevant curricula, poor teaching, and so on), and second, the limitations inherent in the tests and testing situation have been proposed as causing these differences. Both of these are highly related to one another.

For example, people raised in the slums or ghettos do not have the same cultural and educational opportunities as those who are financially more fortunate (see Chapter 13 on "Racism"). Moreover, many of the problems or questions used in intelligence tests presuppose a certain cultural background. If questions concern such things as organs, typewriters, skiing, and so on, then a person who grew up in a culture without these possessions is certainly going to be handicapped on such a test. Mercer (1972) states:

> What the IQ test measures, to a significant extent, is the child's exposure to Anglo culture. The more Anglicized a non-Anglo child is, the better he does on the IQ test. When we controlled for social background there were no differences in intelligence between Anglos and blacks, or between Anglos and Chicanos (p. 44).

Specifically, Jorgensen (1973) lists four critical factors which serve to undermine the IQ test and its administration.

First, the informational content of IQ tests do not take into account the black or Chicano language and vocabulary as a means of assessment. As a result, many minorities are mistakenly placed in classes for the mentally retarded because they are unfamiliar with the English language. Ramirez (1972) reports that when many Mexican-American children were retested in their native language there was an average 13 point gain in IQ. In addition, the vocabulary selected for inclusion on tests tends to be more familiar to whites than blacks or Chicanos.

Second, many of the items included on IQ tests tend to reflect a particular value orientation not held by ethnic minorities. Doing well on the test may only indicate that you prescribe to certain social values, rather than to measure intellective power. If you believe women are weak and need protection, that labor laws are just, and that paying taxes is good, then you may do well on this type of test.

Third, the social setting in which testing occurs affects the performance of subjects. Studies show that the more familiar minorities and lower class students are with the test setting, the better their performance becomes. Since disadvantaged groups are often unfamiliar with the testing situation, they can be unfairly penalized.

Fourth, the cognitive sets of the testers and subjects also affect the outcome of IQ testing. If the tester is operating under certain stereotypes or expectations about the intellectual inferiority of minorities, this may affect the performance of subjects. Rosenthal and Jacobson (1968) found that teachers, who were told that a group of randomly selected students were "intellectual bloomers" and another group not, somehow communicated these expectations to the students. As a result, those expected to do well showed IQ gains while the others did not. Furthermore, the cognitive sets of blacks undergoing IQ testing are not free of strong intense emotions. Such factors as resentment, anger, and alienation which blacks feel toward the tests must affect their performance.

From the foregoing discussion, one would have to conclude that IQ tests may not be valid for various ethnic minorities. However, there can be no doubt that intelligence possesses both a genetic and environmental component. We know that racial differences are strongly affected by environmental and cultural differences. To deny this would be absurd. At the present time, it is difficult to answer the nature-nurture question. A more fruitful channeling of our energies might be aimed at two particular areas.

First, it is obvious that ethnic minorities are raised in social conditions less conducive to optimal intellectual development than their white counterparts. Only when social conditions are equal among the races will we be able to deal with the nature-nurture question. Until then, let us devote our energies toward alleviating these unfair conditions. We can change social problems easier than our genes.

Second, all of us must become aware of the limitations and potential dangers of IQ testing. Decisions based on faulty IQ testing affect thousands of people each year by mistakenly placing incorrect labels on them. Intelligence testing should ideally maximize growth and development in the child. For many minority children as well as others the converse seems to be true. They tend to stigmatize and humiliate many school children with long-term effects by placing them into special classes for the retarded. To label minorities as mentally retarded on the basis of IQs is wrong. As mentioned previously, we must take into account the aspect of social competence. Mercer (1972) finds that many minorities with low IQ have high social competence. Furthermore, whites with low IQs do not have social competence, again suggesting testing bias.

Creativity

In the last section, we discussed certain issues which questioned the adequacy of the IQ concept for ethnic minorities. At another level, we can question whether conventional IQ tests might not measure too narrow a group of abilities and whether it might exclude other important attributes valued by our society. In this section, we shall consider research which deals with this important question. In particular, we shall examine research which shows one important intellectual ability, known as creativity, which is not measured to any substantial degree by conventional tests of intelligence. This state of affairs exists in spite of the great social significance of this type of mental ability.

Creativity is usually thought of as pertaining to the arts. Actually, creativity, or originality, can occur in any field of endeavor, whether one is a doctor, parent, football player, or scientist. Anyone who shows originality and the ability to integrate the elements of a given situation into a harmonious whole are leading creative lives. People who can do this typically manifest a general freedom from rigid thought patterns and an ability to keep looking at situations in fresh ways. A free-roving imagination is essential for obtaining an original idea. But, in order to be effective, the creative person must be able to systematically test and evaluate his idea before shaping it into final form.

Relationship to intelligence

Much current research on creativity has proceeded from a distinction that is made between divergent and convergent processes of thought. Convergent thought processes are those which end in a single, correct response. Standard intelligence tests such as the Stanford-Binet measure convergent thought because each of the items on the test has one correct answer. Divergent thought processes, on the other hand, do not culminate in a single, correct response but yield a variety of different types of appropriate responses. For example, a person may be asked to list all the various uses that he can think of for a rock. Excellence in divergent thinking is measured by the number of statistically unique or original responses given by the individual alone. Tests of creativity attempt to measure divergent thinking ability while conventional intelligence tests, as previously indicated, are concerned with convergent thinking.

A number of studies have reported that the relationship between scores on tests of creativity and measures of intelligence is low. One of the best known studies is reported by Getzels and Jackson (1962). They gave a series of divergent thinking tests to high school subjects who had high IQs. The tests of creativity included a word association test, unusual uses test, and tests of divergent thinking ability dealing with spatial, verbal, and mathematical materials. Getzels and Jackson concluded from the results that intelligence and creativity were relatively independent of each other. For instance, the correlations (mathematical procedures for measuring the degree of relationship between two variables) between the measures of divergent thinking and intelligence were low.

Wallach and Kogan (1965) performed a similar study in which they used a gamelike atmosphere when presenting measures of creativity. Their chief objective was to do away with testlike conditions which they argued interfere with the assessment of creativity. Test conditions normally have some degree of pressure associated with them, as most students will testify. They used five tests of divergent thinking ability in this game-like relaxed atmosphere and, in addition, ten measures of intelligence. Only small correlations were obtained between measures of intelligence and measures of divergent thinking; most of them were insignificant, meaning they could easily have occurred by chance. Thus, Wallach and Kogan's data clearly establish statistical independence between IQ scores and measures of creativity (Figure 7-4).

These results are supported in a later study by Wallach and Wing

FIGURE 7–4
Tests for creativity. Two projective tests which have been used to distinguish between creative and uncreative persons are the inkblot test and the drawing completion test. In order to describe the inkblots, a person must make "sense" or meaning out of an ambiguous configuration. The average person usually describes the inkblot in terms of its most obvious, simple features. On the other hand, the creative person is apt to perceive the figure in a novel, elegant manner which is personally satisfying to him. Similar results are obtained in the drawing completion test (right). The average person is satisfied with a drawing which is "meaningful," but simple (middle), while the creative person not only gives meaning but even emotion to his drawing (bottom).

Common Responses
1. Smudges
2. Dark clouds

Uncommon Responses
1. Magnetized iron filings
2. A small boy and his mother hurrying along on a dark windy day, trying to get home before it rains

Common Response
1. An ape
2. Modern painting of a gorilla

Uncommon Responses
1. A baboon looking at itself in a hand mirror
2. Rodin's "The Thinker" shouting "Eureka!"

Common Responses
1. An African voodoo dancer
2. A cactus plant

Uncommon Responses
1. Mexican in sombero running up a long hill to escape from rain clouds
2. A word written in Chinese

 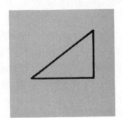 

Source: Frank Barron, "The Psychology of Imagination," *Scientific American*, 1958, 199(50). Reproduced by permission of Frank Barron.

(1969). Having once again established the independence of intelligence and creativity, they went on to explore the relationship between differences on each of the abilities and accomplishments in a variety of diversified extracurricular activities. The clearest and most dramatic finding which emerged is that differences in divergent thinking ability are positively related to talented accomplishments outside the classroom, while differences in intelligence are not. The talented accomplishments studied by Wallach and Wing were leadership, art, social service, literature, dramatic arts, music, and science.

It should be noted, however, in interpreting these results, that their sample consisted of highly intelligent college students. In short, high intelligence appears to be a necessary condition of creative work in many fields. One cannot be creative in many areas of science without the intellectual ability to master the highly complex mathematics involved or one cannot be creative in playwriting without well-developed verbal abilities. But, intelligence, in itself, is not a sufficient condition for creativity. Many highly intelligent people have been unable to make any major discoveries or novel contributions in their chosen line of work.

Personality characteristics of the creative

There is some evidence to suggest that subjects who are high in creativity have traits that differ from those who just have high IQs. Schaefer (1969) conducted a study in which he located creative adolescents within a larger group of students by using both tests and ratings from teachers. All students selected for the study were high in IQ, but they were divided into a higher creative and lower creative group on the basis of the test results and the ratings. Subjects in both groups were then given an adjective checklist in which they were asked to check those adjectives that they thought applied to themselves.

The creative students, in comparison to those not considered creative, perceived themselves as being original, spontaneous, rebellious, complicated, and somewhat introverted (withdrawn from other people). Other studies support these findings. For example, Barron (1965) reports that creative women mathematicians seem in general to be self-centered, individualistic, and original. And creative writers tend to be highly productive, to have many diversified interests, to be independent, and to put great value on self-worth.

In summation, the main theme running through most of these studies is that highly creative people tend to be somewhat dominant, forceful, self-centered, and innovative in ideas and action.

Are creative people strange?

There have been some well-known cases of creative individuals who behaved in peculiar fashions. The renowned artist Vincent van Gogh cut off his ear. Edgar Allen Poe was a narcotic addict who still managed to write great poetry, although many of the poems are somewhat frightening and now form the basis for horror movies.

If you should happen to wander through the corridors of an art school on any campus you are likely to see people whose dress and attire strike you as "far out." Undoubtedly there are some creative people who are mentally disturbed. But most likely only a few creative people are really mentally ill; others are people who may not care about the conventions of society. The viewpoint that bizarreness in behavior is necessarily a sign of creativeness is far-fetched and unreliable. Instead, creative people appear to have superior ego strength and a constructive way of handling difficult problems (Cross, Cattell, & Butcher, 1967).

Can anybody learn to be creative?

Many people would be surprised to know that creativity can be taught in accordance with the basic principles of learning. Not that everyone can become a creative genius—but it is probable that most people can be trained to engage in patterns of thinking that are potentially creative. Maltzman (1960) demonstrated in an experiment that if people are reinforced for creative responses in a preliminary training session, they show more creative behavior in a latter test situation. The study involved reinforcing college subjects by giving different answers to a word association test which was administered on six different occasions. Subjects were forced to go beyond common word associations and to produce more original responses. When these same subjects were later given a creativity test, they received higher scores than a group of control subjects who had not received such training.

One technique for creativity training is the use of "brainstorming," in which members of a group are presented with a problem and asked to think of all possible solutions to it, whether they seem practical or not. Everyone is encouraged to give free flight to his imagination and to get rid of his inhibitions, which often act to stifle creativity. This method has proven useful in generating many good solutions which on first glance appear absurd, but subsequently prove to be remarkably appropriate. If the size of a group becomes too large, however, much effort is wasted and ideas tend to be duplicated (Bouchard & Hare, 1970).

Gordon (1969) describes a very innovative technique that has been used to stimulate creative thinking. Students or employees are encouraged to think about problems from the viewpoint of another organism such as a lion or elephant. Needless to say, this does require one to have an active imagination in order to try to think in terms of some animal. However, at least one important idea was generated by this procedure. The space program was confronted with the problem of devising a way of sealing space suits because zippers are not airtight. During one of these ingenious brainstorming sessions, someone proposed having insects run up and down the zipper area manipulating little hatches. This idea actually led to a workable, airtight latch-zipper (Gordon, 1969).

Summary

Psychologists have used two definitions of intelligence: (1) intelligence is what intelligence tests measure, and (2) intelligence is the ability to think abstractly or solve problems. Although there is confusion about how to define it, intelligence occupies a pedestal in our society. Ever since Binet constructed the first systematic and successful test of intelligence, IQ tests have essentially patterned themselves after his assumptions: (1) intelligence is complex and involves more than simple sensory and motor abilities; (2) intelligence increases with age until maturity; and (3) a dull child will behave on tests like a normal child of a younger age. With the development of an intelligence test, the IQ became popularized.

Some of the better known individual tests are the Stanford-Binet and Wechsler Scales. Because individual intelligence tests are difficult to administer and can only be given to one person at a time, group tests have been developed. Their usefulness as predictors of school performance and other situations provided further impetus for their use.

Is there an overall intelligence, or does intelligence consist of a collection of specific abilities? Some psychologists believe that there is one common intellectual factor (g) and that other abilities are dependent on this basic g. Others take exception to this view and postulate specific intelligences (ss). Thurstone believes that seven independent factors or primary abilities exist: verbal comprehension, word fluency, number, space, memory, perception, and reasoning.

Mental retardation is the term given to individuals with subnormal IQs (70 or lower). In addition to IQ, determination of subnormal intelligence must take into account a person's social competence. About 3 percent of the people in the United States are mentally deficient and they fall into four categories: mild, moderate, severe, and profound. Besides inheritance (primary mental retardation), direct damage to the brain (secondary mental retardation) can cause retardation. Special training for the mildly or moderately retarded has shown benefits.

At the opposite end of the scale are the mentally gifted or those with IQs above 140. In Terman's studies of the gifted, he found them to be physically and medically superior to the average child, better adjusted, and producing outstanding schoolwork. Follow-up studies indicated two-thirds went on to college where they excelled educationally and professionally.

These early studies and the effectiveness of IQ tests predicting school performance did much to elevate IQ onto a pedestal. The fact that many more minorities are found in mentally retarded classes and that blacks, on the average, score 15 IQ points below white samples have led some to conclude that blacks and Chicanos are intellectually inferior to whites and that these differences are mainly inherited. These conclusions are difficult to come by because of our inability to control environmental factors. People raised in the slums and ghettos do not have the same cultural and educational opportunities as those who are financially more fortunate. Moreover, many of the problems or questions used in intelligence tests presuppose a certain cultural background. Inequities in the latter can be found in the informational content of tests, value orientations, social setting in which testing occurs, and the cognitive sets of the tester and subjects.

That environmental and hereditary factors contribute to intelligence cannot be denied. Rather than waste our time debating the nature-nurture issue, we should turn our attention to improving social conditions and guarding against improper uses of testing.

Studies of creativity indicate that other abilities besides intelligence may contribute to productivity. While intelligence tests tend to measure convergent thinking, creativity is divergent thinking. Although it is apparent that a minimal level of intelligence is needed in the creative process, there is a low correlation between intelligence and creativity.

In terms of personality, creative people tend to be somewhat dominant, forceful, self-centered, and innovative in ideas and action. The viewpoint that bizarreness in behavior is necessarily a sign of creativeness seems to be incorrect. Indeed, superior ego strength tends to characterize them. Some studies show that creativity can be taught to most people. One such technique for creativity training is the use of brainstorming.

References

Barron, F. The psychology of creativity. In *New Directions in Psychology*, New York: Holt, Rinehart & Winston, 1965.

Barron, F. The psychology of imagination. *Scientific American*, 1958, **199**(50), 150–156.

Baughman, E. E. *Black Americans.* New York: Academic Press, 1971.

Bouchard, T. J., Jr., & Hare, M. Size, performance and potential in brainstorming groups. *Journal of Applied Psychology*, 1970, **54**, 51–55.

Coleman, J. C. *Abnormal psychology and modern life.* Glenview, Ill.: Scott, Foresman, 1972.

Cox, C. M. Genetic studies of genius. Vol. W. In *The early mental traits of three hundred geniuses*. Stanford, Calif.: Stanford University Press, 1926.

Cronbach, L. J. *Essentials of psychological testing.* New York: Harper & Row, 1970.

Cross, P. G., Cattell, R. B., & Butcher, H. J. The personality patterns of creative artists. *British Journal of Educational Psychology*, 1967, **37**, 293–299.

Dunn, L. M. Special education for the mildly retarded—Is much of it justifiable? *Exceptional Children*, 1968, **35**, 5–22.

Getzels, J. W., & Jackson, P. W. *Creativity and intelligence.* New York: Wiley, 1962.

Gordon, W. J. Synetics. Quoted in G. A.

Davis, Training creativity in adolescence: A discussion of strategy. *Journal of Creative Behavior*, 1969, **3**, 95–104.

Jensen, A. R. How much can we boost IQ and scholastic achievement? *Harvard Educational Review*, 1969, **39**, 1–123.

Jorgensen, C. C. IQ tests and their educational supporters. *Journal of Social Issues*, 1973, **29**, 33–40.

Kirk, S. A. *Early education of the mentally retarded.* Urbana, Ill.: University of Illinois Press, 1958.

Maltzman, I. On the training of originality. *Psychological Reports*, 1960, **67**, 229–242.

Mercer, J. R. Institutionalized anglocentrism: Labeling mental retardates in the public schools. *Race, Change, and Urban Society*, 1971, **5**, 311–338.

Mercer, J. R. IQ: The lethal label. Reprinted from *Psychology Today* Magazine, **6**, 1972. Copyright © Ziff Davis Publishing Company.

Oden, M. H. The fulfillment of promise: 40-year follow-up of the Terman gifted group. *Genetic Psychology Monographs*, 1968, **77**, 3–93.

Ramirez, M. Social responsibilities and failure in psychology: The case of the Mexican-American. *Journal of Clinical Child Psychology*, 1972, **1**, 5–7.

Rosenthal, J., & Jacobson, L. *Pygmalion in the classroom.* New York: Holt, Rinehart & Winston, 1968.

Schaefer, C. W. The self-concept of creative adolescents. *Journal of Psychology,* 1969, **72,** 233–242.

Terman, L. M., & Merrill, M. A. *The Stanford-Binet Intelligence Scale.* Boston: Houghton Mifflin, 1960.

Terman, L. M., & Oden, M. H. *The gifted group at mid-life.* Stanford, Calif.: Stanford University Press, 1959.

Thurstone, L. L. Primary mental abilities. *Psychometric Monographs,* 1938 (Whole No. 1).

Thurstone, L. L., & Thurstone, T. G. Factorial studies of intelligence. *Psychometric Monographs,* No. 2, Chicago: University of Chicago Press, 1941.

Thurstone, T. G. *Examiner's manual: Primary mental abilities for grades 9–12.* Chicago: Science Research, 1963.

Wallach, M. A., & Kogan, N. *Modes of thinking in young children.* New York: Holt, Rinehart & Winston, 1965.

Wallach, M. A., & Wing, C. W., Jr. *The talented student.* New York: Holt, Rinehart & Winston, 1969.

Wechsler, D. *The measurement and appraisal of adult intelligence.* Baltimore: Williams and Wilkins, 1958.

Williams, R. L. Scientific racism and I.Q. *Psychology Today,* 1974, **7**(12), 32–41, 101.

8

Understanding personality

There are few words in the English language that have such a fascination for most of us as the term personality. Everyone uses the term in everyday conversation, but most of us would find it difficult to accurately define. Although the word is used in many ways, most of these popular meanings fall under one of two categories. The first usage equates the term to social skill or the impression we make on others. Schools which specialize in glamorizing the American female, use the term in this sense, when they offer courses in "personality training." Likewise, when we refer to a movie star as having charisma we are using a popular conception of personality.

The second usage considers the personality of the individual to inhere in the most outstanding impression he creates in others. Thus, we label John as having an "aggressive personality" while his sister is called submissive because she behaves in an opposite fashion. In each case, we are selecting an attribute or quality which is highly characteristic of the person and which presumably is an important part of the overall impression made on others. It is quite clear that there is an element of evaluation in both usages of the term. Personalities are often described as good or bad.

What is personality?

Personality as defined by psychologists

Personality may be viewed as the study of the characteristics and ways of behaving that determine an individual's unique adjustments to his environment. The fact that you play, sleep, and work does not define your personality: your personality is defined by how you play, how you sleep, and what is characteristically unique about your work patterns. Since no two people are exactly alike even in the case of identical twins, psychologists consider individuality and uniqueness to be essential to the definition. Apart from predictions about how you will behave in a particular situation, what you actually do because of your characteristics reflect your personality.

In attempting to understand the uniqueness of personalities, we obviously must make choices of what we wish to focus upon in our studies. To a certain extent, these choices are arbitrary, and they are made according to what we are most interested in knowing about a person. Many students of personality stress those qualities that affect an individual's ability to get along with other people and themselves; in other words, they emphasize personal adjustment. Others may choose to emphasize a person's attitudes, motives, or the characteristic way in which a person thinks about themselves, their self-concept.

No matter what personality characteristics are chosen for study, a personality characteristic must be relatively consistent over time. It does us little good, for example, to know that Mr. X was angry on Monday morning. He may have been facing a situation that would have made anybody angry, and this may have been the first time he was angry in a month. What is important to know about Mr. X is whether he is generally a hostile or angry person or whether he normally has a sunny, peaceful disposition. If he is usually serene and only occasionally angry under exasperating conditions, we characterize him as a serene person. By confining ourselves to those aspects of personality which are consistent and unique to a given individual, we simplify considerably the problem of studying personality.

The development of personality

A person's personality traits and their self-concept do not suddenly emerge but, possess a developmental history. Starting from the genetic endowment we inherit at birth, and continuing to death, personality is a developing system. Personality change and development appear to be more rapid early in life but personality growth never ceases. What can be said in general is that several factors seem all important in affecting personality growth. These are heredity, cultural values, and family influences.

Heredity

As is the case with most psychological processes, personality is not directly inherited. What is inherited is a predisposition to develop in certain ways, modified by environmental factors. Before much learning has taken place in infants, it is possible to see some of these predispositions at work. A look through the observation window of a hospital nursery will reveal what experienced nurses and parents already know— babies are born different. Some are extremely active, while others are sluggish. Some sleep a lot, while others cry and fuss. Some have eating problems and are colicky, while others experience no problems in eating. Moreover, some are big and strong, while others are born small and weak.

RECENT STUDIES. In this section, we shall focus on some recent studies on the role of genetics without attempting a comprehensive review which may be found elsewhere (McCleary & Meredith, 1966; Nash, 1970). Two aspects of human behavior considered important in the development of the child is the smiling and fear response. They are important because they may be seen as the beginnings of social behavior. Individual differences have been found in the precise age of onset of these behaviors and in the amount of smiling and the degree of the fear reaction to strangers. Both of these behaviors have been shown to be innate, and

Freedman (1965) reports a high degree of concordance in the character-istics of these responses in identical twins.

In the first month of life, the infant often shows a spontaneous smile for which there is no specific external stimulus. It is considered to be a reflexive motor reaction and not a true social smile because it is not di-rected toward anyone in particular. This usually disappears in the second month and is replaced by the first social smile elicited by an adult face. Interestingly, the smile can also be observed in blind children and is also accompanied by orienting movements of the eyes toward the person holding the child (Freedman, 1965), which is evidence of its innate basis.

Until about the age of five or six months, the infant smiles indiscrimi-nately at everyone, but at this age discrimination between familiar faces and unfamiliar ones begins to occur. Although children will continue to smile at familiar faces, they will now react fearfully to the latter. Both of these behavioral reactions appear to have the adaptive function of strengthening the bond between parent and child and preventing gen-eralization to strangers.

Other behavioral patterns also seem to have an innate basis for their development. Schaeffer and Emerson (1964) have found evidence sug-gesting this to be true for the avoidance of close physical contact on the part of some infants. As a result, the program of cuddling that normal infants receive does not take place. The pattern of noncuddling, a break-down of the normal mother-child interaction, has an early influence that is likely to produce widespread effects on the child's ability to form social relationships.

These findings are also related to the research of Gottesman (1966) which produced evidence from twin studies that personality characteris-tics such as "introversion-extroversion" may be influenced by heredity. An *introvert* may be defined as one who directs his interests and atten-tion upon himself, while an *extrovert* tends to focus attention upon his environment and other people. Gottesman believes these different personality types may be derived developmentally from the noncuddling syndrome.

Cultural forces

Anthropologists have been primarily responsible for investigating cross-cultural differences and their effects on personality development. While psychologists agree that psychological development is not an iso-lated phenomenon apart from sociocultural forces, most theories of personality are culturally exclusive. That is, they do not take into account cultural values as they affect the person's development. That cultural values are important was demonstrated in a series of studies conducted by Sue and Kirk (1972, 1973) on Chinese- and Japanese-Americans. These investigators found that Asian values stressing conformance, respect for authority, and submergence of individuality make many Asian-Americans appear less autonomous and more obedient than their Caucasian counterparts. In addition, Asian emphasis on restraint of strong feelings tends to make many Asian-Americans appear "inhibited and passive." It is unfortunate that negative Western labels are placed upon cultural values held by many minorities, for they indicate an intolerance of differing life-styles. Furthermore, such negative labeling tends to do much harm to the self-esteem of ethnic minorities as we shall see in Chapter 13 on "Racism."

Psychologists are just beginning to study in a systematic way the consequences of being born red, yellow, brown, or black in America. The emerging social consciousness of psychologists is helping to correct this situation. Additionally, we are beginning to realize that many subcultures within our own society need to be reemphasized. For example, socioeconomic class and urban-rural living possess important values that affect many people's development. We can also learn about how internal cultural and socioeconomic differences mold one's personality by listening to what people say who have experienced them. Claude Brown, in *Manchild in the Promised Land* (1965) writes about what it was like to grow up in Harlem:

> As a child, I remember being morbidly afraid. It was like a fever that never let up. Sometimes it became so intense that it would just swallow you. At other times, it just kept you shaking. But it was always there. I suppose, in Harlem, even now, the fear is still there (p. 413).
>
> . . . I always thought of Harlem as home, but I never thought of Harlem as being in the house. To me, home was the streets. I suppose there were many people who felt that. I wonder if mine was really so miserable, or if it was that there was so much happening out in the street that it made home seem a dull and dismal place (p. 415).

Family factors

Perhaps the most dominant force in the environment during your early years when personality is being molded is the socialization given you by your parents. Socialization is accomplished through specific training procedures and through the atmosphere they create in the home. These include such things as social poise, manners, cultural values about right and wrong, good and bad, and the inhibition of socially unwanted behaviors such as aggression and hatred of others (Janis, Mahl, Kagan, & Holt, 1969).

Two main variables emerge as major factors of parent-child interaction. The most important appears to be whether your parents use love-oriented, or physical methods of discipline to control your behavior. A second significant variable concerns the amount of parental control over the child, whether they tend to be strict or permissive in the home atmosphere they provide.

Schaefer (1961) summarized several studies which showed that these two factors account for much of the effects of parents on their children. He devised a model to account for the findings which consists of two dimensions of parent-child interaction: autonomy versus control and hostility versus love. The combination of love and autonomy produces an atmosphere that is free, democratic and accepting of the child. These characteristics of the parents are copied by the child through imitation and become part of his personality. He tends to become active, socially outgoing, creative, and successfully aggressive in obtaining what he wants.

The other combinations produce different atmospheres in the home and subsequently various personality types. For example, parents who control their children and are hostile may produce neurotics (see Chapter 9 on "Abnormal Personality"), who withdraw from difficult situations and their peers, are shy, have a low self-image, and feel guilty most of the time.

Parents who control and love their children may produce submissive, dependent, polite, obedient little boys and girls. These children are typically considered ideal by parents and teachers because they cause few problems. However, boys tend to see these children as sissies. These children demonstrate little creativity and comply with the wishes and demands of almost everyone.

The last combination of parent-child interaction, hostility and autonomy, produces children who tend to become delinquents. The child is maximally aggressive to all except the parents and is in constant trouble with the law. They have little respect for authority and are consistently hostile against the world which they feel is trying to keep them from expressing themselves. They are constantly frustrated because society will not permit them to do everything they want in contrast to the home situation.

Theories of personality development

Theories of personality are attempts by man to explain in a global and comprehensive way the reasons behind the actions of people. There are many theories which vary among themselves because they differ in subject matter and assumptions about the nature of man. Some theories emphasize motivation, others perception, and still others learning. The variations seem strongly related to the fact that we lack much of the scientific data about man to construct a universal theory of personality.

Lest we become bogged down in the multitude of theories, we have chosen to examine four representative theories: psychoanalysis, Carl Rogers' self-theory, behavior theory, and somatotype theory. It is important to keep in mind that these theories are all not universally accepted within the field of psychology.

Psychoanalytic theory

The first steps toward an understanding of personality came about through the astounding contributions of one man, Sigmund Freud (1856–1939). Freud (shown in Figure 8–1) was the first person to develop a broad theory of personality which not only helped us to see similarities and differences in people, but also attempted to explain why people acted in the ways they did.

Although originally trained in neurology, Freud was drawn into the areas of personality and psychotherapy when he discovered, in collaboration with a colleague, Joseph Breuer, that powerful mental processes may remain hidden from consciousness and cause many physical symptoms without an organic base. Both men were intrigued with the discovery that many *hysterical* patients (see Chapter 9) suffering from blindness, paralysis, and so on, could have their symptoms removed when they were forced to talk about traumatic events under hypnosis. The "talking under hypnosis" technique led to Freud's discovery of the unconscious and his subsequent development of psychoanalysis as a formulation of personality and psychotherapy.

Many academic psychologists have vehemently attacked and criticized psychoanalysis as being mystical and unscientific. However justified these criticisms may be, it cannot be denied that psychoanalysis has, and

FIGURE 8–1
Sigmund Freud

The Bettmann Archive, Inc.

still is, an important and pervasive force in the study of personality. Most theories of personality are either variants of psychoanalysis or direct reactions to its assumptions and concepts.

STRUCTURE. Freud believed that personality was composed of three separate but interacting systems. These three systems he called the id, ego, and superego.

Id. The id is the original system of the personality from which both the ego and superego develop. It consists of everything which the person has at the moment of birth and is the reservoir of psychic energy. The id furnishes all the power for the operation of the other two systems. It is said to operate under the pleasure principle in that it seeks for immediate gratification and is undisciplined. It knows not the constraints of the real world and is the inner world of subjective experience. The id cannot tolerate increases of energy because they are uncomfortable and, thus, must be discharged. Like an unsocialized child, it is selfish, undisciplined, and demanding. If left to its own devices, the id would surely destroy itself. For that reason, a guiding or policing agent is necessary for the survival of the organism.

Ego. The ego has frequently been called the "executive" of the personality because it controls the gateways to action. Since the organism requires appropriate transactions with the objective world of reality (environment) in order to survive, the ego makes realistic decisions and is said to operate under the reality principle. It is able to distinguish between the id's subjective world (fantasy, dreams, wishes, and so on) and the real one. The ego is an extension of the id and never independent of its influence. It aids the id in gratifying its impulses by selecting and deciding where and when this satisfaction will occur. For example, if a man was to be momentarily possessed by strong sexual urges, the id would demand immediate gratification. Since it does not distinguish external reality from subjective experiences, the id might have the man fantasize having sexual intercourse or, worse yet, sexually assault the first available female in public. However, both courses of action would not lead to desirable consequences. The first approach does not fulfill the sex drive and the latter action might bring legal charges of rape. As a result, the ego might prevent the expression of sexuality by having the man wait until he arrives home to his wife. Although it may seem like the ego has made an ethical value judgment, this is definitely not the case. The decision not to express the sex urge to the first available female was based upon realistic considerations (punishment by society) rather than moralistic ones. Moralistic considerations are the domain and function of the superego.

Superego. The superego is the moral-ethical arm of the personality and is the internalized values and ideals of society as interpreted to the child by parents. As a result, the superego is idealistic rather than realistic. Hall and Lindsey (1970) have identified three functions of the superego; (1) It attempts to inhibit the impulses of the id (sex, aggression, and so on) which it considers bad; (2) there is an attempt to persuade the ego to substitute moralistic goals for realistic ones; and (3) the superego strives for perfection. Two parts can be identified as conscience and ego ideal. When people engage in behaviors disapproved of by the conscience they are *punished* with feelings of *guilt*. However, if people engage in altruistic behaviors, they are *rewarded* with feelings of *pride* by the ego-ideal. These are the major techniques used by the superego to control the ego and thus, indirectly, the impulses of the id.

DYNAMICS. In order for the personality to operate and perform work, some source of energy must be available. The main source of energy, which is contained in the id, is the instincts.

Instincts. Freud believed that two large classes of instincts existed: the life instincts (Eros) and the death instincts (Thanatos). The life instincts consist of those forces concerned with self-preservation (need for water, food, oxygen, and so forth) and sex (libido). It was this latter instinct which has received the greatest attention.

In his latter years, Freud became convinced that another force in man existed which functioned antagonistically to the life instincts. The overall aim of this instinct is the biological death of the person. Unable to explain such things as murders, wars, and suicides, Freud formulated the idea of death instincts. The death instincts are manifested in many ways and one of the most important is that of aggression. Aggression is seen as turning self-destructive instincts toward other objects and persons.

All instincts have four major characteristics: source, energy, aim, and object. The *source* of instinct lies in the somatic processes of metabolism. For example, the life instincts are rooted in anabolism (building up activity of cell processes) and the death instincts are rooted in catabolism (breaking down processes). Instincts are psychic manifestations (thoughts, wishes, emotions, and so on) of these processes. The *energy* is characterized by a state of deprivation experienced as tension; that is, an instinct's energy indicates that the organism does not have something it needs. Therefore, the *aim* of all instincts is to reduce tension. Reduction of tension is accomplished by *objects* in the environment such as food, water, and sexual partners, which will satisfy or alleviate the tension. Since Freud stressed the importance of the libido, let us apply these characteristics to the sexual instincts.

The *source* of the sexual instincts is the cells differentiated for sexual reproduction such as the genitals. However, the mouth, breasts, anus, and other secondary sexual areas also serve to build sexual energy. The areas of the body which are sensitive to irritation and when manipulated in certain ways produce pleasurable sensations are called erogenous zones because they produce erotic wishes. As we shall see later, the sensitivity of body parts and their importance in psychological development depends on the person's psychosexual stage. The *energy* or driving force of the libido is caused by the sensitivity of the erogenous zones involved in sexual expression. This is felt as sexual tension. The *aim* of the instinct is the discharge of tension through intercourse, orgasm, or ejaculation. The *object* or appropriate goal may be the genitals of a member of the opposite sex.

Anxiety and defense mechanisms. Anytime that stress or stimulation becomes great the person reacts with anxiety. Freud identified three types of anxiety frequently experienced by people. *Reality anxiety* occurs when there is a threat to the person from the environment such as potential physical injury. *Neurotic anxiety* occurs when the individual fears that his impulses or instincts such as aggression will get out of control. *Moral anxiety* occurs when the person is punished by the superego for thinking or doing something considered immoral. In order for the ego to adequately deal with anxieties generated from the environment, the impulses of the id, or the guilt feelings of the superego, it is forced to use certain defense mechanisms to avoid or control these feelings.

All of us use various defense mechanisms in order to maintain psychological integration. However, they are considered pathological when they become the predominant means of coping with stress and interfere with our ability to handle the adjustive demands of everyday life. As pointed out by Hall and Lindsey (1970), all defense mechanisms have three things in common: (1) they distort reality, (2) they operate unconsciously, and (3) they protect the ego from anxiety. We shall now enumerate some of the more widely known and used defenses.

1. Repression. Freud believed that repression is basic to all other defense mechanisms and is generally the first to be used. It is a mechanism by which threatening or painful thoughts and memories are excluded from consciousness as a means of controlling dangerous or unacceptable desires, or protecting the individual from traumatic experiences. During World War II, a number of soldiers were treated for so-called cases of combat neuroses in which they were amnesic to battle experiences which were of a life-threatening nature. It was as if many soldiers found such memories too painful to remember and consequently repressed the incidents. A more complex example of repression was a case treated at a VA hospital by one of the authors.

> Mr. X was a 35-year-old veteran who complained of listlessness, occasional anxiety, and inability to taste the flavor of foods. In addition he complained of numbness throughout his body and a ringing in his ear which was correlated with certain mood states. For example, a high pitch meant he was angry and a low pitch meant he would become elated. A thorough neurological exam revealed no significant organic involvement. As a result, he was referred to the psychology service for further evaluation. Subsequent interviews revealed a strange obsession on the part of Mr. X. For the past two months he had found himself drawn to reading the obituary column of the local newspaper, although he found such activity extremely frightening. He could not make sense of his obsession nor could he ever recall anything related to his preoccupation. Under hypnosis, Mr. X was finally able to recall that as an adolescent he had broken into several cemeteries and would dig up graves as a prank. One night he broke into a coffin containing the body

of a young female and found himself sexually aroused by the body. The thought of being sexually attracted to a corpse was so abhorrent to him that he completely forgot and repressed the entire memory from consciousness. However, his repressive mechanisms were beginning to fail him as seen by his current symptoms.

2. Projection. Projection is a defensive reaction in which unacceptable thoughts or impulses are placed upon others, or a person's shortcomings and mistakes are attributed to others. For example, "Ma, he's making eyes at me" can be substituted for "I am making eyes at him." Extreme cases of projecting unacceptable impulses onto others is often seen in the case of latent homosexuals. The latent homosexual is often an individual who finds these impulses unacceptable to himself and will project them onto someone else; that is, he may believe that the male stranger riding in the elevator with him is trying to pick him up, when in reality these are homosexual feelings which he possesses. Projection is also frequently at work when we blame others for our own failures. In extreme cases, the individual may begin to believe that some force is out to get him. This is the typical defensive maneuver of the paranoid as we shall see in the next chapter.

3. Rationalization. This is a common defense mechanism in which we give socially acceptable and logical reasons for our behavior which are not really true. This is illustrated by the student who explains reactions to a flunked test in the following manner. "I'm not interested in the course and don't really need it to graduate. Besides, I find the teacher really dull." This student is making it seem quite plausible and rational that he flunked. He has not mentioned the possibility that he could not pass the course or simply was afraid that it would be too difficult and did not try.

4. Reaction formation. This is a reaction in which dangerous impulses are repressed and converted to their direct opposite such as feelings of hate to love, sexual desires to rigid morality, and pessimism to optimism. The extremely overprotective mother who is afraid to let her five-year-old son out of the house and into the backyard may actually be masking her resentment and hostility toward the unwanted child which has tied her down for the past five years. Because mothers are supposed to love their children, she cannot admit to these feelings and converts them to the opposite by showering her son with superficial love and attention.

5. Displacement. In displacement, there is a straightforward substitution of one goal or object for another. Often displacement involves unpleasant emotions such as anger or fear. Below is an example.

> John came home from school in a rage. He had been bawled out by his football coach for not going all out in football practice which he felt was unjust because of his many bruises. When he returns home that evening he begins to yell and pick at his younger brother for no apparent reason.

John has vented his anger and rage on a less threatening object, his younger and smaller brother. Although it is unfair to his brother, it is much safer than telling off his coach. As we shall see in Chapter 12, minority groups are often used as scapegoats for the anger and frustrations of other people.

6. Compensation. Many individuals develop certain attitudes, interests, skills, or talents to overcome their deficiencies in other areas. Such may be the case of a physically handicapped person who becomes a great chess master or the aspiring young actress that does not have the talents to make it in Hollywood and becomes a leading commercial artist.

7. Regression. As mentioned in Chapter 6, regression constitutes a retreat to an earlier stage of development and the adoption of less mature types of behavior.

8. Sublimation. According to Freud, sublimation is a form of displacement of instinctual energy from the id into higher social and cultural achievements. It was his belief that sublimation is the most productive of the defense mechanisms and has led to many artistic creations enjoyed by our society and has produced a social organization from which man now lives.

Psychosexual stages of development. Freud was one of the first theorists to emphasize the importance of childhood experiences on the later development of personality. Indeed, he has stated that "The child is father to the man," implying that the basic personality is formed during the first five years of life. He postulated five stages of development which everyone experiences. Each of these stages is organized around a certain zone of the body (erogenous zones) in which the instincts are expressed: oral, anal, phallic, latency, and genital.

1. Oral stage. During the first year of development, called the oral stage, the infant's chief pleasures are derived from such experiences as sucking on the nipple and consuming milk and food. Freud believed that the mouth was the first response mechanism to deal with the outside world. He assumed that the way the infant's oral needs are met sets the stage for later adult personality characteristics. Presumably, if the breast is readily available, the infant is likely to develop trusting and optimistic attitudes. However, if milk is long in coming or delayed, then the infant may develop a pessimistic outlook and lack of trust.

In the latter instances, an infant may show oral-incorporative characteristics such as greed, tenacity, and possessiveness, or he may develop oral-aggressive traits, exhibited in sarcasm, gossip, plus other forms of verbal aggressiveness. On the other hand, an infant who has satisfying oral experiences may show oral optimism, as indicated by his trust of others and expectations of favorable outcomes in the future.

2. Anal stage. This second stage of personality development occurs around the second year of life for the child when he is attempting to gain control over bowel movements. Because parents attempt to teach the

child control over previously involuntary eliminative processes, the child has his first experience with discipline and authority. The actual process of toilet training and the child's reactions can set the stage for later adult personality development. If the mother is excessively strict and repressive, the child may react in one of two ways: the child may defy the mother by holding back the feces or comply anxiously for fear of punishment. If the former approach is used by the child, he will develop an anal-retentive character marked by future traits of obstinancy, meticulousness, and stinginess. If the latter reaction is used, then the child would develop an anal-expulsive character marked by hostility, anger, and destructiveness.

3. Phallic stage. The third, or phallic, stage of development occurs between the ages of three and six. At this time the child discovers pleasures associated with its genitalia and develops such behaviors as stroking, rocking, and various forms of masturbation. This stage is characterized by the *Oedipus* and *Electra* complexes for the boy and girl, respectively. These two terms were taken from the ancient Greek tragedy which symbolized the son's and daughter's sexual attraction to the opposite-sexed parent, and resentment and hostility toward the same-sexed parent. Unresolved problems at this stage are alleged to result in inappropriate sex roles. The resolution of the Oedipal complex for the boy occurs when he experiences *castration anxiety* or the fear that his rival, in this case the father, will castrate him. As a result, the son identifies with the father to remove the anxiety and at the same time vicariously enjoys the mother. For the girl, the Electra complex is resolved when she identifies with the mother. However, the girl believes that she has already been castrated by the mother and develops penis envy. She desires the penis of the father but fears further retaliation by her mother and thus vicariously obtains the father's penis through identifying with the mother.

In traditional theory, the phallic stage is followed by the *latency stage* during which sexual interests are submerged in favor of other activities and then by the *genital stage*, in which the individual achieves independence and mature relationships with the opposite sex. Although there have been many experimental studies designed to test hypotheses regarding the various stages, the research evidence is not conclusive. For the interested reader, there is a review by Hilgard (1968) of the recent literature concerning research on psychoanalysis.

Conclusions

In summary, we see that psychoanalytic theory is both a conflict and tension reduction model of personality. It is a conflict model in that Freud assumes opposing tendencies in man: life versus death instincts, id versus ego, ego versus superego, and id versus superego. It is a tension reduction model because the aim of instincts is to remove tension and return man to a quiescent state of equilibrium, or balance. In addition, psychoanalytic theory is characterized by the importance of past influences on present behavior and the intricate workings of the unconscious.

As the founder of psychoanalysis, Freud attracted many followers who became disciples of his. But because many of these people were quite bright and independent thinkers of their own, some disagreed with Freud's ideas causing animosity between them and Freud. As a result, many of his former disciples broke away and formed separate schools of personality and psychotherapy. For example, Alfred Adler formed what is called individual psychology in which he stressed the importance of purposive goal-directed behavior, striving for superiority and man's innate concern with social interest (Ansbacher & Rowena, 1964); Carl Jung founded the theory called analytical psychology in which he de-emphasized the importance of sex, sees man as more goal directed, and believed that man possesses inherited racial memories; Otto Rank felt that the trauma of birth in which the infant is separated from the mother's womb is all important in determining behavior; Karen Horney was one of the few theorists to stress the importance of social factors in the development of personality. Although forming their individual theories, all of these psychologists were influenced by Freud's thinking. Members of this latter group have oftentimes been referred to as neo-Freudians.

Carl Rogers' self-theory

As we have seen, the Freudian view of personality places a strong emphasis on the unconscious processes in understanding the person's behavior. To a great extent, man is viewed as largely controlled by his unconscious motives and the various defense mechanisms which are placed in operation. The importance of man's conscious experiences is believed by psychoanalysts to be minimal against the power of the unconscious. A number of theorists have taken issue with this view and have developed a concept of man which attaches far greater importance to man's conscious experiences, particularly his conscious experience of himself. As a result, these theorists have used the concept of *self* as critical and focal in personality.

Carl Rogers, an American psychologist, is foremost among this group (Figure 8–2). His concern for the welfare of man and his deep conviction that humanity is positive, forward moving, trustworthy, and ultimately good is reflected in his theory of personality. Rogers believes that the human organism has an innate tendency toward *self-actualization* in that man is not only motivated to meet his biological needs but to grow, maintain, and enhance the self.

THE ACTUALIZING TENDENCY. Rogers calls the energizing force in man the actualizing tendency. Specifically, self-actualization may be defined as the organism's push to become what its inherent potentialities meant it to be. As Maddi (1968) points out, the actualizing tendency is under-

FIGURE 8–2
Carl Rogers

Courtesy of John T. Wood

stood in terms of fulfilling a grand design or a genetic blueprint. It is the thrust of life that pushes man forward and is manifested in many ways such as curiosity, creativity, and the joy of discovery. As a result, we can see that the actualizing tendency is a forward-moving force that involves tension increase rather than reduction.

The psychological manifestation of this force has been called self-actualization because it involves the self. The self is that part of us which forms the "I" or "me" and our perceptions of how they relate to others, various aspects of life, and the values we place on them. In other words, the self-concept can be said to consist of how you view yourself and how you think others see you. Additionally two other learned needs affect our self-concept: the *need for positive regard* and the *need for positive self-regard*. The need for positive regard is our satisfaction at receiving support and approval from others, while the latter need refers to our own approval or disapproval of ourselves. Thus, we are affected and sensitive to the attitudes and opinions of other people. However, our need for positive self-regard will make it probable that our actualizing tendencies will favor the development of a consistent self-concept. The self-concept defines the ways in which our actualizing tendency will be expressed.

DISHARMONY BETWEEN THE ACTUALIZING TENDENCY AND THE SELF-CONCEPT. If we are to become fully functioning persons, then our self-concepts and inherent potentialities must be consistent with one another. Rogers believes that if man is allowed to grow and develop freely in an unencumbered manner, the result will be a self-actualized person. However, if society has not provided a "good" atmosphere for man to develop within, then it is possible for discrepancies to exist between the actualizing tendency and the self-concept. In other words, since the self-concept is socially determined, it is possible that a distorted or repressive form of environment will create a self-concept different from what the person was meant to be as expressed through the actualizing tendency.

Rogers believes that the disharmony between the two is caused by what he calls *conditional positive regard;* that is, significant others in the individual's life accept some, but not all of the person's actions, feelings, and thoughts. The person's self-concept is thus defined as only those actions and attitudes approved by others while other expressions of behavior are considered unworthy. The person has developed *conditions of worth* which lead to defensive maneuvers such as denial and distortion. These tend to prevent people from actualizing their potentials and leads to a crippling life-style. A state of *incongruence* is said to exist between your potentialities and your self-concept.

The consequences of incongruence can be avoided if significant others (parents, friends, and so on) in your environment have given you the opportunity to experience *unconditional positive regard.* Rogers feels that it is important for parents to provide an atmosphere of love and valuing of the child that communicates respect for the person regardless of the child's actions or thoughts. An atmosphere of unconditional positive regard means that the child will evolve into a fully functioning person who experiences harmony between the actualizing tendency which is innately determined and the self-concept. We will have more to say about the characteristics of the fully functioning person later in this chapter.

CONCLUSIONS. Rogers' theory of personality is very different from that presented by Freud. First, his humanistic view of man is more optimistic in that the individual is seen as having more control over his own destiny and possesses innate potential for health. Second, he stresses man's consciousness as opposed to Freud's emphasis on the unconscious. Third, he views man as basically "good" who develops abnormally only when society fails to present an atmosphere conducive to the innate growth of the individual. Rogers sees the behavior of an individual as very much related to his self-concept. If people perceive themselves as inadequate, they will act inadequate. If they perceive themselves as capable and worthy, they will act accordingly and expect others to perceive them in this way.

Behaviorism

Another powerful force in the conceptualization of personality and psychotherapy has been the advent of behaviorism on the American scene. In Chapter 5, we described two types of learning: classical and operant conditioning. We also described how behavior could be shaped, modified, and extinguished through the use of various learning principles such as positive and negative reinforcement, punishment, extinction, spontaneous recovery, shaping, and schedules of reinforcement. However, to say that behaviorists have formulated a cohesive theory of personality would be incorrect. What we see is a body of learning principles which can be used to explain, control, and predict man's behavior. Since behaviorists believe that personality is rooted in behavior, they feel that they have the essential tools to understand man's behavior. Rather than repeating that which was discussed in Chapter 5, we will only attempt to point out some general views held by many behaviorists.

Behaviorists tend to study *overt behavior* and to avoid speculating about internal intrapsychic events. For that reason, they tend to downgrade the importance of concepts such as the unconscious and self-concept in favor of studying observable and quantifiable behavior. This approach is quite antagonistic to that of psychoanalysis and Rogers' self-theory. Among the more outspoken behaviorists that hold to this extreme position is B. F. Skinner who believes that speculating about the existence of an "inner man" and self is fruitless. Since man behaves according to well-known principles of learning, the domain of psychology should be the study of behavior. Man's behavior is shaped by his environment through the rewards and punishments that he experiences.

The popularity of behavior theory in the United States is due largely to major breakthroughs in the successful treatment of abnormal behavior. Reasoning that most behavior is learned through well-known principles of learning, regardless of whether they are labeled as normal or abnormal, many psychologists have successfully applied principles of learning to the "cure" of psychopathology. The use of these techniques, based on learning concepts, have been given the term *behavior modification*. In the next chapter, we shall see how behavior modification has been used in the treatment of behavior disorders.

Sheldon's somatotype theory of personality

For the man in the street, physical characteristics of his fellowman provide an insight into different aspects of his personality. Fat people are considered to be jolly and lazy while lean individuals are shy and morose. However, most American psychologists have resisted the possibility of an intimate association between body and behavior because of the strong belief in environmentalism. In fact, psychologists have largely neglected the study of physical characteristics with the exception of the unique contribution of William Sheldon.

BODY-TEMPERAMENT PRINCIPLE. In its most elementary form, Sheldon has proposed a theory which states that there are three main body types corresponding to an equal number of temperaments.

The somatotype (body type) of the person is the patterning of the primary components of physique as expressed by three numerals derived from some 17 measures. A complete description of the process of measuring the male body is contained in Sheldon et al., *Atlas of Men* (1954), which included representative somatotype photographs of over 1,000 men (Figure 8–3).

In obtaining an overall score for an individual, the first of the numerals always refers to endomorphy, the second to mesomorphy, and the third to ectomorphy. The numerals range from 1 to 7 with 1 representing the absolute minimum of the component and 7 the highest possible amount. Thus an individual with 1-1-7 is extremely high in ectomorphy and very low in endomorphy and mesomorphy. An individual rated 6-1-4

FIGURE 8–3
These drawings show Sheldon's three somatotypes: endomorphy (7-1-1), mesomorphy (1-7-1), and ectomorphy (1-1-7). A balanced physique (4-4-4) is also shown.

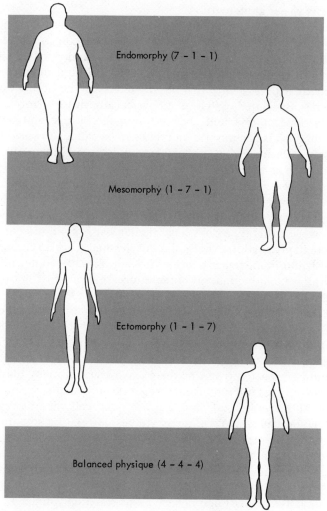

Endomorphy (7 - 1 - 1)

Mesomorphy (1 - 7 - 1)

Ectomorphy (1 - 1 - 7)

Balanced physique (4 - 4 - 4)

Source: Sheldon, 1954.

is high in endomorphy, markedly deficient in mesomorphy, and about average in ectomorphy. Although most people are a combination of all three, each type and accompanying behavior will be described as a pure type in order to draw a clear picture. Why don't you rate yourself and figure out whether you match the following descriptions?

Endomorph-viscerotonia. This individual is characterized by softness, fatness, and a rounded body. Consistent with this softness and fatty quality is an underdeveloped bone and muscle structure. Such an individual has a low specific gravity and floats quite high in water. The viscerotonia temperament (traits are rated on scales from 1 to 7 like somatotype components) is characterized by love of physical comfort, love of eating, relaxation in posture and movement, and slow reactions. In addition, they are very sociable, even-tempered and are generally easy persons to get along with.

Mesomorph-somatotonia. Does the reader know anybody who is all muscle, bone, and very powerful? This type of person usually has the body build of a wrestler or football player. The mesomorph body is capable of absorbing and administering great physical punishment because of its strength. A person with this physique has a somatotonia temperament which is associated with love of physical adventure, vigorous physical activity, love of risk and chance, physical courage and boldness. The individual is also aggressive and tends to be callous toward the feelings of others. Desire for action, power and domination constitutes the life-style of such an individual.

Ectomorph-cerebrotonia. The ectomorph is usually thin, fragile, and characterized by flatness of the chest and underdeveloped muscles. The physique is poorly equipped for competitive and persistent physical action. However, this type does have the largest brain and central nervous system in proportion to body size. An elevated score on cerebrotonia implies restraint in movement, love of privacy, fear of people, and aloofness. Overall, this individual gives the impression of being an introvert and a loner.

THE RELATION OF PHYSIQUE TO BEHAVIOR (PERSONALITY). Great caution must be used in evaluating Sheldon's theory of personality. All of us know of individuals who on the basis of body type would fit into one of these categories but possess completely different temperaments from what would be expected from the theory. We know of many big, powerful athletes who are both intelligent and gentle individuals. It remains for us to look at the empirical data and see how well they fit Sheldon's theory. Sheldon has conducted many studies on relating somatotype to personality, as summarized in Sarason (1972). In his best known study, he related physique and temperament among 200 white male subjects who were willing and able to participate over a long period of time. The results of his work were even more satisfactory than he had hoped; the relationship between body and behavior was startlingly high.

Whether body build determines personality characteristics has always been a topic of debate among laymen and scientists alike. More recently, Harry Edwards (1973) has pointed out how black physical traits have been used to perpetuate notions of intellectual inferiority among black Americans. Additionally, many social scientists believe that the correlation between physical and personality characteristics are learned in our society. For example, a father who has a big, strong son will encourage him to develop his skills and encourage him to be aggressive and competitive. With a much smaller and weaker son he may tend to be much more protective and discourage him from being outgoing and aggressive. Instead, he is encouraged to pursue a more sedentary life such as becoming a doctor or teacher. Even Sheldon does not negate the importance of environmental influences upon people. His great importance for psychology is in demonstrating that biological or physical factors must be taken into account when explaining behavior.

The measurement of personality

Personality assessment is done in a variety of situations for many purposes. Almost all of the modern fields of psychology, which we discussed in Chapter 1, have used personality tests for one purpose or another. All of us are aware that many clinical and counseling psychologists routinely administer tests of personality to patients in order to assess the emotional problems they may be suffering from. Another area in which such tests are frequently used is in the screening and selection of job candidates. For example, a salesman may be tested to evaluate how sociable and at ease he is with people; traits he would definitely need in becoming a successful salesman.

In order to determine the nature of an individual's personality, psychologists use a wide spectrum of psychological tests. These tests not only help to uncover the distinctive traits of an individual but do this in some mathematical form so that individuals can be compared with each other. Many of us possess the same traits and attitudes but in different amounts. Measurement aims at discovering these differences and relating them in a way that is meaningful to other investigators in the field of personality. The two broad categories of personality tests in current use are the projective techniques and the objective personality inventories. Some well-known tests are described in the following sections.

Projective tests

All projective tests have several common features. First, the task which is presented to the person is usually novel and quite ambiguous. As a result, it is difficult to depend upon established, conventional and stereotyped patterns of responding. Second, the nature of the appraisals being made is usually well disguised. The subject is unable to determine the true purpose of the test, or if he does, he does not know which of his responses are significant. Third, the test situation is generally very unstructured and the subject is given great latitude in how he responds to the projective material. Fourth, because of the ambiguous nature of the task, any responses from the subject are believed to be a function of the type of personality he possesses. This is similar to the experience many people have of looking at clouds in the sky and seeing different things in them. Perhaps at one time a cloud will look like a dog, and another time, it will look like the head of a person. Our motivations, impulses, thoughts, and beliefs are believed to determine what we will see. This concept of projection can best be explained by examination of some typical projective techniques.

RORSCHACH INK BLOTS. The Rorschach consists of ten individual inkblots which are presented singly as illustrated in Figure 8–4. The person is instructed to report only what he sees in them. Unlike other tests which you take in school, there are no right or wrong answers. The psychologist is interested not only in what the person sees and reports, but also in a number of other variables such as the number of responses per card, parts of the blot used for the response, and how conventional or original the responses are.

A basic assumption underlying the Rorschach is that there is a relationship between perception and personality. The way in which an individual structures or organizes the inkblots in forming his perceptions, reflect fundamental aspects of psychological functioning. In fact, psychologists have never found two people who give exactly the same responses to the ten Rorschach cards. It is always puzzling to people when others cannot see the same thing they saw in a given situation such as cloud formations or certain animals. However, psychologists would assume that there are different personalities involved, and thus differences in responding.

The Rorschach has been used most often by clinical psychologists who find it useful in diagnostic work-ups on patients. Unfortunately, most of the efforts to obtain demonstrations of validity have been damaging to the test's reputation (Cronbach, 1970). Holtzman (1968) made a systematic effort to improve the reliability and validity of the test by developing many new and different inkblots based on data from research on Rorschach's original blots. They have found interesting interrelationships with other personality measures such as the MMPI (Moseley, Duffey, & Sherman, 1963) which will be discussed below.

THEMATIC APPERCEPTION TEST. The TAT, as it is commonly called, consists of a series of cards depicting people in a variety of situations (Figure 8–5). The scenes are suggestive of many possible interactions, including mother-son, father-son, mother-daughter, father-daughter, husband-wife, and so on. The individual is asked to make up a story for each card with a beginning, middle, and end; he is also instructed to discuss the feelings and thoughts of the characters involved in the story. By

FIGURE 8–4
Four inkblots and some typical responses for each

Inkblot	Typical responses
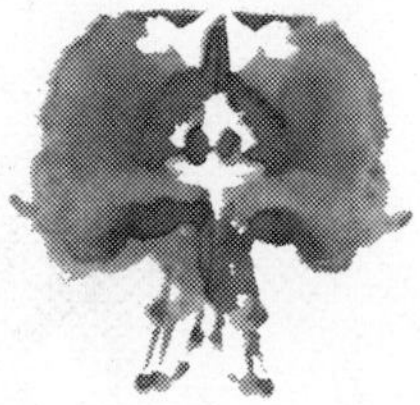	Two bears kissing Two clowns clapping hands A spinning top
	A bear rug A monster sitting on a tree stump
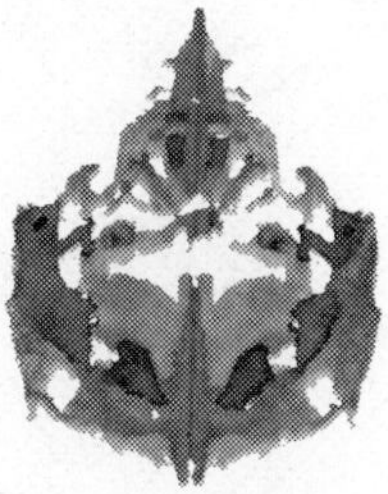	Animals climbing The insides of a person
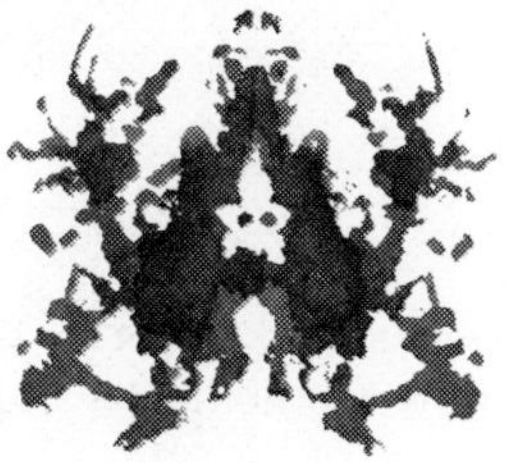	Two bugs biting each other Poached eggs

Source: From Benjamin Kleinmuntz, *Personality Measurement: An Introduction.* Homewood, Ill.: The Dorsey Press, 1967.

FIGURE 8–5
The old and young woman

Source: Reprinted by permission of the publishers from Henry A. Murray, *Thematic Apperception Test*, Cambridge, Mass.: Harvard University Press, Copyright, 1943, by the President and Fellows of Harvard College, 1971 by Henry A. Murray.

analyzing the style, length, language, themes, and so forth, the psychologist attempts to understand how people view themselves and others in interaction.

Objective personality inventories

In contrast to the projective tests, the personality inventories are highly structured and do not allow the individual much latitude of response. The individual is generally presented with a series of descriptions or statements, and is asked to answer true or false or to select from a limited number of choices. The statements which are presented generally deal with aspects of behavior or personality. Based upon a person's responses, the psychologist ascertains whether the overall pattern of answers is similar to those found within people of known personality characteristics. Thus, if an individual gives a set of answers similar to those given by people known to be depressed, the individual is presumed to be depressed or to have depressive tendencies.

The *Minnesota Multiphasic Personality Inventory* (MMPI) is an example of such an inventory (Figure 8–6). One version consists of over 500 items which the individual or subject declares is either characteristic or not of him. The test has a number of scales which include most of the conventional psychiatric categories to be described in the next chapter. These include psychopathic deviate, hysteria, depression, paranoid, schizophrenia, and others, as well. The psychologist then takes all the test's responses and sees which of these categories best describes the person. Thus, if the subject taking the test described himself in a way that schizophrenics describe themselves, then psychologists would suspect schizophrenic tendencies on the part of the person.

The *Edwards Personal Preference Schedule* is another personality test widely used in recent years (A. L. Edwards, 1954). This inventory was not designed to measure abnormal personality traits, as does the MMPI, but is designed to measure one's dominant needs or motives. However, experienced clinicians are frequently able to use this instrument to assess abnormality.

In constructing his test to measure these needs, Edwards wanted to avoid a bias found in many paper and pencil tests; that is, the tendency

FIGURE 8–6
Three sample items from the Minnesota Multiphasic Personality Inventory. The subject is asked to classify 550 affirmative statements, such as below, into three categories: *true, false,* and *cannot say.*

Much of the time I feel as if I have done something wrong or evil.

I easily become impatient with people.

At one or more times in my life I felt that someone was making me do things by hypnotizing me.

Source: Reproduced by permission. Copyright 1943, renewed 1970 by the University of Minnesota. Published by the Psychological Corporation, New York, N.Y. All rights reserved.

for a person to make responses that show him in a socially desirable light. Consequently, Edwards presents items in pairs which have been found, on the average, to be equally desirable. The subject is required to choose one or the other of the two items in each pair. Altogether, 225 pairs of items make up the test. It has been proven quite useful in counseling situations while the MMPI has been considered to be better in clinical situations concerned with the measurement and diagnosis of abnormality.

The healthy personality

In recent years, psychology has begun to emphasize the importance of helping the "normal" person to become more mentally healthy as well as treating those considered to be mentally ill. A humanistic approach has grown in which psychologists are concerned with questions such as: How can man lead a more fulfilling life? Is it possible for man to become more altruistic? How can children be taught to become more creative? Rather than concentrating on behavior disorders, the humanistic movement is concerned with bettering the state of man and helping him actualize his potentials to his fullest. If this goal sounds familiar, it is because Carl Rogers holds a similar view.

It should be emphasized at this point that becoming a mentally healthy person or mentally ill is not an either/or matter. The concept of mental health is discussed as a matter of degree, rather than an "all or none" dichotomy. There is a continuous relationship from mental health to mental illness. All of us differ in our position along this continuum. It should be noted here that the terms mentally healthy and self-actualization are used interchangeably.

Characteristics of mentally healthy people (self-actualizers)

One of the first psychologists to study mentally healthy people was Abraham Maslow (Figure 8-7) who we have already met in connection with his need hierarchy. Much of Maslow's work has focused on what he considers to be mentally healthy or self-actualized persons. Among the mentally healthy and famous people he has identified from biographies are Albert Einstein, Thomas Jefferson, Mrs. Eleanor Roosevelt, and Walt Whitman. However, one does not have to become famous in order to be among the self-actualizers. It is possible to become self-actualized as a housewife, bricklayer, teacher, or clerk. After studying many self-actualizing people, Maslow concluded that most of the following traits may be found in these mentally healthy people.

1. AN ABILITY TO ACCEPT ONESELF, OTHERS, AND NATURE. Self-actualizers accept shortcomings in themselves and are not ashamed of being what they are. They have a positive self-concept and feel they are making con-

FIGURE 8–7
Abraham Maslow

Courtesy Brandeis University

tributions to the world in their own way. They also extend good feelings toward others, and accept them even if they are different.

2. A MORE ADEQUATE PERCEPTION OF REALITY AND MORE COMFORTABLE RE-LATIONS WITH IT. Self-actualizers prefer to cope with even unpleasant truths rather than attempt to avoid them by retreating to pleasant un-realities. Since they perceive reality as it really is they are in a better position to resolve a problem when it arises. Little time is wasted on feeling sorry for themselves and they are able to make decisions in terms of how things really are rather than how they wish they were.

3. SPONTANEITY. The mentally healthy are relatively spontaneous in their behavior, and in their thoughts and inner impulses. Their behavior is marked by simplicity and naturalness rather than artificiality. How-ever, this does not mean they behave in an unconventional manner. It is their ideas or thoughts which are unconventional and spontaneous, not necessarily overt behavior. For example, one student who rated high on self-actualization, accepted an honor which he despised in private. How-ever, he decided to accept it rather than hurt the feelings of the people who voted him the award.

4. PROBLEM-CENTEREDNESS. Maslow's subjects focused on external problems rather than worrying about themselves. They were concerned with the major world issues of the day, and were also interested in de-veloping a philosophy of life. Since they were not overly self-conscious they could devote their attention to a task or mission that seemed peculiarly cut out for them.

5. A NEED FOR PRIVACY. Self-actualizers seem to enjoy solitude and privacy more than most people. This may cause others to perceive them as being somewhat aloof, reserved, and unruffled by events which disturb most people. Actually, they do appreciate other people and enjoy being around them. It is just that they need a certain amount of time to be by themselves in order to collect their thoughts.

6. INDEPENDENCE FROM ENVIRONMENT. Mentally healthy people remain relatively stable in spite of undergoing deprivation and hard times in their current environment. Their attitude may be characterized as follows: "I am going to make the most out of these circumstances now that I am here." With this type of outlook on life, they are able to maintain serenity and happiness in circumstances that might well drive others to suicide.

7. A CONTINUED FRESHNESS OF APPRECIATION. The self-actualizing people show the capacity to appreciate again and again the basic joys of nature. They enjoy sunsets and can get excited over flowers, babies, and animals. They do not dismiss such an event by declaring "If you have seen one flower, you have seen them all." To the contrary, they can see the unique in many apparently commonplace experiences.

In addition, Maslow describes numerous other traits of self-actualizers. They have a strong ethical sense, a democratic character structure, creativeness, a good sense of humor, and a feeling of belongingness to all mankind. More recently, Maslow has attempted to make the concept of self-actualization even more understandable by describing some behaviors that can lead to increased self-actualization.

The fully functioning person

The concept of the "fully functioning person" was introduced by Carl Rogers. From his years of work in the field of psychotherapy, he has become very optimistic about man's inherent nature and his ability to develop in a healthy manner. According to Rogers, the fully functioning person can be characterized by the following consistent behavior patterns.

1. OPENNESS TO EXPERIENCES. Healthier people are more aware of their feelings and attitudes. They make no attempt to disguise their actual sensory and visceral reactions. The more open they can be to their experiences, the healthier they are. By being willing to accept what they experience, the fully functioning person will not be overburdened with self-defense mechanisms which only serve to rigidify them.

2. THE LIKING OF ONESELF. Not only is the healthy person open to experiences, but they even learn to feel a quiet pleasure in being themselves. They are able to develop a tolerant easygoing attitude toward themselves and others; they can even laugh at themselves. Abilities are neither over- or underestimated. They are able to accept their own shortcomings and still have self-respect.

3. WILLINGNESS TO GROW AS A PERSON. The fully functioning person tends to understand that being alive means allowing oneself to grow and to change as a person, rather than reaching some end point and standing there. This can be seen in people who are constantly searching for new ideas, new friends, and seeking new adventures. They refuse to give up searching for new challenges just because they have obtained old goals. Instead, they must plan new directions for their lives to take.

4. THE FEELING THAT MAN IS BASICALLY GOOD. According to Rogers, healthy people possess a positive viewpoint toward human nature. They believe that given good conditions, the nature of man will become constructive and trusting. Humans are rational beings who will work toward positive goals and self-actualization if not hampered by the fetters of society.

From these descriptions by Maslow and Rogers emerges a picture of the mentally healthy person as one who is realistic, open, active, and able to gratify basic needs through acceptable behavior without creating problems. They are also able to devote their energies and thoughts to social interests and problems. Essentially, both theorists see man's fullest state as being human. Most of these traits we have described are the qualities that differentiate man from animals.

How do mentally healthy persons develop?

How can children be raised to become self-actualizers or fully functioning persons? This and related questions interest researchers and parents alike. Although research on the backgrounds of these special people has been quite limited, some trends have emerged. One of the most important prerequisites to becoming a mentally healthy person is having early experiences that convey a positive feeling about oneself. For instance, if a child has successful experiences, confidence will be developed. A child who suffers failure after failure will probably feel that he is an unworthy person. Although having early positive experiences is important to becoming mentally healthy, it is not the only avenue available. Many people have become very healthy who have had anything but rewarding experiences.

A second variable which helps in developing good mental health is having warm, close human relations with someone. A relationship of basic trust with another person in whom you can confide seems to facilitate the process. As a result, one's self-concept, feelings of worthiness, enables the person to better accept reality.

A third way of aiding the growth of mental health is having success in developing vocational, intellectual, social, and recreational skills. This involves the desire to engage in hard work, the willingness to put aside immediate rewards while making long sustained efforts, and learning how to concentrate. Successful experiences in school, on the job, or in other walks of life are vital to good mental health. However, they do not always come easy and require considerable effort.

A fourth method involves staying in contact with new ideas, exploring new philosophies, and meeting new people. This can be done by taking trips to other countries or by visiting new locations within the United States. It also can be achieved by being an active reader, taking new courses in school or by reacting to new drama and music. To maintain good mental health means staying mentally or intellectually active.

Finally, it is important to have outlets for our emotions. Participating in sports, hobbies, and other recreational activities is one way to give vent to our emotions. It is rather obvious that an inability to release one's feelings can result in an emotional breakdown. This will become quite evident in Chapter 9, when we will discuss the unhealthy personality and mental illness.

Humanistic psychologists such as Maslow and Rogers feel that all of the ways to achieve a mentally healthy being can be utilized by everyone. Exciting, meaningful personalities can be built just as a strong body by practice. What is required, however, is that people be relatively free from frustrations and conflicts brought on by poor environmental conditions which distort human nature. One's own basic and innate impetus toward self-actualization will help bring about greater personal growth and self-fulfillment.

Summary

Psychologists define personality as the characteristics and ways of behaving that determine an individual's unique adjustment to the environment. It is constantly developing over time, but early childhood experiences seem to have a particularly important impact. Three such influences are (1) heredity, which may affect social behaviors such as smiling, fear, and cuddling reactions; (2) cultural influences; and (3) factors of parent-child interaction, such as whether the home atmosphere emphasizes autonomy versus control and hostility versus love.

Many theories of personality have been proposed to explain in a global and comprehensive way the reasons behind the actions that people make. We discussed four of these: psychoanalysis, self-theory, behavior theory, and somatotype theory.

Sigmund Freud was the founder of psychoanalysis and stressed the importance of unconscious motivations and early childhood experiences in later adult life. He saw personality as composed of three parts: (1) the id; (2) the ego; and (3) the superego. Behavior is always a product of the interaction among these three.

The energy which is available to these systems comes from the life and death instincts. The life instincts are composed of those concerned with self-preservation and sex. An important manifestation of the death instinct is that of aggression. All instincts have four characteristics: (1) a source, (2) an energy, (3) an aim, and (4) objects.

Freud believed that anxiety was caused by overwhelming stimulation experienced by the ego from the environment (reality anxiety), uncontrolled impulses of the id (neurotic anxiety), and the superego (moral anxiety). To protect itself, the ego uses defense mechanisms. Among the defenses discussed were repression, projection, rationalization, reaction formation, displacement, compensation, regression, and sublimation.

Freud's emphasis on childhood experiences can be seen in his psychosexual stages of development. He postulated five stages of development: oral, anal, phallic, latency, and genital. Each stage is associated with certain personality traits that may be manifested in later adult behavior.

The personality theory proposed by Carl Rogers places great emphasis upon man's inherent and innate tendency to actualize himself to his fullest. The psychological manifestation of this forward-moving push is called self-actualization because it involves the self. We all possess learned needs for positive regard (approval from others) and positive self-regard (approval of self). If man is left to develop in a healthy environment his self-concept, which is socially determined, will be congruent with the actualizing tendency. However, if conditions of worth are developed within the person, a state of incongruence will exist between the self-concept and the actualization tendency. Incongruence is brought on by conditional positive regard which leads to crippling life-styles. What the child needs to experience is unconditional positive regard which leads to the fully functioning person.

Behaviorism, most notably associated with B. F. Skinner is that branch of psychology which stresses the study of overt behavior. For that reason, nonobservables such as the unconscious or the self is downgraded as important topics of study. Behaviorists believe that behavior is developed through principles of learning.

In the personality theory of Sheldon, man's personality characteristics are intimately associated with body build. Three major body types were identified that all humans are seen as possessing varying qualities of these physical attributes. The endomorph is characteristically soft, fat, and has underdeveloped muscles. Such an individual tends to be sociable, easygoing and loves comfort. The mesomorph is big, muscled, and strong. A person with this physique is adventure oriented, loves risks and physical adventure, and is aggressive and dominant. The ectomorph is thin, fragile, and characterized by underdeveloped muscles. This person is restrained in movement, loves privacy, and is aloof and fearful of people.

Personality assessment is an attempt to use certain psychological tests in order to measure personality characteristics. Two broad classes of tests are projective and objective. Projective instruments such as the Rorschach and TAT have several common features. They are relatively unstructured and ambiguous so that the person cannot rely on established, conventional, and stereotyped ways of responding. On the other hand, objective inventories (MMPI, EPPS) are highly structured and generally deal with a self-description. The responses of the person to test items are compared to various identifiable groups.

Many contemporary psychologists have begun to emphasize the need to study normal or healthy individuals and to work toward this goal. After a study of what Maslow considers to be self-actualized people, he has identified what he considers to be characteristics of the healthy personality. They tend to have an ability to accept themselves and others, a more adequate perception of reality, spontaneity, problem-centeredness, need for privacy, independence from the environment, and a continued fresh appreciation of things and experiences. These attributes are similar to Rogers' description of the fully functioning person: openness to experiences, liking oneself, willingness to grow and a feeling that man is healthy.

References

Ansbacher, H. L., & Rowena, R. (Eds.). *Superiority and social interest by Alfred Adler.* Evanston, Ill.: Northwestern University Press, 1964.

Brown, C. *Manchild in the promised land* by Claude Brown. Copyright © Claude Brown, 1965.

Cronbach, L. J. *Essentials of psychological testing.* (3d ed.) New York: Harper & Row, 1970.

Edwards, A. L. *The Edwards personal preference schedule manual.* New York: Psychological Corp., 1954.

Edwards, H. The black athlete: 20th century gladiators for white America. *Psychology Today,* November 1973, 43–52.

Freedman, D. An ethological approach to the genetic study of human behavior. In S. G. Vandenberg (Ed.), *Methods and goals in human behavior genetics.* New York: Academic Press. 1965, 141–161.

Gottesman, I. I. Genetic variance in adaptive personality traits. *Journal of Child Psychology and Psychiatry,* 1966, **7**, 199–208.

Hall, C. S., & Lindsey, G. *Theories of personality* 2d ed. New York: Wiley, 1970.

Hilgard, E. R. Psychoanalysis: Experimental studies. In D. L. Sills (Ed.), *International encyclopedia of the social sciences.* Vol. 13. New York: Macmillan and the Free Press, 1968, 37–45.

Holtzman, W. H. Holtzman inkblot technique. In A. I. Rabin (Ed.), *Projective techniques in personality assessment.* New York: Springer, 1968, 136–170.

Janis, I. L., Mahl, G. F., Kagan, J., & Holt, R. R. *Personality-dynamics development and assessment.* New York: Harcourt, Brace, & World, 1969.

Maddi, S. R. *Personality theories: A comparative analysis.* Homewood, Ill.: Dorsey, 1968.

McCleary, G. E., & Meredith, W. Behavior genetics. *Annual Review of Psychology,* 1966, **17**, 515–550.

Moseley, E. C., Duffey, P. F., & Sherman, L. J. An extension of the construct validity of the Holtzman inkblot technique. *Journal of Clinical Psychology,* 1963, **19**, 186–193.

Nash, J. *Developmental psychology: A psychobiological approach.* Englewood Cliffs, N.J.: Prentice-Hall, 1970.

Sarason, I. G. *Personality: An objective approach.* (2d ed.) New York: Wiley, 1972.

Schaefer, E. S. Converging conceptual models for maternal behavior and child behavior. In J. C. Glidewell (Ed.), *Parental attitudes and child behavior.* Springfield, Ill.: Charles C. Thomas, 1961.

Schaeffer, H. R., & Emerson, P. E. Patterns of response to physical contact in early human development. *Journal of Child Psychology and Psychiatry,* 1964, **5**, 1–13.

Sheldon, W. H., Dupertuis, C. W., & McDermott, E. *Atlas of men: A guide for somatotyping the adult male of all ages.* New York: Harper & Row, 1954.

Sue, D. W., & Kirk, B. A. Psychological characteristics of Chinese-American college students. *Journal of Counseling Psychology.* 1972, **19**, 471–478.

Sue, D. W., & Kirk, B. A. Differential characteristics of Chinese and Japanese American students. *Journal of Counseling Psychology.* 1973, **20**, 142–148.

9

The problem
of mental health:
The unhealthy
personality

I n the previous chapter, we spent some time discussing characteristics of the healthy personality. In this chapter we will be discussing the psychologically unhealthy personality; its causes and treatment. What should be kept in mind is that this chapter is really a continuation of Chapter 8 because we will be describing those persons who fall at the opposite end of the continuum on mental health.

The fact that one out of every ten Americans now living will, at some time, require treatment for mental illness is a frightening thought. However, not everyone who falls victim to a mental disorder is destined to spend the remainder of his life in a psychiatric institution. Actually, many of these people will never be hospitalized at all. Some patients are discharged from institutions within a period of months after their admission and never return. Still others receive treatment at a specialist's office and appear to live a normal life.

But so many people are, have been, or will be mentally ill or seriously maladjusted that none of us can escape some personal contact with it. It represents one of the great social problems of our time, whose tragic significance is reflected both in human suffering and in economic loss. It costs more than $1 billion a year to care for people who are emotionally disturbed, not counting the cost of time and professional services provided by psychiatrists, clinical psychologists, nurses, and others who care for psychiatric patients. As a matter of fact, psychiatric patients occupy approximately 50 percent of all hospital beds in the United States. Even more importantly, an estimate of the cost of psychiatric disturbances cannot ignore the incalculable suffering, not only of the patient, but also of family and friends.

While the scope of mental illness is staggering in this country, the figures on admissions to mental hospitals have remained surprisingly constant for nearly a century as shown in Figure 9–1. These figures were compiled from the records of the state of Massachusetts. You can see that the number of people below the age of 50 who were committed was about the same in the period from 1917 to 1940 as to that of 1885. Other data from additional sources show more or less the same thing. This suggests that the factors that cause the more severe mental disorders, apparently, have not changed appreciably in the last 80 years.

Defining mental illness: Criteria

Mental illness is the term generally used to describe a psychological maladjustment which is serious enough to handicap the afflicted person and to burden other people. Other nearly synonymous terms that will be used interchangeably in this chapter are *mental disease, mental disorder, psychiatric disorder, psychopathology,* and *behavior disorder.* These terms, unfortunately, are not easy to define, as psychological maladjust-

FIGURE 9–1
Admission rates to mental hospitals for the year 1885 and the period 1917–1940.
Are the stresses of modern life causing more behavioral disorders? Actually, for
persons under 50, the statistics have changed little over the years.

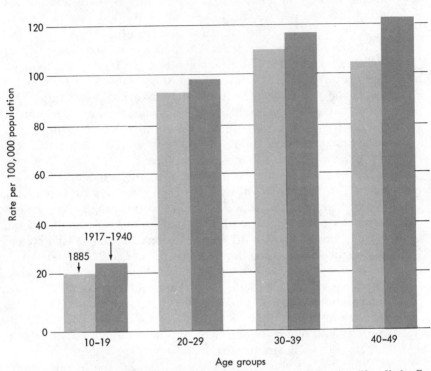

Source: H. Goldhammer and A. W. Marshall, *Psychosis and Civilization* (New York: Free
Press, 1953).

ments are not diseases in the same sense as that of physical ailments.
They are not caused by infections or specific malfunctions. As a result,
experts do not always agree on what represents pathological behavior or
the various varieties of pathology.

Statistical concepts of normality

The statistical concepts of normality state that whatever characteristics or attributes occur most frequently in the population is considered
to be the norm. Any deviation from this norm is considered to be abnormal. People who walk down the street naked, who talk to themselves, or
laugh uncontrollably would be considered abnormal in most situations,
because most Americans do not behave in this manner. At first glance,
this may seem to be an adequate criterion of normality. However, there
are several problems inherent in such a definition. First, such a definition

does not take into account relativity with regard to time, place, and various community standards and cultures. For example, for girls to go braless prior to the mid-1960s would have been considered abnormal. Furthermore, many of the more liberal cities such as San Francisco, Berkeley, and Boston are much more tolerant of different life-styles that may be judged abnormal in other parts of the country. In many historical societies, having hallucinations were considered divine. Indeed, if we were to consider deviations from the majority as being abnormal, then almost all of our ethnic minorities would fit into this category. Asian-Americans, blacks, Chicanos, and native Americans, would all have to be considered abnormal because they hold different values than those held by American society. The detrimental consequences of such a criterion to minorities will be further discussed in Chapter 13 on "Racism." Second, the statistical concept does not supply a basis for determining desirable and undesirable deviations from the norm. Would a child with an IQ of 145 be considered abnormal? According to the statistical notion, a child with an IQ of 70 and that of 150 would both be abnormal. It is clearly evident that the statistical concept of normality and abnormality contains many weaknesses.

Ideal mental health criterion

Using ideal mental health as a criterion for normality has beeen proposed by such theorists as Maslow and Rogers (see Chapter 8). In essence, such a belief stresses the importance of attaining some goal or ideal such as self-actualization. Other goals which have been proposed are insight, resistance to stress, maturity, competence and autonomy. There are several problems with using ideal mental health as a criterion. First, what particular goals or ideals should we use? Unfortunately, it is not clear since the answer to this question varies with the particular person we ask. Second, these goals lack precision and are frequently ambiguous. For example, if we believe autonomy is something that is characteristic of the mentally healthy, is the person who refuses to obey rules and regulations healthy? After all, can we not say that he is independent and free from rules? Third, but most important, is the fact that the use of this criterion would exclude too many people. That is, very few of us would be considered mentally healthy if we were to use self-actualization as the only notion of normality.

Practical criterion of abnormality

The practical or clinical criterion of mental illness is incomplete and subject to many of the criticisms which we have expressed for the other two. However, Buss (1966) feels that this criterion may be somewhat more useful because it inquires into the reasons for labeling people psychologically unhealthy and tends to be much more pragmatic. While recognizing its many weaknesses, we will accept the practical criteria for the purposes of this chapter.

DISCOMFORT.   Many people come to the attention of mental health workers because they are in physical or psychological discomfort. Their discomfort may be manifested physically such as fatigue, pain, and nausea, or psychologically such as constant worry, anxiety, fear, or depression. As we shall shortly see, physical discomforts such as asthma, peptic ulcers, and palpitations of the heart may be caused or exaggerated by psychological conflicts. However, the reader is probably much more aware that discomfort in the mentally ill is generally characterized by extreme or prolonged emotional reactions. It is normal to feel depressed if a loved one has recently passed away. However, if this reaction is extended over a long period of time until it incapacitates one's ability to function adequately, it can be considered abnormal. The same can be said about anxiety. It is normal for us to feel anxious when we are confronted with a poisonous snake, but when this fear is extended to all snakes, poisonous or not, then we may consider this reaction abnormal.

BIZARRENESS.   This concept depends very much on the statistical notion of normality. In essence, it states that bizarre behaviors are abnormal deviations from accepted standards of behavior. These behaviors may be socially defined as abnormal or they may be the result of a failure of biological adaptation expressed through the sense organs. Thus when a person commits murder or engages in sexual perversions, he is considered to be abnormal because he has committed asocial or antisocial acts as defined by our society. As pointed out earlier, this criterion is subject to charges of cultural relativism. A person is also considered bizarre when his sense organs do not function normally. Such is the case for delusions, hallucinations, and disorientation.

Delusions and hallucinations generally only occur in the psychotic reactions and seldom in the more mild disorders. *Delusions* may be defined as strong beliefs which the individual steadfastly maintains despite all evidence of its falsity. *Delusions of grandeur* are quite common in individuals who believe they are some exalted being, such as a president, millionaire, great artist, or even God. One woman patient in a mental hospital, who appeared to be behaving in a normal fashion most of the time, vehemently held onto her belief that she was Jesus Christ. Nothing could shake her delusion, even when it was pointed out she was of the wrong sex.

A second type of delusion is that of *persecution*. Here individuals are constantly on guard against their enemies who are everywhere. Other people are seen as spying on them or that some evil force is plotting to do them in. Recently, Jim Dunbar, a radio-TV personality in San Francisco, had several shots fired at his bulletproof window while broadcasting early one morning. Luckily, the attempted killing was unsuccessful. However, it was later revealed that Dunbar's assailant believed that radio waves were controlling his mind and that it was vital to his safety that the source be destroyed. Unfortunately, it is not always easy to determine whether a particular belief held by a person is delusional or not. Many blacks voice the fear that "The Man" is out to get them. With such widespread prejudice and discrimination, can we really call this a delusion?

Hallucinations, defined as false impressions involving the various sensory modalities, quite often accompany delusions. The patient may hear voices accusing him of all kinds of filthy deeds. Visual hallucinations may predominate in which the individual might perceive the walls of the room closing in on him. One patient was hospitalized because she kept feeling bugs crawling under her skin, which in the patient's own words "are driving me crazy." Religious hallucinations are quite common and patients report seeing and hearing God, Jesus Christ, or other religious figures.

Disorientation as to person, place, and time is also a manifestation of bizarreness. Patients may not remember who they are or forget some aspect of their personal identity, they may not know the day, month, or year, or they may be unable to recall where they are.

INEFFICIENCY. In our everyday life, we are asked to perform many roles and to fulfill the responsibilities of each. Our roles as students, teachers, parents, marital partners, doctors, dentists, lawyers, bricklayers, and plumbers all have certain expectations. When emotional problems begin to interfere with our performance in these roles and render us ineffectual, we are talking about inefficiency. Inefficiency is assessed by either comparing our potentials with our actual performance or comparing our performance with the requirements of the role. A student with an IQ of 150, who is failing in school, can be said to be inefficient. Likewise, we can assess how efficient a salesman is by noting the number of sales he actually makes with how many the company feels he should be able to make.

In the following discussion of specific behavior disorders, you may wish to apply these practical criteria. Note that some of the criteria seem more applicable to certain types of disorders. For example, neuroses are seldom characterized by bizarreness and usually involve only discomfort and inefficiency. Psychoses, however, oftentimes involve bizarreness and the other two.

Neurotic reactions

Neurotic reactions are considered to be ineffectual defense maneuvers in the face of stress or frustration. Although the wide variety of psychological symptoms that result are usually not severe enough to require hospitalization of the patient, work and social adjustment are sometimes affected. The most common symptoms are feelings of inadequacy which lead to anxiety, avoidance rather than coping with stress situations, lack of insight into one's own behavior and reactions, inability to form satisfying interpersonal relationships, and general unhappiness such as depression or guilt.

The American Psychiatric Association has classified a variety of symptom-types of neuroses. We shall briefly describe the following types: anxiety reactions (free-floating and phobic), depressive reactions, hysterical reactions (conversion and dissociative), obsessive-compulsive reactions, and fatigue-hypochondriasis. We must keep in mind that these are only outward signs of neurosis and diagnosis is not made on the basis of known causes. However, the symptoms represent outcomes of stress, frustration, and psychological conflicts.

Anxiety reactions

The most common of all the neuroses is a *"free-floating"* or diffuse anxiety in which the fear stimuli are unknown. The person suffering from this disorder is frightened, apprehensive, and enveloped with a sense of catastrophe for no apparent reason. This mild, chronic anxiety is often punctuated with occasional states of panic in which the individual may believe death to be imminent. Physiological reactions reflect his acute fear: accelerated breathing and heartbeat, trembling of the limbs, elevated blood pressure, gastric upset, excessive perspiration, and inability to sleep regularly.

Anxiety in itself is not necessarily a neurotic symptom. What identifies the neurotic reaction is the intensity and persistence of anxiety in situations that are not dangerous. Anxiety neurotics simply lack adaptive devices that will keep anxiety from emerging, and since they do not remember the specific cause of their anxiety, they feel trapped by unknown forces.

> A young married accountant constantly complained to his therapist about feeling apprehensive and tense. He worried about many things including his ability to keep his job, making monthly mortgage payments, his daughter's safety, etc. His heavy perspiration and constant upset stomach caused him much consternation. Unable to sleep regularly, he often awoke in the middle of the night with his body tense and rigid feeling that death was imminent.

Like free-floating anxieties, *phobic reactions* include persistent and irrational fears. However, the feared object, place, or thing is known to the victim. Phobias are unrealistic fears which are disproportionate to the actual feared situation. For example, a person who possesses a fear of snakes may have good reason especially if the snakes are poisonous. However, if the fear is generalized to all snakes, and even worms, and is so strong that the person is unable to leave home for fear of encountering one, then the fear is abnormal. Other phobias may involve fear of heights, crowds, noise, school, exams and enclosed places. There seems to be no limit to the number of objects that can bring forth phobic reactions.

Unfortunately, phobias tend to generalize, so that as time passes, the fear generalizes to more and more objects. The following cases are examples of people with multiple phobias:

> Jennifer, an 18-year-old freshman, was afraid of loud noises, dirt and many types of potential illnesses. Originally she had been repulsed by her boyfriend holding her close and caressing her for fear of catching a cold. In addition, her aroused sexual urges seemed sinful and wrong. Discontinuing the relationship with her boyfriend did not help matters as her fears became more diversified. She began to develop intense fears of men and social occasions.
>
> Mrs. K's difficulties demonstrate another type of phobic reaction which is both unusual and exotic. She began to fear traveling far from her house until the radius around her house, in which she felt safe, decreased to such an extent that she became housebound. This particular phobia is called *agoraphobia*. Although she would feel perfectly safe and happy while remaining in her own home, Mrs. K would experience strong panic reactions whenever she had to travel.

Depressive reactions

Depressed neurotics are characterized by feelings of sadness, worthlessness, lack of energy, and guilt. Patients often complain of inability to concentrate, lack of self-confidence, apathy, and ill health. Neurotic depression is frequently a reaction to a failure (not being admitted to graduate school, not obtaining a desired promotion, and so on) or a loss of some important person such as a wife, husband, close friend, or relative. The symptoms tend to be vague and diffuse and may represent a kind of surrender. The person has given up in life and blames himself for the results.

The following dialogue between an unmarried, 29-year-old, female patient and her doctor illustrates this type of reaction:

> Pt.: I don't know, I just don't seem interested in anything anymore. I used to like playing tennis, bridge, and going to the plays. Now *(speaking slowly and softly)* they don't do anything for me. I just don't care about anything *(weeps)* . . . I . . . I don't even care about my boyfriend anymore.
>
> Dr.: You feel your condition is due to your brother's death in Viet Nam?
>
> Pt.: Well, things got real bad then. How would anyone get over something like that? He was my only brother and we were so . . . *(weeps)* . . . so close. He was only 18 years old. I wish I would have treated him better. I feel like I'm to blame for his death. Sometimes I can't sleep knowing that he depended on me when our mother died. *(Weeps uncontrollably)* Instead . . . instead of spending more time with him . . . I should have known he needed me. How could I have let him down?

Hysterical reactions

As you will recall, we mentioned in the preceding chapter that Freud's major breakthrough in his conceptualization of personality came about in his studies of hysteria. Hysteria is one of the forms of *conversion reactions* whose symptoms superficially resemble those present in organic diseases but there is no true physical pathology. They may take the form of seizures, motor paralysis, blindness, deafness, anesthesias (loss of some sensation), or other physical symptoms. Usually, the symptoms are gross in character and can be recognized by the fact that the disorder is physiologically incorrect. Patients, for example, may develop an anesthesia and be unable to feel anything in one hand normally covered by a glove. But the pattern of the sensory nerve supply to the part of the body involved in the "glove anesthesia" could not come from a neural disorder (Figure 9–2). In such a case, part of the arm would also be involved.

A dramatic example of a hysterical neurosis, conversion type, is seen in the following example of a married 55-year-old man who developed symptoms of full paralysis of the legs and partial paralysis of the right arm. In addition, he began to stutter heavily when he became angry. Months of observation and exhaustive medical exams failed to reveal any organic causes for his condition. As a result, he was referred to the psychology service where it was discovered that the onset of his symptoms correlated strongly with the separation from his wife. The week before his symptoms appeared, his wife informed him that she was leaving him. Apparently, she had fallen in love with another man. Enraged at his wife for leaving him, he threw a massive temper tantrum

FIGURE 9–2
Glove anesthesia. This illustration of a glove anesthesia is an example of hysteria, described by Freud as an illness in which there is no organic basis for the physical symptoms. The area in the drawing on the right in which the person has no sensation does not correspond with the distribution of nerves, but with the area a glove would cover, as diagrammed on the left.

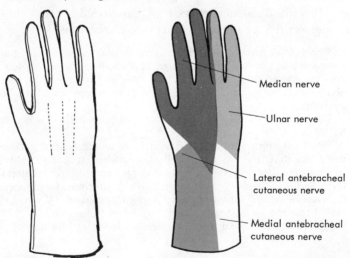

Source: From *Psychology: A Scientific Study of Man, Third Edition,* by F. Sanford and L. S. Wrightsman. Copyright © 1970 by Wadsworth Publishing Company, Inc. Reprinted by permission of the publisher, Brooks/Cole Publishing Company, Monterey, California.

and totally demolished the interior of their home. For several days he was obsessed with pursuing them with his rifle and making them pay for the misery they had caused him. The thought of committing murder, however, was frightening. One morning he woke up and found himself unable to move. It was as if his paralysis served to prevent him from committing this sinful deed.

Some hysterics seem to enjoy their illness and appear to be indifferent to their symptoms. Although the hysteric is not deliberately pretending to be ill, it is apparent that these symptoms serve a useful purpose by removing the person from unpleasant situations and conflicts.

A second manifestation of the hysterical neurosis is the *dissociative type*. These types of neuroses are characterized by a loss of personal identity. Certain aspects of reality may be so painful for the individual to recall that entire episodes from the person's life may be repressed from consciousness (see Chapter 6 discussion of repression). Dissociative reactions may take several related forms including amnesia, fugue, and multiple personality.

Amnesia involves a total or partial inability to recall or identify personal experiences. Amnesiacs may selectively forget their names, addresses, or be unable to recognize friends and relatives. It is believed that amnesia results from psychological conflicts in which the individual represses motives which would expose him to guilt or anxiety. Amnesiacs then act out their repressed desires as "someone else" without exposing their own personal identity to guilt or anxiety associated with their behavior. In using the mechanism of repression, dissociated neurotics not only engage in actions which resolve their conflict, but also avoid their own involvement in it. The following case shows an amnesiac's reaction to a frustrating situation.

> Joan S. was a 35-year-old housewife who was experiencing increasing dissatisfaction with her four children and husband. The two eldest children were constantly in trouble with the authorities and were notorious for setting fires in the neighborhood. In addition, her husband was an irresponsible and unemployed alcoholic. Her strong desires to physically escape the unhappy family situation conflicted with her strong moralistic upbringing. On her way to pick up groceries one evening, she disappeared for three months until a friend ran into her at a shopping center. She failed to recognize her friend and was using a different name when discovered. She had no memory or recollection of who she was or her previous life.

Amnesia is sometimes accompanied by physical flight in which a person wanders off for days or even years and ends up in strange places, completely unaware of how he got there. Such episodes are called *fugues* and represent a way of fleeing from one's problems.

The most well-known and extreme form of dissociation is the *dual or multiple personality*. Multiple personalities have gained a great deal of attention through the mass media and fictional works. Probably the most well-known case is *The Three Faces of Eve* (Thigpen & Cleckley, 1957) in which a young woman exhibited multiple personalities. Recently, a novel has been published entitled *The Sixteen Personalities of Sybil* (Schreiber, 1973) which reports that a young woman possessed 16 distinct personalities! Actually, such cases are extremely rare in clinical practice.

In multiple personalities, the individual may develop two or more distinct personalities which alternate in taking over conscious control of the person for varying periods of time. The relationships between the personalities may be extremely complex. For example, personality A may be aware of B and C but B may only be aware of A while C is aware of neither. In most cases, these personalities are dramatically different from one another and may even behave like the Dr. Jekyll and Mr. Hyde character, opposite values and beliefs.

Obsessive-compulsive reactions

An *obsessive* reaction is an excessive preoccupation with certain topics and is manifested in two forms: doubting and thoughts. In the former, the obsessive person has difficulty in making decisions; and in the latter, the obsessive is unable to stop thinking about recurrent thoughts that usually involve prohibited actions (sexual, aggressive, and so on). Below are two examples illustrating these characteristics.

> John C. was an 18-year-old Chinese-American student who came to the counseling center because of an inability to make decisions which was incapacitating his life. His symptoms included an inability to decide on topics for essays and indecisions about what to wear or eat during the day. His symptoms became so severe that he would lay in bed for days trying to decide whether to get up or not. As a result he was forced to drop out of school and seek professional help in the community.
>
> Margaret G., a young mother of 23, had frightening recurrent thoughts about taking the kitchen knife and killing her 11-month-old son, Joey. To the mother there was no rhyme or reason for her wanting to injure her son, and yet these thoughts continued to occur at all hours of the day. The thoughts became so strong that Margaret finally avoided the child completely for fear of injuring him. Under therapy, it was discovered that prior to the time of Joey's birth, the mother has looked forward to a long vacation in Europe that was disrupted by her unplanned pregnancy.

Compulsions are irresistible urges to carry out a particular behavior sequence involving repetition (repeating a behavior over and over) and/or symmetry (lining objects and things into orderly formations). Examples of compulsions are *kleptomania*, the compulsion to steal and *pyromania*, the compulsion to set fires. If the person fails to perform these motor acts, which are recognized as silly, there will ensue a feeling of anxiety or discomfort.

> Betty K. a young girl of 13, was frequently found wandering around downstairs at all hours of the night by her mother. She was deathly

afraid that a fire would start in the house with faulty electrical cords and would feel compelled to go around the house pulling all cords from their sockets. However, once she returned to bed, Betty would wonder whether there were any sockets she might have missed. Unless she got up in the middle of the night to check, she would be so anxious that it was difficult for her to sleep. As a result, she would frequently repeat this behavior over and over again.

Obsessive-compulsive symptoms often occur together in neuroses and represent another way of reducing anxieties while repressing the motives that arouse them. If you were to have an obsession about dying, it may be because you have anxieties over some past act. Similarly, the compulsive who washes his hands every few minutes may have anxieties over sexual transgressions, and the hand washing may be an unconscious attempt to cleanse himself of guilt. In this way the neurotic may obtain some relief, but it is often incomplete.

Fatigue-hypochondriasis

The last group of neurotic reactions which we will discuss is that of fatigue-hypochondriasis. Individuals suffering from this malady are characterized by an excessive preoccupation with their state of health. Physical complaints are common and many hypochondriacs feel they are suffering from every new disease they read or hear about. What is characteristic about their complaints, however, is that they do not seem restricted to any logical pattern. They are generally vague, diffuse, and involve general areas of the body. Complaints of fatigue and weariness are voiced even though they are usually in good health.

Psychotic reactions

As we learned in the preceding sections, the neurotic develops various habit patterns or symptoms in attempting to reduce anxiety associated with conflicts and other problems of life. Although they overreact to stress and frustration, they are able to function and carry on in life even though inefficiently. On the other hand, psychotics usually cannot maintain their normal role in society because they are seriously mentally ill. There is such a severe personality breakdown that, in most instances, they lose contact with reality and may become quite bizarre. Among the chief symptoms are marked deterioration of cognitive and emotional faculties. Psychotic behavior is sometimes labeled *insanity*. Actually this is a social and legal term that denotes a psychiatric disorder so grave that the individual is deemed incapable of assuming responsibility for his own actions, in which case he is usually institutionalized. Table 9–1 compares neurotic and psychotic disorders.

Psychoses may be divided into three major categories: *organic, schizo-*

TABLE 9-1
Comparison of neurotic and psychotic disorders

Factor	Psychoneuroses	Psychoses
General behavior	Mild degree of personality decompensation; reality contact and social functioning impaired	Severe degree of personality decompensation; reality contact markedly impaired; patient incapacitated in social functioning
Nature of symptoms	Wide range of psychological and somatic symptoms but no hallucinations or other extreme deviations in thought, feeling or action	Wide range of symptoms with delusions, hallucinations, emotional blunting, and other severely deviate behavior
Orientation	Patient rarely loses orientation to environment	Patient frequently loses orientation to environment
Insight	Patient often has some insight into nature of his behavior	Patient rarely has insight into nature of his behavior
Social aspects	Behavior rarely injurious or dangerous to patient or to society	Behavior frequently injurious or dangerous to patient or to society
Treatment	Patient rarely needs institutional care	Patient usually needs institutional care

Source: From *Abnormal Psychology and Modern Life* by James C. Coleman. Copyright © 1972 by Scott, Foresman and Company. Reprinted by permission of the publisher.

phrenic, and *affective.* The latter two are classified as *functional psychoses* because there is no evidence of brain damage or physiological causes for the symptoms. Organic psychoses are those in which some physiological injury or disease is the main factor in causing the illness. Some of the organic conditions associated with them are syphilis, injury to the brain, epilepsy, cerebral arteriosclerosis (hardening of the arteries of the brain) and senile deterioration.

Organic disorders

General paresis is a good example of a disorder with a physical cause which produces a variety of intellectual and personality problems in the afflicted person. It is a mental disorder caused by the infiltration and destruction of brain tissue by syphilis germs. Some paretic patients become euphoric and experience delusions of grandeur, but are not as logical or rational as those often reported by some paranoid patients. Another group of paretics become extremely depressed. They are usually aware of their diminishing abilities and react with despair and apathy.

Mental disorders can also be caused by several types of toxins and metabolic dysfunction. Admiral Byrd's remarkable record of his lonely Antarctic winter vigil is a fascinating account of a man struggling with great fatigue, loneliness, and monoxide poisoning. At many points, he experienced deliria and irrational thoughts common to the toxic disorders (Byrd, 1938).

Excessive drinking of alcohol, as we have seen in Chapter 4 on "Altered States of Consciousness," can also produce psychotic behavior. Delirium tremen is a psychotic reaction resulting from excessive drinking of alcohol. The person's behavior may include disorientation for space and time, hallucinations, tremors of the tongue and hands, and great anxiety.

Finally, a variety of behavior problems are associated with physical damage to the brain from either head injuries or tumors. All of these forms of psychotic reactions have in common some external factor that injures the nervous system. The following psychotic reactions, however, do not possess clear-cut organic involvement.

Schizophrenic reactions

The form of psychosis that is most common and constitutes the gravest problem for psychiatry is schizophrenia, which means splitting of the mind. The term *split personality* has frequently been applied to this disorder but it should not be confused with the neurotic disorder of multiple personality. The term split personality means that the personality has been detached from reality, not that the personality has been split into conflicting parts.

Schizophrenic patients may exhibit a wide variety of symptoms, all of them characterized by disturbances in the patient's contact with reality. The most salient symptoms occur in the cognitive functioning of the person. Symptoms include disturbances of language, thought, self; retreat and detachment; hallucinations and delusions.

Although many types of schizophrenia have been identified, psychiatrists usually divide them into four symptom types. There is much overlapping among the groups and it is not unusual for a patient's symptoms to shift from one subgroup to another during the course of illness. Nevertheless, such a classification system is useful because it does provide a fuller description of schizophrenia and sketches its course of development.

SIMPLE TYPE. Simple schizophrenics are best characterized by withdrawal and isolation from their fellowmen. They are often apathetic, show disturbances of thinking and attention, often accompanied by blunted affect (failure to react with appropriately intense emotion). This form of schizophrenia usually begins in adolescence and is so gradual in onset that families are not aware of the seriousness of the disorder. Since the symptoms are seldom bizarre, many simple schizophrenics are never hospitalized and may live out their lives as vagrants, tramps, and prostitutes. Others may be recognized as town eccentrics, but, because they are harmless, are left alone.

CATATONIC TYPE. In catatonic schizophrenia, psychomotor disorders predominate such as peculiar gestures and postures, and stereotyped actions. Sudden onset of symptoms is one of its hallmarks. When in a *stuporous phase*, the patient may remain in one position for days in which no effort is made to move or talk. However, sometimes the patient may allow the doctor to mold his position by moving an arm or leg. In such a state of *waxy flexibility*, a patient's body can be molded into any odd posture. Many psychologists believe that the stuporous phase of catatonia represents a retreat from the world by the patient who views it as frightening. The odd postures are said to be symbolic of the person's inner conflicts and fears.

In contrast to the more common catatonic stupors are the *catatonic excitements*, marked by uncontrollable bursts of energy. The patient is literally in a frenzied state during which the catatonic may endanger his own life and those of others. Fortunately, these episodes are brief, because they require enormous physical energy.

HEBEPHRENIC TYPE. The hebephrenic type of schizophrenia, like the simple reaction, has an early but slow onset. It is characterized by inappropriate emotional behavior, such as laughter, smiling, giggling, and weeping (Figure 9–3). These patients have bizarre ideas, incoherent, disorganized speech and often lively hallucinations and delusions. The hebephrenic tends to become more and more withdrawn as the years pass and shows marked regression, such as soiling and wetting himself. The picture of the "raving maniac" painted by popular fiction fits the description of the hebephrenic. The following conversation between doctor and patient includes many of these elements.

> The patient was a 38-year-old man who was admitted to the hospital suffering from bizarre hallucinations and delusions. He had a record of alcoholism and possible incestuous relations with his two sisters. Below is a conversation typical of hebephrenic responses.
>
> D.: How are you today?
> P.: The day is fine *(giggle)*.
> D.: When did you get here?
> P.: Two hundred years ago before the hospital was built ... 1515 A.D.
> D.: What are some of the reasons which brought you here?
> P.: I was seriously injured in the War of the Worlds ... I was a spy that got caught and blasted with laser beams *(giggle)*. I'm here to repair my body. Are you friend or foe?
> D.: I'm a doctor.
> P.: I used to be a doctor ... see *(unzips pants and pulls out penis)* ... I was always able to cure my sisters *(silly giggle)*.

PARANOID TYPE. The paranoid schizophrenic has the usual symptoms of flattened affect, withdrawal, and hallucinations: but the most impressive symptoms are his delusional systems (Figure 9–4). As mentioned earlier, delusions of persecution or grandiosity are frequent. The following case history describes such a person:

FIGURE 9-3
Arthur H. Bremer (tie loosened), convicted of the shooting of Governor George
C. Wallace, is shown here at a rally, clapping his hands. He has been pictured
often with a characteristic grin, typical of some hebephrenic schizophrenic
patients.

Wide World Photos

A young schizophrenic man believed that there was an elaborate plot
to kill him because he was, in truth, Jesus Christ. The plotters had discovered his true identity and were themselves agents of Israel. He believed he was sent to earth to save mankind from Communist and Jew-
ish foolishness. He said God had told him personally of his role but re-
quested him to maintain secrecy while saving the world. Somehow word
got out, even to his relatives, who had been corrupted by his enemies
and they were trying to keep him in the hospital.

FIGURE 9–4
Sirhan B. Sirhan, convicted assassin of Senator
Robert F. Kennedy, has been diagnosed as a
paranoid schizophrenic.

Wide World Photos

Affective psychoses

In contrast to the schizophrenias whose major disturbance is in the cognitive realm, the affective psychoses are predominantly disorders of mood. The disorder is characterized by extreme moods from elation to depression. It has frequently been called a *manic-depressive reaction* and considered as an entity for several reasons. First, both mania and depression are mood disorders differing only that both occupy different ends of the continuum. Second, manic behavior is often seen as a last ditch effort to stave off depression. For example, breaking up with a boy friend or girl friend can be extremely depressing. However, much of the sadness and misery can be controlled if we keep ourselves excessively busy so that we have little time to think about our depression. Many individuals who are experiencing a manic episode are believed to be doing just this very thing. Third, many patients afflicted with this disorder tend to alternate between manic and depressive episodes. These psychotic episodes tend to last about six months, the depressed state is generally longer than the manic ones.

The depressed patient is dejected, guilt ridden and feels worthless. The person's past, present, and future looks bleak and gloomy. Many patients become so depressed that they will no longer eat food or drink water and must be forcibly fed through a tube. In addition, daily personal care such as dressing and taking care of toilet needs is left undone. In extreme cases, attempts at suicide may occur so that they must be watched closely. The following case is typical:

> Pauline B. is a fifty-seven-year old widow who graduated from high school, attended business school, and had training as a nurse. She has had three commitments to mental hospitals for depressions. When seen at the hospital on her most recent admission, the patient presented the typical picture of depression. She appeared sad, talked in a somewhat whining voice, and showed psychomotor retardation. She had numerous self-condemnatory ideas, and was preoccupied with thoughts of suicide. Her general attitude was one of hopelessness. She said that life is not worth living, and that she would be better off dead. She had no interest in anything, and there was nothing left to live for. Between her depressive episodes, the patient is regarded as a happy outgoing person, although subject to rather wide swings of mood (Kisker, 1964, p. 374).

In contrast to the depressed patient, the manic individual is highly energetic, optimistic, and self-confident, and sometimes becomes aggressive and obnoxious. He may sing, dance, run, talk a lot, and exhibit delusions of great wealth, status, or competence. In the most extreme manic phase, the patient may become quite dangerous as he may break furniture, attack people, use vile language, and generally put life and property in jeopardy.

Personality Disorders

Neuroses and psychoses represent attempts on the part of the individual to control anxiety and to protect the person from further decompensation under stress. However, *personality disorders* do not necessarily involve personal distress on the part of the person but an acting out of socially inappropriate behaviors. This is a broad category which includes the *antisocial personality* and a variety of *personality pattern disturbances, alcoholism, drug addiction,* and *sexual deviance.* Because Chapter 4 on "Altered States of Consciousness" dealt with alcoholism and drug addiction and Chapter 10 on "Sexuality" will deal with various types of sexual deviance, we will devote this section to a discussion of the *antisocial personality.*

The antisocial personality is characterized by the following behaviors: (1) Such people typically engage in one or more illegal acts that are antisocial or may be considered asocial in nature (stealing, forging checks, and pathological lying. (2) There is an inability to control impulses so that the person usually acts out his aggressive and sexual urges. There is low frustration tolerance and an inability to delay immediate pleasure for future or long-term goals. (3) Although they are able to put up a good front and may appear likable, their friendship is only a manipulative ploy to exploit others. (4) Because they are self-centered, immature and superficial in their relations with others, they are unable to form long lasting friendships. (5) The antisocial personality often has a disregard for conventions and rejects traditional discipline and authority. (6) Finally, there tends to be an inadequate conscience development in that they generally experience little anxiety or guilt for their antisocial behaviors.

Because the antisocial personality is not considered an emotional disorder, many individuals with such a personality rise to occupy positions of importance. Politicians, salesmen, ruthless business executives, as well as the criminal offender and delinquent are often in this category.

Psychosomatic disorders

In Chapter 2, we spent considerable time discussing *psychosomatic disorders*, their symptoms, possible origins, and treatment. As you may recall, we defined this disorder as actually involving organ systems of the body; that is, psychological stress was seen as being intimately associated with actual organic changes in the body (hypertension, asthma, skin problems, and so on). This is in sharp contrast to the symptoms of hysteria, conversion type, in which no actual organic changes occur. Rather than repeat our earlier analysis of the psychosomatic disorders, we strongly urge the reader to review this section in Chapter 2.

Causes of behavior disorders

Because behavior disorders are such an important mental health problem, much research effort is being expended to find its causes. The *etiology* (causes) are sought in genetics, biochemistry, and in psychological stresses. However, research is often contradictory and unclear. Furthermore, the problem is compounded by the fact that explanations of abnormal behavior are linked to the many theories of personality. For example, psychoanalytic, self, and behavior theory all emphasize different causes for the formation of psychopathology. We will explore some of these explanations later in this chapter, but let us now turn our attention to some general explanations.

Genetic factors

In Chapter 2, we discussed the importance of heredity on such characteristics as eye color, birth imperfections, and intelligence. The belief that heredity may also play an important role in the development of psychopathology has also been proposed. Kallman (1959) has presented some striking data in demonstrating that the family history of psychotic patients often show other cases of psychosis. He found that the probable incidence of schizophrenia is closely related to the closeness of the blood tie to the schizophrenic patient. The probability of an identical twin sibling developing schizophrenia, if his or her sibling has the disorder is very high. Furthermore, if one of two parents have schizophrenia, the probability of the offsprings' developing the disorder is 19 times greater than in the general population.

In a more recent study, Gottesman and Shields (1966) studied schizophrenic patients who had twin siblings. Because identical twins share the same heredity while fraternal twins do not, we would expect that the rate of schizophrenia between the former to be much higher if the genetic hypothesis is correct. Gottesman and Shields found that 79 percent of the identical twins, as opposed to 45 percent of the fraternal twins, showed some psychiatric abnormality.

These results suggest a strong heredity component in the development of schizophrenia and similar evidence has been obtained in the case of manic-depressive psychosis. Nevertheless, in spite of such impressive data, few psychologists would label these disorders as solely caused by genetic factors. Not all identical co-twins become mentally ill. Furthermore, it is difficult for us to deny that it is possible for us to learn maladaptive behaviors regardless of a genetic base. Consequently, most investigators take an interactional view of behavior disorders. It is believed that we can inherit a *predisposition* to become psychotic but the eventual manifestation of this disorder depends on how much stress we experience in life.

Biochemical theories

Some scientists feel that schizophrenia and other mental disorders can be understood in terms of biochemical disturbances. As we saw in Chapter 4, several drugs have been found that can produce psychoticlike states when taken. For example, lysergic acid (LSD) often causes disturbances of thought patterns, paranoid ideas, hallucinations, and detachment from reality. The discovery of these drugs has heightened speculation that a metabolic imbalance of some type is responsible for many mental disorders, particularly since many of these drugs resemble normal body substances.

Other researchers have found metabolic differences between psychotics and normals. For instance, Heath and co-workers (1967) were able to process a substance from the blood serum of schizophrenics that they call *taraxein*. They next injected this substance into monkeys and volunteer prisoners. According to Heath, these subjects began to show schizophrenic symptoms and, in the case of the prisoners, disorganized thinking, delusions, and hallucinations. But, in other studies, there has been a notable lack of success in duplicating these findings.

It should be pointed out that biochemical evidence does not in any way refute environmental factors such as stress in psychoses. It is quite possible that early experiences may cause permanent biochemical changes and that these may predispose some individuals to behavior pathology.

Psychological stress

It is difficult to adequately discuss all of the various explanations which have been advanced concerning the importance of environmental forces in the development of behavior pathology. Explanations have utilized maternal deprivation, early psychic trauma, severe stress, poor social conditions, and pathogenic family patterns as causes. In this section we will restrict ourselves to two hypotheses which explores the family environment of those who suffer from mental illness: the double-bind phenomena and marital schism and skew.

DOUBLE BIND. One of the more popular theories proposed for the development of schizophrenia was first advanced by Bateson et al. (1956) and quickly became known as the double-bind situation. In essence, the theory explains schizophrenia in terms of the confused communications which are sent to the preschizophrenic child. For example, all of us are aware that what we say and do can be qualified by other things such as tone of voice and body posture. Saying "I'm not angry" with my teeth together and voice raised is an incongruent message. In this case my denial that I'm angry is negated by the tone of my voice and body posture that tells you I am. Luckily, most of our levels of communication tend to enhance one another. However, Bateson believes that this is not the case in the schizophrenic family environment. The mother is said to express at least two opposing messages to the preschizophrenic child. The first message is a simulated loving and approaching in which the child's responses reaffirms the mother's belief that she is a "good and loving parent." The second message which is communicated is hostile and withdrawing. These conflicting messages are difficult for the child to understand.

If the child accurately discriminates the message, he must face the fact that mother does not love him. Such a thought arouses too much anxiety for him on a conscious level so that the child deceives himself and incorrectly discriminates his own internal messages and those of others. Accurate reality testing is severely distorted. The child is caught in a double bind because he is punished for discriminating messages both accurately and inaccurately. For example, should the child respond to the mother's simulated loving, she will immediately punish the child by withdrawing. However, if he does not make loving approaches to her, the mother will punish the child for being ungrateful and unloving.

A variant of the double bind has also been proposed by Haley (1959) who believes that parents of preschizophrenic children tend also to negate one another's messages. In this case, members of the same household do not have any clear leadership since each contradicts the other. As a result, any firm alliance and relationships become impossible.

The double-bind hypothesis, therefore, explains schizophrenic behavior as an inability to distinguish real from unreal or fantasized events and hallucinations. This inadequacy, in accurately reading reality, is fostered in the family that forces a child to send and receive confused messages.

MARITAL SCHISM AND SKEW. While accepting the double-bind hypothesis as a major contributor to disordered behavior, Lidz et al. (1958) formulated an interpersonal basis for the development of schizophrenia by studying families with schizophrenic children. Families were found to exhibit two types of pathological patterns. In *marital schism,* parents are so engrossed with their own personality adjustment problems that they are unable to relate to one another or show any form of love, affection, or support. The household is characterized by constant bickering among the parents, antagonism and threats of separation. Each parent tends to undercut the other in front of the children. As a result, the child will develop conflicting views of reality and experience a faulty identification. To identify with one parent means a rejection of the other.

In *marital skew,* the dominant pathology of one marriage partner is supported by a weaker more dependent one. The dependent spouse tends to please, and go along with whatever the pathological partner does or says. There is a denial that any difficulties exist and the child is forced to accept the "sick" and distorted interpretations of the family. Under these situations, disordered behavioral and emotional development may be the result. The following psychiatric description of the mother of a schizophrenic man illustrates the extreme pathology of the family that is often discovered in the background of a psychotic (Lidz et al., 1958):

> Mrs. D. was a mother who was dominated with thoughts that her twin sons were geniuses whose development should not be limited in any way. Acts of delinquency by the twins such as robbery, setting fires, etc. were ignored or blamed on other children. She was prone to violent rages whenever her obsession with cleanliness was disrupted but gave inordinate praise to her sons for acts that the twins knew were nonsense. The atmosphere she created in the home for her husband and sons was crazy and distorted. For example, both twins believed for many years that constipation meant disagreeing with mother because whenever they argued with her she would say they were constipated and needed an enema. She would force both twins to lie naked in a prone position on the bathroom floor while she inserted the nose of a nozzle in each boy. The mother made this a contest to see which could hold out longer. The loser was required to dash downstairs to use the basement lavatory. Psychological tests of the mother revealed an unmistakable pattern of schizophrenia.

Alternative views of mental illness

Recently, some mental health professionals have begun to question traditional views of mental illness and have become increasingly dissatisfied with these formulations. Among these questioners, R. D. Laing (1967, 1969) has spoken out consistently and eloquently stating that individual madness is but a reflection of the madness of society. He believes that schizophrenic breakdowns are desperate strategies used by the person to liberate themselves from a "false self" used to maintain behavioral normality in our society. The false self has somehow become divided from the person's true inner self and the presumed "pathology" which we see is an attempt to heal this division. What comes through loud and clear from Laing's writings is that any attempt to adjust the person back to the original normality is denying the individual an opportunity to heal this split. As a result, traditional forms of treatment are viewed as inadequate.

Another vocal proponent of this viewpoint is Thomas Szasz, a psychiatrist, who has written a much circulated article (1960) and book entitled *The Myth of Mental Illness* (1961). Szasz takes a much more political and activistic stance than Laing. He believes that mental illness is not only a myth, but a misnomer, used by society to control the behavior of certain people whose behaviors deviate from theirs. Because the term implies that it is an organic disorder with a real medical origin, mental illness is treated as if it was free from ethical and moral interpretations. However, mental illness is not an illness in the physical sense and really represents "problems in living." Because diagnosis is subjective and requires judgment on the part of the mental health professional, a person is labeled mentally ill on the basis of how closely his behavior matches or deviates from psychosocial, ethical and legal norms. Putting the individual into a sick role is a powerful political ploy used by society and directed against people whose ideas, beliefs and behaviors differ from ours. Szasz likens the role of a psychiatrist to that of a slave master.

> The committed patient must accept the view that he is "sick," that his captors are "well"; that the patient's own view of himself is false and his captors' view of him is true; and that to effect any change in his social situation, the patient must relinquish his "sick" views and adopt the "healthy" views of those who have power over him. . . . Since most patients (like oppressed people generally) eventually accept the ideas imposed on them by their superiors, hospital psychiatrists are constantly immersed in an environment in which their identity as "doctor" is affirmed. The moral superiority of white men over black was similarly authenticated and affirmed (Szasz, 1970, p. 168–169).

This statement regarding the profession of psychiatry has frightening implications for many persons both inside and outside the mental health field. Sue and Sue (1972) point out that ethnic minorities and other disadvantaged groups feel that they live in a highly oppressive environment which attributes their cries of injustices to psychological maladjustments. In this way, such challenges are easily dismissed as being pathological and having no legitimacy. The concern can be best illustrated by a student of ours who made these statements: "Are we assuming that we are dealing with a sick person who cannot adjust to a normal society, or are we dealing with a normal individual who cannot adjust to a sick society? Maybe deviant behavior is a healthy reaction to a sick society. Should therapy be aimed at adjusting people to a society that is fraught with racism?" These are questions which are difficult to answer and pose ethical dilemmas for the mental health practitioner. In our following discussion of psychotherapy, these issues should be kept in mind. For if Halleck (1971) is correct in saying that "therapy is the handmaiden of the status quo," then we need to examine carefully our definitions of abnormality when applying them to others.

Treatment of emotional disorders

It is extremely difficult to talk about treating behavior disorders without reference to our previous discussion of etiology. This is because many of our treatment techniques are based upon the various theories used to explain mental illness. For example, if you believe that the causes of schizophrenia lie in some type of chemical imbalance or deficit, then you would tend to seek a cure via biological means. However, if you believe that environmental stress contributes to the development of disordered behavior, then your attempt at treatment might be a modification of that environment. The number of treatment techniques which have been suggested and used varies with the number of explanations of mental illness. In this section we will explore some of these therapy techniques.

Physical therapies

The *physical therapies* are a group of medical procedures that are used quite extensively with psychotic and to a lesser extent with neurotic patients. As such, the responsibility for using such treatment techniques lies in the hands of medical doctors.

The most recent advance in physical therapy with mental patients involves the use of drugs. Tranquilizers help calm the aggressive or overexcited while stimulants energize the depressed. Perhaps the most important thing about these drugs is that they help people reestablish some contact with the external world; consequently, they also make them more attentive and amenable to psychotherapy.

The use of drugs has also curtailed the use of more drastic medical procedures such as *insulin* and *electroshock* therapy. Insulin shock therapy, which some doctors report reduces schizophrenic confusion, consists of giving the patient an overdose of insulin so that convulsions are produced. However, because it is a dangerous procedure, it is rarely used today and has been replaced with electroconvulsive shock therapy. This medical technique involves producing a convulsion in the patient by passing a mild electric current through the body of the person. Electroshock therapy appears to have its greatest success with depressed patients. Studies indicate that as many as 80 to 90 percent of these patients show full recovery after a course of five to ten treatments. However, future depressions cannot be prevented by electroshock therapy and no one knows, despite its success, why it produces the results it does.

Moral, ethical, and legal issues have frequently been raised in the use of the physical therapies. The fact that use of the physical therapies is more often associated with disadvantaged groups in our society raises political questions similar to those just expressed in the last section. Furthermore, the potential damaging consequences of drugs and electroshock therapy is unclear. Great harm may be inflicted upon the individual without our awareness.

Psychotherapy

Psychotherapy, which literally means "mental treatment," is a term applied to the treatment of mental illness by psychological methods of therapy—in contrast to physical methods such as drugs and electric shock. The types of psychotherapy being practiced today are many and vary with the nature of the individual case and theoretical convictions of the therapists. Although there are major differences, it should be remembered that all techniques of therapy are directed at helping the person live a better life. The road to attaining this goal, however, depends to a large extent on the particular theory of personality held by the therapist.

PSYCHOANALYTIC THERAPY. Let us again briefly summarize some of the important concepts of psychoanalysis discussed in the previous chapter. Freud believed that anxiety-provoking impulses and memories could be hidden from consciousness through the use of certain ego-defense mechanisms (repression, projection, and others). However, unconscious material always seeks for conscious expression and is constantly exerting force toward this end. According to Freud, this repressed material can become conscious in two ways: (1) overcoming the forces of repression, or (2) circumventing the defenses. If the former occurs, the most likely reaction on the part of the person is a full-scale panic attack that results in a psychotic break. The ego is completely overwhelmed by the frightening unconscious material. The second method occurs during states of so-called ego-weakness. That is, for one reason or another, the ego relaxes its guard and during that period some of the unconscious conflicts or impulses leak into consciousness. Ego-weakness can occur if the individual becomes fatigued, relaxed, or sleeps. The conscious guard of the person is lowered. However, the ego is never fully relaxed so even when unconscious material leaks out, the censoring apparatus disguises or alters the material in some way. Slips of the tongue and the pen, dreams, and much of our actions are dictated by unconscious forces. In the case of behavior pathology, disordered behavior is seen as being symptomatic of these deep underlying conflicts.

The role of the psychoanalytic therapist, therefore, is to uncover the repressed material in a graded fashion that does not overwhelm the patient with anxiety. Just like an artichoke, the role of the therapist is to strip away the outer leaves until the heart of the problem is reached. In the process of psychoanalysis, the patient develops insight into the problem through an intensive and prolonged relationship with the therapist. The patient's unconscious motivations are explored, with special importance attached to the earliest sources of conflict and repression. Much of this is accomplished through techniques of free association, analysis of transference, and interpretation.

Free association. In free association, the unconscious is explored by having the patient recline on a couch and be instructed to talk about whatever thoughts, feelings, or topics comes to mind regardless of how embarrassing, painful, or illogical it may be. The attempt here is to facilitate states of ego-weakness so that the repressed material can gain consciousness. The patient, at first, talks about what appears to be an aimless, directionless stream of topics, but eventually the thoughts drift toward the unconscious material. Since these conflicts tend to be highly symbolic, the analyst proceeds to interpret to the patient the meaning of the thoughts, wishes, and attitudes expressed in the free association.

Transference. Transference is the process in which the patient responds unconsciously and emotionally to the analyst in the same fashion as some important people in his life, such as the father or mother. The transference may involve feelings of love and admiration or be negative, hostile and envious. For example, the patient may respond with anger toward his analyst because he feels overwhelmed in his presence. When this anger is analyzed, the patient might discover that the analyst reminds him of his father whom he unconsciously resents.

The interpretation of behavior resulting from transference is the heart of psychoanalytic treatment. It enables the patient to see how his present personality traits and conflicts have emerged from his early experiences, many of which have been repressed. Consequently, when the individual accepts these interpretations and consciously redirects his attitudes and views toward himself and others, restructuring of personality takes place.

Interpretation. The major function of interpretation is to speed up the process of uncovering repressed material which the therapist has been able to put together like a jigsaw puzzle. The analyst listens for gaps in the story, observes the patient's reactions and behaviors, and formulates what is believed to be the unconscious conflicts experienced by the patient. For example, during the course of analysis a patient may evidence *resistance*, an unwillingness or inability to deal with certain topics or thoughts. Resistance occurs because the patient is seen as getting too close to the threatening material and is frightened off. Evidence of resistance is seen in such things as switching topics suddenly, forgetting or being late for appointments, and giving glib incorrect associations.

Interpretation is generally applied in the area of *dream analysis*. The content of dreams is always considered to be very meaningful and to represent disguised expressions of something in the patient's unconscious. Freud believed that there were two parts to dreams: the *manifest content*, that part which we remember and the *latent content*, the actual true meaning of the dream. From the manifest content and the analyst's knowledge of the patient, an attempt is made to interpret the latent meaning. To illustrate, a man who is filled with anxiety about failing on the job and being fired may express his fear symbolically by dreaming that he is running uphill, pursued by wild animals. Or, a boy might have sexual dreams about an older woman, which represents an unresolved "Oedipus complex."

Basic to psychoanalysis is its belief that by making the unconscious conflicts conscious, the person is better able to change his personality structure with consequent changes in behavior (disappearance of symptoms). The belief that insight always leads to behavior change is being challenged and we will discuss this controversy shortly.

CLIENT-CENTERED THERAPY. Carl Rogers has developed a method of psychotherapy that is, in many ways, strikingly different from psychoanalysis. It is called *client-centered* because the therapist will not suggest a solution to the client, but deliberately leaves it up to him. It is nondirective because it is left up to the client what he wishes to talk about; the therapist will not suggest any topics for discussion. This technique, as we have seen in Chapter 8, is based on the premise that an individual who is sufficiently motivated can work through his own problems. Man is considered to be essentially a rational creature, possessed of the capacity to grow and solve his own problems. If provided with the opportunity, goals and acts will be in the direction to effect self-actualization. In nondirective therapy, the role of the therapist is to accept, restate, and clarify the client's feelings. The therapist is simply interested in creating an understanding atmosphere that will at all times encourage the patient to clarify his present feelings about any subject or person. In contrast to psychoanalysis, the patient is regarded as an individual behaving in the present without regard to his past; there is no attempt to uncover repressed drives and fears.

Rogers identifies six necessary and sufficient conditions for effective psychotherapy:

> (1) Two persons are in psychological contact. (2) The first, whom we shall term the client, is in a state of incongruence, being vulnerable or anxious. (3) The second person, whom we shall term the therapist, is

congruent or integrated in the relationship. (4) The therapist experiences unconditional positive regard for the client. (5) The therapist experiences an empathic understanding of the client's internal frame of reference and endeavors to communicate this experience to the client. (6) The communication to the client of the therapist's empathic understanding and unconditional positive regard is to a minimal degree achieved. No other conditions are necessary. If these six conditions exist and continue over a period of time this is sufficient. The process of constructive personality change will follow (Rogers, 1957, p. 96).

These six conditions again emphasize Rogers' belief that man is able to solve his own problems when placed in a healthy environmental situation.

BEHAVIOR THERAPY. One of the newer directions in psychotherapy has been the attempt to link therapeutic processes to learning principles discovered in the laboratory (see Chapter 5). Maladaptive behavior can be classified as a behavior deficit or excess, and therapy should be aimed at either increasing adaptive or decreasing maladaptive responses. For example, an autistic child may lack speech, a withdrawn student may have undeveloped social skills or assertive responses, or a child may be too often engaged in temper tantrums. In all cases, behavior therapists define disorders in terms of observable responses.

While psychoanalysis and nondirective therapy place great emphasis on the patient's gaining insight into his deepest feelings, behavior therapy deals more directly with the disordered behavior. This difference represents one of the greatest differences between the two approaches. Because psychoanalysis believes that symptoms are only the visible results of unconscious intrapsychic conflicts, the cause and not the symptoms should be attacked. If we eliminate the symptoms without eliminating the underlying cause, we have not cured the individual. The belief is that the symptom will either return or another one will take its place (symptom substitution). Let us use an analogy to illustrate this point. Supposing that you have a bacterial infection which causes dizziness, headaches, and a high fever. The infection is the cause of your symptoms and unless you eliminate the bacterial invasion of your body you will continue to be ill. We can use icepacks or other physical means to reduce or even eliminate the high fever. Have we cured you? No! The bacterial infection is still in your body causing internal damage that may result in other symptoms and eventually death, unless it is cured.

Because behavior theory believes that symptoms are learned behavior subject to the principles of learning, the aim of therapy should be to attack the symptoms directly. There is no need to postulate a deep underlying cause since the symptom is the disease. As a result, treatment of symptoms (observable behaviors) will cure the person and no other symptoms will return. The basic belief of the behavior therapist is his assumption that psychopathology, particularly in the case of the neuroses, arises out of learning experiences that have produced persistent and inflexible habits that were acquired initially as means of avoiding anxiety. Because therapy is aimed at behavior change, techniques of classical and instrumental conditioning are used. We shall describe three general techniques of behavior therapy.

Counterconditioning. Joseph Wolpe (1969) has identified three ways in which counterconditioning principles may be used in the treatment of different disorders: *systematic desensitization, assertive training,* and *therapeutic sexual arousal.* As you should recall from Chapter 5, counterconditioning was employed with the case of the little boy who developed an extreme fear (phobia) of furry animals. At the sight of furry animals, the boy would show anxiety by whimpering, crawling away, shaking and trembling. The experimenters were able to eliminate his fear by feeding the child in the presence of the animal. On succeeding days the animal was brought nearer and nearer to the young boy as he ate until all fear of the animal disappeared. This was done gradually in a step-by-step fashion. The principles applied were based on counterconditioning. What the experimenters did was to condition another incompatible response (eating) to anxiety in the presence of the small animal. Because the act of eating is pleasurable and antagonistic to anxiety, anxiety associated with the animal was eliminated.

Wolpe reasoned that any response antagonistic to anxiety could be used to eliminate the fear associated with a particular situation. Because relaxation has behavioral and physiological responses that are opposite to that of anxiety, he felt this to be an excellent response to use in therapy. *Systematic desensitization* is the breaking down of an anxiety response habit in piecemeal fashion through the use of relaxation. Suppose that you have a phobia about taking tests. Wolpe might approach your situation by (1) training you to relax, (2) constructing a hierarchy of the feared events in graded fashion from scenes that elicit the least to the greatest amount of anxiety, and (3) counterimposing relaxation responses to these scenes. Below is a typical anxiety hierarchy which might have been constructed in your case.

1. Taking the test.
2. Waiting for the exam to be handed out.
3. Standing in front of the examination room.
4. The night before the exam.
5. Studying for the exam.
6. One week before the exam.
7. Two weeks before the exam.
8. The professor announces an exam to be given.

These scenes are ordered in such a sequence that the most anxiety-arousing scenes are at the top and the least are at the bottom. The fearful imagined scenes are then presented to you with instructions to relax. The pairing of deep muscle relaxation with the fearful scenes should eliminate your anxiety. Wolpe would systematically move up the steps until they no longer aroused any type of anxiety. In essence, you have been desensitized and should not now experience test-taking phobia. The success of systematic desensitization in the treatment of phobias or fearful situations has led to its increasing popularity as a therapeutic technique.

Similarly, *assertive training* has been used successfully in the treatment of clients who are extremely timid or passive. It is also based on counterconditioning but this time the antagonistic response is assertion. Wolpe believes that those who are unable to assert themselves are prevented from doing this because of anxiety (fear of being punished, and so on). As a result, the anxiety must be overcome by teaching the client to become more aggressive in social situations. Each time the person asserts himself, he weakens the fear associated with different situations.

Although the use of *therapeutic sexual arousal* also is similar in principle to desensitization and assertion, we will discuss this technique in Chapter 10 on "Sexuality."

Aversive techniques. Aversive techniques are those which make use of pain such as electric shocks or nauseating drugs to eliminate maladaptive behaviors. This technique has been used extensively in the treatment of deviant sexual behavior (see Chapter 10) and alcoholism. Lovaas, Shaeffer and Simmons (1965) have identified three ways in which pain can be used therapeutically. First, pain can be used directly as punishment. A prime example is when parents spank or punish their child for misbehaviors. Furthermore, direct punishment has been employed in the treatment of autistic children whenever they have engaged in temper tantrums, or self-stimulation. Second, pain can be removed or withheld contingent upon certain behaviors. A child who has been spanked for not cleaning up his room knows that to avoid such treatment requires him to pick up all the toys. Alcoholics who are given a drug, antabuse, know that to take a drink of any alcoholic beverage will make them deathly ill. Third, any stimulus associated with pain reduction will acquire reinforcing properties. The fact that most parents are viewed positively by their children may be due to their ability to reduce fear and pain in their children. If a child has a frightening nightmare and wakens in a dark room, his fears are considerably reduced when mother comforts him. Most aversive techniques used in therapy are variations of these principles.

Positive reinforcement. Receiving rewards after exhibiting a behavior will increase the probability of its occurrence. In this case, the behavior therapist identifies desirable behaviors that he would like to see strengthened in the person. He then systematically sets out to reinforce these behaviors each time they occur. In the case of autistic children who lack speech, speaking can be reinforced by candy, verbal compliments, and hugs. The choice of a reinforcer is dependent upon what the person finds most rewarding. Teachers who give gold stars to students use these as rewards for their performance in class. The establishment of "Token Economy" systems in many mental institutions operates under this principle. Patients earn tokens for certain things they do during their stay in the hospital. These tokens can be used like money in exchange for leaves, attendance of movies, or highly desirable privileges.

GROUP FORMS OF THERAPY. Throughout our lives we all participate in various groups. Indeed, it is impossible for any of us to escape the influence of the various groups in our social system. Clinicians are beginning to realize more and more that social influence affects personality formation and the manifestation of psychopathology. Much of the current theories of abnormal behavior assumes intrapsychic causes; the newer view, however, is that behavior pathology can evolve from disturbed interpersonal transactions. Indeed, the double-bind theory and the concept of marital schism and skew is such a broader view.

This thinking has led to emphasis on the use of group therapy as a means to treat behavior disorders because it simulates real life more closely than individual therapy. Furthermore, if behavior problems are a result of disturbed relationships with others, therapeutic experiences with groups may help work through such problems. The use of family therapy and the encounter group movements are two such examples. Since we have already discussed some aspects of encounter groups in Chapter 6, we will deal only with the former in this section.

The *family therapy* approach emphasizes the interdependence of all behavior within the family constellation. When one member shows disordered behavior, it is seen as the inevitable outcome of a typical pattern of family interactions. An example of this is revealed below:

Scott B., a ten-year-old boy, was first brought to the clinic by his mother who described his behavior as "disruptive." During the past two weeks he had refused to eat or sleep and would not speak to anyone. The parents were becoming extremely worried about the state of his health. Mr. B. thought that Scott was trying to defy his authority and did not accede to bringing Scott to the clinic any earlier. However, Mr. B.'s son had begun to mutilate himself with sharp objects and this convinced him that Scott was, perhaps, seriously disturbed.

Because of Scott's emaciated condition he was hospitalized and forced fed with a tube. Over a period of two months he made rapid improvements and was finally discharged from the hospital. However, he was brought to the clinic twice a week for treatment on an outpatient basis. During the next two weeks, the therapist began to see evidence of regression in Scott. At the time of the discharge, he was happy, talkative, and outgoing which contrasted sharply with his increasingly sullen and withdrawn mood. Fearful of a relapse, the parents were immediately drawn in for family counseling.

Family counseling revealed a pattern of pathology among its members. Although the parents had originally stressed how well both of them got along with one another, it became increasingly clear that hostile tension existed between the two. What appeared was the picture of frustrated marital partners who disliked one another intensely. Unable to face this fact, both parents would use Scott as a scapegoat for their marital problems. As long as Scott was identified as the "problem," attention was taken away from their own difficulties. During the two months in which Scott was hospitalized, Mrs. B. reported that she and her husband argued frequently. This supported the therapist's belief that Scott was serving a scapegoat role. In his absence, the parents had no one to blame for their difficulties.

This example makes clear several things. First, deviant behavior often is a function of group interaction patterns. Second, it may be futile to treat the individual without treating the entire family. Although the individual may be cured, he may revert back to a "sick" role if no consequent change has occurred in the family. The family member who is seen as being "sick" may be, in disguise, symptomatic of a disturbed family in need of treatment. For that reason, family therapy stresses treating the family as a unit. The manner of treatment can take many forms and depends upon the presenting problems and the orientation of the family therapist.

The effectiveness of psychotherapy

It is extremely difficult to give a precise evaluation of psychotherapy for treating mental illness, or to compare the relative success of particular techniques. Different therapists work with different types of patients, and consequently, do not regularly compare their records. Also, therapists usually do not have access to control groups, who receive no treatment, that would permit them to estimate the number of spontaneous recoveries (patients with the disappearance of symptoms in the absence of treatment). In the case of family therapy, little objective research data has been collected.

One author (Eysenck, 1967) in summarizing the data of several investigators, reports that spontaneous remissions occur in the majority of neurotic cases. Nevertheless, a patient probably has a much better chance to improve with psychotherapy than with no help at all. This is particularly true for neurotics.

Summary

Mental illness is a term used to describe a psychological maladjustment serious enough to handicap the afflicted person and burden others. Although this term appears adequate, it is often difficult to determine what constitutes normality and abnormality. The statistical concept believes that deviations from whatever characteristics occur most frequently in the population is considered abnormal. The ideal mental health criterion states that some goal such as self-actualization, maturity, and insight should be used. Both of these definitions have major weaknesses as outlined in the chapter. Although the practical criteria are also subject to similar criticism, they tend to be more useful because they inquire into the reasons for labeling individuals abnormal. The practical criteria use discomfort, bizarreness, and inefficiency as gauges of abnormality.

Neurotic reactions are most frequently manifested by discomfort and inefficiency rather than bizarreness. Five large classes of neuroses were identified. (1) Anxiety reactions are either free-floating or phobic. (2) Depressive neurotics are characterized by feelings of sadness, worthlessness, lack of energy, and guilt. (3) Hysterical neuroses are of the conversion or dissociative type. (4) Obsessive-compulsive disorders are composed of obsessions manifested in doubting and thoughts, and compulsions, are irresistible urges to carry out a behavior sequence. (5) Fatigue-hypochondriasis is that class of disorders which has symptoms of over-concern with bodily health, and complaints about vague aches and pains.

Not only do psychotic reactions involve discomfort and inefficiency but also bizarreness. Psychotics are usually unable to maintain their normal role in society. Three forms of psychoses were identified: (1) Organic disorders involve an actual physical cause. (2) Schizophrenic reactions involve cognitive dysfunctioning. Four types of schizophrenia were discussed: simple, catatonic, hebephrenic, and paranoid. (3) The affective psychoses are predominantly disorders of mood. This group is commonly called manic-depressive reactions because it is characterized by extreme mood swings.

Besides neuroses and psychoses, personality and psychosomatic disorders were also discussed. Personality disorders do not necessarily involve distress on the part of the person but an acting out of socially inappropriate behaviors. Psychosomatic disorders involve actual organic changes (hypertension, asthma, and others) in the body caused by excessive stress.

Many explanations have been proposed as to the origins of these disorders. Genetic and biochemical theories seek explanations within the body. A more prevalent theory seeks to explain psychopathology as arising from environmental forces. Especially important is the family environment. One popular theory called the double bind states that parents send conflicting messages to their children which makes it difficult to distinguish reality from unreality. Another variant believes that other pathological patterns such as marital schism and skew contributes to behavior disorders.

Recently, many mental health professionals have begun to question traditional views of mental illness. Among these are Laing and Szasz, who believe that (1) individual madness is a reflection of madness in our society, and (2) mental illnesses are really problems in living. There is fear that the label "mental illness" and the use of psychotherapy may become political tools used to control individuals who possess different ideas.

Treatment of emotional disorders is intimately linked to beliefs concerning its causes. Physical therapies (medication and shock therapy) assume biological causes. Psychotherapy, which is the treatment of mental illness by psychological methods, is strongly based on the different theories of personality: (1) Psychoanalytic therapy aims at making unconscious intrapsychic conflicts conscious. There is an attempt to have the individual achieve insight into repressed materials. (2) Client-centered therapy is a nondirective approach which believes that the client, when provided with unconditional positive regard by the therapist can resolve his own problems. The role of the therapist is to accept, reflect, and clarify the client's statements. (3) Behavior therapy attempts to apply learning principles to the cure of behavior disorders. Since maladaptive behaviors are learned, behaviorists believe that elimination of the symptoms constitute a cure. Three general techniques have been used: *(a)* counterconditioning; *(b)* aversive techniques that use pain or discomfort to eliminate or enhance behaviors; and *(c)* positive reinforcement. (4) Group forms of therapy such as encounter groups and family therapy are based on the theory that behavior pathology evolves from disturbed interpersonal transactions. As a result, some psychologists believe treatment should be aimed at groups rather than individuals.

References

Bateson, G., Jackson, D. D., Haley, J., & Weakland, J. Toward a theory of schizophrenia. *Behavioral Science*, 1956, **1**, 251–264.

Buss, A. H. *Psychopathology*. New York: Wiley, 1966.

Byrd, R. E. *Alone*. New York: Putnam, 1938.

Coleman, J. C. *Abnormal psychology and modern life*. Glenview, Ill.: Scott, Foresman, 1972.

Eysenck, H. J. New ways in psychotherapy. Reprinted from *Psychology Today* Magazine, **1**(2), 1967. Copyright © Ziff Publishing Company.

Goldhammer, H. & Marshall, A. W. *Psychosis and Civilization*. New York: Free Press, 1953.

Gottesman, I. I., & Shields, J. Schizophrenia in twins: 16 years consecutive admissions to a psychiatric clinic. *British Journal of Psychiatry*, 1966, **112**, 809.

Haley, J. The family of the schizophrenic: A model system. *Journal of Nervous and Mental Disease*, 1959, **129**, 357–374.

Halleck, S. L. Therapy is the handmaiden of the status quo. *Psychology Today*, 1971, **4**(11), 30–34, 98–100.

Heath, R. G., Krupp, I. M., Byers, L. W., & Liljekuist, J. I. Schizophrenia as an immunologic disorder: Effects of serum protein fractions on brain function, 1967 (unpublished).

Kallman, F. J. The genetics of mental illness. In S. Arieti (Ed.), *American handbook of psychiatry*. New York: Basic Books, 1959, 175–234.

Kisker, G. W. From *The disorganized personality*, by G. W. Kisker. Copyright © 1964 by McGraw-Hill, Inc. Used with permission of McGraw-Hill Book Co.

Laing, R. D. *The divided self*. New York: Pantheon, 1967.

Laing, R. D. *The politics of experience*. New York: Pantheon, 1969.

Lidz, T., Cornelison, A., Terry, D., & Fleck, S. Intrafamilial environment of the schizophrenic patient: VI. The transmission of irrationality. *American Medical Association Archives of Neurological Psychiatry*, 1958, **79**, 305–316.

Lovaas, O. I., Schaeffer, B., & Simmons, J. Q. Building social behavior in autistic children by use of electric shock. *Journal of Experimental Research on Personality*, 1965, **1**, 99–109.

Rogers, C. R. The necessary and sufficient conditions of therapeutic personality change. *Journal of Consulting Psychology*, 1957, **21**, 95–103.

Schreiber, F. R. *The sixteen personalities of Sybil*. New York: Regnery, 1973.

Sue, D. W., & Sue, S. Ethnic minorities: Resistance to being researched. *Professional Psychology*, 1972, **2**, 11–17.

Szasz, T. S. The myth of mental illness. *American Psychologist*, 1960, **15**, 113–118.

Szasz, T. S. *The myth of mental illness*. New York: Hoeber-Harper, 1961.

Szasz, T. S. The crime of commitment. *Readings in Clinical Psychology Today*. Del Mar, Calif.: CRM, 1970, 167–169.

Thigpen, C. H., & Cleckley, H. M. *Three faces of Eve*. New York: McGraw-Hill, 1957.

Wolpe, J. *The practice of behavior therapy*. New York: Pergamon Press, 1969.

SECTION SIX

Developmental aspects of behavior

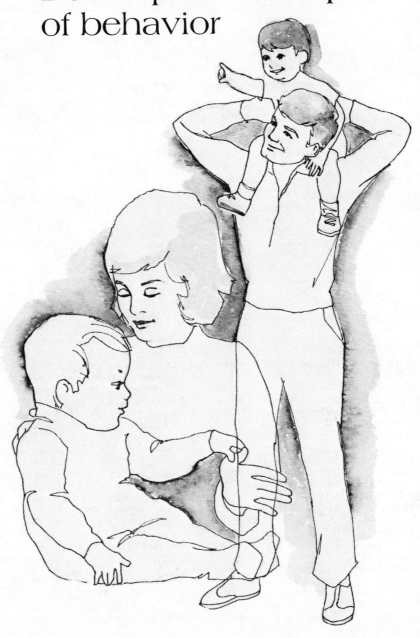

Developmental psychology is that field which attempts to describe changes in behavior and psychological functioning which are highly correlated with age. These changes may be the result of biological and environmental factors. As we saw in Chapter 8, Freud postulated several psychosexual stages in development which he saw all of us experiencing. He emphasized the importance of the libido or the sex instinct in man's behavior and later development. Although the sex motive and its secondary implications occupy a position of importance in our society, it has not been a "proper" area for biological or psychological inquiry. As a result, much misinformation and myth has grown up around this area. Chapter 10 deals with the biological, psychological, and sociological implications of sexuality. Like Chapter 9 in its organization, it follows a parallel in describing disordered sexual development and its treatment.

Continuing with our belief that development is an ongoing process, Chapter 11 discusses youth and old age from a continuity perspective. Although you may not be surprised to see adolescence and adulthood covered in a section on development, it may be surprising to see a discussion devoted to senescence or old age. Most introductory texts do not deal with this topic. As a result, old age and attitudes toward death have been a neglected topic. Why is this so? Perhaps our avoidance of old age and death reflects our negative attitudes toward death. We also seem to fear getting old and believe that the aged cannot be helped. We will do anything to appear youthful and engage in activities which fool us and help us deny our advancing age. Yet, all of us will grow old and die one day. Hiding from our fate does not help us to understand the process of aging.

10

Sexuality

The sex hormones.

Neural mechanisms.

Dysfunctions of the female reproductive system.

The role of personality characteristics.

Eroticism.
  Sexual response cycle.
  Bodily reactions of men and women.

Sex appeal.

Attitudes on sex (generation gap, Kinsey reports, double standard, promiscuity and swinging).

Different cultures and sexual patterns.

Sexual variance.
  Impotency and frigidity.
  Satyriasis and nymphomania.
  Homosexuality and transvestism.
  Incest.
  Rape.
  Exhibitionism and voyeurism.
  Sadism and masochism.

General causes of sexual deviations.

Treatment of sexual disorders.

Summary.

I t is a safe generalization to assert that human sexuality has been until recently a very underresearched topic. It is thus somewhat paradoxical that since sex occupies such an important place in our society, it has only recently been the subject of several investigations. Needless to say, the paucity of research does not reflect any lack of interest on the part of scientists or people in general. Rather, sexual behavior is associated with so many taboos and prohibitions in our society that free discussion of sex, not to mention research, is prohibited in many situations. These taboos are slowly lifting as reflected in recent studies (Gagnon, 1973; Goldstein & Kant, 1973; Weinberg, 1973) and this chapter will cover some of the findings with respect to the several aspects of sexuality. These include so-called normal sexuality on both the behavioral and physiological levels. Also sexual variations and dysfunctions, as well as some of the new therapy techniques developed to aid those with sexual problems, will be presented.

Sex is a powerful motive and thus it is somewhat tragic that such an important aspect of human functioning has been neglected so long. Undoubtedly, many of the problems so rampant in marriage are related to sexual inadequacies which could be improved and helped with the development of more knowledge about sexual relations.

Sex research has a long history, but during the past few decades there have been several important advances. In part, our increase in knowledge is because of a marked increase in the number of scientists from several disciplines investigating problems of sexual behavior. It is also because of the new discoveries in the development of rigorous and sophisticated techniques.

The sex hormones

It has been known for many years that gonadal hormones play a crucial role in the growth of the genital structures in humans and lower animals. But, before we report on how they affect sexual behavior, it is worthwhile to understand the role of sex hormones in the fetus. In this manner, we are in a position to better comprehend how the so-called gonadal hormones exert their effects on subsequent sexual behavior. The evidence indicates that sex hormones influence sexual behavior by directing the early differentiation and development of the central nervous system structures. These are partly genetically controlled and partly shaped by the influence of the different sex hormones during childhood and adolescence.

Androgens and male sexual behavior

The male testes, in addition to producing the sperm necessary for reproduction, secrete the male hormones known as *androgens* and a small amount of the female hormones, *estrogens*. Only a small amount of both hormones are produced prior to puberty; but as a male reaches sexual maturation, the supply of androgens is dramatically increased. There is little doubt that these sex hormones play a crucial role in the growth of the genital organs in man and in the lower species. However, contrary to popular opinion, the anatomical structures do not necessarily determine their function in sexual behavior.

For instance, the gender role of hermaphrodites (people with the genital organs of both sexes) is determined by the social role assigned to them after birth (Zuckerman, 1971). While hormones do not seem to play an important role in determining the direction of sexual interests, they may have crucial consequences for the strength of the sex drive. The actual physiological effects of androgens include the stimulation of the growth and dilation of the blood vessels in the penis enabling a complete erection to take place. A major factor in the sexual decline in later years is a decrease in production of these hormones.

The best evidence for the effect of hormones on male sexual behavior is provided by experimental castration in animals. This procedure involves removing the testes, the chief source of androgens. The general effect of castration is to lower the level of sexual behavior; however, there are two major factors involved that will modify these results. First, the effect is much greater when castration takes place before puberty; as a matter of fact, in ancient times men took advantage of this method to provide eunuchs to guard their harems. Second, the results of castration depend on the evolutionary stage of the species. Lower mammals, such as rats, show a rapid decline in sexual activity after castration. However, higher mammals, such as dogs, may retain potency for several years and chimpanzees even longer. In the case of castrated animals who lose their sexual drive, it can be quickly restored by injections of androgen.

CASTRATION IN MAN. In keeping with the above general principle, the situation at the human level is the most complex of all. Some men have reported a marked decline in sexual interest and capacity after accidental castration, but others report a continued high level of performance for as long as 30 years (Murray, 1964).

One group of hypogonadal males, who had suffered a decline in their sex drive and later had it restored by androgen injections, reported a loss of arousability once again when the shots were stopped (Zuckerman, 1971). The amount of semen was reduced until no fluid was emitted, and the men reported they had fewer erections and little urge to masturbate or initiate heterosexual activity. Even reports of erotic imagery and daydreams were diminished. We should keep in mind, however, that psychological factors are also important in regard to the sex drive. Most cases of impotence in males are not expressions of hormonal insufficiencies and do not respond to treatment with additional androgens. Sex hormones apparently operate to lower thresholds for sexual arousal in men, but as previously stated, some males remain active after castration.

Effects of estrogen on the female psyche

Female sexual behavior is also influenced by hormones, but the relationship is even more complex than in men. Sexual activity, as well as the development of secondary sex characteristics, is increased at puberty by estrogen. These female hormones are secreted by the ovaries along with a small amount of androgen; the latter hormones apparently act to heighten sexual excitability. For example, Money (1961) presents considerable clinical evidence that androgen is also related to sexual arousability in women. Furthermore, many women who receive androgen therapy report increased sexual drive.

At the time of puberty, we also see the beginning of estrual or fertility cycle in female animals. The human fertility cycle lasts about four weeks and is controlled by a complex interaction between the hormones of the ovaries and the pituitary. As we saw in Chapter 2, the pituitary is called the master gland because it affects hormonal activities of other endocrine glands. During the first two weeks of the cycle, one ovary prepares an egg for fertilization and both ovaries produce estrogen; the hormones prepare the uterus for implantation. During the second half of the cycle, ovulation occurs—the fertile egg starts its journey to the uterus, and the ovaries begin to secrete *progesterone*, the maternal hormone. This second female hormone further prepares the uterus for implantation and indirectly prepares the mammary glands for nursing.

The effects of the fertility cycle and hormones on sexual behavior can most clearly be seen in the lower mammals. During ovulation, when the bloodstream becomes enriched with estrogens, female mammals lose their previous indifference to males and become highly receptive or even aggressive in their sexual behavior. This behavior is known as *estrus*, or "heat," and serves as a signal that the female animal is in a condition to be impregnated. As we go up the evolutionary scale, the sexual behavior of the female becomes less closely bound to the fertility cycle. Monkeys and apes have been observed to copulate during all phases of the fertility cycle, although the greatest amount of sexual excitement occurs during ovulation.

The removal of the ovaries, female castration, has the same general effects similar to those found in male castration. In lower animals, this operation completely abolishes sexual behavior in the female, and the male is no longer attracted. But chimpanzees and other apes may continue to show sexual responsiveness even after the ovaries are removed. More likely, though, is that the usual level of sexual activity is considerably lessened.

At the human level, hormonal influence over feminine sexual activity seems to be overshadowed by social and psychological conditions. Unlike lower female organisms, women frequently engage in sexual relations at all times of the fertility cycle, therefore demonstrating independence from hormonal conditions. In fact, many women who have undergone ovariotomies or who have passed through the menopause, do not lose their sexual desire at all.

On the other hand, there is some evidence that estrogen has a tendency to arouse sexual interest. Psychoanalytic observations show that women have more erotic dreams during the first two weeks of the fertility cycle than at other times. During the second half of the cycle when progesterone is dominant, women have more dreams with maternal themes (Murray, 1964).

Neural mechanisms

As we have seen, hormones do not account for all of the sexual behavior, particularly in the case of humans. Sexual behavior is undoubtedly mediated by the central and autonomic nervous systems, including an important role for the hypothalamus. Beach (1958) has noted that there are species and sex differences in dependence of sexual arousal on the higher centers in the brain or hormones. The evolutionary trend is toward more emphasis on structures and less on hormones.

The cerebral cortex

Starting with the highest center in the brain, the cerebral cortex, we find that it is significantly involved in the sexual behavior of animals. This principle holds true to the extent that sensory stimulation, motor coordination, and perception are necessary. There are marked differences between female and male animals. The female rat, cat, and dog readily copulate in spite of complete decortication (removal of the cortex part of the brain). In most gross respects, the behavior pattern is quite normal, although some of the minor components are missing (Morgan, 1965). One important difference, however, is that the female no longer attempts to take an active part in initiating sexual activity.

In male animals the picture is somewhat different. Damage to about 60 to 75 percent of the cortex will entirely eliminate sexual behavior, and even large doses of sex hormones cannot restore it (Beach, 1940). Cortical lesions made on male animals of higher species have even more pronounced effects. For example, the ability of the male cat is greatly impaired by bilateral removal of any one of the major lobes of the cortex, although it still manifests awkward attempts at mounting the female. Apparently, large cortical lesions greatly disturb motor capacities that are essential in the execution of mating behavior but not sexual excitement.

Hypothalamus

Once again, we find the hypothalamus plays an important role in a motivational state, this time sexual behavior. This tiny brain center, interlinked with the autonomic nervous system and pituitary gland, is responsible for organizing various complex components of sexual arousal and behavior. We know of its importance because destruction of the relevant area in the hypothalamus eliminates sexual behavior. For instance, although the genital reflexes remain, a female cat with a hypothalamic injury does not show typical crouching behavior with a male.

Electrical stimulation of the appropriate area in the hypothalamus will directly elicit sexual behavior, which suggests that the normal mechanism of maintaining the sex drive is its direct excitation by hormones. Vaughan and Fisher (1962) obtained exaggerated sexual behavior in the male rat by such techniques. Within a few seconds after the current was turned on, the animals began mounting estrual females and continued their sexual activity at a very high rate until the current was turned off, whereupon the behavior dramatically stopped. Penile erection was virually constant during the stimulation and some rats had as many as 15 to 20 ejaculations an hour.

Spinal cord

The spinal cord possesses the control centers for many of the basic sexual reflexes organized by the hypothalamus. The spinal reflexes which are found also in men include erection, pelvic movements, and ejaculation in the male. They have been observed in many victims of gunshot wounds or car accidents (*paraplegics*) whose spinal cords have been severed. Paraplegics cannot voluntarily move or receive sensations from their lower limbs because of the injury to the sensory and motor nerve tracts. Yet there was one case of a paraplegic who succeeded in impregnating his wife, showing that spinal reflexes are sufficient for minimal sexual activity (Murray, 1964).

Integration of neural and endocrine structures

We have now covered much of the physiological basis for sexual behavior. Although the various neural mechanisms and endocrine glands have different functions, they have a reciprocal relationship as illustrated in Figure 10–1. The central nervous system, including the cortex, hypothalamus, and spinal cord, mediates the effects of environmental changes and exerts a regulatory influence over the pituitary gland.

The pituitary gland, in return, controls the testes and ovaries by the production of its gonadotrophic hormones. The hormones from the gonads, in return, feed back to the CNS and pituitary gland to influence

FIGURE 10–1
The reciprocal relationship between
neural centers and endocrine glands in
determining sexual behavior

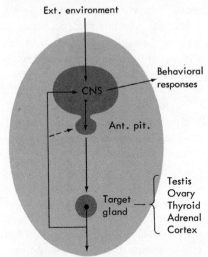

Source: G. W. Harris, "Central Control of
Pituitary Secretion," in John Field (Ed.),
Handbook of Physiology (1960), vol. 2. Copyright 1960 by the American Physiological Association. Reprinted by permission.

both the behavior of the organism and the level of pituitary activity. This
general schema holds true for both man and lower organisms. However,
the highest neural centers become increasingly important for sexual behavior in higher animals and hormones less dominant.

Dysfunctions of the female reproductive system

Emotionally related dysfunctions of the reproductive system in men
seem primarily limited to two types of systems; impotence and premature ejaculation. These male disorders will be covered later in the chapter. In contrast, women experience an astonishing range of ailments
which can involve every one of the reproductive organs. A partial list
of symptoms illustrates the diversity of reproductive dysfunctions: painful menstruation, suppression of or scanty menstruation, painful vaginal
spasms, unexplained infertility, false pregnancy, premature labor, premature rupture of the membranes, spontaneous abortion, and insufficient milk production. Any of these symptoms may have a psychological
origin or a direct physical cause. We shall focus mainly on the role of
psychological factors in contributing to these symptoms.

The role of personality characteristics

The self-concept of many women is closely linked to their appearance and the function of their bodies. Physical attractiveness and sexual and maternal behavior are traditionally stressed as feminine values and largely affect feelings of personal worth. Because emphasis is placed on the bodies of women, their bodily organs become a prime outlet for the indirect expression of aggression and resentment.

Much of the available research does show that gynecological symptoms are associated with certain personality characteristics (Bardwick, 1971). These psychosomatic patients are commonly found to be ambivalent about being female and assuming the traditional feminine role. This identity crisis is related to strong dependency needs, in which the patients are unwilling to give up their excessive dependency upon their husbands. They often are passive and defer to their spouses in order to secure affection. But they are found, at the same time, to resent the affectional needs and role demands of their husbands. In other words, these women want to receive rather than to give in a relationship.

Most psychosomatic patients caught in this bind do not have available social outlets through which they can directly express their hostility. They are not engaged in recreational and vocational activities which provide effective outlets for the releasing of anger and frustrations. Thus, their tensions are expressed in a psychosomatic manner. These symptoms begin early, as the origin of dependency and passivity lie in childhood and adolescence. As we shall see in Chapter 14, much of these problems stem from a rigid role definition given to women in our society.

Obstetric illnesses

Problems in pregnancy, childbirth, and breast-feeding are also more likely to occur in women who are dependent and passive. In the past few years much interest has focused on a possible connection between anxiety, complication of pregnancy and delivery in the mother, and defects in the newborn child. Basically, the theory holds that high levels of anxiety will result in uncoordinated uterine contractions, which cause congenital defects. Many studies have found that as anxiety increases in pregnant women, the greater the likelihood of labor problems. Zuckerman et al. (1963) found a significant correlation between somatic complaints during pregnancy and a history of anxiety and marital conflict. Similarly, patients who suffered excessive weight gain and premature rupture of the membrane scored significantly higher on the anxiety and social introversion scales of a personality test than did pregnant women with no somatic symptoms.

The ability of mothers to breast-feed their babies has also been found to be affected by their psychological states of mind. Doctors have become more aware of feeding problems in the past decade in connection with the "back to nature" movement which has become popular. A number of studies summarized in Newton (1968) indicates that women who are afraid of sex and dislike nudity are averse to breast-feeding. In contrast to women who bottle feed their babies, nursing mothers have a greater tolerance of sex-play in their children (masturbation). Newton found that women who successfully breast-feed infants enjoyed their feminine role and actually had shorter labors during the delivery of their first child.

Eroticism

For many years, myths and misconceptions about the nature of the human sexual response have abounded. This is caused in part by sensationalistic movies and articles that appear in the popular press which are designed to make money rather than to be informational. It is also caused in part by the lack of research on human sexuality because society was not ready for it. It is primarily the work of William Masters, a gynecologist, and Virginia Johnson, a psychologist (1966, 1970), that has yielded much needed information on human sexual responses. These controversial investigators studied nearly 700 males and females in acts of sexual intercourse and self-stimulation. Besides clinical interviews and controlled observations, electrophysiological measures, color movies, and a clear plastic phallus for intravaginal photography was used. Their studies provide an important consideration for a person seeking compatibility with his or her partner.

The sexual response cycle

Biologists have arbitrarily divided the human sexual response into four phases in order to provide a framework for the description of anatomical reactions to sexual stimulation. Accordingly, Masters and Johnson have used this structure to describe in detail the anatomic reactions of men and women to effective sexual stimulation. Some of these reactions are of such a brief duration that they are confined to one phase of the cycle. Other reactions are of such a magnitude they may be seen throughout the entire sexual cycle. Masters' and Johnson's findings for the four phases will be summarized in the sections below and are graphically illustrated in Figures 10–2 and 10–3. Their subject population consisted of 382 women with an age range of 18–78 years and 312 men with an age range of 21–89.

All of us become sexually aroused and excited when we are in the presence of sexual stimuli. The *excitement phase* is initiated by whatever is sexually stimulating to us. A seductive glance, a lingering caress, or a

FIGURE 10–2
Male sexual response cycle

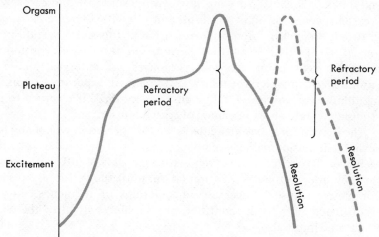

Source: Reproduced by permission from Frank A. Beach (Ed.), *Sex and Behavior* (New York: John Wiley & Sons, Inc., 1965).

FIGURE 10–3
Female sexual response cycle

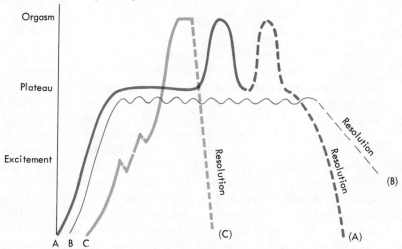

Source: Reproduced by permission from Frank A. Beach (Ed.), *Sex and Behavior* (New York: John Wiley & Sons, Inc., 1965).

pornographic movie may excite and arouse us. Our excitement frequently builds up quickly if the stimulation (physical or psychological) is effective. The length of the excitement phase is dependent on the variations in stimulation which may prolong or disrupt this period. If your date engages you in an exciting good-night kiss, you may become sexually aroused and "turned on." Should your date abruptly terminate the kiss and refuse to engage in further pleasantries, the excitement phase will end quickly. However, if your date continues to kiss and caress you, increased sexual tension is the result and you will enter the *plateau phase* in which arousal is intense. Termination at this point results in a prolonged frustrating resolution period. If stimulation continues and reaches a peak point, the body responses will enter a climatic or *orgasmic phase* in which the man and woman will experience orgasm. During the *resolution period*, following orgasm, there is a return to the unstimulated state and a lessening of sexual tension.

The human male has an acute refractory period in which any form of sexual stimulation will evoke no response or, at best, a delayed reaction. Men over 30 years of age are frequently incapable of full erection, no matter how intense the sexual stimulation, until the refractory period has completely elapsed. Successive ejaculations in all men, claims of extraordinary feats to the contrary, are possible only after the elapse of short time intervals.

In contrast to men, women do not have any distinct refractory periods. After an orgasm, a women's level of sexual tension may not fall below that of the plateau phase if sexual stimulation is continued. She is capable of going from one orgasmic experience to another, as long as effective stimulation is maintained.

General body reactions

MEN. In men, the *excitement phase* is characterized by erection of the penis, erection and swelling of the nipple, and an increase in elevation and size of the testes. As a general rule, younger males achieve full penile erection faster than men over 30 years of age. There is also an increase in the circumference at the corona (ridge along the tip of the penis) not present at the earlier stage of the sexual response, which can be seen with an increase in sexual tension to the *plateau-phase* level. Pre-ejaculatory emissions from the penis that help lubricate the vagina commonly occur during this period. The amount emitted is restricted to two or three drops. A measlelike rash (sex flush) occasionally develops over the rib cage, face, and neck. Increased muscular tension in the face, neck, abdomen, and legs is evident. The muscles of the thighs and buttocks gradually increases the thrusting of the pelvis. As tension increases, the muscular reactions become involuntary.

Ejaculation, the most unique phenomena in the cycle of the sexual response, is the essence of the male *orgasmic experience*. Various contractions in genital and accessory organs and in the external rectal sphincter take place during orgasm.

This experience occurs in two stages. The first occurs prior to ejaculation in which the man has a feeling of inevitability (inability to stop ejaculation), and in the second stage the contractions of the penis force the seminal fluid out. In younger men, the pressure is great enough to expel the semen from the penis two or more feet. Loss of vasocongestion (dilation of the blood vessels) marks the resolution phase and it takes place in two stages. The first stage is characterized by a rapid reduction in the size of the penis, in which it is reduced to one to one-half times its normal size. This is followed by a second, slower stage, as penile size returns to normal. The latter stage may be particularly slow if the sex response has been prolonged.

A widespread superficial vasocongestive sex-tension flush has been observed in 25 percent of the male subjects during individual sex response cycles. Furthermore, all males show numerous voluntary and involuntary movements of the skeletal muscles that can be seen in the arms, legs, abdomen, and in spasmodic facial contractions. Other general bodily reactions that occur are hyperventilation, sweating, and rapid cardiac rates. All of these bodily reactions are the result of involvement of the autonomic nervous system in sexual behavior.

WOMEN. There are several parallels between anatomic responses of the male and female since the autonomic nervous system is involved in both cases. As the woman becomes aroused during the excitement phase, she responds with the production of vaginal lubrication. In addition, the nipples become erect, vaginal walls thicken; there is a flattening and elevation of the major labia as well as expansion of the vaginal barrel as it prepares to accept the penis during intercourse. The sex flush spreads to all areas of the breasts, chest, and abdomen. This is followed during the plateau phase by engorgement with blood in the genital areas that causes a decrease in the opening of the vagina. It corresponds to the increase in size of the coronal area of the penis in males.

The female's orgasm usually lasts longer than in males as shown by the graphs in Figures 10–2 and 10–3. Its onset takes place with contractions of the uterine musculature and are concommitant with the development of contractions of the vagina and uterus. It is these anatomic reactions that provide the sensations of pelvic visceral contraction which women identify with an orgasm. During the resolution phase, women lose the engorgement of the vaginal area and the walls of the vaginal barrel return to their unstimulated width. These reactions are slow in comparison to analogous responses in the resolution phase of the male and may take several minutes. Finally, hyperventilation, perspiration, rapid cardiac rates, and contractions of skeletal muscles occur during the female sex response cycle, similar to those observed in males.

Sex appeal

What are the major factors that make a person attractive to members of the opposite sex? Many students when asked this question would answer by saying "intelligence" and "good personality." How many of you would say "good looks"? Elaine Walster and her colleagues (1966) conducted a large-scale research project to determine the role of physical attractiveness and psychological factors in the dating choices of college freshmen students. A total of 332 men and 332 women participated in the field study that took place in connection with a Computer Dance held on campus. The students were rated on physical attractiveness by four college sophomores working independently of each other. They were then measured on the following four variables: subject's popularity (self-report), nervousness on dates, type of dating partner expected (attractiveness, and so forth), and self-esteem. Finally, the subjects completed personality measures, and intelligence test scores and grade point averages were obtained from their high schools. Later, during intermission at the Computer Dance, the subjects' attitude toward their dates was assessed. The major results of this study are summarized below.

Physical attractiveness

A significant correlation was found between physical attractiveness and how the subjects rated their own social desirability; the more attractive a person was, the more popular he or she said they were. On the other hand, the more attractive they were, the less attractive they thought their dates were. In other words, attractive men and women are harsher than "average" people in the standards they set for their dates.

Follow-up studies were conducted to see if an individual would choose to date a partner of approximately his own level of attractiveness. It was found, in general, that the men had high hopes. They did not make any special effort to date girls similar to themselves. To the contrary, the only important determinant of whether or not the computer date was asked out again was how attractive she was; the most attractive girls were asked out most often. These dating preferences were true for all men regardless of how personally attractive they were. In a closely related finding, individuals of both sexes were found to like the most physically attractive dates best, not dates similar to themselves.

Two surprising results emerged which ran counter to the hypotheses of the investigators. First, a man's physical attractiveness was also found to be the largest determinant of how he was liked by his date. It was just as important in determining the personal appeal of men in the case of women. The more attractive a man was the better his date liked him and the more often she wanted to date him again.

The second surprising result that emerged from this study was a lack of symmetry betweeen a man's liking for his date and her liking for him. Nor was there a significant relationship between whether or not the man wanted to date his partner again and whether she felt the same way. Clearly, liking one's date does not generate reciprocity.

Intelligence and personality variables

The subjects' intelligence and intellectual achievement bore little or no relationship to being liked by one's date. These results demonstrate in a clear fashion that these variables are not nearly as important as physical attractiveness in determining liking. Neither were any of the personality measures such as social skills, masculinity-femininity, or introversion-extroversion found to be good predictors of likability. All of the correlations were small.

What can account for the overwhelming importance of physical attractiveness in determining likability as opposed to personality traits and intelligence? One explanation might be that the findings of this study were limited to a youthful population (average age was 18 years) which might not be typical of older people. As we will see in Chapter 11, this finding is significant because many individuals make their lifelong romantic choices at this age.

Another possible explanation lies in terms of the conditions under which the data were collected. Intelligence and personality variables might have been more important had the dating partners had more time to get acquainted. It may well be that two and one-half hours are too short of a time for individuals to discover much about their partners' other qualities besides physical appeal which is obvious from the start. On more conventional single dates, the individuals are known much better to each other. Nevertheless, physical attractiveness does appear to be an important variable in dating behavior and by implications in the selection of a marital partner.

Attitudes on sex

Everyone is aware that changes are taking place in sexual attitudes and courtship patterns in the 20th century. Even as late as the 1950s or early 1960s, the attempt to teach undergraduate students about sex in the classroom was difficult. Most efforts to lecture about sex were resisted by both college administrators and faculty members alike. Surprisingly, students also tended to reject the objective data on the physiology of the sexual response, petting, and premarital intercourse, topics that should have held their interest. Typically, there would be giggling or silence throughout the lectures, all of which indicated embarrassment at such frank discussions.

Fortunately, times have changed and now courses dealing with sexual behavior are routinely found in college and high school curriculums. The presentation of such topics is no longer taboo in the classroom nor in films, to which any devotee of R and X rated movies can testify. We shall now cover what evidence we have on the changing norms in attitudes and sexual behavioral patterns. As we shall see, the facts are not always in agreement with popular beliefs.

The generation gap

Dramatic evidence of a generation gap can be seen in a comparison of the views of college students on premarital sex and virginity with those of their elders. A Gallup poll (Gallup, 1970), conducted on 55 campuses with 1,114 students, showed that 3 out of 4 college students felt it is not important that the person they marry be a virgin; in contrast, 68 percent of adults 21 and over said premarital sex is wrong. In interpreting these data, it must be pointed out that the question was not worded to reflect a person's feelings about his spouse having premarital relations with someone else besides himself. This will help account for the apparent discrepancy between this poll and later studies to be reported.

Table 10–1 shows the breakdown on the college sample into key groups. As can be seen, there is little difference between the sexes and their views on the importance of virginity in a marital partner. Far more important is the factor of religion; students who say religion is an important part of their lives are far more inclined to stress the importance of virginity than their nonreligious-oriented peers.

TABLE 10–1
Percentage of students who state it is important for themselves to marry a virgin.

	Important	Not important	No opinion
All students	23%	73%	4%
Men	24	71	5
Women	21	77	2
Private colleges	21	75	4
Public or state-supported	21	75	4
Denominational or church affiliated	42	56	2
Freshmen	29	68	3
Sophomores	23	76	1
Juniors	21	70	9
Seniors	16	80	4
Graduate students	15	83	2
"Liberals"	18	79	3
"Conservatives"	39	58	3
Religion is relevant part of life	39	58	3
Not relevant	12	85	3

Source: George Gallup. *Generation gap shown in sex view.* Copyright © 1970 by the American Institute of Public Opinion. Reprinted by permission.

The Kinsey Reports

After World War II, a college professor by the name of Alfred Kinsey became interested in human sexual behavior when some of his students at Indiana University asked him for sexual advice. After conducting an exhaustive review of the literature on sexual patterns and mores, he discovered that the information was primarily all opinion and little fact. So Kinsey became determined to find out what men and women really do in their lives. His research efforts have become a classic in the literature on sexual habits. His data, based on interviews conducted with literally thousands of subjects, show that shifts in American standards are not nearly as dramatic as trumpeted in the popular press or by pessimistic moralists. Apparently, people are primarily more open in talking about sex rather than having changed very much in their sexual practices.

Among other findings, Kinsey and his colleagues found sex habits to vary according to social class and gender, the two main determinants. In a comparison of the sexual norms of young males in the semiskilled labor class and in the professional class, a marked difference was noted. The semiskilled group had a low frequency of masturbation and a high rate of premarital intercourse. These patterns were reversed for the professional group. In general, the semiskilled group was more sexually active, starting at an earlier age (Kinsey, Pomeroy, & Martin, 1948).

Women were found to be much less sexually active than men and also less easily aroused by fantasy, pictures, and other symbols. Masturbation to orgasm was less frequently reported for women than men (25 percent versus 99 percent) as was premarital intercourse. About 50 percent of the women entered marriage as virgins in comparison to 33 percent of the men.

Recent norms

Although not as comprehensive as Kinsey's original work, there have been some later studies reported. Miller and Siegel (1972) in summarizing the recent literature are essentially in agreement with Kinsey's earlier findings on changing mores. They conclude that the so-called generation of the sexual revolution is verbally looser rather than sexually freer in practice and that sexual behavior did not change significantly in the 1960s. For example, Miller and Wilson (1968) in a questionnaire study of sexual behavior found little difference among college students from behavior claimed some 20 years earlier. Also, *Playboy* magazine in a similar study (published in September 1969) found only scattered and uneven evidence for any marked increase in sexual freedom among today's youth.

Decline of the double standard

In line with the above findings, there does not appear to have been a revolution concerning attitudes toward the sexual conduct of women; if anything, there is a decline but not yet the fall of the double standard. In a survey of 2,200 unmarried college juniors and seniors, the majority of women indicated that they would not be troubled by the knowledge that their husbands had premarital sexual experiences with one or more other persons, but over two-thirds of the college men replied that they would be upset to some extent by the knowledge of such experience on the part of their wives (Packard, 1968). Similarly, Mosher and Cross (1971) reported that both men and women endorse more liberal premarital standards for men than for women.

At first glance, these studies appear to be in conflict with the previously reported Gallup poll. However, the disparity may be explained in the manner questions were worded. For instance, these studies queried students about reactions toward their mates having premarital sexual relations with others; the Gallup poll did not. Apparently premarital coitus by women with their prospective husbands is fairly well accepted in college settings, but sexual experiences with other men are still frowned upon. This hypothesis is supported by the fact that the increase in proportion of women who have had premarital intercourse has occurred among women who had intercourse only with their spouses-to-be (Smigel & Seiden, 1971).

Promiscuity

As further evidence of the existence of the double standard are the labels of sexually promiscuous and sexually delinquent applied to young females but rarely to young males. As we shall see in Chapter 14, these labels are indicative of sexism in our society. The term indicates a bias or at least disapproval of repeated transient sexual experiences on the part of young girls which are lacking in men. However, only a relatively small percentage of sexual delinquent girls are ever brought to the attention of juvenile authorities or mental authorities.

Swinging

Extramarital sexual relations have traditionally been regarded as a more serious "deviation" than premarital relations, and adultery has generally been regarded as grounds for separation or divorce. Yet Kinsey et al. (1953) found that 50 percent of the men and 27 percent of the women in his sample have had extramarital relations at some time during marriage. Hunt (1973) reports that such behavior is on the increase, particularly among young women. In fact, marital infidelity has become a way of life for some people and is most noticeable in the modern sexual phenomenon known as "swinging," in which sex practices take place within a group. An organization known as the Sexual Freedom League in the San Francisco Bay Area conducts large-scale parties in which sexual relations may be carried out between couples who know each other minimally.

In a study of wife-swapping and other group sex practices among middle-class Americans, Bartell (1971) has estimated the number of swingers engaging in these practices at two million and increasing. The greatest concentrations of swinging couples are found in the Los Angeles and San Francisco areas with other major metropolitan centers close behind.

An enterprising reporter and his wife once spent two months investigating wife-swapping in California which began with the insertion of an ad in the *San Francisco Chronicle:*

> Attractive couple in late 20s, bored with conventional friendships, wishes to meet couples or singles to exchange unconventional experiences in the unusual/exotic/unique. Both bored (Avery & Avery, 1964).

There were more than 300 replies to this ad, and during their investigation, the Averys corresponded with and met more than 100 couples who were unaware that they were talking to reporters. Many wife-swappers considered themselves to be in the avant-garde. Typically, they boasted about being "broad-minded" and having the ability to enjoy life and have fun in any form.

Bartell's (1971) findings on swingers are similar to those reported by the Averys. They ranged in age from 18 to about 55 with the average for women being about 29 and for men about 32. The majority of the swinging couples exchanged partners with another couple only once and would then seek new contacts. Apparently, their swinging activities did not lead to long-term satisfaction or contentment as can be seen in the fact that most couples drastically curtailed their activities after about two years, or dropped out of swinging altogether.

Psychological determination of erotica

Kinsey et al. (1953) in their questionnaire study found men to be more easily sexually aroused than women. There were also sex differences in the type of stimuli that would elicit arousal. Women were aroused by moving pictures, literary materials, novels and poetry that were more romantic than sexual; on the other hand, men reported that they were aroused by explicit sexual stimuli such as naked pictures of the opposite sex.

A more recent study by Sigusch et al. (1970) undertook the investigation of sex differences in psychosexual stimulation under experimental conditions. Male and female students were shown erotic pictures (Table 10-2) and were later asked to rate the pictures with respect to favorableness-unfavorableness and their sexual-physiological reactions during the presentation of the pictures.

The women, in comparison to the men, tended to judge the pictures as less arousing and more unfavorably. However, the sex difference depended to a large extent on the content of the picture. Pictures of semi-nudes and nudes were judged by the women as much less sexually stimulating and more unfavorably than men. In contrast, they judged pictures with a romantic content (kissing and embracing with affection) more favorably but as erotic as by the men.

In regard to the sexual-physiological reactions in the genital area, the results surprisingly showed little or no significant sex-specific differences. Thirty-five out of the 50 women subjects and 40 out of the 50 men noticed some sort of sensations in the genital area.

These findings suggest that the common belief that women are less aroused through pictures with sexual themes than men is wrong. In fact, when measured by the objective indicators of physiological reactions in the genital area, women are found to be just as easily aroused as men. Sigusch et al. interpret their findings to indicate that women are cul-

TABLE 10–2
List of themes shown to subjects*

Males	Females
1. Girl in a one-piece bathing suit.	Man in a bathing suit.
2. Girl in a bikini.	Man in a bikini.
3. Kissing couple, with naked shoulders.	
4. Couple in bathing suit kissing and embracing.	
5. Couple in bed naked above waist (woman's breasts not seen) showing affection.	same
6. Closeup of female legs from thigh to toes.	Closeup of male legs from thigh to toes.
7. Closeup of girl with open blouse showing breasts.	Man with pants partly open.
8. Girl wearing only panties.	Man wearing shirts but no pants showing genitals, no erection.
9. Naked girl in normal posture.	Naked man in normal posture, no erection.
10. Closeup of female breasts.	Closeup of male genitals, no erection.
11. Naked girl with legs spread apart exposing genitals.	Naked man with erection.
12. Closeup of female genitals.	Closeup of male genitals with erection.
13. Seminude girl showing breasts and genitals.	Man removing pants showing genitals, no erection.
14. Naked girl in posing position.	Naked man in posing position, no erection.
15. Seminude couple with manual-genital contact, female active.	
16. Naked couple with man stimulating girl's breasts.	
17. Naked couple with manual-genital contact, female active.	
18. Naked couple in coitus face to face, man above, showing genitals.	
19. Naked couple in coitus from the rear.	same
20. Naked couple with oral-genital contact, female active.	
21. Naked couple with oral-genital contact, man active.	
22. Closeup of genitals in coitus.	
23. Closeup of oral-genital contact, female active.	
24. Naked couple in coitus (position other than No. 18, 19).	

* In the right column (females) only the variations used are named.
Source: V. Sigusch, G. Schmidt, A. Reinfeld, and I. Wiedemann-Sutor, Psychosexual Stimulation: Sex Differences," *Journal of Sex Research*, February 1970, 6(1).

turally conditioned to emotionally reject erotic pictures, although they are sexually aroused similarly to men.

Different cultures and sexual patterns

How much of a role cultural factors play in determining the type of sexual stimulation and total amount of sexual behavior is becoming increasingly documented in anthropological literature. In many human societies, certain forms of bodily stimulation are so common that they may be considered vital parts of the total sexual intercourse pattern.

They may range all the way from primitive biting and scratching to highly socialized patterns such as mutually grooming the partner's body. The nature of these various sexual activities and differences in cultural norms can be seen as we review some well-known anthropological studies, and then examine the norms for different advanced societies. As will be seen, what is considered to be normal sex behavior is a matter of cultural definition more than a biological phenomenon.

Stimulation of the breasts

AMERICAN CULTURE. In our society, there are some couples that regard any sexual behavior except actual intercourse to be a perversion and to be distasteful (Ford & Beach, 1971). This includes such activities as oral stimulation of the penis (fellatio), of the woman's clitoris (cunnilingus), or by the simultaneous performance of both of these activities.

However, stimulation of the feminine breast by the male is a very common type of foreplay in our culture. Manual stimulation of the breasts was the rule in 96 percent of all college graduates interviewed by Kinsey and his co-workers and 82 percent reported mouth contact. Much lower rates of breast stimulations were reported by males from lower educational levels.

OTHER CULTURES. Breast stimulation is common in most other societies and for some peoples this form of activity constitutes the only form of precoital sex. A case in point is the Lepaha society. Courtship barely exists among them and there is no preliminary stimulation in the way of kisses or embraces; only fondling of a woman's breast takes place before copulation.

There are a few societies in which breast stimulation is reported to be completely lacking such as the Sirione (Ford & Beach, 1971). However, copulating couples may lock in a tight embrace as climax approaches and then the women's breasts are pressed close to the man's chest. The lack of breast stimulation does not necessarily imply the existence of specific prohibitions against the custom since many couples seem almost completely uninhibited in sexual matters.

Stimulation of the partner's genitals

AMERICAN CULTURE. Stimulation of the partner's genitals is a widespread type of extracoital activity for men and women in our society. Handling and rubbing of the women's genital parts was practiced frequently by about 90 percent of the college-educated men and among 75 percent of the males at a lower educational level interviewed by Kinsey, Pomeroy and Martin (1948). Oral stimulation occurs occasionally among many husbands, 45 percent of the well educated and 4 percent of the poorly educated.

American women were found only slightly less likely to handle the penis than are men to manipulate the feminine sexual parts. This practice is performed frequently by the wives of 75 percent of the college-educated husbands and 57 percent of less educated men. Fellatio is much less common in our society being avoided in 58 percent of the cases, and takes place only occasionally in most of the remainder.

OTHER SOCIETIES. Manual stimulation of the partner's genitals is very common in most other cultures. For instance, among the Crow Indians, fingering the genitalia serves as a stereotyped erotic advance. Ford and Beach (1971) report that the male Crows have a quaint custom of crawling up to the tents at night, thrusting their arms under the women's beds and trying to stimulate their genitals. If they are successful by the use of this technique, intercourse will normally be the result.

Oral stimulation is practiced to some extent in a few societies; particularly those situated on the islands of the Pacific Ocean. It is especially elaborate in Ponape, where the men titilate the labia and clitoris in a prolonged foreplay period. In another custom, which must be considered unique by American standards, the Ponapean men place a fish in the woman's vulva and then gradually lick it out prior to coitus.

Free sex in Sweden

Sweden has become well publicized by its movies that are exported around the world for its alleged sexual freedom. Such movies as *I a Woman* and *I Am Curious Yellow*, two big Swedish box office hits in the United States, point to the existence of a single standard of freedom for both sexes.

There have been some studies reported which do show that premarital sex is very common among the Swedes. For example, a 1964 study of 436 military draftees showed that 88 percent had already had sexual intercourse while the others either had never experienced it or declined to answer (Israel, 1965). The average age at first coitus was below 16 years. A parallel study with married women found that 80 percent had experienced premarital intercourse.

Another recent study was conducted on the sexual habits and knowledge of approximately 500 pupils at two separate schools in the city of Örebro (Linner, 1967); the average age at both schools was around 18. The results showed that 57 percent of the males and 46 percent of the girls had already experienced intercourse. The average age of first coitus was 16 for males and 17 for females. It is important to note that most of the boys and girls chose "steady" friends as partners for their first experience, suggesting that they are not completely promiscuous in taking up with just anyone.

As more evidence of a single standard of sexual conduct, the majority of both sexes maintained that their first coitus was by mutual agreement. Along the same lines, the overwhelming majority of both sexes gave as the reason for their first intercourse that they wanted it. Not a single boy or girl acquiesced because of strong pressure from his or her partner, including threats to break off the relationship. When asked about possible feelings of guilt following intercourse, only a few youngsters of either sex expressed remorse over their behavior. Their overall attitude appeared to accept sex as a reality of life and to adopt a corresponding code of morality.

Sexual variance

Coleman (1972) has stressed the point that the development of adult sexual behavior is a long and complicated process often resulting in widespread and individual differences. As we have already seen, norms of sexual conduct vary from one culture to another. Thus, what is considered to be normal or deviant behavior is interwoven into the standards of different societies, but few patterns are universally condemned or rejected. Within our society, we have called anything a perversion or sexual deviation that does not eventually lead to coitus.

There are presently still laws on the books in some states that make oral-genital contact a crime, punishable as a felony in spite of its widespread practice. However, there are many changes taking place within our accepted mores, and many sexual patterns formerly considered perverse or immoral are being redefined as desirable. As a case in point, some people consider homosexuality to be a permissible alternative to heterosexual relationships (the American Psychiatric Association in 1973 revised its stance by no longer considering homosexuality a mental disorder), and many others view premarital sexual relations and even extramarital activities as desirable.

Thus, the question arises as to what range of sexual patterns should be considered normal and encouraged, both personally and socially. This question is difficult to answer because of the fast-changing standards taking place and the great role that learning plays in determining sexual activities. Although, we shall adhere to the traditional classification of deviancy, we should keep in mind that we are speaking actually about sexual variations. Sexual acts may be regarded as varying with reference to: (1) intensity or frequency of drive and gratification as in impotence and satyriasis; (2) mode of gratification as in exhibitionism and sadism; and (3) choice of sex objects as in homosexuality and incest (Coleman, 1972). Much of our following discussion will be based on Coleman's analysis of sexual deviations.

Impotency and frigidity

Impotency and frigidity refer to a general sexual inadequacy in which there is an impairment in the desire for, or ability to achieve sexual gratification. There are wide ranges of physical conditions such as injuries to the genitalia, disease, drugs, and fatigue, which can affect sexual desire or ability. However, the vast majority of prolonged cases of inadequacy are due to psychological factors.

The most common forms of impotency in the male are (1) an inability to attain or maintain an erection long enough to have successful intercourse, and (2) premature ejaculation. Common forms of frigidity in the female are: (1) *vaginismus,* a condition in which the vagina involuntarily clamps tightly shut when attempts are made to enter; and (2) an inability to achieve orgasm. It has been estimated that as many as half of the marriages in America are threatened or damaged by sexual inadequacy (Masters & Johnson, 1970).

A number of psychosocial factors including faulty early learning, anxiety, lack of emotional closeness to a sexual partner, low sex drive, and homosexuality, have been related to impotency and frigidity.

In one study of 49 sexually inadequate males, Cooper (1969) found anxiety over intercourse to be the primary factor in their impotence. In many cases, their anxiety started early in life and developed or was aggravated by being pushed into sexual relations at an early age. Instead of bringing forth the expected satisfactions, such sexual freedom resulted in feelings of inadequacy.

Masters and Johnson (1970) consider faulty early learning to be the predominant cause of frigidity in women. Many of their patients had been taught from childhood that sex is dirty, lustful, and evil. Consequently, they were unable to enjoy intercourse with their husbands because they continued to have feelings of guilt over any type of sexual relations.

Satyriasis and nymphomania

The difficulties inherent in labeling certain sexual patterns as deviant are illustrated by the use of the terms, *satyriasis* and *nymphomania*, to refer to men and women, respectively, who focus their entire lives around sexual activities. Research has demonstrated that there is such a tremendous variation among people, in terms of their sexual desires, as to make the application of these labels almost meaningless. Unless the high incidence of sexual intercourse of a particular person is maladaptive and interferes with one's job, interpersonal relationships, or other life adjustments, it is considered normal.

THE CASE OF THE SUNDAY SCHOOL TEACHER. As previously discussed, there are some CNS brain structures that are important in the regulation of sexual arousal. If certain sections of the limbic section (lying below the frontal lobes) are damaged, the result is an almost insatiable desire for sex.

One interesting case was reported of a Sunday School teacher who complained of developing uncontrollable sexual urges after receiving a head injury in a San Francisco cable car accident (*Los Angeles Times,* 1970). She reported having intercourse with over 100 men since the accident, and of being unable to hold a job because of her overwhelming sex drive. However, diagnostic medical data was unavailable in her case and there has been no research available to indicate the involvement of brain pathology in cases of people with unusually high sexual needs.

Homosexuality and transvestism

Homosexuality involves physical attraction between members of the same sex. It is much more common among men than women; about 2.6 million males and 1.4 million women in our society are exclusively homosexual (Coleman, 1972). There are several million other individuals who combine both heterosexual and homosexual experiences (Figure 10–4). A common misconception holds that homosexuals manifest qualities of the opposite sex; hence, male homosexuals are supposed to be effeminate and lesbians masculine. However, this is the exception rather than the rule and male homosexuals are found in the military, professional sports, so-called masculine endeavors, as well as in so-called feminine occupations such as hairdresser, interior decorating, and art.

One type of sexual deviation sometimes related to homosexuality is the obtaining of sexual gratification by wearing the clothes of the opposite sex known as transvestism. The male transvestite especially likes to have his genitals come into contact with feminine garb, and when dressed in this manner often adopts the ways and mannerisms of women. Although some female homosexuals wear men's clothing, only a few are true transvestites.

The following case history concerns the case of a male transvestite who was inadvertently picked up on the streets of New York on charges of prostitution and vagrancy:

"Miss" D. H., after being picked up by the police was taken to jail where he was searched by one of the matrons. She was astonished to find out that "Miss" D. H. was really a well-developed man. He was 25 years of age, had long dark hair, and with lipstick and eye makeup looked like a young woman. When arrested he was wearing a padded brassiere, nylon stockings, a pretty dress and high-heeled shoes.

He was the son of a school teacher who had to raise him by herself; his father died when he was only one year old. He closely identified with his mother and never formed any close friendships. As a child he took to dressing in his mother's clothing and applying her makeup when she was at work. When he was nine he was seduced at school into homosexual activities by an older schoolmate. By the time he was fifteen, he was skillful enough at female impersonation to go out into the streets and let drunks "pick him up." Interestingly enough, none of the drunks ever discovered that D. H. was a male.

Incest

The majority of cultures prohibit or frown upon sexual relations between members of a family such as parent and child or brother and sis-

FIGURE 10–4
With the changing sexual mores and increasing acceptance of homosexuality
in the United States, many homosexuals are able to accept themselves as
worthwhile human beings.

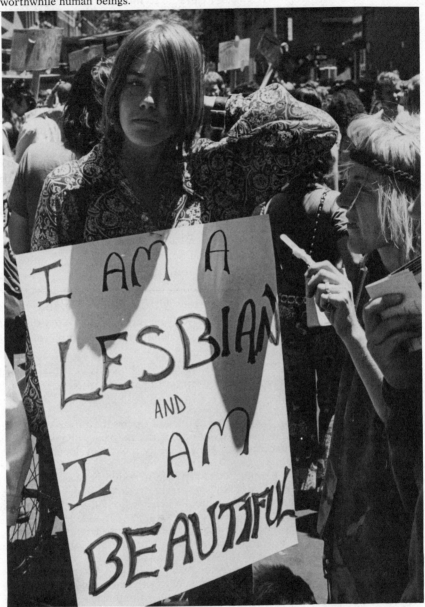

Leonard Freed—Magnum

ter; when relations of this type do occur, they are referred to an *incestu-ous*. Because incest takes place in families and is infrequently reported, its actual incidence is unknown. However, Kinsey and his cohorts reported a rate of five cases per 1,000 persons while Gebhard et al. (1965) found a higher rate of incidence among sex offenders, 30 cases per 1,000 subjects. Studies indicate that brother-sister incest is approximately five times more common than father-daughter relations.

Besides moral ones, the most common objection stated against incestuous relations is the genetic risks involved. That this is not just an "old wive's tale" is born out in a study by Adams and Neel (1967). In comparing the offspring of 18 incest marriages between 12 brother-sister and 6 father-daughter relationships with those of a control group, only 7 of the 18 infants turned out to be normal: 5 died at the end of six months, 6 were either severely mentally retarded or of borderline intelligence, and 1 had a cleft palate. In contrast, only two of the control-group family infants showed indications of abnormality; one showing signs of borderline intelligence and the other suffered from a physical defect.

Rape

More serious to society is forcible rape which seems to be on the increase; there were over 37,000 cases reported in 1970, more than twice as many as in 1960 (FBI, 1971). The actual incidence, based on detailed interviews made by the National Opinion Research Center of the University of Chicago (NORC), is reported to be three and one-half times the reported rate (President's Commission, 1967).

Coleman (1972) reports that (a) the typical rapist is a young anti-social man with a past record of other aggressive acts against society, (b) he is most likely to be married and living with his wife at the time of the crime, and (c) some rapists show very little aesthetic preference in their choice of sexual objects and will attack women who are ugly, pretty, young, or old. There is a case reported in Los Angeles newspapers in 1972 of a man in his early twenties who broke into a 74-year-old woman's apartment, raped, and murdered her. He was not mentally ill, mentally retarded, drunk, or under the influence of drugs.

It is quite common for the victim of the rapist to receive injuries such as broken ribs, fractures, and multiple bruises, particularly if she struggles. Occasionally, several offenders of a juvenile gang join together and rape a victim consecutively. Besides the physical trauma inflicted on the woman, the psychological reactions of the victim and those of her children, husband, and parents, may be very severe. Sutherland and Scherl (1970) investigated the response patterns of the victims, and their descriptions illustrate just how severe the psychological trauma may be. They found that the women in their initial reaction were often agitated, incoherent, and in a highly volatile state.

Exhibitionism and voyeurism

Exhibitionism and voyeurism (peeking) are the two most commonly reported sexual offenses. In exhibitionism the individual gains his primary gratification out of showing his genital organs to other people. The exposure may take place in some secluded location such as on country roads or in more public places such as theaters, department stores, or in front of the window of someone's home. Recently, college campuses have been the setting for a new phenomenon known as "streaking" in which students race through public places with nothing on other than a pair of shoes. Although social scientists disagree as to the meaning of the streaking craze, it contains strong exhibitionistic qualities (Figure 10–5).

Most exhibitionism offenders are young adult males, who come from all different backgrounds; this is relatively rare among women. When it does occur, it is much less likely to be reported as the following case shows.

> A rather pretty young 21-year-old girl had been seen walking nude late in the evenings in the relatively secluded areas of a middle-class neighborhood. Several people, as revealed by a police investigation, had seen her on different occasions. Out of an estimated 20 to 25 exposures she was reported on only two different occasions, both times by women.

In voyeurism, we have the opposite of exhibitionism. The voyeurist gains sexual pleasure from looking at the genital organs of another person or from observing other people engaging in sexual activity. Most "peeping Toms" tend to be secretive in their activities and usually concentrate on females who are undressing or on couples engaging in sexual relations. The profile of peepers shows most are immature young men who are shy and relatively harmless. Voyeurism ordinarily does not have any serious criminal or other unalterable antisocial aspects.

Psychiatrists have noted that most people have some exhibitionistic and voyeuristic tendencies which are well checked by practical considerations and moral attitudes. The majority of American men find some degree of sexual pleasure and stimulation in observing women in various degrees of "undress"—witness the popularity of "girl" shows in night clubs. On the other hand, women below the level of deviancy are more inclined toward exhibitionism than men in this country. The popularity of going braless and wearing bikinis, miniskirts, and "plunging necklines" testify, in part, to these normal tendencies.

Sadism and masochism

In *sadism*, the individual gains his primary sexual gratification through inflicting pain on another person. The term is derived from the infamous Marquis de Sade (1740–1814). To obtain sexual gratification he inflicted such acts of cruelty on his victims that he was eventually com-

FIGURE 10-5
Whether or not exhibitionism is a sexual disorder depends on cultural standards.
Streaking has been a fad, particularly on college campuses; however, this
display of nudity is not considered to be a sexual disorder.

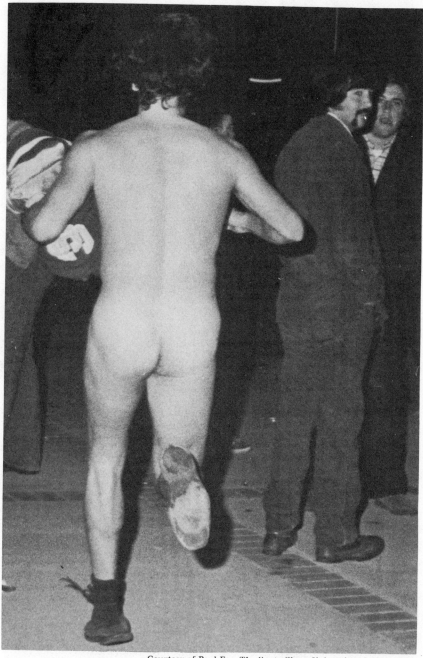

Courtesy of Paul Fry, *The Santa Clara*, University of Santa Clara

mitted to an insane asylum. The pain inflicted by sadists may be achieved by such means as whipping, scratching, and biting; it varies in intensity from pure fantasy to severe mutilation or even murder in some cases.

Sadistic activities sometimes lead to coitus, but in others full sexual gratification is obtained from the sadistic act alone. For instance, a sadistic man was arrested by the police after he was caught in the bedroom of a young woman. He admitted to assaulting women many times before, and the only way he could obtain an orgasm was by beating his victims with an iron. He did not follow up any of his assaults with attempts at intercourse.

Masochism is the opposite condition which consists in obtaining sexual pleasure through being hurt painfully by another person and by remaining passive throughout the act. In contrast to sadism, masochistic activities are more commonly found among women than men. These activities range from stimulating fantasies or brutal treatment to actual pain-inflicting acts such as sticking with pins, spanking, or verbal abuse.

One often cited case (East, 1946) concerns a young woman who frequently cut herself about the legs, arms, and breasts, in addition to inserting pins and needles under her skin. She was unable to get sexual pleasure through any method except by experiencing pain and by viewing blood from the incisions.

Other deviant activities

There are other types of sexual deviancy and sex crimes that are frequently described in the psychiatric literature. Of these, fetishism, pedophilia, and bestiality occur commonly enough to warrant discussion. In *fetishism*, the individual is sexually motivated not toward another person, but toward a part of a person (ankle) or some object that stands symbolically for the person (underwear). The number of objects that become a fetish are almost limitless; however, the ankle, foot, undergarments, and stockings are the usual choices of a fetishist.

Pedophilia is a serious criminal offense in which a child is the object of the person's sexual desire. This is illustrated by the novel *Lolita*, later made into a movie which dealt with the love affair of a man in his thirties and a 12-year-old girl. As in this novel, the pedophiliacs may seek adult-type gratification with the child, but many may engage in various other perversions with the child. Most pedophiliacs have been found to be actually impotent men who are afraid of attempting sexual relations with an adult woman (Cohen & Seghorn, 1969).

Bestiality includes all cases in which an animal is the object of sexual desire. Some deviants derive their gratification from watching animals engaging in coitus, while still others may engage in masturbation by means of friction against the animal, fellatio, masturbation of the animal, or actual sexual intercourse. Practically all large farm animals are involved such as cattle, sheep, and dogs. Occasionally, even ducks, geese, and chickens serve as the sexual objects.

As to be expected, bestiality occurs primarily in rural areas where it is often learned from examples set by other boys or by experimentation after observing coitus among the animals themselves. It occurs more commonly than most people realize; in fact, about 1 male in 12 or 14 has had sexual experience with animals (Kinsey, et al., 1948).

General causes of sexual deviations

As we have noted, adult sexual behavior is the result of a long process of development in which the sex drive potentialities of an infant are undifferentiated. There are no physiological mechanisms that will guarantee that the end result will be "normal" heterosexual interests; an almost infinite variety of sexual patterns exists that are possible for any individual in any society. Psychological factors are recognized as playing a dominant role in determining sexual variance in our society. We are deliberately omitting any reference to biological factors (heredity, hormonal abnormalities, and so on) because they have not been consistently found in any group of sexual deviants (Coleman, 1972; Rosen & Gregory, 1965).

Deprivation of normal sexuality

Under conditions of deprivation, especially when there is prolonged segregation of the sexes, a certain amount of deviant behavior occurs; for instance, homosexuality has long been noted to commonly occur in prisons. Adults deprived of normal sexual outlets may resort to other means of sexual expression. However, when heterosexual opportunities are once again present, most will return to this mode of expression. Inviduals who become involved in such activities because of deprivation at an early age may not abandon them at a later time. Isolation in childhood leads to an overall inadequate development of personality, including faulty heterosexual habits.

Specific episodes in childhood or youth

A sexual episode may profoundly affect the later behavior of any impressionable young child or youth. Homosexuality often begins when a child or adolescent experiments with someone his own age or an older person. If a youngster's needs for affection and sexual gratification are both met by an older homosexual, the newly learned homosexual behavior is rewarded and is, therefore, very likely to become persistent.

Being spanked across the buttocks while lying in an adult's lap is apt to arouse both pain and sexual excitation in some children and masochism may be the result. Fetishism is also likely to begin with specific learning episodes in which a formerly neutral stimulus (see Chapter 5, section on "Classical Conditioning") becomes endowed with sexual arousal properties. For example, Rachman (1966) created a mild fetish under laboratory conditions in an interesting experiment. Subjects were shown a photograph of women's boots on several occasions along with slides of sexually stimulating nude females. The men came to exhibit sexual arousal—to the boots alone; this response also became generalized to other types of women's shoes.

Fear and hostility toward opposite sex

Many people are afraid to approach members of the opposite sex which may be manifested in many forms. Fetishism and voyeurism are methods of avoiding other human beings, homosexuality substitutes a familiar object—one's own sex—for the strange and fearful opposite sex, and pedophilia is contact with an immature and therefore less fearful object.

Sadistic activities serve as a method of expressed hostility and contempt toward members of the opposite sex. Many male sadists are described by investigators as timid, feminine, and undersexed individuals who apparently receive little or no satisfaction if their victims remain passive and show no pain. However, if the victim does respond, the sadist often feels he has great power and superiority over her.

Failure in sex identification

Sometimes children are not provided an adequate model in which they have a chance to learn the appropriate sex-role behaviors. Usually the father or mother serves as the appropriate model for learning such sexual roles. However, in psychosexual development, the individual identifies with a parent or parent substitute of the opposite sex and homosexuality is often the result. The earlier this identification is made and the more intense it is, the harder it is to change such an inversion. This important role played by the parents in homosexuality is well documented in a study by Bieber et al. (1962) of homosexual and heterosexual males undergoing psychoanalysis. They found marked differences in the parental relationships of the two groups.

The mothers of homosexuals did not encourage masculinity and often formed coalitions with the sons against the fathers. They interfered with attempted heterosexual activities on the part of their sons and demanded to be the center of their attention. Closely associated with this was their seductive behavior as they tended to dress and undress with the patient, kiss him sensually and fondle him. In short, the mothers behaved as if they wanted their sons to be homosexual, much as they might deny it. The fathers proved to be inadequate models as they were distant, disliked, and feared by the homosexual patients. It is noteworthy that the differences in parental relationships between the homosexual and heterosexual comparison groups were considerable even though the latter group consisted of patients with neurotic and antisocial disorders.

Provocation by victim

Public opinion and the law have traditionally regarded molested women or children to be the innocent victim of the male. However, it has been repeatedly observed that many victims are known to the offender which raises the question of whether they deliberately invited or unconsciously provoked the sexual act. Although this hypothesis seems farfetched where child victims are concerned, it does appear to have some validity with respect to cases involving adolescents and adults. Evidence for this hypothesis has been reported by Amir (1971), who in a study of 646 cases of rape reported to the Philadelphia police, found 19 percent to have been precipitated by the victims.

An invitation to sexual assault by an adult female sometimes results from deliberately teasing the male with the intention of frustrating him only to discover that he will not accept the frustration. In another pattern, a hysterical female may quite unwittingly provoke a sexual response which she then attempts to reject. In either case, the subsequent hostility of the victim may lead to legal charges and conviction.

Association with psychopathology

Many people arrested for sexual offenses have been found to exhibit other maladaptive behaviors and mental illnesses of various sorts. In a pioneering study of 300 sex offenses, Brancale, Ellis and Doorbar (1952) found 86 percent to manifest other various symptoms of psychopathology. Most of the patients were neurotic but there were also some cases of psychoses, brain damage, psychopathic personalities, and mental retardation. Such pathological conditions often involve the inadequate development of a code of conduct or loss of inner controls. The further a person's preference is from adult genital heterosexuality, the less likely they are to approximate normality in nonsexual areas and the more likely they are to experience reality distortion.

It should be noted, however, that many sexually diverse persons have been extraordinarily creative. Rousseau found heterosexuality repugnant, Swinburne was a sadomasochist, Michelangelo was reportedly a homosexual, and Mozart wrote pornographic letters in addition to his music.

Treatment of sexual disorders

The specific treatment of sexual disorders depends to a large extent upon the particular type of deviation and the general personality organization of the patient. The treatment of impotence in a normal and stable individual is considerably different from the treatment of pedophilia or homosexuality.

Somatic treatments

Various somatic treatment measures have been tried including the use of drugs and more drastic measures as castration. Tranquilizers and antidepressive drugs have been successfully used to provide relief from the anxiety and depression accompanying sexual deviation, but, of course, do not change the patients' underlying sexual motivation. Male sexual activity and desire has been suppressed by the administration of female hormones, but there is no change in the direction of the residual sexual impulses. Similarly, male hormones administered to homosexuals have failed to convert them to heterosexuality. The most drastic somatic treatment of all, castration, has also failed to change the individual's sexual aims although it diminishes the drive. In general, none of the somatic treatments has proven very useful with sexual deviations.

Psychotherapy

The use of psychotherapy has fared somewhat better in treating sexual disorders, particularly patients whose deviation is of recent onset. The types of procedures used in treating sexual deviancy are essentially no different from the treatment of most other types of abnormal behavior, as discussed in the previous chapter. Some procedures, including psychoanalysis, are designed to help the patient gain insight into his motivations and help change his basic attitudes. Other investigators have emphasized the value of group psychotherapy in achieving these treatment goals. Two of the more recent methods, the rapid treatment program of Masters and Johnson and behavior therapy (counterconditioning and aversive conditioning) have been particularly successful in treating certain types of disorders.

Masters and Johnson's Rapid Treatment Program

Masters and Johnson, who are widely known for their studies of human sexual responses, have also been involved in treating problems of frigidity and impotence in marriages. In their version of family therapy, they treat the married couple as a unit rather than as separate individuals. They believe sexual inadequacy is a form of faulty communication which probably extends to other areas of a couple's relationship as well. Consequently, they orient their treatment toward improving communication in marriage and stressing the concept that sex is an experience that both partners must enter into without reservation.

The sequence of events in their treatment program follows a pattern from individual interviews and collection of sexual history information to eventually focusing on the couple's specific sexual problem. Within this context, couples learn to communicate with one another and may discover for the first time how they feel about each other and why. The therapy sessions may also feature the explanation of specific sexual techniques which the couples are encouraged to try. The rapid treatment program is based on the assumption that much of human sexual inadequacy is due to ignorance and improper attitudes rather than mental illness. The treatment consists of a series of educational and therapeutic talk sessions between therapists and patients. There is an attempt to abolish goal-oriented performance by having patients remove themselves from the spectator role. Patients are instructed temporarily to avoid sexual intercourse in order to remove performance fears. They are then instructed to participate in certain sexual activities (not intercourse) such as touching and stroking one another. This assignment frees them of the need to perform and allows them to focus on their own and each others feelings. After a few days, more specific sexual problems are reviewed and concrete techniques are suggested. Five-year follow-up studies of 510 couples and 57 unmarried men and women revealed an overall failure rate of only 20 percent (Masters & Johnson, 1970).

Counterconditioning

Difficulties in sexual behavior are frequently the result of excessive anxiety associated with sexually arousing stimuli. In some way the act of intercourse is associated with strong antisexual attitudes (sex is dirty, filthy, or disgusting) that impair sexual performance. Causes of impotence, premature ejaculation and frigidity may be due to anxiety. Joseph Wolpe (1970) has developed a system of treating human sexual inadequacy through the use of counterconditioning that is very similar to that of Masters and Johnson. Like systematic desensitization and assertive training (see Chapter 9), Wolpe attempts to subtract anxiety from the sexual encounter in a gradual manner. If sexual arousal can be kept stronger than anxiety, it may be possible to overcome and inhibit anxiety. In this case, sexual arousal is used as the antagonistic and competing response to anxiety.

The therapist takes an active hand in directing the course of treatment for his patients. The first step in treatment is to ascertain at what point in the sexual encounter the patient becomes anxious. The situations are developed into a hierarchy (such as systematic desensitization) and the patient is asked to approach his task gradually, never going beyond what is sexually arousing. The patient is constantly monitored by the therapist during the interview sessions and instructed specifically about how to approach the assignment. The following is a typical program used by Wolpe:

1. Whenever the man feels anxious lying next to his partner, he should do nothing more until anxiety has subsided.
2. When anxiety disappears and only sexual arousal is present, he may continue to the next stage—turning and lying next to her, touching her, stroking her genitals, etc. Anytime that anxiety appears, he is to stop until it disappears.
3. Continual movement toward full intercourse is accomplished in stages—insertion of only glans penis in vagina without movement, full insertion, full insertion with movement, etc.
4. The precondition to advancing to the next stage is the absence of anxiety.

The details concerning the use of various behavioral techniques vary from case to case. For example, the following instructions have been found useful in the treatment of premature ejaculation.

1. Lovemaking should never occur when the partners are tired. Should fatigue set in, both partners are told to relax and even sleep.
2. When love play begins and progresses to mutual stimulation of the penis and clitoris, each should inform the other of their excitement level.
3. When the man experiences sensations premonitory to ejaculation, he should inform his partner immediately to desist from further stimulation. This allows the man to gain control over the level of his arousal.
4. Stimulation should only begin when the man is in good control.
5. With the help of his partner, the man should insert his penis part way into the vagina and engage in small movements, keeping well within control. When ejaculation becomes imminent, the man should stop.
6. This procedure is repeated over and over until the man can withhold ejaculation long enough to satisfy his partner.

Aversive conditioning

Although there are a variety of specific behavior therapy techniques, they all are based on principles of learning. Behavior techniques view sexual deviancy and other cases of psychopathology as reflecting faulty learning experiences; the specific technique employed depends upon the exact nature of the sexual disorder.

Aversive conditioning techniques utilize the principles of classical conditioning, as we saw in the case of "Albert" in Chapter 5, where fear of a rat was conditioned. The aim of aversive conditioning is to associate painful or unpleasant experiences (anxiety) to a particular stimulus. Aversive techniques have been used with a wide variety of sexual disorders.

EXHIBITIONISM. In the case of exhibitionism, such therapy usually involves the fostering of more assertive heterosexual patterns and aversive conditioning (Maletzky, 1974). Evans (1967) treated seven exhibitionists by presenting them with descriptive phrases that called up images of their exhibitionistic behavior or heterosexual tendencies. The vivid imagery elicited by the exhibitionistic phrases was then paired with electric shock which could be terminated by the patient changing to a slide describing normal sexual responses. Evans achieved remarkable success as five out of the seven patients no longer had any urges to exhibit themselves following treatment. The two remaining subjects reduced their exhibitionistic activities from 28 to 2 episodes a month.

FETISHISM. Behavior therapy has been particularly useful in the treatment of fetishism where the object of sexual stimulation can be readily identified. Kushner (1965) reported the successful treatment of a 33-year-old male patient with a fetish involving women's panties. The only way he could achieve orgasm was to masturbate while wearing the panties.

Kushner combined the use of electric shock, in association with women's panties with a desensitization program (see Chapter 9) to alleviate the man's fear toward heterosexual relations. These procedures proved to be successful and at last report the patient was married and enjoying heterosexual experiences.

MASOCHISM AND SADISM. There is a dearth of information on the treatment of sadomasochistic reactions. However, as part of the treatment program involving several patients, Abel, Levis, and Clancy (1970) utilized an aversive conditioning technique in treating a young masochistic patient. The initial step involved making a tape describing his masochistic behavior. The tape was then associated with electric shock. By verbalizing normal sexual behavior, the patient could avoid the shocked part of the tape. His masochistic tendencies were inhibited in the laboratory situation, as indicated by penile erections, and were subsequently generalized to real-life situations.

HOMOSEXUALITY. Aversive conditioning is commonly used for homosexual individuals who wish to change their sexual performance. The typical procedure is to show nude male pictures to the homosexual and deliver an unpleasant electric shock to him at the same time. This inhibits the pleasant sexual response usually experienced. This is usually followed by reconditioning; attempts are made to foster approach responses to heterosexual stimuli by giving the subject injections of sex hormones and displaying pictures of attractive nude females when the sex drive is at its peak.

Freund (1960) treated 47 male homosexuals by injecting a noxious drug while they viewed slides of males, and by administering androgen before they viewed films of nude females. A follow-up several years later showed either temporary or permanent weakening of homosexual tendencies in 50 percent of the patients.

Prognosis of sex offenders

The outlook, or prognosis, in the treatment of sex deviancy is generally good, but depends upon the degree and duration of deviancy and the extent of accompanying psychopathology. Inadequate and sexually inhibited people and fetishists have an excellent prognosis as they typically respond well to treatment. The outlook is also favorable for exhibitionists and voyeurists; they both rarely repeat their behavior after therapy (Coleman, 1972). Only in atypical cases usually involving pervasive psychopathology is the treatment likely to prove difficult or unsuccessful in these sexual aberrations.

Hostile psychopaths who are prone to rape and pedophilliacs seem more difficult to treat. However, appropriate treatment for both types of deviancy has proven successful for those offenders who experience a genuine remorse and want to change their maladaptive behavior. For instance, Cohen and Seghorn (1969) have noted that rapists who have relatively normal social and adaptive skills in other areas of life possess good prognosis in group therapy.

The prognosis for homosexuals who want to change to exclusively heterosexual relations is somewhat guarded. The estimates of the success rate in treatment varies to some extent. However, the Task Force on Homosexuality of the National Institute of Mental Health, after reviewing several studies, has estimated that roughly one-fourth of these patients have achieved some measure of heterosexual functioning. Because of the difficulty in making the change, most therapists feel that in many cases it is more practical to encourage the homosexual to accept his homosexuality rather than to try to change (McConaghy, 1971).

Prevention

With sexual deviation and with other abnormal behavioral reactions, effects at prevention are vital. Such efforts are directed toward the alleviation of pathological family patterns which may cause sexual deviation. On the individual level, efforts are organized toward the development of mature, healthy personalities. Prevention depends heavily on proper education concerning behavior.

It is evident that the majority of people who suffer from sexual variance lack adequate information about sexual matters and have very little insight as to the importance and desirability of normal sexual patterns in marital relationships. Examination of their case histories usually shows their education has been confined to vivid ideas of sinfulness and guilt, which tend to make masturbation and heterosexual relations unacceptable outlets for sexual tension. The result, as we have seen, is to discharge sexual energy in undesirable behavioral patterns. Fortunately, society is becoming increasingly aware of the importance of proper education, which is reflected by changes in school curriculums to include instruction on sexual matters.

Summary

The scientific study of sex has been only a recent phenomenon because of the many taboos and prohibitions surrounding it.

Of particular importance in sexual development is the gonadal hormones: androgens and estrogens which influence sexual behavior by directing the growth of the genital organs. Hormones do not seem to determine the direction of sexual interests but influence the strength of the sex drive. Experimental and clinical studies on castration in lower animals and man indicate that the effects depend on the evolutionary level of development. The findings support the contention that many social and psychological factors overshadow the hormones in influencing sexual behavior.

Besides hormonal influence, various neural mechanisms affect sexual activity. Damage to the cerebral cortex greatly disturbs motor capacities that are essential in the execution of mating behavior but not sexual excitement. The hypothalamus contains areas that influence sexual arousal, and the spinal cord possesses the control centers for many of the basic sexual reflexes (erection, pelvic movements, and ejaculation).

Psychological factors can cause human sexual dysfunctions. Because physical attractiveness and sexual-maternal behaviors are traditionally stressed as feminine values, they play an important part in the self-worth of women. The strong emphasis on the body and its organs can frequently lead to using them as a prime outlet to express resentment and anger (gynecological symptoms). Problems in pregnancy, childbirth, and breast-feeding are also more likely to occur in highly anxious women.

In a series of controversial but highly enlightening studies, Masters and Johnson provided important physiological data concerning the sexual response cycle. Four different phases have been identified: (1) The excitement phase is brought about by whatever is sexually stimulating for the person and is characterized by changes in the female (vaginal lubrication, nipple erection, sex flush, thickening of vaginal walls, and so on) and male (penile erection, elevation of testes, and so on); (2) the plateau phase is reached if sexual stimulation continues and produces increased tension in the female (further engorgement of vaginal tissue that decreases the opening of the vagina) and male (increased muscular tension, rapid thrusting of pelvis, preejaculatory emissions); (3) the climactic or orgasmic phase is reached when stimulations reach their maximum intensity and the body reacts involuntarily for the female (contractions of the vagina and uterus) and male (contractions of genital organs that lead to ejaculation); and (4) during the resolution phase a lessening of sexual tensions is experienced although the woman is capable of having another orgasm under effective stimulation but the man goes through a time interval (refractory period) when restimulation is impossible.

In a study of factors determining attractiveness of college freshman in dating, it was found that physical attractiveness was more correlated to liking of the date than either intelligence or personality variables.

With regards to attitudes and practices on sex, it appears that people are primarily more open in talking about sex rather than having changed very much in sexual practices. Nevertheless, important differences in sexual practices can be noted. (1) Differences in the sex habits of various social classes do exist. (2) Women are generally less sexually active than men. (3) There may be a decline but not a fall of the double standard. (4) The phenomenon of "swinging" or wife-swapping is estimated to be increasing. (5) Although they may be culturally conditioned to reject explicit sexual stimuli and prefer more romantic ones, early beliefs that women are less easily sexually aroused than men may be incorrect.

Different cultures tend to influence the manifestation of sexual behavior. Stimulation of the feminine breast in our culture is considered normal in foreplay, however, some societies lack this activity in their practices. Manual stimulation of the genitals is a common practice in our and other cultures. Oral stimulation of the genitals tends to be less frequent in our society. Furthermore, sex identity and educational status influences these practices.

It is extremely difficult to determine normality and abnormality of sexual practices and it may be more beneficial to talk about sexual variance. However, certain sexual dysfunctions and variations have been considered traditionally deviant: (1) Impotency and frigidity are conditions that prevent the individual from achieving sexual gratification. (2) Satyriasis and nymphomania refers to men and women, respectively, who focus their entire lives around sexual activities. (3) Homosexuality involves physical attraction between members of the same sex and transvestism involves wearing female clothes to obtain sexual gratification. (4) Incest is sexual relations between members of a family; brother-sister, parent-child, and so forth. (5) Rape is increasing and is an antisocial sexual act against a woman by a man. (6) Exhibitionism, exposing one's genitals to other people, and voyeurism, peeking at other's genital organs or seeing them engage in sexual activity, are ways of obtaining sexual pleasure. (7) In sadism, the individual gains primary pleasure by inflicting pain on others, while masochism means receiving pain to obtain sexual pleasure. (8) Other deviant types of activities are pedophilia (a child is the sexual object) and bestiality (animals are the objects).

Besides the prospect of biological abnormalities, many social-psychological factors can contribute to sexual deviations. For example, sexual deprivation, early learning influences, fear and hostility toward the oposite sex, failure in sex identification, provocation by the victim, and association with psychopathology have all been proposed as causes.

The specific treatment of sexual disorders depends to a large extent upon the particular type of deviation. Somatic forms of treatment have not proven very useful or successful. The use of psychotherapy utilizing Masters and Johnson's Rapid Treatment Program and behavioral techniques (counterconditioning and aversive conditioning) have fared much better.

Prognosis in the treatment of sexual problems varies with the type of disorder presented. Outlook for the successful treatment of impotence, frigidity, fetishism, exhibitionism, and voyeurism appears good while rape, pedophilia, and homosexuality is guarded.

References

Abel, G. G., Levis, D. J., & Clancy, J. Aversion therapy applied to taped sequences of deviant behavior in exhibitionism and other sexual deviations: A preliminary report. *Journal of Behavior Research and Experimental Psychiatry*, 1970, **1**(1), 59–66.

Adams, M. S., & Neel, J. V. Children of incest. *Pediatrics*, 1967, **40**, 55–62.

Amir, M. *Patterns in forcible rape*. Chicago: University of Chicago Press, 1971.

Avery, P., & Avery, E. Some notes on wife swapping. In H. Grunwald (Ed.), *Sex in America*. New York: Bantam, 1964, 248–254.

Bartell, G. D. *Group sex: a scientist's eyewitness report on the American way of swinging*. New York: Peter H. Wyden, 1971.

Bardwick, J. M. *Psychology of women*. New York: Harper & Row, 1971.

Beach, F. A. Effects of cortical lesions upon the copulatory behavior of male rats. *Journal of Comparative Psychology*, 1940, **29**, 193–245.

Beach, F. A. Normal sexual behavior in male rats isolated at fourteen days of age. *Journal of Comparative and Physiological Psychology*, 1958, **51**, 37–38.

Bieber, I., Dain, H., Dince, P., Drellech, M., Grand, H., Grundlach, R., Kremer, M., Ritkin, A., Wilbur, C., and Rieber, T. *Homosexuality: A psychoanalytic study*. Adapted from *Homosexuality* by Irving Bieber, M.D., and Associates. Basic Books, Inc., Publishers, New York, 1962.

Brancale, R., Ellis, A., & Doorbar, R. Psychiatric and psychological investigations of convicted sex offenders: A sumary report. *American Journal of Psychiatry*, 1952, 193–245.

Cohen, M., & Seghorn, I. Sociometric study of the sex offender. *Journal of Abnormal Psychology*, 1969, **74a**, 249–255.

Coleman, J. C. *Abnormal psychology and modern life*. Glenview, Ill.: Scott, Foresman, 1972.

Cooper, A. J. A clinical study of "coital anxiety" in male potency disorders. *Journal of Psychosomatic Research*, 1969, **13a**, 143–147.

East, W. N. Sexual offenders. *Journal of Nervous Mental Disorders*, 1946, **103**, 526–666.

Evans, D. R. An exploratory study into the treatment of exhibitionism by means of emotive imagery and aversive conditioning. *Canadian Psychologist*, 1967, **8**, 162.

FBI. *Uniform crime reports*. Washington, D.C.: Government Printing Office, 1971.

Ford, C. S., & Beach, F. A. Types of sexual stimulation in various cultures. In B. Lieverman (Ed.), *Human sexual behavior: A book of readings*. New York: Wiley, 1971.

Freund, K. Some problems in the treatment of homosexuality. In H. J. Eysenck (Ed.), *Behavior therapy and the neurosis*. London: Pergamon Press, 1960.

Gagnon, J. H. *Sexual conduct: The social sources of human sexuality*. Chicago: Aldine, 1973.

Gallup, George. Generation gap shown in sex view. *American Institute of Public Opinion*, 1970.

Gebhard, P. H., Gagnon, J. H., Pomeroy, W. B., & Christenson, C. V. *Sex offenders: An analysis of types*. New York: Harper & Row, 1965.

Goldstein, M. J., & Kant, H. S. *Pornography and sexual deviance*. Berkeley, Calif.: University of California Press, 1973.

Hunt, M. Sexual behaviors in the 70s, *Playboy*, October 1973, 85–88, 194–207.

Israel, J. Alder via forsta coitus bland varnpliktiga. *Sociologisk Forskning*, 1965, 30–38.

Kinsey, A. C., & Gebhard, P. H. *Sexual behavior in the human female*. Philadelphia: W. B. Saunders, 1953.

Kinsey, A. C., Pomeroy, W. B., & Martin, C. E. *Sexual behavior in the human male*. Philadelphia: W. B. Saunders, 1948.

Kushner, M. The reduction of a long-standing fetish by means of aversive conditioning. In L. P. Ullmann & L. Krasner (Eds.), *Case studies in behavior modification*. New York: Holt, Rinehart & Winston, 1965, 239–242.

Linner, B. *Sex and society in Sweden*. New York: Pantheon Books, 1967.

Los Angeles Times. Woman awarded damages in cable-car sex accident, May 3, 1970, F. S.

Masters, W. H., & Johnson, V. E. *Human sexual response*. Boston: Little, Brown, 1966.

Masters, W. H., & Johnson, V. E. *Human sexual inadequacy*. Boston: Little, Brown, 1970.

Maletzky, B. M. Assisted covert sensitization

in the treatment of exhibitionism. *Journal of Consulting and Clinical Psychology*, 1974, **42**, 34-40.

McConaghy, N. Aversive therapy of homosexuality: Measures of efficacy. *American Journal of Psychiatry*, 1971, **127a**, 141-144.

Miller, H. L., & Siegel, P. S. *Loving: A psychological approach.* New York: Wiley, 1972.

Miller, H., & Wilson, W. Relation of sexual behaviors, values, and conflict of avowed happiness and personal adjustment. *Psychological Reports*, 1968, **23**, 1075-1086.

Money, J. Sex hormones and other variables in human eroticism. In W. C. Young (Ed.), *Sex and internal secretions*, VIII. Baltimore: Williams and Wilkens, 1961.

Morgan, C. T. *Physiological Psychology.* New York: McGraw-Hill, 1965.

Mosher, D. G., & Cross, H. J. Sex guilt and premarital sexual experiences of college students. *Journal of Consulting and Clinical Psychology*, 1971, **36**(1), 27-32.

Murray, E. J. *Motivation and emotion.* Englewood Cliffs, N.J.: Prentice-Hall, 1964.

Newton, N. Breast feeding. *Psychology Today*, 1968, **2**(1), 34.

Packard, V. *The sexual wilderness.* New York: David McKay, 1968.

Playboy, September 1969, **16**(2), 46.

President's Commission on Law Enforcement and Administration of Justice. *The challenge of crime in a free city.* Washington, D.C.: Government Printing Office, 1967.

Rachman, S. Sexual fetishism: An experimental analogue. *Psychological Record*, 1966, **16**, 293-296.

Rosen, E., & Gregory, I. *Abnormal psychology.* Philadelphia: W. B. Saunders, 1965.

Sigusch, V., Schmidt, G., Reinfeld, A., & Wiedemann-Sutor, I. Psychosexual stimulation: Sex differences. *Journal of Sex Research*, 1970, **6**(1), 10-24.

Smigel, E. O., & Seiden, R. The decline and fall of the double standard. In R. V. Guthrie (Ed.), *Psychology in the world today.* 1971, 361-371.

Sutherman, S., & Scherl, D. L. Patterns of response among victims of rape. *American Journal of Orthopsychiatry*, 1970, **49**(3), 503-511.

Vaughan, E., & Fisher, A. E. Male sexual behavior induced by intracranial electrical stimulation. *Science*, 1962, **137**, 758-760.

Walster, E., Aronson, V., Abrahams, D., & Rottman, L. Importance of physical attractiveness in dating behavior. *Journal of Personality and Social Psychology*, 1966, **4**, 508-516.

Weinberg, G. *Society and the healthy homosexual.* Garden City, N.Y.: Doubleday, 1973.

Wolpe, J. *The practice of behavior therapy.* New York: Pergamon Press, 1970.

Zuckerman, M. Physiological measures of sexual arousal in the human. *Psychological Bulletin*, 1971, **75**, 297-329.

Zuckerman, M., Nurnberger, J., Gardiner, S., Vandiver, J., Barrett, B., & Breeijen, A. Psychological correlates of somatic complaints in pregnancy and difficulty in childbirth. *Journal of Consulting Psychology*, 1963, **27**, 324-329.

11

Youth and old age:
The present and future

W here you are now—your typical patterns of behaving, ways of viewing the world, and acquired skills—is the result of earlier stages of development. We have already discussed various principles of growth, including biological factors such as genetics and maturation of the brain, and psychosocial determinants such as learning, intelligence, and the role of the family. The orientation of this chapter is that one's personal and social development cannot be separated from his past or future. However, many psychological and social changes do take place during the period of transition, adolescence, and also during the declining years, or old age. We will focus on those problems that are peculiar to these special times in our lives, although always keeping in mind the principle of the continuity of development.

Adolescence

As a social phenomenon, adolescence is better understood by making a distinction between it and puberty. *Puberty* refers to the beginning of maturation of the physical aspects of sex, including development of adult sex organs, and the growth of hair in the pubic and other areas. The onset of puberty is easily ascertained and clearly definable.

In contrast, *adolescence* refers to the process of growing up, the period of transition from childhood to adulthood. It begins with puberty and ends with maturity. Although the definition of adolescence is clear, its duration is not. Maturity is difficult to define because it varies with respect to different physical and psychological attributes (see Figure 11–1). In some places, times, and societies, a person may be considered to be an adult at the age of 16. In our society, it is quite possible to be still dependent and not socially defined as an adult until the late twenties or early thirties. An example would be the young man or woman who is studying for a medical career. In other instances, a person will be considered an adult at the age of 18. Consider the case of the young man who is married and holding down a job. He is independent from his parents. In addition, he is also financially able to care for his own family.

The point made by many social scientists is that adolescence is a product of the times and culture (Bernard, 1971; Strange, 1968). Social mores and cultural settings also determine how long this period of transition will last.

In highly developed technological societies, adolescence may be stretched out for as long as 15 years in extreme cases. However, in some lesser developed societies, there may be no period of adolescence at all. Young people go right from childhood to functional adult roles, and the child is taught adult roles as soon as he begins to understand the world about him.

FIGURE 11-1
Curves representing growth toward maturity of various functions

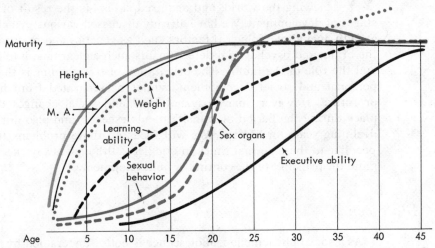

Rationale for representative curves:

1. Height. Probably the easiest curve to draw. In general the child at two years of age is about half as tall as he will be as an adult.

2. Mental age. The consensus is that in terms of retentivity, plasticity, and modifiability the biological basis for learning reaches its peak at about 20–25 years.

3. Weight. Increase in weight slows up in later childhood (wide individual variations), accelerates just before puberty, and tapers off during adolescence. Weight often continues to increase into the middle years (and middle section).

4. Learning ability. Learning requires a brain and preparatory experience. The adult with a background of knowledge has more "apperceptive mass" with which to attack new meanings and concepts. He has an operational advantage over the "callow" youth.

5. Sex organs. Rapid growth from pubescence, but may begin as early as 10 (there are cases on record when it has begun at 3 years) and as late as 20 (also exceptions which are still later).

6. Sex behavior. Perhaps the line should not go above the line of maturity. It is so drawn to show that sex activity, though less vigorous in the middle years, should (and often does) become an aspect of mature love. Sex behavior in early marriage is often an end in itself.

7. Executive ability. In a complex society, experience is more important than physical maturity. Professional men are reaching their peak in the forties. Statesmen and judges are beginning to reach (in their forties) the prominence they will achieve as senior citizens.

Source: From Harold W. Bernard, *Adolescent Development* (New York: Intext Educational Publishers, 1971). Copyright © 1971, Intext Educational Publishers.

The development of identity

More than anyone else, Eric Erikson deserves credit for elaborating the concept of personal identity, particularly critical to any discussion on adolescence. Paradoxically, although Erikson has written much on the subject, he does not provide a simple definition of identity. Instead, he uses examples and general descriptions in his published works. One of the best and simplest definitions is provided by Rappoport (1972), in which identity is used as meaning a continuing sense of who and what one is. The identity concept is important because it ties together many diverse elements that determine the adolescent's self-concept—his ideas about himself as a person, student, and leader. A sense of identity emerges at the core of the self, its central feature.

Identity does not begin at adolescence, for, during childhood, identities are being formulated and reformulated. The self-concept of the child and young teen-ager is relatively plastic, as it can develop and be organized in different ways depending upon various experiences. For example, a young teen-age girl who is both a bright scholar and an Olympic prospect as a swimmer can go either way. Her sense of personal identity can follow either from her image of herself as a scholar or as a world famous athlete.

It is during adolescence that the final self-identity becomes crystallized or finalized as life-styles become organized around a few major activities; in the case of our example, it would be difficult to be both an outstanding scholar and champion athlete; both are very time consuming. Coincidental with the further development of one's self-identity at this period in life is a strong desire for change in one's self. This fervent wish for self-transformation can be seen in the adolescent's changing clothes, hair style, mannerisms, figure, attitude, and beliefs. This yearning to change the self is a reflection of the heightened self-consciousness of adolescence. The conflict brought on by this increased self-awareness and related changes often results in what has been called by Erikson, the *identity crisis*, roughly defined as not knowing "who you are." He considers it to be the major crisis of adolescence.

THE REFLECTIONS OF GEORGE BERNARD SHAW. The retrospective interpretation of George Bernard Shaw, the famous Irish playwright, of his own early identity crisis at the age of 20, is recognized as an analytical masterpiece interpreting youth (Erikson, 1968). As might have been expected of such a witty man, he describes his youth in a most entertaining but informative manner (Shaw, 1952). Shaw, the man, describes the young Shaw as disagreeable, undesirable, and not at all reticent of diabolical opinion. He concludes, "that all men are in a false position in society until they have realized their possibilities and imposed them on their neighbors. They are tormented by a continual shortcoming in themselves; yet they irritate others by a continual overweening. This discord can be resolved by acknowledged successes or failures only: everyone is ill at ease until he has found his natural place, whether it be above or below his birthplace."

Shaw proceeds to describe his youthful identity crisis in terms of not being able to find his place in society. He found himself being trained in an occupation he detested, from which he felt an overpowering need to escape. He "broke lose," which meant leaving his family, friends, business, and Ireland. Shaw thereby granted himself a prolongation of the interval between youth and adulthood, which is called a "psychosocial moratorium" by Erikson. Shaw eventually settled down to studying and writing as he pleased, and then his extraordinary mind came to the fore. Although, he had managed to abandon the previous type of work he had been doing, he had not relinquished the work habit.

Origins of identity

We have described identity as being formulated in childhood and depending on experience. In searching for the actual specific determinants of one's personal identity, Douvan and Adelson (1970) suggest that sex-role factors play the most important part (Figure 11–2). They point out that a major common threat found in all adolescent problems such as puberty, family relations, peer relations, and intellectual growth has to do with sexual identity. Boys tend to construct identity around their vocational choice, but in most cases, girls do not. For most boys, the question of "what to be" begins with the job, and the male is likely to define himself and to be identified by his occupation. In contrast, girls tend to keep identity diffuse, and hazy; they ordinarily do not have the opportu-

FIGURE 11–2
Traditional sex roles assigned by society, which are changing, enter into adolescent self-identity. Occupational choice has commonly influenced young males' perceptions of themselves, while raising children, being a homemaker, have kept young women's personal identity more diffuse.

Courtesy of Paul Fry, *The Santa Clara*, University of Santa Clara

nity to concretize identity through vocational choice. As a result, the identity of the girl is not so much tied in with what she is as with who she knows; her identity is a social one.

A second major component of the sense of identity is a person's social class. It is well documented that lower class children are less well accepted by their peers than middle-class children which has important ramifications for the child's feeling of personal worth. In fact, poor emotional adjustment is often associated with low popularity among children. The effects of social status on identity become even more intensified at adolescence, as the young man or woman becomes increasingly aware of their place in society.

Not only does social class enter into identity, but also an individual's expectations, hopes, and fears concerning their class-to-be. The emerging identity of the adolescent is not so much "plumber's son" as it is "plumber's son who will be a medical doctor; or janitor's daughter who may marry a dentist; or even college president's son who is no good and will not amount to anything." Hence, identity may encompass who your parents are, their status in the community, and what your own place will be in the future.

While there has not been a large body of experimental work done on the concept of identity, it is possible to evaluate the concept in a clinical manner in order to see if it seems to help us understand recognized problems and patterns of behavior.

One such pattern of behavior occurs at the college level and involves the students for whom choosing a major apparently presents a most challenging and anxiety laden dilemma. Choosing a major is a critical step for the student because it may determine his daily activities for life. To decide to work in a scientific laboratory or to enter the world of business is not a small decision. To the amazement of their friends, some students seem to know what they want to do and unhesitatingly plunge into a course of studies designed to lead them to that goal. In the authors' experiences most premedical students stand out as having had no problems deciding on being physicians. Indeed, their study habits often reflect the firmness of their commitment. However, this decision is not so easy for all students, and the reason for this difficulty seems clear; a well-defined choice for a vocation would seem dependent on an equally clear, well-defined self-concept or identity. Not knowing what to major in may be a reflection of a diffuse, undeveloped self-concept. Saying, "I don't know what to major in" is roughly equivalent to saying "I don't know who I am." Identity crises are undoubtedly behind the turmoil and experience as they grapple with this lifetime decision.

For some students, this problem extends beyond academic significance. Schizophrenia has its highest incidence in the 20–35 age range. The schizophrenic usually manifests signs of withdrawal, apathy, and loss of interest in the world around him, associated with deterioration of his ability to think rationally. These individuals quite likely never developed firm, clear identities capable of sustaining them in the demanding adult years. Adolescents choose a major and select dates for their social life, while adults select a vocation and a spouse, both ostensibly for life. Life is no longer filled with tentative, reversible decisions. These enormous decisions obviously come easier for those with a well-developed sense of identity; that is, those who know themselves well and have a realistic sense of self-worth. The ancient adage "Know thyself" seems to have great psychological significance.

Peer group relations

All of us must identify with or feel part of something in order to be able to form some kind of identity. If we are excluded from recognized societal groups, we have no recourse but to start a group of our own, with which we strongly identify. Herein lies the importance of peer relationships during adolescence. It is generally recognized by psychologists and sociologists that there is no period during our lives in which group involvement or peer relations are more important than adolescence (Figure 11–3). As the influence of the family gradually weakens during this time of life, the peer group comes into its own as an autonomous social organization with purpose, values, standards of behavior, and means of enforcing them.

PEER GROUP STRUCTURE. The peer group's influence is now strong enough to compete with the adolescent's parental ties in furthering development. However, it should be recognized that there is no single adolescent subculture; instead adolescent groups vary in structure and

FIGURE 11–3
The importance of peer or group relationships for identity and personal growth has been strongly stressed by many psychologists.

Courtesy of Paul Fry, *The Santa Clara*, University of Santa Clara

nature. The small, close-knit cliques which emerge consist of members who share common interests, problems, aspirations, and secrets. They are bound together by a high degree of personal compatibility and mutual admiration in which they follow the definite socioeconomic class lines of the parents.

In a famous study, the adolescent cliques in a midwestern community, "Elmtown," were investigated (Hollingshead, 1949). Using a social-class classification system, it was found that approximately three out of five friendships were between boys or girls of the same class position. Two out of 5 clique ties were between adolescents who belonged to adjacent classes, and only 1 out of 25 involved individuals who belonged to classes twice removed from one another. Thus, it can be noted from these statistics that the polar classes are largely isolated from one another insofar as intimate, personal, face-to-face relations are concerned. Recent studies have yielded similar findings (Bernard, 1971).

If a girl should form a close friendship with a member from another class, her parents and those from her own class disapprove, ostrasize, or advise her to mend her ways. The dual operation of the parents and peers in the clique is well illustrated in the case of Judy Small's (Class III) relationship with her clique and especially with her friend Jackie Strong (Class III).

> We're all together a lot and she influences me almost as much as my parents. I listen to them somewhat, but I don't agree with them on everything they say about my friends. They really gave me a bad time about some of the girls and guys I wanted to go around with or maybe Jackie did. Most parents seem to get upset about their kids running around with certain other kids, and they'll give them advice; some kids will listen, others don't. If my parents really get uptight and put their foot down, I have to listen.
>
> I know that my parents want what is best for me, but sometimes they just don't understand what kids are doing these days and they think we ought to act like they did thirty years ago. My folks influence what I do, but Jackie influences me just as much, if not more.
>
> Some of the kids are real drags, who are just not my or Jackie's type; they'd like to run around with us but we won't let them. I shouldn't run them down but we just don't have anything in common.
>
> Betty Johnson (Class IV) and her bunch are who I am referring to. They are so wild and run around all night with boys; they even cut school and their folks don't seem to care.
>
> There are some other kids we try to be nice to, but they are such snobs they act like they are better than us. Betty and I tried to get invitations to parties given by Jane Allen (Class II) and her bunch, but they just snubbed us. They seem to have so much money given to them by their parents, although they dress like the rest of us. For example, Jane has gone to Europe with her parents three years in a row.

Traits associated with acceptability. The characteristics which form the basis of friendships are uniformly high on social desirability, which in turn is reflected in popularity. Wenar (1971) summarizes the results of several studies and finds kindness, cooperativeness, generosity, and honesty are ranked highest. What unfolds in general as one looks at the objective data on social acceptability is an ideal picture of the personality traits of the middle-class adolescent. Besides possessing the above characteristics, the socially desirable person is vigorous, tolerant, dependable, neat, clean, and sensitive to the feelings of others. He also provides new experiences for his peers, is above average in intelligence and scholastic achievement, and is emotionally stable. The adolescent low in popularity or social acceptability is retiring and low in tolerance and adaptability. In addition, he is undependable, negativistic, individualistic, quarrelsome, overbearing, and usually insensitive to others or socially maladjusted.

As previously noted, the socially acceptable adolescent and child is the one who reflects middle-class values via his traits. These values have now become more or less permanently implanted in the United States in spite of the fact that we live in an era of rapid transition. They serve as a broad frame of reference and give continuity and direction to the lives of middle-class children and adolescents. Young people coming from different backgrounds and value systems are at a disadvantage.

Whether middle-class values are the best ones for the preservation and growth of society or for the individual is open to discussion. Certainly such values are not intrinsic to human nature. Thus, it is important to guard against the assumption that our values are the right ones, and that others are wrong.

DATING AND MARRIAGE. In our society, dating is a rather ritualized social institution in which the heterosexual skills are learned and perfected. The age at which dating begins is getting lower and too early, according to many authorities (Mead, 1965). Dating may begin as early as age 13 for some girls, and at ages 13–14 for boys. Early dating takes two different forms; it may be an informal matter of pairing off within larger groups so that others are available for moral support. Or it might take the form of one boy dating one girl as the desire to be "alone together" asserts itself. The latter pattern for a great many couples culminates in an early marriage.

However, there is evidence that the dating patterns in this country do provide such positive functions as developing heterosexual skills, providing opportunities to meet opposite-sex peers, and serving as outlets for sexual experiment and discovery within mutually acceptable limits. American adolescents exhibit "a degree of poise and nonchalance in striking contrast to the social backwardness, shyness and embarrassment of European young people of equivalent ages (Douvan & Adelson, 1966).

The average girl goes through three general stages with respect to dating, as outlined by Douvan and Adelson (1966):

> The preadolescent group treats dating as a more or less intellectual issue and gives no real indication of emotional involvement with boys except for occasional signs of anxiety about their imminent introduction

to dating. Early adolescents are very much involved in beginning dating, have considerable anxiety about it, and take a defensive rather than an interactive stance toward boys. Only in late adolescence, as initial anxiety subsides, do girls begin to have true interactive relationships with boys, and bring understanding, sensitivity, and feeling to these relationships. In her early dating, the girl is likely to be absorbed with the problem of integrating new role demands and an image of femininity to this self-concept. As she gains some assurance that she is measuring up to a style of feminine behavior, the girl can begin to seek and find emotional gratification in friendships with boys.

Similar dating patterns exist with boys. However, one notable difference is that they place less stress on the intimate, emotional, interpersonal aspects of dating relationships, and more on commonly shared interests and activities. In brief summary, the significance of dating lies in the provision of social experiences with members of the opposite sex. It is a phase of preparation for a later successful marriage. The young person who has not been able to try out a variety of social and personal roles will be ill-prepared for the adult roles in marriage. One danger of too much stress on early dating is that teen-agers may decide to marry before they are really mature enough.

Adolescent marriage. In spite of the possible dangers of early marriage, more young people than ever before are getting married in their teen years (Bernard, 1971). For example, in 1890 approximately 54 percent of the males over age 15 were married and 57 percent of the women, but in 1967, the figure stood at about two-thirds for each sex. In addition, in the last 50 years, the average age at first marriage has decreased almost two years for both men and women. The median age for women's marriage now is 18 and about 20 for men.

Many of these adolescent marriages are complicated by the fact that they are more likely than older marriages to have resulted from pregnancy. It is estimated that 35 percent of teen-age brides are pregnant at the time of marriage, and one-half of those married before age 18 will be divorced within five years. In such cases, the young couple may not be marrying the person he or she would ultimately choose, and even if they are, they have less time to become adjusted to each other and to the demands of marriage.

Another disadvantage of an early marriage is the danger of childbirth to the mother. There are proportionately five times as many mothers between the ages 10–14 who die in childbirth as those between 20–29. One of the difficult problems for adolescents is to deny sexual gratification for a period of time because of cultural pressures. Nature has established puberty or sexual maturation at the early teen-age years; but, at the same time, the increasing complexities of society make it difficult to have a successful marriage at such young ages where sexual gratification has normally taken place.

Although we have described the hazards of adolescent marriages, significant numbers of teen-age marriages are successful. The marriages which do turn out to be stable involve partners who are personally well-adjusted and relatively mature. It is interesting to note in a study on adolescent marriages that 60 percent of the subjects stated that if they had it to do over again at the same age they would. However, only 23 percent said they would advise their children to marry at the age they did.

Hence, because individuals and circumstances differ, it is not possible to prescribe an optimum age for marriage. Too long a delay also entails certain risks. Marriages contracted after age 30, for either spouse, on the average turn out to be less stable than those occurring for couples in their twenties. In addition, according to available evidence, the longer a person delays marriage after the middle twenties the less chance there is of getting married (Bernard, 1971).

The selection of a mate. In the majority of the cultures in the world, the selection of a marital partner is not made alone by the young person entering into marriage. Most often, the possible mates are determined by the parents, usually the father, or other elder males in the family. The two main reasons for this are: (1) in a patriarchal society the father makes most of the important decisions, and (2) the choice of a marriage partner is often related to economic factors. In most cases, the family sets a limit on the choices available to the young person; he or she then usually has a certain amount of freedom to choose from within this circle of available mates.

In the United States, the shift from a patriarchal family to one more democratically oriented has been related to the emergence of romantic love as a prerequisite for marriage (Figure 11–4). However, parents still have some influence over the selection of their son's or daughter's spouse by passing on values which will affect mate selection. Interestingly, there is some evidence that the mother is more apt to be consulted than is the father, in contrast to the patriarchal system of the past. In one study, reported in Adams (1968), the mother was consulted by 62 percent of the men and 70 percent of the women. The father, on the other hand, was consulted by 44 percent of the men and 32 percent of the women. About 43 percent of the males discussed their choice of a marital partner with a friend or friends, as did 43 percent of the females. The same study also found that 51 percent of the men and 42 percent of the women did not consult anyone on the wisdom of their choice.

Probably the most important impact that parents have on their children's future marriage is that they serve as marriage role models. Generally, the parents are the only adults that children have to observe in the wide range of intimate values and behavior associated with marriage. In most cases, children's ideas on how a husband performs or wife acts are formed by observing the interrelationships between their parents.

Marital happiness. Terman (1938), drawing conclusions from an old but classic study, states a conclusion that is still heartily agreed upon by marriage experts:

FIGURE 11-4
The selection of a mate in our society, unlike many other cultures, is based
primarily on romantic love rather than dictated by one's parents

Courtesy of Paul Fry, *The Santa Clara*, University of Santa Clara

Our theory is that what comes out of a marriage depends upon what
goes into it and among the most important things going into it are the
attitudes, preferences, aversions, habit patterns, and emotional response
patterns which give to or deny the aptitude for compatibility.

In accordance with this statement, one of the most important background factors on marriage has been found to be the happiness of

parents. This finding can be readily understood in light of the parents serving as marriage role models. It is through observation of the parents that children have a chance to learn the important attitude of give-and-take that is so crucial to happiness. Hence, children who have learned this attitude are happy while growing up and are apt to be happy with their marriage.

The impact of parents on their children's chances or capacity to have a successful marriage can be shown in several ways. Over the years, a number of studies have shown that children coming from homes where their parents' marriage has ended in divorce have a greater probability of their own marriage ending in divorce than do children coming from homes where their parents' marriage has remained intact (Adams, 1968). Correspondingly, there is some evidence that a young person has a better chance of success in his own marriage if his parents' marriage was successful. In addition, research also shows that children from homes where their parents' marriage ended through death have a higher probability of divorce than do children whose parents' marriage remained intact. When one of the parents is missing, it often means that the remaining one is no longer filling a marriage role, but is now playing a combined parental role. As a consequence, children growing up under these circumstances may not develop a true image of what marriage is really like and also may fail to learn the appropriate role of a father or mother.

For those whose home background and parents' marriage has been unfortunate all hope need not be abandoned. Sometimes a younger person, who has seen the unhappiness in his parents' marriage, becomes all the more determined to make his own work. Many learn from their parents what *not* to do if they want to get along with their spouses. One girl expressed a prevalent attitude among some in the following manner, "I am not going to make the same mistakes my parents did; my marriage will be a happy one."

Problem behavior in young people

Many young people find it difficult to cope with the adolescent period of development in a manner that is emotionally satisfying to them, and, at the same time, acceptable to society. Each year thousands of these youths get into trouble which takes many forms. They may underachieve in school or terminate their education altogether at an early age. Others may become juvenile delinquents, turn to drugs, or become alienated from adult society and its values. We shall take a look at school problems, juvenile delinquency, and alienation; the use of drugs has already been discussed in Chapter 4.

THE UNDERACHIEVING ADOLESCENT. In the past, an *underachiever* was quite likely to be considered lazy. Today, a more sophisticated approach takes a look at the personality and temperament factors in such a student, along with an examination of the learning situation in school with which he is confronted. The term "underachiever" refers to a student who seems to have the potential to earn far better grades than his current scholastic record shows. This includes not only above-average intelligence students, but those below average as well, and they can be found at all academic levels, from first grade through college.

Much of underachievement seems to be an attack on adults, and is probably one of the most subtle and insidious forms of rebellion. It is subtle in the sense that it may go untreated, and thus a promising academic career is destroyed. Elkind (1968) suggests that among middle-class adolescents, underachievement may be closely related to a breach of contract by the parents. If the parent fails to live up to his contract to take care of the emotional welfare of his child, the only revenge a conforming young person possesses is to do poorly in school.

Kotkov (1965) has described a series of personality traits typically found in underachievers. There is the passive receiver type who believes that good students achieve without any effort at all. He believes such people are just fortunate to be born with skill and intelligence; therefore they do not have to work hard for anything. Such young people are often the victims of maternal overprotection and, are ill-prepared for independent achievement. They are unlikely to be able to tolerate any frustrating situation and tend to react by displaying apathy, a lack of interest, and helplessness.

Another type of underachiever according to Kotkov is that of the youth with a high level of aspiration and a high degree of perfectionism who faces each learning task with a fear of failure. This is exemplified by the case of Jack B. He refused to spend much time studying for any class he had, and as a consequence, he was barely making passing grades. After several counseling sessions with a high school counselor, he admitted that he didn't put forth a wholehearted effort because he was afraid he could not make superior grades. Thus, he withdrew from classroom competition to avoid embarrassment and also to spite his demanding parents. According to Blaine (1966), this pattern is particularly common among children who arrive late in the ordinal rank in the family. Often the parents and teachers compound the problem by comparing them with their older brothers and sisters.

Besides these personality characteristics of two different types of underachievers, other youths may perform poorly in school because of emotional problems. Undue anxiety can cripple or interfere with intellectual functioning because of conflicts existing outside the classroom. Many adolescents are so preoccupied with inner conflicts and emotional stress, it is almost impossible for them to pay attention in class. For example, sexual "hangups" and romantic problems of adolescents can seriously affect their academic performances.

Role of teacher. Educators have become increasingly aware of the problems of underachievers and are making efforts to "humanize" the traditional curriculum. Some underachievers definitely need encouragement from instructors in order not to become disheartened. Their discouragement may actually trigger a vicious cycle wherein they avoid the subject matter, only to have others assume that they lack motivation. In reality, their low motivation is a secondary reaction to their lack of confidence in their ability to learn.

Others who underperform because they are highly distractible or are simply hyperactive can be helped in other ways. They sometimes respond to a well-structured academic environment with a high degree of stimulus intensity within the framework of the subject matter in the classroom, combined with a minimum of outside distractions. This technique is often augmented by the use of carpeted classrooms, acoustical tile, and elimination of windows to reduce outside stimulation.

All of these techniques, plus the use of counseling, are based on the principle of individualizing the formal classroom education as much as is feasible. Educators cannot overlook student temperament and its impact on learning, particularly in the case of underachievers.

SCHOOL DROPOUTS AND SOCIETY. Greene (1968) states a commonly accepted definition of school dropouts: they are those students who leave school without graduating. He goes on to point out that this definition includes both those who are expelled from classes by school officials and those who leave school voluntarily. He notes that this definition, has a weakness in overlooking the fact that some dropouts continue their education in private trade schools, in adult education classes, or in the Armed Forces. For purposes of our discussion, these students who get high school equivalency diplomas will be omitted.

The nation is currently much preoccupied with the problem of youth who drop out of school before graduating, and with youth who receive high school diplomas without having moved much beyond the point of illiteracy. Society is particularly concerned with these young people because they are seriously disadvantaged in terms of future employment, especially in this era of rapid technological change. Although the affluency of the United States is widespread and overall unemployment rates stay between 5 and 6 percent, the opportunities for those without either education or vocational skills continue to decline. A sobering fact is that the proportion of young people who are unemployed is currently greater than it was during the depression of the 1930s. Many of the kinds of jobs that previously existed and which provided an opportunity to gain a foothold on the socioeconomic ladder for the native-born poor, and young people without education, no longer exist. Unskilled workers, farm laborers, and many basic service workers have been replaced by automation. Other occupations have been upgraded and now require the skills provided by education and technological training. Complicating the job outlook further is the vast number of youths looking for jobs, which is the result of the high birthrates following World War II.

Antecedents of dropping out. The tragic irony of school dropouts is that they are most likely to come from the lower socioeconomic classes and ethnic groups already discriminated against socially. This is reflected in the high dropout rate in the slums and among members of minority groups. The dropout rate is highest among blacks, twice that for whites, even though four out of five dropouts are white.

In identifying the adolescent who is likely to drop out, the following major background factors have been cited, as summarized by Lambert et al. (1972):

(1) The potential dropout is often older than his classmates, usually as a result of his having been retained in a grade at least once during his school career. Because of this age difference he has trouble relating to his peers and gaining their approval.

(2) The dropout is usually failing in his school work at the time he decides to leave school, and has a history of consistent failure in his regular courses.

(3) During high school, the potential dropout increases his truancy rate over what it was in elementary school.

(4) Most dropouts are severely retarded in reading.

(5) Although most dropouts are below average in intelligence, that is not necessarily the major factor for his dropping out.

(6) The dropout generally lacks interest in school and is usually unhappy with the curriculum, the faculty, and the various school activities. This is considered to be the *primary factor* responsible for students leaving school.

(7) Potential dropouts tend not to become involved in school activities. In one study of 212 dropouts in Kansas, 144 of the dropouts were found not to have participated in a single activity; in contrast, non-dropouts showed an average of four activities per student in large high schools and six activities per student in small high schools (Bell, 1967).

(8) The family plays a critical role in determining whether a youth stays in school or becomes a dropout. Often parents of dropouts see little value in education and provide no support to their children.

In summary, the typical dropout is likely to come from an emotionally troubled and socially isolated home, frequently located in an ethnically or economically segregated ghetto. He is likely to have had academic trouble in school for many years and to be below average in intelligence. He is not only academically frustrated, but socially isolated as well because of his advanced age.

Programs to help solve the dropout problem. A number of imaginative beginnings have been made in certain areas to help solve the dropout problem. Several summer and school work programs have been started in some major cities to help disadvantaged youths. Both the government and industry have become involved in providing training and jobs for deprived dropouts. For example, there are special school training programs with a strong vocational orientation and individualized counseling. Also available are the Job Corps and the Teacher Corps, and preschool health and social enrichment programs such as Head Start. However, at this date, these programs have been undertaken on only a token basis because of their high costs. Sufficiently intensive and extensive programs will be enormously expensive, but the question is, "Do we have any viable alternatives?" in light of the tremendous loss in human resources that results from the lack of proper education and training.

JUVENILE DELINQUENCY. Although it is basically a legal concept, the term "juvenile delinquent" is very broad. Depending on state and local laws, the term is generally applied to youths ranging anywhere from a maximum age of 16 to 21, and includes those committing offenses that would be considered criminal if performed by an individual legally classified as an adult. Although most delinquents are adolescents when they come to the attention of the authorities, they generally begin their illicit activities during middle childhood.

The extent of juvenile delinquency has become one of the primary domestic problems existing in the United States today. It has been on the increase every year since 1948, and is greater than the general rise in population growth within this age range (Lambert, Rothschild, Altland, & Green, 1972). According to current estimates, at least 12 percent of all children are likely to turn up in juvenile court before the end of adolescence. Delinquency rates are highest in deteriorated neighborhoods and slums near the centers of large cities. There are many opportunities for learning antisocial behavior from delinquent peers in areas which are characterized by general disorganization, economic deprivation, and rapid population turnover. Unfortunately, as is too often the case, delinquent behavior becomes the approved social norm for these adolescents.

Psychological types of delinquency. Several attempts have been made to classify delinquents on the basis of their social characteristics. One system that is frequently used was devised by Hewitt and Jenkins (1941). On the basis of their research, they were able to isolate three psychological types of delinquents: (1) socialized, (2) unsocialized, and (3) the maladjusted or withdrawal type.

The socialized delinquent is relatively well adjusted and is likely to become an emotionally mature adult. As the name implies, they are socialized and show no signs of maladjustment; hence, they are classified by many psychiatrists as "normal." They participate in groups or gangs that are usually found in the deteriorated neighborhoods of the larger cities. The range of behavior of this group is wide, ranging from selling protection to younger children to stealing automobiles for joyriding or committing robbery. The case of Jack W. illustrates one who is a "normal" or socialized delinquent.

> Jack W., the third of four brothers, was 16 years of age. He played hooky from school frequently, and was part of a gang of boys who stole automobiles and also committed holdups with a loaded pistol. He frequently came home late at night, and his mother, who was deserted after her youngest child was born, had little parental control over him.
> The center of Jack's life activities and interests was the gang of adolescents he ran with. His home offered little of interest to him. His

brothers went their separate ways and his mother worked at a laundry in an effort to provide for the family's needs. Her work and social life (visiting with her friends) occupied most of her time. Jack had few educational goals and strongly disliked school. He was friendly with his teachers and the school counselor.

The type of delinquent referred to as unsocialized has not developed social forming behavior in which he has reconciled his individual desires with the demands of society. He is impulsive, emotionally immature, and tends to act the part of a younger child insofar as judgment and sense of values are considered. The lack of self-restraint which can lead to delinquent behavior can be seen in the case of Bruce D.

> Bruce D., 15, the second in a family of three children, was referred to a psychiatrist after being arrested for the fourth time. The first two times he was arrested for burglary and the last two times for petty stealing. All of these acts were committed on the spur of the moment as well as his running away from home.
>
> His mother reported that he was unmanageable, and spent most of his time running around in the streets with undesirable companions. He did poorly in his school subjects as he couldn't concentrate for any length of time. His overall impulsiveness and lack of concern over the consequences of his actions, was more like the actions of an 11-year-old.

The maladjusted delinquent is generally regarded as an insecure person with low self-esteem, or as a highly aggressive and hostile person. He tends to withdraw from social participation and is often a "lone wolf offender." Most of these delinquents give clear evidence of being very unhappy and discontented in their life circumstances, or extremely disturbed because of their emotionally provoking situations or experiences. Their unhappiness and feelings of being unloved or rejected are reflected in personality deviations and many symptoms indicative of maladjustment. The following case described by Topping (1941) illustrates a confused delinquent.

> Harold, white, 14½. One of probably identical twins of a family of seven children. When he was four, his mother died and his father deserted. The twins, two brothers, and a sister were placed in an orphanage where they remained four years, until the sister died. The other twin became delinquent. Harold stated his own delinquent conduct was due to his desire to be with his brother. His studied efforts to emulate the gangster smack of adolescent theatricals. He has a warped and scarred personality and is capable of deadly attack. Bitter hostility and a philisophy of futility became an integral part of his personality. Outstanding in his reactions were disappointment and bitterness arising from the loss of his parents; dread of being thought a sissy by his twin; loss of emotional security through separation from his siblings; determination to rejoin his twin by becoming delinquent.

The treatment of delinquency. When a juvenile delinquent is apprehended one or more of the following procedures take place; (1) there is a court hearing in which no final disposition of the case occurs, a method sufficient to deter some from future delinquency; (2) the court assesses a fine and restitution for any property which has been damaged or destroyed, a relatively mild form of punishment; (3) the youth is placed on probation, wherein he may be required to undergo psychotherapy or be placed under serious surveilance; and (4) an adjudged delinquent is placed in a state institution for various periods of time.

Recently, several new treatment programs have been started in the United States, many of them centered in the community where the youth resides, as alternatives to commitment to a reformatory or a training school. Some programs involve a treatment center where delinquents participate in daily group therapy while still living at home and working or attending school. One ten-month experimental vocationally oriented psychotherapeutic program was undertaken with 20 adolescent boys (10 in an experimental group and 10 in a control group). One psychotherapist served each youth in the experimental group in all therapeutic capacities during the experiment. The program was flexible and geared to the needs of each youth with an emphasis on his acquiring a sense of responsibility. In addition, preemployment counseling was undertaken with the goal of preparing the youths for various jobs. Furthermore, remedial education was introduced when the subject was ready to improve his skills on the job.

The results of this study were encouraging as those subjects in the experimental group tended to improve, first, in their self-image; second, in their control of aggression; and finally, in their attitude toward authority. In addition, they improved in their school performances and showed a much better employment record than the control group; seven out of ten were still in jobs and the other three back in school at the end of the ten-month period. On the other hand, members of the control group showed little improvement on the personal, educational, and vocational dimensions described above (Massimo & Shore, 1963).

Other treatment programs require institutionalization of juvenile delinquents, in which they are sent away from the community. For example, in one institution for delinquent girls, a three-month pilot project was undertaken which was based on the theory that much antisocial behavior is the result of educational failure because of a learning disability. Referred to as *educotherapy*, the program stressed both remediation of the academic deficits and a modification of the maladaptive behavior of the girls. The program was undertaken with ten of the delinquents who were considered to have educational or learning disabilities, or behavior disorders related to such problems. The philosophy underlying the treatment was fourfold: (1) each girl should experience some successes in school; (2) each should learn socially acceptable modes of behavior; (3) each girl should enhance her self-concept; and (4) each should learn to accept responsibility for her actions, including the consequences (Rice, 1970).

Interestingly enough, the delinquent girls improved their reading skills within 2 to 13 months with a corresponding increase in their intelligence as a result of this three-month educationally oriented thera-peutic technique. In addition, there was a noted improvement in the girls' personal appearance and social behavior, less aversive behavior and hostility, and a spirit of group cohesiveness among the ten with each helping one another. As a result, three girls were released from the insti-tution at the end of the program. Also encouraging was the tendency of the other institutionalized girls to imitate the behavior of the girls under-going educotherapy. Thus, this and other related programs which stress psychological, vocational, and educational approaches show promise of being much more effective in treating juvenile delinquency than the tra-ditional reformatories and training schools.

ALIENATION. It is fashionable these days to speak of youth who do not fit in within the normal modes of society as being "alienated." Halleck (1967, p. 642) more specifically defines alienation as "an estrangement from the values of one's society and family and a similar estrangement from that part of one's history and affectual life which links him to his society or family." Viewed in this context, it becomes obvious that aliena-tions differ in several ways. Some youths feel an alienation from what had previously appeared to be a meaningful and orderly universe with a personal God as its center. This has become common as a result of the rapid decline in a clearly defined religious faith wherein adolescents feel an essential lack of any absolute meaning in the universe as a whole. Other youths share *developmental estrangements* (Keniston, 1965), a feeling of alienation that comes with the abandonment of childish ties to one's parents. Sometimes, these severed emotional ties with the family are not replaced by new ones and the adolescent loses his sense of belonging.

While many adolescents may share both these and other forms of alienation, the most common type of alienation currently involves an ex-plicit rejection of the traditional American culture. Some youths become bohemians or social dropouts while others become radicals and may en-gage in violence. Still others become political activists and work within the system for change. Strictly speaking, the latter group is not really alienated; they have already been described in Chapter 1.

The alienated dropout is characteristically pessimistic and too op-posed to the system to even express his disapproval. He responds by dis-senting privately and passively through his nonconforming behavior, dress, and ideology. Unfortunately, he frequently depends upon and gets hooked on drugs in order to intensify his subjective experiences and as another way of expressing his distaste for the normal conventions of so-ciety. The only solution many youths feel available to them is to "drop out"; they typically feel that any meaningful change is impossible.

Alienated radicals who have been involved in student demonstrations of the past decade, sometimes leading to violence, frequently advocate the overthrow of "the Establishment." Rather than respond in a passive manner like social dropouts, they feel that changes in society can be brought about through revolution and violent techniques. Many of their characteristics are similar to those of student and political activists already described; they just tend to be more extreme.

Characteristics of social dropouts. In contrast to many other alienated young people who remain within the physical confines of the middle-class society although rejecting its values, social dropouts move to a life outside of the formal structure of society. This movement involving people dropping out is not really a new phenomenon. Every society has had its social dropouts who did not share the values of the dominant social order, and even in the United States the "hippy" movement was preceded by the "beatnik" generation. What is more noticeable about the new movement is the considerable attention it has received from the public and popular press. In light of the small number of youths that actually participate in the movement, the reaction is wholly disproportionate with its actual significance.

Where do these young people come from? Although there is no single type of social dropout, they characteristically come from white middle-class families in large urban areas. Often they come from families that are unstable as can be seen by the fact that one or both of the parents has probably at some time experienced emotional difficulties requiring psychiatric treatment (Halleck, 1967). This is in spite of the fact that their parents may be viewed as pillars of the community. Thus, although their parents have achieved success in terms of their occupational level and amount of money they earn, many are not psychologically capable of establishing close family ties with their children.

The fathers of the alienated youths are usually absent from their homes for extended periods of time, or leave for work early and come home late so that they spend little time with their children. The mother, on the other hand, is characteristically a talented individual who has sacrificed her career for marriage and her children (Keniston, 1965). Often she overcompensates for a lack of a career by becoming so wrapped up in her family that she discourages her son's independence, thereby causing him to feel "suffocated" in terms of developing his own identity. As a result, he is apt to resort to apathy, inertia, and withdrawal as a means of hurting the older generation.

These youths possess a mutual antagonism of dislike for what they consider to be the aggressive, highly competitive, conformity-demanding, dehumanizing nature of modern society. They view such values as social status and material success to be meaningless and hollow, or in their words, "a real hang-up." What values do they consider to be important? According to Brown (1967), they stress such human values as love, gentleness, immediate relatedness and sharing with people, individual self-expression, appreciation of nature, and heightened sensory experience. However, what they advocate and actually do are not necessarily congruent. For example, Halleck (1967) describes seven characteristics which consistently appear in the personality constellation of these alienated youth:

1. They show a tendency to live only in the present and avoid any commitment to people, causes, or ideas. They are reluctant to relate their current problems to any of their past experiences and will not accept adult responsibilities.
2. They exhibit an almost total lack of communication with their parents and other adults. They distrust adults and their resentment toward authority is reflected through such behavior as cheating on exams.
3. They tend to possess poorly defined self-concepts, and are unable to resolve their identity crisis during their adolescent years.
4. Alienated youths manifest tendencies toward severe depressions which are elicited by relatively minor stresses. Such emotionality is accompanied by a tendency to project their problems on the world, blaming society for their failures. As a consequence, they have little insight into the nature of their hardships.
5. Although they are usually bright, they are unable to concentrate on their school subjects for any length of time. Thus, they believe education is irrelevant and largely meaningless.
6. They tend to engage in promiscuous sexual experiences, but find them largely ungratifying, with intimacy and orgasm generally missing.
7. The alienated strongly emphasize the use of drugs in order to enhance their "inner lives" and sensory experiences. They are fully aware that their parents and authorities disapprove of their usage of these drugs and, therefore, they serve as another weapon of defiance.

Programs to counteract alienation. Contrary to the beliefs of some adults, alienation is neither inevitable nor irreversible. One method of combating it is to have young people take an active role in the formulation of programs pertaining to their future and current needs. Many colleges, for example, have students serve on various university committees along with professors and administrators. Also, at the college level, young people are increasingly given the opportunity to grow through a minimum of required courses in which they are given the chance to enhance their knowledge through extensive use of the library, participation in community affairs, and self-initiated productive work.

Similar programs have been advocated at the high school level. In 1965, several thousand northern California high school students were invited to meet at a conference on youth. Eisner (1969) has summarized the major suggestions proposed by the delegates as follows:

Education:
  (1) Provide students with more responsibility for their own affairs in school.
  (2) Encourage young people to take an active role in establishing school standards and rules by upgrading the functions of the Student Council.
Community Action:
  (1) Invite schools and youth organizations to participate in community action programs and in the solving of community problems.

(2) Encourage youths to work on civic projects, for which they would be given recognition.

(3) Give young people an active voice in community government, possibly by the election of a youth official.

(4) Appoint youths to serve on committees with adults.

(5) Invite young people to participate in youth services agencies, where they could help bridge the gap between agency adults and recipients of agency services.

Jobs:

(1) The school curriculum should be expanded to expose students to the world of work, particularly college-bound youth.

(2) Provide job opportunities for all adolescents, not just dropouts.

(3) Include youths on school or district committees in liaison with industry to facilitate the development of jobs for young people.

As stressed by Eisner (1969), young people usually will become alienated only when they have failed to become part of society. When provided with opportunities by adults to assume meaningful roles in society they are unlikely to choose alienation. Instead, when given a chance to make pertinent decisions and partake in roles that provide a certain amount of status and recognition, youths will become assimilated into the mainstream of society.

The golden years

As man ages, he is said to become "more like himself." This simply means that an individual increasingly shows a pattern of appearance and behavior that is characteristic of him. (See Figure 11–5.) The dynamics of transformation are such that there are some changes that are mixed in with stable features. In addition, in describing the life-span, each period of life has special problems and crises. The child's first steps, learning to talk and his first date are critical events of growing up, as are finding a job and learning its skills, getting married, and raising a family. We have already discussed earlier phases of the life cycle, including childhood and adolescence. The rest of this chapter will be devoted to the psychosocial and biological aspects of aging, in addition to the final act itself, death.

The psychology of aging

Aging is a natural phenomenon with not only broad scientific implications for all living forms, but also with profound implications for every person. Historically, the interest in aging can be seen in the pursuit of the most enthusiastic cures for old age and attempts at rejuvenation. This has ranged from that of inhaling the breath of young girls (Burstein, 1955) to Ponce de León's historic search for the fountain of youth. Today, many people are still looking for a way of slowing down the effects

FIGURE 11-5
Picture of one-egg twins before and after long separations (between the ages of 18 and 65).

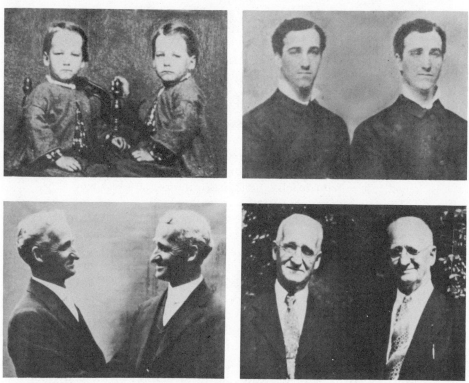

Source: Franz J. Kallman and Lissy K. Jarrick. Individual differences in constitution and genetic background. In J. E. Birren (ed.) *Handbook of Aging and the Individual.* (Chicago: University of Chicago Press, 1959), pp. 216–63.

of aging by resorting to food fads or the extravagant use of vitamins. Still others have "face-lifts," to remove the telltale signs of aging, or special cosmetic preparations to cover up wrinkles.

The scientific study of aging, nevertheless, did not really begin to take place until the 19th century. In fact, the field showed a very slow growth in factual information until after World War II. The psychology of aging involves the description and explanation of the evolution of adult behavior over the life-span. This includes the study of capacities, skills, emotions, and social behavior as they change in the adult with age.

Biological characteristics of the elderly

Senescence connotes the process of becoming aged, and the arbitrary cutoff point for the beginning of old age is usually taken as 65. However, the time of onset of senescence is variable from individual to individual; some people show evidence of senescence in their fifties but others appear "relatively young" in their seventies and eighties. Biologically, the reason all organisms grow old is that with increasing age the various bodily systems lose their capacity for self-repair. For example, younger organisms including man can repair the effects of an infection and resist it on subsequent exposures. But with increasing age, individuals appear to grow more susceptible to deleterious conditions, and self-repair does not return the individual quite so near his previous level of functioning. It should be recognized that the various organ systems may age at their own rate and vary in their capacity for self-repair. Some tissues, such as the skin, are able to repair themselves quite well at any age and form new cells by the division of older ones. In contrast, other tissues, like the brain, are relatively stable and cannot produce new cells when damaged. Although we know that bodily organs lose cells with age, and have a lessened functional capacity, biologists still do not know why.

The favored explanation of cell death which causes aging is that with time damage or accidents occur to the nucleic acids of the cell chromosomes which have the ultimate control over the biochemistry of the cell. With damage to the deoxyribonucleic acids (DNA) or to the ribonucleic acids (RNA), the necessary enzymes for maintaining cell division cannot be synthesized. Thus, such cells would presumably die, and for those cells that can continue to divide, death of the cell may occur at the time of attempted cell division.

We shall now briefly review the age-related changes that take place in various organs and systems of the body. Structural changes in organs, such as atrophy and degeneration will result in alteration of function. Aging is particularly noticeable in the structures of the body that contain highly differentiated cells, those that do not have the capacity for division. Besides neural tissue, highly differentiated cells are also found in the vascular, muscular, and the immunological systems (Birren, 1964).

THE BRAIN. Because of its integrative role in the physiology of the organism and in behavior, the brain and the nervous system are in a particularly crucial position to pass on the influences of aging. With age, the brain cells show an increased accumulation of particles known as pigments (Bondareff, 1959). They appear to be insoluble compounds, as suggested by their persistence, which begin to interfere with vital cell functions. In spite of their frequent presence in old cells, little more is known about the chemical composition of the pigments or how they are formed.

With senescence there commonly occurs increasing interference with blood circulation in the brain. Because the brain is particularly sensitive to the lack of oxygen, there is reason to believe that a common cause of changes in older brains is poor circulation. Such changes, however, tend to be limited to localized regions in the brain rather than being diffuse. There also appears to be a general loss of cells in the brain with aging. The older brain is found to be somewhat lighter in weight than the young brain, which is caused by the loss of cells in the cerebral cortex as well as in the cerebellum. These changes in the brain, besides being associated with various psychological changes to be discussed later, are partly responsible for a slowing in psychomotor behavior.

THE HEART AND BLOOD VESSELS. The cardiovascular system is affected by such age-related changes as degeneration and "wear and tear." The heart gradually becomes less capable of responding to the extra demands involved in the stress of heavy work. Arteriosclerosis, narrowing of the blood vessels, is one of the most important conditions in the aged. It leads to increased resistance to the flow of blood, and the heart is forced to compensate for this by an increase in the systolic blood pressure. Many different signs and symptoms are related to cardiovascular changes. Besides possible brain damage, arteriosclerosis may cause heart disease or result in inadequate blood supply to the legs and kidneys.

Some medical progress is being made in the treatment of cardiovascular disease, a major killer of man, which will reduce morbidity and mortality rates among the aged. Adequate treatment consists of treating or attending to a great number of factors which influence the patient's condition such as proper diets and optimal physical exercise, negative emotions, and stressful family relationships and living patterns. Although little can be done to prevent certain diseases in this area such as cerebral thrombosis (stroke), many disabilities can be avoided by intensive treatment and by vigorous rehabilitation, based on a comprehensive psychosomatic approach.

RESPIRATORY SYSTEM. Respiration, which serves the function of exchanging oxygen and carbon dioxide between lungs and blood, typically may be less efficient with aging. This may be caused by emphysema (changes in the elastic fibers of the lung) as well as by arteriosclerosis of the lung vessels.

Damage to the respiratory system is becoming increasingly common, because of high incidence of lung cancer and emphysema, and is a major cause of death. However, on a lesser level in which actual disease is not present, older people have difficulties in breathing and shortness of breath only when engaging in excessive exercise. Only in clear-cut and severe lung and/or heart disease is shortness of breath present in relaxed older people.

One practical implication of the reduced efficiency of the respiratory and cardiovascular systems is that the aged person has a reduced ability to adjust to extreme temperature variations. Furthermore, it is not uncommon for younger and older members of the family to quarrel over what the room temperature should be. Aging individuals typically like it warmer than younger people.

GASTROINTESTINAL AND URINARY SYSTEMS. As you may have noticed on observing your grandparents, older people become more interested in and preoccupied with food, eating, and elimination. In general there is a decrease in the sense of smell, taste, vision, and hearing; loss of teeth and problems with dentures; reduced motility of the stomach and intestines; and a decrease in production of the digestive juices of the stomach. The usual age-related changes in eating patterns include an increased liking for sweets and a decreased fluid intake. At this time in life, the body actually needs a lesser amount of calories because its overall metabolic rate is lower.

Constipation frequently occurs in older people and may be further complicated by the appearance of hemorrhoids. Extreme constipation as well as its counterpart, bowel incontinence, may represent daily living problems even to healthy aged persons. That older people can psychologically overreact to such a problem can be seen in the case of one elderly man, much to the chagrin of other members of his family, who insisted upon stopping at service stations on vacation trips in order to take his daily enema. He never gave nature a chance to take its own course.

A common problem in old age is more frequent urination. In men, this is frequently caused by enlargement of the prostate gland, where cancer commonly occurs, while in women infection of the urethra and bladder is responsible. Urinary incontinence, like bowel incontinence, is a major practical living problem to many old people and may cause them not to leave their homes. In addition, these problems may rob them of valueable sleep as they sometimes have to get up several times during the night.

SKIN AND CONNECTIVE TISSUES. The changes that take place in the external appearance of the elderly are due to age-related changes in the skin itself such as loss of elasticity and pigmentary changes. In addition, there is also the loss of tissue immediately below the skin. One of the effects of these skin changes is the tendency of older people to bruise easily or to develop skin sores.

It is well known that exposure to sunlight tends to accelerate aging of the skin; therefore aged people are advised to avoid too much exposure to the sun. This advice from medical doctors also applies to young people. People who spend many long hours in the sun in order to get well-tanned, are risking premature aging of the skin, much to their regret later.

MUSCULAR AND SKELETAL SYSTEMS. As older people can testify to, stiffened joints and changes in the structure of bone commonly occur with the onset of old age. This may cause a reduction in height and a stooped posture, as well as curtailment in movement. Closely related are changes in the muscular system which cause a loss of muscle power and a decrease in the ability to perform rapid movements at will. Routine daily tasks become more difficult, but more importantly, such vital functions as breathing, urination, and defecation are impaired. Another common change with senescence is that of osteoporosis, the bone structure becomes lighter and more porous. The practical implication of this change is that old people are susceptible to broken bones with any fall. Fortunately, although this condition may also be painful and disabling, it can be helped with medical treatment.

One general treatment that is recommended for older people suffering from these problems is moderate and regular exercise in order to prevent further disability from musculoskeletal changes. For example, aged people who are bedridden and suffer from lack of exercise often have permanent joint contractions. Walking is considered to be one of the best types of exercise for older people. Also, depending upon the physical condition of the individual, swimming, or nonstrenuous activities such as gardening or shuffleboard are recommended.

Mental ability

The stereotyped image of an older person is that of a rigid, ultraconservative, intellectually weak, and uninteresting person who will avoid the new and the unfamiliar. The evidence continues to mount, however, that this simplistic notion is not supported by actual research. Much depends on the nature of the intellectual task, physical health, and level of motivation of the older person. Another important factor is the level of education which correlates more highly with intelligence test scores than does chronological age. When the educational level is held constant for all age groups, measures of information tend to increase with age while measures of perceptual ability decline. Old people particularly decline in performance on mental tests involving speed. But when it comes to such matters as vocabulary which can only be acquired with time, older persons have given the superior performance (Baltes & Schaie, 1974).

Another factor that is related to IQ scores in old age is the original level of intelligence. The "haves" sometimes improve their scores and the "have-nots" lose. People who were originally brighter typically increase their scores more than those who were less intelligent. Nevertheless, in one study of professional men, there was a drop in IQ (Carp, 1969a). This decline can be mostly attributed to their relatively poor performance on the IQ subtests demanding speed.

As previously indicated, poor health can greatly affect IQ. In fact, a very clear drop in intelligence test scores usually heralds death, and is the best predictor that an individual is going to die (Carp, 1969a). In one sense, the decline in IQ with age is an artifact. The older the age group, the higher the death rate. Therefore, when we take averages of IQ scores, the older the group, the more of these suddenly dropped scores are included. If we eliminate from the average those people who are within a year of death, intelligence test scores do not change very much.

Perhaps the real test of the powers of older persons to adjust to changed conditions should not be based on intelligence tests, but rather upon such meaningful tasks as adapting to industrial changes in occupation. A study was undertaken at an oil refinery, in which retraining was required of all production workers and instrument operators because of their change to automation (Koller, 1968). The grades obtained by older workers in retraining did not suffer essentially from the younger employees. By contrast, when long-distance telephone operators had to be retrained to use an IBM card instead of the more familiar paper form, the older employees did not do as well as the younger ones. This is because rapid changes in psychomotor activity were required which have generally been found to work against older people.

Personality in aging

One of the important questions concerning aging is, "Are there personality types that make a better adjustment to old age than others?" and "Are there some personality traits that remain relatively stable with advancing age, while others change?" In an attempt to partially answer such questions, a group of investigators at the University of California at Berkeley, investigated reactions to retirement as a measure of adjustment to old age (Reichard, Livson, & Petersen, 1962). They classified individuals according to their personality and found that three clusters of individuals appeared to adapt well to aging and forced retirement. These were (1) the "armored type" who were maintaining high well-developed defenses against anxiety, (2) the "mature group" having a constructive approach to life, and (3) the "rocking chair type" of somewhat passive individuals who depended heavily on others. The two types of individuals who adjusted poorly to aging were (1) the "angry," who were hostile and characteristically blamed others for their problems, and (2) the "self-haters," who had been more or less poorly adjusted all of their lives.

While these personality types probably do not have universal properties, they do suggest that certain behavioral or personality traits are related to how well individuals are likely to adjust to old age. In general, the Berkeley investigators concluded that men who adjusted successfully to retirement were psychologically better equipped to stand up under stress; found satisfaction in their activities; accepted changed circumstances of their lives; and importantly, sought out social contact rather than withdrawing into themselves. The differences in adjustment to old age, hence, reflect lifelong differences between those who successfully adjusted in contrast to those who did not.

Similar studies have been carried out by researchers at the University of Chicago, as summarized by Birren (1966). Collectively, the studies indicate that other things being equal, those persons who have the highest satisfaction with their lives are those who maintain close interpersonal relationships. Although disposition to move toward close interactions with other individuals is a general personality trait, some individuals with advancing age tend to reduce their participation in many activities. This has been referred to as a "disengagement" from social roles. There are two different viewpoints as to why social disengagement occurs in some older people. One viewpoint is that the changes in the environment of the older individual make it difficult for him to participate in his characteristic activities, and therefore he becomes disengaged from his social roles. In contrast, an opposing theory maintains that as individuals age, they, themselves, wish to become disengaged from their various social roles.

It is likely that both internal and external processes are involved. The elderly, being retired, may have limited income and little opportunity to maintain their previous social roles. On the other hand, other older people may lack the energy to maintain their previous level of functioning, and hence prefer to be involved in only a limited number of activities. The following case history illustrates both psychological and social forces at work, leading to social disengagement:

> Jack B., a 75-year-old professor emeritus at a large university, had been a leader in education for the greater part of his life. He authored numerous articles and once served as the Dean of Humanities. Upon retiring at the required age of 65, he lost his sphere of influence at the university, which had always been very important to him. He was allowed to keep his office so that he could continue to write. However, he no longer seemed to have the energy to publish as he did when he was younger.
>
> His wife died five years after his retirement, and as a result, he no longer had anybody he was very close to. He took to spending more and more time visiting the faculty club on campus, in which he reminisced to younger faculty members about his many experiences. After a while many attempted to avoid him because they had heard the same old stories on several occasions. As a consequence, Jack B. found himself becoming increasingly socially disengaged; he lacked the energy to keep up on the latest theories and innovations in education and, in addition, many of his former social roles were no longer available to him upon retirement.

AGING AND THE SELF-CONCEPT. Results of projective tests suggest that there is less "ego involvement in life" as people grow older. For instance, older people make up less complex, and emotional stories in response to TAT pictures than younger individuals. Other studies, show a broadly negative trend concerning the self-concept (Rappoport, 1972). The results from one projective task ("draw a person"), for example, show that once past the age of 40, progressively older samples of men and women draw increasingly smaller pictures which is interpreted to mean decreased self-confidence. This is supported by questionnaire studies in which elderly men seem more cautious and less self-confident than those of college age in responding to items involving risk-taking. Finally, comparative studies in which older and younger samples are asked to rate themselves and the "ideal person" reveal a greater discrepancy for the older people between self and ideal.

CHANGES IN MOTIVATION. Studies of interests and activities of adults over the life-span show that there are some changes that take place in motivation. Some activities become more popular with increasing age while interest in others declines. Interest in participating in sports and playing bridge, for example, declines during the adult years while visiting museums, gardening, and relatively solitary activities increase (Birren, 1966).

An interesting trend with aging is the older person's increased interest in "cultural" activities and lessened interest in just being amused. For instance, adults over 50 show more interest in reading books than in listening to popular and dance music in contrast to young adults. In addition, an even greater age difference is seen in movie attendance; 50 percent of the individuals between the ages of 20 to 29 went to a movie at least once a week in 1957, whereas only 8 percent of those over 50 went that often (Birren, 1964). This does not mean that older people sit around and simply vegetate, however, as can be seen by Figure 11–6, showing the amount of time spent watching television. These data indicate that the average amount of time spent in television viewing remains more or less constant for life. In regard to program preferences, once again we find age differences. Older people tend to like variety shows while younger individuals prefer suspense and mystery dramas. Overall, older people tend to like nonfictional entertainment.

SEXUAL BEHAVIOR. Evidence on sexual activity of older people comes primarily from the Kinsey reports and Masters and Johnson (1966).

FIGURE 11–6
Audience composition of selected prime time program types. Suspense and mystery dramas ranked first among adults under 50, while those over 50 preferred variety programs. Situation comedy programs were tops with children, but teens preferred general drama.

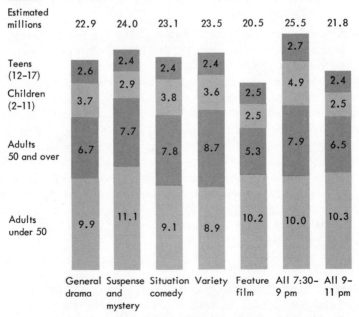

Data courtesy of Television Bureau of Advertising, Inc.

Using the sensation of orgasm as the criterion of sexual behavior, the survey of Kinsey et al. (1948) reported that the frequency of orgasms declined for men from the late teens almost linearally throughout the life-span. Regarding their findings on the frequency of orgasms per week for males and its relationship to age, Kinsey and his co-workers noted that the effects of novelty associated with a new sex partner is such as to increase the frequency of orgasm in older males. However, these effects do not last long and the previous rates of orgasm frequency are soon re-established. This would imply that while novelty may have a stimulating effect on the sex drive, there is still an overall drive reduction throughout the life-span.

Nevertheless, as one man put it, "to be old does not mean I am dead." Some men in their nineties continue to have marital intercourse. The actual statistics show that only about 5 percent of the male population is impotent by the age of 60, and only 30 percent by the age of 70 (Dengrove, 1961). Even in the case of impotency, older males retain their fertility and could father children if they had some way of delivering the sperm.

One of the great limitations on the sex drive of the older age group is the relative unavailability of an appropriate mate. This factor is particularly important in the case of women, since only about one-third of the women over 65 live with a husband. It is also quite likely that the reported decline in marital intercourse of the wife may be more a function of the lack of potency of her husband than her own sexual drive or capacity. Kinsey suggests that because of the greater dependency of the female upon the availability of an appropriate mate during old age, that frequency of masturbation might be a better measure of female sexuality. Although the overall rate of masturbation is lower in women than in men, the decline in masturbation frequency with advancing age is less in females than males (Kinsey, Pomeroy, & Martin, 1953). This suggests that sexual desire changes very slowly and only to a small extent in the female.

It would be instructive to end this section on sex and aging by summarizing briefly the conclusion reached by Masters and Johnson (1966) in their research on the human sexual response. They stress that there is every reason to believe that regular sexual expression combined with good physical well-being and a healthy mental orientation to the aging process will provide a sexually stimulative climate within a marriage. Hence, in this manner, a proper climate is established which will provide for the enjoyment of sex to and beyond the 80-year age level.

Individual differences

In spite of the normative data we have been reporting which suggest negative changes in personality, physical deterioration and reduced social status with age, some encouraging findings are reported by Butler

(1963). He undertook an intensive study of "normal" men above the age of 65 years using 47 subjects who were given detailed medical and psychological tests. According to the medical examination results, the majority of the men were judged to be in optimal health while the rest showed only minimal traces of disease such as minor arthritis or other conditions that were well under control. The psychological test data obtained from these men were compared with those obtained from a young normal-control group. The only notable difference between the two groups involved performances on intellectual tests, in which the younger men scored higher. However, this was mostly because of the slower working speed of the older men, similar to findings we have noted before.

As stressed by Butler, "the significance of these findings, is that many of the impairments ordinarily thought to be a consequence of old age actually result from disease, personality variables, and social-cultural effects. In addition, in the case of otherwise normally functioning older people, the primary physical source for psychological deterioration is arteriosclerosis causing reduced arterial blood flow to the brain." Thus the Butler report indicates that when elderly people are in reasonably good health they are not much different from younger people and can lead active, constructive lives.

A more recent study by Carp (1969b) supports many of the findings of the Butler report. She tested 295 persons ranging in age from 52 to 92 using a senility questionnaire which measures personality changes associated with old age and the MMPI (see Chapter 8). Carp strongly stressed that items in the senility questionnaire reflect the effects of physical deterioration as well as psychological problems.

She reports the following results: (1) no significant relationship between senility scores and chronological age was found; (2) a control group of college students surprisingly made a higher average score on the senility index than did the older group; (3) in a subsample of 100 of the older subjects, senility scores were negatively related to ego strength scores obtained from the MMPI; the lower the senility score, the higher the ego strength. Thus, her findings, like Butler's work, show that chronological age per se is not as important as are physical and psychosocial factors.

Another study which holds out hope for the elderly concerns the description of a subjective age (Rappoport, 1972). When a group of over 300 people, 70 years or older, were asked to describe themselves, about half used the term *middle-aged*. Further study showed that these "underestimators" were people who have made very good adjustments to the problems of growing old. Studies of this type indeed point out that the old adage "you are only as old as you feel" is not meaningless rhetoric. Those individuals who adjust well to old age apparently do so by remaining active as emphasized by Havighurst, Neugarten and Tobin (1968, p. 161):

The older person who ages optimally is the person who stays active and who manages to resist the shrinkage of his social world. He maintains the activities of middle age as long as possible and then finds substitutes for those activities he is forced to relinquish. . . .

Dying and death

Facing terminal changes in health and death itself is the final task of life, which nobody can avoid. Freud once stated that "the goal of life is death." It is only in the last 20 years or so, however, that there has been much interest in the natural process of life on the part of social scientists as reflected in the number of studies concerning attitudes toward death, and other psychological and sociological aspects of dying. This sudden boom of interest in this research area probably stems from the realization that how we end our lives may be just as important a source of knowledge as the way we begin them. Just as studies of birth and infancy have led to better procedures for handling the very young, work on dying may lead to better methods of handling the very old. Also we are seeing a gradual lifting of the cultural taboos associated with discussing the topics of dying and death. However, the removal of these taboos is still relatively incomplete as illustrated by the experience of Pearson (1969), who started teaching a course on the subject:

> Soon I became the object of a curious interest on the part of colleagues. At a social gathering of faculty one evening, the host greeted me at the door and led me to the living room, where he introduced me: "And here is our Minister of Death." Students who were studying with me began to acquire a campus reputation as eccentrics . . . (Pearson, 1969, p. vii).

FACING THE THOUGHT OF DEATH. How do people face the thought that they are going to die? Many studies have been done with elderly people to determine if they are actively afraid of death. Munnichs (1966), a Dutch psychologist, performed one of the best research effects in this area in which he investigated the attitudes toward the death of 100 Dutch elders (70 years of age and beyond). As might be expected, he found a variety of orientations. However, the most important conclusion to come from his findings is that only a small category of old people were afraid of the "end." By far the most frequently observed attitude expressed toward death was one of *acceptance*, with *acquiescence* next. Overall, approximately two-thirds of these elderly people had come to terms with their finitude. It was also found that psychologically mature elders were most apt to accept death in a positive manner. Conversely, fear of death tended to be associated with an immature personality. Munnichs concludes that orientation toward death is a central theme in the early phases of the aging process.

These results are supported in a study by Weisman and Kastenbaum

(1968). Their findings were obtained with relatively sick elders, in a geriatric hospital in the United States, while Munnichs' findings were based on relatively healthy elders. The former found that *apprehension* or fear was less often observed than *acceptance*, and they also noted responses of *anticipation* and *apathy*. Two typical orientations toward the preterminal phase of life was observed in the patients. Some patients accepted their fate quietly, and gradually reduced their activities. The patients themselves initiated this preterminal disengagement which allowed them to bring their affairs to order by focusing on fewer events. Other patients, although recognizing that death was close at hand, opted to remain involved with daily life activities. This could not be considered neurotic, in the sense of denying reality. They were simply continuing to live as they had been living, wherein death would come and have to tap them on the shoulder to interrupt the business of life.

Attitudes toward death among younger adults. Questions about death were included in a public opinion pole of 1,500 adults in the United States under the direction of Jack Riley (reported in Kastenbaum & Aisenberg, 1972). He reports that among adults of all ages only about 4 percent gave evidence of fear or anxiety in connection with their own eventual deaths. His data, thus suggest that chronological age is not a crucial variable per se in determining attitudes toward death. The amount of education a person has seemed to be more important in this survey. For instance, people with limited educational attainment, regardless of their age, were more likely to agree with negative propositions about death.

Among other interesting findings in Riley's study is that the great majority of respondents at all age levels agree with the propositions that "death is sometimes a blessing," and "death is not a tragedy for the person who dies, only for the survivors." The overall trend of Riley's findings shows that the large majority of adults have a positive or accepting attitude toward death in the adult population of the United States.

Along these same lines, it is interesting to note that there seems to be more fear toward death among the relatives and physicians of a terminally ill patient than in the patient himself (Dempsey, 1971). As a consequence, many hospitals are designed and organized in such a way as to prevent the patient from discovering his fate. This would seem to be an outmoded practice in light of the data on the acceptance of death by most people. Even those dying patients who do have some fear of death seem to experience great relief from emotional tension when allowed to express some of their fears. The illuminating personal experiences of Pearson (1969) illustrate this well:

> I first became aware of death as a clinical entity with special psychological impact when consulting at a home for the aged in Chicago some years ago. One day one of the residents failed to appear for our group-therapy session. When I asked about him, the staff member serving as cotherapist with me looked startled. With her face reddening, she said she would tell me about it later. Then one of the other residents calmly

spoke up: "He died last night." This led to a discussion of attitudes toward death as well as toward the dead man. It became apparent that most of the older persons had made some resolution of their feelings toward death. Subsequent talks with staff members, however, revealed much reluctance to discuss the concept (Pearson, 1969, p. vii.).

THE LIFE REVIEW. It has been postulated that one phenomenon that universally occurs with aging is the mental process of reviewing one's life. It is characterized by the return to consciousness of past experiences wherein the older person reminisces about his memories in the past. In fact, the older person is often experienced as "living in the past" much to the dismay of his younger listeners. It is presumed that this process is prompted by the realization of approaching dissolution and death, and by the inability to maintain one's sense of personal invulnerability. In addition, an increased sense of self-awareness is thought to be partly responsible for this phenomenon. As death nears, people again turn to the perennial questions of identity and meaning: "Who am I?", "Has my life been significant or worthwhile?"

Generally, the content of one's life unfolds slowly as the life review process takes place. In its mild form, the process is reflected in increased reminiscence, mild nostalgia, and mild regret; in its severe form it may involve anxiety, guilt, despair, and depression. Other clues to its existence range from reminiscence itself to dreams or nightmares concerning the past and death, an increased concern for religion, and by the strange phenomenon of mirror-gazing. Butler (1963) describes the apparent commonness of mirror-gazing in which a concern for the changes in physical appearance is often expressed by the aging. The following comment of an old man is in line with their attitude: "I was passing my mirror. I noticed how old I was. My appearance, well, it prompted me to think of death—and of my past—what I hadn't done, what I had done wrong." (Havighurst et al., 1968, p. 489).

Sometimes the immediate consequence of living on with the memories, as manifested in the life review, is guilt and shame. As can be seen in the above quotation, the old man started by glancing in the mirror, and quickly ended by thinking of what he had done wrong. In another case, a 70-year-old woman in a mental hospital is quoted: "Some nights when I can't sleep, I think of the difference between what I'd hoped for when I was young and what I have now and what I am" (Butler, 1963). Since these emotional reactions are in most cases not caused by definitive losses, it may be difficult for the observer to comprehend. However, they can be more easily understood when looked at in the following manner. Suppose that you remember a funny incident that happened when you were a child, such as may have occurred at your birthday party, and then conjure up all those old friends. You might have acted more decently to some of them particularly when it may have involved having fun at the expense of the awkward types. Would it help to think about it if you knew they were dead or decrepit? Of course it wouldn't in this hypothetical case, but this is what older people face so often when they reminisce about the past. A better illustration can be provided by reading the real stuff in Alexander Solzhenitsyn's novel *The First Circle* (1968). One of the chief characters is an old communist revolutionary named Rubin. While ill, he found himself plagued with memories of the time he was in charge of collectivizing a peasant village and the men he had to kill. Philosophically, he still believed that his actions were necessary, but he no longer could accept the killings emotionally. Hence, he became very disturbed.

Constructive outcomes to the life review. Maladaptive outcomes to the life review are not invariable. Some older people actually experience new and significant meanings to their lives upon reflecting over their life. The following case represents an occasion in which the life review was creative and resulted in positive, constructive effects.

> An 80-year-old woman, optimistic, contemplative, and creative, and who had become increasingly egocentric, became significantly more interested in the affairs of her husband, children and grandchildren. These changes corresponded with the writing of her autobiography, upon the suggestion of a friend. She wrote down some of her most memorable experiences which she expected her children and grandchildren to read when she was gone. To give herself greater motivation in writing her life story, she pretended to be telling the story directly to them.

Probably, in the majority of the elderly, a substantial reorganization of the personality does occur as the result of attempting to reconcile one's values with the behavior of one's life and to leave behind an acceptable image. In many cases, a favorable and adaptive end result may be enhanced by propitious environmental circumstances such as freedom from major crises and losses. However, it is more likely that a successful reorganization occurs largely as a function of the personality. Those individuals who remain flexible, resilient, and active are most apt to profit from the life review.

Summary

While puberty has many biological correlates (maturation of sex organs) that make it definable, adolescence refers to the process of growing up. It is difficult to determine when a person has reached maturity and adulthood because it varies with regard to the times and culture. An important aspect of adolescent development is that of identity; who and what you are. Although personal identity begins in childhood, it is during adolescence that identity becomes of utmost importance. Several factors tend to influence identity development. First, there is a tendency for boys to construct their identity around their vocational choice while girls are more influenced by a social role definition. Second, social class and the values transmitted to us by parents greatly affect our attitudes, beliefs, and aspirations. Third, peer group influences during this period allows us to interact with others and to clarify sex roles by acting and being responded to, which allows us to learn social competition, cooperation, and values.

The learning of social roles is especially important in peer group interactions. Social desirability or popularity seems strongly linked to middle-class values. Dating is one form of social interaction which allows us to develop heterosexual skills and sexual experimentation. According to authorities, the dating age is lowering and may be the reason for increasingly early marriages. There are fears that teen-agers may decide to marry before they have reached maturity.

In the majority of cultures in the world, selection of marital partners is often made by the parents. However, in our society romantic love has become a prerequisite for marriage and there is a direct lessening of parental influence. The most important impact from parents is the marriage-role model they provide for the children. Another source of parental influence is in marital happiness. Children who come from homes in which the parents are happy, tend also to be happier in their marriage. Likewise, children coming from homes where their parents' marriage ended in divorce are subject to higher divorce rates.

The adolescent period is a stressful one that may cause problems in adjustment. Such is the case of the underachiever, high school dropout, juvenile delinquent, and the alienated student. Although not engaging in antisocial acts, the alienated person tends to reject traditional values of the society. The so-called hippie is a prime example.

At the other end of the youth continuum is that of senescence, the process of becoming aged. The psychology of aging involves the description and explanation of the evolution of adult behavior over the life-span. Biologically, the reason all organisms grow old is that with increasing age the various bodily systems lose their capacity for self-repair. For one reason or another, increasing interference with blood circulation in the brain occurs during senescence. Loss of cells is also characteristic. Other biological changes associated with aging are cardiovascular degeneration, less efficiency of the respiratory system (loss of lung elasticity), gastrointestinal and urinary problems, loss of elasticity of skin tissue, stiffening of joints, and susceptibility to broken bones.

Contrary to many stereotypes of the aged, they need not be rigid, ultra-conservative, intellectually weak, and uninteresting. Rather than declining intelligence of the aged, what we see is rapid changes in psychomotor activity that contributes to lowered performance scores involving speed. Intelligence does not seem to drop when such variables are held under control.

Studies have shown that adjustment to old age is related to personality. Three personality types were found to adjust well to aging and forced retirement: (1) the "armored type" who maintains defenses against anxiety, (2) the "mature" group having a constructive approach to life, and

(3) the "rocking chair type" who are passive and dependent. Two types were associated with poor adjustment: (1) the "angry," and (2) the "self-haters," who were poorly adjusted to begin with.

Interests and activities also change as we grow older. Participating in sports and bridge decline while visiting museums, gardening, and solitary activities increase. Nonfictional entertainment is preferred. In terms of sexual activity, frequency of orgasms decline although very few individuals over 60 are impotent and sex can be enjoyed beyond the 80-year age level.

In spite of these normative data, studies indicate that when elderly people are in reasonably good health they are not much different from younger people and can lead active constructive lives.

None of us can escape death. Only recently have interests focused upon dying and our attitudes toward it. Studies on older people facing death reveal that the most frequent attitude is acceptance and acquiescence. Furthermore, chronological age does not seem to be a crucial variable in determining attitudes toward death. Indeed, most people agree that the tragedy of death is not for the person who dies but the survivors. The life review is a common occurrence among the aged. Mild regret, turning to religion, and positive results often occur as a result of this process.

References

Adams, J. F. (Ed.). *Understanding adolescence: Current developments in adolescent psychology.* Boston: Allyn and Bacon, 1968.

Baltes, P. B., & Schaie, K. W. The myth of the twilight years. *Psychology Today,* 1974, **7**(10), 35–40.

Bell, J. W. A comparison of dropouts and non-dropouts on participation in school activities. *Journal of Educational Research,* 1967, **60**, 248–251.

Benedict, R. Continuities and discontinuities in cultural conditioning. In P. Mullahy (Ed.), *A study of interpersonal relations.* New York: Hermitage Press, 1949, 297–308.

Bernard, H. W. *Adolescent development.* Scranton, Pa.: Intext Educational Publishers, 1971.

Birren, J. E. *The psychology of aging.* Englewood Cliffs, N.J.: Prentice-Hall, 1964.

Birren, J. E. Adult development and aging. In I. A. Berg & L. A. Pennington (Eds.), *An introduction to clinical psychology.* New York: Ronald Press, 1966.

Blaine, G. B., Jr. *Youth and the hazards of affluence.* New York: Harper & Row, 1966.

Bondareff, W. Morphology of the aging nervous system. In J. E. Birren (Ed.), *Handbook of aging and the individual.* Chicago: University of Chicago Press, 1959, 136–172.

Brown, J. D. (Ed.). *The hippies.* New York: Time-Life Inc., 1967.

Burstein, S. R. Papers on the historical background of gerontology. *Geriatrics,* 1955, **10**, 189–193, 328–332, 536–540.

Butler, R. N. The life review: An interpretation of reminiscence in aged. *Psychiatry,* 1963, **26**, 65–76.

Carp, F. M. The psychology of aging. In R. R. Boyd and C. G. Oakes (Eds.), *Foundations of practical gerontology.* Columbia, S.C.: The University of South Carolina Press, 1969. (a)

Carp, F. M. Senility or garden-variety maladjustment. *The Journal of Gerontology,* 1969, **24**, 203–208. (b)

Dempsey, D. Learning how to die. *New York Times Magazine,* 1971.

Dengrove, E. Sex differences. In A. Ellis & A. Abarbanel (Eds.), *The encyclopedia of sexual behavior.* New York: Hawthorn Books, 1961, **2**.

Douvan, E. A., & Adelson, J. *The adolescent experience.* New York: Wiley, 1966.

Douvan, E. A., & Adelson, J. The adolescence experience and identity. In M. Wertheimer

(Ed.), *Confrontation: Psychology and the problems of today.* 1970, 24–34.

Eisner, V. Alienation of youth. *The Journal of School Health.* 1969, **39**(2), 81–90.

Elkind, D. Exploitation and the generational conflict. Paper presented at the meeting of the American Psychological Association, San Francisco, 1968.

Erikson, E. *Identity: Youth and crisis.* New York: W. W. Norton, 1968.

Greene, B. I. *Preventing school dropouts.* Englewood Cliffs, N.J.: Prentice-Hall, 1966.

Halleck, S. L. Psychiatric treatment for the alienated college student. *American Journal of Psychiatry,* 1967, **124**(5), 642–650.

Havighurst, R. J., Neugarten, B., & Tobin, S. S. Disengagement and patterns of aging. In B. Neugarten (Ed.), *Middle age and aging.* Chicago: The University of Chicago Press, 1968.

Hewitt, E., & Jenkins, R. L. Case studies of aggressive delinquents. *American Journal of Orthopsychiatry,* 1941, **11**, 485–492.

Hollingshead, A. B. *Elmtown's youth.* New York: Wiley, 1949.

Kastenbaum, R., & Aisenberg, R. *The psychology of death.* New York: Springer Publishing Co., 1972.

Keniston, K. *The uncommitted: Alienated youth in American society.* New York: Harcourt Brace Jovanovich, 1965.

Kinsey, A. C., Pomeroy, W. B., & Martin, E. E. *Sexual behavior in the human female.* Philadelphia: W. B. Saunders, 1953.

Koller, M. R. *Social gerontology.* New York: Random House, 1968.

Kotkov, B. Emotional syndromes associated with learning failures. *Diseases of the Nervous System,* 1965, **26**, 48–55.

Lambert, B. G., Rothschild, B. F., Altland, R., & Green, L. B. *Adolescence: Transition from childhood to maturity.* Monterey, Calif.: Brooks/Cole Publishing Co., 1972.

Massimo, J. L., & Shore, M. F. The effectiveness of a comprehensive vocationally oriented psychotherapeutic program for adolescent delinquent boys. *American Journal of Orthopsychiatry,* 1963, **33**, 634–642.

Masters, W. H., & Johnson, V. E. *Human sexual response.* Boston: Little, Brown, 1966.

Mead, M. Early adolescence in the United States. *Bulletin of the National Association of Secondary School Principals,* 1965, **49**, 5–10.

Munnichs, J. M. A. *Old age and finitude.* Basel, Switzerland and New York: Karger, 1966.

Pearson, L. (Ed.). *Death and dying: Current issues in the treatment of the dying person.* Cleveland, Ohio: Case Western Reserve University Press, 1969.

Rappoport, L. *Personality development: The chronology of experience.* Glenview, Ill.: Scott, Foresman, 1972.

Reichard, S., Livson, F., & Petersen, P. G. *Aging and personality: A study of eighty-seven older men.* New York: Wiley, 1962.

Rice, R. D. Educo-therapy: A new approach to delinquent behavior. *Journal of Learning Disabilities,* 1970, **3**(1), 16–23.

Shaw, G. B. *Selected prose.* New York: Dodd, Mead, 1952.

Solzhenitsyn, Alexander. *The first circle.* New York: Harper & Row, 1968.

Strange, R. The transition from childhood to adolescence. In James F. Adams (Ed.), *Understanding adolescence.* Boston: Allyn and Bacon, 1968.

Terman, L. M. From *Psychological factors in marital happiness,* by L. M. Terman. Copyright 1938 by McGraw-Hill, Inc. Used with permission of McGraw-Hill Book Company.

Topping, R. Case studies of aggressive delinquents. *American Journal of Orthopsychiatry,* 1941, **11**, 485–492.

Weisman, A. D., & Kastenbaum, R. The psychological autopsy: A study of the terminal phase of life. Behavioral Publications, Monograph No. 4 of *Community Mental Health Journal.* 1968.

Wenar, C. *Personality development: From infancy to adulthood.* Boston: Houghton Mifflin, 1971.

SECTION SEVEN

Social psychology and social issues

We have come a long way from our earliest discussions of psychology. Starting from viewing man as a biological organism operating under basic psychological processes, we followed him through to an integration of the person. The focus throughout the earlier sections concerned man as an individual, his commonalities and differences to others. However, we do not function in a vacuum. In this last section, we are concerned with an even broader perspective. We will concentrate on man as a social animal influencing and being influenced by others.

In Chapter 1, we posed the question "What can psychology do for society?" Although we briefly touched upon this subject in earlier chapters, we did not go into depth concerning implications of psychological research on broader social issues. Chapter 12 is most closely related to the field of social psychology, which can be broadly defined as the study of social influence. We are all influenced by other people whether real or imaginary. Other people exert pressures on us to believe or behave in a certain way. In Chapter 12, we will discuss some general principles of social influence. In addition, we will raise many moral and ethical issues of high relevance to our society. For example, all of you are, no doubt, familiar with the My Lai massacre and Lt. William Calley's claim that he was not guilty of war crimes because he obeyed orders from a higher authority. What would you do in a similar situation? Other issues involve such questions as "When will people help in a crisis?" and "How do police interrogation techniques work?"

Two of the most important social problems facing us today are racism (Chapter 13) and sexism (Chapter 14). Both are similar because they tend to subjugate and discriminate against a group of people on the basis of some common characteristic: race and sex. This discrimination may manifest itself in a lower standard of living (education, housing, employment, and income) and its psychological costs. The latter concept is clearly seen in women believing they indeed are inferior to men and in ethnic minorities who become ashamed of who and what they are. The rise of the women's liberation movement and increasing pride in racial identity can be seen as attempts to reverse this trend of negativity.

Terms such as racism and sexism evoke strong emotional reactions among people. These strong feelings are legitimate and we hope that some of you will experience and empathize with them. However, let us not allow such emotions to prevent us from exploring racism and sexism in a rational and fruitful manner. We have attempted in the last two chapters to present not only the emotional component of racism and sexism but also a rational and scientific discussion of its causes, effects, and potential elimination. Let us approach these topics in an atmosphere of mutual trust and cooperation and view each opinion or issue from all perspectives before we accept or reject them. Only in such an atmosphere can such pressing social problems be changed or eliminated.

12

Social influences on behavior

Several years ago, a highly popular TV program called "Candid Camera" provided some interesting and humorous film clips to the American public. The producer of the series, Allen Funt, set up unexpected situations which confronted naïve citizens. Unbeknown to them, their reactions were filmed by a hidden camera. The unusual behaviors exhibited by these victims illustrate our next topic nicely; that of social influence.

In one film sequence, several men are standing in front of an elevator waiting for its arrival. As the doors swing open, all the men enter the empty elevator. All but one of the men are aware that they are being filmed, and that they (stooges) have conspired to create a most unorthodox situation. The naïve person enters and turns to face the front of the elevator. But to his surprise, all the other men continue to face the rear of the elevator! Looking confused and perplexed, the man finally also turns to face the rear. Several seconds later, all the stooges turn in unison to the right. They repeat this movement in intervals until a complete circle is made, and they once again face the rear. With each of these turns, the naïve subject, looking anxious and confused, follows suit.

Another sequence filmed a man who enters a restaurant and seats himself at the counter. He orders a sandwich and while waiting for its delivery sees a sign in front of him. Next to the sign is a red light bulb. The sign reads "Please *do not* eat while light is on!" Several minutes into eating his sandwich the light suddenly goes on. The man appears puzzled and looks around trying to determine what to do. He finally puts his sandwich down and stops chewing, although his mouth is still full. At this point the light goes off and the man, relieved, continues eating. However, the light again comes on. The man immediately puts his sandwich down and waits for the light to go off. This time, however, the light flashes off and on in quick succession and the man is shown bringing the sandwich up to his mouth and putting it down on his plate at an equally rapid pace.

Social norms and conformity

These examples demonstrate the power and effectiveness of *social norms*. A social norm may be defined as a rule or standard of conduct which implicitly or explicitly tells us how to behave. They are defined by either a group, society, or culture. The man in the elevator was operating under implicit norms created by the stooges, while the man in the restaurant was influenced by an explicit rule written clearly on a sign. In our everyday lives, we constantly observe both implicit (it's not polite to stare at others) and explicit (traffic rules) norms. We would not function effectively without norms to guide our behavior.

There are essentially three purposes for the existence of norms. First, they help us create order and predictability and, thus, facilitate the occurrence and effectiveness of group behavior. For example, suppose that there were no rules or regulations governing driving. Besides huge traffic jams, the number of traffic accidents would increase radically. Second, norms enable us to compare ourselves against others. If you were to obtain a score of 100 on a test, this information alone would not be of much help in evaluating how you did. If the average score was 150, you certainly have not done very well. On the other hand, if the average score was 65, you could pat yourself on the back for such an outstanding performance. Last, conformity to group norms often provides us with a sense of personal identity. Membership in a particular group whether it be the family, clan, tribe, fraternity, or Hell's Angels means that we adopt the standards, values, and norms of that group. Most of us are influenced by the groups we aspire to join. These groups exert strong pressure upon its members to conform to its rules and regulations.

This discussion now leads us into one of the most fascinating topics in the field of psychology, that of *conformity*. We shall use Kiesler and Kiesler's (1969) definition of conformity: "a change in behavior or belief toward a group as a result of real or imagined group pressure" (p. 2). The change in behavior seen in the two individuals on "Candid Camera" would be defined as conformity. Rather than elaborate on this formal definition of conformity, what we will do is discuss five social-psychological studies illustrating the phenomenon of conformity. These studies have been chosen for several reasons. First, some are considered classic studies in conformity that have high relevance in illustrating principles of social influence. Second, each study will give you an idea of how social psychologists conduct experiments. Indeed, many of these studies are not dissimilar to the "Candid Camera" situations. Of course, social scientists have taken much more care in controlling and designing their studies. Third, many of these studies raise moral and ethical issues of high relevance to our society. As such it demonstrates how social psychology is, indeed, concerned with real-life issues and problems.

Sherif's autokinetic effect

When a person is seated in a completely darkened room and is shown a pinpoint of light, the light appears to move. This apparent movement of light called the *autokinetic effect*, in reality, does not really occur. However, almost everyone in a similar situation would see some movement whether up or down, left or right. The amount of movement which subjects report varies with the individual. Some people tend to report large, others moderate, and still others minimal movements.

In a pioneering study of conformity, Sherif (1935, 1936) used the well-known autokinetic effect to learn the extent to which individuals and groups establish their own social norms. He had college students individually and in groups make estimates as to how far they believed the light to move. He found that students who were individually exposed to this phenomenon developed a subjective frame of reference or norm which was idiosyncratic to them. For example, suppose that student A is invited into a darkened room and seated near a telegraph key. He is instructed to press the key whenever the light moves and to shout out the distance. A series of judgments are taken. What Sherif found was that student A would inevitably develop an individual norm, say 4 inches, around which all his judgments would fall. Suppose that we now put student A in a room with one other subject who has developed a norm of 8 inches. We have both of them alternate calling out the distances over a series of trials. At first subjects A and B call out distances very similar to their individual sessions, but as the series continue their judgments begin to converge until relatively high agreement is reached. For example, student A now calls out movements averaging 6½ inches and subject B distances of 7 inches. Apparently, some consensus or a group norm has been established. Each has been influenced by the other. Furthermore, when tested alone, the subjects tend to continue calling out the group average. We will have more to say about this phenomenon shortly.

Asch's line judgments

Imagine yourself in the following situation. As part of receiving credit for your introductory psychology class, you are asked by the professor to participate in a psychology experiment investigating visual judgments. When you report to the experimenter the following morning, you are seated in front of a circular table with seven other students. The experimenter informs the group that you will be comparing the lengths of lines which he will show you on large white cards. On one card is a single vertical line and on the other card are three other lines of which one is identical to the standard line. You are told that you must choose one of the three which matches the single standard line.

Suppose that the investigator now pulls out the cards. The task appears ridiculously easy. You are sure that line number two is the correct choice. Since you are seated at the end of the table, your turn will be last. To your utter astonishment the first student, when asked by the experimenter, calls out number one. How can this be? Does the student need glasses? He has obviously made a mistake! In bafflement you lean forward looking at the lines once again. Can you possibly be wrong? No, line number two is clearly the most similar of the three. To your further amazement, all of the other students also call out line number one. Now it is your turn. What do you do? (See Figure 12–1.)

Asch (1951, 1952) used almost an identical situation to investigate the effects of social pressure on opinions of students. Like the man in the elevator and restaurant, you have been the victim of a planned conspiracy. All of the other students in the room were stooges or con-

FIGURE 12–1
The classic Asch study on group pressure. Subjects are asked to state which of three comparison lines (1, 2, 3) is most similar to line X.

federates of the experimenter. That is, they were in league with the experimenter and instructed to unanimously choose the incorrect line. Asch found some very interesting results from using this experimental design. While subjects exposed to this task seldom made mistakes individually, over one-third of the subjects were influenced in the line they chose in the group situation. Furthermore, approximately 75 percent of the subjects at some time made an erroneous judgment in favor of the group, while only 25 percent chose the correct line in spite of unanimous group pressure.

Why did so many subjects conform to the incorrect judgments when it was clearly obvious that a mistake was being made? This is a question which we will return to later in this chapter.

Compliance and private acceptance

The two experiments by Sherif and Asch illustrate, nicely, two aspects of conformity. Recall that we defined conformity as a change in *behavior* or *belief* toward that of the group because of real or imagined group pressure. In the Asch experiment, the correct answer is usually very obvious and the subject is certain that the group is wrong. He is placed in a situation of conflict between the physical evidence of his senses and the social pressure exerted by members of the group. Asch's technique clearly tests for *compliance;* that is, a change in overt behavior without consideration of private convictions. Many subjects who called out the wrong answers stated afterward that they knew the correct answer. Perhaps many students complied because they did not want to appear different or were fearful of ridicule from the group. We can all easily find examples in which we have conformed to pressure without a change in opinions or beliefs.

However, Sherif's study tends to be more of a measure of *private acceptance* or belief change. As you recall, the situation we are talking about represents that of total ambiguity. The subject perceives the light as moving but has no real idea of how far it moves. As a result of tentative guesses, he establishes a frame of reference. When another person is present, the frame of reference is disrupted and a new one is provided. The answer is not obvious and the subject attempts to solve the problem. Recall that group norms persisted even when one subject was alone. The subject has adopted the new frame of reference and accepted the change privately. It is important for us to distinguish between these two types of conformity.

Milgram's studies of obedience

Earlier we stated that studies being reviewed oftentimes have broad implications for our society and raise moral and ethical issues. Such is the case with a series of studies reported by Stanley Milgram (1963, 1964, 1965a, 1965b, 1972) which appears to represent a case of compliance in an Asch-like situation. Milgram's experiments explore the limits of obedience to commands that may violate a person's basic ethical feelings. It had the task of setting up in the subject a conflict between two conformities: conformity to the experimenter's orders, and conformity to the human value that inflicting harm on others is wrong. Let us turn our attention to how Milgram set up his study.

METHOD. Imagine that you are a poor male freshman student in desperate need of money to spend on a "hot" date for this weekend. While reading the newspaper you run across an advertisement which promises $4.50 per hour to participate in a psychology experiment at your university. You volunteer your services and meet with the experimenter and one other student volunteer. You are told by the experimenter that this is a study investigating the effects of punishment on the learning of paired words. Both you and the other student draw lots in order to determine who will be the *teacher* and the *learner*. The results are that you become the teacher and the other student the learner. The learner is taken into another room and strapped into an "electrified chair" apparatus to apparently prevent escape. Electrodes are attached to his wrist along with electrode paste to prevent blisters and burns. In response to a question by the learner, the experimenter assures him that although the shocks may be extremely painful no permanent tissue damage will occur.

You are now taken into an adjoining room full of electrical gadgets. Before you is a huge instrument panel consisting of 30 lever switches each labeled with a voltage designation from 15 to 450 volts. You are told that this apparatus delivers shocks to the learner in the other room. In addition, some of the levers are designated by words such as "SLIGHT SHOCK," "MODERATE SHOCK," "VERY STRONG SHOCK," "INTENSE SHOCK," "EXTREME INTENSITY SHOCK," "DANGER: SEVERE SHOCK," and finally the last two switches are marked by a "XXX." As a sample of what the learner will supposedly experience if he makes mistakes, you are given a 45-volt shock which is noticeably painful. You are then instructed to administer progressively stronger shocks for each successive mistake made by the learner (Figure 12–2).

As the experiment progresses, the learner begins to make mistakes. Each time you throw a switch to punish the subject a red light flashes, an electric buzzing is heard, and a dial on the voltage meter swings to the right. You know that you are hurting the learner and begin to have doubts about what you are doing. At the switch labeled 300 volts, a loud

FIGURE 12–2
Milgram's obedience study

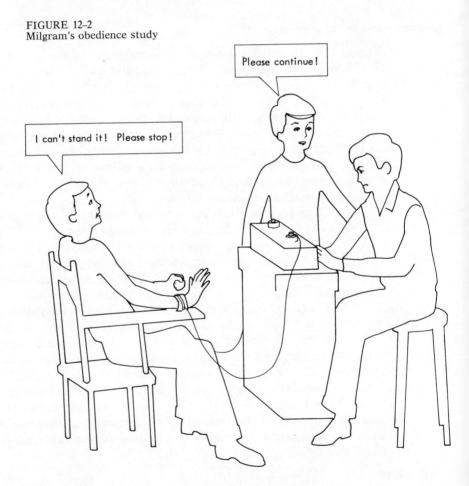

pounding is heard on the adjacent wall from the learner. You hesitate and turn to the experimenter who urges you to continue. What do you do? Do you obey the experimenter and continue potentially injurious punishment to the learner, or do you refuse to go on? This was the dilemma in which many of Milgram's subjects found themselves.

RESULTS AND DISCUSSION. In describing his procedure to 40 psychiatrists, Milgram had the group predict how many subjects would go all the way to the highest shock. The group predicted that less than 1 percent would do so. However, Milgram found that of 40 subjects who participated, 26, or 65 percent continued on to 450 volts!

These results are indeed chilling and frightening. Ever since the end of World War II, many people have wondered how and why the Nazis had been able to carry out their campaign of mass extermination against the Jews in Europe. One popular theory was that a special trait inherent in the German character made them more obedient to orders. However, Milgram's findings indicate that Americans may be equally as willing to obey such orders. It is Milgram's beliefs that for many persons, obedience may be so deeply ingrained that it overrides even training in ethics. We have learned from childhood through parents, teachers, institutions, and other authority figures to obey commands. To disobey an order is an extremely difficult task, especially if the authority appears legitimate. This difficulty in disobeying was aptly demonstrated in other variations of Milgram's study.

Milgram had originally expected that most subjects would disobey his orders especially when the delivery of shocks entered the painful range. Intrigued by his subjects' willingness to comply to his orders, Milgram set out in an attempt to elicit disobedience. He found the following results.

1. More disobedience was elicited the closer the subjects were to the victim. For example, Milgram ran three other conditions: *(a)* a condition in which grunts and groans could be heard from the learner, *(b)* a condition in which the teacher was in the same room as the learner and could see and hear his agony, and *(c)* a condition which forced the teacher to place the hand of the learner on a metal plate to receive the shock. The last condition caused the greatest amount of disobedience to occur.

Let us take the example of a bombardier who releases bombs without any personal experiences of what he is doing to the people below. This situation is similar to Milgram's conditions in which the teacher is physically separated from the learner. Inflicting damage or harm on people may be much easier. He does not see the damage and may find it easy to deny that he is inflicting harm or doing anything wrong. However, in hand-to-hand combat, execution of hostages, or torture of prisoners the damage is obvious. Such denial is difficult when you are physically close to the victim. As a result, empathy or guilt may be so overwhelming that you would find it difficult to comply with orders to hurt another human being.

2. The more removed the authority figure is from the teacher, the greater are the chances for disobedience to occur. Again Milgram created situations in which the experimenter was present in the same room or absent. More disobedience occurred in the absence of the experimenter.

ETHICAL ISSUES. Milgram's work generated more controversy and interest than perhaps any study in psychology. There are essentially two major issues raised in his studies.

1. When does conformity cease to perform a beneficial social function and become destructive, as in unquestioning obedience to authority? This question applies very aptly to historical and current military situations. A soldier is taught to obey orders from superiors and to follow the rules of the military. "A soldier's duty is not to reason why, but to do and die." Kelman and Lawrence (1972) in their analysis of American response to the trial of Lt. William Calley point out some interesting paradoxes (Figure 12–3).

In 1946, an International Tribunal tried and convicted 19 Nazis of war crimes against humanity. Their defense was that they were following orders from their superiors. However, the Tribunal decided that there is a point in which morality must override obedience. Most people considered at that time that the verdicts were just and wise. However, in 1971, the United States convicted Lt. William Calley for the massacre of unarmed Vietnamese civilians at My Lai. Instead of considering this conviction just, the American public was outraged, and many did not consider him responsible for the massacre. His defense rested on the assumption that legitimate orders from superiors must be obeyed and carried out.

Was Calley responsible for his actions? Were the 19 convicted Nazis guilty of wartime atrocities? Who is responsible, the individual or the "legitimate" authority that tells another to act against a third person? What would you do if you found yourself in a similar situation? Stanley Milgram's experiments suggest a frightening answer. People seem willing to allow an authority figure who is perceived as legitimate (Emperor, President, commander, or experimenter) to determine what kind of behavior is right or wrong. Instead of worrying about your own moral demands, there is a shift to concern about how well or poorly you are meeting the expectations of the legitimate authority. At times, actions which are considered normally "bad," i.e., killing or hurting others or even yourself, may appear necessary and "good." For example, Japanese Kamikaze pilots deliberately killed themselves in order to inflict damage on the enemy. Just as Milgram's study had a legitimate purpose of "contributing to the fund of scientific knowledge," the Japanese pilots killed themselves to "save their nation." We can see many examples of appeal to higher "good." The Watergate Affair seems to be such a case in which many high administration officials, including former President Nixon, invoked "national security" as the reason for some of their behaviors.

2. The second major ethical issue in this experiment can be posed

FIGURE 12–3
Lt. William Calley

in the following way. What was Milgram's ethical justification for exposing subjects to such an intense emotional experience? We take up this question because of its importance in all psychological research. Let us now return to a brief discussion of Milgram's experimental design.

Earlier, we proposed a hypothetical situation in which you, the reader, found yourself as one of Milgram's subjects and played the role of the teacher. What you did not know, however, was that you were deceived about the purpose of the experiment (a study of obedience rather than learning and punishment) and as to the situation. The other student, who played the role of the learner, was actually an accomplice of the experimenter. Furthermore, a rigged drawing of lots was held so that you, the naïve subject, always became the teacher. Additionally, *no* electric shocks are ever administered to the learner. Again, you have been a victim of another "Candid Camera" hoax.

A group of social scientists have begun to question the ethics of such psychological experiments. Among some of the more vocal of these is Diana Baumrind (1964, 1971). Baumrind's ethical critique of Milgram's experiments can be summarized as "the ends do not justify the means." She points out a number of alleged ethical violations in Milgram's studies.

First, the experiment exposed the subjects to possible permanent psychological damage. That the experiment placed subjects under extreme and intense emotional stress is attested to by a description given by Milgram (1964).

> He reports witnessing a mature and poised businessman enter the lab in a smiling and confident manner. After 20 minutes of the experiment, Milgram reports that the man was reduced to a twitching, stuttering wreck who approached a point of nervous collapse. "At one point he pushed his fist into his forehead and muttered: 'Oh, God, let's stop it.' And yet he continued to respond to every word of the experimenter and obeyed to the end (Milgram, 1964, p. 377)."

Other subjects were observed to laugh hysterically, bite their lips, sweat, tremble, and groan as they *thought* they delivered the shocks. Subjects in Milgram's studies did not volunteer to undergo the kind of psychological pain inflicted upon them. Furthermore, Milgram did not know anything about his subjects and used no screening procedures to weed out emotionally unstable individuals who might be damaged by such an experience. He also did not provide any professional therapeutic experience directly after the study.

Second, the potential generality of the results of the experiment was not sufficient to justify the drastic methods Milgram used. Baumrind believes that the experimental situation was unreal and is not generalizable to the military situations we have previously discussed concerning Milgram's studies.

These criticisms must be studied carefully because they may contain real merit. Recently, a Revised Code of Ethics has been proposed by the *ad hoc* Committee on Ethical Standards in Psychological Research of the American Psychological Association (Cook, Kimble, Hicks, McGuire, Schoggen, & Smith, 1971). The revision, which is being hotly debated, advocates a risk/benefit approach. In essence, it states that any undertaking of research must carefully consider potential risks to the subject and weigh it against the benefits that the research has in furthering psychological knowledge.

We strongly believe that Milgram's study has broad generality to the human condition. Milgram had a serious purpose: to find out what makes people obey orders. However, some of Baumrind's criticisms, especially those concerning harm to the subject, need stronger consideration lest harm to the subject is justified in the interest of science. We are reminded of studies in the South which investigated the effects of advanced syphilis on man. Is it ethical to leave these individuals untreated to further the knowledge of science? Think about it!

Freedman and Fraser's foot-in-the-door technique

The basic problem in securing conformity is how to get people to do something they might not want to do. Milgram's study uses orders or commands. To be successful this method depends on the experimenter being close to the subject, the giving of orders, and maintaining verbal pressure. However, Freedman and Fraser (1966) suggest another technique utilizing minimal pressure.

The principle behind this technique is that if we are able to get a person to comply to a small request, then he will be much more amenable to agreeing to much larger ones. This principle is familiar to the door-to-door salesman who gets his foot in the door by making a small request, such as demonstrating the operation of a vacuum cleaner, and then winds up by selling it to you. Freedman and Fraser were able to illustrate this principle in the following study.

The experimenters identified a number of housewives in the Palo Alto telephone directory and divided them into two groups: the experimental and control. In the morning, women in the experimental group were called and told that the person was a representative of the "California Consumer's Group" and that they were interested in conducting a survey to find out what products she used in the home. Her help was asked and if she agreed, a series of eight innocuous questions were asked, such as the brand of soap she used. The control group did not have this initial contact.

Several days later, both groups were contacted and subjected to a related but larger request. They were told that the organization would like to send five or six men into the women's home for two hours to classify all the products used in the house. The men were to have complete freedom to seek out and record every product for a survey to be published in a "Guidebook." Imagine having six grown men running all through your house poking into every drawer and cabinet! What an ordeal!

The results were not surprising. Of the experimental group (those who complied to an earlier request), 53 percent agreed to cooperate while only 22 percent of the control group agreed. Freedman and Fraser offer two general explanations of their results. First, it is possible that the subjects who complied with the second larger request are people who see themselves as doers, devoted to causes and willing to make sacrifices for a good cause: a consumers guide. Second, a person may feel that he must be *consistent* in his dealings with others. Many people find it difficult to say "no" after they have already said "yes" to a similar request. Take the example of John Doe, a freshman, who has a "hot date" this weekend. Suppose that John has made careful study of the foot-in-the-door technique and plans to apply this principle to his forthcoming date. He has acted as a perfect gentleman during his first date and plans to make "The Big Move" tonight. To seduce his date he must carefully grade his moves which represent larger and larger requests upon his date. If he is able to get his date to accept handholding, kissing, and finally petting, he may have a fair chance of success. Does John succeed? That is a question best left unanswered. For it is possible that his date has also read the foot-in-the-door technique, and is ready for him!

Studies of altruism: Who will help in a crisis?

On November 16, 1971 in Rochester, New York many motorists were driving home from a hard day's work. Suddenly from out of nowhere a little girl appeared along the shoulder of the road waving as if trying to hail passing cars. She was nearly naked and appeared frantic and hysterical. However, cars continued to speed by and no one stopped to find out why the girl was there. Two days later her body was found in a ditch two miles away. She had been raped and strangled (*Monterey Peninsula Herald*, 1971).

Rosenthal (1964) reports the case of Kitty Genovese, a young woman, who on a March night was set upon and murdered by a madman. She was returning home from work and about to enter her home when attacked viciously. She screamed for help as the murderer took over half an hour to kill her. Reporters for the *New York Times* found that 38 people witnessed her cries for help but none came to her aid or even called the police.

The popular press offered various reasons for the failure of witnesses to help the victim. Some writers spoke of the moral decay of our society. Others wrote of the dehumanization of modern urban life, conditions which make people indifferent to the distress of others and apathetic in times of personal crisis (Figure 12–4).

In this section, we will summarize studies of three psychologists, Latané and Darley (1968, 1969, 1970), Darley and Latané (1968, 1970) and Latané and Rodin (1969). In addition to offering a different explanation

FIGURE 12–4
Who will help in a crisis?

than that of the press, they are interested in aspects of conformity. As Aronson (1972) points out, "nonintervention can be viewed as an act of conformity (p. 39)."

These investigators in a series of experiments, tested the general hypothesis that the *immediate situation* and not the prevalent moral decay of our society, nor defects in the personality of the witnesses produced the results evident in the Genovese case. Darley and Latané maintain that a person who may or may not intervene to help someone in a crisis has three crucial choice-points. He must *(a)* notice the event in question, *(b)* interpret the event as an emergency, and *(c)* take responsibility for doing something. In all of these choice-points the presence of other bystanders affects a person's willingness to help.

NOTICING THE EVENT. In order for a person to act in an emergency situation, he must first notice that something is happening. To test this hypothesis a situation was created in the laboratory. Students were asked to be interviewed about their reactions to urban living. Under this guise they were given a questionnaire to be filled out. Some of the students waited in groups of three, and others individually, as they filled out the form. After a few minutes, an apparent emergency arose in which puffs of smoke began emanating from a vent in the wall. Those subjects waiting alone noticed the smoke much faster than those waiting in groups of three as evidenced by a startle reaction or an inspection of the vent. The presence of other people, apparently, delayed some individuals from noticing the smoke.

How can we explain this difference? Darley and Latané state that in our society it is considered bad manners to invade another's privacy. It is considered unmannerly to stare at people or to pay close attention to what they are doing. Subjects who were alone are free to look around the room without intruding into the life space of others. Those in groups of threes, usually did not look around as often, and paid close attention to their questionnaires. As a result, they did not notice the smoke as quickly.

INTERPRETING THE EVENT. Many years back, when he was much younger, one of the authors can recall taking his first airplane ride. Never having flown, he was naturally quite excited and anxious at the same time. Sometime during the trip, the plane hit some mild turbulence that made the ride quite jerky. He began to become quite fearful that the plane might crash. Not wanting to appear "scared," he pretended casually to glance around the plane at the other passengers. He could remember how relieved he was that the other passengers were so nonchalant about what was happening. They continued to read their magazines and joke with one another even though they may have also been anxious. To him, however, their nonreaction to the situation meant that there was nothing to be afraid of.

In a situation where ambiguity exists, we tend to seek out other people for confirmation of what really is happening. If other people seem indifferent to the situation, we may conclude that no emergency exists. Taking our cue from other people, however, can be quite misleading and harmful in some critical situations. Let us now turn to two studies which illustrate these points.

Darley and Latané used an identical situation as the one described earlier, with one exception. In some of the groups of threes, only one of the subjects was naïve while the other two were stooges. These stooges showed no alarm when the smoke appeared and paid no attention to it. If the naïve subject asked the others what they thought of the smoke, they replied that they didn't know and went on working on their questionnaire.

Subjects who waited alone usually inspected the vent and told the experimenter in 75 percent of the cases. Subjects accompanied by stooges reported the smoke about 10 percent of the time! Where only three naïve subjects were present without stooges, at least one subject reported the smoke 38 percent of the time. This group acted more like the one with two stooges present. When interviewed, subjects who reported the smoke *defined* the situation as a possible emergency. Those who had not acted, even when the smoke got so thick they could not see the questionnaire, had other explanations such as "a leak in the air conditioning," "steam pipes," and "smog." One student thought it was truth gas to make individuals give true answers! Not one mentioned the possibility of a fire. In other words, they accepted a group definition of a nonemergency.

In our society, a person is under considerable social pressure to "maintain his cool" or to hide emotions and not overreact. The two apparently unconcerned stooges exerted *social pressure* upon the other subject not to react. Even in the groups of the three naïve subjects, this pressure was exerted on one another; they looked at one another with passive expressions and concealed their alarm. As a result, each believed that the inactivity of the others meant that an emergency was not present.

In another experiment conducted by Latané and Rodin to test the generality of this phenomenon, the investigators simulated a "Lady in Distress" situation. Subjects were told that a market research project was being conducted to determine people's preference for games. They were met at the door by a woman who had them fill out a questionnaire. The woman then left the room into an adjoining one separated only by a collapsible curtain. Four minutes into the experiment, subjects heard simulated sounds of the woman climbing upon a chair to reach for papers on a bookcase. The collapsing of the chair as the woman fell with a loud crash, followed by a scream and moans were played on a tape recorder. Very few people who waited in groups of twos volunteered to help while 70 percent of those who waited alone went to the assistance of the "victim." Again, the noninterveners defined the situation as a nonemergency and offered other explanations. However, most passive subjects stated that their inactivity was not influenced by the presence of others!

TAKING RESPONSIBILITY. The mere fact that one has *noticed* an event and *defined* it as an emergency does not mean that the individual will take any action to help. Many motorists on the evening of November 16, 1971 did not see the naked girl because they may have been engrossed in deep thoughts. Others who saw the girl may have thought she was playing a game or had to make a quick trip to the rest room. In this case, they did not define the situation as an emergency. However, in the Genovese case, some 38 people who had noticed the lady's distress and interpreted it as an emergency declined to taken any action. Darley and Latané believe that the presence of other witnesses may inhibit intervention by causing a diffusion of responsibility. If you are the sole witness to an emergency, you would probably feel responsibility for helping that person. However, if many witnesses are present, this responsibility may be diffused and diluted. In the case of Genovese, witnesses may have felt it was someone else's duty to respond or that someone else had called the police. In order to test this hypothesis, Darley and Latané set up the following experiment.

Male and female students were recruited and told that they would participate in a highly personal discussion with one another. They were further informed that since participants would be asked to reveal personal information about themselves which might prove embarrassing, precautions would be taken to ensure anonymity. Each subject would be placed in a cubicle and speak over an intercom system so that face-to-face confrontation would be eliminated. Each subject who participated was led to believe that either one or six other subjects were in other booths. In reality, only the subject was in the booth. The other voices which were heard were tape recorded.

As the subject is seated in his booth, the tape recorder starts and a voice comes over the intercom. Very hesitantly, the voice discusses one of his major problems, that he is subject to mild epileptic seizures when under emotional stress. Sometime during the discussion, he feigns an epileptic attack and cries for help.

To the experimenter's surprise, many individuals sat through the entire seizure without coming out of their cubicle to offer help. Most of these people were in the larger sized discussion groups. In the situation in which the subject thought that only he and the victim were present, 85 percent of the students left their cubicle. In the three-person group, only 62 percent tried to help. Individuals who thought they were in groups of six, only 31 percent of the subjects tried to help. Again, it is apparent that the more people present, the less likely a person will take responsibility for action. In the case of Kitty Genovese, the old adage that "there is safety in numbers" proved to be incorrect.

APATHY? Were the people who witnessed the Genovese murder indifferent to her plight? Did the students who failed to help the apparent epileptic victim show apathy? Has society become so mechanized that we are no longer capable of feelings toward others in distress? Darley and Latané believe not. On the contrary, they found that the students who did not offer help showed strong concern and reactions about the victim. Many inquired about health afterward, trembled and perspired. Unlike those students who passively saw smoke because they defined it as a non-emergency, students in their cubicles knew an emergency existed. Why then did the subjects not intervene? The experimenters believe that subjects were placed in an avoidance-avoidance conflict situation and thus thrown into indecision. On the one hand, they did not want to overreact or ruin the anonymity of the experiment. On the other, they were worried about the shame and guilt at not helping the victim.

Principles of social influence

Besides raising moral and ethical issues of high relevance to our society, the five classic studies we have reviewed all point to one fact: our behavior and beliefs are influenced by other people. That is what we mean by social influence. In this section, we will attempt to draw out some general concepts regarding social influence which will help us organize these studies. We will (a) attempt to identify some general principles of social influence, (b) discuss characteristics of the source which facilitate influence, and (c) use police interrogation techniques to illustrate their operation.

Subject sets in conformity

How does it feel to be subjects in conformity experiments and why do people conform? Barry Collins (1970) recently provided some interesting speculations on these questions. He proposed five hypothetical "sets" or "frames of mind" that are often elicited in people when social pressures are placed on them. We will now examine these sets in more detail.

1. THE PROBLEM-SOLVING SET: INFORMATION ORIENTATION. In the problem-solving set, the person is concerned about getting correct information from the communicator. The person accepts or rejects information on the basis of its truth or falsity. This process is rational and logical. However, when a situation appears ambiguous with no clear-cut answer, people turn to others for confirmation about their beliefs. Apparently, the existence of ambiguity motivates people to clarify the situation. The more ambiguous a situation, the more we turn to others as sources of information.

In Sherif's autokinetic effect, the physical situation provides the subject with no frame of reference to make his judgments. He does not know the answer and, thus, is easily influenced by others. Remember that Sherif's subjects adopted a new frame of reference when placed in the room with another subject. As indicated this was an example of private acceptance.

Likewise, Darley and Latané demonstrated the operation of the problem-solving set in their studies. Subjects who saw the puffs of smoke and did not report it, seemed to be operating under this set. Many who saw the smoke appeared puzzled and curious. However, when the other students remained passive and unconcerned, these students processed this information and concluded that it was a nondangerous situation.

2. THE CONSISTENCY SET. People are operating under the consistency set whenever they change an opinion, belief, or behavior in such a way as to make it consistent with other opinions, beliefs, or behaviors. This principle is best illustrated in Leon Festinger's *A Theory of Cognitive Dissonance* (1957). Stated simply, the theory says that when a person's attitudes, opinions, or beliefs are met with disagreement (inconsistencies), cognitive imbalance or dissonance will be created. The existence of dissonance is psychologically uncomfortable and produces tension with drive characteristics. The result is usually an attempt to reduce this dissonance. Let us give you an example of cognitive dissonance in action.

Suppose that you are a 55-year-old man who has smoked cigarettes for the past 35 years. Suddenly you are exposed to the Surgeon General's report that smoking is harmful to your health. This piece of information is inconsistent with your knowledge that you smoke three packages per day. The logical thing to do is to stop smoking. However, Aronson (1972) observes that the theory of cognitive dissonance does not picture man as a *rational* animal but rather as a *rationalizing* one. At times, his need to be right and his rationalizations are in harmony. But more often than not, they are at odds. For example, the middle-aged man may have too much invested in cigarette smoking to stop. He may begin to seek justification for his smoking through the use of rationalizations. First, he may seek support for his position: "Cigarette advertisers say there is no direct cause-effect relationship between cancer and smoking." "I only smoke filter cigarettes." Second, he may devalue the importance of the topic: "We all die sometime. I could get killed walking across the street. What else is new?" Last, he could discredit or derogate the source: "He doesn't know what he's talking about. He's biased."

A person's need to be consistent is a powerful influence upon his behavior. In the experiment conducted by Freedman and Fraser with the so-called foot-in-the-door technique, the consistency set was placed in operation by the experimenters. For those subjects who granted a small request, denying a much larger but similar one would have been inconsistent with their previous behavior. Similarly, subjects in Milgram's experiment may have found it difficult to stop administering shocks after pulling the first few levers. To refuse may have meant that they would have to acknowledge that they were hurting someone. Most people will say that they would never willingly or deliberately hurt someone. To pull the first few levers is inconsistent with this self-concept. As a result, some subjects may have rationalized their participation.

3. THE IDENTITY SET. In the identity set, the individual generally desires to be like or similar to a person or group which they hold in high esteem. Much of our identity is formed from those reference groups to which we aspire. We attempt to take on their characteristics, beliefs, values, and behaviors because they are viewed favorably. An individual who strongly identifies with a particular group is likely to accept the beliefs, and conform to the behaviors dictated by that group. Subjects in Milgram's study may have been operating under this set. Suppose that you are a student aspiring to become a psychologist. You are aware that Stanley Milgram is a famous social psychologist who has done important research in the field. He tells you that this is an important study and that you must continue to shock the learner. Because you have so strongly identified with him and what he represents, you may be much more predisposed to obey his commands. Similarly, the cooperation with requests made by Freedman and Fraser may illustrate this principle. It is possible that many housewives defined themselves as civic-minded citizens involved in consumer protection such as Ralph Nader. Participation with the experimenters may have been facilitated because they were perceived as consumer advocates.

4. THE ECONOMIC SET. In the economic set, Collins refers to perceived rewards and punishments. In this set, a person performs a behavior or states a belief in order to gain rewards or avoid punishments. Your professor can pretty much dictate your behavior in the classroom because he has the power to give you a good or bad grade. If that power is removed, the behavior may disappear. People who conform under these conditions are said to be showing compliance. Private acceptance

is generally not present. For example, in the line judgment experiments of Asch, students who yelled out the incorrect line might have been trying to avoid being disliked or ridiculed. Some students cooperated with Milgram because they may have wanted to be paid money.

5. THE AUTHORITY SET. Under this set, some individuals are thought to have a particular position which gives them a legitimate right to influence or tell us what to do. Studies conducted by Stanley Milgram are prime examples of this principle. Students obeyed Milgram because he was an authority figure and the overseer of the study. Likewise, as we have mentioned, military situations tend to evoke this type of response.

Social influence and source characteristics

It should be quite clear at this point that characteristics of the influencing source are all important in eliciting types of conformance. In addition, the type of set placed in operation oftentimes dictates the permanency and degree of attitude change. For example, the primary component in getting *compliance* is *power* which the person holds over you; the ability to reward or punish. In *identification*, it is the *attractiveness* or liking of the persuader and in *internalization, credibility* or truthfulness is important. We shall now turn our attention to defining characteristics of the source that have been found to be effective in causing change.

CREDIBILITY. Many investigators have studied the effects of communicator characteristics on opinion change by varying the *expertness* of the source. Berkowitz (1957) found that there was greater conformity to a person who exhibits *behavioral evidence* of *past proficiency* on a related task. This was aptly demonstrated in a field study by Brock (1965) involving two salesmen in the paint department of a large retail store. The salesman who was perceived to have more familiarity with the paints was more able to induce a buyer to switch price levels.

In addition, it makes sense to us that individuals who are *famous* or have known *reputations* influence us to a greater extent than those who are not. Aronson, Turner, and Carlsmith (1963) found more opinion change on a task involving rating alliteration value of poems when the source was said to be T. S. Eliot rather than "Miss Agnes Sterns," a student at Mississippi State Teachers College (Figure 12–5).

Another factor which adds credibility to the communicator is the perceived *trustworthiness*. Hovland and Mandell (1952) found that when a communicator was introduced as belonging to a group that would have a motive to convince the audience of his position, he was perceived suspiciously and thought to have given a more one-sided presentation of his argument. There was a tendency for the impartial communicator to effect more opinion change than the suspicion-arousing person. Mills (1966) found that when a communicator likes the audience and states he wants to influence them, more change occurred. Apparently, the source was viewed as being sincere and honest. Another study by Walster, Aron-

FIGURE 12–5
Harry Reasoner, ABC News anchorman, is seen delivering a commencement address at the University of Santa Clara. Reasoner is able to exert strong influence on attitudes and opinions of the American public because of his high credibility.

Courtesy of Paul Fry, *The Santa Clara*, University of Santa Clara

son, and Abrahams (1966) showed that regardless of a communicator's general prestige, he will be more effective in changing opinions when he argues for a position opposed to his own opinion.

In summary, the highly credible communicator is usually more effective in causing conformance. Credibility is usually defined in terms of two general dimensions: expertness and trustworthiness. Perceived expertness is typically a function of reputation, behavioral proficiency and/or evidence of specialized training (degrees, certificates, and so on). Trustworthiness encompasses such factors as sincerity, openness, honesty, or perceived lack of motivation for personal gain. All of these characteristics of the source are most important to individuals who are operating under the problem-solving set.

ATTRACTIVENESS. Another important dimension in social influence is interpersonal attraction. The more we like someone, the more influence that person has over us. Aronson (1972) has summarized conditions which oftentimes lead to increased liking. He feels that these conditions fit under what he calls a reward-cost theory; that is, we tend to like people who bring us maximum gratification at minimum expense.

1. *Propinquity.* People who are close to each other physically tend to like one another more than those who are far away. It costs less in time and effort to receive benefit from them when they are nearby. Propinquity has been found to be an important factor in marital selection (Katz & Hill, 1958) and in friendship patterns (Festinger, Schachter, & Back, 1960).

2. *Reciprocity of liking.* Dale Carnegie (1937) wrote a book on *How to Win Friends and Influence People* in which one of his advices was to show people you like them by lavishing praise on them. Although there are exceptions to this rule, we tend to like people who like us.

3. *Similarity.* People who share similar beliefs, attitudes, and personality traits tend to like one another. It is entirely possible that people who are similar to us provide us with social validation that we are right, and thus, they are rewarding. People who disagree or are dissimilar tend to pose the possibility that we may be wrong and are thus punishing to us.

4. *Exceptions to the rule.* In summarizing conditions which lead to liking, we have necessarily simplified our analysis. There are many exceptions to the rule. For example, Berscheid and Walster (1969) state that proximity may lead to interpersonal hostility. Aggravated assaults, killings, and robberies tend to occur among neighbors, families, or acquaintances. Also, when a person lavishes too much praise upon us, we may question his sincerity and wind up disliking him. Furthermore, the old adage that "Birds of a feather flock together" is not always correct. Many times we prefer individuals who are quite different from us. People with complementary but dissimilar personalities may like one another. Such is the case of a man who has a need to be dominant and his wife who possesses a need to be submissive, or couples locked into a sadist-masochistic relationship.

As mentioned earlier, all of these conditions lead to increased liking of the person. The greater the attraction of the person, the greater is his ability to influence you. Attractiveness of the communicator is most important for the operation of the identification set.

POWER. A person who holds a great deal of power can influence your behavior because of the rewards and punishments which he is able to administer. Oftentimes the power which a person holds is because of his credibility or attractiveness (Raven, 1965). This form of power is much more subtle. However, we can identify two other forms of power which seem to operate under the authority and economic sets. These forms of power may or may not be associated with a person's credibility or attractiveness.

Legitimate power is that form in which individuals accept the right of the person to dictate what they will or will not do. Lt. William Calley claimed that he carried out legitimate orders from his superiors. He was not responsible for his actions and was operating under the authority set. Similarly, the defendants in the break-in of Daniel Ellsberg's office used the same argument.

Coercive power is that form in which a person can influence you not because of its legitimacy, but solely because he is able to punish or reward you. Prisoners of war are frequently the victims of raw coercive power. Here the prisoner conforms to the guards, not because he believes it is right, but because of the potential consequences. The economic set is such an example.

None of the five sets or frames of reference and their corresponding relationship with characteristics of the source are mutually exclusive. These sets frequently interact and any number of them can operate at the same time. For example, it is possible that you are influenced by a person who you find highly credible. It is also possible that you like this person or find him very attractive. Are you influenced by him because he is credible (problem-solving set), attractive (identification set), or both?

Let us pose another difficult dilemma. What we have thus far stated is that the communicator who is viewed positively will cause greatest conformity. As mentioned previously, people who operate under the consistency set expect that traits attributed to the communicator will be consistent with their behavior. Good guys say and do good things while bad guys do and say nasty things. Subjects frequently distort information to fit the source's characteristics. However, cognitive dissonance theory also predicts that it is possible for a negatively perceived communicator to affect more opinion change than a positive one. Recall that earlier we stated that in man's attempts to react consistently, he often acts irrationally. Zimbardo, Weisenberg, Firestone, and Levy (1965) had a communicator who treated an assistant either harshly (negative) or positively (positive), subsequently attempted to induce subjects to eat a highly disliked food, i.e., fried grasshoppers. They found that the negative communicator was much more effective in changing attitudes in the desired direction than was the positive communicator! However, this was *only* true for those who *ate* a grasshopper. Those individuals who ate a highly disliked food under the urging of the negative communicator experienced greater dissonance than subjects in the positive one. In the positive condition, you can rationalize your actions by saying "I tried the grasshoppers because I like the man." Thus, no dissonance is created. On the other hand, the thought that you performed an act which you did not want to do at the urging of someone you dislike, is inconsistent and creates dissonance. As a result, the individual can justify his actions by convincing himself that, indeed, he did like the fried grasshopper!

Social influence: The case of police interrogation techniques

Thus far we have come a long way in our discussion of social influence. We started by reviewing a number of classic studies in the field of conformity and were able to identify five principles which can and have been used to induce behavior or attitude change. Now we turn our full attention to the implementation of these principles. The effectiveness of social influence is most frighteningly and fascinatingly revealed by Philip Zimbardo in his study of police confessions. For our analysis, we will draw heavily from the articles of Zimbardo (1970) and Zimbardo and Ebbesen (1970).

The fact that more than 80 percent of court convictions are obtained with the aid of the defendant's confession makes many court trials a mere formality. The suspect, in essence, has testified against himself. Can a person be induced to confess against his will, even if he is innocent of the alleged offense? Police often claim that their methods cannot induce a suspect to confess to a crime he did not commit and, thus, are valid and acceptable. Yet there are many instances in which innocent people have confessed to crimes against their will. Zimbardo (1970) states that

> Not only are police methods likely to make a guilty man incriminate himself against his will, but I am convinced that they can also lead to false confessions by the innocent. . . . It is my professional opinion as a psychologist concerned with the modification of attitude and behavior that current police techniques represent a highly sophisticated application of psychological principles that for many people are more compelling and coercive than physical torture (Zimbardo, 1970, p. 106).

In the following pages, we will apply Collins' (1970) sets to police interrogation techniques in order to illustrate Zimbardo's contentions.

The police environment

Standard police interrogation manuals frequently stress the importance of interviewing the suspect in an unfamiliar environment so as to remove his usual support systems. The room should be free of distractions such as pictures, windows, and ashtrays. Only the bare minimum of two chairs and a desk are recommended.

Removing the suspect from familiar surroundings places the suspect in a situation that may be fearful, ambiguous, and confusing to him. In this situation, the problem-solving set is placed in operation. Individuals in this situation are unsure of what to expect and may turn to other people, in this case a policeman, for information and orientation.

Behavior of the interrogator

The interrogator is instructed at all times to behave in such a manner as to suggest the invincibility of the law. His authority should be established immediately by directing the subject into the room, telling him where to sit and not to smoke. He is instructed to stand physically close to the suspect in order to be psychologically close. In this case the interrogator's behavior is aimed at eliciting the authority set. By being near the suspect at all times, as we saw in Milgram's study, greater compliance is the result. In addition, when a suspect agrees to go to the police station and follows the orders of the interrogator (where to sit and not to sit), he has taken the first step in confessing. The police have gotten a foot in the door (consistency set) leading to a confession. By submitting to orders of the interrogator, the suspect is psychologically being prepared to accept further suggestions of guilt from the police. After all, who but guilty people are questioned by the police? The use of the consistency set is also seen in subtle statements made by the police. Although it is a constitutional right not to speak and to have an attorney present at the questioning, police often suggest that the refusal to talk and the need of an attorney is indicative of guilt (Figure 12–6).

Distortion techniques

Distortion techniques used by the police generally provide an excuse for the suspects behavior. In this case, the interrogator suggests that the suspect's behavior, although illegal, was the result of an accident, mistake, or even that the victim contributed to the crime. Presumably if the suspect accepts these suggestions, he is more likely to confess (consistency set).

For example, if an older man is questioned about an alleged sexual indiscretion with a child, the interrogator might suggest that she was well developed for her age and that she tried to excite him. In cases of forcible rape, the suspect might be offered a suggestion that the rape victim acted like a prostitute.

Deceitful methods

In some interrogations, the interrogator may simply lie in order to frighten the suspect into a confession. For example, police may tell the suspect that his fingerprints were found at the scene of the crime or that witnesses have come forward and identified him. Occasionally, a suspect may be brought into a lineup for identification. A stooge is implanted in the audience who shouts out "That's the man, the one on the left!" In cases of alleged embezzlement or forgery, falsified records may be shown to the suspect.

In many cases, the police may make the crime appear worse than it

FIGURE 12–6
The presence of police officers often elicits fear, guilt, and confusion even in innocent bystanders. After all, who else but the guilty are questioned by the police? Such a question facilitates the consistency set.

Courtesy of Paul Fry, *The Santa Clara*, University of Santa Clara

actually is. For example, suppose that a man is charged with statutory rape. This charge carries with it a lesser punishment than forcible rape. Police may lie by telling the suspect that the victim claimed that she was forcibly raped and that "you better tell your side of the story if you want to avoid that charge." Such misrepresentation often elicits confessions because of the economic motive, such as pleading guilty for a reduced charge.

The deceitful techniques are especially evident in what is called "The Bluff on the Split Pair." When two or more persons are suspected of complicity in some crime, they are often separated upon arrival at the station. One of the suspects is left alone while his partner is apparently being questioned. Actually both are left alone, each believing the other is being questioned. After some time, the policeman returns and informs each that his buddy has "squealed." Each is led to believe that his partner suggested he was the ringleader. The technique has proven highly successful in eliciting confessions.

Variations of this theme are frequently employed. Police may often fake sounds which the suspect believes are screams and groans coming from his partner being given the "Third Degree." The suspect may confess in order to save his partner from further physical abuse or to save himself from a similar fate. The split-pair bluff is aimed at eliciting an economic set in the suspects.

Identification games

Police interrogators often make use of the identification set by establishing a false relationship with the suspect. The attempt is to make the suspect like and identify with them. A friendly manner at all times is suggested. The interrogator may pat the suspect on the shoulder and offer him water or cigarettes as a means of gaining the confidence of the person. The interrogator is advised to assume the characteristics of the population from which the subject comes. For middle-class suspects, the officer is asked to assume a professional role of dignity, politeness, understanding, and sympathy. For lower-class suspects, police are advised to be familiar with their language and customs in order to assure identification. Praise is often used to this end. For example, interrogators are instructed to compliment the alleged driver of a getaway car on his driving skill.

Police interrogators often use what is called the "Mutt and Jeff" approach which adds the element of fear. Two interrogators assume opposite roles toward the suspect very similar to the comic-strip pair, Mutt and Jeff. Jeff is a big, hostile, and abusive character who threatens the suspect. "We're gonna keep bastards like you off the streets. If you don't tell me what I want to know I'll break every bone in your body." At this point the officer who is playing Mutt, orders Jeff to leave the room. Mutt behaves toward the suspect in a kind, friendly, and sympathetic manner. He informs the suspect that Jeff is a bad cop and that he should be dismissed from the force. He further tells the suspect that there is real reason to fear Jeff. "I go off duty very shortly and I'm afraid he'll come in and work you over. I've seen him badly cripple an old man before." Mutt then advises the suspect to confess in order to save himself from being abused. Not only is the identification process used, but this ploy gives an economic motive for confessing.

Conclusions

Techniques which we have reviewed operate under sound social-psychological principles that, as we have seen, can exert strong influence over people. A suspect has no logical reason to confess and yet we have shown that even an innocent man may confess for any number of reasons. Police like confessions because they simplify the case and make their work easier. However, when obtaining confessions is placed above the truth, then we, as citizens, are in dire danger. Many innocent individuals may be convicted for crimes they did not commit. Furthermore, a recent ruling by the Supreme Court has sharply reduced the impact of the 1966 *Miranda* v. *Arizona* confession decision. The *Miranda* ruling states that police must inform suspects that (1) anything they say may be used against them in a court of law, and (2) they are entitled to have an attorney present during all questioning. The new ruling states that illegally obtained confessions (not warning the suspect of his rights) may now be used by prosecutors to discredit a defendant's testimony, *if he takes the witness stand*. There is fear that such a ruling will weaken the *Miranda* decision and encourage police interrogations.

In addition, people most likely to suffer or succumb to such pressures come from the ranks of the disadvantaged because they are less familiar with their rights and the subtleties of interrogation techniques. Zimbardo (1970) states his fears quite well.

> I am convinced that these methods are psychologically coercive; that they deprive the individual of his human dignity and fundamental rights; and that they debase the police who use them even though the police are trying to be fair as well as efficient (Zimbardo, 1970, p. 103).

There is nothing inherently good or bad about the social influence principles which we have discussed. How we use them, however, is a heavy responsibility.

Summary

Our beliefs and behaviors are influenced by other significant persons in our lives. Social influence is clearly seen in the power and effectiveness of social norms. A social norm may be defined as a rule of conduct which implicitly or explicitly tells us how to behave. The three functions of norms are to create order and predictability, to enable us to have a standard of comparison, and to provide a sense of personal identity.

When our behavior or belief changes in the direction of a group which exerts real or imagined pressure on us, we are talking about conformity. Five important studies on conformity were reviewed in this chapter. Sherif's experiments, using the autokinetic effect, provided an ambiguous situation in which subjects who had established an individual norm, reestablished a group norm in the presence of others. Asch, in his line judgment study, was able to show that many subjects who knew the correct answer could be induced to call out an incorrect response under group pressure. These two studies illustrate that there are two types of conformity: private acceptance, as in the case of Sherif's study; and compliance, as in Asch's study.

One of the most important studies conducted on conformity was that of Stanley Milgram's experiments on obedience. Subjects were placed in a situation of conflict between obeying the experimenter's orders to hurt someone, and the human value that one ought not to hurt others. His ingenious study revealed some chilling findings. Two major ethical issues were raised by Milgram's studies: (1) When does conformity cease to perform a beneficial social function and become destructive as in unquestioning obedience to authority? (2) What was Milgram's ethical justification for exposing his subjects to such an intense emotional experience? All of us must ponder these questions carefully.

In contrast to the use of commands, Freedman and Fraser, using the foot-in-the-door technique, showed that if a person complies with a small request then he will be much more amenable to agreeing to a much larger, but similar one. Apparently, individuals may feel that they must be consistent in their behaviors or dealings with others.

In a series of interesting experiments, Darley, Latané, and Rodin were able to show that the nonintervention of bystanders in emergency situations may be acts of conformity. For example, they found that the more people present, the less likely the victim will receive help. They identified three crucial choice-points in which the presence of others inhibits helping behavior. First, we must notice the event. Second, we must interpret the situation and define it as an emergency. Third, even if we notice and define the situation as an emergency, we must take responsibility for helping.

These classic studies on conformity operate under well-established social psychological principles. Barry Collins has identified five such principles: (1) The problem-solving set occurs when we are motivated about obtaining correct information in order to solve a problem. (2) The consistency set means that we attempt to make our beliefs and actions consistent with one another. (3) In the identity set, the individual generally desires to be like or similar to a person or group which he holds in high esteem. (4) The economic set is in operation when we perform behaviors in order to gain rewards or avoid punishments. (5) In the authority set, some individuals are thought to have a particular position which gives them a legitimate right to influence us or to tell us what to do.

All of these sets are highly influenced by certain characteristics of the communicator who tries to influence us. The problem-solving set is most influenced by credibility; the identification set by attractiveness; and the economic and authority set by power. Credibility is usually defined by two dimensions: expertness (reputation, behavioral proficiency, evidence of specialized training) and trustworthiness (sincerity, openness, and honesty). Attractiveness of a person generally is affected by such things as propinquity, reciprocity of liking, similarity, and so forth. The power the communicator holds may be legitimate or coercive in nature.

The fact that social influence can be used in a highly systematic fashion is most clearly seen in Zimbardo's studies of police interrogation techniques. Among those discussed which operate under the social-psychological principles we have discussed are the police environment, behavior of the interrogator, distortion techniques, deceitful methods, and identification games.

References

Aronson, E. *The social animal.* San Francisco: W. H. Freeman Co. 1972.

Aronson, E., Turner, J. A., & Carlsmith, J. M. Communicator and communication discrepancy as determinants of opinion change. *Journal of Abnormal and Social Psychology*, 1963, **67**, 31–36.

Asch, S. E. Effects of group pressure upon the modification and distortion of judgments. In H. Guetzkow (Ed.), *Groups, leadership, and men.* Pittsburgh: Carnegie Press, 1951.

Asch, S. E. *Social psychology.* New York: Prentice-Hall, 1952.

Baumrind, D. Some thoughts on ethics of research: After reading Milgram's "Behavioral study of obedience." *American Psychologist*, 1964, **19**, 421–423.

Baumrind, D. Principles of ethical conduct on the treatment of subjects: Reaction to the draft report of the Committee on Ethical Standards in Psychological Research. *American Psychologist*, 1971, **26**, 887–896.

Berkowitz, L. Liking for the group and the perceived merit of the group's behavior. *Journal of Abnormal and Social Psychology*, 1957, **54**, 353–357.

Berscheid, E., & Walster, E. *Interpersonal attraction.* Reading, Mass.: Addison-Wesley, 1969.

Brock, T. C. Communicator-recipient similarity and decision change. *Journal of Personality and Social Psychology*, 1965, **1**, 650–654.

Carnegie, D. *How to win friends and influence people.* New York: Simon-Schuster, 1937.

Collins, B. E. *Social psychology.* Reading, Mass.: Addison-Wesley, 1970.

Cook, S. W., Kimble, G. A., Hicks, L. H., McGuire, W. J., Schoggen, P. H., & Smith, M. B. Ethical standards for psychological research: Proposed ethical principles submitted to the APA membership for criticism and modification (by the) ad hoc Committee on Ethical Standards in Psychological Research. *APA Monitor*, July 1971, **2**(7), 9–28.

Darley, J. M., & Latané, B. Bystander intervention in emergencies: Diffusion of responsibility. *Journal of Personality and Social Psychology*, 1968, **8**, 377–383.

Darley, J. M., & Latané, B. When will people help in a crisis? In *Readings in social psychology.* Del Mar, Calif.: CRM, 1970.

Festinger, L. *A theory of cognitive dissonance.* Stanford, Calif.: Stanford University Press, 1957.

Festinger, L., Schachter, S., & Back, K. *Social pressures in informal groups: A study of human factors in housing.* New York: Harper, 1960.

Freedman, J. L., & Fraser, S. C. Compliance without pressure: The foot-in-the-door techniques. *Journal of Personality and Social Psychology*, 1966, **4**, 195–202.

Hovland, C. I., & Mandell, W. An experimental comparison of conclusion drawing by the communicator and by the audience. *Journal of Abnormal and Social Psychology*, 1952, **47**, 581–588.

Katz, A. M., & Hill, R. Residential propinquity and marital selection: A review of theory, method, and fact. *Marriage and Family Living*, 1958, **20**, 327–335.

Kiesler, C. A., & Kiesler, S. B. *Conformity.* Reading, Mass.: Addison-Wesley, 1969.

Kelman, H. C., & Lawrence, L. H. American response to the trial of Lt. William L. Calley. Reprinted from *Psychology Today Magazine*, June, 1972. Copyright © Ziff Davis Publishing Company.

Latané, B., & Darley, J. M. Group inhibition of bystander intervention in emergencies. *Journal of Personality and Social Psychology*, 1968, **10**, 215–221.

Latané, B. & Darley, J. M. Bystander "apathy." *American Scientist*, 1969, **57**, 244–268.

Latané, B., & Darley, J. M. *The unresponsive bystander: Why doesn't he help?* New York: Appleton-Century-Crofts, 1970.

Latané, B., & Rodin, J. A lady in distress: Inhibiting effects of friends and strangers on bystander intervention. *Journal of Experimental Social Psychology*, 1969, **5**, 189–202.

Milgram, S. Behavioral study of obedience. *Journal of Abnormal and Social Psychology*, 1963, **67**, 371–378.

Milgram, S. Group pressure and action against a person. *Journal of Social Psychology*, 1964, **69**, 137–143.

Milgram, S. Some conditions of obedience

and disobedience to authority. *Human Relations*, 1965, **18**, 57–76. (a)

Milgram, S. Liberating effects of group pressure. *Journal of Personality and Social Psychology*, 1965, **1**, 127–134. (b)

Milgram, S. Interpreting obedience: Error and evidence. In A. G. Miller (Ed.), *The social psychology of psychological research*. New York: Free Press, 1972, 138–154.

Mills, J. Opinion change as a function of communicator's desire to influence and liking for the audience. *Journal of Experimental Social Psychology*, 1966, **2**, 152–159.

Monterey Peninsula Herald. And no one stopped—Girl's mystery death. November 29, 1971.

Raven, B. H. Social influence and power. In I. D. Steiner & M. Fishbein (Eds.), *Current studies in social psychology*. New York: Holt, Rinehart, & Winston, 1965.

Rosenthal, A. M. *Thirty-eight witnesses*. New York: McGraw-Hill, 1964.

Sherif, M. A study of some social factors in perception. *Archives of Psychology*, 1935, **27** (187), 1–60.

Sherif, M. *The psychology of social norms*. New York: Harper, 1936.

Walster, E., Aronson, E., & Abrahams, D. In increasing the persuasiveness of a low prestige communicator. *Journal of Experimental and Social Psychology*, 1966, **2**, 325–342.

Zimbardo, P. The psychology of police confessions. In *Readings in social psychology today*. Del Mar, Calif., CRM, 1970.

Zimbardo, P., & Ebbesen, E. E. *Influencing attitudes and changing behavior*. Reading, Mass.: Addison-Wesley, 1970.

Zimbardo, P., Weisenberg, M., Firestone, I., & Levy, B. Communicator effectiveness in producing public conformity and private attitude change. *Journal of Personality*. 1965, **33**, 233–255.

13

Racism: Prejudice and discrimination

What is racism?
Prejudice.
Stereotypes.
Discrimination.
Racism.

Theories of prejudice and discrimination.
The political-economic competition theory.
Scapegoat theory.
The prejudiced personality theory.
Social conformity theory.

Effects of racism on minorities.
Standard of living.
Psychological costs of racism.
Racial pride and identity.

Changing prejudice and racism.
Symptom theory approach.
Sociocultural approach.

Summary.

Several events occurred during the mid-1960s in epidemic proportions that left the American people dazed and puzzled. Rochester, Chicago, Los Angeles, Cleveland, Newark, Detroit, and other cities were all struck by a seemingly senseless wave of collective violence in the black ghettos. The scenes of looting, sniping, assaults, and burning homes and property filled TV screens and sickened the public. In light of these frightening events, many Americans searched for explanations about what had happened (Figure 13–1). What brought on these tragic events? Why should black Americans riot? After all, reasoned many, the conditions of blacks have never been better. Income, housing, and education have definitely risen, so why should they be unhappy?

Many political authorities blamed the riots on the militant-criminal elements of the ghetto. Nathan Caplan (1970) labels this the "riffraff" theory which explains riots in terms of the work of the emotionally disturbed, deviants, criminals, or the unassimilable migrants. In Chapter 9, we saw how such labels can potentially be used by those in power as a political instrument. Sue and Sue (1972) assert that the use of such derogatory labels tends to invalidate many legitimate and constructive criticisms of our society by various ethnic minorities. For example, because change is a difficult process for many institutions, the attribution of pathological motives to protesting forces serves to dismiss such challenges and perpetuates the status quo. In his review of empirical studies dealing with characteristics of black protesters and militants, Caplan (1970) concluded that "militants are no more socially or personally deviant than their nonmilitary counterparts. In fact, there is good reason to believe that they are outstanding on some important measures of socioeconomic achievement" (p. 60).

In light of these tragic events, President Lyndon B. Johnson appointed

FIGURE 13–1
Scenes of ghetto riots which occurred in Detroit; looting, burning of property, assaults, and sniping.

429

a National Advisory Commission on Civil Disorders which published its findings in 1968.

> Of the basic causes, the most fundamental is the racial attitude and behavior of white Americans toward black Americans. Race prejudice has shaped our history decisively; it now threatens our future. White racism is essentially responsible for the explosive mixture that has been accumulating in our cities . . . (p. 10).

This statement supports another viewpoint, that the underlying causes of the riots are due to the social, economic, and political conditions in our society and not the fault of "pathological" protesters. Second, it asserts that the history of the United States is the history of racial prejudice. That this prejudice is not limited to only black Americans, but to other minority groups as well.

In order to understand the full implications of these statements, we will turn our attention to several areas. First, we will need to define terms such as prejudice and racism. Second, we will discuss some of the more common theories which will seek to explain prejudice. Third, we will explore some of the effects which prejudice and discrimination have had upon minority-group members. Last, we will propose some courses of action which may lead to an alleviation of prejudice.

What is racism?

Asian-Americans:
> The Chinese are the least desired immigrants who have ever sought the United States . . . the almond-eyed Mongolian with his pig-tail, his heathenism, his filthy habits, his thrift and careful accumulation of savings to be sent back to the flowery kingdom.
> The most we can do is to insist that he is a heathen, a devourer of soup made from the fragrant juice of the rat, filthy, disagreeable, and undesirable generally, an incumbrance that we do not know how to get rid of, whose tribe we have determined shall not increase in this part of the world (Wagner, 1973, p. 43).

Black-Americans:
> They are like children; the state of their mental development is low. . . . In spite of that, I like the darkie. You may think I am prejudiced, and I am, but they are likeable. . . . Wits weren't developed in the tropics. . . . I have a feeling of aversion toward a rat or snake. They are harmless, but I don't like them. I feel the same toward a nigger (Jones, 1972, p. 30).

Mexican-American:
> If they even take a shower once a month they'd consider it too often. I don't want any of these unclean bastards touching my daughter! No sir, stay away. . . . They're always drunk . . . you can see them unconscious in the streets. They never work. All they do is fuck, drink and steal (white male)!

Prejudice

The examples given above and the countless thousands which we could give are illustrative of the widespread prejudices which have been directed against minorities in America. Gordon Allport (1954) has defined *prejudice* as

> . . . an antipathy based upon a faulty and inflexible generalization. It may be felt or expressed. It may be directed toward the group as a whole, or toward an individual because he is a member of that group. The net effect of prejudice, thus defined, is to place the object of prejudice at some disadvantage not merited by his own conduct (p. 9).

Thus, prejudice can be considered to be a set of hostile and negative attitudes directed at an identifiable group or members of the group. Second, it places the object of prejudice in an unfair and unjust disadvantage.

Stereotypes

When one comes to expect that all members of a particular group possess identical characteristics, what we are talking about are *stereotypes*. Stereotypes are overgeneralizations that are attributed to members of a group. The belief that Asian-Americans are sneaky, inscrutable, and backstabbers; blacks are stupid, athletic, and full of natural rhythm; and Chicanos are dirty, filthy, immoral characters, represent stereotyping (Figure 13–2). Unlike prejudice, however, some stereotypes are frequently helpful in ordering and structuring our world. To the extent that they blind us to individual differences within a group, they can become extremely harmful and maladaptive.

Discrimination

The term *discrimination* has frequently been a source of confusion with the concept of prejudice. While prejudice is an attitude, discrimination refers to an overt act that places an individual at a disadvantage. This is an important distinction to make because it is possible for a person to possess prejudicial attitudes without discriminating. An employer may hire blacks because of legal pressures but still dislike them. On the other hand, an employer who may not be prejudiced will discriminate against blacks because the rest of his friends might accuse him of being a "nigger lover." As in Chapter 12, the distinction is the same as that of compliance and private acceptance.

Racism

When we refer to racism, we are talking about an attitudinal component, prejudice, and its behavioral component, discrimination. Jones

FIGURE 13–2
A prevalent stereotype of black Americans is that
they are inclined to be naturally athletic. Why do
you think that some white Americans are willing
to acknowledge black superiority in sports?

Athletic News Bureau, University of Santa Clara

(1972) has identified three forms of racism: individual, institutional, and
cultural. A person who believes that blacks are racially inferior and will
not hire them for high executive positions can be called a racist. He is
practicing what we call *individual racism*. However, racism can take
many subtle forms which may not be intentional or conscious.

An example of *institutional racism* is given by Carmichael and Hamilton (1967):

> When white terrorists bombed a black church and killed five black
> children, that was an act of individual racism, widely deplored by most
> segments of the society. But when in that same city—Birmingham,
> Alabama—five hundred black babies die each year because of the lack
> of proper food, shelter, and medical facilities, and thousands more are
> destroyed and maimed physically, emotionally, and intellectually be-
> cause of conditions of poverty and discrimination in the black com-
> munity, that is the operation of institutional racism (p. 4).

When societal institutions (economic, educational, legal, and so on) are
structured in such a manner as to subjugate and mistreat large classes
of people, then we are talking about institutional racism. For example,
the improper use of culturally biased test instruments on minorities

have led to a biased determination of what constitutes pathology and cure in therapy (Braginsky & Braginsky, 1973; Halleck, 1971; London, 1964), to discriminatory educational decisions (Russell, 1970), and to an exclusion of minorities in jobs and promotion (APA, 1969). An example of the latter was seen in the *Griggs v. Duke Power Company*, in which Griggs and several other black employees were not allowed to move up to better jobs because they lacked high school diplomas and did not score well on intelligence tests. Luckily, the Supreme Court ruled that no educational requirements or tests can be used to rule out a job for a man or woman unless it is related to attributes needed for that position.

Most test instruments are constructed and standardized according to white middle-class norms. To use them as the sole yardstick in placing Asians, blacks, Chicanos, native Americans, and other disadvantaged groups in jobs or special educational classes for the retarded or to use these results as criteria for entrance to college, graduate or professional school is, nevertheless, racism. These school policies must be changed for they fail to recognize the multicultural background of minorities in evaluating the individual.

This last statement leads us into another form of racism; that is, *cultural* racism. Jones (1972) has defined cultural racism as the "individual and institutional expression of the superiority of one group's cultural heritage over that of another race" (p. 6). It is the most transparent of the forms of racism but it is the basis for the expression of the other two. Its basic manifestations have three parts: (1) a strong belief in the superiority of the achievements, activities, arts, crafts, economics, religion, traditions, language, and history of one group of people (white America); (2) a belief in the inferiority of all different cultural achievements (nonwhite); and (3) an attempt to impose standards, beliefs, and ways of behaving from the dominant to the minority group through the exercise of power. Simply stated, this means that anything white is good and beautiful while anything black, yellow, red, or brown is bad or ugly. We will return to this theme in a later section when we discuss the black, brown, and yellow movement in the United States. But, first, let us turn now to some theories which have been proposed as to how and why prejudice and discrimination are caused.

Theories of prejudice and discrimination

The political-economic competition theory

This theory proposes that prejudice is the result of limited resources in which two ethnic groups compete for goals. These goals may be political or economic in nature and is most evident in competition for jobs. As a result, the dominant group develops hostile, prejudiced attitudes toward the minority group and actively discriminates against them by making it difficult for them to obtain jobs. Such is the case when blacks or minority groups are excluded from trade unions.

Historically, this theory seems to hold much merit. Derald Sue (1973) in his analysis of early Chinese and Japanese immigration to the United States found these early immigrants much welcomed. During the 1840s, there was a large demand for cheap labor in mining and in the building of the transcontinental railroad. However, during the 1850s and 1860s, a series of business recessions dried up the labor market in California and made the Chinese immigrants no longer welcome. Sentiments about the Chinese took a turn for the worse as labor leaders agitated against them. They were called "subhuman aliens" whose ways of living was seen as undesirable and detrimental to the well-being of America. Laws were passed to harass the Chinese and denied them the rights of citizenship and ownership of land. At the height of the anti-Chinese movement, many Chinese were assaulted and murdered by mobs of whites. This anti-Chinese movement culminated in the passage of a racist immigration law, the Chinese Exclusion Act of 1882.

The early Japanese immigrants fared no better than their Chinese counterparts. Although originally welcomed, their fantastic success in the agricultural fields enraged many white citizens who saw the Japanese as a threat to their own economic security. Battle cries such as "The Japs Must Go!" were echoed throughout the newspapers. Individual and mob violence against the Japanese were repeated.

Scapegoat theory

The scapegoat theory of prejudice states that a person who experiences frustration and is unable to direct the source of his anger toward the real source attempts to eliminate frustration by venting anger on others who are (1) less powerful, and (2) different from himself. For example, Mr. Jones is constantly being chewed out by his boss at the office. He experiences frustration because he cannot tell his boss off for fear of losing his job. As a result, he comes home one evening and assails his gardener for not doing his job properly.

The practice of blaming our troubles upon a victim or object which had nothing to do with the original problem has been used throughout history. Ancient Hebrew priests frequently used this technique in transferring the sins and evils of the tribe onto a goat which was then driven off into the wilderness. The goat, philosophically, was made to suffer the sins of the people just as Jesus Christ did. The persecution of the Jews in Nazi Germany and the blacks in the United States are outstanding examples of this phenomenon which engenders economic frustration. Hovland and Sears (1940) found that it was possible to predict the number of lynchings of blacks from the fluctuating price of cotton from the 1880s to 1930; that is, when the price of cotton for a particular year was low, the number of lynchings would increase. Increase in prejudice in the laboratory has been produced experimentally by frustrating subjects. Miller and Bugelski (1948) found the prejudice toward Mexicans and Japanese increased after frustrating subjects by having them fail difficult tests.

Allport (1954) was able to identify certain characteristics which he believed made certain groups more vulnerable as victims of scapegoating. First, the groups used as scapegoats can be identified readily through observable differences in physical appearance or cultural characteristics. The dark skin of blacks and the physical and cultural characteristics of Chicanos and Asian-Americans make them good targets. Second, members of the outgroup must be readily accessible. Third, groups discriminated against are less powerful and cannot retaliate effectively.

The prejudiced personality theory

Related to the scapegoat theory of prejudice is the belief that some people become frustrated and displace aggression more readily than others. It is postulated that certain individuals have a constellation of personality traits that predispose them to prejudicial thinking. Adorno et al. (1960) published a book entitled *The Authoritarian Personality* which summarized a series of important studies that served to break important ground in this area. Essentially, Adorno and his colleagues presented evidence that prejudice was rooted in an authoritarian personality structure. The individual who is labeled authoritarian possesses such characteristics as rigidity in beliefs and values, intolerance of weakness in himself and others, and he is suspicious and punitive toward others and extremely respectful of authority. The instrument used to measure these traits is called the "F" scale, which consists of items which are answered true or or false. Below are examples:

1. A person who has bad manners, habits, and breeding can hardly expect to get along with decent people.
2. Sex crimes, such as rape and attacks on children, deserve more than mere imprisonment; such criminals ought to be publicly whipped, or worse.
3. Too many people today are living in an unnatural, soft way; we should return to the fundamentals, to a more red-blooded, active way of life.

Agreement with these and similar items would indicate high authoritarianism. Furthermore, these people tend to show a high degree of prejudice toward most minorities. The investigators went on to imply that parental behavior was a primary component in fostering this personality type.

Parents of individuals with an authoritarian personality tend to use harsh punitive treatment in disciplining them and frequently threaten to withhold their affection as a means of control. At the same time, dependency and hostility is fostered in the child. Unable to express anger toward parents, it is hypothesized that these individuals displace their aggression onto outgroups. It is also possible that children pick up these attributes from their parents because of modeling behavior. The child learns prejudiced thinking from his parents and is rewarded for such beliefs.

Social conformity theory

In the preceding chapter considerable discussion was devoted to the concept of conformity to group norms. The social conformity theory of prejudice states that the child is socialized into a prejudiced society and conforms to local group norms. These social norms are transmitted to the child via parents, peers, schools, and the mass media. Aronson (1972) gives an example which illustrates this point. Southern coal miners would frequently mix freely with black miners while working underground but would immediately segregate upon coming out of the mine. The miners had developed completely different norms while underground but, upon leaving, the larger norms of the South would prevail.

Effects of racism on minorities

The effects of racism upon minorities in America tend to be both dramatic and highly damaging in two ways. First, the standard of living among many ethnic minorities is inferior to that of white Americans. Second, there is tremendous psychological costs associated with racism.

Standard of living

The standard of living for Asian-Americans, blacks, Chicanos, Indians, Puerto Ricans, and other minority groups is much below that enjoyed by whites. Discrimination can be seen in the areas of housing, employment, income, and education. Taeuber (1965) calculated a segregation index for many American cities and concluded that black Americans were by far the most segregated of the minorities. His data also seems to indicate that it is not so much free choice or the poverty of blacks that led to their living in inferior residential areas so much as discrimination in housing. This inequity in housing also applies to Chicanos, Indians, Puerto Ricans, and Asian-Americans. Sue and Sue (1973) point out that contrary to popular belief, such as the "success myth" of Asian-Americans, Chinatowns in San Francisco and New York represent ghetto areas with high rates of suicide, tuberculosis, juvenile delinquency, unemployment, and poverty.

Minority groups also suffer from discrimination in the form of inferior jobs, higher unemployment rates, and a much lower income than that of their white counterparts. Jones (1972) in analyzing census figures concludes that the median black family's income is approximately 60 percent as large as the white family's and that in our society a white college-educated skin is worth $2,668 annually more than a black college-educated one! Thus, lower income cannot be primarily attributed to inequity in education.

Despite the fact that the present black generation is economically better off than past generations, the gap between whites and blacks has not narrowed. Figures indicate that although the income gap is closing between whites and blacks in the higher income levels, the gap is widening for lower income blacks. Unfortunately, the lower class represents 45 percent of the black population!

According to the Coleman report (1966), blacks also suffer from segregated and inferior education. Class size, qualification of teachers, physical facilities, and extracurricular programs place minorities at a disadvantage. As a result, much of the difference in intellectual achievement between blacks and their white counterparts can be attributed to educational inequities.

As pointed out by Wrightsman (1972), extreme acts of racism can wipe out a minority group. Indian tribes witnessed massacres which destroyed their leadership and peoples. The number of American Indians has dropped from 3,000,000 to 600,000. Furthermore, their life expectancy is 44 years compared to 71 for white Americans. Wrightsman warns that the American Indian may soon disappear from the face of the earth.

Psychological costs of racism

In the late 1940s, Kenneth and Mamie Clark (1947) published their findings dealing with racial awareness and preference among black and white children. What they found was very disturbing. The sample of black children, when presented with a white and colored doll, preferred playing with the white doll. In addition, the colored doll was perceived to be bad and approximately one-third of the black children, when asked to pick the doll that looked like them, picked the white one. The Clarks concluded that many black children possessed a confused sense of self-identity.

The inferior status of blacks as manifested through individual, institutional, and cultural racism can be seen as a major contributor to these results. Constantly bombarded on all sides by reminders that whites and their way of life are superior while blacks and their way of life are inferior, many blacks are simply brainwashed into accepting the prejudices of society. Minorities begin to incorporate the standards of the larger society and react negatively toward their own racial and cultural heritage. They become ashamed of who they are and attempt to identify with and behave like the "good" white majority. In the *Autobiography of Mal-*

colm X recall that Malcolm X tried desperately to appear as white as possible. He went to extreme painful lengths to straighten and dye his hair so that he would appear more like males from the dominant society (Haley, 1966).

The development of a negative self-image and the fostering of racial self-hatred by an intolerant society is not unique to blacks. Weiss (1969) in an anthropological field study of Chinese-Americans found that this incorporation of white standards by a minority member can harmfully affect their social life. Weiss states that:

> Perhaps the most damaging indictment of Chinese-American male "dating ineptness" comes from the dating-age, Chinese-American female. Girls who regularly date Caucasians can be quite vehement in their denunciation and disapproval of Chinese-American males as dating partners. But even the foreign-born Chinese girls—who do not usually interdate—also support a demeaning courtship image of the Chinese-American male. Moreover, "Chinese inadequacies" and "failures" are contrasted with Caucasian "confidence" and "success" in similar situations (Weiss, 1969, p. 14).

It is evident that many minorities do, indeed, accept white standards as a means of measuring physical attractiveness, attractiveness of personality, and social relationships. Among the more ethnically conscious members of a minority these individuals are labeled Oreos (a cookie with white cream filling with dark wafers on the outside) for blacks or bananas (white inside yellow outside) for Asian-Americans. These terms imply that the minority person is white inside and a sellout to his race.

Two strong factors seem to account for the phenomenon of self-rejection among minorities. The first is a positive valuation placed upon white American society which manifests itself most blatantly in color. White is pure, wholesome, and good while black, brown, yellow, and red represent negative characteristics. This is especially true for the color black (blackmail, blackeye, black magic, and blacklist) which is associated with evil and sinister forces or traits. On a broader scale this manifests itself in white *ethnocentrism* or the belief that one group's way of life is better, and all other life-styles are compared to this standard. Second, is the negative valuation placed on other life-styles. For example, African, Chinese, Japanese, Mexican, and Indian cultures are viewed as inferior when compared to the white American norms.

These beliefs are perpetuated by our educational institutions and by the mass media through television, movies, newspapers, radio, books, and magazines. For example, there is a notable deficient coverage and fair portrayal of minority groups in all levels of education. Kane (1970) in his study of the treatment of minorities in social studies textbooks states that:

> A significant number of texts published today continue to present a principally white, Protestant, Anglo-Saxon view of America's past and present, while the nature and problems of minority groups are largely neglected (p. 138).

With respect to specific racial and ethnic minorities, Kane goes on to say that while the blacks are no longer ignored, their treatment is weak and noncommittal; Chinese and Japanese-Americans are portrayed in unfavorable stereotypes; Mexican-Americans have replaced the black man as the invisible minority; Puerto Ricans fare only slightly better.

Sue and Sue (1972) conclude that in higher levels of education, the social sciences have generally ignored the systematic study of certain ethnic groups in America (Asian-Americans) or tended to concentrate on the psychopathological problems of minorities (blacks and Chicanos). Billingsley (1970) notes that "White Social Science" has tended to concentrate on the pathological and unstable black families instead of the many stable ones. He believes that such an orientation leads to distorted perceptions of blacks and reinforces a negative view of them among students, scholars, and the public.

The portrayal of minorities on movies, television, radio, and magazines also contributes to widespread stereotypes. Blacks have traditionally been portrayed as superstitious, childlike, ignorant, fun loving (Amos and Andy); Mexican-Americans are seen as dirty, sneaky, and criminals (Frito Bandito); and Asian-Americans as sneaky, sly, cunning, passive (Fu Manchu). Such portrayal causes widespread harm to the self-esteem of many minorities who incorporate these stereotypes (Table 13–1). Male students should ask themselves this question. How would you feel if all of your TV male characters were portrayed like Don Knotts and Gomer Pyle?

TABLE 13–1
Changing stereotypes

Group	Characteristics	Percent of students attributing trait to the group		
		1932	1950	1967
Americans	Industrious	48	30	23
	Intelligent	47	32	20
	Materialistic	33	37	67
	Ambitious	33	21	42
	Pleasure-loving	26	27	28
Blacks	Superstitious	84	41	13
	Lazy	75	31	26
	Happy-go-lucky	38	17	27
	Ignorant	38	24	11
	Musical	26	33	47
Japanese	Intelligent	45	11	20
	Industrious	43	12	57
	Progressive	24	2	17
	Sly	20	21	3
	Imitative	17	24	22

This table summarizes how three different generations of Princeton students in 1932, (Katz & Braly, 1933), 1950, Gilbert, 1951), and 1967 (Karlins et al., 1969) stereotyped three different ethnic groups. Notice that Americans are seen as becoming much more materialistic while notions of blacks as being superstitious, lazy, ignorant have decreased. Notice that the Japanese are now considered much more industrious than in 1950. Can you explain why these stereotypes have changed over the years? Does it mean that Americans are becoming less prejudiced?
Source: Data from Katz and Braly (1933), Gilbert (1951), and Karlins et al. (1969). Abstracted from Karlins et al., 1969. Permission granted by American Psychological Association.

That these expectations can set up a self-fulfilling prophesy has been demonstrated by Rosenthal and Jacobsen (1968). These investigators told teachers that certain children who were chosen at random in the class were either potential intellectual bloomers or not. They found that those children who were identified as bloomers showed marked IQ gains as compared to those who were not so identified. Just how these expectations were transferred from the teacher to the pupils is not known. However, it is not too far askew to suggest that when people have preconceived beliefs of different groups in our society, these groups will be influenced by their expectations and thus may behave accordingly.

Racial pride and identity

There is no doubt that widespread prejudice and racism has served to severely place minorities in an unenviable position in life as well as damaging their self-esteem. No group can live in harmony by itself if made to be ashamed of who and what they are. For that reason, many minorities have begun to attempt a redefinition of their existence by stressing consciousness and pride in their own racial and cultural identity.

Most evident of this redefinition is the "Black is Beautiful" statement and the symbolic relabeling of identity from Negro and colored to black American and Afro-American. It is felt by many blacks that such terms as Negro and colored are white labels and symbolic of a warped identity given them by society. As a means of throwing off these burdensome shackles, the black individual is redefined in a positive light. All peoples of color have begun this process in some form and banded together into what has been called the "Third World Movement." Since all minority groups share common problems and experiences, there is an attempt in this movement to band together (Asian-Americans, blacks, Chicanos, native Americans, and others) into a political force and to expose and alleviate the damage which racism has dealt. Problems such as poverty, unemployment, and juvenile delinquency are seen as arising from racism in society. There is an attempt to enhance feelings of group pride by emphasizing the positive aspects of one's cultural heritage. That this emphasis may be effective is seen in a recent study by Hraba and Grant (1969). Recall the earlier study of the Clarks who found negative associations given to a black doll? Hraba and Grant found that doll preferences of black children are no longer white oriented. It is intuitively possible that programs stressing black pride and racial identity could lead to such changes. Other evidence indicates that the self-hatred fostered in many minorities may be weakening and being directed to legitimate external sources such as our society. Paige (1970) found that antiwhite attitudes were highly related to feelings of black pride and identity. The Sues (1971) have also noted this trend among Asian-Americans.

As black consciousness and pride began to develop in the mid-1960s, many black leaders called for changes in our society. This is not to deny that blacks have historically fought in various ways to free themselves. But the movement in the sixties was more massive and organized than ever before (Figure 13–3). Unlike the civil rights demonstrations of the fifties and early sixties against segregation in public facilities, the move-

FIGURE 13–3
Racial protests in sports

Wide World Photos

ment entered another stage of escalation when it struck many northern cities. The frustrations against subordination coupled with a sense of black pride escalated the violence in confrontations. A large segment of the black population was no longer willing to wait for changes to occur. They wanted an end to racism *now* and were willing to risk violent confrontations to attain their goal.

As long as the blacks were peaceful and did not physically fight back during the civil rights movement of the fifties, the American public sympathized with their cause. Once riots in the cities began, however, many people became frightened and a backlash developed. Goldschmid (1970) points out that mass media again focused on those individuals who used the most revolutionary rhetoric, and discussions afterward served to paint a distorted image of black militancy and activism. In order to avoid facing the fact that racism created the situation, many individuals rationalized the riots away as the work of a small criminal element (riffraff theory) or Communist agitators. We have seen, however, that this explanation is false and the blame for what occurred lies with *white racism*. The pessimistic conclusions of the Kerner Commission states that:

> Our nation is moving toward two societies, one black, one white separate and unequal. Reaction to last summer's disorders has quickened the movement and deepened the division. Discrimination and segregation have long permeated much of American life: they now threaten the future of every American (p. 1).

Changing prejudice and racism

With this dire warning to the American people, it becomes increasingly clear that the destructive effects of racism must be changed. But how does one go about reducing or eliminating prejudice and discrimination? This is a question which has plagued us for years. Richard Ashmore (1970) has identified two solutions which have been proposed to reduce prejudice: the symptom theory approach and the sociocultural one.

Symptom theory approach

In the symptom theory approach, the assumption is that prejudices are symptom manifestations of psychological conflicts rooted in the personality. The scapegoat and prejudiced personality theories of prejudice are consistent with this belief. The person is prejudiced because of unresolved conflicts or a too rigidly developed personality structure. To eliminate prejudice requires such things as psychotherapy, catharsis, self-insight training, or changes in child-rearing practices. If an individual through psychotherapy can be made to see that his hostility toward blacks are really the results of strong unresolved feelings toward parents (see Chapter 8, section on "Psychoanalysis"), then the prejudice will disappear.

Unfortunately, this manner of eliminating prejudice has not proven exceptionally successful for several reasons. First, the causes and origins of prejudice tend to be multiple rather than unitary. Although psychotherapy might work for some individuals, it definitely does not affect others. Second, the efficacy of using psychotherapy as a technique to end prejudice is not promising because of the masses of people that would have to be reached. Third, social scientists are beginning to realize that attitude change does not necessarily imply behavior change. A reduction in prejudice, as we have seen, does not mean an end to discrimination.

When the U.S. Supreme Court in 1954 handed down its orders for school desegregation, many educators and social scientists argued that it was not possible to legislate morality. The only way of accomplishing the elimination of discrimination was to change attitudes and it was better to wait until this occurred before attempts at integration. What these people did not realize was that social scientists are discovering that attitude change frequently follows behavior change. As Aronson (1972) notes, favorable attitudes toward integration among whites has arisen from 30 percent in 1942, to 49 percent in 1956, and to 75 percent in 1970.

Sociocultural approach

Although the Supreme Court Justices were probably not aware of it, they were essentially advocating a sociocultural approach. The approach assumes that ethnic prejudices can be changed without first reorganizing the personality. Early attempts using this approach attempted to provide correct information about various ethnic groups. Since prejudice was frequently the result of incorrect information through socialization, attempts at dispelling prejudice consisted of providing accurate information on the particular ethnic minority. If Japanese-Americans are seen as sneaky, sly, and inscrutable individuals, we would simply show the prejudiced person a movie or play depicting them as open, honest, and sincere. Or we could give him books and articles to read that would contradict this stereotype.

Unfortunately, such approaches were too simplistic and therefore highly unsuccessful. Lazarsfeld (1944) reports that during World War II, a series of radio programs attempted to reduce intergroup hostility by providing information about various ethnic groups in a favorable manner. However, there was a tendency for many of those who listened to be members of the ethnic groups being portrayed. The lesson learned was that people tend to avoid information inconsistent with their beliefs. As we saw in the previous chapter, cognitive dissonance theory predicts that people will go to extremes to distort or invalidate information even if they could not evade the source. However, it is still possible that providing correct information is a necessary but not a sufficient condition for combating prejudice. Other conditions such as group interaction are needed along with information before prejudice will be affected.

Muzafer Sherif (1956) reports on a series of field studies which he conducted over a number of years. These experiments may shed much light on race relations and we will describe his study in some detail.

THE ROBBER'S CAVE EXPERIMENT. Sherif was very interested in investigating the conditions which lead to harmony and friction among different groups. To study this, he brought normal, healthy, well-adjusted boys who did not know one another to a summer camp in which they were to engage in camp activities. No one knew that they were part of a psychological study. The boys, aged 11–12, were divided into two different groups and placed in different cabins. Each member engaged in activities such as hiking and swimming only within their own group. As a result, each group developed its own jokes, symbols, secrets, and jargon. For example, some members were given nicknames like "Lemon Head" and "Baby Face." Each group developed its own chain of command among its leaders and called themselves the Rattlers and Eagles, respectively. Much "esprit de corps" developed within each group.

Sherif assumed that group hostility would arise if two groups have conflicting aims that can only be obtained at the expense of the other. Note the similarity of his assumption to that of the economic-political theory of prejudice. In order to produce friction, Sherif designed a series of games and events that pitted one group against another in a tournament such as baseball, football, and tug-of-war. The contests soon degenerated into a personal grudge between the two groups. Name-calling (stinkers, sneaks, cheaters) and scuffling became quite overt. At one point the Eagles burned a banner left behind by the Rattlers and the next morning the latter group retaliated by seizing and burning the Eagle's flag.

Sherif then turned his attention to another aspect of group relations. How can groups in conflict be brought into harmony? We saw in the preceding chapter that proximity was highly correlated with interpersonal attraction. If the competitive situation could be eliminated and we could substitute pleasant social events such as going to the movies together and eating in the same room, maybe hostility could be reduced. Far from reducing the conflict, however, this method only provided an opportunity for both groups to attack one another. In the dining hall, shoving, throwing food at one another, and using vile names were the order of the day. Again, proximity might be a necessary but not a sufficient condition for promoting intergroup harmony.

Reasoning that if competition can produce conflict might not its opposite, cooperation, to achieve a desired goal reduce it? Sherif contrived a series of emergencies in which the groups would have to help one another in order to obtain what they all wanted. In one situation the camp managers informed the boys that a water pipe had broken and unless it was located and fixed immediately, they would all have to leave camp.

Both groups volunteered to search the water line and fixed it by the afternoon. In another situation, a large truck that was supposed to go into town and pick up food for the camp broke down. In order to start it, both groups together used a rope to pull the truck until it was able to start. Gradually, these joint efforts lessened the tension and hostility between the groups. A member of one group who had previously been much disliked for his sharp tongue and skill in defeating them became a "good egg." New friendship patterns emerged and the name-calling that characterized earlier meetings disappeared. Toward the end, they decided to hold a joint campfire and to ride home together in the same bus.

CHARACTERISTICS OF THE CONTACT SITUATION. The study by Sherif seems to indicate that intergroup conflict can be reduced through contact situations which stresses *cooperation* in order to achieve *shared goals*. However, how analogous is this situation to racial conflicts and the elimination of prejudice? Stuart Cook (1970, 1971) has taken some of Sherif's findings and created an experimental situation by which to test some of these hypotheses on subjects with known anti-black attitudes. He identified five characteristics of contact situations between black and prejudiced white subjects that would facilitate attitude change.

4. *The acquaintance potential.* The range of possible human relationships is vast. In one way or another, people in the United States are exposed to contact with black Americans. However, these contacts are often brief and dictated by formality or ritual which makes getting to know the person an impossibility. If you are living in a large dormitory or apartment complex, it is often difficult, if not impossible, to be well acquainted with all of the neighbors. You may see them at the mailbox, hallway, or dining room and even chat with them occasionally, but in essence you are unaware of their hopes, aspirations, and fears. As we saw in the Robber's Cave Experiment, mere contact does not mean lowering of prejudice. Only if we get to know someone is there a chance for attitude change to occur.

2. *Status of participants.* Contact between blacks and whites must also be equal; that is, the minority person must have the same status as the prejudiced one. In everyday life, most white Americans occupy roles which have greater status and power than their black counterparts. Contacts of this kind does not facilitate prejudice reduction. Contacts in which blacks are in subservient roles such as porters, shoeshine boys, dishwashers, and attendants increases stereotyping and tends to generate greater prejudice in the attitudes of anti-black persons. Morton Deutsch and Mary Collins (1951) conducted a well-known experiment in a federally funded housing project in which black and white families were either integrated or segregated. Theoretically, the black and white families in the integrated project were of "equal status" and the acquaintance potential was good. Deutsch and Collins did find that white housewives in the integrated housing project expressed greater positive responses toward blacks than did the segregated white housewives.

3. *Norms of the community.* The existence of favorable norms

toward contact between groups also serves to facilitate reduction of prejudice. This is especially true when people have expectations that relationships have social implications as opposed to strictly business ones. Aronson (1972) labels this the psychology of inevitability. When a prejudiced person believes that integration is inevitable, his feelings that he dislikes blacks and the fact that he must interact with them sets up dissonance. In order to reduce the dissonance, he may search for positive characteristics of the minority group member or minimize their perceived negative traits (see Chapter 12). This reasoning derives from cognitive dissonance theory. However, this occurs only under ideal conditions in which the norms of the community favor such a response. If public officials, as many did, state that they do not like integration but will enforce it because of the law, a norm is created that discourages favorable relations but allows another means of dissonance reduction.

4. *Cooperation versus competition.* As we saw in the Sherif study, competition can create conflict when victory for one group means the loss or defeat of another. However, when two groups must cooperate in order to achieve a common goal, prejudice reduction is the result. This is particularly true when mutually interdependent tasks must be performed to obtain a goal.

5. *Characteristics of the contacting individuals.* If contacts with minority group members destroy negative and unflattering stereotypes, prejudice reduction is enhanced. The belief that blacks are lazy and stupid is most easily changed if prejudiced individuals meet blacks who are hardworking and intelligent.

These five conditions were created by Stuart Cook in a laboratory study designed to reduced prejudicial feelings in strongly anti-black subjects. Preliminary analysis indicates that after 40 hours of laboratory contact, approximately 35 percent of the subjects changed to a more favorable attitude toward blacks, 40 percent remained unchanged, and 20 percent had become more prejudiced. These results are astounding when one considers that only 40 hours were used with strong anti-black subjects. However, why some subjects became more prejudiced is difficult to explain. We will have to wait for more research to explain this latter finding. In any case, it seems clear that all Americans must work toward eliminating racism. There is no simple explanation or solution to this problem, and each of us must contribute in his or her own way.

Summary

In the mid-1960s, a series of explosive riots in the black ghettos rocked the American "democratic" foundation. Original explanations which were offered blamed the riots on the militant-criminal elements of the ghetto. However, later investigations concluded that the basic cause was because of widespread prejudice and discrimination. Prejudice may be defined as a set of hostile and negative attitudes directed at an identifiable group or members of a group. Prejudice is facilitated by stereotyping, the belief that all members of a particular group possess identical characteristics. While prejudice is an attitude, discrimination refers to an overt act that places an individual at a disadvantage.

The combination of prejudice and discrimination is termed racism. Three forms of racism are identifiable: (1) Individual, which is directed from one individual to another; (2) institutional, which refers to policies of economic, educational, and legal organizations that subjugate and mistreat large classes of people; and (3) cultural, which is manifested in the belief that the achievements of one group of people is superior to that of another.

Many theories of prejudice and discrimination have been proposed. One of these, the political-economic competition theory, states that prejudice is the result of competition for limited resources. Another explanation has been called the scapegoat theory. A person who experiences frustration and is unable to direct his anger toward the real source attempts to eliminate his frustration by venting anger on others who are less powerful and different. The prejudiced personality theory stresses that certain people have a personality constellation that predisposes them to prejudicial thinking. Individuals who are labeled "authoritarian" tend to be in this category. The social conformity theory states that we are socialized into a racist society that provides norms fostering prejudice and discrimination.

Whatever the reasons for prejudice and discrimination, racism is highly damaging to minorities in America. First, the standard of living among many ethnic minorities is inferior to that of white Americans. Second, there are tremendous psychological costs associated with racism.

Many minorities are now beginning to stress pride in racial and cultural identity in order to reverse the trend of negativity. The "Black is Beautiful" emphasis is symbolic of this movement. All peoples of color have begun this process of raising red, yellow, black, and brown consciousness.

For years, social scientists have attempted to find ways of reducing prejudice and discrimination. Two approaches can be identified: the symptom theory and the sociocultural approach. In the former, there is an assumption that prejudices are symptom manifestations of psychological conflicts rooted in the personality. The sociocultural approach holds the greatest promise because it attempts to attack the problem on a wider basis. However, early attempts such as providing correct information about ethnic groups and giving them a chance to interact in noncompetitive situations did not work. It was postulated that these are *necessary* but *not sufficient* conditions in eliminating prejudice.

The Robber's Cave Experiment conducted by Sherif provided interesting insights into the origins and possible reduction of intergroup hostility. His study indicated that intergroup conflict can be reduced through contact situations which stress *cooperation* in order to achieve *shared goals*. Stuart Cook's study also supports this viewpoint. He identified five characteristics of contact situations between black and prejudiced persons that facilitate attitude change. First, contact between individuals must be more than casual in character. Second, the status of the participants must be approximately equal. Third, the norms in the community must favor interracial contact. Fourth, mutual interdependence or cooperation must exist to obtain a goal. Fifth, if prejudiced persons meet individuals who destroy unflattering stereotypes, then prejudice reduction will be facilitated.

References

Adorno, T. W., Frenkel-Brunswik, E., Levinson, D. J., & Sanford, R. N. *The authoritarian personality.* New York: Harper, 1950.

Allport, G. W. *The nature of prejudice.* Reading, Mass.: Addison-Wesley, 1954.

American Psychological Association. Task Force on Employment Testing of Minority Groups. Job testing and the disadvantaged. *American Psychologist,* 1969, **24,** 637–649.

Aronson, E. *The social animal.* San Francisco: W. H. Freeman Co., 1972.

Ashmore, R. D. Prejudice: Causes and cures. In B. E. Collins, *Social psychology.* Reading, Mass.: Addison-Wesley, 1970, 243–339.

Billingsley, A. Black families and white social science. *Journal of Social Issues,* 1970, **26**(3), 127–142.

Braginsky, D. D., & Braginsky, B. M. Psychologists: High priests of the middle class. *Psychology Today,* **7**(7), 1973, 15, 18–20, 138–142.

Caplan, N. The new ghetto man: A review of recent empirical studies. *Journal of Social Issues,* 1970, **26**(1), 59–74.

Carmichael, S., & Hamilton, C. V. *Black power: The politics of liberation in America.* New York: Vintage Books, 1967.

Clark, K. B., & Clark, M. Racial identification and preference in Negro children. In T. M. Newcomb & E. L. Hartley (Eds.), *Readings in social psychology.* New York: Holt, 1947.

Coleman, J., et al. *Equality of educational opportunity.* Washington, D.C. Government Printing Office, 1966.

Cook, S. W. Motives in a conceptual analysis of attitude-related behavior. In W. J. Arnold & D. Levine (Eds.), *Nebraska symposium on motivation, 1969.* Lincoln, Neb.: University of Nebraska Press, 1970, 179–231.

Cook, S. W. The effect of unintended racial contact upon racial integration and attitude change. Final report, Project No. 5-1320, Contract No. OEC-4-7-051320-0273. Washington, D.C.: U.S. Office of Education, Bureau of Research, August 1971.

Deutsch, M. & Collins, M. E. The effect of public policy in housing projects upon interracial attitudes. In E. Maccoby, T. M. Newcomb, & E. L. Hartley (Eds.), *Readings in social psychology.* New York: Holt, 1951, 612–623.

Gilbert, G. M. Stereotype persistence and change among college students. *Journal of Abnormal and Social Psychology,* 1951, **46,** 245–254.

Goldschmid, M. L. *Black Americans and white racism.* New York: Holt, Rinehart & Winston, 1970.

Haley, A. *The autobiography of Malcolm X.* New York: Grove Press, 1966.

Halleck, S. L. Therapy is the handmaiden of the status quo. *Psychology Today,* 1971, **4**(11), 30–34, 98–100.

Hovland, C. I., and Sears, R. R. Minor Studies of aggression: *VI,* Correlations of lynching with economic indices. *Journal of Psychology,* 1940, **9,** 301–319.

Hraba, J., & Grant, G. Black is beautiful: A reexamination of racial preference and identification. *Journal of Personality and Social Psychology,* 1969, **16,** 398–402.

Jones, J. M. *Prejudice and racism.* Reading, Mass.: Addison-Wesley, 1972.

Kane, M. B. *Minorities in textbooks: A study of their treatment in social studies texts.* Chicago: Quadrangle, 1970.

Karlins, M., Coffman, T. L., & Walters, G. On the fading of social stereotypes: Studies in three generations of college students. *Jour-*

nal of Personality and Social Psychology, 1969, **13**, 1–16.

Katz, D., & Braly, K. Racial stereotypes of one hundred college students. Journal of Abnormal and Social Psychology, 1933, **28**, 280–290.

Lazarsfeld, P. F. (Ed.). Radio and the printed page. New York: Duell, Sloan, & Pearce, 1944.

Leavitt, H. J., & Mueller, R. A. Some effects of feedback on communication. Human Relations, 1951, **4**, 401–410.

London, P. Modes and morals of psychotherapy. New York: Holt, Rinehart, & Winston, 1964.

Miller, N. E., & Bugelski, R. Minor studies in aggression: The influence of frustration imposed by the in-group on attitudes expressed toward out-groups. Journal of Psychology, 1948, **25**, 437–442.

National Advisory Commission on Civil Disorders. Report of the National Advisory Commission on Civil Disorders. New York: Bantam, 1968.

Paige, J. M. Changing patterns of anti-white attitudes among blacks. Journal of Social Issues, 1970, **26**, 67–86.

Rosenthal, R., & Jacobsen, L. F. Teacher expectations for the disadvantaged. Scientific American, 1968, 218.

Russell, R. D. Black perceptions of guidance. The Personnel and Guidance Journal, 1970, **48**, 721–728.

Sherif, M. Experiments in group conflict. Scientific American, 1956, **195**, 145–157.

Sue, D. W. Ethnic identity: The impact of two cultures on the psychological development of Asians in America. In S. Sue & N. N. Wagner (Eds.), Asian-Americans: Psychological perspectives. Ben Lomond, Calif.: Science and Behavior Books, 1973.

Sue, D. W., & Sue, S. Ethnic minorities: Resistance to being researched. Professional Psychology, 1972, **2**, 11–17.

Sue, D. W., & Sue, D. Understanding Asian-Americans: The neglected minority. Personnel and Guidance Journal, 1973, **51**, 386–389.

Sue, S., & Sue, D. W. Chinese-American personality and mental health. Amerasia Journal, 1971, **1**(2), 36–49.

Taeuber, K. E. Residential segregation. Scientific American, 1965, **213**, 12–19.

Wagner, N. N. A white view of American racism. In S. Sue & N. N. Wagner (Eds.), Asian-Americans: Psychological perspectives. Ben Lomond, Calif.: Science and Behavior Books, 1973.

Weiss, M. S. Selective acculturation and the dating process: The patterning of Chinese-Caucasian interracial dating. Journal of Marriage and the Family, 1969, **32**, 273–282.

Wrightsman, L. S. Social psychology in the seventies. Monterey, Calif.: Brooks/Cole, 1972.

14

Men and women: The psychology of sex differences

The serious study of sex differences in personality, ability, and behavior is less than a hundred years old, and yet both occupational and status segregation of the sexes has existed since time immemorial. Woman's less strength and greater dependency have forced her into a passive, homemaking role near the campfire while the man has gone out hunting. The difference in role expectations has been taken for granted in most societies and seldom questioned. Plato, however, was a notable exception as he strongly argued in his famous book, *The New Republic*, that the only difference between the sexes was that men are physically stronger. As he pointed out, among animals such as dogs, the females are not kept from hunting and participate in watching over the pack. Therefore, women should have similar roles in human societies and could best serve as "guardians" for his utopian Republic. But few people accepted the validity of Plato's arguments, and for centuries, society has continued to maintain homemaking roles for women, and occupational roles for men.

The traditional role for women within our own society may be best summed up by a statement from Jacqueline Kennedy Onassis, who was once quoted as saying, "There are two kinds of women: those who want power in the world and those who want power in bed." Many social critics such as Paula Stern (1970) believe that in our society the latter alternative is more acceptable. She argues that women in America have been brainwashed into thinking in this manner and most men believe it to be the mark of womanhood. Children are taught these stereotypes early, as well as the appropriate behavior that goes with each sex-determined role in life.

Sexism: Prejudice and discrimination against women

Jack was walking down the street when he bumped into an old friend. This dialogue followed:

> JACK: Hi!
> FRIEND: Hi! How are you?
> JACK: Fine. What have you been doing since you graduated from high school? I haven't seen you since then.
> FRIEND: Well, I tried college for a few years but didn't like it, so I went to work. I really enjoy being involved in a job.
> JACK: What do you do?
> FRIEND: I got a job five years ago with a construction firm in their drafting department. You remember that was the one thing I really liked in school.
> JACK: Yes.
> FRIEND: I also got married three years ago, and this is my daughter.
> JACK: What's her name?
> FRIEND: It's the same as her mother's.
> JACK (*to daughter*): Hi, Sally!

451

How did Jack know the daughter's name was Sally? (Delworth, 1973, p. 672.)

If you have difficulty with answering this question, you may be reflecting unconscious sexism. Jack knew the daughter's name because his friend is Sally.

Like racism, sexism is any attitude, action, or institutional structure that subordinates a person because of some dominant characteristic, in this case sex. The majority of sexist attitudes and actions are directed against women and the examples are numerous. As Sandra and Daryl Bem (1970) point out, our religious heritage and language perpetuates the belief that God is a man and that man is superior to women:

> For a man . . . is the image and glory of God; but the woman is the glory of man. For the man is not of the woman, but the woman of the man. Neither was the man created for the woman, but the woman for the man (1 Cor. 11).

The subjugation of women has been shown to take place early in life through stereotyped role portrayals. Children's toys, movies, and literature depict girls playing with dolls or sewing, and boys playing with toys and mechanical objects. In addition, adult roles show mothers keeping house and involved with domestic duties while fathers work in offices or factories (Figure 14–1).

The task of bearing and nursing children provides a biological reason for keeping women at home, and man's greater muscular strength makes possible his participation in more strenuous activities. Once the division of labor is established, however, complex regulation by social pressure sets in, and familiar ways of doing things are enforced by taboo and prejudice. As a consequence, members of one sex may do exclusively what members of the other sex could do equally well. This may be seen in the historical prejudice against women that shows up in the academic jobs and in other professions. Most of the jobs can be done equally well by either sex.

For example, of nearly 30 million women in the work force, nearly two-thirds work as service, clerical, domestic, or sales workers. A woman, in 1968 with four years of college training earned an average income of $6,694 a year, the same as a man with only an eighth-grade education. In contrast, men with the same amount of education earned an average of $11,795.

The investigation of the career status of women psychologists in universities clearly shows a lower status in comparison to their male colleagues (Astin, 1972). When women hold doctorates, receive their degrees from top-rated departments, and publish as much as men, they are still paid lower salaries than the men and are promoted to higher ranks at a slower rate (Table 14–1). In a related finding concerning prejudice, a recent survey revealed that in one large western university, only 3.8 percent of the professors were women—a lower proportion than 50 years before.

FIGURE 14-1
Girls are increasingly entering activities traditionally thought to be masculine, such as sports. This picture was taken of college coeds playing basketball.

Courtesy of Paul Fry, *The Santa Clara*, University of Santa Clara

TABLE 14-1
Salaries of male (M) and female (F) psychologists at universities

	Less than $10,000		$10,000–$13,999		$14,000–$16,999		$17,000–$19,999		$20,000 or more	
Articles published	M	F	M	F	M	F	M	F	M	F
None	51	72	42	28	7	0	1	0	0	0
1–2	16	48	64	49	18	4	2	0	0	0
3–4	19	29	73	63	5	7	2	0	1	0
5–10	5	11	79	62	10	26	6	0	1	0
11–20	3	0	54	66	27	28	13	5	3	0
20 or more	1	0	14	17	27	53	24	30	33	0

Note: In percentages. Salary is based on a nineteen-month appointment.
Source: H. S. Astin, "Employment and Career Status of Women Psychologists," *American Psychologist*, May 1972, 27, p. 379. Copyright 1972 by the American Psychological Association. Reprinted by permission.

The psychology department was found to have last appointed a woman to its staff in 1924.

One study indicates that even women tend to perceive males more favorably than they do other females (MacBrayer, 1971). Male and female college students participated in an experiment in which they were administered four sentence completion items concerning the opposite sex along with other incomplete sentences. In classifying the completions into favorable and unfavorable categories, both sexes were found to be much more favorable toward men than women. This perception is also reflected in a study by Phillip Goldberg (1968) who asked college females to rate a number of professional articles from each of six fields. One group of students were told that the author was John T. McKay and the other was told that Joan T. McKay had written the articles. Female students rated the articles attributed to the male author as better than the identical articles attributed to the female author. It is apparent that many females have accepted the values of our society that equate masculinity as more desirable than femininity.

That this type of sexist thinking is present in psychotherapy and has become an area of concern for many people is reflected in current writings. As we saw in Chapter 9, psychotherapy can be viewed as a tool to maintain societal values. Broverman and Broverman (1970) point out that concepts of mental health vary with the sex of the person. Since men and women are systematically trained from birth to fulfill different social roles, a double standard of mental health is maintained. Psychotherapy forces women to adjust to a feminine role dictated by society. Even though masculine roles are seen as more desirable, a woman who does not want to stay home and raise a family but pursue a career can be seen as mentally unhealthy.

Impact of women's liberation

Many young women are no longer willing to accept the traditional sex roles in which a woman is supposed to gain all the skills associated with the custodial care of the children and living quarters—such as cooking, keeping house, sewing, and caring for children—so that she can succeed in her roles as a wife and mother. The resistance to these stereotyped roles can be seen in the growing women's liberation protest movement.

Among their demands and suggestions are: (1) removal of barriers for women who want to raise their status by entering high-prestige occupations; (2) development of child-care centers and other facilities to relieve women of some family responsibilities; (3) increasing the prestige of housekeeping and child care, by recognizing them as real occupations and providing them with pay; (4) eliminating many of the current distinctions between "masculine" and "feminine" activities by having both men and women spend part of the day at work and part at home with the children; and (5) making housekeeping functions, such as cooking or cleaning into cooperative enterprises so there are no clearly defined roles.

A current advertisement proclaims "You've come a long way, baby." In fact, the new feminist movement has resulted in a blurring of the distinction between tasks that are "feminine" and those that are "masculine." Women are now seen as mail carriers, bus drivers, and even as construction workers. Men, on the other hand may be airline stewards, interior decorators, or hair stylists. And at conventions, the leader of an individual session in which scholarly papers are presented is now commonly referred to as "chairperson" rather than chairman.

However, it would be a mistake to believe that the status of women in America is equivalent to that of men who are still predominant in medicine, law, religion, science, and politics. Although the number of women is numerically increasing in these professions, the number of women achieving eminence in these fields is slight.

Theories of sex-role differences

Penis envy and masculine protest

Early psychoanalysts such as Sigmund Freud and Alfred Adler believed that different processes operated in structuring the personality development for boys and girls. Freud's theory is psychosexually oriented in contrast to Adler's belief in inferiority complexes.

As we saw in Chapter 8, Freud believed that as the small girl becomes familiar with the father, she notices the differences between her body and the father's. In particular, she notices the lack of a male organ in herself. Because of alleged rivalry between her and her mother for the father's love, the child comes to blame the mother for her lack of a penis. She attributes the loss to her mother's jealousy, which removes the child as a love object with the father. At the same time, she identifies quite strongly with the father because he possesses something neither she nor her mother has. To this state of affairs, Freud gave the name *penis envy*. The girl continues to feel envious or ambivalent over her "inferior" biological position until adolescence where her conflict is usually resolved. It must be stressed at this point that "penis envy" is an unconscious event, as is most behavior in Freud's theories.

Adler believed that man is born into the world feeling incomplete and with a deep sense of inferiority. The neonate is confronted by a world which appears more competent, bigger and better than he and, as he grows, be becomes increasingly aware of his inferior role in society. A part of this general inferiority complex is the so-called masculine protest. By a somewhat devious route in this thinking, Adler equated being inferior with weakness and femininity. Inferiority, thus, was akin to femininity, the compensation for which was called the masculine protest.

Later, however, he subordinated this view to the more general one that feelings of inferiority for men and women, arise from a sense of unfulfilledness in any sphere of life.

Role theory: Sex typing

During the preschool years sex typing (adoption of behaviors, values, attitudes, and interests appropriate to one's own sex) figures prominently in the socialization and personality development of the child. Most parents pay considerable attention to the sex appropriateness of their child's behavior by rewarding responses considered appropriate to their sex and discouraging those that are not. As a result, parents are more likely to encourage a boy to engage in "rough house" play, behave aggressively, and "fight back" if attacked by a peer, than they are for their daughter (Sears, Maccoby, & Levin, 1957). Girls are not encouraged to participate in major sports, and if they should happen to be athletic are apt to be considered "masculine." (See Figure 14–2.) It is all right for

FIGURE 14–2
A kiss for the champ. Bobby Riggs leans to kiss Billie Jean King after his loss in a tennis match billed as "the Battle of the Sexes."

Wide World Photos

preschool girls to cry, since women are supposed to be more emotional than men; but a boy who shows tears is likely to be told "quit acting like a baby, men don't cry." Strangely, if the same boy shows anger, he is not apt to be considered to be behaving emotionally. By age five, most children are keenly aware of sex appropriate behaviors and attitudes. For example, boys prefer guns, cowboys, and Indians for toys while girls choose dolls and kitchen utensils, considered appropriate for their sex (Mussen, Conger & Kagen, 1969).

Role of parents

The basic components of sex typing are acquired at home, largely through identification with, and imitation of the parent of the same sex. Theoretically, the degree to which the child adopts a parent's behavior is a function of that parent's nuturance, affection, competence, and power (to reward and punish). Thus if parents do not possess these characteristics, the child would not want to be like them. The ideal situation for the adoption of culturally approved sex-role behavior would be one in which (1) the same sex-parent is seen as nurturant and possessing desirable characteristics, and (2) both parents consistently reward sex-appropriate responses and discourage inappropriate ones.

A number of studies have yielded data supporting the above hypotheses. In one experimental study, groups of generally nurturant and nonnurturant mothers (categorized on the basis of their responses to an interview on child-rearing practices) served as models, teaching their daughters to solve maze problems (Mussen & Parker, 1965). During the teaching session, the mother made novel, irrelevant responses in accordance with directions from the experimenter such as drawing her lines very slowly and making unnecessary marks in her tracing (e.g. hooks or curves in her lines).

As would be predicted from the theory, the daughters of the nurturant group imitated many of their mother's irrelevant responses while the nonnurturant girls copied relatively few. Similar results between parental nurturance and sex typing with boys have been found; boys identify with their fathers if the latter are perceived as nurturant and masculine (Hetherington, 1968).

Munzinger (1971) reports that the power relations among family members strongly affect sex typing. Masculine boys see their fathers as being very masculine and competent, in contrast to feminine boys. A dominant father also accelerates his daughter's femininity as well as his son's masculinity. In a mother-dominated home, sex-role identification is affected in a reverse manner; boys become more feminine and girls more masculine and domineering.

It is important to note that role theory does not view sex typing as a product of identification; to the contrary, identification is viewed as a consequence of sex typing. Boys model themselves after males because they already have masculine response tendencies; as a result, masculine values and ways of behaving and feeling are therefore imitated and adopted.

Cultural influences

Sex roles and stereotypes vary widely in different times and places and are apparent from anthropological studies as well as our own cultural history. Anthropologists and sociologists stress the preeminence of cultural factors in the determination of sex differences and believe that even if there are basic predispositions that differ, cultural factors do much to mask them. The following sections explore the ways in which social factors operate to determine "feminine" and "masculine" behavior.

Cross-cultural studies of sex roles

EMOTIONALITY. Margaret Mead has formulated many important theories in anthropology and conducted many extensive field studies of different cultures. A vivid illustration of the role of cultural factors in sex differences is furnished by her description of the traditional emotional characteristics of men and women in three societies of New Guinea (Mead, 1949).

Among a mountain dwelling tribe, the *Arapesh*, both men and women display emotional characteristics which in our society would be considered distinctively feminine. Both sexes are trained to be unaggressive, cooperative, kind, noncompetitive, and responsive to the needs of other people. The river-dwelling *Mundugumur*, however, present a sharp contrast. In their society, both men and women are violent, combative, ruthless, and competitive; fighting has become a way of life with them, in which they take great delight.

Perhaps the most interesting pattern is that of the lake-dwelling *Tchambuli*, among whom there appears to be a complete reversal of the sex stereotypes typical of our culture. The women hold the position of power in Tchambuli and are responsible for the fishing and manufacturing of mosquito bags, which are the tribe's chief articles of trade. The men, on the other hand, are engaged predominantly in the arts and have become skilled in dancing, carving, and painting. In terms of general personality traits, Tchambuli women are described as impersonal, practical, and efficient, while the men are reported to be humanistically oriented, artistic, timid, and submissive. Interestingly enough, the "masculine" man and the "effeminate" women are considered to be deviants in the Tchambuli society!

In a more recent study, the emotional behavior of Iranian men and women was investigated (Hall, 1966). Men in Iran, in contrast to America, are considered to be more emotional than women; they cry more easily and have trouble concealing their feelings. Iranian men also read poetry, are sensitive and, in most cases, are not expected to be very logical.

However, Iranians consider men to be superior to women, and they definitely have a patriarchical society. This primarily reflects that emotionality in Iran is considered both natural and desirable in men, and, in fact, is highly valued.

OCCUPATIONS. Jobs and professions have traditionally provided one of the principal cultural areas of sex differentiation. In cultures where modern technology is lacking, work is necessarily physical, and sharp division of labor is usually observed. A study of 224 nonliterate tribes throughout the world shows that men gravitate toward work requiring muscular strength (mining, hunting, warfare, and boatbuilding). Women tend toward occupations centering around the home and children such as clothes making, water carrying, and the gathering of fruits and nuts. However, there are some exceptions to these rules which can be seen. In one African culture, women do the heavy agriculture field work because men are considered too delicate for such a task. A woman even continues to work in the fields during pregnancy, right up to the day a child is to be born. The brave husband then gets into bed and groans as if he were in great pain while the wife bears the baby. He will stay in bed with the baby to recover from his terrible ordeal while the mother goes back to take care of the crops (Melzack, 1961).

Muscular strength aside, many studies also tell us that men and women do not have a natural affinity for some task nor repugnance toward others. The famous third-century Greek writer, Athenaeus, was quoted as saying, "Whoever heard of a woman cook?" Mead (1935) called attention to the convention of one Philippine tribe that "no man can keep a secret" and to the Manus tribe in New Guinea who believe that only men enjoy playing with babies.

SOCIAL CLASS. In recent years, psychologists, anthropologists, and sociologists have become increasingly interested in studying the differentiation of sex roles within our own culture. The process of socialization of the child varies within the different social classes of American society. Lower occupational groups differentiate sex roles earlier and to a greater extent than do middle and upper economic groups (Rogers, 1969). In one well-known study, children were divided by sex into middle- and lower-class groups (Rabbin, 1950). Lower-class boys were the first to clearly identify themselves with the sex appropriate roles whereas middle-class girls were the last. Lower-class girls and middle-class boys were intermediate between these two extremes in taking on feminine and masculine roles, respectively. The average lower-class little boy manifested sex-typed behavior quite clearly (choice of masculine rather than feminine toys), by the age of four to five, some three to four years earlier than the average middle-class girl manifested feminine behavior.

What are the reasons for this discrepancy? It seems likely that masculine and feminine roles are more clear-cut among the working-class population than they are in the middle-class, and in addition, the masculine role is more atractive to both sexes than the feminine one. Several studies show, in regard to the latter, that both sexes rate boys more favorably, indicate a preference for boy's toys, and show a preference for being the father in the family rather than the mother (McCandless, 1961; Rogers, 1969). These results have been found at every grade level up to the fifth.

There is also evidence, based on child-rearing practices, that lower-class fathers provide clearer masculine models for their sons than middle-class fathers. For example, open aggression, a masculine trait is frowned upon in middle-class society, but more accepted in lower-class society. On the other hand, girlish or sissy behavior on the part of the lower-class boy will be firmly discouraged by both parents; whereas in the middle-class boy such behavior is more likely to be tolerated.

The lower-class girl, like the lower-class boy, is more apt to have a clearer model for feminine identification than the middle-class girl. She may also be punished more often than the middle-class girl for showing tomboyish behavior. On the whole, the overall push toward her appropriate behavior is weaker than her brothers; but the model is clearer than that for middle-class girls.

THE EFFECT OF SIBLINGS. So far we have considered the influence on sex typing of parents, social class, and various cultures. It can also be demonstrated that the presence of older siblings affects sex typing. As might be expected, children with an older sibling of the same sex seem to have their sex typing speeded up. In comparison to only children, they more often choose activities appropriate to their sex (Fouls & Smith, 1956). On the other hand, the girl with an older brother often comes to view his sex role as more appropriate than her own. She is more likely than the girl with an older sister to have a masculine profile on vocational interest tests (Sutton-Smith, Roberts, & Rosenberg, 1964).

A PERSPECTIVE ON SEX ROLE. A proper evaluation of the foregoing discussion should take into account the fact that social sex roles are in a state of flux and that considerable disagreement exists concerning their present status. Many people see a narrowing gap between the sexes, but others insist that basic male and female biological differences mean that the trend toward unisex can only go so far. At any rate, in America more than in most European countries, sex differences are blurred. Evidence for this can be seen in everyday dress which is almost identical in some cases for both sexes, while feminine frills are reserved for special dress-up occasions. Further evidence of this depolarization which has been taking place in the last 40 or more years can be seen in similar studies conducted years apart by Terman and Miles (1936) and Kelly (1955). In the older study, it was found that women become more feminine with age. However, in the more recent study, it was reported that women's masculinity increases with age.

Two of the often discussed reasons for decreasing polarization are the invention of machinery to do the heavy work and the advent of the women's liberation movement. Whether society should consciously modify sex roles in order to reduce the differences, including the disadvantages, is in dispute. Probably the middle course is favored by the majority of both sexes: women should be allowed to have a choice of different careers. A homemaking role can be viewed as a career. By and large, women do not desire to engage in the most vigorous physical activities as do men; similarly men are unwilling to concede to them the most masculine attributes such as action, aggressiveness, and dominance (Rogers, 1969).

Biological influences

We have examined how social factors affect sex roles in different cultures. Mead, on the basis of her anthropological findings, has taken the unconventional view that sex differences in personality are unrelated to physiological factors and are entirely the result of cultural determinants. The existence of matriarchal societies has also been taken as evidence for the cultural nature rather than biological basis for sex differences, especially in aggression and dominance. However, as pointed out by Nash (1969), matriarchal societies are very unusual and may be the result of the existence of atypical conditions, such as the young men being killed off by war or by the men being away long periods of time in connection with ocean fishing. Nash argues that whether or not a society should be feminine oriented is another question, but the fact seems to be that the male-dominated society is a universal phenomenon, particularly in advanced countries.

The debate over biological versus cultural factors in sex differences, as exemplified by Nash and Mead, continues to run unabated. We shall next examine biological factors that have been noted in determining psychological differences between the sexes. They may be reflected either (1) directly by inherited traits or (2) indirectly through socially learned reactions to physical differences.

SEX-DETERMINING CHROMOSOMES. A major source of general sex differences is provided by the X and Y sex-determining chromosomes. It will be recalled from Chapter 2 that each cell in the body receives a complete set of chromosomes. For the female, each body cell contains an X pair. This means, then, that the two sexes differ in every cell in the body. Not every body cell, of course, must necessarily develop differently in men and women, since not all genes may be active in the development of every cell. But these sex differences in gene constitution, repeated in every body cell, undoubtedly must account for many of the physical differences between the sexes. Sex differences have been reported for almost every physical dimension, including body-build and size, and physiological functioning (Nash, 1969).

BODY SIZE AND DEVELOPMENT. In all human societies known to us, men are taller and heavier than women. The men have been found to average approximately 5 percent heavier than women at birth and 20 percent heavier by age 20; in height, the male excess increases from about 1.5 to 6 percent taller. In addition, men have broader shoulders and larger bones and muscles.

During a few years in earlier adolescence, however, girls are on the average taller and heavier than boys, and reach physical maturity earlier (Figure 14–3). Girls, in general, are found to be developmentally accelerated throughout all childhood. Studies have shown that at each year, girls have attained a greater percentage of their adult height and weight than boys. Other aspects of physical development show similar acceleration of the female sex. Skeletal development, as measured by bone ossification (hardening of the bones), is well advanced for girls, in comparison to boys, at all ages. Dentition differences are also noted; girls shed their deciduous teeth sooner and get their permanent teeth at an earlier age than boys. It is noteworthy that the general developmental acceleration of girls begins even before birth. Girls on the average are born more mature than boys and also tend to have a shorter fetal period.

MUSCULAR STRENGTH AND VITALITY. The greater muscular strength of the male is well known. This difference, in spite of the accelerated development of the female, is apparent at birth. Bell and Darling (1965) found that male neonates raise the head higher and for longer periods

FIGURE 14–3
Age of maximum growth rate. The age of greatest growth in height was determined for each boy and each girl and then plotted to make this figure. As can be seen, girls typically mature earlier than boys.

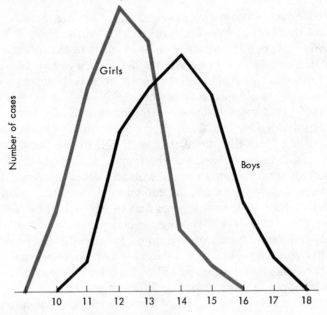

Age of maximum growth (in years)

Source: Data from several sources.

than do females. The differences in the musculature are reflected in the typical manner of throwing as seen in young boys and girls. No doubt with training these patterns can be modified, but girls spontaneously throw a ball overhand by holding the ball at the back of the shoulder and throwing with a forward and downward movement (Nash, 1969). In contrast, boys spontaneously tend to throw with a horizontal motion at shoulder level, and twist the body so that the shoulders actually enter into the throwing movement.

In keeping with the above differences in muscular strength and development are metabolic differences. Anderson and Langham (1959) have noted sex differences in potassium (K) concentrations, much higher for males, which is related to muscular development. In addition, men have a higher metabolic rate, produce more physical energy, and thus require more food. Similarly, the male heart beats more strongly and the male blood is richer in red corpuscles. These physiological differences have an obvious relationship to the greater vital capacity of males (vital capacity is the total volume of air that can be expelled from the lungs following maximal inhalation). This difference is especially significant because vital capacity is an important factor in sustaining energy output. This, of course, is one of the main reasons that men can perform physical feats, such as long-distance running, better than most women. On the average, men will simply have greater endurance.

All these physical differences may play an important part in sex differences in play activities and interests. For example, S. Goldberg and M. Lewis (1969) studied one-year-old children in a standard play situation and found the boys to be more exploratory and active in overcoming obstacles. Girls, however, were more likely to passively accept barriers that kept them from play areas and more often responded by crying.

THE BIOLOGICAL VULNERABILITY OF THE MALE. Although males have the advantage over females in terms of immediate physical strength and endurance, they are at a disadvantage in terms of viability and sex-linked defects. At all ages, the female shows more viability or capacity to maintain life than does the male as reflected in her greater life expectancy (Table 14–2). The interpretation of mortality rates in adulthood are, of course, complicated by differential hazards met by the two sexes in their traditional occupational and recreational activities. However, the higher mortality rate of males cannot be explained entirely on this basis, as can be seen by examining several facts.

First, prenatal and infant deaths are much more common among boys than among girls. For unclear reasons, various statistical sources indicate that although the ratio of male to female conception lies between 120:100 and 150:100, only 5 to 6 percent more boys than girls are born. Thus even before birth, death has already taken a considerably greater toll of the male sex. Second, this greater mortality rate among males is

TABLE 14—2
Life expectancy rates by age, color, and sex: United States, 1971.

Life table value and age	Total	White		All other	
		Male	Female	Male	Female
Expectation of life:					
At birth	71.0	68.3	75.6	61.2	69.3
At age 1	71.4	68.6	75.8	62.3	70.2
At age 21	52.3	49.6	56.4	43.6	51.0
At age 65	15.1	13.2	17.0	12.9	16.1
Percent surviving from birth:					
To age 1	98.1	98.1	98.5	96.8	97.4
To age 21	96.7	96.4	97.6	94.3	96.0
To age 65	72.3	66.9	81.8	49.5	66.3
Median age at death ..	74.9	71.8	79.7	64.8	71.9

Source: Department of Health, Education, Welfare.

maintained throughout life as well. He is more susceptible to infection and is more often afflicted with physical defects than his female counterpart.

SEX-LINKED DEFECTS. One reason for the sex difference in viability and in physical disorders lies in the nature of sex chromosomes. Since the female receives two X chromosomes, the effects of a defective gene in one is likely to be counterbalanced by a normal gene in the other chromosome. As we saw in Chapter 2, the male receives only one X chromosome and a smaller Y chromosome with relatively few genes in it. It is unlikely that a defective gene will have a normal counterpart from the X chromosome to check the effect. This relationship between corresponding genes in each pair of chromosomes can best be understood by noting that a defective gene is probably one lacking in certain vital chemical substances. Such a deficit can be overcome by the presence of the same ingredients in the corresponding normal gene.

The most notorious example of such a "sex-linked disease" is *hemophilia*, a condition in which the blood fails to clot properly. A woman with a defective gene which produces hemophilia will probably not have it herself because of a normal gene at the same position in the other X chromosome. She will, however, be a carrier and pass on this trait which may show up in some of her male children.

The most eminent hemophilia carrier in history was Queen Victoria of England. Her son, Edward VII, from whom later British monarchs were descended, escaped from the disease so there is no hemophilia now in the British royal family. However, one of her daughters who was a carrier, married Czar Nicholas II of Russia. As a result, their only son was a hemophiliac; his condition helped alter the history of Russia for it was through influence over him that the monk Gregory Rasputin gained power in Russia and helped bring on the discontent that eventually led to revolution. Another daughter of Victoria was also a carrier and is of historical interest. She herself had a daughter also a carrier who married into the royal house of Spain producing hemophilia there. Because of its presence among the Spanish Bourbons and the Russian Romanoffs, hemophilia has become known as the royal disease. However, it has no particular connection with royalty, except for the unfortunate descendants of Victoria.

A less serious sex-linked disorder is color blindness which is far more common among males than females. The presence of only one X chromosome which makes males susceptible to this and related diseases may also cause a general weakness in men. In this manner, we can account for the fact that when women are protected against death from childbirth problems they tend to live longer than men. The 23d complete sex pair of chromosomes appears to make women "the sounder biological organism."

DIFFERENCES IN MALE-FEMALE SYSTEMS. Recent evidence suggests the development in the embryo of a male and a female brain which may result in different psychological modes of functioning. It is hypothesized that this differential development is the result of the action of the sex hormones.

Harris (1964) claims that the female-type brain is the more basic of the two. In the fetus, the CNS is at first sexually undifferentiated but in the absence of hormonal influence develops into a female-type nervous system. There is, however, in the development of nervous systems a critical period when the presence of male hormones causes the development of a male-type brain. In contrast, the growth of a female-type brain seems to be dependent only on the absence of androgen and not on the presence of estrogen. The female-type brain develops if male hormones are absent whether female hormones are present or not.

As noted by Harris, there is a spiraling effect concerning this development. The prenatal presence of androgens modifies the course of CNS development, including the development of the hypothalamus which directly influences the endocrine system; the modified CNS in turn influences further hormonal secretions. The research is still recent and most of the work to date in this area has been done on the lower animals. However, similar mechanisms apparently operate in primates. Harris is not specific as to the nature of the male and the female CNS, but Phoenix et al. (1959) have suggested that the sex hormones may affect the organization of the nervous system and thereby ultimately cause sex differences in behavior. In experiments performed on guinea pigs, they were able to produce hermaphroditic (bisexual) female offsprings by injecting pregnant mothers with male sex hormones. Subsequently, they engaged in mating behavior patterns which approximated that of normal males. Evidently, the nervous system of the hermaphrodites had become masculinized.

INFANT DIFFERENCES. In the preceding section, we explored the related evidence that there are differences in the central nervous system of males and females. Many researchers have looked for corresponding differences in the behaviors of male and female animals and children. In the latter case, they have looked for measurable differences before socialization has had a chance to occur.

Nancy Bayley (1968) and her colleagues at the University of California, Berkeley, examined 56 "normal" people from birth to age 36. They found evidence for differences in the course of cognitive or mental growth for boys and girls as well as different relationships between cognitive development and various personality variables. Only a few examples can be reported here.

Several consistent and stable correlations were found for boys between behaviors during the first three years of life, and personality variables, and verbal intelligence at a later age. However, for girls there were no striking consistencies between childhood behaviors and either concurrent or later intelligence. For both boys and girls, there were few exceptions to the general rule. For example, at age one, shyness and unhappiness were predictive of later high verbal scores for girls, but for boys at the same age, happiness was a predictor of later high verbal scores.

The quality of maternal behavior was found to affect the development of intelligence and personality-related behaviors. For boys, how mothers responded to them during the first three years had a permanent effect on their IQ scores as measured at 18 and 36 years of age. Hostility in mothers was related to low adult intelligence in their children while mother love was positively related to adult intelligence. In contrast, the girls' intelligence were not related to the maternal *handling* they received, but rather were correlated with measures of parental *ability*.

To summarize the above results and other findings of the Bayley report, it is suggested that hereditary factors may be more potent contributors to cognitive and related personality factors for females than for males. On the other hand, boys and men appear to be more susceptible to environmental influences than girls and women. This finding is supported by other evidence already discussed, such as males being more apt to develop physical or mental illnesses, to commit acts of violence, and to commit suicide. In addition, it has also been reported that after the atomic bombing of Hiroshima, male fetuses were more likely to be born dead or defective than female fetuses (Maccoby, 1966).

If we look at other primates, we find that the sex differences are consistent with the findings for humans. Within a month after birth, male rhesus monkeys are aggressive as manifested by wrestling, tugging, and biting. On the other hand, the female monkeys begin to behave in a shy manner and avoid fights with the males. Harlow (1962) similarly observed that male monkeys are much more aggressive and more likely to make threatening gestures in the face of attack than females. Grooming and play behavior were also found to sharply differentiate the sexes: caressing was more often initiated by the females but rough-and-tumble play was strictly for the males.

Harlow made some observations of human play at a second-grade picnic and found very similar sex differences to those he had seen in the monkeys. He concluded that the secondary sex differences in behavioral patterns probably exist throughout the primate order, and moreover, they are innately determined by biological factors regardless of cultural differences. The differences theorized in male and female brains and determined by genetic factors, hence, are reflected in the sex differences in behavior.

THE INTERACTION OF BIOLOGICAL AND CULTURAL DETERMINANTS. We have now covered the theories and evidence on the role of both biological and cultural factors that influence sex differences. These two categories of determinants, at first glance, seem to be in opposition to each other. However, the discrepancy is more apparent than real when we recognize that behavior is multidetermined; hence, these various cited factors usually appear to interact together rather than by themselves in determining sexual differences.

Children are not born with a built-in set of responses that will determine their behaviors irrespective of environmental influences. Neither is it true that children are born without any constitutional behavioral predispositions, destined to be molded solely by methods of socialization. Predispositions by the sexes to respond and act differently to stimuli are genetically determined and have their roots in physiology. The behaviors of children are then shaped and modified by the process of socialization. We suggest that most cultures reward the natural different predispositions of the sexes, thereby setting up different sex roles. In the remaining section of the chapter, we shall examine the observed sex differences in older children and adults without concentrating on the nature-nurture controversy. The concluding discussion on achievement will be an exception.

Sex differences in intelligence and aptitudes

General intelligence

Most authors today would probably agree that no difference in general intelligence exists between males and females, although many of the tasks that might be used in tests of general intelligence are known to involve a sex difference. The established measures of general intelligence have attempted to avoid those tasks that show a sex bias, and where sex biases still exist on certain subtests, they have been carefully balanced by opposite biases on other items. Thus, the most widely used tests such as the Binet and Wechsler are claimed to be unbiased in regard to sex.

In general, it would probably be valid to say that neither sex shows an overall superior intellectual ability. However, qualitative differences do appear to exist when we examine specific cognitive abilities. We shall look at those sex differences in cognitive abilities, but in so doing, we must not lose sight of the extensive overlapping which characterizes the distributions of the two sexes.

VERBAL SKILLS.   On the average, girls surpass boys in verbal or linguistic functions. This difference is found in almost every aspect of language development that has been investigated and has been reported with remarkable consistency by several investigators (Parlee, 1972). Observations on normal as well as on gifted and mentally retarded children show that girls begin to talk at an earlier age and have a larger vocabulary than boys before entering school. Girls learn to read at an earlier age than boys and throughout the school years maintain an advantage in grammar, spelling, and word fluency.

The accelerated articulatory patterns of girls, in comparison to boys, may provide a clue to the general female superiority in linguistic functions. The greater physical maturity of girls probably accounts for their more rapid progress in articulation, a motor function. This in turn may give them a large initial advantage in mastering all language functions and account, in part, for the much greater frequency of reading disabilities, stuttering, and stammering found among boys. The estimated ratios of male to female stutterers varies from 2:1 to 10:1, and from 1.6:1 to 2:1 in reading disability cases (Maccoby, 1966).

With the development of multiple-factor intelligence tests, which break down mental ability into its basic components or factors, it has proven possible to analyze sex differences in verbal functions more precisely. Studies of high school age groups with Thurstone tests of primary Mental Abilities show a significant difference in favor of girls in Word Fluency (W), but not in Verbal Comprehension (V), in which sex differences are insignificant and unreliable. Similar results are obtained with use of the Differential Aptitude Tests; girls excel in Language Usage but no sex difference is found on the Verbal Reasoning Test (Tyler, 1965). Hence, it is apparent that girls do relatively better in word fluency and in mastering the mechanics of language than they do in verbal comprehension and verbal reasoning tests.

NUMERICAL ABILITIES.   Males show greater superiority in solving mathematical tasks as noted by several investigators (Parlee, 1972). Boys typically do better on school achievement arithmetic tests requiring reasoning (story problems). However, at the lower age levels of kindergarten and below where only simple computation or mechanical arithmetic is involved, no sex differences are found. Likewise, among elementary school children and older subjects, computation tests most often show negligible sex differences. It is in mathematical reasoning or problem solving that males excel.

A few studies throw additional light upon sex differences in problem solving, and help account for the sex differences in numerical reasoning. Tyler (1965) suggests that females are usually less likely than men, in solving problems, to use the technique of restructuring; this involves discarding the first approach and reorganizing facts in new ways. For example, Sweeney (1953) reported a series of studies in which college males were significantly superior to coeds on a variety of problems requiring restructuring. This difference between the sexes persisted in spite of the fact that the groups had been equated for general intelligence, mathematical ability, relevant knowledge, and various background factors. Gall and Mendelsohn (1967) present some evidence that this difference is primarily a matter of attitude, and is susceptible to training. As one feature of their study, they used a technique that facilitated restructuring and proved very beneficial to the female subjects in problem solving; men, because they traditionally use it, were found to have benefited less.

Kostick (1954), in a study on high school seniors, found that boys were better able to transfer skill and knowledge in science and home economics to new situations. All of the above studies furnish promising leads for further research on sex differences. The extent to which these sex differences are due to ability to use restructuring and transfer basic skills to new situations also needs to be further explored.

MEMORY. Most studies agree that females outperform males on rote memory tasks. These tests, in general, require the exact repetition of a group of digits or words immediately after presentation, the recitation of a short story that has been read aloud, or the reproduction of geometrical figures that have been studied for a short time (Parlee, 1972). In all of these types of tasks, female superiority is the rule, although the sex differences are not nearly as large as in verbal or mathematical skills.

It is possible that these results are due to the role of verbal functions in facilitating retention or due to the fact that women seem to have more vivid mental imagery (see Chapter 5, on "Eidetic Imagery") than men in every sense modality (Nash, 1969). However, when we look at other memory tasks which involve general information or are of a quantitative nature, boys usually turn out to be superior to girls (Miele, 1958). To what extent these sex differences in memory reflect female superiority in verbal abilities, vivid imagery, or just the traditionally different sex roles cannot be ascertained from the data.

Motor skills

Different investigators have found that males generally surpass girls not only in muscular strength, but also in speed and coordination of gross bodily movements (Nash, 1969). This difference has been noted from infancy; Gesell and his co-workers (1940) found boys achieved superiority in walking a series of narrow boards and in throwing a ball over girls of the same age (preschool). Males have also been found to have shorter and more consistent reaction times (Kling & Riggs, 1971).

On the other hand, in tasks involving *manual dexterity*—light, swift movements of the hands—the advantage is with girls and women. This can be seen in early childhood as girls are usually able to dress themselves faster, and are also better able to wash their hands and turn door knobs (Nash, 1969). All of these everyday tasks involve "fine" movements of the fingers and wrists.

The greater manual dexterity of females is further indicated by the results of standardized tests used to predict success in different occupations requiring fine muscle movements. For example, women average consistently better than men on the O'Connor Dexterity Test, Crawford Small Parts Dexterity Test, and the Purdue Pegboard (Figure 14–4). It seems safe to conclude that on any job requiring dexterity and speed rather than strength, women can be expected to do at least as well as men, and probably better.

Spatial and clerical functions

In judgment and manipulation of spatial relationships, men consistently outperform women (Garai & Scheinfeld, 1968). Tests that require a subject to fit differently shaped pieces into the correct places on a form board show that from preschool levels to adult, males are generally more successful than females. In related findings, Witkin and associates (1962) report that females are much more prone to having their spatial orientation upset by conflicting visual cues than males. In his terms, females are more field-dependent and more apt to have their

FIGURE 14–4
The O'Connor Finger Dexterity Test. Women typically do better on tasks involving manual dexterity, shown below, than do men.

Courtesy of the Stoelting Company

perceptual judgments influenced by the context of a task than males. For example, women make larger errors on such tests as perception of the vertical within a tilted frame when given misleading visual cues. This work has received confirmation in a number of other cultures as well (Goodenough, 1963).

On clerical aptitude tasks, which involves the rapid perception of details and frequent shifts of attention, we find that women are definitely superior. Differences are large and unquestionably significant as illustrated by the fact that only 21 percent of employed male clerical workers reach or exceed the average for female clerical workers on the widely used Minnesota Clerical Test. Tyler (1965) in summarizing the evidence, reports that at all ages and grade levels, about 20 percent of the males exceed the average for females. Similar results have been demonstrated on other tests that emphasize perceptual speed.

Mechanical aptitudes

Mechanical aptitude tests cover a variety of functions, including dexterity, perceptual, and spatial aptitudes. But on some of the tests, mechanical reasoning and sheer mechanical information items predominate. We shall focus our discussion of sex differences only on the findings associated with the latter two mechanical functions.

A difference in favor of males has been repeatedly observed on tests depending upon mechanical information or comprehension. This is illustrated by the results of a study with the Bennett Test of Mechanical Comprehension (Form AA), administered to high school and adult groups. The males averaged much higher than the females as a group and made fewer errors on all the picture items (Bennett & Cruikshank, 1942).

An examination of the test manual for the Minnesota Mechanical Aptitude Tests shows sex differences in favor of males from seventh-grade children up to college sophomores. The largest sex difference appears on the Assembly Test, which requires subjects to put together common objects such as a spark plug or a bottle stopper from the given parts. Mention may also be made of the superiority of boys that has been found for assembling objects, puzzle boxes, and working slot mazes. These tasks probably demand spatial orientation as well as mechanical reasoning ability.

Creativity

It has been noted by many authors that males are more frequently recognized for creativity in the arts and other fields than are women. McCormack (1967) has written, concerning the life-styles of educated women in Eli Ginzberg's study of women who held fellowships at Columbia University from 1945 to 1951, that nothing emerges as clearly as their lack of style. Her overall impression of this group of women was that while they are intelligent and competent, they are rarely creative; performing necessary and useful services, but rarely critical. McCormack, in summing up her findings, states "they are in every sense of the word—socially, intellectually and economically—underemployed."

Many hypotheses have been put forth to account for the above common findings. Some theses support the idea that the bearing of children limits artistic creativity, with the biological creativity of pregnancy becoming the artistic-creativity of child-rearing. Others claim that the preoccupation of a woman with household work results in her inability to formulate a self-identity, making creativity impossible. Bardwick (1971), however, hypothesizes that while these may be contributing factors to the lack of feminine creativity, they are not the major ones. She believes the core factors to be sex differences in personality and differences in sex roles.

There are a few studies available that show many of the skills and personality qualities that relate to creativity also relate to sex differences. Hammer (1964) studied male high school students who had won art scholarships and found that the really creative males manifested high feminine characteristics, such as a high degree of sensitivity, and also male characteristics including independence, determination, and desire for power. Helson (1966) did a similar study on creative female college students and found they were also characterized by bisexuality, including such masculine traits as impulsiveness, rebelliousness, a mistrust of personal relationships, and an independence of judgment.

Both of these studies are supported by Getzels and Csikzentmihalui (1964), who found less difference between the male and female art students than between art students and other college students. The art students tended to be more socially reserved than other students and to avoid close personal contacts. Bisexuality was again exhibited by the art students; the females were more dominant than college women in general, while the males was more timid and sensitive.

Helson, like Bardwick, concludes from these studies and others that the main reason why more women are not creative is that they lack the masculine characteristics of assertiveness, independence, and use of logical thinking. Like the creative male, the creative female must have bisexual qualities including masculine traits of independence, ambition, dominance needs, and basic analytical skills. It is a fusion of masculine and feminine characteristics that marks the truly creative individual.

Sex differences in personality and motivation

We have frequently alluded to sex differences in nonintellectual traits in previous passages, and indeed, we find greater difference between males and females in terms of personality and motivation than in intellectual functions. This is reflected in Kimble, Garmezy and Zigler's (1974) summation of sex training differences and expectancies of parents in regard to personality traits of boys and girls. Boys are encouraged to be aggressive and to take responsibilities, while girls are encouraged to be dependent and helpless toward others; "tomboyishness" typically gains them few rewards.

Masculine and feminine tests of personality

An often used historical approach to sex differences has been to compare women and men on those responses which have proved to be most characteristic of each sex in our culture. A form of item analysis is used in which items are chosen that best differentiate between the sexes. Only those items marked by a significantly greater proportion of males or females are included on the test. Thus, if 50 percent of the men and 48 percent of the women indicated that they like modern jazz, the item would be discarded because it does not reflect sex differences.

The Terman-Miles study

The most thorough and comprehensive study of this type was that of Terman and Miles (1936). Their investigation had its origin years before in their discovery that gifted boys and girls differed markedly from each other along many personality dimensions. As a consequence, they developed a personality inventory called the Attitude-Interest Analysis Blank, which included seven different kinds of information: information, emotional and ethical response, word association, introversive response, inkblot association, interests, and opinions. This scale proved to be very useful in differentiating between men and women of all ages, occupational levels, and degrees of education. Overlapping of male and female distributions proved to be very slight. However, as Terman and Miles themselves pointed out, the method they used tends to exaggerate differences because items on which there were no differences were excluded from the final version of the scale.

Examination of their major findings revealed that the males evinced a strong interest in adventure, in physically strenuous occupations, in tools, inventions, physical phenomena, and sometimes, business. On the other hand, females showed a distinctive interest in domestic affairs, sedentary occupations, social welfare jobs, and aesthetic objects.

Closely paralleling these differences in choice of occupations and related activities were dissimilar emotional dispositions and directions. The males manifested greater self-assertion and aggressiveness, fearlessness, and more roughness of language, manners, and sentiments. The females, in contrast, manifested more emotional behavior, and greater compassion, aesthetic sensitivity, and timidity.

These masculine-feminine traits, of course, are not absolute in the sense that a person either has a trait or has not. Among men, athletes and engineers have the highest "masculine" averages while journalists, artists, and clergymen average the lowest. Among women, domestic employees have the most "feminine" profiles; athletes and doctors, the least "feminine." Differences are also found between age groups. In general, 8th-grade girls are more "feminine" and 11th-grade boys more "masculine" than any other age groups. We must be reminded again that individuals within any one of the occupational or age groups differ among themselves, and what we have is a continuous distribution rather than an exact classification.

A supplementary study was conducted by Terman and Miles in which they investigated the attitudes of male homosexuals. They report a marked difference between the homosexuals classified as passive (those who play the female role in homosexual relationships) and those classified as active (ones who play the male role). The PHM (passive male homosexuals) obtained significantly more feminine scores than average, while the AMH group (active male homosexuals) tended to be more masculine. Terman and Miles, after examining the case histories of several of the passive homosexuals, concluded that environmental rather than constitutional factors led to the development of homosexuality. Many of the subjects reported having been treated as a girl when growing up, and in many cases no adequate male model was available for them to emulate. These subjects further reported that their mothers overemphasized neatness and niceness of behavior.

CURRENT PERSPECTIVES. A number of M-F scales have been constructed since Terman and Miles' original work. For example, several of the general personality and interest inventories include M-F scales, such as the Strong Vocational Interest Test, and the MMPI (see Chapters 1 and 8, respectively). Research with these scales has shown repeatedly that masculinity or femininity is not a unidimensional trait. For instance, Barrows and Zuckerman (1960) found only low correlations between scores on the Strong and MMPI, and in addition, separate parts of the Terman and Miles test show little correlation with one another (Tyler, 1965). These investigators conclude that masculinity-femininity is not a clearly defined concept.

Because of the ambiguity about what any particular M-F scale is measuring we must be cautious about drawing psychiatric diagnostic conclusions from M-F scores or labeling someone either masculine or feminine. While general masculinity-femininity scales are still used in some research investigations, most investigators are currently focusing on more specific personality and motivational traits in regard to sex differences.

Emotional adjustment

A major personality area in which large differences are reported between the sexes is that of "neuroticism" or "maladjustment." This can be seen by examining the norms on several inventories. These show a tendency for women's averages to be closer to the maladjusted end of the scale than men's. For example, on the Bernreuter Personality Inventory, and Woodworth-Mathews Test of Emotional Instability, women score higher on neuroticism than men (Tyler, 1965). R. B. Cattell (1965) also found, in related findings, that women were far more emotionally sensitive than men. The women were more anxious, more impatient, and much more easily brought to tears by discouraging circumstances. These clear-cut sex differences, however, do not show up in groups younger than high school age. Just what these findings mean are not clear. One possible explanation is that as males and females learn more about their places in life, more women are dissatisfied with their sex role than men. Another equally plausible explanation put forth is that women are simply more willing than men to confess their emotional difficulties, since they are not taught to inhibit their feelings as are men. Both of these culturally based hypotheses make sense as opposed to strictly biological explanations, since statistics show more men have certain emotionally caused disorders, such as ulcers, than women (Coleman, 1972).

Some other investigations of children by nonquestionnaire methods, including field observation techniques, show that girls report more fears and worries than boys (Anastasi, 1958; Tyler, 1965). In addition, they present evidence that girls manifest more "nervous" habits, such as nail-biting and thumb-sucking. On the other hand, "behavioral" problems, such as juvenile delinquency, are much more common among boys (Coleman, 1972). These various findings may mean that the total amount of instability is no different between the two sexes during childhood, but is just manifested in other ways. Girls may simply resort to milder and less violent ways of expressing maladjustment than boys, because of socially placed restrictions and differences in sex roles.

Differences in interpersonal relationships

It is almost a universal finding that females are more interested and dependent upon people than are males. A large number of studies based on a variety of measuring techniques and subjects of all ages from preschool to adulthood could be cited to show this (Smith, 1968). For example, girls typically reflect more need for affiliation, as shown in their stories for the Thematic Apperception Test pictures (see Chapter 8). In an interesting study that further reveals the extent of the affiliation need in females, a psychologist devised an experiment in which women students at a university upon arriving at his laboratory to take part in his study found a frightening looking piece of apparatus and were told that its function was to deliver electric shocks. After being made anxious about the nature of the experiment, they were told that they could either wait alone or in the company of other subjects. As it turned out, the majority of the women indicated they preferred to wait in the company of others rather than alone, thereby demonstrating a high affiliation need (Kagan & Havemann, 1972).

As would be expected because of their greater social responsiveness, women are found to be more considerate than men, and more observant of the rights and feelings of others. This superiority was evident in a well-known experiment where men and women performed three observational tasks (Witryol & Kaess, 1957). Two relatively easy tasks required males and females to recall the names associated with photographs; the women proved to be the better on both. In the third more difficult task, five men and five women were given aliases and assigned to a group in which the experimenter conducted an interview with each subject. In every interview the interviewee spoke his or her alias at least once. The results showed, again, that the women were much better in remembering names than men, when asked later to match the person with the correct alias. Witryol and Kaess concluded that their data was a reflection of society's greater emphasis upon the acquisition of social skills for females than is the case for males.

As previously noted, the greater interest of females in people and in interpersonal relationships is evident early in infancy (Bakan, 1966). In play activity, girls tend to use more family figures, fewer vehicles, and prefer stories about family life more than the stories of adventure preferred by boys. Girls are more concerned with personal attractiveness and family relationships while boys are more interested or worried about physical health, safety, and money. Furthermore, girls show more motherly behavior and more often have fantasies concerning people.

Differences in male-female outlooks

One of the most comprehensive analyses of masculinity-femininity was made by Bennett and Cohen (1959). They conducted a study of 1,300 subjects, ranging in age from 15 to 64, wherein each participant was asked to choose sets of words that described him most and least well. All of the words had to do with wishes, values, and the social environment. Although the choices made by the men and women were more similar than different, some characteristic sex differences did show up on some of the words. After analyzing all of the differences in detail, Bennett and Cohen summarized their findings under five general principles. They are as follows:

1. Masculine thinking is a modification downward in intensity of feminine thinking.
2. Masculine thinking is oriented more in terms of the self while feminine thinking is oriented more in terms of the environment.
3. Masculine thinking anticipates rewards and punishments determined more as a result of the adequacy or inadequacy of the self while feminine thinking anticipates rewards and punishments determined more as a result of the friendship or hostility of the environment.

4. Masculine thinking is associated more with desire for personal achievement; feminine thinking is associated more with desire for social love and friendship.
5. Masculine thinking finds value more in malevolent and hostile actions against a competitive society, while feminine thinking finds value more in freedom from restraint in a friendly and pleasant environment.

Interests and values

That specific interests and values, besides overall social orientation, vary between adult men and women, is apparent from everyday observations. A comprehensive early study was carried out by Strong (1943), which supports this conclusion. He tabulated item responses made by representative samples of men and women and attached scoring weights to those that showed large differences, thereby obtaining an M-F (masculinity-femininity) key on his Strong Vocational Interest Test. Strong found more similarities than differences in scoring most items. However, he did find that certain kinds of items differentiated between the sexes. The distinctly masculine interests show up in (1) mechanical and scientific activities; (2) physically strenuous and adventuresome activities; (3) certain forms of entertainment such as smoking and chess; and (4) legal, political, and military occupations.

Strong feminine interests, on the other hand, are indicated on items having to do with (1) literary activities; (2) musical, artistic activities; (3) certain kinds of entertainment, e.g., fortune-tellers, full-dress affairs, and movies dealing with human or social problems; and (4) social work, clerical work, and teaching.

As would be expected, men and women also differ considerably on the occupational scales of the Strong Vocational Interest Test. Men score higher on the scales for science and business whereas women usually average considerably higher on the scales for occupations involving art, social service, and writing. However, if groups of men and women of the same profession are compared instead of sample groups representing all males and females, the interests of the two sexes are practically indistinguishable. Men and women doctors, for instance, have comparable interests, as do life insurance agents of both sexes.

Similar findings have been obtained on the *Kuder Preference Record*, also designed to measure vocational interests, in which various types of activities are presented in groups of three. Women and men of the same occupational groups again show very similar interest patterns, but most males and females in general do not.

As previously alluded to in the chapter, there is evidence that there is a shift taking place in the interests of girls; their interests are becoming more like those of boys. Rosenberg and Sutton-Smith (1960) have presented evidence that the trend toward the masculinization of the interests of girls continues to increase. In their checklist experiment involving traditionally male and female play activities, girls checked many of the "masculine" activities as characteristic of them. These results were confirmed in a more comprehensive experiment performed later by the same authors (Rosenberg & Sutton-Smith, 1964).

Study of values

The Allport-Vernon-Lindzey *Study of Values* was designed to measure the prominence of six basic evaluative attitudes: theoretical, economic, aesthetic, social, political, and religious. Each item requires the preferential rating of either two or four alternatives falling in different value categories; sample items are illustrated in Figure 14–5.

Significant sex differences have been obtained on the *Study of Values*. Women typically score highest in the aesthetic, social, and religious values. This suggests that artistic experiences, the social welfare of others, and spiritual values are relatively important in the life-style of the women. In contrast, the profile for men shows an emphasis on theoretical, economic, and political values. Such a profile reflects an interest in the intellectual or rational approach, a desire for practical success and money, and a drive for personal power, influence, and prestige. These differences in values, however, are not very great and there is considerable overlapping between the sexes. As in the case of occupational interests,

FIGURE 14–5
Sample items from the Allport-Vernon-Lindzey *Study of Values*, 3d ed.

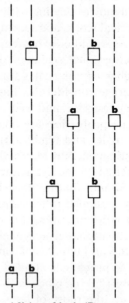

17. The aim of the churches at the present time should be: (a) to bring out altruistic and charitable tendencies; (b) to encourage spiritual worship and a sense of communion with the highest.

18. If you had some time to spend in a waiting room and there were only two magazines to choose from, would you prefer: (a) <u>Scientific Age</u>; (b) <u>Arts and Decorations</u>?

19. Would you prefer to hear a series of lectures on: (a) the comparative merits of the forms of government in Britain and in the United States; (b) the comparative development of the great religious faiths?

20. Which of the following would you consider the more important function of education? (a) its preparation for practical achievement and financial reward; (b) its preparation for participation in community activities and aiding less fortunate persons.

Source: G. Allport, Vernon, and Lindzey, *Study of Values*, 3d ed. (Boston: Houghton Mifflin Company, 1960).

far larger differences have been found between various occupational groups of the same sex than between men and women in general.

The results obtained from the *Study of Values* and the occupational interests tests all show the greater underlying social orientation or sensitivity of women. These differences develop very early, not only in American children but also in English and Finnish children (Tyler, 1965). One possible explanation of the greater social values of girls may be their accelerated language development, which gives them an advantage in communicating with other children. Also of prime importance are the subtle social pressures that exist in Western cultures, which stress socially oriented interests for females, more so than is the case for males.

Aggressiveness and dominance

One of the most pronounced sex differences is to be found in the area of aggressiveness. A large number of studies have shown that males are more aggressive than females. Oetzel (1966) in his comprehensive bibliography, included more than 60 studies based on observation, rating, experiments, projective techniques, and self-report inventories. The great majority of these reported that males of all ages turned out to be significantly more aggressive than females. Only in a few cases did girls turn up with higher aggression scores, and these were in terms of verbal rather than physical aggression. Moreover, women and girls consistently gave evidence of greater anxiety and guilt about aggression than did men and boys.

Sex differences in aggressiveness may help to account for the fact that more boys are referred to clinics for treatment of behavioral problems and the fact that the bulk of all violent crimes are committed by males. Homicide rates are 5 times as high for males as compared to females, and for robbery the figure is 20 times as great (Johnson, 1972).

SEX HORMONES AND AGGRESSION. For centuries, it has been common knowledge that castrated male animals become relatively tame. For instance, castration reduces a savage bull into a plodding ox, and many pet owners have their dogs and cats "fixed" to render them more docile. Analogous castrations have also been carried out with humans for therapeutic purposes. LeMaire (1965) writes about such operations performed on prison convicts in Indiana, in which their successes in reducing criminality led to the passage of the first castration laws (later repealed). Germany, Switzerland, and Denmark have legalized such treatment although the number of cases reported is relatively small. Based on the few hundred cases studied, it would seem that castration leads to docile behavior and low incidence of recidivism (Johnson, 1972).

The importance of sex hormones for humans as well as for animals can also be seen in the dramatic increase in competitive behavior which usually accompanies puberty. The most important hormone with respect to aggression is testosterone, one of the male androgen sex hormones that initiates puberty in males when it begins circulating in quantity. This is readily seen in most species of animals and a multitude of experiments show that the aggressive behavior of both sexes increases with injections of testosterone. In the case of humans, the role of hormones in aggression, as we have seen with sexual behavior, is less important.

SEX TYPING AND AGGRESSION. As previously discussed, social norms dictate what is masculine and feminine behavior. Sex roles are so defined in Western civilizations that aggressiveness is considered to be a masculine trait while women are supposed to be more submissive. Hence, aggressiveness is more apt to be rewarded for young boys than for young girls.

The importance of sex-role development and its relation to aggressive behavior is illustrated by an experiment involving binocular rivalry with a stereoscope (Moore, 1966). Males and females were shown two pictures simultaneously, a different picture for each eye. One picture depicted a man with a dagger in his back whereas the other, considerably more passive in theme, showed a mailman. The pictures were flashed on and off a screen very rapidly which created a "rivalry" over which elements would be best seen. Males were found to perceive violence significantly more than females, and the difference increased with age. Hence, the results showed the importance of previous experience (as reflected in age) and type of experience (reflected in age) in affecting the perception of aggression. A similar experiment was conducted by Toch and Schulte (1961) in comparing men who had just completed a program in police administration with others who were just starting. They discovered that the men just finishing the program were more likely to see violence or aggression.

Thus, society exerts its influence on the observed sex differences in the amount of aggression by its definitions of sex roles. It is interesting to note, in regard to this interpretation, that where cultural roles are more nearly equal for males and females, the sex differences in criminal offenses are fewer.

Achievement

For many years, one set of facts on sex differences has challenged various investigators. The question is, "Why have women made so few major contributions to civilization in contrast to men?" History has recorded the names and achievements of many men, but only a relatively few women have become famous. J. McK. Cattell's (1903) list of the 1,000 most renowned persons in the world includes only 32 women, some of which were emininent because of circumstances of royal birth rather than from achievements of their own. His findings were supported by Ellis (1904) who found only 55 women in his total group of 1,030 British geniuses. Similar findings have been recorded on famous Americans. For example, the 1927 edition of *American Men of Science* lists only 725 women out of 9,785 entries. Nash (1969), in summarizing more recent findings, notes that males are much more frequently recognized for feats in the arts and other fields than are women. This is true even in the fields traditionally assigned to women such as dress designing, interior decorating, and cooking. In the latter case, the greatest chefs of all time have been men, in spite of the fact that in most cases the preparation of meals is done by women.

In contrast to all of the data showing greater achievement for adult males, most studies of school achievement agree that girls consistently outperform boys in classroom work. More of them receive higher grades and fewer of them receive unsatisfactory marks. These differences are very large, as is shown in a typical survey (Northby, 1958) of high school graduates in Connecticut high schools. In breaking the distribution of grade point averages down into tenths of percentages, the predominance of girls in the high categories and boys in the low categories is very striking. For instance, girls constituted 72 percent of the top tenth and only 36 percent of the bottom tenth.

Several major types of explanations have been put forth to explain these differences in achievement. The first has to do with differences in special aptitudes as already discussed. As we have seen, girls consistently do better in verbal tasks, which probably results in feminine superiority in almost all school subjects, most of which depend upon language functions.

The differing rates of maturation between the sexes has also been offered as a hypothesis to explain the differences in school achievement. The fact that girls are accelerated in physical development and reach puberty earlier than boys may be reflected in more mature study habits. Although physical and mental traits do not correlate highly, Ames and Ilg (1964) found that girls in kindergarten through second grade scored significantly higher on four school aptitude learning tasks. The most popular, or favored, interpretation of differences in school performance relates them to sex differences in motivation.

NEED-ACHIEVEMENT MOTIVATION. As you will recall, need achievement may be simply defined as a desire to be successful. The person with a high-achievement motivation has developed an internal standard of excellence and takes pride in doing tasks well; but while men typically show a higher need achievement than women, this model has been proven to predict well the direction and persistence of achievement behaviors in male students; it has not in females. This discrepancy is probably because of different standards of success for males and females. In most industrial societies, success for men is defined in terms of the marketplace, whereas women are rewarded for social success. Hence, because of these cultural value judgments, females may feel ambivalent about any accomplishments on the job for fear of alienating others who might consider them "masculine." This ambivalence, according to most theorists, is resolved in many girls by their internalization of the cultural standards. They add feminine-role activities to the usual academic grade-point indicator of success. After school, women may strive to be the best possible housekeeper, to excel in charity causes, to raise outstanding children, or to be the wives of very successful men. None of these activities, of course, will get them listed in *Who's Who in America*, or in the history books.

To summarize the above theory on need achievement for women, many internalize the sex-role related definitions of success. Interpersonal accomplishments replace earlier academic-vocational deeds as the relevant measures of success. Men, of course, maintain the latter standard.

ACHIEVEMENT MOTIVES IN BOYS AND GIRLS. Evidence for this hypothesis may be obtained by examining measures of achievement taken with children. Do boys and girls show a similar desire to excel and, if so, at what age do differences emerge similar to the adult patterns?

In one comprehensive study of children in the first to third grades, no sex differences were found in test measures of achievement or in competition, intellectual, and play activities. Other differences, however, were found. The girls were found to lack confidence and expected to fail in various tasks in which the boys expected to succeed. The girls tended to blame themselves for intellectual failure while boys projected the blame onto others. In related findings, the brighter the girl, the less expectations she had of being successful on intellectual tasks, while boys, overall, set higher standards for themselves (Crandall, Katkowsky, & Preston, 1962). These results are supported in a study made of children in nursery school, ages three to five. No sex differences were found in achievement efforts, but in contrast to the boys, the girls lacked confidence in their work and looked for help and approval from adults. (Crandall & Rabson, 1960).

Relative changes in need achievement, however, take place in adolescence, as seen by the significant strides made by boys in their academic efforts. They become more involved in specific content areas and began to see academic and vocational success as part of their masculine role. Girls, on the other hand, although they do not necessarily suffer a decline in academic performance, do not become committed to a vocational identity. For many girls, academic competition threatens a more valued social prestige. As Margaret Mead so aptly stated, in our culture boys are unsexed by failure and girls by success (Rostow, 1964).

From our discussion, it seems quite evident that the greater vocational successes of men are primarily because of cultural sex-role expectations, as manifested in sex differences in the motive to achieve. High-speed achievers also tend to have "masculine" personality characteristics which will be reflected in vocational success, such as self-confidence, enjoyment of taking moderate risks, and the liking of individual responsibilities.

Summary

The fact that many women in our society are no longer content with their traditional sex roles may indicate that it occupies a less desirable position in our society than roles assigned to men. Sexism is the label used to denote any attitude, action, or institutional structure that subordinates a person because of sex. This second-class citizenship for women is seen in religion, language, income, career status, and even psychotherapy. The task of bearing and nursing children provides a biological reason for keeping women at home, and man's greater muscular strength makes possible his participation in more strenuous activities. Once the division of labor is established, complex regulation by social pressure sets in and familiar ways of doing things are enforced by taboo and prejudice.

First, many theories of personality perpetuate the belief that women are inferior to their male counterparts. Freud believed that the female suffers from "penis envy" and Adler stressed the "masculine protest" in which inferiority and weakness is equated with femininity. Second, sex typing by parents and society has set up artificial distinctions between sex-appropriate roles. Boys are reinforced for aggressive behaviors while girls are discouraged from them. Third, anthropological studies indicate how cultural values affect sex-role identity. Emotionality and occupations (apart from those requiring muscular strength) of people throughout the world have strong cultural components. Fourth, social class also influences sex-appropriate roles. Findings indicate that lower-class boys are usually the first to clearly identify themselves with sex roles whereas middle-class girls are the last. Fifth, the presence or absence of siblings is important. Children with an older sibling of the same sex tend to have their sex typing speeded up.

Many individuals believe that segregation of the sexes is the result of biological and not exclusively social determinants. To understand the impact of biology on sex differences, we must turn to biological studies conducted on men and women.

The fact that females inherit two XX chromosomes as opposed to an X and Y for the male may account for many physical differences. In all human societies, men are taller, heavier, stronger, and have greater vitality. Women, on the other hand, are accelerated developmentally throughout childhood and reach physical maturity earlier. Furthermore, they show greater viability and capacity to maintain life over the male.

Recent evidence suggests the development in the embryo of a male and female brain that may have effects on psychological functioning as a result of the sex hormones. These findings along with others indicate that hereditary factors may be more potent contributors to cognitive and related personality factors for females than males.

The nature-nurture controversy cannot be easily resolved. Evidence suggests that behavior is multidetermined. Predispositions by the sexes to respond and act differently to stimuli are genetically determined and have their roots in physiology. The behaviors of children are then shaped and modified by the process of socialization. Most cultures tend to reward natural predispositions by sex typing. Many of these sex roles, however, go far beyond the natural boundaries set by our physiology.

Differences between the sexes have not been found in overall intelligence although qualitative differences seem to exist. On the average, girls surpass boys in verbal or linguistic functions while males show greater superiority in solving mathematical tasks. Females are also superior on tasks of memory which may be because of more vivid mental imagery.

With respect to motor skills, males surpass females in strength, speed, and coordination of gross bodily movements: they also excel in tasks of spatial relations. Women are superior on tasks involving motor dexterity, rapid perception of details, and frequent shifts of attention. On tests of mechanical comprehension and information, men perform much better.

It has been noted by many people that males are more frequently recognized for creativity in the arts and other fields. Many hypotheses have been put forth to account for these findings. Sex-role differences in personality and motivation have been proposed as one dominant theory.

Differences in occupational interests and personality (assertiveness and adventurous) and emotional adjustment have been observed between the sexes. Other findings are that women tend to be more socially and interpersonally oriented than men.

Achievement differences between the sexes indicate that girls consistently outperform boys in classroom work which may be a manifestation of earlier maturation or superior language functions. However, achievement in later life tends to favor males. It seems quite clear that greater vocational successes of men are primarily because of cultural sex-role expectations as manifested in sex differences in the motive to achieve.

References

Ames, L. B., & Ilg, F. L. Sex differences in test performance of matched girl-boy pairs in the five-to-nine-year-old range. *Journal of Genetic Psychology*, 1964, **104**, 25–34.

Anastasi, A. *Differential psychology: Individual and group differences in behavior*, 3d ed. New York: Crowell-Collier-Macmillan, 1958.

Anderson, E. C., & Langham, W. H. Average potassium concentration of the human body as a function of age, *Science*, 1959, **130**, 713–714.

Astin, H. S. Employment and career status of women psychologists. *American Psychologist*, 1972, **27**, 371–381.

Bakan, D. *The duality of human existence: An essay on psychology and religion*. Chicago: Rand McNally, 1966.

Bardwick, N. *Psychology of women*. New York: Harper & Row, 1971.

Barrows, G. A., & Zuckerman, M. Construct validity of three masculinity-femininity tests. *Journal of Consulting Psychology*, 1960, **24**, 441–445.

Bayley, N. Behavioral correlates of mental growth: Birth to thirty-six years. *American Psychologist*, 1968, **23**, 1–17.

Bell, R. Q., & Darling, J. F. The prone head reaction in the human neonate. *Child Development*, 1965, **36**, 943–949.

Bem, S., & Bem, D. J. Case study of a non-conscious ideology: Training the woman to know her place. In D. J. Bem, *Beliefs, attitudes, and human affairs.* Monterey, Calif.: Brooks/Cole, 1970.

Bennett, E. M., & Cohen, L. R. Men and women: Personality patterns and contrasts. *Genetic Psychological* Monograms, 1959, **59**, 101–155.

Bennett, G. K., & Cruikshank, R. M. Sex differences in the understanding of mechanical problems. *Journal of Applied Psychology*, 1942, **26**, 121–127.

Broverman, I. K., & Broverman, D. Sex-role stereotypes and clinical judgments of mental health. *Journal of Consulting and Clinical Psychology*, 1970, **34**, 1–7.

Cattell, J. M. A statistical study of eminent men. *Popular Science Monographs*, 1903, **62**, 359–377.

Cattell, R. B. *The scientific analysis of personality.* Chicago: Aldine, 1965.

Coleman, J. C. *Abnormal psychology and modern life.* Glenview, Ill.: Scott, Foresman, 1972.

Crandall, V., Katkowsky W., & Preston, A. Motivational and ability determinants of young children's intellectual achievement behaviors. *Child Development*, 1962, **33**, 643–661.

Crandall, V., & Rabson, A. Children's repetition choices in an intellectual achievement situation following success and failure. *Journal of Genetic Psychology*, 1960, **97**, 161–168.

Delworth, U. Raising consciousness about sexism. *Personnel and Guidance Journal*, 1973, **51**, 672–674.

Ellis, H. A. *A Study of British genius.* London: Hurst, 1904.

Fouls, L. B., & Smith, W. S. Sex-role learning of five-year olds. *Journal of Genetic Psychology*, 1956, **53**, 105–116.

Gall, M., & Mendelsohn, G. A. Effects of facilitating techniques and subject-experimenter interaction on creative problem solving. *Journal of Personality and Social Psychology*, 1967, **5**, 211–216.

Garai, J. E., & Scheinfeld, A. Sex differences in mental and behavioral traits. *Genetic Psychology Monographs*, 1968, **77**(2), 169–299.

Gesell, A., et al. *The first five years of life.* New York: Harper, 1940.

Getzels, J., & Csilzentmihalui, M. *Creative thinking in art students.* Chicago: University of Chicago Press, 1964.

Goldberg, P. A. Are women prejudiced against women? *Trans-action*, 1968, 20–28.

Goldberg, S., & Lewis, M. Play behavior in the year-old infant: Early sex differences. *Child Development*, 1969, **40**, 21–31.

Goodenough, D. R. Sex differences in psychological differentiation. Paper read at the Society for Research in Child Development, biennial meeting, Berkeley, California, 1963.

Hall, E. T. *The hidden dimension.* Garden City, N.Y.: Anchor Books, 1966.

Hammer, E. Creativity and feminine ingredients in young male artists. *Perceptual and Motor Skills*, 1964, **19**, 414.

Harlow, H. F. The heterosexual affectional system in monkeys. *American Psychologist*, 1962, **17**, 1–9.

Harris, G. W. The central nervous system and the endocrine glands. *Triangle*, 1964, **6**, 242–251.

Helson, R. Personality of women with imaginative and artistic interests: The role of masculinity, originality, and other characteristics in their creativity. *Journal of Personality*, 1966, **34**, 1–25.

Hetherington, E. M. The effects of familial variables on sex-role typing, parent-child similarity and imitation in children. In J. P. Hill (Ed.), *Minnesota symposia on child psychology*, Vol. 1, Minneapolis: University of Minnesota Press, 1968.

Johnson, R. N. *Aggression in man and animals.* Philadelphia: W. B. Saunders, 1972.

Kagan, J., & Havemann, E. *Psychology: An introduction.* New York: Harcourt Brace Jovanovich, 1972.

Kelly, E. L. Consistency of the adult personality. *American Psychologist*, 1955, **10**, 659–681.

Kimble, G. A., Garmezy, N., & Zigler, E. *Principles of general psychology.* New York: Ronald Press, 1974.

Kling, J. W., & Riggs, L. A. *Woodworth and Schlosberg's experimental psychology.* New York: Holt, Rinehart & Winston, 1971.

Kostick, M. M. Study of transfer: Sex differences in the reasoning process. *Journal of Educational Psychology*, 1954, **45**, 449–458.

Le Maire. Castration of sexual offenders. *Journal of Criminal Law and Criminology*, 1956, **47**, 294–310.

MacBrayer, C. T. Differences in perception of the opposite sex by males and females. In D. L. Schueffer (Ed.), *Sex differences in personality readings.* Belmont, Calif.: Brooks/Cole, 1971.

Maccoby, E. E. (Ed.). *Development of sex differences.* Stanford, Calif.: Stanford University Press, 1966. (a)

Maccoby, E. E. Sex differences in intellectual functioning. In E. E. Maccoby (Ed.), *The development of sex differences.* Stanford Calif.: Stanford University Press, 1966.

McCandless, B. R. *Children and adolescents: Behavior and development.* New York: Holt, Rinehart & Winston, 1961.

McCormack, T. Styles in educated females. *The Nation 23,* January 17, 1967.

Mead, M. *Sex and temperament in three primitive societies.* New York: Morrow, 1935.

Mead, M. *Male and female.* New York: Morrow, 1949.

Melzack, R. The perception of pain. *Scientific American,* 1961, **204**(2), 28, 41–49.

Miele, J. A. Sex differences in intelligence: The relationship of sex to intelligence as measured by the Wechsler Adult Intelligence Scale and the Wechsler Intelligence Scale for Children. Dissertation Abstracts, 1958, **18**, 2213.

Moore, M. Aggression themes in a binocular rivalry situation. *Journal of Personality and Social Psychology,* 1966, **3**, 685–688.

Munzinger, H. *Fundamentals of child development.* New York: Holt, Rinehart, & Winston, 1971.

Mussen, P. H., Conger, J. J., & Kagen, J. *Child development and personality.* New York: Harper & Row, 1969.

Mussen, P., & Parker, A. Mother nurturance and girls' incidental imitative learning. *Journal of Personality and Social Psychology,* 1965, **2**, 94–97.

Nash, J. *Developmental psychology: a psychobiological approach.* Englewood Cliffs, N.J.: Prentice-Hall, 1969.

Northby, A. S. Sex differences in high school scholarship. *School and Society,* 1958, **86**, 63–64.

Oetzel, R. Annotated bibliography. In E. E. Maccoby (Ed.), *The development of sex differences.* Stanford, Calif.: Stanford University Press, 1966.

Parlee, M. B. Comments on "Roles of activation and inhibition in sex differences in cognitive abilities" by D. M. and W. Vogel. *Psychological Review,* 1972, **79**, 2, 180–184.

Phoenix, C. H., Goy, R. W., Gerall, A. A., & Young, W. C. Organizing action of prenatally administered testosterone propionate on the tissues mediating mating behavior in the female guinea pig. *Endocrinology,* 1959, **65**, 369–382.

Rabbin, M. Sex role identification in young children in two diverse social groups.

Genetic Psychological Monograms, 1950, **42**, 81–158.

Rogers, D. *Child psychology.* Belmont, Calif.: Brooks/Cole, 1969.

Rosenberg, B. G., & Sutton-Smith, B. A revised conception of masculine-feminine differences in play activities. *Journal of Genetic Psychology,* 1960, **96**, 165–170.

Rosenberg, B. G., & Sutton-Smith, B. The measurement of masculinity and femininity in children: An extension and revalidation. *Journal of Genetic Psychology,* 1964, **104**, 259–264.

Rostow, E. Conflict and accommodation. Spring 1964, 93.

Sears, R. R., Maccoby, E. E., & Levin, H. *Patterns of child rearing.* New York: Harper & Row, 1957.

Smith, H. C. *Personality development.* New York: McGraw-Hill, 1968.

Stern, P. The womanly image: Character assassination through the ages. *The Atlantic Monthly,* March 1970.

Strong, E. K., Jr. *Vocational interests of men and women.* Stanford, Calif.: Stanford University Press, 1943.

Sutton-Smith, R., Roberts, J. M., & Rosenberg, B. C. Sibling associations and role involvement. *Merrill-Palmer Quarterly,* 1964, **10**, 25–38.

Sweeney, E. J. Sex differences in problem solving. Stanford, Calif.: Department of Psychology, Stanford University Technical Report 1, Dec. 1, 1953.

Terman, L. M., & Miles, C. C. *Sex and personality: Studies in masculinity and femininity.* New York: McGraw-Hill, 1936.

Toch, H. M., & Schulte, W. H. Readiness to perceive violence as the result of police training. *British Journal of Psychology,* 1961, **52**, 389–394.

Tyler, L. E. *The psychology of human differences.* New York: Appleton-Century-Crofts, 1965.

Williams, R. J. *Biochemical individuality.* New York: Wiley, 1956.

Witkin, H. A., et al. *Physiological differentiation: Studies of development.* New York: Wiley, 1962.

Witryol. S. L., & Kaess, W. A. Sex differences in social memory tasks. *Journal of Abnormal and Social Psychology,* 1957, **54**, 343–346.

GLOSSARY

Glossary

Acetylcholine A transmitter chemical in the nervous system.

Achievement motive A motive to accomplish something difficult or to excel.

Acute refractory period A time interval usually following orgasm in which the man will not respond to sexual stimulation.

Adolescence A term used to refer to the process of growing up, the period of transition from childhood to adulthood.

Affective psychosis A form of psychosis in which the predominant disorder is one of mood.

Affiliation A social motive involving the desire to be with other individuals.

Aggression A social motive that takes such form as direct physical attack or occurs in a more symbolic nature as trying to destroy the opposition with words.

Aging The biological and psychosocial aspects of change in a person from birth to death.

Agnosia The inability to recognize familiar objects after damage to an association area.

Alcoholism Physiological dependence on alcohol.

Alienation An estrangement from the values of one's society, family, or self.

Alpha rhythm A regular wave pattern in the EEG, found in most subjects when they close their eyes and relax.

Altruism A social motive involving the helping of others as an end in itself.

Amnesia A total or partial inability to recall or identify personal experiences.

Amphetamine One type of drug that produces a psychologically stimulating and energizing effect.

Amphetamine psychosis A psychotic disorder brought about by excessive usage of amphetamines.

Anal stage The second stage of personality development according to Freud's psychoanalytic theory of personality development. It occurs around the second year of life for the child when he is attempting to gain control over bowel movements.

Analytical psychology A school of personality and psychotherapy, formed by Carl Jung who broke away from Freud and his psychoanalytic theory of personality development. Jung de-emphasized the importance of sex and stressed that man is goal oriented in his behavior. In addition, he believed man inherited racial memories.

Androgen A male sex hormone.

Antisocial personality A disorder characterized by illegal acts and immature forms of behavior.

Anvil Small bone in the middle ear located between the hammer and the stirrup.

Apathy An apparent indifference to the plight of others.

Aphasia A language disorder normally caused by damage or disease of the brain.

Aerial perspective Clearness of details under different atmospheric conditions. Objects with clear details appear nearer than hazy objects, thereby serving as a cue for depth perception.

Assertive training A behavioral technique using aggressive responses to counteract anxiety.

Association area A general term for areas of the cortex outside the primary, sensory, and motor areas.

Astigmatism A visual defect characterized by clear vision in one dimension and unfocused, fuzzy vision in the other.

Attention The process of psychological selectivity or perceptual focusing on certain stimuli.

Attractiveness The factors that make an individual likable.

Auditory canal Part of the outer ear which receives the sound wave.

Authority set See sets.

Autokinetic effect The apparent movement of light when one is in a darkened room and shown a pinpoint of light.

Aversive conditioning Using classical conditioning to associate painful or unpleasant experiences to a particular stimulus.

Axon A nerve fiber that transmits impulses from the cell body to an adjacent neuron or to an effector.

Barbiturate Depressant drug that causes sedation and sleep.

Basilar membrane A membrane at the base of the cochlear canal. Its movements play an important role in stimulating the auditory nerve.

Beatnik See social dropouts.

Behaviorism A systematic position, vigorously expounded by John B. Watson, which maintains that the subject matter of psychology is behavior, not conscious experience.

Behavior therapy A method of therapy in which learning principles are applied to the treatment of behavior disorders.

Bestiality A state in which individual's primary sexual desire is directed toward animals.

Beta rhythm Fast irregular small waves in the EEG, characteristic of mental activity.

Biofeedback Voluntary bodily regulation through the feedback of information from internal organs.

Bizarreness Abnormal deviations from accepted standards of behavior that are usually dramatically different and unique (hallucinations, murder, etc.)

Brain The part of the nervous system encased in the skull. It contains the centers for sensory experience, motivation, learning and thinking.

Brightness The intensity aspect of light; the visual dimension represented by the black-white continuum.

Brightness constancy The tendency for an object to be seen as maintaining the same intensity of brightness despite the different sensations it emits, depending upon the amount of illumination present.

Castration The removal of male or female sex organs.

Castration anxiety According to Freud's psychoanalytic theory of personality development, the boy resolves his Oedipus complex during the phallic stage by experiencing fear that his father will castrate him. As a result, the son identifies with the father to remove his fear of castration over his sexual desires for the mother.

Catatonic schizophrenia A form of schizophrenia in which psychomotor disorders predominate such as peculiar gestures and postures.

Central nervous system One main division of the nervous system that consists of the brain and spinal cord.

Cerebellum A structure in the hindbrain that controls body posture, and coordinates body movements and equilibrium.

Cerebral cortex The gray matter covering the cerebrum.

Cerebrotonia A dimension of personality characterized by love of privacy, aloofness, and introvert tendencies.

Chromosome A long chainlike structure found in cells containing genes.

Clairvoyance The claimed ability to perceive what is happening elsewhere without the use of the regular senses.

Classical conditioning The experimental method of learning used by Pavlov. A conditioned stimulus is paired with an unconditioned stimulus.

Client-centered therapy A method of therapy in which the therapist accepts, restates, and clarifies the client's feelings. The whole process is aimed at giving the client an opportunity to solve his own problems.

Cochlea A coiled structure on the basilar membrane of the inner ear where the sound wave stimulates receptors.

Coercive power See power.

Cognitive dissonance A theory which states that a person will change an opinion, belief, or behavior to make it consistent with others.

Cognitive processes Thinking and associated processes that play a vital role in complex learning.

Color blindness A weakness or defect in sensitivity to hue; the most common type is red-green blindness in which the individual has difficulty in distinguishing red and green from grays of the same brightness.

Color solid A means of showing the relationships between the three qualities of color.

Compensation A defense mechanism in which individuals may develop certain attitudes, interests, or skills to overcome one's deficiencies in other areas.

Compliance A change in *overt behavior* because of social pressure that occurs without regard for private convictions.

Compulsions See obsessive-compulsive reactions.

Conditioned response The response which is evoked by the conditioned stimulus after conditioning has taken place.

Conditioned stimulus The "neutral" stimulus which is paired with the unconditioned stimulus and subsequently acquires the capacity to evoke a response similar to the one made to the unconditioned stimulus (e.g., a tone paired with food will elicit salivation).

Cone A receptor in the retina primarily for color vision.

Conformity A change in behavior or belief toward a group as a result of real or imagined group pressure.

Consciousness Refers both to the state of being normally awake and responsive, and to the complex thought processes guiding the behavior of the higher animal when awake and responsive.

Consistency set See sets.

Construct A hypothetical concept not directly observable but invented by the scientist to account for some series of actions or events.

Consumer psychology That branch of psychology specifically concerned with the buying habits of the American public.

Contact comfort The inborn need or motive to seek something soft and warm.

Continuous reinforcement The reinforcement of every correct response.

Control group A group used for comparison with the experimental group. The groups must be as similar to one another as possible.

Controlled observation Techniques used by the scientist to ensure that what he sees is actually there and not a function of his desires, wishes, or biases.

Convergent thinking Thought processes involved in arriving at a single correct solution to a problem.

Conversion hysteria See hysterical reaction.

Cornea The transparent covering over the eye through which light passes.

Corpus callosum A band of fibers which connects the two cerebral hemispheres together.

Cranial nerves The nerves serving the brain. There are 12 pairs of cranial nerves which are involved in motor or sensory functions, or both.

Credibility The expertness and trustworthiness of a person.

Cultural racism See racism.

Cunnilingus Oral stimulation of the woman's clitoris or vulva.

Dark adaptation Increasing visual sensitivity as one remains in darkness or low illumination.

Dating A ritualized social interaction between a boy and a girl, usually having a strong romantic flavor.

Death The biological termination of life.

Decibel The unit of measurement used in determining sound intensity.

Defense mechanism A process, generally believed to be unconscious, in which the purpose is to protect the individual's self-esteem and defend him against excessive anxiety when confronted with continuing frustrations.

Delirium tremens Acute delirium, state of mental confusion, associated with prolonged alcoholism; characterized by intense anxiety, tremors, and hallucinations.

Delta rhythm Large slow waves in the EEG; characteristic of deep sleep or brain damage.

Delusions Strong beliefs which the individual steadfastly maintains despite all evidence of its falsity.

Dendrite A nerve fiber that is normally stimulated by a physical stimulus or by the impulse brought to it by an axon.

Dependent variable The event observed to determine if any changes have occurred as the result of manipulation of the independent variable.

Depressive reactions A neurotic disorder characterized by feelings of sadness, worthlessness, lack of energy, and guilt.

Discrimination An overt act that places an individual at a disadvantage.

Disorientation A person who may become confused as to person, place, and time.

Displacement A defense mechanism in which one goal or object is substituted for another one more attainable.

Dissociative reaction See hysterical reaction.

Disuse Lack of practice; the theory that forgetting occurs merely because of the passing of time.

Divergent thinking Thought processes involving the use of information to discover a variety of ideas or solutions to a problem.

Dominance A social motive involving a need to maintain one's power over others, as seen in animals and man.

Double bind A theory used to explain schizophrenia in terms of confused communications sent to the preschizophrenic child.

Dream analysis The process of interpreting the meaning of a dream.

Dying The process of death.

Economic set See sets.

Ectomorph A body type characterized by a tall, thin, fragile frame.

Educotherapy A treatment program which emphasizes the fact that many delinquent individuals are the result of educational or learning disabilities.

Edwards Personal Preference Schedule Personality questionnaire designed to measure one's dominant needs or motives; it consists of 225 pairs of items and the subject is required to choose one or the other item of each pair.

EEG—Electroencephalogram The record of "brain waves" changing potentials in the cortex measured by electrodes attached to the scalp.

Effectors Organs such as muscles and glands that are capable of producing responses.

Ego According to Freud's psychoanalytic theory of personality development, the rational self that satisfies the needs of the id and directs and controls the libido into effective behavior.

Ego-weakness A state in which the ego relaxes or lowers its defenses.

Eidetic image An exceptionally detailed and vivid memory image.

Electra complex According to Freud's psychoanalytic theory of personality development, the tendency of a girl in the phallic stage to have sexual desires for her father.

Emotion A general term referring to powerful physiological and psychological responses that influence perception, learning and performance. It consists of both subjective feelings or affective states and bodily changes.

Endocrine glands Ductless glands that secrete small amounts of chemical substances called hormones directly into the bloodstream or lymph system.

Endomorph A body type characterized by fat, particularly in the abdominal region.

Engram The hypothetical physiological changes associated with learning; the memory trace.

Estrogen Female sex hormone.

Estrual Fertility cycle in female animals.

Etiology A term used to mean "causes."

Excitement phase The first phase identified by Masters and Johnson in the sexual response cycle. It is initiated by whatever is sexually stimulating to the individual.

Exhibitionism An individual who gains primary gratification from showing his or her genitals to other people.

Experiment A scientific method in which the experimenter makes a careful and controlled study of cause and effect by manipulating an independent variable and observing the effect on a dependent one.

Experimental group A group of subjects whose behavior is observed while the experimenter manipulates an independent variable.

Extinction The process in which the conditioned response tends to disappear because the unconditioned stimulus or reward is withheld.

Extraneous variables Variables which may affect and contaminate an experiment unless properly controlled.

Extrasensory perception (ESP) Awareness of thoughts and objects without direct participation of the senses.

Extrovert A person who directs his attention upon his environment and other people.

Factor analysis Statistical method used to identify the minimum number of variables that account for the intercorrelations in a number of tests or other forms of observation.

Family therapy An approach which emphasizes the interdependence of all behavior among family members. As a result, treatment is geared to the whole family.

Farsightedness (hyeropia) The inability to see objects close up although objects in the distance can be seen quite well.

Fatigue-hypochondriasis An excessive preoccupation with the state of your health.

Fellatio Oral stimulation of the penis.

Fetishism An individual who is sexually motivated toward some object such as an ankle, foot, undergarment, or stocking.

Field study A method used by the scientist in which the researcher goes into a natural setting to observe his subjects without any effort to control the behavior under investigation. Behaviors which naturally occur are observed and systematically recorded.

Fixed interval schedule An interval reinforcement schedule in which the first response after a fixed, predetermined time interval is reinforced (e.g., after every three minutes).

Fixed ratio schedule A ratio reinforcement schedule in which the response is reinforced after a fixed number of previous responses have been made (e.g., after every five responses).

Flashback The recurrence of a drug experience, such as from LSD, without further ingestion of the drug; usually of a negative nature following a "bad trip."

Foot-in-the-door technique A technique which stresses that if you are able to get a person to comply to a small request, he will be more likely to agree to a larger related one.

Forebrain The most forward of the three main divisions of the brain. It includes the cerebrum, thalamus, and hypothalamus.

Forgetting A loss of retention of material previously learned.

Fovea A small part of the retina which is the area of sharpest vision. It contains only cones.

Free association A technique used by psychoanalysts in exploring the unconscious by having the patient talk about whatever thoughts, feelings, or topics come to mind.

Free-floating anxiety A diffuse anxiety in which the fear stimuli are unknown.

Frigidity Women who experience an impaired ability to enjoy sexual activity.

Frontal association area The nonmotor areas of the frontal lobes involved in complex behavioral functions.

Frontal lobotomy The surgical interruption of pathways from the frontal association areas, sometimes performed in extreme cases of behavioral disorder.

Frontal lobe The part of the cerebral cortex that lies in front of the central fissure.

Frustration The blocking of goals by an obstacle which leads to unpleasant feelings.

Fugue A term used to indicate a form of amnesia in which the person wanders off for days or even years.

Functional psychoses Psychotic reactions produced by psychological factors.

Gene The essential substance in the transmission of hereditary characteristics, carried in chromosomes.

Genital stage The fifth stage in Freud's psychoanalytic theory of personality development in which the individual achieves independence and mature relationships with the opposite sex. The genital stage starts at the beginning of adolescence.

Germ cell An egg or sperm cell.

Gonads The sex glands which are the testicles in the male and the ovaries in the female. They determine secondary sex characteristics, such as growth of the beard, change of the voice, growth of the breasts, and beginning of menstruation and also affect sexual motivation.

Gonadotropic hormones Hormones secreted from the gonads.

Hallucinations False sensory impressions in the absence of stimulation of receptors. They are present in certain behavioral disorders such as schizophrenia.

Hammer A small ossicle of the middle ear attached to the eardrum.

Hebephrenic-schizophrenia A form of schizophrenia in which inappropriate emotional behavior such as laughter, smiling, giggling, and weeping may be pronounced. Bizarre ideas, incoherence, disorganized speech, hallucinations, and delusions are also present.

Hedonism A theory of motivation that considers the attainment of pleasure and the avoidance of pain to be the primary motivators of human behavior.

Hemophilia A condition in which the blood fails to clot properly.

Hermaphrodites People with the genital organs of both sexes.

Heterozygous The condition that results when both members of a pair of genes dictate different characteristics; i.e., one gene becomes dominant over the other.

Hindbrain One of the three divisions of the brain. It includes the medulla, cerebellum, and pons.

Hippie See social dropouts.

Homosexuality Physical attraction between members of the same sex.

Homozygous The condition that results when both members of a pair of genes dictate identical characteristics.

Horizontal-vertical illusion The tendency to perceive a vertical line next to a hori-zontal line as longer, even though they are of the same length.

Hue The characteristic of visual experiences related especially to the wavelength of light—e.g., red, green, blue, and yellow. Color in the everyday sense of the word.

Hyperkinetic children Disorder of childhood characterized by overactivity, restlessness, and distractibility.

Hyperphagia Overeating caused by damage to the hypothalamus.

Hypnodisk An apparatus that consists of rotating geometrical patterns. Subjects are asked to fix their gaze on it by a hypnotist in the induction of hypnosis.

Hypochondriasis See fatigue-hypochondriasis.

Hypophagia Undereating, or starvation, caused by damage to the hypothalamus.

Hypothalamus A region of the forebrain which contains centers for the regulation of hunger, thirst, sleep, sex, and body temperature.

Hysterical reaction A neurotic disorder which may take the form of *conversion* in which symptoms superficially resemble those present in organic diseases without true organic involvement or *dissociation* in which there is a loss of personal identity.

Id According to Freud's psychoanalytic theory of personality development, the reservoir of man's basic instinctive, animal urges.

Identity crisis The conflict brought on by individuals not knowing who they are. Usually it manifests itself during adolescence when the young begin to search for an identity whether it be personal, social, or vocational.

Identity (personal) A continuing sense of who and what one is.

Identity set See sets.

Illusion A false perception because it does not agree with the objective measurement of the physical form, which is regarded as more fundamental.

Imitation learning (modeling) A special type of learning that is social in that another organism is involved. An organism learns new behavioral patterns simply by imitating others.

Impotency Impairment of the man's

sexual response manifested by inability to attain or maintain an erection long enough to have successful intercourse.

Imprinting A form of learning which occurs very early in life and determines the form which behavior will take, as in the case of ducklings which follow the first moving object they see and remain closely attached to it.

Incest Sexual relations between members of a family such as parent and child or brother and sister.

Independent variable The factor manipulated in order to determine if it has any effects on the dependent variable.

Individual psychology A school of personality and psychotherapy, formed by Alfred Adler who broke away from Freud and his psychoanalytic theory of personality development. Adler stressed the importance of purposive goal-directed behavior, striving for superiority and man's innate concern with social interest.

Individual racism See racism.

Inefficiency The inability to perform adequately the responsibilities of a role.

Inner ear The innermost part of the ear, containing the cochlea and the semicircular canals.

Insanity A social and legal term that denotes a psychiatric disorder so grave that the individual is deemed incapable of assuming responsibility for his own actions.

Insight A general term used to describe the sudden solution of a problem.

Instinctive behavior A complex, unlearned pattern of behavior such as the nest building of birds.

Institutional racism See racism.

Instrumental conditioning A form of conditioning or learning in which the organism's response is instrumental in obtaining reinforcement.

Intelligence An abstract term, actually consisting of several definitions; generally used to describe a person's general ability to learn or abilities in a number of different areas, including verbal and motor skills.

Intelligence quotient (IQ) Numerical value of the ratio of mental age to chronological age, multiplied by 100; the score 100 is the average IQ.

Interposition A monocular cue for depth perception, involving the overlapping or partial obscuring of one object by another.

Interpretation A technique used by the therapist to help patients make sense of their problems and conflicts.

Introvert Person who directs his interests and attention upon himself.

Iris The flat circular muscle which controls the amount of light admitted to the retina.

Juvenile delinquent Basically a legal concept to refer to youths ranging in age from 16 to 21 who commit criminal offenses.

Kleptomania A compulsion to steal.

Klinefelter's syndrome A condition that results when a male inherits an extra female sex chromosome. These infants fail to mature sexually.

Latency stage The fourth stage in Freud's psychoanalytic theory of personality development during which sexual interests are submerged in favor of other activities. The latency stage occurs between the age of five and the beginning of adolescence.

Legitimate power See power.

Lens A structure behind the iris of the eye which is involved in changing the focus of light on the retina.

Libido According to Freud's psychoanalytic theory of personality development, the energy that serves the basic instincts and motivates every aspect of a person's behavior; it is basically sexual energy.

Life review A term used to refer to the phenomenon that occurs during aging or prior to death in which people review their lives.

Light adaptation A gradual decrease in sensitivity in bright illumination.

Limbic system A series of related structures in the forebrain concerned with emotion and motivation.

Linear perspective Perception of the distance of objects through apparent convergence of lines toward the horizon and through decrease in size with increasing distance.

Location constancy The tendency to perceive objects in a setting that remains essentially fixed although the retina is receiving changing impressions as the result of our own movement.

LSD—Lysergic acid diethylamide A hallucinogenic drug that can induce vivid perceptual experiences, hallucinations, and disorganized thinking.

Manic-depressive reaction A disorder characterized by extreme mood swings from one of elation to depression and vice versa.

Mantra An ancient Hindu incantation used in transcendental meditation.

Marijuana A drug derived from the hemp plant which produces changes in perception and perceptual sensitivity.

Marital schism A form of family interaction marked by extreme conflict and antagonism between the parents.

Marital skew A family situation where the dominant pathology of one marriage partner is supported by a weaker more dependent one.

Masculine protest Adler's earlier belief that femininity was equated with weakness and masculinity with strength. The masculine protest refers to an individual's attempt to be strong and to avoid inferiority.

Masochism Obtaining sexual pleasure through being hurt painfully by another person and by remaining passive throughout the act.

Mediating process The element of thought, capable of holding an excitation and, thus, of bridging a gap in time between stimulus and response.

Medulla Lowest part of the hindbrain; it regulates breathing, heartbeat, and blood pressure.

Megalopolis A term used to describe huge metropolitan areas in which large cities have engulfed the smaller towns around them.

Mental age (MA) Measuring unit of intelligence based on a norm; an MA of eight means the individual has performed as well as the average eight-year-old.

Mental illness A term generally used to describe a psychological maladjustment which is serious enough to handicap the afflicted person and to burden others.

Mental retardation Also commonly known as *mental deficiency,* or *mental subnormality,* refers to individuals with IQs below 70; approximately 3 percent of the population.

Mescaline One of the hallucinogenic drugs, made from peyote, a small spineless cactus.

Mesomorph A body type characterized by muscularity and well-developed bone structure.

Methadone An orally administered narcotic which kills the craving for heroin and paves the way for rehabilitation of heroin addicts.

Method of savings A method of measuring retention in which the subject is simply asked to relearn a task that he learned some time before. The number of trials required to relearn the task is compared with the number of trials required for original learning of the task.

Mnemonics A variety of techniques of organizing memory, often employed by memory experts.

Midbrain The middle of three divisions of the brain. It contains tracts which connect the cerebral cortex with lower structures in the brain, and "primitive" centers for visual and hearing functions.

Middle ear Part of auditory mechanism between the eardrum and cochlea containing the ossicles.

Minnesota Multiphasic Personality Inventory (MMPI) Personality questionnaire developed as an aid to diagnosing pathological behavior; each subject responds to 550 sentences by labeling each "true," "false," or "no reply."

Mongolism A mild to moderate form of mental retardation in which the facial features resemble somewhat those of mongoloid people. Also known as Down's syndrome.

Monocular cues Cues for depth perception that are used with one eye, as distinguished from binocular cues (cues used by both eyes).

Montessori methods A form of educational philosophy which utilizes well-developed equipment and materials to facilitate learning.

Moon illusion The fact that the moon looks larger near the horizon than it does high in the sky.

Motivation A general term referring to the forces regulating behavior that is undertaken because of drives, needs, or desires and is directed toward goals.

Motor area An area of the cerebral cortex lying around the central fissure. Movements can be elicited by stimulation of this region.

Müller-Lyer illusion A line of a given length appears shorter or longer by the addition of lines, such as enclosing arrowheads or arrowheads extending outward from its end.

Multiple personality (dual) Development of two or more distinct personalities which alternate in taking over the conscious control of the person.

Nearsightedness (myopia) The inability to see objects well in the distance.

Nerve net A primitive nervous system found in some lower animals that is simply a network of nerves functioning somewhat independently of each other. They are located in different parts of the body without any particular central point.

Nervous system The brain, spinal cord, and nerves which serve the various sense organs, endocrine glands, and muscles of the body.

Neural impulse An event, both electrical and chemical in nature, which is transmitted by neurons. These complex biochemical events underlie all behavior.

Neuron The cell that is the basic unit of the nervous system. It consists of dendrites, cell body, and axon.

Neuroses A group of disorders characterized by defensive maneuvers in the face of frustration and stress. The symptoms usually involve discomfort and inefficiency but rarely are bizarre.

Normality

Statistical concept of normality Normality is the norm of characteristics which occur most frequently in the population.

Ideal mental health concept This criterion of normality stresses the importance of attaining some goal or ideal such as self-actualization, in-

sight, and resistance to stress.

Practical criterion A pragmatic definition of normality and abnormality which utilizes such characteristics as discomfort, bizarreness and inefficiency in determining mental illness or health.

Nude marathon One of the more radical types of encounter groups. People are encouraged to take off their clothes so that they will be more open about themselves and less defensive about expressing their feelings.

Nymphomania A term used to label women who focus their entire lives around sexual activities.

Objectivity An attempt to look at the world without bias or prejudice.

Obsessions See obsessive-compulsive reactions.

Obsessive-compulsive reactions A neurotic disorder composed of two reactions: (a) an *obsession* which is an excessive preoccupation with certain topics to the exclusion of others, and (b) *compulsions* which are irresistible urges to carry out a particular behavior sequence.

Occipital lobe The part of the cerebral cortex lying at the back of the head. It contains the major sensory areas for vision.

Oddity problem A problem to test learning ability in which three or more stimuli are presented and the subject is asked to indicate which stimulus is different.

Oedipus complex According to Freud's psychoanalytic theory of personality development, the tendency of a boy in the phallic stage to have sexual desires for his mother.

Operant behavior Responses that "operate" on the environment and not directly elicited by a stimulus. Normally the type of response worked with in instrumental conditioning as opposed to reflexive behavior in classical conditioning.

Operational definition A definition of an abstract concept framed in terms of the operations used for observing it. For example, hunger might be defined as the number of hours since you last ate.

Optic chiasm The partial crossing of fibers in the optic nerve. This crossing makes it possible for the right visual field to be projected on the left hemisphere and vice versa.

Oral stage The first year of development, according to Freud's psychoanalytic theory of personality development, in which the infant's chief pleasures are derived from such experiences as sucking and consuming milk and food.

Organic psychoses Psychoses brought about by a physical injury or biological disease.

Organization The grouping of items together according to some rules to facilitate learning.

Organ of Corti A structure on the basilar membrane of the inner ear where the sound wave stimulates receptors.

Orgasmic phase The period of time in which the man or woman will experience an orgasm.

Ossicles The three small bones in the middle ear which play a role in the perception of movement.

Outer ear That portion of the ear outside the cranium and extending inward to the eardrum.

Overlearning Continued practice after some criterion of mastery has been achieved.

Ovulation The process in which the fertile egg starts its journey to the uterus and the ovaries begin to secrete progesterone.

Ovum The female egg formed in the ovary.

Paranoid schizophrenic A form of schizophrenia in which the usual symptoms of flattened effect, withdrawal, and hallucinations are present but the most impressive symptoms are delusions of grandeur or persecution.

Paraplegics Individuals who have suffered injury to their spinal cords and are unable to voluntarily move or receive sensations from their lower limbs.

Parietal lobe The part of the cerebral cortex that lies immediately behind the central fissure.

Partial reinforcement Schedules of reinforcement employed in which not every correct response is reinforced.

Pedophilia A serious criminal offense in which a child is the object of the person's sexual desire.

Penis envy According to psychoanalysis, an unconscious desire on the part of females to possess the penis of the male and the consequent feelings of biological inferiority.

Perception The ordering experience that lends coherence and unity to sensory input.

Peripheral nervous system Includes all the nerve cells and nerve fibers that lie outside the central nervous system.

Personality An abstract term used in several ways, generally refers to the organized characteristics and ways of behaving that determine an individual's unique adjustments to his environment.

Personality disorders A group of disorders which encompass the acting out of socially inappropriate behaviors.

Phallic stage The third stage of development which occurs between the ages of three and five, according to Freud's psychoanalytical theory of personality development.

Phobic reactions Unrealistic fears which are disproportionate to the actual feared object or situation.

Physical therapies A group of medical procedures used quite extensively by medical doctors in the treatment of the mentally ill and involves the use of medication, electroshock therapy, and so on.

Pitch The qualitative aspect of sounds, which may be determined as high or low; determined chiefly by sound wave frequency.

Pituitary gland A gland located beneath the hypothalamus that secretes a number of hormones affecting other glands of the body. It also secretes a growth hormone that controls the general rate of growth of the body.

Plateau phase The second phase of sexual arousal following the excitement phase.

Political-Economic Competition Theory A theory which proposes that prejudice is the result of limited resources for which two ethnic groups compete.

Pons A group of nerve fibers which connects the two sides of the cerebellum together and also transmits impulses upward and downward within the central nervous system. It also helps regulate breathing and is responsible in part for the rapid eye movements that take place while dreaming.

Posthypnotic suggestion A suggestion given to a hypnotized person that he will perform in the waking state some command given by the hypnotist during the hypnotic state.

POT association area The large association area of the cortex which includes parts of the parietal, occipital, and temporal lobes not involved in movement or sensation. It is responsible for complex behavioral functions.

Power A person's ability to influence another's behavior because of the rewards and punishments he is able to administer.
    a. *Legitimate power* Power which is wielded because of that person's right to do so.
    b. *Coercive power* A form of power in which a person can influence others not because of its legitimacy, but because he is able to punish or reward others.

Precognition The claimed ability to know what is going to happen before it occurs.

Prejudice A set of hostile and negative attitudes directed at an identifiable group or members of the group.

Prejudiced personality theory A theory which postulates that certain individuals have a constellation of personality traits that predispose them to prejudicial thinking.

Premarital coitus Sexual relations prior to marriage.

Primary colors The colors out of which all other hues can be derived by mixing them in appropriate proportions.

Primary mental abilities According to Thurstone, the basic elements of intelligence, including perceptual speed (P), numerical ability (N), word fluency (W), verbal comprehension (V), spatial visualization (S), memory (M), and reasoning (R).

Private acceptance A change in *belief* toward that of the group because of social pressure.

Proactive thinking Forgetting that is a weakening of learning caused by prior learning.

Problem solving Deals with an organism's or subject's ability to discover a correct response to a new situation. Unlike simple tasks, the response is not obvious and usually involves ideas or other mediating processes.

Problem-solving set See sets.

Progesterone The maternal hormone secreted during ovulation. It prepares the uterus for implantation and indirectly prepares the mammary glands for nursing.

Programmed learning A teaching technique using a textbook or teaching machine which breaks down learning into a series of small controlled steps. This self-instructional method requires the learner to become actively involved in a process that provides immediate feedback and reinforcement as to the accuracy of his responses.

Projection A defense mechanism in which unacceptable thoughts or impulses are placed upon others, or a person's shortcomings and mistakes are attributed to others.

Projective tests Tests using ambiguous stimuli to determine underlying personality factors and to uncover unconscious conflicts.

Promiscuity A term used to describe people who freely engage in sexual activity with members of the opposite sex.

Propinquity A term describing physical proximity to other people.

Psychoanalysis A school of psychology originated by Freud, which emphasizes the study of unconscious mental processes; also a comprehensive theory of personality and a method of psychotherapy which seeks to bring unconscious desires into consciousness and make it possible to resolve conflicts which have their origin in early childhood experiences.

Psychokinesis (PK) Mind over matter phenomenon whereby a mental thought affects a physical body or an energy system.

Psychology A science which studies the behavior of man and other animals.

Psychoses A severe mental illness marked by impairment in the cognitive and emotional realm so that contact with reality is often lost.

Psychosexual stages According to Freud's psychoanalytic theory of personality development, the sequence of stages through which the child progresses. Each stage has its "zone of gratification."

Psychosomatic disorder A bodily disorder instigated or aggravated by emotional disturbance.

Psychotherapy Treatment of mental illness by using psychological principles.

Puberty The beginning of sexual maturation, especially the adult sex organs and the growth of hair in the pubic and other areas.

Pupil The opening in the iris through which light enters the eye.

Pyromania A compulsion to set fires.

Racial pride An attempt by many minorities to redefine their existence by stressing consciousness and pride in their own racial and cultural identity.

Racial self-hatred Being ashamed of your own race, resulting in a dislike for yourself.

Racism A term referring to an attitudinal component, prejudice; and its behavioral component, discrimination.
   a. *Individual racism* Racism directed from one individual to another.
   b. *Institutional racism* Discriminatory policies which exist in institutions (economic, educational, legal).
   c. *Cultural racism* The individual and institutional expression of the superiority of one group's cultural heritage over that of another race.

Rape A male offense in which the victim is forcibly made to have sexual relations with the offender.

Rationalization A common defense mechanism in which we give socially acceptable and logical reasons for our behavior which are not really true.

Reaction formation A defense mechanism in which dangerous impulses are repressed and converted to their direct opposite. For example, feelings of hate may be converted to love.

Reasoning The spontaneous integration of separate habits to solve a problem.

Recall A method of measuring retention in which the subject is instructed to reproduce what he has previously learned.

Receptors Cells that receive stimulation.

Recognition A method of measuring retention in which the subject is required to discriminate between what he has seen from what is new.

Regression The return to more primitive modes of behavior which characterize a younger age. Often seen as a reaction to frustration.

Reinforcement A stimulus that will affect the probability of occurrence of the preceding response.

REM (rapid eye movement) Eye movement that occurs during dreaming.

Repression A defense mechanism in which threatening or painful thoughts and memories are excluded from consciousness as a means of controlling dangerous or unacceptable desires, thereby protecting the individual from traumatic experiences.

Resistance An unwillingness or inability for patients to deal with certain topics or thoughts during the actual course of therapy.

Resolution period This phase follows orgasm in which the person returns to the unstimulated state with the lessening of sexual tension.

Retina The innermost part of the eye, which contains the cone and rod receptors and is thus photosensitive.

Retinal disparity The slight difference between the retinal images perceived by the two eyes when a nearby object is viewed; helps make depth perception possible.

Retroactive inhibition Forgetting caused by interference between what is learned and subsequent learning.

Ribonucleic acid (RNA) Complex molecules found within cells, involved in the production of proteins. It is hypothesized that learning experiences change the detailed chemical structure of RNA within neurons.

Riffraff theory The belief that ghetto riots could be explained as the work of the emotionally disturbed, deviants, criminals, or unassimilable migrants.

Rods Receptors in the retina primarily for achromatic (black and white) vision.

Rorschach inkblot test Projective test consisting of 10 symmetrical inkblots in shades of gray or black or in color.

Sadism An individual who gains primary sexual gratification through inflicting pain on another person.

Saturation The degree to which color of a given hue is present; i.e., the degree to which it differs from gray of the same brightness.

Satyriasis A term used to label men who focus their entire lives around sexual activities.

Scapegoat theory In prejudice, a theory stating that a person who experiences frustration and is unable to direct the source of his anger toward the real source attempts to eliminate frustration by venting anger on others who are (a) less powerful, and (b) different from himself.

Schedules of reinforcement The program governing the sequence of reinforcements and nonreinforcements of a response.

Schizophrenia A psychotic disorder which constitutes the gravest problem for psychiatry and is characterized by cognitive deterioration.

School dropouts Students who leave school without graduating.

Secondary reinforcement A previously neutral stimulus that acquires reinforcing properties.

Second-chance family A type of encounter group in which students meet and form families so that they can learn what an actual family is like. It provides new opportunities for the development of the self which may have not been available in their actual childhood families.

Self-actualization Uniquely human drive to discover one's self and fulfill one's real potential, emphasizing the whole of human life; advocated by Rogers and Maslow.

Self-theory Theories of personality that stress the importance of conscious experiences and man's conscious experience of himself in determining personality. Theorists, such as Carl Rogers, view the concept of self as critical and focal in personality as opposed to unconscious processes.

Senescence The process of becoming aged; the arbitrary cutoff point for the beginning of old age is usually taken as age 65.

Sensitivity training A rather new approach that has been developed to help people better understand the emotions of frustrations of their fellowman including their own. It involves a group of people who interact together on many different levels over an extended time period. Also known as encounter groups.

Sensory area Area of the brain concerned in sensory functions such as vision, hearing, and touch.

Sets A term used to describe an individual's frame of mind.

   a. *Authority set* A belief that a person has a legitimate right to influence or tell us what to do.

   b. *Consistency set* The changing of an opinion, belief, or behavior to make it consistent with other opinions, beliefs, or behaviors.

   c. *Economic set* Changing of behaviors or beliefs in order to gain rewards or avoid punishments.

   d. *Identity set* A desire to be like or similar to an attractive person or group.

   e. *Problem-solving set* A concern for obtaining correct or truthful information.

Sex appeal Attributes that make a person attractive to members of the opposite sex.

Sex flush A measlelike rash appearing on the body of the man or woman during sexual tension.

Sexism Any attitude, action, or institutional structure that subordinates a person because of sex.

Sex typing The process during socialization in which boys and girls are rewarded for sex appropriate behaviors and discouraged from inappropriate ones.

Shadowing A monocular cue in which the three-dimensional effect is enhanced by the variation of the pattern of light and shadow on an object.

Shape constancy The tendency to perceive objects as maintaining their shape despite the marked changes in the retinal image.

Shaping A method of modifying behavior by reinforcing successive approximations of the kind of behavior the experimenter desires. Used by animal trainers to get animals to perform complicated acts.

Simple schizophrenia A form of schizophrenia characterized by withdrawal and isolation from others. Although the symptoms are seldom bizarre, there are disturbances of thinking and effect.

Size constancy The tendency for an object to be seen as maintaining its absolute size despite changes in the size of the retinal image.

Skeletal muscle Class of muscles attached to the bones of the skeleton by tendons that contract and then relax again to move the trunk and limbs.

Smooth muscle Class of muscles found in blood vessels, intestines, and certain other organs.

Social conformity theory In prejudice, a theory which emphasizes the fact that the child is socialized into a prejudiced society and conforms to local group norms.

Social discord A term used to describe unrest, conflict, and disharmony among large segments of our society.

Social dropouts Individuals alienated from the values of middle-class society who move to a life outside of the formal structure of society. Terms such as "beatniks" and "hippies" have been used to describe these people.

Social norm A rule or standard of conduct which implicitly or explicitly tells us how to behave.

Sociocultural approach A belief that prejudices can be eliminated by a wider social approach as opposed to individual psychotherapy.

Somatotonia A dimension of personality characterized by love of physical adventure, vigorous physical activity, aggressiveness, physical courage and boldness.

Somatotype Body type of a person. Shelton stressed in his somatotype theory of personality that body type determines personality.

Spinal nerves The 31 pairs of nerves that extend outward from the spinal cord to various parts of the body. They are involved in sensory and motor functions.

Split-brain preparation A surgical procedure severing the neural connections between the two hemispheres of the brain.

Spontaneous recovery The reappearance of an extinguished conditioned response after a time interval in which no practice occurred.

Stanford-Binet test An intelligence test originally devised by Binet and Simon, and later revised by Terman. This test, used for children and adults, heavily weighs verbal skills.

Stereoscopic vision The experience of perceiving depth in flat pictures as the result of the presentation of artificial depth cues to both eyes.

Stereotyped behavior The repeating of some action over and over again in spite of the fact that it does not serve any useful purpose. Often a reaction to frustration.

Stereotypes Overgeneralizations that are attributed to members of a group.

Stimulus A physical energy of some type impinging upon our bodies, detected by our sense modalities.

Stirrup A small bone in the middle ear, attached to the oval window marking the beginning of the inner ear.

Streaking A recent fad in which individuals race through a public place with nothing on other than shoes or socks.

Student activism A broad term to indicate student unrest, protest, demonstration, and agitation usually over some social issue and occurring at a college or university campus.

Subjectivity A human tendency to consider things in light of our own point of view and to make evaluations from that framework. In science, it may bias our findings.

Sublimation According to Freud's psychoanalytic theory of personality development, a form of displacement of instinctual energy from the id into higher social and cultural achievements.

Subliminal advertising Presentation of advertising material below the conscious threshold of people in an attempt to affect attitudes and behaviors.

Subliminal perception Refers to a threshold or intensity level below which a stimulus cannot be detected consciously; however, possibly "observers" respond to a stimulus which is below that threshold.

Superego According to Freud's psychoanalytic theory of personality development, the moral-ethical part of the personality which consists of the internalized values and ideals of society as interpreted by parents to the child.

Swinging A contemporary term denoting free sexual experimentation and experience by single and married individuals. The conventional codes governing sexual behavior tend to be ignored.

Synanon game Is a special type of encounter group experience sponsored by the Synanon Foundation. Full-time residents live together and a whole way of life is provided for them. The Synanon game players attack each other's faults in a surgical fashion in order to break down resistance.

Systematic desensitization A behavioral technique involving the breaking down of anxiety responses in piecemeal fashion through the use of relaxation.

Symptom theory approach The belief that prejudices are symptom manifestations of psychological conflicts rooted in the personality.

Taraxein A substance found in the blood serum of schizophrenics and believed to be related to that disorder.

Technology A term used to describe major inventions and advances in our society that may have large-scale implications for our quality of living.

Telepathy The claimed form of extrasensory perception in which what is perceived depends upon thought transference from one person to another.

Temporal lobe The part of the cerebral cortex lying on the side of the cerebrum beneath the lateral fissure. Contains the major sensory centers for hearing.

Tests for Primary Abilities A battery of intelligence tests, developed by Thurstone and based on factor analysis, which measures several abilities.

Thalamus Located in the forebrain, it is the brain's major relay station. It connects the cerebrum with the lower structures of the brain and spinal cord.

Thematic Apperception Test (TAT) Projective personality test in which the individual is shown a set of pictures, each deliberately drawn to serve as a stimulus for the telling of a story. Often a subject's narrative will reveal the nature of his problems.

Therapeutic sexual arousal A behavioral technique using sexual arousal to overcome anxiety associated with sexual performance.

Thyroid gland An endocrine gland located in the neck that influences the general level of bodily activity.

Timbre Sound quality, as in the difference between the same note played on a piano or violin. A function of the complexity of sound waves, the overtones produced.

Tone deafness Type of hearing defect in which the individual cannot perceive differences in tone; one note sounds like another to him.

Transcendental meditation (TM) A method of altering consciousness by relaxation and controlled breathing.

Transference A process in which patients respond unconsciously and emotionally to an analyst in the same fashion as some important figure in their life.

Transvestism A term describing an individual who obtains sexual gratification by wearing the clothes of the opposite sex.

Trapezoidal illusion An illusion involving an apparatus that consists of a rotating trapezoidal window. The subject tends to perceive the longer end as always closer to him as the window appears to oscillate or sway rather than to rotate.

Turner's syndrome A genetic defect in women in which only one X chromosome is inherited. Victims of this defect have a defective body structure in addition to mild mental retardation.

Tympanic membrane (eardrum) Part of the outer ear that vibrates and passes the sound to the middle ear.

Unconditioned response The response that is made to the unconditioned stimulus in classical conditioning (e.g., salivation is the response to food).

Unconditioned stimulus The stimulus (an "exciting" event) that automatically elicits the unconditioned response in classical conditioning (e.g., food elicits salivation).

Unconscious A large segment of the mind considered by psychoanalysts to contain a great deal of forgotten material (ideas, wishes, and motives) that cannot be recalled at will.

Underachiever An individual, usually in a school setting, who is performing well below his or her potential.

Vaginismus A condition in which the vagina involuntarily clamps tightly shut when attempts are made to enter.

Variable interval schedule An interval reinforcement schedule in which the first response after a variable time interval is reinforced. The time interval is designated by the average length of these intervals (e.g., in a variable schedule of three minutes the response is reinforced once every three minutes on the average, with some intervals being as brief as a few seconds and others much longer than three minutes).

Variable ratio schedule A ratio reinforcement schedule in which the response is reinforced after a varying number of responses have been made. The ratio is designated by the average number of responses that precede a reinforcement (e.g., a variable interval schedule of 10 responses would be one in which reinforcement occurs on the average after every 10 responses but varies from 1 response to 30 or more responses).

Vasocongestion Dilation of the blood vessels.

Viscerotonia A demension of personality characterized by extrovert tendencies, love of physical comfort, slow reactions, and love of eating.

Visual acuity Sharpness of vision measured by standardized charts.

Visual cliff An apparatus, consisting of two surfaces, that is used in experiments on the development of depth perception.

Visual imagery The occurrence of mental activity corresponding to the visual perception of an object, but when the object is not presented to the eyes.

Voyeurism A person who gains primary sexual pleasure from looking at the genitals of another person or from observing people engaged in sexual activity.

Wavelength The linear distance between two corresponding positions in a wave, as from crest to crest.

Wechsler Adult Intelligence Scale (WAIS) An intelligence test for individuals above the age of 16 that combines verbal and performance problems; IQ measures are derived from a comparison of the subject's score with scores of other individuals of the same chronological age.

Wechsler Intelligence Scale for Children (WISC) A test for children from ages 5 through 15 that combines verbal and performance problems; IQ measures are derived from a comparison of the subject's score with scores of other individuals of the same chronological age.

Weigl principle oddity test A special type of oddity task used clinically to test a patient's ability to engage in abstract thinking.

White light The light obtained by mixing all the light wave frequencies together.

White noise The noise obtained by mixing all of the frequencies of the sound spectrum, corresponds roughly to the sound of a hissing steam radiator.

Wife-swapping Exchanging marital partners for the express purpose of sexual relations.

Women's liberation A movement among females to unite and eliminate sexism in our society.

X chromosome Female sex chromosome; the male has only one, the female two.

Y chromosome One of the sex chromosomes, possessed only by males.

Zygote The product of the union of a sperm cell and an egg.

Indexes

Name and reference index

Subject index